P9-EDR-223

THE GOSPEL ACCORDING TO ST JOHN

RUDOLF SCHNACKENBURG

THE GOSPEL ACCORDING TO ST JOHN

VOLUME ONE
INTRODUCTION AND COMMENTARY
ON CHAPTERS 1—4

CROSSROAD · NEW YORK

1982
The Crossroad Publishing Company
575 Lexington Avenue, New York, NY 10022

Original edition: *Das Johannesevangelium,* Part I
Herder, Freiburg, 1965
Herders theologischer Kommentar zum Neuen Testament IV/I
General editors: Serafin de Ausejo, Lucien Cerfaux, Béda Rigaux,
Rudolf Schnackenburg, Anton Vögtle

This translation by Kevin Smyth, © 1968 by Herder KG

Printed in the United States of America

Library of Congress Cataloging in Publication Data

Schnackenburg, Rudolf, 1914–
The Gospel according to St. John.

Translation of: Das Johannesevangelium.
Includes bibliographies and indexes.
Contents: v. 1. Introduction and commentary on chapters 1-4—v. 2. Commentary on chapters 5-12.
1. Bible. N.T. John—Commentaries. I. Title.
BS2615.3.S313 1982 226'.507 81-22157
ISBN 0-8245-0311-2 (v. 1) AACR2

Preface

After many years of preparation, a beginning may be made, I think, with the publication of this commentary on the Gospel of St. John. Like every human undertaking, it is a child of its times. It would not have been possible without the theological labour of earlier centuries and the scientific research of the last decades. I should like the commentary to make its contribution to the present state of studies, without abandoning Catholic tradition or the scientific method used by New Testament scholars of all confessions. Dealing as we are with one of the most mature and, at the same time, one of the most controverted products of early Christianity, in which some find the supreme and crowning testimony of the faith of the primitive Church, and others a work of pious speculation with no historical value, one can only use all available means to "explain" it, that is, to make it understandable to the mentality of the present-day reader. The tension which is now so strongly felt between "faith and history", "history and myth", "historical knowledge and the understanding of faith" comes out perhaps more strongly than elsewhere in the Gospel of St. John. Every commentary on it represents a scientific decision and a personal confession of faith. My own effort claims to be no different.

Anyone who now undertakes to write a "major commentary"—an enterprise which grows more and more laborious every year—must consider well what he proposes to offer and what limits he imposes on himself. A long introduction seemed desirable for many reasons, and almost indispensable in the present work. The general purpose of the series is to provide the reader with an adequate amount of scientific information about the problems which arise; further, the introduction is meant to indicate the scientific and theological standpoint of the author and to prepare for the commentary. As regards the materials available for the comparative history of religions, I have concentrated on the texts from Qumran and the new Coptic Gnostic finds, insofar as they have been made accessible. What I owe to other authors, either the Fathers or older exegetes or modern research, will be easily recognized by scholars, as will my effort to make the scientific discussion a counter-poise to certain tendencies. What matters above all, as the Johannine kerygma tells us, is the duty of listening to the words of God's envoy himself, as he speaks from the fullness of the Spirit (Jn 3:34).

Rudolf Schnackenburg

Contents

EXCURSUSES

BIBLIOGRAPHY AND INDICES

Abbreviation

ATANT	Abhandlungen zur Theologie des Alten und Neuen Testaments
BZ	Biblische Zeitschrift
CBQ	The Catholic Biblical Quarterly
CSCO	Corpus Scriptorum Christianorum Orientalium
CSEL	Corpus Scriptorum Ecclesiasticorum Latinorum
DBS	Dictionnaire de la Bible, Supplément
DTC	Dictionnaire de Théologie Catholique
FRLANT	Forschungen zur Religion und Literatur des Alten und Neuen Testaments
GCS	Die griechischen christlichen Schriftsteller der ersten drei Jahrhunderte
JBL	Journal of Biblical Literature
JTS	The Journal of Theological Studies
KT	Kleine Texte für theologische und philologische Vorlesungen und Übungen
LTK	Lexikon für Theologie und Kirche (2nd ed.)
NRT	Nouvelle Revue Théologique
NTS	New Testament Studies
PG	Migne, Patrologia Graeca
PL	Migne, Patrologia Latina
RAC	Reallexikon für Antike und Christentum
RB	Revue Biblique
RGG	Die Religion in Geschichte und Gegenwart
RSR	Revue de Science Religieuse
TLZ	Theologische Literaturzeitung
TU	Texte und Untersuchungen zur Geschichte der altchristlichen Literatur. Archiv für die griechisch-christlichen Schriftsteller der ersten drei Jahrhunderte
TWNT	Theologisches Wörterbuch zum Neuen Testament E. T.: Theological Dictionary of the New Testament
ZAW	Zeitschrift für die alttestamentliche Wissenschaft
ZKT	Zeitschrift für katholische Theologie
ZNW	Zeitschrift für die neutestamentliche Wissenschaft
ZTK	Zeitschrift für Theologie und Kirche

NOTE: The sources (Bibliography I) are generally quoted by editor's name only. The works listed in Bibliography II and III are quoted by author and (short) title. Book titles are given in italics, and articles from periodicals, dictionaries, collective works, etc., in quotation marks. For full references see the bibliography.

INTRODUCTION

CHAPTER I

The Gospel of St John as a Written Gospel

The fourth and last Gospel to be admitted into the canon of the New Testament, which has never been known except as the Gospel "according to John" (or "the Gospel of John"), presents critical and historical research with the greatest problems, and a solution of the "Johannine question", agreement on the complicated network of particular questions which it contains, cannot be foreseen. Since the first critical investigations into its origin and authorship, its special quality and its contrast with the synoptic Gospels,[1] it has been the subject of a literature too vast for survey, which now promises to grow still greater, stimulated by new literary finds (the Qumran literature, the texts from Nag-Hammadi) and by new methods, which are being tested on this unique literary work.[2] It cannot be the task of the introduction to the "theological commentary" here presented to discuss all these questions at length. Its object can only be to lay a scientific foundation for the principles used in the exposition. Every commentary on the Gospel of St John represents a decision, which cannot be arrived at without a verdict on these "introductory" questions. And the commentary itself will be a contribution to such questions, in so far as it succeeds in bringing to light and explaining the contents of the Gospel itself. In keeping with the object of the series of which this work forms part, the emphasis will be laid on positive theolog-

[1] A survey of critical research on the "Johannine problem" since the Enlightenment is given by Loisy, *Le Quatrième Évangile*, pp. 18–39; Merlier, *Le Quatrième Évangile*, pp. 52–98; Kümmel, *Einleitung*, pp. 132–35, E. T.: *Introduction*, pp. 139–42. More recent research is listed by Bauer, "Johannesevangelium und Johannesbriefe"; Haenchen, "Aus der Literatur zum Johannesevangelium"; Behm, "Der gegenwärtige Stand der Erforschung des Johannesevangeliums"; Howard, *The Fourth Gospel in Recent Criticism and Interpretation;* Menoud, *L'évangile de Jean d'après les recherches récentes;* id. , "L'évangile de Jean d'après les recherches de Bultmann à Barrett"; Mollat, "Rassegna di lavori cattolici su S. Giovanni dal 1950 al 1960".

[2] See the survey given by Schulz, *Untersuchungen zur Menschensohn-Christologie im Johannesevangelium*, pp. 39–81, with extensive bibliography, pp. 13–36.

ical exposition. But this again is not possible without consideration of the literary problems, comparative religion (as far as this background can be discerned) and the historical circumstances of the origin of the Gospel. For further discussion of the problems concerned with the origins of the Gospel, the reader is referred to recent Introductions to the New Testament[3] and to particular works.[4]

The work with which we are dealing is a Gospel, even though the words εὐαγγελίζεσθαι, εὐαγγέλιον, εὐαγγελιστής do not occur at all in the Johannine writings, except in Revelation. It is in fact the most mature fruit of Gospel composition, and the perfect embodiment of all that "Gospel" implies by its very nature. Research into this central concept of the Christian religion[5] has eliminated many older notions: "the Gospel" is not originally a literary product, but the message of salvation which Jesus Christ has brought as God's eschatological bearer of good tidings (cf. Is 52:7) — hence the verbal form at the beginning (cf. Mt 11:5 par.; Lk 4:18; 16:16 etc.) — and which the early Church understands further, in keeping with the situation after Easter, as the word of salvation about Jesus Christ, the crucified and risen Lord and Messiah, exalted at the right hand of God (cf. Acts 2:36; 5:42 etc.; Rom 1:1–4, 16 etc.).[6] Jesus Christ, who "preached the Gospel of God" (Mk 1:14), which was "the Gospel of the kingdom (of God)" (Mt 4:23; 9:35; 24:14), becomes himself the "Gospel of God" (cf. 1 Thess 2:2; Rom 1:1) as the Church proclaims its faith in him. This proclamation of salvation was only committed to writing in books known as Gospels at a comparatively late date, to record and attest Jesus's words and works, his death and resurrection, and to present them to the acceptance of faith. The fact that these writings had a new and special purpose brought with it the

---

[3] Catholic: Meinertz, *Einleitung in das Neue Testament;* Schäfer, *Grundriss der Einleitung in das Neue Testament;* Wikenhauser, *Einleitung in das Neue Testament,* E. T.: *New Testament Introduction;* Robert and Feuillet, *Introduction à la Bible,* vol. II: *Nouveau Testament,* E. T.: *Introduction to the New Testament.* Protestant: Jülicher and Fascher, *Einleitung in das Neue Testament;* Michaelis, *Einleitung in das Neue Testament;* Kümmel, *Einleitung in das Neue Testament,* E. T.: *Introduction to the New Testament.*

[4] Along with the works mentioned in n. 1, see especially the list given in Wikenhauser, *Einleitung,* p. 200 and pp. 429 f., E. T.: *Introduction,* pp. 278, 520, 530; Kümmel, *Einleitung,* pp. 127 ff., E. T.: *Introduction,* pp. 134–7; also de la Potterie, *Getuige van het Woord;* Dodd, *Historical Tradition in the Fourth Gospel.*

[5] Cf. Schniewind, *Euangelion;* Friedrich, "εὐαγγέλιον"; Asting, *Die Verkündigung des Wortes im Urchristentum,* pp. 300–457; Huby and Léon-Dufour, *L'évangile et les Évangiles;* Schmid, "Evangelium"; Léon-Dufour, *Les évangiles et l'histoire de Jésus.*

[6] Cf. Origen, *Comm. in Jo.,* I, 5: "Thus the gospel is a discourse which contains a present good for believers, or proclaims that the expected good is present. This is true of the books which we call gospels. For each gospel is a collection of messages which mean salvation for believers and they are salutary for those who do not take them in a wrong sense."

creation of a special *genus litterarium*,[7] which is first met with in the Gospel of St Mark. The genre is not without affinities in other writings originating at "sub-literary" levels.

The aim of the evangelists was gravely misapprehended, with consequences which also affected the "Johannine question", when the gospels were taken to be principally chronicles and histories of the life and work of Jesus of Nazareth. The result was that consciously or unconsciously a "Gospel" was judged by the amount of historically reliable information it gave or could give about the memorable events in Palestine at the beginning of the Christian era. One must, of course, never overlook the fact that the aim of Gospels also includes the historical element, a characteristic which is particularly marked in the work of St Luke (cf. Lk 1:1–4), and that this aim was an intrinsic interest of the evangelists, imposed on them by the historical nature of the revelation of salvation in Jesus Christ.[8] But the writing of history is not the predominant and ultimate goal of our canonical Gospels. Ever since it was seen that this principle applied to our oldest document, the Gospel of St Mark,[9] and that it was confirmed not only by the more doctrinal and systematic Gospel of St Matthew, but also by the diptych of St Luke, with its theological tendencies,[10] the way was open to do more justice to the Gospel of St John as another record of the Gospel.

1. Connection with earlier Gospel writing

Biblical criticism engaged with the "Johannine question", in the form in which it was raised since the Enlightenment,[11] was strongly dominated

---

[7] Cf. Wendland, *Die urchristlichen Literaturformen*, pp. 258–314; K. L. Schmidt, "Die Stellung der Evangelien in der allgemeinen Literaturgeschichte". Cf. also the method of "form-criticism" which bases itself explicitly on these suppositions.

[8] In contrast to the "Kerygma theology" which only allows significance to the kerygma of the crucified and risen Jesus, this is also admitted by critically-minded scholars; cf. Käsemann, "Das Problem des historischen Jesus"; Conzelmann, "Jesus Christ", especially cols. 648 ff.; Bornkamm, "Glaube und Geschichte in den Evangelien". Among Catholics, cf. Rigaux, "L'historicité de Jésus devant l'exégèse récente"; Mussner, "Der historische Jesus"; Léon-Dufour, *Les évangiles et l'histoire de Jésus*.

[9] Wrede, *Das Messiasgeheimnis in den Evangelien;* Schmidt, *Der Rahmen der Geschichte Jesus;* Wellhausen, *Einleitung in die drei ersten Evangelien;* Léon-Dufour, *Les évangiles*, pp. 178–87.

[10] Cf. Conzelmann, *Die Mitte der Zeit*, E. T.: *The Theology of St. Luke;* Haenchen, *Die Apostelgeschichte*, on which see J. Dupont in *Revue biblique* 64 (1957), pp. 102–7; O'Neill, *The Theology of Acts in its Historical Setting*.

[11] The first critical approaches were made in England by Evanson with *The Dissonance of the Four Generally Received Evangelists* (1792); in Germany, by Eckermann with *Theologische Beiträge* (1796) and then in particular by Bretschneider with *Probabilia de evangelii et epistularum Johannis Apostoli indole et origine* (1820).

by a comparison of the synoptic Gospels with the Gospel of St John. This approach, which was also suggested by the possibilities of exact comparison of these literary works, could not but make the Gospel of St John appear as an "outsider". It offered a striking number of tensions and indeed "contradictions" with regard to the synoptic Gospels, which were far more in agreement with each other and on the whole unanimous. Since then, the relationship between "the Synoptics and St John" has been part and parcel of all investigations of the "Johannine question", and we shall have to discuss it in due course (see below, ch. ii). But these investigations entailed, and still entail, the danger of obscuring the common structural elements of the four canonical Gospels, precisely as "Gospels". Here Christian antiquity, which did indeed miss many of the points raised by modern criticism, was in a happier situation. For Irenaeus, the four-fold canon of the Gospels represented a profoundly significant fact,[12] foreseen and willed by God, while Clement of Alexandria could express the difference he felt between the synoptics and St John in the words: after the "corporeal" had been revealed in the first three Gospels, St John produced the "spiritual" Gospel.[13] But even this statement points to a gap which no longer exists according to our present understanding of the matter. Even the Gospel of St Mark is not content to present only the external events of Jesus's work. Its aim is to make the hidden divinity shine through, at least in "secret epiphanies" (M. Dibelius). And the fourth evangelist in turn makes the flesh the very dwelling-place of the divine glory present in Jesus and makes it visible only to those who believe (1:14; 2:11; 11:40). The oldest Gospel, like the last, is a document of faith in the service of faith, and merely uses other means in its presentation of the "history of Jesus", the Son of God, to its readers. Its intentions are the same.[14]

Further special traits which associate the Gospel of John with its forerunners and give it the character of a written Gospel, at least in its traditional form (on the question of its origins see below, ch. iv), are as follows:

a) The whole narrative is in all essentials contained within the framework of the event which ran its course between the baptism of Jesus in the Jordan (cf. 1:32 ff.) and his Resurrection (ch. 20). But this is precisely

---

[12] Irenaeus, *Adv. haer.*, III, 11, esp. para. 11 (Harvey, vol. II, pp. 46–52); he forged the expression τετράμορφον τὸ εὐαγγέλιον (*ibid.*, p. 47).

[13] Clement of Alexandria in Eusebius, *Hist. eccles.*, VI, 14, 7.

[14] Cf. Schäfer, *Grundriss*, p. 85: "We only see the figure of Jesus as through a transparency, as in the Synoptics ... The notion that partially blinded many scholars not so long ago, that Jesus was God only in John, but a mere man in the Synoptics, has been practically eliminated today; we have again learned to see that the Jesus of the Synoptics, even the Jesus of Mark, is also a divine figure."

the eschatological moment of history in which the great salvific event announced in "the Gospel" took place, the event which forms the real object of "the Gospel", as it is summarized in the missionary discourses of the Acts of the Apostles (cf. Acts 10:37–41; 13:23–31) and developed in the Gospel of St Mark. All that precedes it in the Gospel of St John is the prologue (1:1–18), which allows the believing reader an early glimpse of the divine pre-existence of the bringer of salvation, and enables him to understand his work from his divine origin. St Matthew and St Luke likewise give a "pre-history" of Jesus, for other reasons, before they recount his public appearance.

b) Historically well attested, and intrinsically meaningful, Jesus's "progress from Galilee to Jerusalem", which has its own role to play in each of the synoptic Gospels, with a different theological emphasis in each case, is retained in the fourth Gospel. This remains unmistakable, in spite of the "calendar of feasts" at Jerusalem (cf. 2:13; 5:1; 6:4; 7:2,14; 10:22), and the relatively small space allotted to the Galilean ministry of Jesus, compared with the Synoptics — though attention is in fact paid to the beginning (2:1–13; 4: 46–54) and the climax (ch. 6).

This geographical orientation has also its deep theological grounds in John; indeed, the importance of Jerusalem as the centre of Judaism (cf. ch. 5; 7; 11f.), and as the holy city of God enshrining the temple (so at the very beginning, 2:13–22) is also strongly underlined. Even from the point of view of presentation, emphasis is laid on the (Judean or) Jerusalem ministry of Jesus by his repeated visits to Jerusalem and his debates there with the leading representatives of Judaism. This is the summit of a trend which could be noticed earlier, especially in Luke.

c) In spite of the deep spiritual interests which dominate the presentation, the Gospel of John attaches importance to certain external circumstances in the ministry of Jesus. Several localities are named, which are not known from the synoptic tradition, and this can hardly be explained except by the fact that they belong to the "Johannine tradition". K. Kundzinš maintained that the topographical traditions of John stem from the interest taken in these places by later Christian communities who had settled there.[15] But this cannot be proved, and it also fails to explain all the concrete data, as, for instance, the exact localities named in Jerusalem. The geographical and topographical informatiou given in John, apart from what is also in the Synoptics, is by no means slender, as the following survey shows:

---

[15] Kundzinš, *Topographische Überlieferungsstoffe im Johannesevangelium;* contrast the works of Potter, "Topography and Archaeology in the Fourth Gospel" and Merlier, *Itinéraire de Jésus et Chronologie dans le Quatrième Évangile.*

Bethany beyond the Jordan, as a place where John the Baptist baptized, 1:28; cf. 10:40;
Bethsaida, also mentioned several times in the Synoptics, is named 1:44 as the home of Andrew, Peter and Philip;
Cana in Galilee, where the first miracle of Jesus took place (2:1–11) and also the healing at a distance of the official's son (4:46–54), and where Nathanael came from (21:2);
Aenon near Salim, 3:23, another place where John the Baptist baptized;
Jacob's well in Samaria, along with Sychar, 4:5, 11f., 39f.;
the pool of Bethesda with the porticoes, in Jerusalem, 5:2;
Tiberias by the lake of Gennesareth, 6:1,23; cf. 21:1 (not mentioned in the Synoptics);
the pool of Siloam in Jerusalem, 9:7, 11 (cf. Lk 13:40);
Ephraim in Peraea, 11:54;
the Lithostroton (Gabbatha) near the praetorium, 19:13;
Golgotha explained as "the place of a skull", 19:17;
the tomb of Jesus in a garden, 19:41; cf. 20:15.

d) The fourth evangelist gives careful attention to the beginnings of Jesus's activity. He tells of an official mission from the authorities in Jerusalem to John the Baptist, of John's description of himself, his testimony to Jesus (1:19–34), the winning of the first disciples of Jesus, who came from the school of the Baptist (1:35–51), and then gives some episodes from the early activity of Jesus: the first miracle, at the marriage feast of Cana (2:1–11), the cleansing of the temple in Jerusalem (2:13–22), the conversation with the councillor, Nicodemus (3:1–12), baptisms in Judea (3:22–30), return to Galilee with a stay in Samaria (4:1–42), and a second miracle in Galilee (4:46–54). Though the emphasis is on the individual scenes and their intrinsic importance (especially in the conversations with Nicodemus and the Samaritan woman), it is all presented as a connected narrative, which stands out clearly as a sort of preliminary survey of the whole work of Jesus. The themes envisaged are: the self-revelation of Jesus in word and "sign", and the forces of belief and unbelief (see the commentary).

There is a dramatic element in this opening section (cf. 2:17–22; 4:1–3). But the fuller account which follows, though it uses very little "action", is still more dramatic, as has often been observed. The climax in Galilee, when the masses are stirred by the multiplication of the loaves, becomes the turning-point (cf. 6:66), and after the public failure in Galilee, the whole interest is concentrated on Jerusalem. There is a struggle between faith, on the part of the people, and unbelief, on the part of the leading circles (ch. 7), and the rift between Jesus and the rulers grows wider and wider (ch. 8). It is certainly not the intention of the long chapters 9–11 to recount the actual course of the controversy between Jesus and the Jewish authorities. They are dominated by the thought of the self-revelation of Jesus, as light and life of the world. Still, the background remains his historical and permanently significant clash with Jewish unbelief, which is manifested as blindness (9:39 ff.), deception (cf. the imagery of the shepherds in ch. 10) and mortal enmity on the part of the leaders (11:45–53). Thus another dramatic climax is reached in connection with Jesus's greatest "sign", the raising of Lazarus. Popular enthusiasm mounts once more (Jesus's entry into Jerusalem, 12:12–19), but the forces of unbelief are also mobilized for determined action (cf. 11:53, 57; 12:10). More clearly than even in the Synoptics, we are presented with a "history of Jesus", whose aim, however, is to disclose, under the mantle of the historical, the deep and permanent meaning of the event.

e) With this purpose in mind, the evangelist decided to make a considerable change, with regard to his predecessors, in the whole lay-out of his Gospel. The "public ministry" of Jesus is followed by a sharp break, which the evangelist marks by giving a retrospect, a "balance-sheet" (12:37–43), to which he adds further a summary of the revelation given in public (12:44–50). The Passion and Resurrection of Jesus do not follow at once. The evangelist inserts a special section, of not inconsiderable length, which gives the farewell discourses of Jesus to his disciples (ch. 13–17), which represent in his Gospel all Jesus's "intimate" instruction of his disciples. Compared to Mark, where the "private" instructions are scattered throughout the public ministry of Jesus, this represents an important change, not due to historical perspectives, but still the continuation of a tendency which could already be noted in the Synoptics. At the same point of the lay-out in Mark we have the great eschatological discourse (Mk 13), which, though its theological intention is different, still opens up the perspective of the time of the community after Jesus's departure. There is actually the start of a collection of "farewell words" of Jesus in Luke, in the account of the Last Supper (22:24–38). This procedure is again linked up with historical fact: Jesus's last hours together with his closest disciples at their farewell meal. But the historical viewpoint is left behind, for inner reasons: what Jesus has to say to "his own", in contrast to the unbelieving "world", are special matters, pointing on to the future (cf. in particular the Paraclete sayings). But even this section is linked with the Gospel narrative (cf. 13:1, 27–30; 18:1).

f) Jesus's public work in John consists of words and "signs". These two expressions for his activity as revealer are closely connected and reciprocally related. John still speaks of his "teaching", as does Mark, though less frequently (6:59; 7:14 ff., 28; 8:20; 18:19f.), but links it up much more intrinsically to his great miracles, which are regarded as "signs", through which believers get a glimpse of Jesus's "glory" and of the deeper salvific meaning of his external actions (see excursus iv). But it would be a grave misapprehension to see in these signs (according to the mind of the evangelist) merely vivid representations or symbolic illustrations of certain Christological and soteriological truths. It is remarkable how strongly he emphasizes their real and factual nature. Not only do they appear as unmistakable sign-posts and symbols, but they are anchored as far as possible in the basic history; hence the observation that the servants at the marriage feast of Cana knew where the wine came from (2:9). So too the father of the sufferer healed from a distance was informed of the exact moment when the fever left him, the moment, that is, when Jesus uttered the healing word (4:52f.). Hence too the repeated interrogations of the man born blind, so that there can be no doubt about his identity and the fact of his being cured (9:8–34), and the statement that corruption must already have set in, at the raising of Lazarus (11:17, 39). Thus, under another aspect, the "signs" are also characterized as "works" of Jesus, which testify to his mission from the Father (cf. 5:36; 10:25, 37f.; 14:11; 15:24). The evangelist, therefore, wishes that the great miracles which he records should be regarded as proofs of the Messiahship of Jesus (cf. 7:31; 9:32f.; 10:41; 11:47; 12:37), even though as such "proofs" as alone are possible in the realm of history and for the believer, that is, as "testimonies". But this concept of "testimony" also includes the historical experience, the statement of those who have "seen" it, and cannot be reduced to the general experience of believers, who are certain of their faith in the person of Jesus Christ.[16] No matter how criticism judges the historical credibility of the events attested by the fourth evangelist, it cannot fail to admit his intention of attesting and confirming actual events. But with this, the evangelist is in the line of his predecessors, and displays the same intention of attesting and handing on what happened once and for all. The same tendency is also to be seen in his account of the Resurrection (cf. especially 20:7f., 20, 24–29).

g) This is finally confirmed by the evangelist's own statement about the object of his Gospel (20:30). At the end of his work, he expressly returns to the "signs" which he has recorded, and emphasizes that Jesus performed many more in the sight of his disciples. But those recorded in the Gospel are to lead to faith in Jesus as Messiah and Son of God, obviously not merely by the riches of their meaning and their thought-provoking quality, but above all by their reliable attestation. They are works which must convince every man of good will that Jesus is one

[16] Cf. Cullmann, "Εἶδεν καὶ ἐπίστευσεν"; de la Potterie, "La notion de témoignage dans s. Jean" (with further lit.); Schnackenburg, *The Letters of St John*, excursus i.

with the Father (cf. 10:38). If 20:30 already formed the conclusion of a "σημεῖα-source" used by the evangelist (see below, ch. iii), he certainly made the thought his own, when he ended his Gospel with these words, affirming on his own part that the "signs" which he had incorporated had the value of testimony. This means that he understood them as real events, still capable of arousing faith in Jesus the Messiah and Son of God, through the testimony of tradition and the preaching based on it.

The difference, therefore, between the Synoptics and the fourth Gospel is not such that it can be ranged under another *genus litterarium:* either of "revelation discourses" detached from history, with symbolic "signs" to explain them,[17] or of liturgical homilies in which certain words and actions of Jesus were pondered and proposed to faith,[18] or of narratives taking up certain primitive Christian traditions and spinning them out in the manner of the midrash.[19]

2. *The special character of John*

It remains true, however, that the literary genre of "Gospel" needs to be reconsidered and examined theologically, especially in its relationship to "history writing". After recent studies and discussions,

[17] Cf. Strathmann, *Das Evangelium nach Johannes*, p. 22: "The Johannine discourses of Christ are Johannine discourses about Christ. John uses them as a way in which he cast his preaching about Christ . . ."; *ibid.*, p. 23: "Like the discourses, the narratives about the ministry of Jesus have also been kerygmatically stylized, that is, they have been shaped to serve the kerygma." The verdict of Jülicher and Fascher, *Einleitung*, p. 408, is still more radical: "But none of the miracles recounted only in John—the change of water into wine, the healing of the incurable at Bethzatha and of the man born blind, the raising of Lazarus —have any trace of real experience. They are the enhancement of wellknown synoptic narratives, artificially thought out and impressively recounted."

[18] The thesis of the "cultic setting" of John has often been put forward and in various forms. See especially Raney, *The Relation of the Fourth Gospel to the Christian Cultus;* Cullmann, *Urchristentum und Gottesdienst*, E. T.: *Early Christian Worship;* Guilding, *The Fourth Gospel and Jewish Worship*, which maintains that John follows the three-year cycle of Jewish worship: "In the Fourth Gospel the use of the Old Testament lections is entirely systematic and explicit; indeed, the Gospel might fairly be described as a Christian commentary on the lections of the triennial cycle. The Evangelist seems to have wished to preserve a tradition of Jesus' synagogue sermons that has found no place in the synoptic Gospels, and to present them in a form which would be familiar and acceptable to Christian Jews who had been recently excluded from the synagogue" (p. 231). Miss Guilding holds that such discourses as that of the bread of heaven (ch. 6) render faithfully Jesus's own doctrine (*ibid.*).

[19] We must also mention the attempts to explain John according to a typological pattern, e.g. that of the Exodus; cf. Sahlin, *Zur Typologie des Johannesevangeliums;* Enz, "The Book of Exodus as a Literary Type for the Gospel of John"; Smith, "Exodus Typology in the Fourth Gospel". Cf. also Ziener, "Weisheitsbuch und Johannesevangelium".

taking in especially the problem of "the historical Jesus and the kerygmatic Christ",[20] it should be clear that the interests of the evangelists are not primarily "historical", but much rather theological, kerygmatic, catechetical and didactic. In most of these discussions, the Gospel of John is deliberately left aside, on the grounds that it is open to the suspicion of being "non-historical" from the start. Scholars are not lacking, on the other hand, who insist on the amount of valuable historical tradition in John.[21] With regard to the question of the chronology of the Passion in particular, where John can hardly be harmonized with the Synoptics, not a few scholars are inclined to give preference to John, and hence to fix the date of Christ's death as the 14 Nisan—before the "eating of the Pasch", cf. 18:28.[22] In another old controversy, namely as to whether the Jews then possessed the right to inflict capital punishment *(ius gladii)*, opinion also seems to be coming down on the side of Jn 18:31 ("It is not lawful for us to put any man to death"), though here again contradiction is not lacking.[23] The secret meeting of the council, reported only in Jn 11:47–53, at which the death of Jesus was decided, also deserves credence, at least with regard to the (political) motives given there for Jesus's removal. Other elements, however, such as the placing of the cleansing of the temple at the beginning of Jesus's public activity (2:13–22), leave the historian sceptical. Each of these questions must be examined on its merits, and hence are reserved for the commentary. It is also to be considered that the author may have had

---

[20] Cf. the collective works Ristow and Matthiae, ed., *Der historische Jesus und der kerygmatische Christus*, and Schubert, ed., *Der historische Jesus und der Christus unseres Glaubens;* also Robinson, *The New Quest of the Historical Jesus;* Bultmann, *Das Verhältnis der urchristlichen Christusbotschaft zum historischen Jesus* (with lit.); Hahn, Lohff and Bornkamm, *Die Frage nach dem historischen Jesus;* Schnackenburg, "Zur Formgeschichtlichen Methode in der Evangelienforschung".

[21] See e.g. Michaelis, *Einleitung*, pp. 104 f.; Edwards, *The Disciple Who Wrote These Things;* Gyllenberg, "Die Anfänge der johanneischen Tradition"; Stauffer, "Probleme der Priestertradition"; Potter, "Topography and Archaeology in the Fourth Gospel"; Robinson, "The New Look on the Fourth Gospel"; Higgins, *The Historicity of the Fourth Gospel* (independent of the Synoptics, early traditions, perhaps not the "last" of the Gospels); Merlier, *Itinéraires de Jésus et chronologie dans le quatrième Évangile* (finds that it has been re-edited); Stauffer, "Historische Elemente im vierten Evangelium"; Dodd, *Historical Tradition in the Fourth Gospel.*

[22] So e.g. Dibelius, *Jesus*, pp. 115 f., E. T.: pp. 118 f.; Olmstead, *Jesus in the Light of History*, pp. 279 f.; Bornkamm, *Jesus von Nazareth*, p. 147; Stauffer, *Jesus. Gestalt und Geschichte*, p. 86; Blinzler, *Der Prozess Jesu*, pp. 78–81, E. T.: *The Trial of Jesus*, pp. 72–80; Strobel, "Der Termin des Todes Jesu"; Ruckstuhl, *Die Chronologie des letzten Mahles und des Leidens Jesu*, p. 17.

[23] The correctness of Jn 18:31b is defended at length in Blinzler, *Der Prozess Jesu*, pp. 163–74, E. T.: pp. 157–63, but attacked again recently by Winter, *On the Trial of Jesus*, pp. 67–74, 75–90.

certain reliable items of information, not available to the Synoptics, and inserted them into his work, but aimed on the whole at a presentation entirely dominated by theological thinking, with little interest in the historical. Finally—and this is the most attractive solution, which we shall pursue in this commentary—he may have used a foundation of good historical and topographical knowledge on which to develop a profounder theological vision of the "history" of Jesus, which uses the eyes of faith to go to the root, as it were, of the historical events and external things and strives to reveal the secret divine thoughts which they enshrine.

That the fourth evangelist did not aim at a "historical" presentation in the modern sense may be seen from his rendering of Jesus's words. When we compare the simple, vivid language of Jesus in the Synoptics, so full of images and parables, with the profoundly theological discourses in John, we feel ourselves in another world with the latter. The whole diction is transposed to a higher plane, enriched with new concepts (key theological concepts like "life", "light", "truth", "being born of God", etc.), characterized by highly significant formulae ("I am", "you in me and I in you", "abide in", etc.) and by dualistic-sounding contrasts ("light—darkness", "life—death", "to be from below—from above", "truth—lie"). Ambiguous expressions recur—"to raise up", "to see", in a material and a spiritual sense, etc.;[24] the whole movement of thought is different (see below, ch. vi). This cannot be explained, though the attempt was sometimes made earlier, by the Johannine discourses being addressed to different sets of hearers, under different circumstances and taking up new subjects of debate. The Synoptics often show Jesus engaged in debate with opponents, in theological controversy and the like, but we never hear the language of John. And then, the Johannine Jesus speaks the same type of language as the evangelist himself (cf. the prologue, the summary in 12:44–50 and 3:13–31, 31–36 according to the explanation given in the commentary), and—what is still more telling—as the author of 1 John. It cannot, therefore, be doubted that John presents us with the theological language of the author. His faithfulness in rendering the thoughts and words of Jesus is not thereby decided; it is merely presented as a problem.

That the fourth evangelist does not conform to our "historical" norms in presenting his version of the words of Jesus, may be seen not only from formal, external criteria, but also from their subject-matter. The Johannine Jesus is the bringer of a revelation which apparently retains little contact with the proclamation of the kingdom of God on the

[24] Cf. Cullmann, "Der johanneische Gebrauch doppeldeutiger Ausdrücke als Schlüssel zum Verständnis des vierten Evangeliums".

lips of the Jesus of the Synoptics. (The expression ἡ βασιλεία τοῦ Θεοῦ occurs only in 3:3, 5, and even there with a palpable shift of meaning; see *ad loc.).* We say "apparently", because here too a proper theological estimation of the eschatological thought of John can lead to profounder insight, which reveals what is common to both.[25] But then one would have to presuppose a transposition of the message of Jesus in terms of Johannine theology, which is precisely the problem posed by the discourses of Jesus in John, and anticipates the answer we are looking for. What the Johannine Jesus reveals, constantly and indeed exclusively, is himself, and the theological principle behind this procedure is disclosed with all desirable clarity in the discourse on "the goal and the way" (14:4–11): no one attains the Father and hence salvation, except through him. He himself, in his person, is the "way", because he is the only true and full revelation of the Father (v. 9b), and he alone can lead those who believe in him to the realm of the divine and heavenly (cf. v. 2f.). This role of Jesus as mediator of salvation is indeed presupposed in the Synoptics and (at least according to the faith of the primitive Church) also contained implicitly in the preaching of the Jesus of the Synoptics. But it is scarcely audible in the words and discourses of Jesus transmitted by the Synoptics, and, historically speaking, probability is all on the side of the fact that Jesus never spoke publicly of himself in the way in which he constantly does in John.[26] The self-revelation of Jesus in John—which must be carefully weighed in each concrete utterance, with regard, for instance, to his Messiahship,[27] to avoid over-hasty rejection of all historical basis—stems from a theological interpretation of the evangelist, which must be recognized as such. Whether it is legitimate or not is another question.

Once one has noticed this basic feature of the Johannine discourse, one is no longer surprised that sometimes the various matters treated of in them have no "historical" coordinates. The difficulty of Jesus's speaking at the very beginning of his activity about the mystery of his "exaltation" (on the cross), when addressing the Jewish councillor, Nicodemus, disappears in the hypothesis of the literary history of the passage put forward in the commentary. But even so the dialogue remains difficult enough, historically speaking, with regard to its subject-matter (cf. 3:3–8), unless we keep in mind the theological interpretation of the

---

[25] Cf. Stählin, "Zum Problem der johanneischen Eschatologie"; Müller, *Das Heilsgeschehen im Johannesevangelium;* van Hartingsveld, *Die Eschatologie des Johannesevangeliums;* Blank, *Krisis. Untersuchungen zur johanneischen Christologie und Eschatologie.*

[26] The "Johannine logion", Mt 11:25 ff., Lk 10:21 f., is important for the Johannine term "Son", but is specifically stated to be a special revelation for the disciples (the "little ones"). It is only at the end, before the Sanhedrin, that Jesus openly proclaims his Messiahship (Mk 14:62 par.).

[27] Cf. Schnackenburg, "Die Messiasfrage im Johannesevangelium".

evangelist, whose interest goes beyond the historical to envisage the Christian reader. This is also true of the dialogue with the Samaritan woman, especially with regard to the theme of "adoration in spirit and truth" (4:21–24). It is likewise hardly possible, in view of the Synoptics, that Jesus should have spoken openly, in front of unbelieving Jews, of the power given him (the Son) to give life and to judge (cf. 5:20–30), though some connection with the "Son of Man" sayings in the Synoptics cannot be ruled out. The situation of at least one of the discourses allows of a comparison with the Synoptics—the discourse about the bread of life which follows the great miracle of the loaves (ch. 6). Apart from other difficulties, the allusion to the sacrificial death of Jesus (6:51b), made at the climax of the Galilean ministry, is in conflict with the fact that according to Mk 8:31 par., it is only after Peter's confession of faith at Caesarea Philippi (cf. Jn 6:68f.) that Jesus begins to unveil the mystery of his death. And this is to his disciples, not to the people, with even Peter reacting strongly against it. These examples, which could easily be increased, suffice to prove that the discourses in John cannot and do not intend to be historical reporting or a word for word record.

But then what are they? Are they "words of the Christ", inspired by faith and placed on the lips of Jesus, because according to the faith of the writer Jesus could and must have spoken in this way? Or are they perhaps the words of the risen Lord from on high, addressing his community on earth through an inspired evangelist, conscious of his charismatic enlightenment from the Holy Spirit? This idea was chiefly suggested by the farewell discourses, and proof for it was sought in the "high priestly prayer" (ch. 17). The thesis that it is Christ ascended into heaven who speaks in the Johannine Jesus needs serious testing.[28] Whatever one thinks of the "historical" character of his words, it cannot be proved from the evangelist's presentation, from the tenses he uses and the subject-matter, that Jesus *must* already be speaking as the risen and glorified Lord. It is more correct to say that in the mind of the evangelist the earthly Jesus speaks, though always fully conscious of his imminent "exaltation" which begins with the Crucifixion. To be even more exact, one should say that he is fully conscious of his divine origin (meaning also

[28] Cf. Strathmann, *Das Evangelium nach Johannes*, p. 22; Michaelis, *Einleitung*, p. 118. Kundziņš, "Character und Ursprung der johanneischen Reden" and "Zur Diskussion über die Ego-Eimi-Sprüche im Johannesevangelium" looks for the origin of the discourses in the first person to the primitive Christian experience of revelation and considers them as utterances of the risen Christ. Schulz, *Komposition und Herkunft der johanneischen Reden*, explains the *Ego-Eimi* sayings, and likewise the parabolic discourses, as the authoritative self-manifestation of the exalted and present Lord (cf. pp. 128 ff., 144–9). On Jn 17 cf. George, "'L'heure' de Jean XVII".

pre-existence, cf. 1:1f.; 8:58), and his return to the Father, which means regaining his ancient glory (17:5), and a new glorification by transmitting the divine life to all who believe (17:2). In other words, he speaks in full consciousness of his unity with the Father, which does not cease on earth, but is merely presented otherwise in the incarnate Word. But this gives us the real principle at the base of the "Johannine" re-moulding of the discourses of Jesus. The deep faith of the writer moved him to clothe the thoughts and words of Jesus in their present dress, but his intention is to let the earthly Jesus speak and express his own thoughts. This may look from outside as if the evangelist put his own words on the lips of Jesus, and the critic has every right to test the historicity of the thoughts thus expressed. But he must first take cognizance of the intention of the evangelist (who is writing a "Gospel") and admit that he wishes Jesus to be heard, and not himself.

There is a big difference therefore between the two approaches. One holds definitely that the discourses of Jesus in John have been freely (and consciously) invented as "discourses of Christ". The other holds that according to the intention of the evangelist they are discourses of Jesus, which have indeed passed through the medium of faith. In the second case, the question of historicity is secondary and in the nature of a corollary, and need not necessarily be answered in the negative, as long as one keeps in mind the type of "historicity" which the evangelist himself envisaged.[29] It is basically the same category which the Synoptics also force on our attention, since their presentation of the historical event is also penetrated by faith in Jesus, the Christ and Son of God. Tradition was permeated and interpreted by the light of faith, and the only difference in John is that this process has here reached its climax, so that the fourth Gospel is a presentation completely dominated by the vision of faith.

Catholic exegesis must also be prepared to think out these questions anew. Catholics were warned by the answer of the Biblical Commission of 29 May 1907 not to take the discourses of Christ in the fourth Gospel as mere "compositiones theologicas scriptoris, licet in ore Domini positas" *(Enchiridion Biblicum,* 189). But they were also urged, by Pope Pius XII's encyclical on the Bible, 30 September 1943, to investigate "quid dicendi forma seu litterarum genus ab hagiographo adhibitum, ad veram et genuinam conferat interpretationem" *(Enchiridion Biblicum,* 560). The task now urgently imposed by present-day problems is to study the peculiar nature of the Gospels as historico-kerygmatic accounts of the work of Jesus. More precisely, it is to examine the intermingling of the historically relevant and the kerygmatically challenging, according to the

---

[29] Cf. Brown, "The Problem of History in John"; Léon-Dufour, *Les évangiles*, pp. 112–43.

intention of the evangelists. What matters is the intention of each writer, not our ideas of how he ought to have written his history, according to our historical norms. In the case of the fourth evangelist, it was clearly not his intention to offer his readers a purely historical chronicle of events. He above all is most profoundly convinced that the mere facts, including even the greatest miracle in Jesus's work, are impotent to lead closed minds to faith (cf. 9:30–34; 10:37ff.; 11:45–50; 12:37, 42f.). He places his reader from the very beginning in the perspective of his own faith (cf. 1:14 b–c, 16), to produce new faith by his own believing testimony—which is in fact a salutary piece of instruction for those who imagine that they can provide faith with its surest foundation by the reconstruction of historical facts. This does not, of course, absolve us from the duty of testing his assertions as far as possible, which obliges us to explore every avenue opened up by modern scientific methods. This includes a comparison of the matter used by the fourth evangelist with that of the Synoptics, the investigation of his sources and of the genesis of the fourth Gospel in general, the question of authorship, which is, of course, not of itself decisive, and other matters which will be dealt with below.

The purpose of these investigations, however, is not primarily to gain greater historical certainty, but to get a better and profounder understanding of the evangelist's own way of thinking, of his theological language and assertions. The fourth Gospel too has a historical situation which must be determined exactly. As the Gospel itself strives to make the eschatological revelation audible by narrating and bearing witness to the historical coming and work of the incarnate Logos, so too, in its temporal dress, we must perceive the eternal message which the Gospel wishes to bring us.

CHAPTER II

Relationship to the Synoptics

We have been considering the structural relationship between John and the Synoptics as written Gospels. We must now give an account of the matter embodied in his narrative in relation to the Synoptics, that is, of the contacts and differences which ensue from his choice and presentation of his matter, and of the reason for them. Was the author acquainted with the Synoptics, so that he could draw on them at least from memory, or does he provide a completely independent tradition? In the first case, the further question of his attitude to them arises. Did he intend to complete them,[1] to compete with them, to surpass them[2] or even to replace them?[3] It might also be that he knew only one or other of the synoptic Gospels, or that he had sources similar to them. Finally, what is the relationship of his special traditions, where the Synoptics offer no comparable matter, to the parts which have contacts with the Synoptics? Why did he insert these rather than other elements into his Gospel?

This is a difficult set of problems, on which there is as yet no agreement among scholars, in spite of exact comparisons being possible. It may be

---

[1] So the Church writers, cf. Clement of Alexandria in Eusebius, *Hist. eccles.*, VI, 14, 7; Origen, *Comm. in Jo.*, 3 f.; Eusebius, *Hist. eccles.*, III, 24, 7–13 (his own verdict); Epiphanius, *Pan.*, 51; Augustine, *De consensu evangelistarum*, IV, 11–20. More recently cf. Zahn, *Einleitung*, vol. II, p. 513, who holds that John always has the Synoptics in mind and proceeds on the assumption that their narratives are known, eliminating possible misunderstandings, clarifying what they have left obscure and correcting inexactitudes, but on the whole confirming their account, both by what he repeats and what he omits but takes for granted as known from their presentation. This notion of "supplementing" the Synoptics, however, can take various forms, cf. Sigge, *Das Johannesevangelium und die Synoptiker*, pp. 10–16, 26–34.

[2] Cf. especially Overbeck, *Das Johannesevangelium*. But the intention of outdoing the Synoptics is said to imply that of displacing them (pp. 113–16), which opens up the hypothesis of "displacement"; cf. Sigge, pp. 34–40.

[3] Here the most important work is that of Windisch, *Johannes und die Synoptiker*, which is discussed by Sigge.

said in general that earlier scholars were rather inclined to think that John knew the Synoptics, and then tried to define the relationship on this basis. But more recently, there is a greater tendency to deny all literary relationships and to assert the independence of the Johannine tradition, whose contacts with the Synoptics would be explained by the oral tradition existing before or alongside of the creation of the synoptic Gospels.[4] No verdict can be arrived at with any sort of certainty without an exact comparison of the individual passages. This cannot be attempted here, and must be left to special studies. What follows should be considered merely as an orientation and a cautious effort to form a judgment. For practical reasons, the longer passages in the narrative matter may be treated first, and then the minor contacts which occur in certain ("synoptic") logia.

1. Common narrative passages

We can learn much about the procedures of the fourth evangelist from his account of John the Baptist, a figure whose impact was also described by the Synoptics. On the whole, John gives new and independent matter: the synoptic description of the desert preacher's mode of life disappears, and there is no account of his preaching repentance or baptizing; even the baptism of Jesus is not reported. The interest is concentrated instead on the "testimony" given to Jesus by this "man sent by God": Jesus is the promised Messiah, he who baptizes with the Spirit. However, it is taken for granted that the readers know about Jesus's baptism (cf. 1:32f.), so that one might think that here the author meant to "complete" the story: so too in the following passage about some disciples of John going over to Jesus (1:35–41). But the evangelist is not concerned with completing our historical knowledge. He tells us nothing, for instance, about why Jesus submitted himself to the baptism of repentance, though this was a question which the early Church was asking, according to Mt 3:14f. We learn nothing about the exact words of the voice from heaven, though this is not given in the same form by each of the Synoptics.[5] Nor does the localization in Bethany, 1:28, betray any tendency to fill up the gaps left

[4] Sigge presupposes knowledge of the three Synoptics, but holds that John is substantially independent and pursues its own goal. Knowledge of Mark and Luke is assumed by Barrett in his commentary, pp. 34–45; Kümmel, *Einleitung*, pp. 136 ff. (from memory). The contrary position is maintained by Gardner-Smith, *Saint John and the Synoptic Gospels;* Noack, *Zur johanneischen Tradition;* Dodd, *Historical Tradition*. Cf. the account of research given by Mitton, "The Provenance of the Fourth Gospel".

[5] The voice from heaven may be deduced from Jn 1:34, cf. Cullmann, *Urchristentum*, pp. 64 f.; Jeremias, "παῖς θεοῦ", p. 699; see the commentary.

by the Synoptics, because it seems to be rather in the character of a final note, indicating that the account of the interrogation of the Baptist by the mission from Jerusalem is in the nature of trustworthy testimony. The Christological interest, the effort to display John the Baptist as a "witness" for Jesus, dominates so strongly that conscious reflection on the synoptic narrative must be ruled out.

The cleansing of the temple (2:13–22) is the next passage which has contacts with the synoptic tradition. Here we notice first of all that, in contrast to the Synoptics, it is placed at the beginning of the public ministry. But there is no indication that the evangelist meant to challenge the synoptic presentation. In John too, the menacing situation in which Jesus found himself is explained not so much by the immediate interrogation by "the Jews" (2:18) as by the scriptural prophecy behind 2:17, which, in conjunction with 2:22, undoubtedly points to the death of Jesus (see commentary). In putting the cleansing of the temple at the beginning, the author must have had other reasons than a wish to correct the Synoptics. The description of the action taken against the traders and money-changers has features of its own (sellers of sheep and oxen, a whip of cords, Jesus's words) and some special vocabulary (κερματισταί, ἀνατρέπω), so that knowledge of the actual text of the Synoptics cannot be deduced. The account of the healing at a distance (4:46–54), which modern research is inclined to identify with the event recorded in Mt 8:5–13 and Lk 7:1–10, differs so much from the Synoptics that there can be no question of literary dependence. When we also take into account the fact that this miracle is said to be the "second sign" after the miracle of the wine at Cana, it becomes practically certain that the fourth evangelist had information of his own, independent of the Synoptics—perhaps a "σημεῖα-source".[6] This makes it all the more difficult to reduce the healing of the cripple in ch. 5 to the synoptic narrative of Mk 2:1–12 or the like, or the healing of the man born blind, ch. 9, to one of the miraculous cures of blindness in the Synoptics. In any case, real synoptic parallels are more readily recognizable.

A serious problem in this connection is presented by the complex of narratives in Jn 6. Here we have not merelys imilarities in the presentation of the multiplication of the loaves and the walking on the waters, but the same sequence of events as is given in the "Marcan framework":

Multiplication of loaves Jn 6:1–13; Mk 6:34–44
Walking on the waters Jn 6:16–21; Mk 6:45–52
Return to west shore Jn 6:24f. (Capernaum); Mk 6:53 (Gennesaret)
Demand for a sign Jn 6:30; Mk 8:11
Confession of Peter Jn 6:68f.; Mk 8:29

[6] Schnackenburg, "Zur Traditionsgeschichte von Joh 4:46–54".

Did the fourth evangelist know the Marcan presentation and re-mould it in his own way? It must, of course, be remembered that in our canonical Mark some items are inserted between the return to the west shore and the demand for a sign: the more doctrinal section, 7:1–23; the Syro-phoenician woman, 7:24–30; the healing of a deaf mute, 7:31–37; the feeding of the four thousand, 8:1–10; so too before the confession of Peter Mark has the discourse on leaven (8:14–21) and the healing of the blind man of Bethsaida (8:22–26). Did our evangelist have the narrative in a shorter form—which contained only one multiplication of bread?[7] Did he create a continuity for his own purposes? A detailed comparison also brings out some awkward points. The multiplication of the loaves provides some notable coincidences: there is "green grass" (Mk 6:39) or "much grass" (Jn 6:10) in the place; five loaves and two fishes are available (Mk 6:38; Jn 6:9); the comment of the disciples (Mk 6:37; Jn 6:7) alludes to "two hundred denarii"; the left-overs fill "twelve baskets" (Mk 6:43; Jn 6:13); the number fed and contented was about "five thousand" (Mk 6:44; Jn 6:10). But along with this there are notable differences: in John the whole initiative comes from Jesus, it is not yet evening, Jesus tests the attitude of his disciples, at the end of the scene the participants try to make Jesus the Messianic king[8] and so on. The walking on the waters is, on the whole, recounted differently, the only element remaining unchanged being the central theme, Jesus's saying to his disciples, "It is I, fear not" (Mk 6:50; Jn 6:20). In contrast to the account of the bread miracle, that of the walking on the waters, as given by John, gives the impression of being more independent, and perhaps more primitive.[9] The rest of the group of narratives, however, is completely Johannine in its handling, including the demand for a sign and the confession of Peter. So all sorts of explanation are possible: direct knowledge of the Marcan presentation, with deliberate re-moulding; a passing acquaintanceship, based solely perhaps on hearing it as it was rendered, say, in the liturgy; contacts confined to oral tradition, which at this point retained the sequence fairly rigidly; use of a special source (a σημεῖα-source) with a similar account of the events, though with some differences (as in the walking on the waters). In considering these solu-

---

[7] Schmid, *Das Evangelium nach Markus*, pp. 126–9, 145–8; Blinzler, "Brotbrechen", cols. 709 f.; Ziener, "Die Brotwunder im Markusevangelium", are inclined to think of only one multiplication of loaves; contrast Knackstedt, "De duplici miraculo multiplicationis panum"; id., "Die beiden Brotvermehrungen im Evangelium".

[8] This is historically probable, cf. Blinzler, "Eine Bemerkung zum Geschichtsrahmen des Johannesevangeliums"; id., in *Novum Testamentum* 2 (1957), pp. 44 ff.; Gärtner, "John 6 and the Jewish Passover", pp. 38 f.

[9] Cf. Goodenough, "John a Primitive Gospel", esp. pp. 156 ff.; Mendner, "Zum Problem Johannes und die Synoptiker", esp. pp. 289–94.

tions, one must of course also keep in mind the evangelist's own modifications—especially with regard to the discussion and discourse in the synagogue of Capernaum, and the confession of Peter.

The anointing at Bethany (Jn 12:1–8) displays still closer associations with the Marcan narrative. The oil is described in terms not found together elsewhere as νάρδος πιστική (Mk 14:3; Jn 12:3); the indication of its value, "(more than) three hundred denarii", is found only in Mk 14:5 and Jn 12:5; Jesus's answer to his indignant companions (or to Judas) contains the same turn of speech, ἄφετε αὐτήν (Mk 14:6), ἄφες αὐτήν (Jn 12:7), which fits in badly in John, though not in Mark.[10] These are strong indications of knowledge of Mark in its written form; but then again, the Johannine account diverges considerably from Mark in the general presentation and orientation. These remarkable verbal parallels to Mark remain exceptional, so that we are not perhaps justified in assuming a literary acquaintanceship with Mark. Nowhere else, either at the entry into Jerusalem or in the Passion narrative, do we meet with such clear echoes of Mark.

Special contacts between Matthew and John are rare and unimportant. Only two special traits are to be noted in the narrative: at the moment of his arrest, Jesus says to Peter according to Mt 26:52: "Return your sword to its place"; according to Jn 18:11, "Put your sword into its sheathe". Matthew continues with matter of its own, while John has the saying about the chalice to be drunk, a metaphor familiar from the synoptic tradition (cf. Mk 10:38 par.; Mt 20:22; Mk 14:36 par.); the agreement need not mean very much. More important are the contacts in the account of the appearance of the risen Lord to Mary Magdalene (Jn 20:14–17), to the women (Mt 28:8ff.). It is most probably the same tradition, which is given more exactly by John where the apparition is confined to Mary Magdalene. In Matthew's (summary) account, it is to the women returning from the tomb. There are remarkable parallels (the adoration, Jesus's words: "Go and tell my *brothers*"), but also discrepancies: in Matthew the women embrace Jesus's feet (v. 9), while according to John Jesus says to Mary Magdalene, "Let me go!" (v. 17). The passage probably comes from the same strand of oral tradition, and the Johannine version seems to be the more primitive.[11]

The Lukan tradition, however, has affinities with the Johannine which deserve closer attention.[12] The following list refers only to the longer narrative passages:

---

[10] Cf. Blinzler, *Der Prozess Jesu*, pp. 301 f.; Dodd, *Historical Tradition*, pp. 167 ff.

[11] Cf. Benoît, "Marie-Madeleine et les disciples au tombeau selon Jean 20:1–18".

[12] Cf. Schniewind, *Die Parallelperikopen bei Lukas und Johannes;* Osty, "Les points de contact entre le récit de la Passion dans saint Luc et saint Jean"; Léon-Dufour, "Récits de la Passion", cols. 1438–44; Bailey, *The Traditions Common to the Gospels of Luke and John.*

a) The Messianic preaching of the Baptist. In Lk 3:15, as in Jn 1:19f., the question arises as to whether the Baptist is the Messiah.

b) The great catch of fish. Only Lk 5:1–11 tells of such a catch, at the beginning of Jesus's activity. There is a certain parallel in the Johannine "appendix", 21:1–19.

c) The anointing. In the anointing done by the unnamed sinner (Lk 7:36–50) there are two features which also stand out in the Johannine story of the anointing of Jesus in Bethany by Mary, the sister of Lazarus and Martha. The sinner wets Jesus's feet with her tears and dries them with her hair, and then anoints them (Lk 7:38); in Jn 12:3, Mary likewise anoints Jesus's feet (in Matthew and Mark the head), and dries them with her hair.

d) The sisters of Bethany. At the anointing in John, we hear of the sisters Martha and Mary, the former of whom "served" (12:2), while the latter poured out the precious oil (12:3), which reminds us of the specifically Lukan episode (Lk 10:38–42). It is remarkable that the two women are named only by these evangelists. Then there is the account in John of the raising of their brother Lazarus from the dead (ch. 11), and the name occurs only here and in the parable in Lk 16:19–31. Critical research has sometimes sought in the final sentence, Lk 16:30f., the "basis" of the "symbolic" narrative of Jn 11—a very dubious hypothesis. But there could be some connection.[13]

e) Jesus's entry into Jerusalem. A special feature of Luke and John is that the crowd expressly acclaims Jesus as "the king (of Israel)", Luke 19:38; Jn 12:13. The mention of the Pharisees (only Lk 19:39; Jn 12:19) has, however, a different ring in each case.

f) At the last supper. Luke already gives a grouping of farewell words (Lk 22:24–38), which looks like the first stage of the farewell discourses in John. They are different in content; but the saying about service (Lk 22:27) recalls the washing of the feet in John (13:4–15).

g) Judas and the arrest. According to Lk 22:3, Satan enters Judas Iscariot; according to Jn 13:2, the devil puts it into his heart to betray Jesus. At the arrest, Jesus says in Lk 22:53, "This is your hour and the power of darkness", which is a Johannine idea (cf. Jn 13:30; 19:11; also 9:4; 11:10; 12:35). Some agreement in external detail may also be noted, e.g., Lk 12:39 and Jn 18:2; the traitor's kiss, contrary to Mark and Matthew, is not mentioned; Annas, before whom Jesus is led

---

[13] Two recent works reject a purely symbolic explanation and hold that there is a good traditional basis: W. Wilkens, "Die Erweckung des Lazarus"; R. Dunkerly, "Lazarus", who sees the relationship between Jn 11 and Lk 16 inversed: "But the parable might have been told and written with the knowledge of an actual incident in mind, before any report of it had been written down" (p. 322).

according to John 18:13, 24, is given the title of "the high priest" in Acts 4:6.[14]

h) Jewish proceedings against Jesus, Peter's denial. Neither of the evangelists speaks of a formal night session of the Sanhedrin to judge Jesus's case; the examination of the witnesses drops out; nothing is said of silence on the part of Jesus. Does this go back to a different tradition from Mark-Matthew? (This problem cannot be discussed here). In the denial scene, in Luke and John, the second denial is not occasioned by a maidservant; Lk 22:58 makes it a ἕτερος, Jn 18:18, 25 servants and police; the third is not occasioned by the bystanders, but in Luke 22:59 by an ἄλλος τις, in Jn 18:26 by a servant of the high priest, a kinsman of Malchus (cf. 18:10).

i) The trial before Pilate. Both evangelists say that the Roman governor declared three times that Jesus was innocent, not at the same point of their narrative (Lk 23:4, 14f., 22; Jn 18:38; 19:4, 6), but in similar terms. The general picture displays a certain uniformity, in spite of divergence in the actual sequence: the people, not its leaders, are the chief actors; more accusations are made against Jesus; less blame is attached to the Roman judge than even in Mark-Matthew.

j) The Passion. Here Luke and John agree against Mark-Matthew only in their omissions: they say nothing of a drink to induce numbness, nor of the mockers under the cross. But the presentations as a whole are differently orientated.

k) Burial and Resurrection. Lk 23:53 and Jn 19:41 stress more strongly than Mt 27:60 that Jesus's tomb was a new one, not yet used for a burial. An important point is the fact that in Luke and John the appearances of Jesus after the Resurrection are confined to Jerusalem or its neighbourhood. The reasons for this in Luke are clearly theological (cf. Lk 24:6 and Mk 16:7; Mt 28:7); but John too is preoccupied with Jerusalem. The agreement between the third and fourth evangelists on this point is certainly not accidental. It stems from their whole theological attitude.

In view of all this, it is hardly possible to deny links between Luke and John in the history of tradition; but they are not so close as to allow us to affirm that the fourth evangelist had the Gospel of St Luke before his eyes and made use of it.[15] The idea that the fourth evangelist knew Luke and

---

[14] Does Luke think that Annas was the official high priest? Cf. Wellhausen's commentary, p. 81; Conzelmann, *Apostelgeschichte* on Acts 4:6. But deposed high priests retained their title; cf. Jeremias, *Jerusalem zur Zeit Jesu*, vol. II, pp. 14 f.; Blinzler, *Der Prozess Jesu*, pp. 87 f., E. T.: p. 83. On the relationship between the Lucan and Johannine tradition on the proceedings, cf. Schniewind, *Parallelperikopen*, p. 40.

[15] This is considered possible by Barrett in his commentary, pp. 36 f.; Bailey, *Traditions*, argues in many cases for John's direct knowledge of Luke, as regards the anointing at Bethany (p. 8) the prediction of Peter's denial (p. 39), the thought of the farewell discourses

drew on it from memory,[16] is also open to serious doubt. His Bethany tradition, with the brother and two sisters, is more detailed and definite, and so can hardly be merely a subsequent combination and elaboration of Lukan data. He is also more exactly informed about Jerusalem, and probably bases himself on a particular group of disciples there (cf. Nicodemus, 3:1; 7:50; 19:39; the disciples from Judea, 7:3; the disciple known to the high priest, 18:15). His account of the trial and Passion is independent. If he knew Luke, it would be hard to understand why he passed over the scene with Herod (Lk 23:6–16), which could have been of use to him in his portrayal of Jesus's kingship. We should probably envisage an earlier stage in the pre-history of the composition of these gospels, and assign the formation of the common tradition with its various contacts to this previous stage, which is no longer accessible to us. It is clear that both writers drew heavily on a tradition concentrated on Judea and Jerusalem. If the existence of a "pre-synoptic" form of John, independent of the Synoptics, may be deduced,[17] it is easy to think that St Luke had access to sources close to this "Johannine tradition" (see further below). The explanation that he heard the author of the tradition himself, and was influenced by him for many of his basic concepts,[18] presupposes, however, certain ideas about the former (John the son of Zebedee) and about Luke himself (a stay in Judea), which would need to be examined further. An adequate explanation would be that Luke was in a position to make use of sources of information from these regions and from these Christian circles. There are episodes in Luke which have to some extent a more primitive ring and provide more exact details, as for instance the anointing (Lk 7:36–50); the information about the women, especially Mary Magdalene (8:1 ff.); these could be explained by the fact that here his sources were more abundant than the "Johannine tradition" in its early form. So too for Mt 28:8 ff. an isolated item of such tradition could be assumed as known to the first evangelist. In any case, the narrative episodes in John, even where they furnish notable contacts

(p. 45), the arrest (pp. 51 ff.), important traits of the discussion with Pilate (pp. 64–67), the story of the Passion (pp. 78–84), the account of the Resurrection apparitions (pp. 92 f.).

[16] As regards Mark, Lee, "St Mark and the Fourth Gospel", says: "These literary parallels seem to us strong enough to reach the conclusion that John had use of the Gospel of Mark and had Mark's programme in mind during the writing of his narrative" (p. 58). As regards Mark and Luke, Kümmel says, *Einleitung*, p. 138: "The author clearly has the Gospels of Mark and Luke in mind and draws on them from memory as far as it serves his purpose."

[17] This view is gaining ground, cf. Osty, "Les points de contact", p. 154; Lee, "St. Mark and the Fourth Gospel", p. 50; Benoît, "Marie Madeleine", p. 152; Braun, *Jean le Théologien*, pp. 396 f.; Dodd, *Historical Tradition*, pp. 424–32.

[18] Osty, "Les points de contact", p. 154: "Luc a donc du entendre Jean, recueillir quelques-uns de ses propos et s'en inspirer."

with the synoptic tradition, can hardly go back to a reading of the synoptic Gospels or to the memory of such reading.

2. Common logia

Apart from parallels and contacts in the narrative, there are also brief sayings in John which are remarkably close to the text of the Synoptics, and hence have been called, not without some justification "synoptic logia".[19] An exact comparison demands the use of a synopsis; here it must suffice to indicate the type of relationship, that is, the common matter and the divergencies.

First there are the words of the Baptist in Jn 1:27 (cf. Mk 1:7 par.). The metaphor of "untying the shoe-laces" is common to John and to Matthew and Luke, while Mt 3:11 reads "carry his shoes"; John agrees with Mark and Matthew in the expression "he who is coming" (Mk: ἔρχεται). It is to be noted that John uses the word ἄξιος (with a ἵνα-clause) for "worthy", while the Synoptics have ἱκανός (with the infinitive). In the same logion in Acts 13: 25, St Luke also uses ἄξιος; hence his ἱκανός in the account of the baptism points to literary influences (cf. also Mt 8:8, par. Lk 7:6), to which John did not yield. The fourth evangelist knows the same logion, but gives it in his own way. He certainly takes it from the tradition (unless Jn 1:27 is to be regarded, for reasons of literary criticism, as a redactional addition), and uses it in such a way that we are given to think that the words of the Baptist (1:15, 30), which he alone gives, may be an interpretation of the ἰσχυρότερος (cf. the commentary).

From Jn 1:33 (cf. 26 a, 31 c) we may deduce the same saying as is transmitted in Mk 1:8 (hence in conjunction with the above): "I have baptized you with water, but he will baptize you with holy Spirit" (where Mt 3:11 and Lk 3:16 add "and with fire"). Once more knowledge of a synoptic logion is confirmed, as is also the freedom of its handling. Jn 1:34 is probably based on the voice from heaven at the baptism, as given in the Synoptics (cf. the commentary).

Jn 1:42 (the name Cephas for Simon-Peter) mentions the same fact as Mk 3:16 and Mt 16:18, but in a different context. A deliberate correction, pointing out that the name was not first given at the choice of the twelve (Mk) or at Caesarea Philippi (Mt) does not seem to be intended.

The logion Jn 1:51 has given rise to many conjectures, as for instance that it is a Johannine re-moulding of Mk 14:62 par. The Johannine

[19] Cf. Noack, *Zur johanneischen Tradition*, pp. 89–109.

"Son of Man" logia may certainly be considered to be part of a definite tradition,[20] in which the synoptic tradition represents an intermediate stage. But the form and content of the logion Jn 1:51 make direct dependence on Jesus's answer to the Sanhedrin, as attested by the Synoptics, quite improbable.

But the logion on the temple, Jn 2:19, is certainly the same as that transmitted in varying forms by Mk 14:58 with Mt 26:21; Mk 15:29 with Mt 27:40; cf. Acts 6:14. Such a saying about "destroying the temple" and "re-building in three days" was current in the early Church; but here in particular the fourth evangelist shows the freedom of his rendering and interpretation, so that there can be no presumption of a reading or reminiscence of the Synoptics. He may also have derived the logion from oral tradition—or another source.

A connection between Jn 3:3, 5 and Mt 18:3 (cf. Mk 10:15; Lk 18:17), such as has often been asserted in recent times, cannot be ruled out, but cannot be strictly proved (see *ad loc.*). If the fourth evangelist has re-shaped this synoptic logion, he has done so freely, on a deeper theological level. It hardly allows of conclusions as to his knowledge of the Synoptics.

A really "synoptic logion" is found again at Jn 4:44, cf. Mk 6:4; Mt 13:57; Lk 4:24. The verse is difficult in its context, and many exegetes take it to be a redactional gloss from a later hand (see *ad loc.*). The wording does not coincide with and of the Synoptics, and is a free rendering of the same thought. Nonetheless, it clearly records a traditional saying of Jesus (the πατρίς here is not Nazareth, but his "homeland", Galilee). Here John and the Synoptics are certainly tributary to the same tradition, as is proved by the further saying, 6:42, which is part of the same context (cf. Mk 6:2 par.).

From here on, there are no more "synoptic logia" for a long time. All comparable sayings occur in the framework of the narrative passages dealt with above (under 1) and are to be explained on the same terms. The command given by Jesus to the sick man in 5:8, which coincides almost word for word with the words addressed to the cripple in Mk 2:9, is natural in the circumstances, which are, however, different from those in the Synoptics. At the walking on the waters, John coincides with the Synoptics in the saying: "It is I, fear not" (Jn 6:20; Mk 6:50 par., but with the added θαρσεῖτε). But the rest diverges widely. Peter's confession of faith, 6:69, actually uses a different title for the Messiah. It must also be remembered that in the same chapter of John, 6:51c, 53 ff. seem to presuppose an account of the institution of the Eucharist characteristi-

[20] Cf. Schulz, *Untersuchungen*, pp. 96–124 (apocalyptic expectations taken over by Jewish-Christian communities).

cally different in terminology (σάρξ instead of σῶμα), which is an important indication of an independent Johannine tradition.

There are some sayings which were part of the passion narrative but which may have found their way in John into the public ministry of Jesus. Jn 8:28 is said to reflect Jesus's answer before the Sanhedrin, particularly in the form given by Lk 22:69f., while the peculiar phrasing of Lk 22:67 is referred to Jn 10:24b–25a; but a possible reminiscence, either in Luke or John, is the most that can be deduced. But there can be little doubt that Jn 12:27 is the Johannine form of the synoptic "Gethsemane". The "troubling" of Jesus's soul (ταράσσειν, cf. 11:33; 13:21; 14:1, 27) points back to the mortal anguish of Jesus in the synoptic account, the dialogue with the Father which follows echoes Jesus's prayer in Gethsemane, and the pregnant ὥρα is mentioned here in John as in the Synoptics (Mk 14:35, 37, 41 par. Mt; cf. Lk 22:53). But the whole scene is transformed in the light of the Johannine theology, and the hour of anguish merges into the "glorification".

At the Last Supper, Jesus announces his betrayal by Judas, Jn 13:21, in the same words as Mk 14:18 and Mt 26:21 ("one of you will deliver me up"); but previously (13:18) Ps 41:10, only echoed in Mk 14:18 (ὁ ἐσθίων), is expressly quoted, though not word for word. And the synoptic saying about the traitor who "is dipping into the dish with me" (Mk 14:20 and Mt 26:23) becomes an action of Jesus in Jn 13:26. Indeed, the whole scene is more pointedly delineated as the unmasking and dismissal of the traitor (v. 27). John also places the prediction of Peter's denial in the supper room (13:36 ff.); according to Mk 14:29 ff. and Mt 26:33f., it only takes place on the way to Gethsemane. Luke, however, already includes it in the leave-taking (Lk 22:34, after a word addressed to Simon in particular). Luke is also closest to John in the formulation of the saying about the cock crowing, which is in all four Gospels. The saying about the scattering of the disciples, omitted by Luke in keeping with his theological perspective, is still among the farewell discourses in John (16:32), in contrast to Mk 14:27f. and Mt 26:31f. But the formulation is quite different. Here and throughout one notes the influence of Johannine theology.

There are also some general words to the disciples, undeniably akin to synoptic logia, which are of particular interest. These include the saying, Jn 12:25, about "losing one's life and saving it", cf. Mk 8:35 parr.; Mt 10:39 with Lk 17:33. The fourth evangelist uses a different contrast (love—hate), says φυλάσσειν instead of σῴζειν or εὑρίσκειν, and introduces the distinction ἐν τῷ κόσμῳ τούτῳ—εἰς ζωὴν αἰώνιον, which is a deliberately "Johannine" re-modelling. The saying which follows, about serving and following, probably takes up the saying about carrying one's cross after Jesus, which occurs in the context in the Synoptics

(Mk 8:34 parr.; also in "Q", Mt 10:38 and Lk 14:27). But it is greatly altered, especially by the Johannine thought: "Where I am, there also shall my servant be" (cf. 14:3; 17:24 and also 13:36). The notion of "serving" has perhaps been introduced from another logion, which also has parallels in the Synoptics: "The servant is not greater than his master..." (15:20), cf. Mt 10:24—Lk 6:40. The same saying occurs in Jn 13:16, with the addition: "and the messenger is not greater than him who sends him".[21] The thought recurs in still another saying with synoptic parallels: "He who receives my messenger, receives me, and he who receives me, receives him who sent me" (13:20; cf. Mt 10:40; Lk 10:16; Mk 9:37—Lk 9:48). The general idea of the envoy and the sender (see further Jn 9:4; 17:18; 20:21) appears in varying forms and was echoed in many ways in the primitive Church. It is not a reason for affirming that the fourth evangelist knew the Synoptics or was dependent on their tradition. The Johannine logia have their own special stamp (cf. the typically Johannine λαμβάνειν τινά for the synoptic δέχεσθαι) and only show that the Johannine and the synoptic traditions have a common basis.

In the Passion, we may recall the metaphor of the chalice (18:11b) which we have already touched on briefly. It is also found in the synoptic tradition, in the answer to the sons of Zebedee (Mk 10:38—Mt 20:22), and in the Gethsemane scene (Mk 14:36 parr., here in a prayer to the Father: Jn 18:11 ὃ δέδωκέν μοι ὁ πατήρ). A borrowing from the Synoptics is again unlikely, but some connection in the development of tradition is unquestionable. So too in the case of the logion in which the risen Lord gives power to forgive sins, 20:23: it is undoubtedly connected in some way with the saying about "binding and loosing" in Mt 18:18; cf. 16:19.[22]

It is theoretically possible to deduce from the data of the logia that John knew the Synoptics, at least from having heard them in public reading, or from his own earlier reading. But the better solution seems to be that both "traditions" coincided for several sayings of Jesus, both ultimately going back to the original oral tradition. But the fourth Gospel, in its present form, may also have drawn on a brief written source for these sayings, which the evangelist exploited in his own way: the "synoptic logia" stand out distinctively enough from the main stream of the longer discourses of a "Johannine" type.

---

[21] Hence knowledge of Matthew is deduced by Sparks, "St John's Knowledge of Matthew: The Evidence of Jn 13:16 and 15:20"; contrast P. Gardner-Smith, *Journal of Theological Studies* 4 (1953), pp. 31–35.

[22] Cf. Vögtle, "Ekklesiologische Auftragsworte des Auferstandenen", esp. pp. 292 f.: "But it is quite understandable that the primitive Church should have reached the formula of Jn 20:23, in its desire to explicitate the content of the power of binding and loosing, under a certain aspect, very essential for the attainment of salvation."

3. Further observations

All this suggests that behind John there is an older tradition, going back to "synoptic" or "pre-synoptic" times, with many contacts with the synoptic tradition, but still an independent one. Some further observations will help to confirm this view.

a) The O.T. quotations in John are far from being as numerous as in the Synoptics, but they have several instructive features. Attention is called expressly to O.T. texts, by a wide variety of formulae introducing a quotation, at the following places: 1:23; 2:17; 6:31, 45; 7:38, 42; 8:17; 10:34; 12:15, 38, 40; 13:18; 15:25; 17:12; 19:24, 28, 36, 37—eighteen times in all. We are not interested for the moment in the many problems posed by the origin and wording of the texts, but simply in their contacts with synoptic quotations.

Only five of these texts have a clear parallel in the Synoptics:

1:23 (cf. Mk 1:3 parr.) "A voice crying in the wilderness" (Is 40:3), said of the Baptist in the Synoptics, attributed to the Baptist in John;

12:15 (cf. Mt 21:5) "Behold, your king is coming" (cf. Zech 9:9), used at the entry into Jerusalem;

12:40 (cf. Mk 4:12 parr.), the hardening of hearts, from Is 6:9f.;

13:18 (cf. Mk 14:18, merely an allusion; indirectly at most in Lk 22:41), the quotation about the traitor from Ps 41 (40):10;

19:24 (cf. Mk 15:24 parr., where, however, there are no quotation marks), the casting of lots quoted from Ps 22 (21):19.

None of these quotations, however, agree word for word with the Synoptics (we need not go into details). The text of Is 40:3 is quoted by the Baptist himself in John, as a testimony to himself, while in the Synoptics it is used as an instance of the Scripture being fulfilled in his regard. The Synoptics give the quotation about the hardening of the heart in the context of the parables, while in John it occurs in the retrospect of the public ministry. All the evangelists had Zech 9:9 in mind, undoubtedly, as the theological background of Jesus's entry into Jerusalem on an ass. But in Matthew it is one of the special "reflective quotations" of the evangelist, who seems to have also had Is 62:11 in mind; and it appears in another form in John, probably as a free quotation of Zech 9:9 only. At the casting of the lots, only John quotes exactly, and takes the *parallelismus membrorum* literally as two elements, which are applied to the distribution of the clothes and the drawing of lots for the seamless garment.[23]

---

[23] Cf. Dodd, *Historical Tradition*, pp. 122 f.

Further contacts (in subject-matter) may be found at Jn 7:42 (the origin of the Messiah in Bethlehem, cf. Mic 5:1), with Mt 2:6 (in the very different context of the infancy narrative); also at Jn 8:17 (the validity of two witnesses), with Mt 18:16 (after Deut 19:15, but in a completely different context). Here there can be no question of the fourth evangelist's depending on the Synoptics.

The other quotations are proper to John. But a closer inspection of the texts invoked by the fourth evangelist allows us to draw, with Dodd,[24] the following important conclusion. They are nearly all taken from Psalms or chapters of the prophets which play a part elsewhere in the N.T. writings. The texts quoted in John (in so far as a quotation can be verified) are taken from contexts to which the primitive Church attached importance. The text quoted in 2:17 is taken from the widely-used psalm of suffering, Ps 69 (68), v. 10;[25] v. 5 is quoted in 15:25, and v. 22, probably, in 19:28 ("I thirst"—the connection with the vinegar in Jn 19:29 suggests Ps 69 rather than Ps 22:16. Jn 6:31 refers to Ps 78 (77):24, the same psalm which may be behind the enigmatic text of Jn 7:38 (cf. Ps 78:16 and 20). A glance at the *index locorum* in Nestle shows that nearly all the quotations in John are from Psalms or sections of prophetic writings which are drawn on directly or indirectly elsewhere in the N.T.: Jn 6:45 echoes Is 54:13; Jn 7:38 may include Zech 14:8 among its sources;[26] Jn 12:38 is after Is 53:1; Jn 19:36 after Ps 34 (33): 21; Jn 19:37 is probably after Zech 12:10 (cf. Mt 24:30; Rev 1:7). Only Jn 10:34, after Ps 82 (81):6, invokes a psalm not quoted elsewhere; as the peculiar nature of the passage also suggests, this could be a special reflection of the evangelist on the Scriptures. It is not too bold to conclude from all this that John did not pick his texts at random, but conformed to a primitive teaching tradition in which certain parts of the O.T., and not just isolated verses, were used as the scriptural basis of Christology.[27]

The evangelist sometimes contents himself with a general allusion to the testimony of Scripture, cf. 1:46; 2:22; 5:39, 46; 20:9, to which 17:12 might perhaps also be added. But even these general comments show how closely he was linked with primitive Christian tradition. The

---

[24] *Ibid.*, pp. 47 ff. Similar considerations and conclusions in Lindars, *New Testament Apologetic.*

[25] Cf. Lindars, pp. 104 ff.

[26] Cf. Grelot, "Jean 7, 38: Eau du rocher ou source du Temple?", which contains an account of the previous discussions of the biblical theology behind this text.

[27] Cf. Lindars, *New Testament Apologetic*, pp. 251–86. "John's use of Scripture shows an awareness of the living tradition from which he derives his choice of texts, and this differentiates him from Matthew" (p. 271); "The selection of scriptures for apologetic needs in the early Church is governed by a single factor, the established use of the Prophets and Psalms in eschatological speculation" (p. 283).

whole early Church was convinced that the messiahship of Jesus (cf. 1:46; 5:39) was attested by Scripture (cf. Lk 24:27; Rom 1:2f.; 1 Pet 1:11, etc.). The special testimony of Scripture to the Resurrection of Jesus (20:9; cf. 2:22), which we find difficult to trace, was an incontestable fact from an early date, according to 1 Cor 15:4. The testimony of Moses (5:46) is to be sought no doubt in Deut 18:15, 18, especially as "the prophet", as a Messianic figure, is mentioned more than once in John (1:21, 25; 6:14; 7:40; cf. 7:52 v. l.). And this messianic doctrine has also left traces in other parts of the N.T. (Mk 9:7 parr.; Acts 3:22; 7:37). All this supports the view that John was independent of the Synoptics, but drew on the biblical theology of the early Church, in his use of the O.T., with a common fund of O.T. testimonies at his disposal, though certainly not a *testimonia*-collection.

b) Short parables, figurative sayings, aphorisms. Normally, great stress is laid on the very striking difference between the teaching method of parables in the Synoptics and the figurative discourses of John. And the specifically Johannine discourses, with such figurative elements as the shepherd and the sheep (10:1–18), the vine and the branches (15:1–8) or the light (8:12; 9:4f.; 12:35f., 46), have a completely different character, marked by theological reflection. This is chiefly due to their connection with the ἐγώ εἰμι of the self-revelation of the Johannine Jesus, and it is certainly this "Christological" principle which has brought about the change, as a comparison between 10:1–5 and 10:7–18 will show. But there are also shorter sayings of a parabolic or even allegorical type, much closer to the synoptic, which are often overlooked. C. H. Dodd has collected seven such "parabolic forms":[28]

3:29	The bridegroom and the friend of the bridegroom;
5:19–20a	The son "apprenticed" to his father (?);
8:35	Slave and son in the house of the father;
10:1–5	The shepherd, the thief and the watchman;
11:9f.	The traveller overtaken by night;
12:24	The grain of wheat;
16:21	The woman in labour.

Doubts may be cast on 5:19–20 a, since Jesus may be speaking directly of himself and his heavenly Father when he uses the terms "son" and "father" (cf. v. 17). But there are other texts, mentioned by Dodd elsewhere, which may be added to this group:

3:8	The parable of the wind;
5:35	John the Baptist, the burning lamp;
10:11b–12	The Good Shepherd and the hireling;
21:18	The metaphor of girding oneself.

[28] *Historical Tradition*, pp. 366–87 (on Jn 5:19–20a, see p. 386, n. 2).

Finally, some aphorisms and proverbs may be added, which are likewise typical of the synoptic tradition:[29]

3:27	"No one can take anything . . .";
4:35a	The proverb about the harvest(?);
4:37	Sower and reaper;
4:44	The prophet in his own country (already discussed among the "synoptic logia");
7:4	"No one does anything in secret . . .";
13:16	Servant and master, envoy and sender (already discussed among the synoptic logia);
15:13	"There is no greater love . . ."

c) Established sayings. Certain other logia merit consideration for our present purpose. In their present form, they are completely Johannine in stamp. But their taut formulation, their definite contours and their characteristic content suggest strongly that they have been taken over from somewhere else, and merely further elaborated. This type of logion has been studied by S. Schulz, who has analyzed their "tradition of themes".[30] His results are not entirely convincing, least of all for the "Son Sayings". But we must mention at least two groups, in which the logia stand out from their context, the Son of Man sayings 1:51; 3:14; 5:27; 6:27 with 53; 6:62; 8:28; 12:23; 12:34; 13:31f.; and the Paraclete sayings 14:16f.; 14:26; 15:26; 16:8–11; 16:13f. In the Son of Man tradition, which John sees in a very definite perspective (see excursus v), there is no need to postulate a special logion for each text. There may be simply one particular form (e.g., "the Son of Man must be lifted up") which is the original basis of the various sayings in John. It has long been recognized that the five Paraclete sayings form a unified group, and their possible origin is the subject of investigation. Without going into this question, it is possible to affirm that we have here a pre-Johannine or a "primitive Johannine" tradition—one which existed before it was inserted into our canonical Gospel.

4. Conclusions

The foregoing considerations allow us to draw the following conclusions, with all due reserves:

a) A direct literary dependence of John on the Synoptics is improbable. The occasional verbal agreements with Mark could suggest knowl-

[29] Cf. Bultmann, *Geschichte der synoptischen Tradition*, pp. 73–113, esp. pp. 77–82, 107 f., E. T.: *History of the Synoptic Tradition*, pp. 69–107, 73–76, 102 f.

[30] Schulz, *Untersuchungen*, pp. 85–93 (Method of "history of themes"), pp. 124–42 (tradition of the theme of Son); cf. my review in *Biblische Zeitschrift* 4 (1960), pp. 293 ff.

edge of this Gospel, but they may perhaps be explained by oral tradition. The connections with the Lukan tradition are certainly not due to direct literary contacts; the basis of the unmistakable similarities in traditional matter, presentation and theological themes should probably be sought in an earlier stage of the history of tradition.

b) The Johannine tradition is on the whole independent, and even where it deals with matters also found in the Synoptics, it does not seem to pass any judgment on them. The fourth evangelist has his own style of narration and formulation, and does not show any tendency to correct or replace the Synoptics.

c) Whether the fourth evangelist had some knowledge of the traditional matter behind the Synoptics is another question. He supposes his readers' knowledge of several matters which are known to us from the synoptic tradition, as for instance, the baptism of Jesus, more miracles than he himself narrates, discussions or deliberations of the Sanhedrin. But such information need not be derived from the synoptic Gospels. It may have been available also in the oral tradition. Here we must certainly assume the existence of cross-currents between the "Johannine" and the "synoptic" traditions.

d) As regards the number of external facts recorded, the Johannine tradition is in many respects poorer than the synoptic, but it gives a not inconsiderable amount of extra information, which merits respect even from the historical point of view. This is true above all of the tradition concerning the Baptist, and the passion narrative. The dating of the Crucifixion, the interrogation before Annas and Pilate's negotiations with the Jews command confidence. From the geographical point of view, there are the items about the places where John baptized, and about Cana and Samaria. But the information about Jesus's activity in Judea and Jerusalem, which could be derived from local groups of Jesus's disciples, is of particular interest.

e) John shows many traces of an old tradition of the words and deeds of Jesus, which seems to be as weighty as that of the Synoptics, and is even similar in style to it, when these bits and pieces are sifted out of the ubiquitous theological presentation of the evangelist or when their original form is assessed. This early stage or sub-stratum of the Johannine tradition may be contemporaneous with the synoptic tradition. What we have before us at present in John is, of course, a later stage of development, with a long evolution of tradition behind it, quite apart from the literary processes out of which the Gospel grew.

f) The fourth evangelist has a special aim in view in his presentation, and this is the readiest explanation of the remarkable relationship which obtains with regard to the synoptic tradition. At times he is in partial agreement with the synoptic accounts, but more often he diverges from them in choice of matter, structure and order, idiom and narrative form. He offers information of his own which is sometimes in conflict and indeed in contradiction with the data of the Synoptics. But he does so, not merely because he has a different and independent tradition at his disposal, but also because he is intent above all on his own theological purpose. However this may be envisaged,[31] his main interest is clear. It is to delineate boldly the majestic figure of the eschatological bringer of revelation and salvation, to display the radiant glory of the Logos as he lives on earth and dwells among us, to disclose the ever-present significance of the saving events which lie in the past. The words once spoken by the Son of God when he came into the world, are to become audible as his unremitting and ever urgent interpellation. The earthly Jesus is understood as the Christ who continues to be present in his community, in its preaching, worship and sacraments he is the *Christus praesens*. In other words, the evangelist desired, in the Holy Spirit (16:13f.), to link up the time of Jesus, the bearer of the Spirit (1:33), with the time of the Spirit (7:39); but the Spirit is imparted to the faithful in the words of Christ (6:63), in the sacraments which realize and render fruitful the saving events (cf. 19:34; 1 Jn 5:6 ff.), through the mediation of the Church, which takes over with the mission of Jesus his preaching and his authority, for the salvation of mankind (cf. 20:22f.).

---

[31] Hoskyns, *The Fourth Gospel*, pp. 83 f., finds the immediate occasion in the deficiencies of the synoptic type of presentation, which was inadequate to the times of the fourth evangelist: "This presentation of the life of Jesus in fragmentary episodes must have been a grave danger at the turn of the first century, for the scattered Christian communities had no generally accepted creed that would keep the evangelical episodes in a strict theological context, nor was their worship, whatever forms it may have taken, held to its final theme by an authoritative reading, say, of the opening verses of the Fourth Gospel." This brought with it the risk of a merely "historical" understanding of Jesus. "From so grave a misunderstanding of the Jesus of history, and of the tradition, oral and written, of His life, the author of the Fourth Gospel determined to save his readers." This motivation may not be altogether certain, but the authors have correctly recognized the problem of "history" and "faith" which is seen and answered so profoundly in John. Cf. the whole section "The Historical Tension of the Fourth Gospel" (pp. 58–85) and Davey's contribution, "The Fourth Gospel and the Problem of the Meaning of History" (pp. 107–28).

CHAPTER III

Literary Criticism of the Gospel of St John

Apart from the comparison with the Synoptics, there is also the literary structure of the Gospel itself to provide a field of investigation which may also throw light on the special character and the genesis of John. Literary criticism has long been busied with the fourth Gospel, but in spite of intense exertions, has not led to any definite and accepted result. We need not recount the history of this branch of research here.[1] It will suffice to note the type of questions that have been asked and the methods developed to solve them. This will clarify the problem as far as it seems relevant to the interpretation and to the standpoint there adopted.

1. Literary unity and literary criticism

Is there any need at all for literary criticism of John? Much more than the Synoptics, it presents on the whole a transparent structure, with a theological language and a characteristic style which give an immediate impression of great unity and purposefulness. The sharp-sighted criticism which has scrutinized the Gospel chapter by chapter for tensions, contradictions and "aporias",[2] seems to overlook the fact that the author could have envisaged his task differently from us, that he was not bound to apply the strict rules of logic, continuous development and unimpeach-

---

[1] For older efforts see Bousset, "Ist das vierte Evangelium eine literarische Einheit?"; for recent works see Howard, *The Fourth Gospel*, pp. 95–127; Menoud, *L'Évangile de Jean*, pp. 12–26; id., "L'Évangile de Jean d'après les recherches de Bultmann à Barrett", pp. 14–18; Haenchen, "Aus der Literatur zum Johannesevangelium", pp. 302–313; Kümmel, *Einleitung*, pp. 139 f.

[2] Cf. esp. Schwartz, "Aporien im vierten Evangelium"; Wellhausen, *Das Evangelium Johannes;* Spitta, *Das Johannesevangelium als Quelle der Geschichte Jesu;* Wendt, *Die Schichten im vierten Evangelium;* Hirsch, *Studien zum vierten Evangelium;* Macgregor and Morton, *Structure of the Fourth Gospel.*

able history in his presentation, and that he could have proceeded in a way strange to us, but adapted to his own form of thought and kerygmatic intention. Since he could suppose that much of what he wished to recall was known, and needed merely to be seen in a new light, in the perspective of his faith, why should he not introduce Mary as the woman "who anointed the Lord with oil and dried his feet with her hair" (11:2), even before he came to the story itself (cf. 12:1–8)? Having developed his own style of "parabolic discourse" (shepherd and flock 10:1–18; vine and branches 15:1–10), it must be granted that he could first have given a sort of general sketch (10:1–6; 15:1–2), and then have applied some elements of the imagery to the real subject, and indeed expressed it in terms of the figurative elements already present. Could he not approach the theological ideas which seemed to him important by making a number of fresh starts—omitting other elements of the imagery, shifting the perspective, introducing new traits and so on (cf. 10:7–18; 15:4–10)?[3] It is the task of exegesis to adapt itself to his movement of thought, and not to be too hasty in signalling discords and discontinuity which would imply confusion in the course of the writing. This explains why so many exegetes are now sceptical with regard to all efforts to find a "better" order by transposing either large blocks or small elements of the text, and prefer to do their best with the present arrangement, which they try to show is that of the evangelist.[4] But there are limits to such efforts, and there are places which simply cannot be understood as the deliberate or spontaneous arrangement of the evangelist, their collocation being incompatible with the original general plan, and unthinkable in terms of a continuous literary composition. If we consider the most important of such points, the general picture is as follows, though taken singly each point has not the same probative force:

a) We prescind from places which are shown by textual criticism not to have been originally part of the work, as for instance 5:3b–4 and the pericope of the adulterous woman 7:53–8:11, since they need not be considered in this connection (see below). But ch. 21, which is unimpeachable from the point of view of textual tradition, shows that

[3] This matter of the structure of the parabolic discourses has not yet been adequately investigated. On Jn 10, see Schneider, "Zur Komposition von Joh. 10"; more recent discussions have paid too little attention to the literary work of the evangelist, as Robinson, "The Parable of Jn 10:1–5" (conflation of two parables); Meyer, "A Note on Jn 10:1–18". On Jn 15 see Borig, *Der wahre Weinstock*.

[4] So at present English commentaries of Hoskyns, Barrett, Lightfoot and Dodd, *Interpretation*, pp. 289 f.; Catholic commentaries of Lagrange, Tillmann, Durand, Braun; there is also an increasing number of German Protestant exegetes who urge reserve, cf. Kümmel, *Einleitung*, p. 140. On the other hand, Catholic exegetes also welcome a moderate form of literary criticism, cf. commentaries of Mollat, Schick, Wikenhauser.

an "epilogue" has been added to the Gospel, which ended originally with 20:31. Both the contents (an apparition of the risen Lord in Galilee) and the notable divergence in style[5] show that it can hardly have come directly from the evangelist, though it may be based on his material. Further, the definitive ending 21:24f. proves that a later editor was at work, who spoke for a group who supported the testimony of "this disciple" "whom Jesus loved" (cf. 21:20, 23, 24) and looked back on the whole presentation of the gospel (v. 25).

b) In the farewell discourses, the signal for departure is given as early as 14:31 — "Stand up, let us leave". But there follows at once, starting with 15:1, a series of long leave-takings and the "high priestly prayer" (ch. 17), before Jesus's actual departure is recounted (18:1). All efforts to fit in the intervening discourses "on the way", or to understand the command to go other than literally (note the ἐντεῦθεν), are unconvincing and sound like counsels of despair. But the matter is easily explained, if we have here a collection of farewell discourses (all from the same author, as is shown by their unity), which were ultimately inserted here, not by the author (who could easily have omitted the little phrase in 14:31) but by the editors, who decided that this was the place for the extra material which they had at their disposal.

c) The sequence of what now forms chs. 5 and 6 seems to have been inverted. As early as the *Diatessaron* of Tatian, the order is reversed, and though the problem is still debated, it cannot be gainsaid that 7:1 in particular sounds very strange after ch. 6 which is devoted to Galilee. Why the emphatic remark that "after this, Jesus went about in Galilee", if he has just been described as working in Galilee? And why the explanatory reference, skipping back over the long ch. 6, to the murderous plan of the Jews, which was put before the reader in 5:16, 18? At a pinch, this could still be explained by the peculiar narrative procedures of the evangelist, who needed the note to introduce the next episode. But if the reverse order is used as a test-case, not only is this difficulty solved, but other points are easier to understand (see commentary).

d) This brings up another problem, which can be solved satisfactorily by a further re-arrangement of the text. The section 7:15–24 can be fitted into its present context to some extent, but it is still surprising to find it here, on account of the matter-of-fact reference to the healing of ch. 5 (cf. 7:21, 23). Historically speaking, one would have to assume that at the Feast of Tabernacles Jesus is referring to a healing performed in Jerusalem during an earlier feast (5:1), as if his action on the Sabbath were still "topical" and bound to cause excitement. It might indeed be urged that the evangelist does not think historically but simply challenges

[5] Cf. Boismard, "Le chapitre 21 de s. Jean"; Merlier, *Quatrième Évangile*, pp. 151–60.

the reader. But even so, the allusion to something so far back in the past remains strange. The whole matter takes on an different aspect if 7:15–24 was originally attached without a break to 5:47 (according to the arrangement of the evangelist). This is also suggested by the "key-word" γράμματα, which links up 5:47 and 7:15, and again by the notion of "seeking one's own glory" which links up 7:18 with 5:41–44, as indeed by the whole set of themes here treated. On the other hand, 7:15–24 would not be missed from its present context, since the comment of the people in 7:25 could well be a reaction to Jesus's "teaching in the temple" as noted in 7:14 (cf. 7:28; 8:20); no episode is needed in between. Have we not here a secondary arrangement of the text, which does not correspond to the original intention of the evangelist? The displacement is, of course, not completely accidental, since the section has a meaning even in its present context. But how the present arrangement came about is a problem which can only be discussed later.

If we reverse the order of chs. 5 and 6, and put 7:15–24 after 5:47, the two moves lend support to one another, and we arrive at the simple result: that ch. 4 was followed at once by ch. 6, and that after this climax and turning-point in Galilee, the reader learns of the equally dramatic but even more menacing developments in Jerusalem. Ch. 5, continued by 7:15–24, tells of the event which started the clash, a healing on the Sabbath, then of a "revelation discourse", of a decisive nature, followed by a controversy on fundamentals. We learn then in ch. 7 the reactions of the various groups to Jesus. Their mood is described in a series of brief and quickly changing scenes, obviously grouped around the beginning, middle and climax of the Feast of Tabernacles, and of increasing intensity. The skill displayed by the evangelist in this dramatic presentation is further justification of the literary criticism offered above.

e) A further problem is presented by the "unattached" sections of discourse found in ch. 3. Since the evangelist—contrary to a fairly widespread opinion—always marks off Jesus's discourses clearly, that is, nowhere else allows the words of Jesus to pass over imperceptibly into his own or someone else's words, the question arises as to where the dialogue with Nicodemus actually ends, and how it happens that the section 3:31–36, which on the face of it (cf. 3:27) is still part of the words of the Baptist, but which from its contents, as almost all agree, cannot and does not intend to be such, has taken up its present position. Whatever be the explanation of the enigma,[6] one can scarcely maintain that the present form of the text corresponds to the intention of the

---

[6] Where displacement of leaves is assumed to have taken place, 3:31–36 is joined to 3:21, cf. commentary of Wikenhauser, p. 35; but even so there are difficulties, cf. Schnackenburg, "Die 'situationsgelösten' Redestücke in Joh 3".

evangelist. The literary criticism undertaken at this point, in the hope of explaining the text and improving its arrangement, is not an arbitrary procedure. It is called for by observation of the literary procedures of the evangelist himself.

f) The prologue too, in its present form (1:1–18), has long held the attention of literary criticism. The interpretation may and must follow the actual lines of its structure to give its meaning, since at least the final redaction of the Gospel treated it as a unity. But the question of its original form cannot be avoided. "Interpolations" about John the Baptist have been inserted into the structure (cf. 1:6–8, 15). Its pattern of concepts include the "Logos", found only here, "grace and truth", "his own" in a different sense from 13:1. The style in many verses lacks all the usual "Johannine" criteria. Last but not least are the difficulties posed by part of the contents: do vv. 5, 9–11 speak of the pre-existent or the incarnate Logos? Was there perhaps a hymn to the Logos already in existence, which the evangelist incorporated into his work?[7] No solution up to the present has met with general agreement, but this does not absolve one from facing the literary problem.

g) Finally, there are shorter items which arouse misgivings, by their complicated construction, strangeness of style or questionable subject-matter. They may not correspond to the original text of the evangelist, that is, they may have been re-touched by the redactors. Such items would include 4:2 (a parenthesis correcting 3:22), possibly 4:44, certainly 6:22f., and possibly other short parts of the text. But this argument must be used very cautiously, as the evangelist himself can produce very complicated pericopes.

We omit other questions, as for instance section 12:44–50, which comes in surprisingly after the final reflections of the evangelist 12:37–43, but may still be explained by his intention of giving still another summary of the public discourses of Jesus. That a moderate and prudent literary criticism is needed should be clear enough from the facts adduced above.

2. Theories of multiple sources

The text of John is admittedly in disorder to some extent. How is this to be explained? This is a more difficult question, because the facts are not

[7] See for instance Green, "The Composition of St John's Prologue"; de Ausejo, "Es un Himno a Cristo el Prólogo de San Juan?"; Schnackenburg, "Logos-Hymnus und johanneischer Prolog"; Käsemann, "Aufbau und Anliegen des johanneischen Prologs"; Schulz, *Komposition*, pp. 7–57; Haenchen, "Probleme des johanneischen Prologs". See below, introduction to the prologue.

all of the same nature, and still a comprehensive answer is called for. Every "theory" runs the risk of not catering for the data as a whole, or of failing to satisfy when applied in practice to the actual texts. This is not a reason for rejecting all "theories" out of hand, but it is a warning against too ambitious blue-prints.

First of all there are the efforts to reach a Johannine *Grundschrift*—a basic document from which later deposits can be distinguished, or where the hands of editors who carried on the work may be traced. The writings of J. Wellhausen (1908),[8] F. Spitta (1910),[9] B. W. Bacon (1910),[10] E. Hirsch (1936),[11] and G. H. C. Macgregor—A. Q. Morton (1961)[12] may be taken as representative of this approach. Their findings differ notably in detail and cannot be reproduced here;[13] they have in common the notion of an "original" Gospel which was expanded by redactional additions till it reached finally its present form. J. Wellhausen, an epoch-making name in pentateuchal criticism, who later turned to Gospel criticism, describes as follows the main lines of his observations on John: "But from this monotonous and shapeless mass, certain elements emerge like stepping-stones, to indicate a traceable but not uninterrupted line. They stand out from the whole, but still form its backbone, and may be designated as the basic document. Layer by layer, additions have been made to it. . . . The basic document is only the thread of the warp, a minor element compared to the filling" (p. 6). Spitta's work goes more carefully into details, and though it rejects the results of E. Schwartz[14] and J. Wellhausen, it uses the same methods. It actually starts off with a German translation of the whole Gospel, which divides John into a "basic document", "editorial additions" and "elements taken over from other writings" (e.g., "Galilean narratives"). B. W. Bacon aimed chiefly at determining the "editorial stratum", basing himself on ch. 21, but reached different results again. One of the last efforts in this direction is the work of E. Hirsch, who prints a continuous Greek text, and uses typographical means to distinguish the original gospel[15] from "additions of the ecclesiastical redaction" and ancient glosses on this. He also signals re-arrangements supposed to have been made by the redactors.

---

[8] See above, n. 2. [9] *Ibid.*

[10] *The Fourth Gospel in Research and Debate.*

[11] See above, n. 2.

[12] *Ibid.*

[13] See the summary of the results in Howard, *Fourth Gospel in Recent Criticism*, pp. 297–302; Macgregor and Morton, *Structure*, pp. 93–135, have themselves summarized their results.

[14] See above, n. 2.

[15] See his more popular work, *Das vierte Evangelium in seiner ursprünglichen Gestalt verdeutscht und erklärt.*

The resulting picture is extremely complicated, and is open to the suspicion, like all these attempts, of subjective views and judgments.[16]

Misgivings at the very different results of the various analyses give rise to the question as to whether the method of literary criticism is not being asked to do too much in this field. Sharp-sighted though criticism may be, is it really capable of distributing the various elements with certainty among the so-called strata, or of allotting them to the various editors? Can the strata be credibly determined in their historical sequence, and perhaps be assigned to certain individuals or Church circles?[17] Or are these efforts not based very often on a preconceived notion of history, the life of the Church and theological development? This suspicion is nourished by the fact that the authors of such theories often placed the final stages of the Gospel as late as the middle of the second century, whereas recent manuscript finds (P^{52}, Papyrus Egerton 2, P^{66}, P^{75}) make such a date for the final redaction unlikely (see below). The proof from the "breaks and patching", the "aporias and contradictions" is open, as we have said, to the suspicion of applying too modern notions and demands to this ancient piece of literature. The linguistic observations which might have offered the most reliable criteria have lost much of their force since the style was investigated. But before we turn to this type of work, we must discuss another approach which has been made to the literary criticism of John.

Instead of one basic document, a number of sources are assumed for the start of the literary process which gave rise to the Gospel. The work of the evangelist in collecting and dove-tailing them did not succeed in concealing the multiple nature of the underlying tendencies. Efforts on these lines began early, but the most important is that of R. Bultmann.[18] He finds two main sources as the basis of the Johannine presentation throughout: a σημεῖα-source and a source containing Gnostic "revelation discourses". As he provides no comprehensive summary, it is not easy to group the passages which he assigns to the two sources. An effort to do so was made by E. Ruckstuhl.[19] R. Bultmann assigns to the σημεῖα-

[16] Cf. Michaelis's criticism, *Einleitung*, p. 112: "It may be seen from this example (the analysis given by Bultmann) how subjective, as a rule, are such decisions." On Macgregor and Morton, *Structure*, see the review by A. F. Parker-Rhodes in the *Journal of Theological Studies* 14 (1963), pp. 467–70.

[17] Thus Wendt, *Die Schichten*, ascribed the prologue and the longer discourses to the Apostle John, but the narrative portions to an evangelist other than John; Soltau, *Das vierte Evangelium in seiner Entstehungsgeschichte dargelegt*, distinguished three levels: Johannine legends, written down about A.D. 80, which go back to the Apostle John; episodes taken over from the Synoptics; discourses added later. He tried to date the levels, and also the later writers who worked on the Gospel.

[18] Exposition and criticism in Michaelis, *Einleitung*, pp. 109–13.

[19] Ruckstuhl, *Literarische Einheit*, pp. 25 and 31 f.

source not only the seven miracles expressly recorded, but other passages which he finds akin in vocabulary and style: 1:35–50, as the introduction to the source (cf. p. 78); 4:5–42 (less several passages, p. 131); 7:1–13 (p. 217, n. 1) and its conclusion, 12:37f. and 20:30f., where E. Faure[20] had already sought the end of the source. There are certain considerations which tell against the immediate rejection of a σημεῖα-source (see below, ch. iv), but there are grave objections to Bultmann's reconstruction, particularly on stylistic grounds.

Bultmann's pupil H. Becker has made a close study of the group of (Gnostic) "revelation discourses". He tries to determine more exactly the character and extent of the source, which he compares with other examples of Gnostic revealers' discourses, and produces a reconstruction based on many verses and parts of verses from John which are ascribed to the source.[21] According to this view, "the thanksgiving of the community of believers, in the prologue" was followed by an "introduction to the body of the discourses", which Becker puts together from elements of ch. 3. Then came a series of "crisis discourses": "the bread of life", "life", "the light of the world", to which were annexed the farewell discourses: "the good shepherd", "the true vine", and a discourse on "the way, the truth and the life". The whole collection was then terminated by "the farewell prayer of the revealer". The three discourses on "life", "the light of the world" and "the way, the truth and the life" in particular appear as a mosaic of single verses or short groups of verses dispersed over several chapters. The question is unavoidable: how could the evangelist have treated so well-articulated a collection merely as a "quarry" for the discourses of Jesus? But there is also the question of scientific method. Is it possible to disentangle this source from the gospel merely on grounds of style and content? For here we must listen to the verdict of the latest researches into style-criticism, which uses the best-attested elements of style as a criterion of the essential unity of the Gospel as a whole (see below). This type of argument is very impressive and cannot be easily dismissed. And we must also ask whether the "Gnostic revelation-discourses", in spite of the abundant material for comparison, provide enough constants in form and content to allow of certain verses and parts of verses in John to be assigned to them with certainty? Is it not also possible that the evangelist adapted himself to a certain type of discourse then current, in order to transmit his own thought? Bultmann complicates his theory further by assuming other sources and the insertion of several other texts by an "ecclesiastical redaction", especially those of the old

[20] "Die alttestamentlichen Zitate im vierten Evangelium und die Quellenentscheidungs-hypothese", esp. pp. 107–12.

[21] Becker, *Die Reden des Johannesevangeliums*. He gives the reconstructed text of the source, pp. 129–36.

type of "dramatic eschatology". The general result of the analysis is so complicated that it has hardly found any acceptance.[22]

It seems, therefore, that none of the various theories put forward in the line of analysis of sources can be considered acceptable. Proof of this is also offered by the investigations into the stylistic uniformity of John which have already been touched on. The first to undertake this task was E. Schweizer, in his study of the *Ego-eimi* sayings. His object was to determine what were the certain criteria of Johannine style, of which he noted thirty-three, which he then sorted into groups, studying their distribution over the Gospel and its strata, in order to test the various hypotheses of distinct sources (especially those of Spitta, Wendt and Hirsch).[23] With this method, which excludes as far as possible subjective sources of error, Schweizer came to the conclusion that "if such sources are to be supposed, they have been worked over to such a degree that they form a uniform whole; they have been worked over so well that for the present at any rate it has been impossible to demonstrate them" (p. 108). He does not radically exclude the presence of sources which the evangelist may have re-modelled, but sees little possibility of recognizing and disentangling them, in view of the way the evangelist assimilated and recast them. This critique of style was then taken up with even greater precision by E. Ruckstuhl in his *Literarische Einheit des Johannesevangeliums* (1951), and applied in particular to R. Bultmann's literary criticism of the Gospel as a whole, as well as to the "eucharistic" section, 6:51b–58, which had been described as secondary by even such moderate critics as J. Jeremias. Ruckstuhl revised Schweizer's list of stylistic criteria and expanded it to embrace fifty items.[24] Applied to Bultmann's division of sources, he found the result was entirely negative. He was not inclined to admit written sources even for individual passages which contain few Johannine characteristics, as for instance 2:1–10; 4:46–53; 12:1–8 (pp. 217ff.). The investigation of the style of 6:51b–58, on the other hand, proved positive, so that this section must also be ascribed to the evangelist —a result to which J. Jeremias has since subscribed.[25] Thus the older method of literary criticism seems to be ineffective with John, at least on the level at which it was formerly applied.

---

[22] Even pupils of Bultmann are unable to follow him here, cf. Käsemann's review of Bultmann's commentary in *Verkündigung und Forschung, Theologische Jahresberichte 1942–46* (1946–47), pp. 182–201, esp. 188.

[23] Schweizer, *Ego eimi*, pp. 87–109.

[24] pp. 180–205; Jeremias, in his valuable essay "Johanneische Literarkritik" accepted in principle the statistical procedure of Schweizer and added some stylistic criteria on his own account, but assigned 6:51c–58 to the redactor of 21:24, on grounds of style.

[25] Jeremias, "Joh 6, 51c–58—redaktionell?"; id., *Die Abendmahlsworte Jesu*, p. 101, E. T.: *The Eucharistic Words of Jesus*, p. 73.

3. Hypotheses of displacements

Much play was made with re-arrangements of the text even in the theories of disparate sources discussed above. It was not unusual to break up large unities, and to re-assemble the bits and pieces to form completely new unities in complete disregard of the original order, as for instance the "Discourse on the light of the world" in the theories of Bultmann and Becker.[26] The procedure seems arbitrary and finds no support in the evangelist's methods of work.[27] A different view must be taken of hypotheses which make less drastic assaults on the present state of the text, and only propose occasional rearrangements, when suggested by weighty reasons. Here it is a matter of larger blocks, as we have shown above (under 1) when dealing with the inversion of chs. 5 and 6, the proper place of 7:15–24, and the question of the "unattached discourses" in ch. 3, vv. 13–21, 31–36.

To explain the dislocations, the theory that some leaves were accidentally interchanged was put forward long ago. After initial studies by some other English scholars, J. H. Bernard decided in its favour in his large-scale commentary (1928).[28] He counted an average of 750 letters to a page, and tried to explain the displacement of various sections in terms of this number or a multiple of it (e.g., 7:15–24 = 763 letters). Other scholars such as E. Schweizer,[29] J. Jeremias,[30] A. Wikenhauser[31] followed his lead. Some dislocations of pages did occur in antiquity. This was the reason why Ecclus 33:16b–36:10a LXX (in Rahlf's enumeration) lost its original place between 30:24 and 25, as can be proved by a comparison with the Hebrew text and with other versions (Syr., Lat., Arab., Slav.). In the Ethiopie Book of Enoch, in the "Apocalypse of Weeks", the displaced section, 91:12–17, which deals with weeks 8 to 10, must be

---

[26] According to Becker's reconstruction, *Die Reden des Johannesevangeliums*, p. 132, this discourse was composed as follows in the source (with brief excisions in the verses): 11:9; 9:4, 39, 41; 8:12; 12:44, 47 f., 49 f.; 8:21, 23, 28b, 29; 12:35 f.; 8:31 f., 34–36, 38, 44a, 42b, 41, 44 f., 47, 51. Can such a mosaic be convincing?

[27] An early precursor of such efforts may be seen in the famous change of order in the text of the Codex Syro-sinaiticus at 18:12–24. Probably to turn it into the trial of Jesus before Caiaphas, the scribe put v. 24 near the beginning, and kept the trial neatly apart from Peter's denial, so that the sequence is 12–13, 24, 14–15, 19–23, 16–18, 25–27. The cursive 225 (A.D. 1192) puts v. 24, less skilfully, between v. 13a and 13b. Against the mass of witnesses, these are clearly emendators who claim to have a better view of the history; whether they are correct is another question (see commentary).

[28] Vol. I, pp. xvi–xxx.

[29] *Ego eimi*, pp. 109 ff.

[30] "Johanneische Literaturkritik", p. 46; but he has since abandoned this view, cf. "ποιμήν", p. 494.

[31] *Evangelium nach Johannes*, pp. 34–37.

inserted after ch. 93 (weeks 1 to 7). But there are grave difficulties against the hypothesis of an interchange of leaves: a) the dislocation must have occurred very early, possibly even in the original, since the original order of the text has been preserved in no ancient manuscript. But it is very likely that rolls were used for writing in the earliest days, and if so, the hypothesis breaks down from the start. b) In the early codices, the length of the line and the number of lines to a page varies widely, so that calculations based on the average number of letters to a page are very questionable.[32] c) Above all, it remains inexplicable that the "accidental" dislocations never broke up sentences. They preserved a well-marked unity, so that even the present order makes sense.[33] One would have to assume that the worst damages were repaired at once by the first copyists. But this still does not explain why the section in question fits in relatively well to its present context. Hence the theory is being more and more abandoned.[34]

But may there not be another explanation besides this purely accidental one? Once it is admitted that some sections should be transposed, for strong reasons based on the present text, and once it can be shown that there are some plausible reasons for the present secondary state, it seems obvious that editorial work must be responsible for the disorder. That there was such a redaction is proved by 21:24. But then the question is how it was possible for the editors to produce an arrangement which we no longer find convincing. Several considerations come to mind: the evangelist might have died while his work was still unfinished, leaving his disciples with a certain amount of material which still had to be incorporated into the text. The objection to this would be that he would not have made his notes on loose leaves but, more probably, on a longer papyrus roll (see above). However, we cannot be so certain as that about writing habits in antiquity, and he might have preferred the cheaper papyrus leaf for his drafts. This theory can also be combined with the idea that he only produced his work "in sections, with a general framework in mind into which they would later be inserted",[35] these sections being written in his own hand or dictated to someone else. It would hardly advance matters to suppose that there was a secretary who arranged and

---

[32] See Roberts, "The Christian Book and the Greek Papyri", esp. p. 163.

[33] See for instance 3:30 and 31, so that the impression is given (perhaps intentionally) that what follows is also part of the Baptist's testimony; or the insertion of 7:15–24 in its present context, dealing with Jesus's teaching in the temple.

[34] See along with Jeremias, "Johanneische Literaturkritik", Parker, "Two Editions of John", pp. 304 f., Teeple, "Methodology in Source Analysis of the Fourth Gospel", p. 286, "Beware of rearranging the material"; Kümmel, *Einleitung*, p. 140: ". . . and hence the hypothesis of a later re-arrangement cannot solve the literary problem of John."

[35] Feine and Behm, *Einleitung in das Neue Testament*, p. 121.

expanded the text.[36] It would be easier to suppose that certain units of text were produced by the evangelist primarily for liturgical use and were only grouped in the form of a written Gospel by his disciples or the editors.[37] Against this is the fact that most of the narrative episodes and discourses in John are fairly long, and do not give the impression of being self-contained "pericopes". And there is also the fact that an overall plan is recognizable, which allows us to conclude that the writer intended from the start to produce a Gospel (see above, ch. i). But there are no serious objections to the idea of editorial work on a limited scale, which treated the partially disordered material delicately and respectfully. This solution is, of course, also a "theory" and one which does not, and indeed does not try to, resolve all the literary problems, as, for instance, the present form of the prologue. But as here defined, it seems to be acceptable.

To place our results exactly, and demarcate them against the hypothesis of an interchange of leaves, we examine the list of transpositions which Wikenhauser finds necessary:[38]

a) 3:31–36 is in the wrong place and should be inserted after 3:21. The problem is there, but it should be solved differently. The redactors put the section, and probably 3:13–21 as well, into its present place, which is unsuitable.[39]

b) The inversion of chs. 5 and 6. This is correctly noted, but should be explained as the deliberate choice of the redactors.

c) 7:15–24 is the continuation of 5:19–47. This is correct, but the present order is not accidental.

d) 10:1–18 should come between 10:29 and 30, which would give a good text sequence: ch. 9; 10:19–21; then a new section 10:22–29, 1–18, 30–39. This transposition creates new problems, as the Good Shepherd discourse is more intelligible *before* 10:26–29, and does not seem called for by the method of the evangelist.[40] It is better to ignore it.[41]

e) 12:44–50 seems to be misplaced, after the evangelist's reflections in 12:36b–43. But this objection to the structure of the Gospel is likewise not

---

[36] The hypothesis of a secretary was maintained by Gaechter, "Strophen im Johannesevangelium", on the basis of his investigations into the Johannine discourses, which seemed to him to be composed of strophes. A helper translated the sermons of the Apostle John into Greek, inserted a number of additions (from the Apostle's material) and put the whole Gospel together (with the Apostle inspecting and approving). Criticized by Michaelis, *Einleitung*, p. 116.

[37] So, in various ways, Stauffer, *Die Theologie des Neuen Testaments*, E. T.: *New Testament Theology*; Raney, *The Relation of the Fourth Gospel to the Christian Cultus* (assumes the existence of various "prose hymns", 1:1–18; 3:14–21, 31–36; 10:1–18; 14; 15; 16; 17, which were then built into a Gospel); Pernot, *Les quatre Évangiles*, pp. 241 ff.

[38] *Evangelium nach Johannes*, p. 35.

[39] See above, n. 6.

[40] See Schneider, "Zur Komposition von Joh. 10."

[41] Cf. Jeremias, "ποιμήν", p. 494.

decisive, since the evangelist could have wished to sum up the discourses in which Jesus presented his revelation to the "world".

f) The farewell discourse comes to an end with the command to the disciples in 14:31, and the presentation is continued in the Passion narrative 18:1 ff. This is true, but the insertion of chs. 15–17 is best explained by the editorial work of the disciples.

It seems, therefore, that only a few transpositions and interpolations need be assumed. There are a few minor additions which may also be due to the editorial work of the disciples, as we shall now see.

4. Further literary criticism

In spite of the relative uniformity of John in style and structure, there are still some units of the text which give rise to the question of authorship. Not long after the investigations of Schweizer, J. Jeremias saw that the question was unavoidable, and tried to use 21:24 as a criterion of style.[42] He makes a noteworthy distinction between ὁ Ἰησοῦς (evangelist) and Ἰησοῦς (redactor), according to which 4:2, 44; 7:39b; 12:16 would be brief additions made by the redactor.[43] There are also other reasons for considering these verses to be editorial glosses, as for instance that they appear in the context as merely secondary comments, though the matter is not quite clear (see *ad loc.*). In any case, 21:24 is hardly a sufficient and certain criterion. Jeremias's observations on the use of ἀληθής and ἀληθινός (redactor: interchangeably; evangelist: distinctively) are open to question.[44]

Where characteristic elements of the Johannine style are lacking, one may conclude that a source has been used, as in the two Cana miracles,[45] or that editorial additions have been made. Thus it can be shown that the verses of the prologue which are "poetic" and rhythmical contain few indications of the hand of the evangelist, while the other verses which disrupt the strophic structure show many characteristics of the Johannine style.[46]

One must, however, be on one's guard against a one-sided and exaggerated estimation of style-criticism. E. Hirsch took a stand against it in an essay in which he subjected the methods of E. Schweizer to a

---

[42] "Johanneische Literaturkritik".

[43] But it seems from the variants in P^{66} and P^{75}, where Ἰησοῦς appears with or without the article for no apparent reason, that it is very questionable whether this criterion is valid.

[44] See Ruckstuhl, *Die Literarische Einheit des Johannesevangeliums*, pp. 235–42.

[45] See Schnackenburg, "Zur Traditionsgeschichte von Joh. 4:46–54", esp. pp. 63 ff. and 76–82.

[46] See Schnackenburg, "Logos-Hymnus", pp. 77–82.

counter-criticism.[47] He takes the view that the redactor was at pains to imitate the style of the evangelist. But this is hard to verify, blurs all the distinctions and thus becomes a weapon which can be turned against Hirsch himself. He is right, however, in maintaining that the contents must be weighed as well as the formal stylistic criteria. But here great prudence is called for, if one's own particular concepts are not to be read into the mind of the evangelist or redactor.

Where considerations of style are reinforced by arguments from vocabulary and extrinsic elements, it is easier to accept redactional additions. This is true of the involved construction of 6:22f.

We can disentangle a single thread of narrative, if we skip from the εἶδον in v. 22 to the εἶδεν in v. 24 and treat the intervening matter as a later interpolation of the editor. Perhaps even the εἶδον is part of his interpolation.[48] His purpose is clearly to explain how the people on the far shore of the lake of Gennesaret, the eastern side, where the miracle of the loaves had taken place, could have started out the next day and reached Capernaum. The procedure is intelligible if we take only v. 24 as part of the original narrative of the evangelist. There it is said that they saw that Jesus and his disciples were gone, and then, that the people got into τὰ πλοιάρια and came to Capernaum. What boats were these? The redactor explains in vv. 22f.: the people had noticed (εἶδον must now be a pluperfect) that there was only one boat by the shore and that Jesus had not boarded it with his disciples when they put out. However, other boats from Tiberias landed close to the scene of the miracle, and the people boarded these. From the point of view of vocabulary, εὐχαριστήσαντος τοῦ κυρίου is also suspect as a gloss of the redactor. The evangelist usually uses ὁ Ἰησοῦς in his narrative. Except when others are speaking, he rarely uses ὁ κύριος (4:1; 11:2—which may, however, be a redactional gloss; the only other instance is after the Resurrection 20:20). Further, εὐχαριστήσαντος—in itself a superfluous comment—sounds like a standard term used to allude to the Eucharist. Another pointer to the fact that the parenthesis was added later is that the redactor takes up once more the thread of the narrative with an οὖν in v. 24. Here the particle is not the οὖν *historicum* which is characteristic of the evangelist, but the conjunction usually used elsewhere.

A similar verdict may be given on 4:44. The parenthesis, exegetically difficult (see commentary), and notable for the anarthrous Ἰησοῦς (see above), becomes more intelligible if the redactor wished to direct the reader's attention to Jesus's reception in his homeland, Galilee. He recalls, therefore, a saying of Jesus which leads one to expect that the attitude of Jesus's compatriots would be rather hostile; but, as the evangelist records in v. 45, they welcomed him, though only because they had seen all that Jesus had done at the Passover feast in Jerusalem. Hence v. 44 is only a gloss, after which the redactor takes up again the narrative thread of the evangelist with ὅτε οὖν.

---

[47] "Stilkritik und Literaturanalyse im vierten Evangelium".

[48] The plural εἶδον after ὁ ὄχλος *(constructio ad sensum)* is also possible for the style of the evangelist, cf. 6:2 (though only in the subsequent subordinate clause); cf. Funk, *Grammar*, para. 134, 1.

There are perhaps other brief comments which are to be attributed to the editors. But this is a way out which will only be taken where subject-matter and vocabulary make it imperative, since the evangelist himself is not averse to brief comments (cf. 3:24; 4:9c; in 4:46 the reference to Cana, "where he had turned the water into wine" etc.). Thus one might ask, with a number of critics, whether the short section 2:23–25 is not also from a redactor.[49] But in spite of the "vague and diffuse expressions" of which one modern critic complains,[50] and in spite of many awkwardnesses, including the singular expression οὐ πιστεύειν ἑαυτόν, there are enough characteristic elements of Johannine style to make it hazardous to affirm that the text does not come from the evangelist. Otherwise one relapses too easily into the faults of the older, hypercritical approach.

Still greater caution is called for when one is tempted on purely theological grounds to deny the evangelist's responsibility for certain texts, e.g., those which speak of the future resurrection of the body (5:28f.; 6:39, 40, 44, 54), and of the judgment on "the last day" (12:48; cf. 5:29). No doubt the stereotyped remark made four times in ch. 6 sounds formal; but why should it not have been used as a formal expression even by the evangelist? To be too hasty in postulating an "ecclesiastical" redaction intent on correcting the evangelist, is to expose oneself to the suspicion of theological prejudices.

Recent attempts to refurbish the older type of literary criticism as applied to the fourth Gospel are not completely convincing. Several articles of S. Mendner, for instance, have been devoted to a close examination of individual pericopes.[51] But in spite of sound observations on particular points, his findings will hardly gain wide acceptance. And the most recent effort to establish a general theory for the literary genesis of John that of Macgregor and Morton (see above, p. 44), seems on the whole too artificial and complicated, though it incorporates shrewdly the best results of previous research. Literary criticism must now be combined with other methods and be used in the wider framework of the history of tradition and of redaction. H. M. Teeple has put forward some principles of methodology,[52] but their concrete application is difficult enough. However, we shall discuss further the problem of tradition and redaction in John in the following section.

---

[49] See esp. Mendner, "Johanneische Literarkritik", pp. 420 ff.

[50] See *ibid.*, p. 421.

[51] "Johanneische Literarkritik"; "Die Tempelreinigung"; "Zum Problem Johannes und die Synoptiker" (multiplication of loaves and walking on the waters); "Nicodemus".

[52] "Methodology in Source Analysis of the Fourth Gospel".

CHAPTER IV

Tradition and Redaction

Contrary to the conviction of earlier centuries that the fourth Gospel was the work of a great author, the Apostle St John, the son of Zebedee, who composed and wrote it in a substantial continuity,[1] the opinion is now fairly widespread that the Gospel is the aggregate result of a long process of literary formation, comprising "strata" of diverse age and origin. It was, therefore, subject to the same laws of growth, and calls for the same methods of research, as the synoptic Gospels, which have been studied in this perspective, recognized today as legitimate, especially since the development of the method of "form-criticism".[2] This type of research, mainly engaged on the traditions incorporated and transmitted by the evangelists, has begun again in recent years to pay more attention to the contribution of the evangelists themselves, that is, to the "redaction", which afforded them many opportunities of shaping the traditional material and of charging it with their own theological insight. There is a certain tension between "tradition" and "redaction", especially when the evangelist is an independent theological thinker, who recognizes at the same time that he is bound by the tradition which he must repeat and transmit.

1. The relationship of tradition and redaction

Thus in all study of the Gospels it is important to distinguish the traditional elements from the superimposed redaction, to determine the strength and

[1] This opinion was held very early; according to Clement of Alexandria, John was the last evangelist who composed his "spiritual" Gospel, at the urging of his friends and enlightened by the Spirit (Eusebius, *Hist. eccles.*, VI, 14, 7); the legend given in the Muratorian Canon, lines 9–16, supposes a similar view; according to the Latin prologue to the Gospels (date disputed), the Gospel of John was produced and published *(manifestatum et datum est)* while John was still alive, and Papias wrote it down at John's dictation (texts in next chapter).

[2] Cf. Wikenhauser, *Einleitung*, pp. 182–99, E. T., pp. 253–97; Schnackenburg, "Formgeschichte"; id., "Zur Formgeschichtlichen Methode in der Evangelienforschung".

influence of both components and to give an account of their mutual relationships. For the synoptic Gospels, the synoptic comparison is very helpful in enabling one to recognize what is proper to each evangelist. For the "special matter" of each synoptic, and for Mark, which is a special case on account of its general priority, other methods are available, such as the historical investigation of the various genres of discourse and narrative, the distinction of these units from the framework which introduces and closes them, the recognition of redactional summaries and so on. Here the "redaction" coincides substantially with the work of each evangelist, and in spite of the keen interest now taken in the theology of each of the synoptic Gospels, the demarcation of the traditions which they incorporated remains a major interest.

In the case of the fourth Gospel, this problem presents itself in a different and a very special way. From what has been said up to this, especially about the relative homogeneity of the Gospel, it is certain that the evangelist gave his work its characteristic form and that it is completely penetrated by his theology. But we must still ask to what extent he used certain traditions, available perhaps only to himself, and also to what extent his work underwent modifications in subsequent revisions and a final redaction. The question of the redaction is particularly important for John in the form in which we have it at present, and it is a special problem, compared with that of the Synoptics: was the original character of the work of the evangelist obscured and overlaid by one or more redactions? The question of what traditions were used seems to be less important. But it may not be lost sight of, if a proper judgment is to be formed on the origin and trustworthiness of the Johannine tradition. The earlier tradition worked over by the evangelist and the subsequent editorial work done on his text must first be distinguished from his own work, if this is to be accurately determined. This is the only basis on which an answer can be given with some sort of assurance to the question of the identity of the evangelist.

There are a number of difficulties in determining the three strata, existing tradition, work of the evangelist, subsequent redaction. Thus, for instance, recent investigations of the second Cana miracle, the healing of the official's son (4:46–54), have arrived at different results. Many scholars take v. 48 as a saying of Jesus inserted by the evangelist into an episode taken over by him in essentials from tradition or some other source, while one scholar regards this verse—and some others—as a later redactional addition.[3] Similar doubts arise with regard to other questions

---

[3] See Schnackenburg, "Zur Traditionsgeschichte von Johannes 4:46–54", pp. 60–70.

which present greater difficulties: are the texts which contain a "futurist" eschatology (5:28f.; 6:39, 40, 44, 54; 12:48) a sign that the evangelist retained the ordinary eschatology with only a shift of emphasis, or do they betray the presence of another hand, an older stratum or a later redaction? Were the great "signs", with their symbolical interpretation, created by the evangelist himself as aids to contemplation, or is he responsible only for the profound theological explanation, of which the groundwork was provided by a straightforward miracle story taken from current tradition or from a written source? In the "eucharistic homily" of 6:32–58, is the evangelist giving his own theology or is he basing himself on a preceding tradition? Is he reflecting a fully-formed Christian tradition in the Paraclete sayings,[4] merely inserting them into the farewell discourses, or is he christianizing a traditional theme which already existed before and outside Christianity? Is the section 12:44–50 the "kerygmatic" conclusion with which the evangelist had himself intended to round off the first part of his work, or was it only added by a redactor (or transferred here from somewhere else)? And finally, is the "epilogue", ch. 21, based wholly or in part on material supplied by the evangelist and merely manipulated to a greater or less extent by the redactors, or is it a purely redactional addition? These and other questions depend to some extent on the way the three strata are determined and demarcated. This is not the place to discuss them in more detail, but they serve to delineate the problems and to throw light on the hypotheses which must now be discussed.

2. Considerations on the history of forms and of tradition

Though the fourth Gospel cannot compare with the Synoptics as a reservoir of traditional items selected and shaped by the early Christian preaching, catechetics and liturgy, and hence is not amenable to the method of form-criticism to the same extent, still, in the light of what was said above (under ch. ii), this method is not completely inadequate or irrelevant when applied to John.

The most thorough effort in this line is the work of O. Merlier, who puts forward the following classifications: in narrative matter: "Johannine" narratives (such as the dialogue with the Samaritan woman, ch. 4, the healing of the man born blind, ch. 9, the raising of Lazarus, ch. 11), which are of a distinct type, compared either to the Passion narrative or the shorter and purely narrative stories such as the marriage

---

[4] On the history of tradition see esp. Windisch, "Die fünf johanneischen Paraklet-Sprüche"; Schulz, *Untersuchungen*, pp. 142–58 (lit.); Betz, *Der Paraklet*, pp. 5–35 (history of research); pp. 210 f. (his own views).

feast of Cana (2:1–12), the healing of the cripple at the pool of Bethzatha (5:1–15), the healing at Capernaum (4:46–54) and so on; then "synoptic" stories, short narratives such as are told in ch. 1 about John the Baptist, the Jews and Jesus, in ch. 2 the purging of the temple, in ch. 7 the scenes in Jerusalem, in ch. 12 the anointing at Bethany and the entry into Jerusalem; in the discourses: Dialogues as in chs. 3, 4, 6, 13; discourses with a minimum of introduction (7:14–38; 8:12–19; 8:23–59; 10:1–19), then the farewell discourses in chs. 14–17; "fragments" of discourses: 1:35–52 (*sic*, should be 51); 2:13–21; logia grouped without any apparent unity: 3:11–21, 31–36; 5:19–47.[5] This division of the material, obviously modelled on the work done by form-criticism on the synoptic Gospels, will hardly be found satisfactory. The grouping of the stories appears to be artificial, if for no other reason than that the author must assume transitional forms between the "Johannine" and the "synoptic" types; he attaches the Passion narrative to the second type, while he attributes the fairly long healing narratives (Cana etc.) to an author "who copies the synoptic rather than the Johannine narratives" (p. 427). The grouping of the discourse is also strange. It is dominated by the question of how far logia of Jesus have been incorporated, linked up or elaborated in Johannine style. In reality, it is the discourses which show a much greater unity, a prevailing "Johannine" style, whether they are presented in dialogues or monologues, in shorter or longer pericopes. The author's method leads him to the following diversified picture of the process of composition: a) logia taken from an anonymous collection; b) a story of the life, death and resurrection of Jesus, treated in a "Johannine" way; c) a work of harmonization; d) discourses aiming at edification and apostolic preaching; e) a final redaction. He therefore assumes an evangelist who composed account "b" and enriched it with logia "a"; a redactor who harmonized the whole, "c"; a second redactor, who added in the great discourses in chs. 14–17, "d"; a final redactor, who left us our present Gospel, "e". This complicated picture can hardly be convincing, since even the method by which it was built up is questionable.

In the narrative matter, the two miracles linked with Cana are distinctive (2:1–11; 4:46–54), by reason of their style (no particularly Johannine characteristics), their presentation (practically no word of comment) and their enumeration (2:11; 4:54). But it may also be asked whether the longer narratives of the "signs" are not also based on briefer miracle stories which were taken up by the evangelist, expanded according to his method and enriched with words of Jesus. Then form-criticism would have to be combined with the history of tradition: the evangelist came upon "miracle-stories" of the synoptic type, took them over in part, but also re-modelled others for his theological purposes. In other words, it is less a question of form-criticism and the distribution over various types of presentation, than of existing traditions or sources on which the evangelist drew, creating something new by breaking up existing forms. Contrary to the synoptics, he did not simply take over items in their existing form, but used them with sovereign freedom for his way of presenting the Gospel, which is therefore characterized by short scenes and longer expositions, as well as episodes where the story-telling is taken

[5] *Le Quatrième Évangile*, pp. 426–29.

farther and parts enlarged by discourses. The various "forms" need not be distributed over different stages of a literary process, but may be attributed to the approach of the evangelist himself, who used these varying styles, often very artistically, to shape his account of the earthly work of the Son of God. Thus, for instance, he preferred for his "enunciation of themes" rather short narrative episodes (chs. 1–2), which he continued with two important dialogues (chs. 3–4), and then for the climax in Galilee (ch. 6) and in Jerusalem (ch. 5) gave long "revelation discourses", after which he illustrated the situation in Jerusalem by brief, swiftly changing scenes (ch. 7). Redactors to combine or "harmonize" the various literary strata are superfluous. The main work was accomplished by the evangelist himself, who worked over the traditions at his disposal and moulded them into a relatively unified Gospel.

The same is true of the material of the discourses. Here again, with the help of form-criticism, one can certainly sift out several logia and call some "synoptic logia" (see above) on account of their affinities with the sayings of Jesus in the synoptics, others "Johannine" on account of their singularity and their "Johannine" character ("Son of Man" sayings, Paraclete sayings, *ego-eimi* parabolic forms). But it is hardly possible to reconstruct a set of logia which existed as a closed collection at an earlier stage.[6] The most one can say is that such logia were at the disposal of the evangelist, either as elements formed by earlier tradition, or as the fruits of his own preaching, and that he incorporated them into the scenes and discourses of his Gospel. Their distribution is so irregular that it is hard to imagine any other reason for it. Some of these logia stand in isolation (e.g., 1:51; 8:12; 13:31; 14:16f.). Others, and indeed the majority, are inserted into larger contexts. They are found in lengthy discourses such as the "homily" on the bread of life (6:32–51), in the two parabolic discourses (10:1–18; 15:1–10), in the final farewell discourse (where the Paraclete sayings are intimately linked with the dominant thought of Jesus's departure, 16:7–15). They also occur within the framework of the narrative of a "sign", as in ch. 9 (cf. vv. 4f. and 39) and ch. 11 (cf. vv. 4, 40 and 25f.). As in the construction of the narrative, certain stereotyped logia were used in various ways, and the fact is no doubt to be attributed to the evangelist. Thus the noting of various stylistic genres does not lead here to distinct literary strata, but only to matter perhaps already available to the evangelist, which he made use of with sovereign

[6] Merlier, p. 430; cf. pp. 438–42. He thinks that P. Egerton 2 (the "Unknown Gospel") contains extracts from this anonymous collection, including Jn 5:39. But the "Unknown Gospel" is not a collection of logia and probably represents a later stage of Gospel composition (cf. its knowledge of the canonical Gospels); see Jeremias, "An Unknown Gospel with Johannine Elements".

freedom for his presentation of Jesus's work as revealer. The question of the history of tradition takes precedence in John over form-criticism. The problem is rather that of the sources which he perhaps used. The intermediate stage, the re-shaping of the matter by the evangelist, is central and all-important, and one can only ask what elements and materials he worked on, and investigate whether and how far his presentation, which prevails on the whole, was subjected to the work of redactors.

3. The question of possible sources

In spite of the great uniformity of style apparent in John, which has been discussed above, the question of the sources which the evangelist may have used remains relevant, and is of importance for the trustworthiness of the tradition and the identification of the author. The notion of a source for the miracle-stories has most in its favour. Even though the division of sources proposed by Bultmann is not convincing in general, his various observations in favour of a σημεῖα-source have considerable weight. Other more recent investigations of individual narratives in John (see below) likewise favour this assumption. A brief examination of the seven "signs" which are recounted more or less fully, gives the following picture:

a) The marriage feast at Cana (2:1–11), proper to John, contains hardly any characteristics of Johannine style in the narrative as such, that is, except v. 11. It is briefly told and resembles synoptic miracle-stories, even though it probably contains a Johannine meaning on a deeper level (cf. commentary). But the sense thus given it is not made explicit: there is not a single word of comment to bring it to the fore (except the general remark in v. 11b–c).

b) The same formal analysis may be applied to the second miracle of Cana (as the evangelist wishes it to be understood), the healing at a distance of the sufferer in Capernaum (4:46–54). Here, however, there is reason to think that the illness is the same as that in the story of the "centurion of Capernaum", preserved in the special tradition common to Matthew and Luke (Mt 8:5–13; Lk 7:1–10). The narrative diverges so strongly that it cannot be taken from the Synoptics or their source. Yet it seems to be derivative in the fourth Gospel, where it has merely been "fitted in" to the evangelist's narrative.[7]

The numbering of these two detailed "signs" (2:11; 4:54) may certainly be attributed to the evangelist, especially as the last verse in each case contains signs of his writing. The numbering is not continued,

[7] Cf. the essay "Zur Traditionsgeschichte von Joh. 4:46–54", esp. pp. 62–67.

but this may be explained by the fact the evangelist relied on his reader "to go on counting himself after 2:11 and 4:54 till he reached the number of seven, and then recognize that the significance of the *semeia* included their being seven".[8] However, as the evangelist is quite ready to indicate numbers, it is not easy to understand why he did not suggest this symbolism more strongly to his readers. The readier explanation is that he found the two first miracles already linked up (cf. 2:12, which may have formed the transition) and that he wished to emphasize them as the "beginning" of the revelation of Jesus's glory by his miracles.

c) The multiplication of the loaves (6:1–15), also part of the narrative material of the Synoptics, has notable associations with the Markan narrative[9] which have led many scholars to assume direct dependence here. More recent investigations, however, have questioned this view,[10] and it remains possible that this Johannine "sign" was also taken from a special source which chimed with the Synoptics for this complex (see also above, pp. 28f.).

d) The walking on the waters (6:16–21) is not given specifically as a σημεῖον, but it is of the same genre of miracle-story, and has so many special traits which distinguish it at once from the Synoptics that a special source is likely. Since the feeding of the multitude and Jesus's appearance on the lake are closely connected, and were probably always recounted together, the peculiarities of the second story reinforce the probability that both come from the same source. The notion that the evangelist followed his own independent tradition only for the walking on the waters,[11] hardly finds support in the procedure of the evangelist elsewhere. Apart from the story of the anointing (12:1–8), no other narratives give the impression of dependence on Mark, and the anointing is not one of the σημεῖα. It would be surprising if the evangelist had followed the Markan presentation for the multiplication of the loaves, but not for the walking on the waters. There is no difficulty, on the contrary, in supposing that the hypothetical σημεῖα-source contained the miracle of the bread as well as the miracle of the wine.

e) In the miracle at the pool of Bethesda, the actual story of the healing (5:2–9) is given very briefly, in the style of a miracle-story and without special Johannine characteristics. It has a certain affinity with the synoptic healing of the cripple (Mk 2:1–12 parr.), but the differences are so great—especially the exact description of the "health

---

[8] Michaelis, *Einleitung*, p. 111.

[9] See for instance Mendner, "Zum Problem Johannes und die Synoptiker", pp. 285–9; Haenchen, "Johanneische Probleme", pp. 31–34 (dependence on same tradition).

[10] So esp. Wilkens, "Evangelist und Tradition im Johannesevangelium"; Johnston, "The Johannine Version of the Feeding of the Five Thousand—An Independent Tradition?"

[11] See Mendner, "Zum Problem Johannes und die Synoptiker", pp. 289–95.

resort" at Jerusalem—that the synoptic narrative is ruled out as a source.

f) The same is true of the healing of the man born blind, at the pool of Siloam in Jerusalem (ch. 9). Though the event is expanded into a long story of the Johannine type, here too the basis may have been a brief miracle-story taken from a source (cf. 9:1,6f.). But even the beginning must have been re-modelled in the Johannine style (especially vv. 4f.), and the interrogations and the changes of scene, including the confession of faith of the subject of the cure, must be Johannine expansions, possibly derived from oral tradition. Thus the miracles of ch. 5 and ch. 9 would correspond to some extent in the presumed source: both are healings at a pool in Jerusalem, both involve chronic illnesses causing grave distress.

g) The raising of Lazarus from the dead (ch. 11) also falls within the perspective of the history of tradition, though with the healing of the man born blind it is the "sign" most heavily charged with "Johannine" feeling, since the realistic description is both an attestation and a symbolic presentation of Jesus's significance, as conqueror of death and giver of new life. The story has constantly come under the fire of historical criticism, as a free creation of the evangelist's theology, linking up with the cautionary tale of the rich man and the beggar Lazarus in Luke, especially the ending (Lk 16:30f.). But literary analysis enables us to detach from the whole a simpler and briefer miracle-story, which, according to W. Wilkens,[12] comprised more or less the following verses (from which some Johannine traits must be omitted from their present form): 1 a, 3, 17, 33–34, 38, 39 a, 41 a, 43–44. From the point of view of size and genre, this would be the same type of miracle-story as the others, but their climax from the point of view of content.

All this is of course merely hypothetical, but it allows us to attach the Johannine narratives to a source which gave straightforward miracle-stories with no pretensions to deep theological significance, and certainly more numerous than the seven recounted in John. That the number was far larger may perhaps also be indicated by the following points: a) the frequent mention of σημεῖα *en bloc* in the Gospel,[13] which surely implies that the evangelist claimed to know others; b) the important role allotted to the miracles of Jesus in the discussions with the Jews;[14] c) the final remark, 20:30, which is not an allusion to the appearances of the risen Lord, but envisages the whole Gospel narrative, more particularly the first main section dealing with the public ministry of Jesus.

---

[12] "Die Erweckung des Lazarus", esp. p. 27; see also Dunkerley, "Lazarus".

[13] Cf. 2:23; 3:2; 6:2, 26; 7:31; 11:47; 12:37; 20:30.

[14] Cf. 7:31; 9:16, 30–33; 10:41; 11:47.

It may have already formed the conclusion of the source,[15] since the reference to Jesus's work on earth is remarkable, after the words addressed to Thomas in 20:29 and the long chapters containing the farewell discourses, the Passion and the Resurrection. But the remark is readily intelligible as conclusion of the σημεῖα-source, and in its present context, is obviously meant by the evangelist to encourage the reader to believe (cf. v. 31, for the full meaning of faith in John), on the basis of the testimony to Jesus which he wished to give by recounting these (selected) σημεῖα. In their character of "sign", they were meant to reveal the hidden glory of the incarnate Logos to the reader who does "not see" (v. 29), but through the apostolic preaching accepts what once happened as present in faith. And this is the ultimate reason why the evangelist chose only a limited of σημεῖα, but disclosed the profound Christological significance of these few, in some cases presenting them at greater length, both to certify their unquestionable reality and to bring out the full riches of their meaning.

To extend the presumed source beyond the recorded miracle-stories (cf. Bultmann) would not be wise, as criteria are lacking. It might, however, be asked whether the "miraculous draught of fishes" in the epilogue, ch. 21, does not perhaps come from the same source. It agrees remarkably with the Lukan tradition which recounted, though in a different manner, a great catch of fish at the beginning of the earthly work of Jesus. This is a difficult question from the point of view of the history of tradition, and this is not the place to discuss it. But in any case, the Resurrection appearance in Galilee, Jn 21, is so peculiarly interwoven with various themes that the oldest form of the narrative can hardly be disentangled from the redactional elaboration. Hence the question of whether the tradition of the miraculous draught of fishes, which it records, also formed part of the σημεῖα-source is better left in suspense.[16]

While the σημεῖα-source may be allowed some probability, a logia or discourse source must be rejected. In view of what has been said above (in ch. iii) on the hypothesis of Bultmann and Becker, no solid reasons can be adduced to buttress such an assumption. The clearly defined complexes of discourse which interrupt the flow of the presentation and suggest mistakes of arrangement (3:13–21, 31–36; cf. 12:44–50) or later insertion (chs. 15–17), can be explained by redactional work on the material left by the evangelist. The rest of the discourses are often loosely attached to their contexts (cf. 8:12, 21, 30f.; 10:1–18). Possibly the evangelist had meant to make their situation clearer in the final stage of his Gospel

---

15 Cf. Schnackenburg, "Zur Traditionsgeschichte von Joh. 4:46–54", pp. 77–79.

16 *Ibid.*, pp. 84–88.

which he never arrived at. But they all fit in with the general lines of the gospel narrative, and there is no serious reason to doubt that they were formed by the evangelist himself, like all the revelation discourses of the Johannine Jesus—whether he used "models" or not. The *ego-eimi* sayings and the parabolic discourses, the Son of Man and the Paraclete sayings all carry his personal stamp, and here too one can hardly postulate written sources.

If we remind ourselves of the fact that this book is in the nature of a Gospel, with its own peculiarities (see above, ch. i). we may assume a close connection between the evangelist and the traditions at his disposal, but we shall not expect him to have wished to make his sources recognizable. They were probably of the oral type on the whole, and even where he relied perhaps on written ones, he used them freely, as is also suggested by the way in which he used the books of the Old Testament in his quotations.[17]

4. History of tradition: recent theories

The recognition of the fact that the work of the evangelist is the dominant factor in the fourth Gospel and that even so his work does not give the impression of being a fully harmonious unity, has led to new hypotheses which try to solve the discrepancy by analysing the history of the tradition. The dissertation of W. Wilkens on the history of the genesis of the fourth Gospel represents a concrete effort in this direction.[18]

Wilkens disassociates himself from the start from the efforts of source-criticism, since the whole Gospel is to be ascribed to one and the same author. He assumes instead a long process of growth through which the Gospel was taken at the hands of the evangelist. He takes as his starting-point the "Passover framework of the fourth Gospel", which he delineates by means of the "Passover formulae of transition" in 2:13; 6:4; 11:55 (pp. 9–24) and holds to be secondary (pp. 25–30). Having eliminated this framework, he tries to penetrate to the "basic Gospel" of John (pp. 30f.), which he tries to reconstruct (pp. 32–93) and presents finally in the form of a survey (pp.92f.). The Gospel started with Jesus's work in Galilee (the two Cana miracles, the loaves and the walking on the waters). Then came Jesus's work in Jerusalem (chs. 7; 5; 10:40–11:57, but without the discourses), parts of ch. 13, the cleansing of the temple, finally the Passion and the Resurrection appearances. At a second stage, the evangelist expanded this basic Gospel by means of discourses, where Jesus spoke of the bread of life (ch. 6), of judgment (fragments of ch. 7; 5; 8), of the light (chiefly parts of chs. 8 and 12), of "the resurrection and the life" (ch. 11). Then came the farewell discourse of ch. 14 and the prologue (pp. 94–122). But the work which definitely gave the Gospel its present-day form was undertaken only at a third stage,

[17] Cf. Goodwin, "How Did John Treat His Sources?"

[18] *Die Entstehungsgeschichte des vierten Evangeliums*, to which the page numbers in brackets refer.

when the evangelist re-modelled it as a Gospel of the Passion. He re-distributed the various elements with the Passover in mind, and inserted new matter: the dialogues with Nicodemus and the Samaritan woman; the division within the circle of the disciples (6:60–71), the division within the ruling circles (7:31f., 45–52; 12:42f.), the discourse on the children of Abraham (ch. 8), the parable of the good shepherd and the scene at the feast of the Dedication (ch. 10), warnings to the disciples (11:7–10), the washing of Peter's feet (13:6–11), the farewell discourse of ch. 15–16, the high priestly prayer (ch. 17), the race to the tomb (20:2–10), the appearance of the risen Lord in Galilee (ch. 21). This thorough-going re-shaping was undertaken on theological grounds: "The whole work of Jesus in word and deed is made part of the Passion. This is a deliberate theological effort, undertaken in the struggle against docetism. The Cross of Jesus is the focus of the gospel . . ." (p. 171). Externally, the chief effect was as follows: "The external framework of the Gospel of the Passion is provided by the Passover formulae of transition 2:13; 6:4; 11:55, with their corresponding pericopes, the cleansing of the temple (2:14–22), the eucharistic discourse (6:51c–58) and the anointing (12:1–8), and by the passage 19:31–37 within the Passion narrative. Jesus's visits to Jerusalem are the consequence of this new reconstruction" (p. 172).

In sharp contrast to earlier hypotheses of different sources, the various strata and phases which occur in the genesis of the Gospel are attributed to the evangelist himself. The author does in fact do justice thereby to the uniformity of style and language in the Gospel and its dominant "Johannine" theology, and succeeds at the same time in eliminating some awkwardnesses in the structure, above all, the occurrence of the cleansing of the temple at the beginning of Jesus's work, the fact that brief narrative episodes alternate with passages into which long discourses have been inserted, the completion of the brief original farewell discourse (ch. 14) by further discourses belonging to the same situation (chs. 15–17), the addition of ch. 21. But the effort remains unconvincing in practice. The stereotyped phrase: "and the Passover of the Jews was near at hand" (2:13; 6:4; 11:55) is hardly a secondary formula of transition, and cannot bear the burden of the proof for the radical transformation into a "Passion Gospel". Does not the author take offence too quickly—like earlier literary analysts—at many items which may well be accounted for by the style and intention of the evangelist? The three stages of composition are unnecessary, if the evangelist did not proceed as systematically as is here supposed. Why should his "basic Gospel" have been an unpretentious narrative, which he gradually filled out with discourses and finally gave a constructive orientation for theological reasons? He could have started with a different conception of his task. Perhaps he decided at once to combine various narratives with revelation discourses, and to present the mystery of the Passion, which he saw as the "exaltation" of Christ, the entry upon "glorification",[19] at the very beginning of his work. An investigation

[19] See Thüsing, *Die Erhöhung und Verherrlichung Jesu im Johannesevangelium.*

of Johannine theology in terms of its leading ideas and principles, prescinding from the structure of the Gospel, rather goes to show that Jesus's way to his predestined death also stirred this evangelist deeply and was the great preoccupation of his theological thinking. Hence he never planned his Gospel except in the perspective of the Cross and Resurrection, both of which were most intimately bound up with one another in his theological thought. It is quite true that the evangelist cannot have written his Gospel in one piece without break or pause. But it would be difficult to prove that it was composed by stages, spread presumably over a long period, in which the theological thought developed progressively. But Wilkens too supposes that he could not give his Gospel its final form.[20] Any unevennesses which may be noted should, therefore, rather be ascribed to the final redaction.

Another view of the history of tradition is arrived at if one follows M.-É. Boismard, who studies the eschatological texts of John and finds there two different theological strata, adjoining one another but remaining distinct.[21]

Boismard bases himself on texts which seem to take different eschatological viewpoints: 12:46–50, compared with 3:16–19a; 5:26–30a, compared with 5:19–25. The texts mentioned first in each case reflect the standard (futurist) eschatology, the others give the "realized eschatology" which is mostly taken to be specifically "Johannine". He considers the former to represent the earlier stage (in contrast to Bultmann, who ascribes it to a later ecclesiastical redaction), while the latter came later. "We may therefore conclude that there was an evolution in the Johannine traditions. The concept of an eschatological judgment was replaced by that of a judgment already realized" (p. 514). He raises the question of our having here two different renderings of the same saying of Christ, which the redactor of the Gospel arranged as a diptych (p. 516), considers the development explained by the "re-reading" *(relecture, passim)* of the text, and thinks that the developed texts show contacts with 1 Jn (p. 516). He finds further examples of two theologically disparate strata in 5:30b–32, 37, compared with 8:14–18 (p. 518); 14:1–3, compared with 14:18–21 (pp. 520 ff.), and refers briefly to 7:33–36, compared with 8:21f.; 6:35–50, compared with 6:51–58; 8:37–39, compared with 8:40–42a (p. 523). He offers a choice of two explanations for the "re-readings". There may have been two different authors, the younger, who also revised the Epistles, being possibly a disciple of the older. Or the "re-readings" may be due to the same author, whose own style and theology had developed over a long period. Briefly, our criticism is as follows: the arguments from the analysis of the style are not effective; there is indeed a certain tension in the thought, but it need not point to two strata. It can be supposed to have persisted in the thought of the same theologian.[22] It is misleading to identify

---

[20] *Entstehungsgeschichte*, p. 172.

[21] "L'évolution du thème eschatologique dans les traditions johanniques".

[22] The difficulties of the divergent lines of thought in John should not be ignored; one of the most striking examples is perhaps the juxtaposition of the Paraclete logion, 14:16 f., with the promise of Jesus's own coming 14:18 ff. There could be reasons in tradition for this, not that two literary strands have been combined, but because the evangelist possibly

the "younger" theologian (of the realized eschatology) with the author of 1 Jn, since the older eschatology stands out strongly once more in the great Johannine Epistle (cf. 2:28; 3:2; 4:17[23]). If the two "strata" are to be attributed to the same author, it is impossible to understand why he allowed the two views to stand (sometimes immediately side by side). It would be better to suppose two different authors, whose separate texts were combined but not reconciled in the process of redaction. But this too is very improbable.

There are undoubtedly considerable tensions in the texts of John, but they hardly allow us to conclude to two different "strata". One should rather ask whether they are not part of the evangelist's own thinking, resolved by him in the sense that they were both preserved and overcome. Thus, for instance, the Johannine Jesus can claim that his own "testimony" is fully sufficient (8:14), and still have recourse a little later to the testimony of two witnesses demanded by the law, given by his Father and himself (8:17f.). He can affirm that he judges no one (8:15), and again, that his judgment is true (8:16; cf. 5:30). These "tensions" grow out of the Johannine Christology, which is as fully aware of the contrast between Son and Father, and of the Son's obedience, as of his perfect inner unity with the Father. Something similar must be supposed in the eschatological texts: realized eschatology is the real interest of the evangelist, but it does not exclude the futurist. It merely means that he rarely envisages the "day of judgment" and the resurrection of the body. Thus even these considerations do not point with certainty to different strata in the history of tradition, but rather to the evangelist, who must, however, have himself adopted diverse traditions and worked them into his theology.

A subsequent revision and expansion of the Gospel by the evangelist is also accepted by P. Parker.[24] His starting-point is ch. 21, which he ascribes to the same hand as chs. 1–20, and he thinks he can prove from ch. 6, ch. 4 and 2:1–12 that the evangelist undertook a "new edition" for certain reasons (the unbelief of the Jews, a stronger interest in the Eucharist, the role of Peter). This attempt is also unconvincing in its practical application. But the main idea, that the evangelist allowed his work to mature slowly, is surely correct.

S. Temple's study of 6:24–71 is also noteworthy.[25] Basing himself on elements of style and vocabulary, he tries to disengage three layers: the "core", which goes back to the tradition of eye-witnesses, a theological

---

took up a ready-made Paraclete logion and inserted it along with the other. But he could well connect the coming of the Paraclete intrinsically with the (spiritual) coming of Jesus, just as a little later he speaks of the coming of Jesus and of the Father (v. 23).

[23] See Schnackenburg, *The Letters of St John*, Introduction, ch. vi, 2.

[24] "Two Editions of John".

[25] "A Key to the Composition of the Fourth Gospel".

revision by the evangelist intended to convince the reader of the Messiahship and divine Sonship of Jesus (vv. 36–40, 44, 46f., 61–65, 71), and a "homily" (vv. 48–59), which may have been inserted into the Gospel when ch. 21 was added. The three strata still seem to be envisaged too one-sidedly from the aspect of literary criticism. He supposes an "early and independent Palestinian source" for the core,[26] and would assign the "homily" to the redaction. But the three strata are all equally well characterized by the style and vocabulary of the evangelist. But if the findings are envisaged from the point of view of the history of tradition, one recognizes the same tendency as has directed our own enquiries so far: the evangelist had at his disposal ancient, independent traditions, probably oral; he also made use of a "eucharistic homily", but moulded all into a unified whole.

These examples may suffice to indicate present-day approaches; in discussing the various attempts, our own standpoint has been made sufficiently plain. It remains, finally, to give an outline of the origins of the fourth Gospel as far as they can be ascertained.

5. The history of the origins of the fourth Gospel

We may perhaps sum up the results of our investigations as follows:

a) Literary criticism does not enable us to distribute the fourth gospel over various independent literary strata, which were then combined by one or more redactions. It is essentially the work of the evangelist, who relied, however, on diverse traditions, and allowed his gospel to grow and mature slowly, but did not finish it completely.

b) It is difficult to point to written sources among the traditions upon which the evangelist worked. Apart from some doubtful cases, direct use of the Synoptics cannot be proved. But he must have had some knowledge of the synoptic tradition by word of mouth, and have taken it for granted in his readers. In the course of their history, his traditions had striking associations with the special tradition of Luke (see above, ch. ii). The use of a written "σημεῖα-source" may be maintained with some probability.

c) For his special traditions, the evangelist could draw on independent and original oral narratives, which may be considered to be of high antiquity and to contain good information. This is a stage of tradition for which efforts have been made to disengage a "basic document" or a "basic Gospel". Though literary criticism is unable to detach and establish such a basic Gospel as an independent piece of writing, it may be

[26] *Ibid.*, p. 220.

presupposed with some assurance as an early stage in the history of tradition.

d) These early traditions must also have contained logia and other utterances already couched in fixed form, which the evangelist made use of for the sayings and discourses of Jesus in his Gospel. A special source for logia or discourses is improbable, but there is reason to think that when shaping the revelation discourses of Jesus, the evangelist utilized formulae which were already fixed, and many established units of discourse. But he inserted them into the dialogues and discourses of Jesus as he constructed them, combining all so well that it is the discourses which bear most clearly the stamp of his mind.

e) It is also possible that at certain places he incorporated liturgical or kerygmatic matter which was circulated and preserved in the communities. This is true of the prologue in particular, the basis of which may be assumed to be a Christian hymn to the Logos, and may also be true of the "eucharistic homily" (linked with Ps 78:24) in 6:31–58, or of its last part, 6:51–58.

f) The evangelist was unable to give his work its final form, and also left some items among his material—particularly discourses of Jesus—which represented further drafts, as perhaps 3:13–21, 31–36; chs. 15–17. These were inserted into the Gospel only at the final redaction, sometimes not quite relevantly (the "unattached" passages of discourse in ch. 3), sometimes with traces of the secondary addition (farewell discourses and high priestly prayer, chs. 15–17).

g) The redactors are certainly responsible for ch. 21, where they may have used material from the evangelist, and perhaps the σημεῖα-source (for the great catch of fish). They are also responsible for certain collocations of text which do not correspond to the original intentions of the evangelist: the inversion of chs. 5 and 6; the displacement of 7:15–24 to its present place, instead of after 5:47; the insertion of one of the fundamental revelation discourses, 3:31–36, 13–21, at two places in ch. 3; perhaps also 12:44–50 at the end of the first main section. Elsewhere the redactors confined themselves to brief glosses and additions (4:2 or 4:1f.; 4:44; 6:22f.; 7:39b; 11:2; perhaps 12:16). It seems unnecessary to suppose major interventions or re-arrangements on the part of the redactors; it likewise seems superfluous to postulate several redactions one after the other.

These results may seem meagre and disappointing after all the sharp-sighted criticism which has been done on John. But if they serve to underline the evangelist's predominant role in the making and shaping of the fourth Gospel, and as the distinctive theologian who gave its doctrine its unified character, then the detours and labours of research have not been in vain. At the same time, John no longer appears as the "single-storeyed" work of an author who wrote it in one piece. It displays a pre-history in tradition, just as it can be seen to have undergone a subsequent redaction. Finally, it must be emphasized that the solution offered to this difficult and intricate question is only the personal and debatable view of the author of this commentary. But it had to be definitely outlined, so that the reader could recognize clearly the direction that has been taken.

CHAPTER V

The Question of Authorship

The "Johannine question" in the narrower sense is concerned with the author of the fourth Gospel. Can it be maintained, as was held throughout the centuries in the Church, demonstrably since the last decades of the second century, that this Gospel was written by John, the son of Zebedee, the brother of James, an outstanding personage in the circle of the Twelve, hence "Apostle" in the sense of one of the "Twelve Apostles"? Or is this view no longer tenable in the light of critical research? This problem has harassed theologians and historians,[1] professional exegetes and laymen,[2] down to recent years, and the answer to it is often considered as a confession touching the faith itself, or at least as the assertion of a definite theological standpoint — and demanded from the scholar on these terms. We have left the question in abeyance up to this, to allow the investigation of the literary character of John to make one thing clear to start with: that this work cannot simply be treated as the work of an author in the modern sense. To give a solution tenable in the light of all scientific methods of investigation, we should have had to postpone the question still further, and first try to describe exactly its style and language, its conceptual framework and its spiritual environment. These aspects cannot be neglected, if one wishes to ascribe the fourth gospel to the Galilean fisherman, the Palestinian whose mother-tongue was Aramaic, the companion and disciple of Jesus born and bred in Judaism. Having examined, however, the literary characteristics of the work, we came to the conclusion that, though not composed in one piece, it testified in the main to the workmanship of one single individual, whom we simply

---

1 See Eckhardt, *Der Tod des Johannes als Schlüssel zum Verständnis der johanneischen Schriften;* on which see L. Martyn in the *Journal of Biblical Literature* 81 (1962), p. 314; W. Michaelis in *Theologische Literaturzeitung* 89 (1964), pp. 133 ff.

2 See Green-Armytage, *John Who Saw*. Among theologians, the authorship of the son of Zebedee was defended recently in particular by Nunn, *The Authorship of the Fourth Gospel;* Edwards, *The Gospel according to St John*.

call "the evangelist". Hence we shall discuss the question of authorship at once, to check our results in the light of the viewpoints just mentioned. Another reason for doing so now is not to delay too long the presentation of the external evidence of tradition to the authorship, so that the reader may be in a position to compare the conviction of the early Church with the observations of modern biblical scholarship on the nature and structure of the work.

But first it seems necessary to put the "confessional" angle, the significance of this question for the faith, in its proper light, and to rid the debate of unnecessary acrimony. Why do some champion so vigorously the authorship of the son of Zebedee, and why has the magisterium taken the abandonment of this position so seriously?[3] Certainly not because it might mean the end of a long-cherished notion, a "Church tradition". On the question of authorship with regard to other books of the Bible, as for instance whether the epistle to the Hebrews was the work of St Paul, the opinion of earlier centuries has been revised. But what seems at stake here is the authority of the Bible, and in particular the reliability and binding force of the tradition preserved in the fourth Gospel. It is a matter of the "apostolicity" of the last canonical Gospel. Historical conditions also conspired to render scientific criticism suspect, because many radical critics—in the nineteenth and at the beginning of the twentieth century—denied that John had any historical value at all, and treated it as a late work of doubtful origin. Hence its authority as "Gospel" in the sense described above (in ch. i) was at stake, and Christianity was threatened with the loss of an important witness for the coming of Jesus Christ, for his message and history and revelation. In the meantime, however, the most radical verdicts have had to be modified in the light of scientific findings: the late dating, for instance, well into the second century, has had to be revised since the discovery of very early papyri, especially P^{52} of about A.D. 130, and the historical value of many of the data of John is also esteemed more highly. So it seems to be time to correct also any too narrow apologetical or fundamentalist views, as if what mattered was to have a work written by the Apostle's own hand as far as possible, coming straight in its original form from his desk. We have long since learned to recognize and accept the fact that

[3] Cf. the Responsum IV of the Pontifical Biblical Commission, 29 May 1907: "Joannem Apostolum et non alium quarti Evangelii auctorem esse", is to be affirmed both in accordance with tradition *(Enchiridion Biblicum*, p. 187) and the internal evidence *(ibid.*, p. 188). It must be considered, however, that researches into the history of tradition which have made a slow genesis of the Gospel probable, had not then been sufficiently advanced, and that in the meantime the historical and apologetic questions (especially that of authorship) have been thrown open to enquiry, in so far as they do not affect the faith itself (cf. *Biblica* 36 [1955], pp. 564 f.).

this is not so in the case of other biblical books, the gospel of St Matthew, for instance. Once the Gospels may be rightly considered "apostolic", that is, the testimony of the authorized guarantors of the primitive Christian kerygma, of the legitimate envoys sent out to preach by Jesus, the question of the actual writer becomes less pressing. It makes no difference whether they were composed directly by the companions of Jesus and the witnesses of his resurrection, or by disciples of the Apostles (cf. Mark and Luke) or by other authors who wrote at their mandate, by their authority, and in their spirit. From the theological point of view, therefore, the question of authorship really comes down to the "apostolic authority" behind the Scriptures which were then recognized and proclaimed by the Church as inspired and canonical. Without further discussion of this dogmatic question,[4] which is still being debated on many points, we must reject the alternative: is John the son of Zebedee author of the "Gospel of St John" or not? as wrongly put and misleading. It is more correct to ask, as we do more or less with regard to our present Gospel of St Matthew: does the Gospel of St John have apostolic authority behind it, in particular, that of the Apostle St John? The fact that there may still be a history of tradition and redaction between the Apostle and the final form of the Gospel is of less significance for the faith.

Having thus taken our bearings, we now turn to the external evidence, given in the testimonies of tradition, and the internal evidence, drawn from the Gospel itself. For a closer study of the texts we must refer the reader to the special works on the subject.[5]

1. The tradition of the ancient Church about the author of the fourth Gospel

We have several witnesses to tradition from the fourth quarter of the second century, which show that in various regions (Asia Minor, Egypt and Rome) the fourth gospel was traditionally ascribed to the Apostle St John. The clearest and most important testimony comes from St Irenaeus, Bishop of Lyons († c. 202), a native of Asia Minor. He was not, however, the originator of this view. He is merely the most pre-eminent witness to the tradition of Asia Minor, to which he had his own contribution to make. It is also attested independently by Polycrates of Ephesus (see below). The view held in Rome can be seen from the

[4] Cf. for instance Benoît, "Inspiration"; Rahner, *Über die Schriftinspiration*, E. T.: *Inspiration in the Bible;* Congar, "Inspiration des Écritures canoniques et apostolicité de l'Église".

[5] Along with the Introductions, see esp. Zahn, *Forschungen zur Geschichte des neutestamentlichen Kanons und der altkirchlichen Literatur*, pp. 175–217; Lagrange, *Saint Jean*, pp. xii–lxvi; Braun, *Jean le Théologien*, pp. 331–55.

Muratorian Canon, and that of Egypt in Clement of Alexandria, though here it is possible that this much-travelled man may have acquired his information elsewhere, perhaps also in Asia Minor. Thus discussion of the value of St Irenaeus's testimony[6] loses some of its urgency, though it is still important enough to ask how far he understood Papias and St Polycarp correctly, when they spoke of their authorities.

(a) St Irenaeus: his testimony and his authorities

The Bishop of Lyons expresses his conviction unmistakably: "After that, John, the disciple of the Lord, he who had leaned on his breast, also published the Gospel, while living at Ephesus in Asia".[7] He gives his view in greater detail in another text, where he enlarges upon the age of Jesus (cf. Jn 8:57): "And all the presbyters who had met in Asia around John, the disciple of the Lord, testify that this (Jesus's being 40 to 50 years of age) was handed on by John. For he lived among them till the time of Trajan".[8] He is assured of the authority of the Church of Ephesus, because "it was founded by Paul, and John lived there till the time of Trajan", which makes it an authentic witness of the tradition of the Apostles.[9]

St Irenaeus, therefore, bases his conviction on the "presbyters", among whom St John was supposed to have lived. He names one of them in particular, St Polycarp, Bishop of Smyrna († 156), whom he himself heard when still a child. Polycarp always taught what he had heard from the Apostles, and there were people who had heard him tell the story of how John, the disciple of the Lord, arriving at Ephesus and wishing to take a bath, saw (the heretic) Cerinthus inside, and fled from the building, refusing to take a bath along with this enemy of the truth.[10] Of St Polycarp of Smyrna, who is known to us from his letter to the Philippians and the ancient account of his martyrdom, we learn more from St Irenaeus in his letter to Florinus, which is preserved in Eusebius.[11] Here we are told that he heard Polycarp speaking of his "association with John" (τὴν μετὰ Ἰωάννου συναναστροφήν), and with the "others who had seen the Lord", and how well he used to recall what John had related of the Lord, his miracles and his doctrine. Polycarp, therefore, could be said to have been a hearer of the "eye-witnesses of the Word of Life".

[6] Gutjahr, *Die Glaubwürdigkeit des irenäischen Zeugnisses über die Abfassung des vierten kanonischen Evangeliums;* Zahn, *Forschungen*, pp. 53–94; Chapman, *John the Presbyter and the Fourth Gospel.*

[7] Irenaeus, *Adv. haer.*, III, 1, 2 (Harvey, vol. II, p. 6).

[8] *Ibid.*, II, 33, 3 (Harvey, vol. I, p. 331); also quoted by Eusebius, *Hist. eccles.*, III, 23, 3.

[9] *Ibid.*, III, 3, 4 (Harvey, vol. II, p. 15).

[10] *Ibid.*, III, 3, 4 (Harvey, vol. II, pp. 12 f.).

[11] Eusebius, *Hist. eccles.*, V, 20, 4–8.

Prudent historical criticism does not doubt that St Irenaeus, as a child, still heard St Polycarp speaking of disciples of the Lord, including one named John. But reserves are made as to whether this John must have been the Apostle, the son of Zebedee, as St Irenaeus supposed. The reasons for this scepticism are: a) In the letter to Florinus, John is not called an Apostle. However, as St Irenaeus elsewhere affirms that some of "the presbyters saw not only John, but other Apostles as well",[12] he must certainly have considered him to be the Apostle. b) St Polycarp himself, in his letter to the Philippians, gives no indication of having known the Apostle John or any other of the Apostles.[13] But at the end of his letter to Florinus, St Irenaeus says that Polycarp wrote letters (a number of them) to the neighbouring communities and to individual Christians, so the silence of the Bishop of Smyrna in his letter to the Philippians must not be over-stressed, especially as he wished to honour St Paul, on account of the recipients. c) St Irenaeus also calls Papias of Hierapolis a "hearer of John and companion of Polycarp",[14] but is contradicted by Eusebius, who also knew the writings of Papias, quotes the decisive passage (see below), and accuses St Irenaeus of having confused the Apostle with the "presbyter John". This is the most important argument, because, as we shall see, Eusebius was probably correct about Papias. This does not of course prove that St Irenaeus was wrong about St Polycarp. But the suspicion remains that he could as a child have also been confused about the John mentioned by St Polycarp, especially as he mostly speaks of John as "the disciple of the Lord", without calling him an Apostle.

Papias thus appears as another of St Irenaeus's authorities. He nowhere says that he knew the Bishop of Hierapolis personally, but we can check the passage that he must have read in Papias's work on the gospels, since it is explicitly quoted by Eusebius. It may be translated as follows:

"(a) I shall be glad to tell you, in the course of my exposition, everything that I once learned from the presbyters. I remember it all very well, and I can guarantee its truth . . .

(b) But if it happened that someone who followed the presbyters came this way, I used to ask for the words of the presbyters, what Andrew

---

[12] *Adv. haer.*, II, 33, 3 (Harvey, vol. I, p. 331).

[13] For this argument, which is constantly invoked, the date of Polycarp's death is important. It has been suggested that the data given by Eusebius point to the reign of Marcus Aurelius (161–180), but the accepted date (155 or 156) is still the most probable; cf. Baus, *Von der Urgemeinde zur frühchristlichen Grosskirche*, p. 161, E. T.: *From the Apostolic Community to Constantine*, p. 136. Irenaeus affirms expressly that Polycarp spoke of his acquaintance with those "who had seen the Lord" *(Ep. ad Florinum)*; see also Braun, *Jean le Théologien*, pp. 334–8.

[14] *Adv. haer.*, V, 33, 4 (Harvey, vol. II, p. 418); also Eusebius, *Hist. eccles.*, III, 39, 1.

or Peter said, or what Philip or Thomas or James or John or Matthew or any other of the Lord's disciples (said),

(c) and what Aristion and the presbyter John, the disciples of the Lord, were saying. For I considered that I should never gain as much from books, as from the living and abiding voice".[15]

A John is named twice in this text: first in the list of the seven Apostles mentioned by name (b), and then along with the disciple of the Lord, Aristion (c). The primary sense of the text seems to be that given by Eusebius: a distinction is made between two persons called John, one an Apostle, the other a "presbyter". There are, however, defenders of the other view, according to which Papias meant the same person in both cases.[16]

The first reason given is the different tenses in (b) and (c): Papias used to ask what one of the Apostles whom he mentioned had said (εἶπεν), and also what Aristion and the "presbyter John" were still saying (λέγουσιν), both being alive at the time of his enquiries. The Apostle John, mentioned once already, is mentioned again because he lived longer, and given the title "presbyter" at the second mention, to distinguish him from Aristion. The order of the names is strange, the Apostle coming after Aristion. But this argument is countered by pointing out that the list of the Apostles is also given in ascending order, the two evangelists, John and Matthew, coming at the end.[17] It is of particular importance for the interpretation to determine who the πρεσβύτεροι were. In this view, they are always Apostles: Papias was able to learn some things from the Apostles themselves (a), then included what he had learned about them from their disciples (b), and also got information about what the survivors, Aristion and the Apostle John, were saying (c).

But this interpretation gives rise to serious misgivings. The main objection is that the πρεσβύτεροι can hardly be the Apostles themselves, but only, as in St Irenaeus,[18] bearers of tradition in an earlier generation, mostly disciples of the Apostles. Taken this way, the passage also gives a good sense: Papias did not get information from the Apostles themselves, but from men close to them (a); he was so interested in the words of these disciples of the Apostles that he also interrogated those who had been in touch with them, to have further information about what they had heard from the Apostles (b); finally, he also tried to learn what two surviving "disciples of the Lord"[19] had to say (c). The fact that only John, and not Aristion, receives the title of ὁ πρεσβύτερος, may be due to the fact that this was the favourite way of speaking of this particular John (on which see below). The idea that Papias himself was a hearer of the Apostles (a) is also open to doubt on other counts (compare the other traits which Eusebius quotes from his works).

---

[15] *Ibid.*, III, 39, 3 f.

[16] Zahn, *Forschungen*, pp. 112–52; Meinertz, *Einleitung*, pp. 218 f.; Feine and Behm, *Einleitung*, pp. 107 ff.; Michaelis, *Einleitung*, pp. 93 ff.; Nunn, *Authorship*, pp. 52–70; Edwards, *The Disciple*, pp. 3 ff.

[17] Michaelis, *Einleitung*, p. 93.

[18] See Chapman, *John the Presbyter*, pp. 13–19; Lagrange, *Saint Jean*, pp. xxxiv–xlii; Bornkamm, "πρεσβύτερος", pp. 676 ff.; Braun, *Jean le Théologien*, pp. 361 f.

[19] This designation of Aristion and the "Presbyter John" causes difficulty, since it clearly means that they were companions of Jesus, like the Apostles named under (b). Some

Thus the two Johns in the quotation from Papias should be kept apart, and personal contact with the Apostle John seems to be excluded. Then Irenaeus was wrong in appealing to this authority as a "hearer of (the Apostle) John", which does not mean that his testimony to tradition becomes worthless. He still offers security for the view of his times that John the son of Zebedee was the author of the fourth Gospel.

(b) Polycrates of Ephesus

There is still further proof that the Church of Ephesus felt itself closely associated with the Apostle John. We have the testimony of Bishop Polycrates, who, when writing to Pope Victor I (about 190) about the date of Easter, pointed to the great "stars" (στοιχεῖα) who were buried in Asia and would rise on the last day, the Apostle Philip in Hierapolis, and "John, who leaned on the breast of the Lord, who was a priest and bore the breastplate (πέταλον), a witness (μάρτυς) and a teacher: who is buried in Ephesus".[20] Nothing is said of the authorship of the fourth Gospel, but the tradition that the son of Zebedee lived at Ephesus and died there is perfectly plain. Eusebius also heard of the tomb of John at Ephesus—of two tombs in fact, each with the name of John.[21]

The value of Polycrates's testimony is, however, lessened by the fact that this second-century bishop confused the "evangelist" Philip, one of the seven deacons (cf. Acts 6:5; 8; 21:8), whose two daughters he refers to, with the Apostle Philip ("Philip, one of the twelve Apostles"). He could also have made a mistake about the Apostle John, and Irenaeus may have been misled from the start by the error of the Church of Ephesus. There is also something strange about the remark: "He was a priest, who bore the (high priestly) breastplate". This can hardly be seen as a vague reminiscence of some relationship of the Apostle John with high priestly circles (cf. Jn 18:15). The statement is probably to be understood as a symbolic expression for the priestly activity of John of Ephesus.[22]

---

scholars think of an interpolation, as the words are missing in the Syriac version; cf. Mommsen, "Papianisches"; also Lagrange, *Saint Jean*, p. xxxiii; Bardy, "Jean, le Presbytre", col. 844; but see Munck, "Presbyters and Disciples of the Lord in Papias", esp. pp. 230 and 239 f. It can hardly be correct that the "Presbyter John" was an immediate disciple of the Lord, as has often been held in connection with the hypothesis of his authorship (see text, section g).

[20] In Eusebius, *Hist. eccles.*, III, 31, 3.

[21] *Ibid.*, III, 39, 6; he suggests that the other "John" might be the author of Revelation, no doubt influenced by Denis of Alexandria, whose opinion he cites elsewhere (VII, 25, 6 ff.).

[22] See Zahn, *Forschungen*, pp. 209–13; Lagrange; *Saint Jean*, pp. liv f.; Stauffer, *Die Theologie des NT*, p. 25 (John a sacred minister); Braun, *Jean le Théologien*, pp. 339 f.

(c) Clement of Alexandria

The frequently quoted passage from the Hypotyposes[23] is valuable, not merely because it designates "John" as the author of the fourth Gospel, but because it attributes this tradition to "the ancient presbyters".[24] "Presbyter" here can hardly mean any thing very different from what it means in Papias and Irenaeus: bearers of tradition in an earlier generation, mostly disciples of the Apostles. One may even suspect that here the learned Alexandrian is dependent on the tradition of Asia Minor.[25] Clement did in fact know the Ephesus tradition, as is clear from a passage in his *Quis dives salvetur*, which says that the Apostle John came to Ephesus from the island of Patmos after the death of the tyrant (Domitian) and visited the surrounding country, where he installed bishops and set up close bonds between all the communities.[26] Then follows a long and edifying story about a young man, converted by John, who afterwards became chief of a band of robbers and was finally brought back once more to repentance by the aged Apostle. It is at least an indication that legends were soon formed about John of Ephesus.

(d) The old Latin Gospel prologues and the Muratorian Fragment

There is a prologue attached to the Gospels in several Latin manuscripts, which goes back, according to the studies of De Bruyne and Harnack to the second half of the second century, though brought down later in a more recent study.[27] The text, not uniform in all the manuscripts, reads as follows:

> "Evangelium Johannis manifestatum et datum est ecclesiis ab Johanne adhuc in corpore constituto, sicut Papias nomine Hierapolitanus, discipulus Johannis carus, in exotericis (id est in extremis) quinque libris retulit, descripsit vero evangelium dictante Johanne recte; verum Marcion hereticus, cum ab eo fuisset improbatus eo quod contraria sentiebat, abiectus est ab Johanne. Is vero scripta vel epistulas ad eum pertulerat a fratribus qui in Ponto fuerunt".[28]

---

[23] Eusebius, *Hist. eccles.*, VI, 14, 7. [24] *Ibid.*, VI, 14, 5.

[25] Cf. Bornkamm, "πρεσβύτερος", p. 679, who calls attention to the contrast with Irenaeus, that "the doctrinal succession of the presbyters is never linked with the succession to the episcopal office". Origen remains in this line, *ibid.*, pp. 679 f.

[26] *Quis dives salvetur*, 42, 1 f. (Stählin, vol. III, pp. 187 f.); also in Eusebius, *Hist. eccles.*, III, 23, 6.

[27] Heard, "The Old Gospel Prologues", esp. p. 15, places them as late as 5/6th century, on account of the legendary traits in the last part; see also Haenchen, *Apostelgeschichte*, p. 10 with note.

[28] Cited according to Aland, p. 533; on the MSS variants cf. Braun, *Jean le Théologien*, pp. 345 ff.

The appeal to the writings of Papias is important ("exotericis" may be a mistake for "exegeticis"), but whether the information given in the first sentence actually comes from him is doubtful, on account of the silence of Eusebius. If the sentence was originally written in Greek,[29] it would make it still more probable that the writings of Papias were known in Rome at an early date. As to the John here mentioned (see above on Irenaeus), the quotation itself does not allow us to draw any precise conclusions. The author of the prologue certainly understood him to be the Apostle.

The following sentences, however, diminish considerably the value of the prologue. We observe here again the growth of legend, as in Clement of Alexandria. The assertions, whose source is unknown to us, cannot be defended historically. It is improbable (cf. the preface of Papias's work, given in Eusebius) that John dictated his work to Papias, and impossible that the heretic Marcion (born about 85, proclaiming his doctrines in Asia Minor about 130) was condemned by John himself. It is arbitrary to try to correct "by John" into "by Papias" or "by (an appeal to) John", or to explain it as a later interpolation by a copyist. Hence the assertions after "retulit" at least, must be considered as anachronisms. This does not exclude the fact that the first sentence contains a record of a tradition widespread in Rome, which possibly reached there from Asia Minor.

This idea is also supported by the Muratorian Canon, which is from the last decades of the second century. The part of this famous fragment dealing with John reads as follows (with corrected spelling):

> (Lines 9–16) "Quartum evangeliorum Johannis ex discipulis. cohortantibus condiscipulis et episcopis suis dixit 'Conieiunate mihi hodie triduo, et quid cuique fuerit revelatum, alterutrum nobis ennarremus'. eadem nocte revelatum Andreae ex apostolis, ut recognoscentibus cunctis Johannes suo nomine cuncta describeret." (Lines 26–33) "quid ergo mirum, si Johannes tam constanter singula etiam in epistulis suis profert dicens in semetipsum 'Quae vidimus oculis nostris et auribus audivimus et manus nostrae palpaverunt, haec scripsimus vobis'. sic enim non solum visorem se et auditorem, sed et scriptorem omnium mirabilium domini per ordinem profitetur".[30]

This is the oldest list of canonical books in existence, and is generally taken to be of Roman origin, composed possibly by Hippolytus of Rome. The author reckons John among the "disciples", that is, among the

---

[29] Heard, "The Old Gospel Prologues", pp. 11 f., gives some older opinions; Braun, who appeals to J. Donovan, points to the fact that a Greek ἐκηρύχθη must be behind *manifestatum*.

[30] Text according to Lietzmann, pp. 5–7.

companions of Jesus (as follows from line 22), and also ascribes the epistles to him (cf. line 69: *Johannis duae in catholica habentur*). Papias or the Asia Minor tradition could again be behind it,[31] but the account of the composition is accompanied by a legend which tries to confer a very special apostolic authority on the fourth Gospel ("under the auspices of all" the Apostles), and, in addition, commits the anachronism of imagining that John's "fellow-disciples" were still alive. The same tendency can be recognized in the more or less contemporaneous *Epistula Apostolorum*, when it puts John first in the catalogue of the Apostles.[32] Thus in the oldest canon, as in the old Latin prologue, we can recognize a received tradition, to which tendentious legends have been attached.

(e) Further testimonies

Later testimonies (from the second century on) add nothing substantially new, and generally build on the texts already known. We note here only a few interesting particulars.

At the end of the second century, Tertullian († after 220) is already emphasizing against Marcion that two Gospels come from Apostles, John and Matthew, and two from disciples of the Apostles, Mark and Luke.[33] And he has a further legend to tell, obviously of Roman origin: at Rome, the Apostle John was plunged into boiling oil but came out unhurt and was banished to an island.[34]

Eusebius (†339), in spite of his interpreting Papias in the sense of two Johns, accepts the Apostle John as the author of the fourth Gospel, and remarks, as he does about the Gospel of St Matthew, that the Apostle confined himself for a long time to oral preaching, but finally also committed his words to writing.[35] This shows that Eusebius had his own ideas on the origins of the two "Gospels of Apostles" and perhaps even at this early stage had some understanding of the "history of tradition".

The following statement is attributed to St Ephraim the Syrian (†373): "Johannes scripsit illud (sc. evangelium) graece Antiochiae, nam permansit in terra usque ad tempus Traiani." But it is found only in the appendix to his commentary on the *Diatessaron* of Tatian, and not even

---

[31] Cf. Braun, *Jean le Théologien*, pp. 354 f.

[32] *Ep. Apost.*, 2 (13), according to Duensing in *New Testament Apocrypha*, vol. I, p. 192. The same arrangement of the names of the Apostles is also found in the "Apostolic Church Order", which is probably dependent on the *Epistula apostolorum;* cf. Schmidt, *Gespräche Jesu mit seinen Jüngern nach der Auferstehung*, pp. 230 f., 240–46; Horner, *Statutes of the Apostles*, p. 9.

[33] *Adv. Marc.*, IV, 2 (Kroymann, vol. III, p. 426).

[34] *De praesc. haer.*, 36, 3 (Kroymann, vol. II, 2, p. 46).

[35] *Hist. eccles.*, III, 24,5 ff.

in all manuscripts; very probably the whole appendix was only added later.[36] The transfer of the Apostle's place of residence from Ephesus to Antioch is probably due to the local patriotism of the Syrians. There is, however, also another tradition (also attested by St Jerome) which affirms a close link with St Ignatius of Antioch: "Post quem (Johannem) auditores insignes fuerunt Papias Hierapolitanus episcopus et Polycarpus Zmyrnaeus et Ignatius Antiochenus."[37] The relationship of John to Syria and to Ignatius in particular is a difficult matter, which must be reserved for discussion later (see below, g); but these witnesses hardly offer reliable tradition.

Finally, no historical value can be attached to the apocryphal Acts of John. They were known to Eusebius, but cannot be traced back beyond the fourth century. The first part, which, however, did not originally form part of the work, mentions the exile in Patmos and then the Apostle's stay in Ephesus; the main section of the work is completely legendary.[38] The so-called Monarchian prologues to the Gospels (probably not earlier than the fourth to fifth century) show contacts with the Acts of John, in the legend of the death of the Apostle (leave-taking from his disciples by the open grave).[39] The Latin prologue also repeats the tradition about Patmos and Ephesus, and stresses strongly the life-long virginity of the Apostle.[40]

Thus tradition offers a clear picture to the historian, in so far as it shows the conviction of the Church, in the last decades of the second century, that the Apostle St John wrote the fourth Gospel. Originating probably in Ephesus and Asia Minor, the tradition appears almost at the same time in Asia Minor, Egypt and Italy (Rome), and appeals to the tradition of the "Elders" (πρεσβύτεροι), bearers of tradition in an earlier generation, probably disciples of the Apostles. The chief links in the tradition are Papias and Polycarp, but no certain proof can be given of their having had contacts with the Apostles, John in particular, and the possibility of confusion with another John (the "Presbyter") makes the contact questionable (see further below). Legends grew up early about John of Ephesus, and later texts often give clear signs of anachronisms and tendentious accretions. Still, the relatively early conviction in the

---

[36] See Conybeare, "Ein Zeugnis Ephräms über das Fehlen von C 1 und 2 im Texte des Lukas"; Leloir in his edition of the Armenian translation, p. 248, and in his recent edition of the Syriac text in the Chester Beatty MS 709, p. 251, where the remark is missing.

[37] Chronicle (Helm, pp. 193, 25 – 194, 2).

[38] The first part with the story of Patmos and Ephesus in the edition of Bonnet, pp. 153–60; on the *Acts of John* in general see now Schäferdiek.

[39] The "assumption" (metastasis) is found in the *Acts of John*, pp. 106–15 (trans. Schäferdiek, pp. 254–8; James, pp. 257–70); it is told briefly in the prologue (ed. Lietzmann, p. 14).

[40] Ed. Lietzmann, p. 13.

Church of the authorship of the son of Zebedee remains a factor which must be taken seriously into consideration. This is a point, however, which must be examined further, by asking what sort of general recognition was accorded to the fourth Gospel in the Church since the end of the second century (see below, ch. x).

(f) The supposed early martyrdom of the Apostle St John

It would be practically certain that the Apostle John was not the author of the fourth Gospel, even in a basic form, if this great figure of the circle of the Twelve had already suffered martyrdom at an early date. This has been maintained by a number of scholars since E. Schwartz published his studies on "the death of the sons of Zebedee" in 1904, and has been as sharply rejected by others.[41] The controversy is by no means finished yet, but it has lost much of its keenness, since at least the fragility of the arguments has become more apparent. They have recently been re-examined by F.-M. Braun, who has shown that the ostensible arguments from tradition are untenable.[42] A brief summary of them will suffice. But first we must consider another argument, which is drawn from the Gospels themselves: it is "difficult to explain why the prediction of Mk 10:39 par. was retained. . . , if it had been belied by the facts".[43]

According to Mk 10:39b, Jesus says to the two sons of Zebedee: "You shall drink the cup that I drink, and you shall be baptized with the baptism with which I am baptized." These words give rise to many problems, only one of which interests us here. Does the two-fold metaphor mean death, and in fact a violent death, in view of the parallel with Jesus, or can it be understood otherwise? Mt 20:23 has only the metaphor of the cup; the whole pericope is absent in Luke. But the image of baptism has an important parallel in Lk 12:50, where Jesus says of himself: "(But) I have a baptism with which I must be baptized, and how I am in anguish, till it be completed!" It occurs here in conjunction with the mention of the fire which he came on earth to kindle (v. 49).[44] Here we can only outline the earlier usage of these metaphors in the Old Testament. The image of being plunged in a flood occurs frequently in the Old Testament for dire tribulation (cf. 2 Sam 22:5; Ps 32:6; 42:8; 69:2f.; 124:4f.; Is 43:2), the "cup" is "the cup that makes men reel" when God in his anger makes his enemies drink it (Is 51:17, 22; Jer 25:15f.: Lam 4:21; Ps 75:8). Delling thinks that Jesus uses these images to signify the wrath of God which he takes freely upon himself, and into whose ambit the disciples will also be drawn. "Hence death cannot be the only meaning of the chalice and the baptism. The point is not how far the fire will embrace the disciples, or how deeply they will be immersed in the flood. The

---

[41] The literature on the controversy and the sides taken by scholars are given in Braun, *Jean le Théologien*, p. 375, nn. 1–3.

[42] *Ibid.*, pp. 378–85; cf. pp. 407–11.

[43] Kümmel, *Einleitung*, p. 171.

[44] Cf. Jeremias, *Die Gleichnisse Jesu*, pp. 163 f., E. T., pp. 122 f., where there are important pointers to the understanding of the text.

important thing for the disciple is his readiness."[45] The text may undoubtedly contain a "theology of martyrdom", but in the same sense in which Jesus demands that all his disciples should follow him on his way to death (cf. Mk 8:34f. parr.), and the endurance of hate, persecution and distress is enough for this. There can be no question of the logion's conferring the "distinction" of martyrdom on the sons of Zebedee.[46] On the contrary, they are reminded of the destiny of all disciples, and the reference to the Father's power of disposing all things actually excludes any such distinction for the sons of Zebedee. It is, therefore, highly doubtful that the text contains any sort of "prediction", except that of the path of suffering which awaits all disciples of Jesus.

If Mk 10:39 par. does not contain a certain *vaticinium* of the martyrdom of the two sons of Zebedee, one cannot deduce from it with certainty that the early Church had any knowledge of the violent death of the Apostle John at an early date. His brother James soon fell a victim to King Herod Agrippa I (A. D. 44). But John was still alive, and a "pillar" of the Church, when Paul met the first Apostles in Jerusalem, which can only have been at the "Council of the Apostles" of Acts 15, which must be dated about 49. If John died a martyr's death, it would have had to be later (at the hand of Jews); to connect it with the martyrdom of James "the brother of the Lord", in 62, is an arbitrary procedure.

For the early martyrdom of the Apostle John, two later writers of Church history are invoked, who claim to have read in the second book of Papias's work that "John the Theologian and his brother James were killed by Jews". The older of the two, Philip of Side (about 430) did not go about compiling his "Christian History" very conscientiously, as his younger contemporary, Socrates of Constantinople, already complained, and as can be verified in the present case, because the Apostle John had not been given the title of "the Theologian" in the time of Papias. The second "witness" for the supposed testimony of Papias, the monk George Hamartolos (842–847), seems in fact to have said that the Apostle John died a peaceful death in Ephesus. Only one of the twenty-seven manuscripts of his "Chronicle" (*Codex Coislinianus*, 134) reads instead as in Philip of Side—probably an interpolation based on the latter.[47]

Some ancient martyrologies or menologies are also invoked. The *Breviarium Syriacum* (of A.D. 411) gives for 27 December: "John and James, Apostles, in Jerusalem", and the Armenian calendar (probably earlier, third century): "St James the Elder and St John the Evangelist", for 28 December. Such notices vary in the different calendars, and all they intend to do is to fix the date for the liturgical remembrance of the

---

[45] Delling, "βάπτισμα βαπτισθῆναι", p. 112. See also Kuss, "Zur Frage einer vorpaulinischen Todestaufe", pp. 9 ff.

[46] So Lohmeyer, *Das Evangelium des Markus*, p. 223.

[47] See the documentation in Braun, *Jean le Théologien*, pp. 407–11.

saints, which is celebrated under various headings: not only martyrdom but consecration as bishop, transfer of relics etc.; feasts of different saints were celebrated on the same day, and no further conclusions are possible.[48]

In view of all this, the hypothesis of the martyrdom of the Apostle John may be pigeon-holed without misgivings.

(g) The hypothesis of the "Presbyter John"

At the end of our survey of the testimony of tradition to the authorship of the fourth Gospel, we must deal with a hypothesis which must be carefully considered, and which has had many supporters, since it was put forward by A. von Harnack at the end of the last century,[49] down to the present day.[50] It is the hypothesis that the "Gospel of St John" was really written by someone called John, but that this was not the Apostle, son of Zebedee, but the "Presbyter John" mentioned in the quotation from Papias, who was the "John of Ephesus" who lived till the reign of Trajan. He was soon confused with the Apostle, on account of having the same name, but actually belonged to the second generation of bearers of tradition. Hence he is still a man of great authority.

This hypothesis has appeared again and again in various forms, which we cannot go into here.[51] For von Harnack himself, it was linked to the conviction that the Apostle was behind the Gospel in one way or another, and hence that it should be regarded as "the Gospel of John (the Presbyter) according to John (the son of Zebedee)."[52] From the present-day standpoint with regard to the "apostolicity" of the New Testament writings, there need be no serious misgivings against the acceptance of the hypothesis as it stands. If the "Presbyter" possessed good and reliable tradition, which ultimately went back to the Apostle St John himself, why should the ancient Church not have recognized his Gospel as "apostolic", when it found its faith in Christ attested in it? Would the confusion of the two historical personages be really such a

[48] Cf. Braun, pp. 381–5, appealing to H. Delehaye.

[49] *Die Chronologie der altchristlichen Literatur bis Eusebius*, pp. 659–80.

[50] The hypothesis of the "Presbyter" has again received decided support from Merlier, *Le Quatrième Évangile*, pp. 220–45, 446 ff.

[51] See for instance Streeter, *The Four Gospels*, pp. 433–6: the Presbyter was acquainted with Jerusalem and had some personal connections with the Apostle John; Bernard, *Commentary*, vol. I, p. lxiv: he was a disciple of Jesus, though not one of the Twelve and derived his narrative matter from John the son of Zebedee; Edwards, *The Disciple*, pp. 200–11: he was the "other disciple" of Jn 18:15, then a young man, belonging to the priestly families of Jerusalem, a disciple of the Apostle John, whose teachings and recollections he gathered and published, known later as "John the Presbyter (Elder)"; Eckhardt, *Der Tod des Johannes*, pp. 113–26: The Presbyter was only the translator; Ignatius of Antioch was the redactor of the work of the son of Zebedee.

[52] *Chronologie*, p. 677: εὐαγγέλιον Ἰωάννου (τοῦ πρεσβυτέρου) κατὰ Ἰωάννην (τὸν Ζεβεδαίου).

monstrous error as conservative theologians try to make it? In any case, the Church historian Eusebius already accused Bishop Irenaeus of making such a confusion, though he himself likewise considered that the Apostle John had written the fourth Gospel. In recent years, of course, it has often been denied that the Apostle John had any part in the composition of the Gospel.[53] But this is on grounds which are sought in the contents of the Gospel itself. And here it must be asked whether too much attention is not paid to the characteristics which seem to plead for the "Presbyter", and too little to the stratum of tradition which might go back to the Apostle himself. This point can only be discussed when we are dealing with the inner evidence of John (see below, 2). But the possible confusion of the two "Johns" remains primarily a historical problem.

The existence of a "Presbyter John", of the same rank and importance as the otherwise unknown Aristion, is accepted by many scholars, including Catholic ones, from their reading of Papias as quoted by Eusebius.[54] It is also accepted in these pages, in the light of our analysis of the text. But this involves some other questions, which are not without their importance for the problem of the composition of the fourth Gospel: was this "Presbyter" himself an immediate disciple of Jesus? What was his relationship to the Apostle St John? Can he be considered the evangelist, that is, the author to whom we must ascribe substantially the essential stratum of John, the presentation strictly speaking and hence the composition? Is he the same "Presbyter" who introduces himself anonymously, but by the same title, as the sender of 2 and 3 John?

Some scholars still hold that the "Presbyter John", who is named with Aristion in the quotation from Papias, was himself an immediate disciple of the Lord.[55] But this is improbable on the following grounds: a) He must have lived into the first decades of the second century. According to the quotation from Papias, there were contemporaries of his who heard the Presbyter (and Aristion); if the λέγουσιν is also to be referred to the time of Papias's enquiries, it seems that these enquiries (in contrast to the interrogation of the group mentioned earlier) may have gone on for a long time, perhaps till the writing of his work, the date of which, however, is the subject of debate.[56] Both of these "disciples of the Lord", as they are called (on the added title, perhaps an interpolation, see above), must

[53] Cf. Merlier, *Le Quatrième Évangile*, p. 446: "It seems certain to us that he took no part in the redaction of the first text"; Parker, "John the Son of Zebedee and the Fourth Gospel" (twenty-one reasons against, drawn from the character of the son of Zebedee in the New Testament); Kümmel, *Einleitung*, p. 171: "Thus John cannot have been composed by John the son of Zebedee."

[54] So Lagrange, in his commentary, pp. xxix–xxxiv; Bardy, "Jean le Presbytre"; Wikenhauser, *Einleitung*, p. 207; E. T., p. 287; Braun, hesitantly, *Jean le Théologien*, pp. 357–64.

[55] Munck, "Presbyters", pp. 239 f.; Kümmel, *Einleitung*, p. 169; Braun, pp. 360–3 ("probably").

[56] Mostly taken to be about 125–30; but see Gutwenger, "Papias" (about 90); Munck, "Presbyters", pp. 226, 240 (before 100).

have lived to a great age. b) It is probable that Papias himself heard Aristion and the "Presbyter John", as Eusebius was surely right in thinking. "At any rate", writes Eusebius, "he often mentions them by name and gives their traditions in his writings"[57]—an example of which is his explicit quotation of what "the Presbyter"said about Mark.[58] This confirms our previous observation. c) According to Eusebius, the writings of Papias also contained other διηγήσεις of Aristion and παραδόσεις of the Presbyter John.[59] Thus we must probably think of this "Ancient" as a bearer of tradition, who handed on what he had himself heard, but can hardly have been himself an immediate witness of the deeds and words of the Lord.[60] The Aristion named along with him played a still more modest role as "interpreter". Both of them can certainly only be men of the "second generation".

But this provides us with an important preliminary basis on which to answer our next question. We have no idea at all of the relationship, if any, between the "Presbyter John" and the Apostle John. It is improbable, however, in view of the characteristics ascribed to him above, that he was the author of John. And there are further reasons against it: according to external evidence (the papyri), John must have been published early in the second century, presumably before Papias wrote. But given the close contacts between Papias and the "Presbyter", the writings of the latter (or their contents) could not have been unknown to him. But this is hard to reconcile with what Eusebius has to say about the five books of Papias. He was undoubtedly an uncritical collector and compiler of oral traditions, including "extraordinary parables and doctrines of the Redeemer and other still more fabulous things".[61] But if he followed the "Presbyter John" in particular, many difficulties arise, on the supposition that the latter wrote the Gospel. Papias was a chiliast, which was the main reason for Eusebius's vigorous polemics; he also used 1 Jn, as Eusebius explicitly states.[62] But there is no sign of his having used John, or of his being affected by its spirit.

We are left with the dubious statement of the old Latin prologue, that Papias maintained in his writings that the Gospel was published (or proclaimed) and given to the Churches by John while he was still alive. Let us suppose that something of the sort was to be read in fact in Papias. But then he would have certainly described his "Presbyter John" more clearly, if he regarded him as the author of the Gospel,

---

[57] *Hist. eccles.*, III, 39, 7.

[58] *Ibid.*, 39, 15.

[59] *Ibid.*, 39, 14.

[60] See Lagrange in his commentary, p. xxxi: "en style rabbinique, Jean était un Tannaïte, un anneau, non le point de départ des récits relatifs au Seigneur".

[61] *Hist. eccles.*, III, 39, 11.

[62] *Ibid.*, 39, 17.

and the general confusion could not have started so quickly. Or it may also be argued that some such statement may have been made by Papias, with reference to the Apostle, and that Eusebius did not quote it, because he took this view for granted. Papias would then be an early witness for the composition of the fourth Gospel by the son of Zebedee. But the argument remains hypothetical because the testimony of the prologue itself is so questionable.

Strictly speaking, the "Presbyter John" could be the same as the anonymous sender of 2 and 3 Jn. The close affinities between these short letters and the "great" Epistle of St John, and through this with the Gospel, would then buttress the view that the "Presbyter" was also the author of the Gospel. But again the argument is not stringent. There were clearly several "Ancients" at the time, that is, respected bearers of tradition. He need not have been identical with the John mentioned by Papias, and he needed to use only his honourable title of the "Presbyter" when presenting himself to the readers of his letters.[63]

Looked at as a whole, what we know about the "Presbyter John" is too little to base a certain judgment on it. It is, however, probable that he was only a bearer of tradition, one among many, "with the modest role of handing on traditions of secondary rank" (Lagrange). The hypothesis of his having been confused at an early date with the Apostle John, and of his being the author of the Gospel, is much more fragile than is sometimes admitted, and it would be better to drop it.

But if we look back once more at the tradition of the early Church as a whole, the one view that remains solidly founded is that the fourth Gospel was composed by the Apostle John in Ephesus. But we are sure of this only for the closing years of the second century, and it is difficult to trace it back earlier. Supporting evidence for Irenaeus cannot be found in his assertion that Papias was "a hearer of John". But the other factor, his appeal to Polycarp, whom the Bishop of Lyons, while a child, still heard speaking of "John" (the Apostle, to his mind), still has its weight. The less convincing one finds the hypothesis of a confusion between two Johns, the more seriously must the testimony of Irenaeus be taken, even though other problems remain (the recognition and use of John). The insufficiency of the external evidence means that the question of authorship must be investigated in terms of the inner testimony of John itself.

2. The inner evidence

The question of whether the fourth Gospel as we have it could have been written by the Apostle John, son of Zebedee, in view of its nature and

[63] See Schnackenburg, *Letters of St John*, Introduction to 1 and 2 John.

contents, also has many aspects which it is best to consider separately, before forming a general opinion on the matter. And here above all it should be admitted that the personal element cannot be entirely excluded from the verdict on the particular issues.

(a) The son of Zebedee as known from the New Testament, and the narrative of the fourth Gospel

Possibly the most complete collection of the reasons which seem to exclude the authorship of the son of Zebedee, from what we know of him otherwise, is to be found in the stimulating essay of P. Parker.[64] Some of his twenty-one arguments are weak, as for instance that this "Galilean" would have told more about Jesus's activity in Galilee, and that this "fisherman" would have shown more interest in fishing, or that he was an "active" type, a "son of thunder", a man of strong emotions, which he displayed once in his indignation against the Samaritans (Lk 9:54). These and similar "psychological" arguments overlook the fact that the Easter experience and his human and Christian maturation could have brought about a change in him, which we are simply unable to follow. But the arguments on the other side, which are sometimes based on his great age and his spiritual growth, are equally questionable. It cannot be proved that we have in John a typical product of old age.[65] And it cannot be assumed without more ado that the simple man, without higher spiritual culture, whom we know from the Synoptics, the Acts and Gal 2:9, did in fact undergo such a remarkable spiritual development.

Other reasons have more weight. In the Synoptics, Simon Peter and the two brothers James and John play an outstanding part, especially at the raising of the daughter of Jairus, the Transfiguration and Gethsemane, while the sons of Zebedee are never mentioned in the fourth Gospel, except in the epilogue, 21:2. John, of course, might be concealed behind the figure of "the disciple whom Jesus loved". But it is still remarkable that his brother James is not mentioned, though other disciples are, who play little part in the Synoptics. If, however, one recalls that James, the son of Zebedee, died a martyr at an early date, the omission may be occasioned by the actual interests of the later Church. If John is "the disciple whom Jesus loved", his connection with Simon Peter is in fact strongly underlined in the fourth Gospel. The omission of the scenes where the trio come to the fore in the Synoptics may be easily explained on theological grounds, especially the omission of the scene on the Mount of Olives, cf.

---

[64] "John the Son of Zebedee and the Fourth Gospel"; see also Merlier, *Quatrième Évangile*, pp. 200 ff.

[65] See Hoffmann, *Das Johannesevangelium als Alterswerk*.

12:27 ff. The Transfiguration, a scene told in the style of a theophany, could also be omitted, because, for the evangelist, it is the "signs" which reveal the glory of Jesus, and a direct theophany is not to be thought of (cf. 14:8 ff.). The exorcisms, in which, according to Parker, John the son of Zebedee took a great interest, could also be omitted from the fourth Gospel, in keeping with its theological purpose, which is to show how the supernatural and divine dignity of Jesus found expression in his immediate self-revelation. And it cannot be proved from the Synoptics that John, called to discipleship in his early youth, had any particular leanings towards apocalyptic, more perhaps than the other companions of Jesus. We shall return to such questions, which are more theological in nature, in the next section, which is also the place to discuss the oft-quoted remark of Acts 4:13, that Peter and John were "uneducated and simple" folk, as well as the argument from the language of the evangelist.

Most of the reasons adduced remain *argumenta e silentio:* if the fisherman's son from Galilee had written the fourth Gospel, he would have had to tell this or that, which is passed over in silence. But in such cases the actual situation—the *Sitz im Leben*—of the evangelist must first be considered, his purpose in writing, and the concomitant circumstances. The Gospel itself makes it clear that it offers only deliberately selected episodes (20:30), and its purpose is to arouse or strengthen faith in Jesus, the Messiah and Son of God, among a definite circle of readers. It was no part of the purpose of the evangelist to provide a predominantly historical account of the work of Jesus.

Another difficult question is whether the Gospel itself gives signs of having been written by an eye-witness. There is in fact one scene where it makes this claim. Having described how the side of Jesus was opened and how blood and water flowed out, it says: "And he who saw it bears testimony, and his testimony is true, and he knows that he speaks the truth, that you also may believe" (19:35). Views differ, indeed, about the ἑωρακώς and the ἐκεῖνος; there are so many possible interpretations that it is difficult to gauge the bearings of this attestation.

That an eye-witness under the Cross is presented here cannot be doubted: as C. H. Dodd says, "You cannot 'see' a theologumenon; you can see only sensible facts". It is more difficult to decide whether the ἐκεῖνος is meant to introduce someone who guarantees the truth of the testimony, Jesus (so Bultmann etc.) or God, or whether the same witness affirms once more the truth of his statement. According to Johannine usage the latter (ἐκεῖνος taking up ἑωρακώς) is quite possible, and in this case the most obvious.[66] Then the eye-witness can hardly be anyone but the "disciple

---

[66] See the examination of the linguistic usage in Dodd, *Historical Tradition*, pp. 133 f. Bultmann, in his commentary, p. 526, assumes that the text is corrupt: it read originally καὶ ἐκεῖνον οἴδαμεν ὅτι. This emendation is doubtful in the light of 21:24, and arouses misgivings, since it substitutes an easier text for a more difficult one.

whom Jesus loved", mentioned in 19:26. But there is a further question. Is 19:35 a redactional gloss, like the comment of the final redaction 21:24, which likewise ascribes the Gospel to this disciple, or does this verse come from the evangelist himself? In the second case, we should have to suppose that he is speaking of himself in the third person (so Zahn, cf. Schlatter), or again, that he is appealing to someone else to endorse his testimony. One should keep an open mind about this last possibility. But the difficulties of interpretation here listed are such that the verse cannot be used as a sure basis for the discussion of the authorship.

From the narrative passages of the Gospel itself, no certain arguments can be drawn either for or against the author's being an eye-witness. There are many details, indications of persons and places, minor descriptive traits and chronological notes which might point to someone who took part in the events,[67] but other elements are awkward. The supposedly insoluble "aporias" noted by earlier literary criticism, the observations made by the newer history of tradition[68] and the suspicion that sources have been worked over (see above, ch. iv) —all combine to make us less confident that we have the immediate account of an eye-witness before us, even though some items of information (such as in 19:34f.) may go back to a first-hand account. There is not much to be done with this uncertain argument.

(b) The son of the Galilean fisherman and the theological character of the fourth Gospel

One of the main arguments against the authorship of the son of Zebedee is the high spiritual level on which the Gospel is written, in terms, namely, of a theology which is in contact with Hellenistic thought. Can a simple fisherman from the lake of Gennesaret have acquired such a degree of culture?

Too much weight should not be attached to the remark of Acts 4:13. The expression ἀγράμματος need mean no more than "unlearned", that is, in Torah studies, as was also said about Jesus (cf. Jn 7:15), and the second epithet ἰδιώτης confirms this view, since it means the "layman" in contrast to the "expert".[69] One must also consider the context, which stresses the astonishment caused by the eloquence of Peter and John, including their use of Scripture. Their "cultural deficiencies" did not prevent either of them from working as missionaries among the Jews.

If John stayed for many years at Ephesus, as the tradition of the ancient Church maintains, he could have learned much at this centre of spiritual activity, where the most diverse currents of religious life ran

---

[67] See Westcott, *The Gospel according to St John*, pp. xviii–xxi.

[68] See Haenchen, "Johanneische Probleme"; he thinks it is "a fixed tradition, already obscured" (p. 52).

[69] Cf. Arndt and Gingrich, *Lexicon*.

together and mingled and came into conflict with each other. The Gospel itself shows knowledge of rabbinical Judaism (interpretation of the law), Hellenistic Judaism (Wisdom speculation) and indeed a general contact with the thought and language of pagan Hellenism (the Logos concept, "Gnostic" attitudes etc., on which later): but no one could see there any great learning, as for instance in Philo of Alexandria or indeed the author of the Epistle to the Hebrews. Here too one will be inclined to distrust any overall verdict for or against the possible authorship of the Galilean Apostle, and to accept rather the opinion of C. H. Dodd: "It is not impossible to imagine that a Galilean fisherman may have grown into the accomplished theologian whom we meet in the Fourth Gospel, but I find it difficult".[70]

A special problem is presented by the peculiar "realized" eschatology of John which transposes the last things into the present time. It is in fact easier to imagine that one of the first and closest disciples of Jesus, captivated as they were by an earthly Messianism and apocalyptic notions, could have written a work like Revelation, which is so unlike John in language and theology that the difference was already noted in antiquity. But then again, there are so many contacts between the two works that it seems that they must have come from the one school or from similar circles. There seems to us to be a very strong tension between eschatology as present and realized and an eschatology which looks forward to a dramatic end of the world. But the early Church need not have felt it as an irreconcilable contrast in its spirituality, as may be seen from the great Epistle of St John. The question remains, of course, as to whether one and the same author could have written such different works, or whether it is not much more likely that one Christian circle of great vitality produced two different personalities, one speaking with more of a prophetic voice, the other more contemplative. That the two spiritual attitudes are not mutually exclusive can also be seen from the texts of Qumran, where an apocalyptic and bellicose work like *The War of the Sons of Light against the Sons of Darkness* is preserved alongside of the *Thanksgiving Hymns*, which strive for a profound and intimate fellowship with God. But here too one can hardly think that both works come from the same author. The relationship between John and Revelation is part of our problem, but it is impossible to go into it more deeply here.[71]

There is something else to consider with regard to the acknowledged use of "rabbinical" arguments (cf. 7:22f.; 8:17, 56; 9:31; 10:34 etc.) and

---

[70] *Historical Tradition*, p. 16.

[71] See Wikenhauser, *Einleitung*, pp. 394–8, E. T., pp. 547–53; Boismard, "L'Apocalypse", pp. 739 ff.; Merlier, *Quatrième Évangile*, pp. 215–20; Braun, *Jean le Théologien*, pp. 43–59.

"messianological" information (cf. 1:21, 25; 7:27, 42, 52; 12:34) in the fourth Gospel.[72] The queries and controversies also reflect very clearly the conflicts between Jews and Christians at the end of the first and the beginning of the second century. A Christian who had been born a Jew, even if he came from Palestine, could hardly avoid such controversies if he found himself in an environment where the two fronts met. He would have had to learn and handle the arguments and answers used by each side. If one of the intentions of John was to be topical polemics and propaganda, it is understandable that an able Jew from Palestine, arriving in the Greek diaspora (cf. Jn 7:35), should have acquired the necessary knowledge and intervened in the struggle. The author cannot have grown up in the diaspora: he is too well acquainted with the geography and other details of Palestine, as is clear from the whole of John; and it is hard to imagine that a pilgrim coming for the Passover or the like would have ever seen some of the places mentioned (e.g., the sites where the Baptist worked). But these are only possibilities. They do not furnish a positive proof that the son of Zebedee was the author of John.

But what of the "Gnostic language" of the discourses of Jesus in John, which are supposed to "make it impossible that John was composed by an eye-witness"[73]? First of all, this description needs to be considerably restricted. We have already maintained that it seems unwarranted and unnecessary to suppose a source containing "Gnostic revelation discourses" (see above, ch. iii). There is a growing tendency to revise or indeed reject the thesis put forward by Bultmann and his disciples, and also by other scholars, with regard to the "Gnostic" background of the discourses of Jesus. Nonetheless, it is hardly possible to deny entirely the influence of certain Gnostic queries (cf. 7:28, 34; 8:14 etc.: πόθεν ἔρχομαι καὶ ποῦ ὑπάγω), presuppositions and terms ("see" in the sense of "know", redemptive "knowledge", perhaps "light and life" and so on). But a comparison with really Gnostic ("Christian") writings like the texts of Nag-Hammadi or the Odes of Solomon show how notably different was the fourth Gospel. Anything in the line of Gnostic questioning and language which may occur, can be sufficiently explained, like the "rabbinical" information, by actual contacts with the environment, and polemic against early Christian heresies of the Gnostic type (cf. 1 John). Again, it cannot be excluded that a mentally alert Jewish Christian from Palestine could have acquired such knowledge. In this case it would be easier to suppose someone who had grown up in a syncretist environment, fully acquainted with its ideas and language and able to pass a sure judgment on them.

---

[72] See Dodd, *Interpretation*, pp. 74–96; on the Messianic notions, Schnackenburg, "Die Messiasfrage im Johannesevangelium".

[73] Kümmel, *Einleitung*, p. 204.

Thus once more the argument leads to no certain conclusion, except that the idea must be rejected that the simple Galilean fisherman could not possibly be responsible for the spiritual heights of the fourth Gospel.

(c) The problem of "the disciple whom Jesus loved"

In the Gospel itself, the strongest statement with regard to the authorship is to be found in 21:24, where the editors affirm: "This is the disciple who testifies to these things, and who has written them down, and we know that his testimony is true." The disciple spoken of here can only be "the disciple whom Jesus loved", mentioned previously (21:20), with regard to whom a saying was current to the effect that he would not die. This opinion is corrected—probably because he had died in the meantime.

The testimony of the redactors and disciples in the epilogue should neither be overrated nor underrated. It is not the direct testimony of the evangelist, but merely reflects the conviction of the redactors, who also added the whole of ch. 21 or gave it the final touches. But it may be deduced from vv. 20–23 (and from the οἴδαμεν of v. 24, if it includes the recipients) that "the disciple whom Jesus loved" was not unknown to the communities, or at least that they had heard of him (cf. the saying which was current about him among the "brothers", v. 23). His death must have been fairly recent, because the saying in question was obviously still causing upsets. A confusion, as in the case of the Presbyter hypothesis, cannot be excluded, but there is no proof of it; and v. 24 contains a decided affirmation about knowledge of the composition of the Gospel, to which περὶ τούτων and ταῦτα must refer. A collective interpretation of the γράψας ταῦτα[74] is untenable.

The text in the epilogue (21:20) expressly identifies "the disciple whom Jesus loved" with the disciple "who leaned on (Jesus's) breast at the supper", and this brings up the texts in the Gospel itself where this disciple is mentioned: 13:23 (at the Last Supper); 19:26 (under the Cross); 20:2 (on Easter Sunday morning—here with ἐφίλει instead of ἠγάπα, probably just a variation). It is noticeable that the designation occurs only in the second part of the Gospel; but this could be due to the fact that it is only there that the evangelist concentrates on the group who are "his own". It has been suggested that "the disciple whom Jesus loved" (the expression "beloved disciple" is better avoided) is also silently indicated in two other places: 1:40f., as the unnamed disciple who had come to Jesus along with Andrew, whose name is given; and 18:15, as "the other disciple" who followed with Simon Peter after the arrest, and managed to enter the courtyard of the high priest because he "was known" to the latter. These suggestions are not unwarranted, though there is no proof for them either. It can hardly be claimed that it follows from the πρῶτον of 1:41 that just as Andrew "first" found his brother Simon, the other

[74] Kragerud, *Der Lieblingsjünger*, pp. 115–19.

also sought out *his* brother (James)—(cf. commentary). Nonetheless, if the silence of the Gospel in his regard is intentional, it is the son of Zebedee who is most likely to have been the unnamed disciple. It is different again in 18:15, where the identification with "the disciple whom Jesus loved" could be suggested by the fact that elsewhere he is always named along with Simon Peter. He need not have been present at the arrest of Jesus; no proof can be drawn from "the other disciple" in 20:2ff.[75] (the article in 18:15 should be eliminated for reasons of textual criticism). The mention of his being known to the high priest is important. With regard to the son of Zebedee, it is surprising, but not impossible, but it rather points to a follower of Jesus from Jerusalem. In any case, all hypotheses based on these texts are very shaky.[76]

If we prescind from the doubtful cases and confine ourselves to the certain texts, "the disciple whom Jesus loved" was definitely present on the following important occasions: the Last Supper, the death of Jesus, the finding of the empty tomb and (in the epilogue) at an appearance of the risen Lord in Galilee. The main question is whether he is to be identified with the Apostle John. We give the main reasons for and against:

For the identification:[77] the "disciple whom Jesus loved" must have belonged to the inner circle of the disciples, since he was present at the Last Supper and even lay on the breast of Jesus. Here, as elsewhere, no serious objections can be brought against the presence of the son of Zebedee. The mention of his standing under the Cross and running to the tomb may go back to special traditions; the close association with Simon Peter is also confirmed by the Acts (Acts 3:1–4,11; 4:13,19; 8:14); no mystery is made about his appearing along with the other disciples, except that his name is not given (though in 21:2 he may be one of the "sons of Zebedee"); the omission of his name is best explained by the fact that it is the evangelist himself; finally, the importance of John the son of Zebedee in the circle of the disciples tells in favour of this solution.

---

[75] *Ibid.*, p. 12, n. 2, Kragerud considers the article in 18:15 as original, and attributes the text with certainty to the "beloved disciple" passages (cf. pp. 25 f.). The article in 20:2 is correctly explained by Bultmann in his commentary, p. 530, n. 3: "and to that other whom . . ."; contrast Westcott's commentary, pp. xxiv and 289: the ἐφίλει was chosen deliberately, because Simon Peter is also included in this friendly love; hence he was one disciple whom Jesus loved, John was "the other . . ."; so too Sanders, "Those Whom Jesus Loved", p. 33. But this is not convincing, since the verbs can also vary elsewhere, cf. 3:35 with 5:20; 11:5 with 3; 14:23 with 16:27.

[76] See Edwards, *The Disciples*, pp. 200–11 (distinguishing him from the "disciple whom Jesus loved", identifies him with the young man of Mk 14:51 f. and considers him the evangelist); so too earlier Strachan, *The Fourth Gospel*, pp. 84–87; see further Kragerud, *Der Lieblingsjünger*, p. 46 with n. 19.

[77] Still most impressively given in Westcott, *St. John*, pp. xxi–xxv.

Against the identification there are also a number of arguments which can be adduced: the omission of the name, and the substitution of the clause with its high pretensions are inexplicable, if the speaker is an Apostle of the rank of John; the self-presentation by the phrase "the disciple whom Jesus loved" is strange, and certainly not a sign of modesty, as might otherwise be suggested to explain the anonymity; the mention of the sons of Zebedee in 21:2 tells rather against than for the identification of "the disciple whom Jesus loved" in 21:7, 20 with John the son of Zebedee, since it violates the principle of anonymity. Here too the disciple in question is rather to be sought behind the two unnamed disciples at the end of the list;[78] in any case "the disciple whom Jesus loved" is a pale and shadowy figure, "not a man of flesh and blood" (Jülicher)—hence an ideal or symbolical figure; this suspicion is confirmed by the clear and undoubtedly deliberate challenge to Simon Peter.

When one considers the reasons for and against, it becomes apparent that there are basically two conflicting opinions: the interpretation as an individual, which is then practically bound to recognize in him the Apostle John, and the interpretation as an ideal or symbolical figure, which is then determined in various ways. It may be the type of the ideal disciple,[79] the ideal bearer of apostolic testimony,[80] gentile Christianity as the perfect form of Christianity,[81] Johannine prophesy in contrast to Church offices.[82] Many scholars see the dilemma which the opinions present: the son of Zebedee, who is practically imperative in the "individual interpretation", must, they feel, be rejected for other reasons, chiefly because the Gospel cannot have been written by an eye-witness;[83] but the "symbolical inter-

---

[78] Cf. Kragerud, *Der Lieblingsjünger*, pp. 43 f.; contrast Jülicher and Fascher, *Einleitung*, p. 401: "The very fact that the sons of Zebedee are mentioned only here (the names James and John do not occur at all in John) gives the impression that here the author, without abandoning entirely his cherished obscurity, wished to hint a little more clearly who the great witness for the gospel might be; the two unnamed disciples of 21:2 are included merely to bring the number up to seven."

[79] Jülicher and Fascher, *Einleitung*, pp. 404 ff.; Kraft, "Die Personen des Johannesevangeliums", pp. 25 f.

[80] Käsemann, "Ketzer und Zeuge", p. 304.

[81] Bultmann, *Johannes*, pp. 369 f.

[82] Kragerud, *Der Lieblingsjünger*, pp. 67–83.

[83] Jülicher, *Einleitung*, p. 407: "But the simplest observations of literary and historical criticism exclude at once an eye-witness as author of this book, and John the Apostle, as depicted in the Ephesus legend, must be ruled out from the start. Hard work was being done between A.D. 70 and 100 in Palestine and the neighbouring countries on written sources; the best possible documentation was being gathered with great trouble, as may be seen from Lk 1:1, and as the very existence of Mark and Matthew show in another way. How is this thinkable if one of the 'pillars', the great authority on the matter, was still alive in Ephesus and could have swept all this paper work into oblivion at any moment by the publication of his memoirs?" See further, section (d).

pretation" also leaves them dissatisfied. In 19:35 and in ch. 21 he is clearly understood as an individual; but this could be dismissed as a mistake of the redactors. However, the symbolic explanation also breaks down even in the texts which are certainly the work of the evangelist, "because his challenge to Peter leads inexorably to the conclusion that Peter too is an ideal figure".[84]

This is also the main objection to the monograph of A. Kragerud, who decides in favour of a symbolic and collective interpretation. He holds that "the disciple whom Jesus loved" is a symbol of the "prophecy" which is behind the whole group of Johannine writings, and which came to compete (in practice, not in theory) with the official authority in the community as represented by "Peter". The figure stands for the "charismatic" ministry in the Church, the "apostolate of the wandering prophets", a well-knit group which thought of itself as mediator between Christ and his community, bearer of revelation, teacher of life and leader of the Church. The office-bearers in the Church were not rejected, but subordinated to the charismatic prophets. This circle produced (collectively) the Gospel of St John. In spite of its many acute observations, this explanation cannot be sustained; the idea of the Gospel as a collective work also breaks down at the singular in 21:24.[85]

Thus the redactors cannot be blamed for a "mistaken" view of the individual interpretation: the Gospel itself suggests it clearly. On the supposition that "the disciple whom Jesus loved" was a historical figure, various proposals have been made to identify him with someone else than the Apostle John;[86] but these efforts only sound like ingenious guesswork. On the other hand, the difficulties in the way of interpreting the disciple as the son of Zebedee must not be overlooked. The embarrassment caused by this dilemma has often led to the resigned confession, that we do not know the author of John. But is there not a way to solve it which will take these difficulties into account and still allow us to maintain the basic authorship of John the son of Zebedee and so the apostolic origin of John?

(d) Attempt at solution; general verdict on the authorship

At the end of his careful monograph, F.-M. Braun writes: "on the supposition that it (John) was produced at a single effort, if we had to ascribe it to a Galilean whose formation was exclusively Hebrew, the book would be unthinkable. But the problem is not to be envisaged this way." He then gives his own idea of the origin of the Gospel: the kerygma

---

[84] Kümmel, *Einleitung*, p. 165.

[85] See my review in *Biblische Zeitschrift* 4 (1960), pp. 302–7.

[86] Mark: Weiss, *Das Urchristentum*, p. 612; Paul: Bacon, *The Gospel of the Hellenists*, pp. 301–31; Lazarus: Filson, "Who Was the Beloved Disciple?"; Sanders, "Those Whom Jesus Loved", pp. 33 f.; Matthias: Titus, "The Identity of the Beloved Disciple".

of John was first crystallized in small literary units, after which a long period of time ensured before John decided to produce a major work. This he did with the help of secretaries and collaborators, giving them only the main lines of his thought, and leaving the rest to the redaction. He probably called on more than one of his disciples in succession. After this preparatory work, and with the situation in Asia Minor in mind, he brought in a competent writer of Greek, who is immediately responsible for our present text. This writer, probably a Jew born and bred in the diaspora, had not finished his work before the Apostle died, and only gave it the finishing touches later, without removing certain difficulties. But we owe it to him that we know of the real author, "the disciple whom Jesus loved", the Apostle John.[87]

Cautiously, therefore (so as not to restrict unduly the Apostle's share), Braun affirms that John does not come directly from the hand of the fisherman's son from Galilee, even though the contents go back to him. The actual writer is someone else, someone familiar with Hellenistic Judaism, whom the aged Apostle made use of as his secretary. The general idea, that we must distinguish between "the primary spiritual cause", so to speak, and the "evangelist", who committed the Gospel to writing, is correct enough; but the hypothesis of a "secretary" is still unsatisfactory. Braun clearly supposes that the writer of the body of the Gospel also made the final comment in 21:24. But this is hard to accept, because the style and character of the epilogue suggest another hand, a special redaction at work subsequently. This is a minor point, however, compared to the recognition of the fact that even the written Gospel as such had a pre-history, and that the son of Zebedee has his place in it, but not in the actual writing of the Gospel. This is basically the way in which we think of the origins of our Gospel of St Matthew. Here too most Catholic scholars postulate a long development from the "basic Matthew" to our present Gospel, which is clearly the work of an author who wrote in Greek.[88]

Braun is very anxious to reduce the contribution of the evangelist who was ultimately responsible for the work, the "redactor" of the Johannine material, to that of a "secretary". But since he makes much of the fact that he was a writer with roots in the Jewish diaspora, he is obviously inspired by the idea that the style and language have a character of their own which cannot be associated with the Apostle John. We must surely concede a far greater measure of independence to the Hellenistic disciple of the Apostle who committed the Gospel to writing, because form and

---

[87] *Jean le Théologien*, pp. 396 f.

[88] Cf. Meinertz, *Einleitung*, pp. 173 f.; Schäfer, *Grundriss*, pp. 59 f.; Wikenhauser, *Einleitung*, pp. 140 f., E. T.: pp. 178 ff.; Léon-Dufour, "Évangile selon Matthieu", pp. 194 f.

content, language and thought, cannot be separated. There is no need, of course, to suppose that all he had at his disposal was the purely factual information from the Apostle which had been long since collected and handed on and to some extent already fixed in writing. We may also assume that he also absorbed the thought which permeated the account of the words and deeds of Jesus, that is, the "apostolic interpretation" of the salvific event. Still, it would be wrong to deny that the evangelist himself re-cast the matter in his own consistent mould of thought, since otherwise he could hardly accomplish his task, which was to make the Apostle's story and message accessible to his readers in the appropriate kerygmatic form. Thus the evangelist would have been both the spokesman who transmitted the tradition and the preaching of the Apostle John, and a theologian in his own right and teacher of the readers whom he addressed.[89]

This is of course merely a hypothesis, but one which tries to do justice both to the tradition of the ancient Church about the authorship and what we know from the work as we have it before us. Let us test it again briefly, in the light of the results now acquired. When examining the external evidence of tradition, we found ourselves constantly forced to distinguish the basic conviction, going back to the "Ancients" (Presbyters), that John the son of Zebedee lived to a great age in Asia Minor or Ephesus, and was the author of the Gospel of St John, from the teeming legends which sprang up around it. The idea that he "dictated" the Gospel and published it under his name before his death is already part of the embroidery and "objectification" of the tradition; for it is practically certain that he was already dead when the final redactors wrote down their testimony in 21:24, and the notion of a solemn promulgation of the Gospel must face the almost insuperable difficulty that John was not readily accepted everywhere in the second century (see below, ch. x). It is a different matter if a work appeared after his death, whose origin was not obvious on the face of it, and if there was no sure information about its publication.

The inner evidence noted in John itself is likewise compatible with this hypothesis. The topographical data, concrete narrative details and other information about the events of Jesus's life point to a bearer of tradition who was in a privileged situation, while the more highly organized state of much of the presentation, and also some vagueness and inconsistency at times, indicate a long process of tradition. Finally, the theological

[89] An analogy, though only a faint one, may be seen in the Epistle to the Ephesians, for which Benoît assumes a secretary also, who put the thought of Paul into a special form, in imitation of Colossians. See "Rapports littéraires entre les épîtres aux Colossiens et aux Éphésiens", pp. 21 f.

tendencies and emphases suggest a work of interpretation (done by the Apostle) and a theological shaping (done by the evangelist), both of which may be accounted for by the purpose of the written Gospel and the conditions in which it was preached. So too certain logia and some elements of discourse already stereotyped must be part of the early tradition, while the typically "Johannine" discourse of Jesus again display the influence of an interpreter, either the venerable preacher, who remains more in the background, or the evangelist who gave the final form to the whole. Or perhaps it would be better to speak of the theological school or trend which is recognizable here, and which was also responsible for the final redaction of the Gospel, and to which the rest of the "Johannine" writings must also be ascribed. It is of course difficult in individual cases to assign a particular item to a given stratum of tradition or a given writer. But we are provided at least with a mental framework into which we can fit our somewhat disparate observations: independent and early traditions, secondary traits, late theological formulations.

The hypothesis is also important for the relationship between the Johannine and the Lukan traditions which was noted above (see pp. 30 ff.). If there is ancient apostolic authority behind John, and the work grew out of the preaching of John the son of Zebedee which was gradually committed to writing, the many contacts with the tradition assembled by St Luke become more readily understandable. They come from a time when the "Johannine tradition" was also in its early stages, and are to be explained partly by echoes of the oral tradition, partly perhaps by written sources, now lost, to which St Luke had access. That the third evangelist could and must have turned to the Apostle John if he lived for a long time in Asia Minor is not so certain as some critics imagine, because we know far too little about how things stood in the last years of the first century. What we have said of the Lukan tradition also holds good for the relationship between John and Mark. Finally, the hypothesis does not rule out the occasional use of other sources, such as a σημεῖα-source, by the fourth evangelist. Why should the Hellenistic Christian who worked on the Apostle's material not also have made use of a written version at his command—and possibly also in the possession of the Apostle? Here, however, it must be conceded that we are well into the region of the merely possible.

The hypothesis appears, however, to be particularly valuable for the problem of "the disciple whom Jesus loved". The difficulty of the evangelist having made such high claims for himself disappears. The designation would rather be due to his disciples, including the evangelist, who were accustomed to speak in this way of their master, John. This is what must have happened in fact: where the narrative goes back to the Apostle, he spoke of himself simply in the first person when he had to mention himself.

His disciples who noted his words and retailed his narratives could, no doubt, have inserted his name; but it is also understandable that they did not use his name among themselves or that they chose respectfully to use a periphrasis.

This hypothesis will find no welcome among those who reject the whole ancient tradition of the Church as legendary, take a very sceptical view of the fourth Gospel and think of its author as an unknown theologian of later times whose "Gospel" is of no value for the "history" of Jesus,[90] or as a collector of traditions handed down in certain communities, perhaps also in the liturgy, which have a certain interest alongside of the synoptic tradition.[91] The state of research at the present day hardly justifies such low esteem of the Johannine tradition. Nonetheless, the "Johannine problem" remains a complicated one and cannot be solved as easily as the conservative defenders of the authorship of the son of Zebedee imagined. Hence we put forward this "intermediate" solution for discussion.

---

[90] Cf. Jülicher and Fascher, *Einleitung*, p. 414.

[91] Cf. Haenchen, "Johanneische Probleme", pp. 53 f.

CHAPTER VI

Language, Style, Movement of Thought

It is important for many reasons to form a clear idea of the language, style and movement of thought of the fourth evangelist. The language could tell us something about his origins and environment; the style and stylistic criteria also have important bearings, as we have seen, on questions of literary criticism, the unity of the work, the use of sources and redactional additions; the movement of thought allows of conclusions about the distinctive mentality of the author and is of importance directly for exegesis. Of these three aspects which affect one another so constantly and profoundly, the first is the most problematical, as may be seen from the different positions taken up by scholars. We shall first try to form a picture of the linguistic situation.

1. The linguistic character of John

In 1902, A. Schlatter published a work[1] in which he had assembled linguistic parallels to the Johannine writings from the two ancient Tannaitic Midrashim, Mekhilta on Exodus and Siphre on Deuteronomy, both written in Hebrew. This collection of material, which is still impressive today, was meant to counter the tendency of the time to range John within the spiritual setting of Hellenism, by giving palpable proof that the "language and homeland of the fourth evangelist" was to be sought for in Palestine. C. F. Burney went further with his thesis of the Aramaic origin of the fourth Gospel,[2] claiming that the author's mother-tongue was Aramaic, and that the work had been composed originally in Aramaic. He was followed by C. C. Torrey, who put forward similar views based on his

[1] Schlatter, *Sprache und Heimat des vierten Evangelisten.*

[2] Burney, *The Aramaic Origin of the Fourth Gospel*, which was examined by Lagrange in his commentary, pp. ciii–cxvi.

own researches,[3] but went beyond Burney by maintaining that all the Gospels were translated from Aramaic. That such an eminent Semitic scholar could put forward such extreme and unacceptable views was a warning for caution, and scholars continued to be sceptical about the Semitic original of John. In 1931, E. C. Colwell put forward the opposite thesis, that there were no traces of Aramaic influence in the Greek of John;[4] his observations on the Greek of John were good, but failed to do justice to many turns of phrase. J. de Zwaan took up again the Aramaic thesis,[5] but criticized many of the supposed mistranslations and other points from which Torrey had argued. The matter was taken a step further by the careful work and nuanced judgments of M. Black, who came to the conclusion that John used perhaps an Aramaic logia-tradition, probably in the form of an early Greek translation, but that the rest of the Gospel, especially the longer discourses, was written in Greek.[6] Many of his observations and findings with regard to various texts are important. The whole matter was again thoroughly investigated by J. Bonsirven,[7] who confirmed to some extent the work of Black. Bonsirven first showed by a number of arguments that John was written in Greek, and then noted certain Semitisms (Hebrewisms and Aramaisms), almost exclusively in the vocabulary. These Semitic concepts and phrases (examples below) are embedded in a sufficiently idiomatic Greek, from which Bonsirven concluded that they reflect the words of the Lord, on which the evangelist had meditated. K. Beyer took up a special field of study, the conditional clauses, and tried to show by the minute analysis of detail, supported by copious material from other sources, whether the Semitic substratum was Hebrew or Aramaic. He claimed as his most important findings "that a greater number of definite Hebrewisms could be found in the Gospel and letters of John than Aramaisms. This means that the main influence was Hebrew, just as it was the sole influence in Revelation."[8] He pointed out further that in this matter the Johannine writings were strongly reminiscent of the Qumran texts written in Hebrew, though it was unlikely that John was a translation of a Semitic original, since Graecisms were abundant. One could only describe it as a Greek strongly coloured by Semitisms.[9] This result, based on concrete material, is surprisingly like that of Schlatter, who also collected his material from Hebrew sources, though now, of

---

[3] Torrey, "The Aramaic Origin of the Fourth Gospel" (on Burney); id., *Our Translated Gospels.*

[4] Colwell, *The Greek of the Fourth Gospel.*

[5] De Zwaan, "John Wrote in Aramaic".

[6] Black, *An Aramaic Approach*, esp. pp. 207 ff.

[7] Bonsirven, "Les araméismes de s. Jean l'Évangéliste".

[8] Beyer, *Semitische Syntax*, p. 17.

[9] *Ibid.*, p. 18.

course, the Qumran texts are available. But Beyer also confirms the view put forward by other scholars for many years,[10] that the fourth evangelist wrote a simple Greek, without solecisms, and used Greek for his Gospel from the start.

These lines of study are still being pursued.[11] Before we draw any conclusions about the author, we shall adduce at least some examples which may throw light on the language of the fourth Gospel. For the arguments which go to show that the Gospel was originally written in Greek we may refer to the work of Bonsirven.[12] Here we turn our attention rather to the Semitic colouring of the language of the evangelist.

As regards the vocabulary, some caution is needed in accepting Bonsirven's findings, since a number of his Semitisms are also to be found in the Koine, while new parallels for many expressions can now be found in the texts of Qumran.

We note first of all the expressions which are given in the original Semitic form and then translated: ῥαββί (1:38 and seven other places, as against four occurrences in Matthew and four in Mark; ῥαββουνί (20:16; cf. Mk 10:51); Μεσσίας (1:42; 4:25, only in John); Κηφᾶς (1:42); Σιλωάμ (9:7, interpreted of Christ); Θωμᾶς (11:16; 21:2); some names are expressly described as "Hebrew": Βηθζαθά or Βηθέσδα (5:2); Γαββαθά (19:13); Γολγοθά (19:17); other expressions are already known from the Synoptics: ἀμήν (see below), ὡσαννά (12:13); μάννα is new (6:31, 49; elsewhere only Heb 9:4; Rev 2:17).

Words and phrases of a strongly Semitic colouring are:

ἀπεκρίθη καὶ εἶπεν (or the plural), 31 times; but this might also be to lend a solemn character to the style;

1:14, 17 χάρις καὶ ἀλήθεια; but this was probably taken over along with the hymn to the Logos;

1:12; 2:23; 3:18 πιστεύειν εἰς τὸ ὄνομα;

12:28; 17:6, 11, 12, 26: ὄνομα referring to God and his nature; there are, however, comparable phenomena in the religious language of Hellenism, cf. Arndt and Gingrich, pp. 573 ff., s. v., 4;

3:21 ποιεῖν τὴν ἀλήθειαν;

3:29 χαρᾷ χαίρειν, cf. Funk, *Greek Grammar*, para. 198,6;

3:35; cf. 13:3 διδόναι ἐν τῇ χειρί;

7:42; 8:33, 37 σπέρμα for descendants;

---

[10] Abbott, *Johannine Vocabulary*; id., *Johannine Grammar;* Moulton and Howard, *A Grammar of New Testament Greek*, pp. 31 ff.; Commentaries of Lagrange, pp. cxvii f., and Barrett, pp. 10 f.; Merlier, *Quatrième Évangile*, pp. 175–87.

[11] See Smith, "The Sources of the Gospel of John"; Brown, "From Burney to Black: The Fourth Gospel and the Aramaic Question".

[12] "Les arameïsmes", pp. 411–25.

words governed by υἱός: 12:36 υἱοὶ φωτός; 17:12 ὁ υἱὸς τῆς ἀπωλείας; 13:2 τοῦ διαβόλου ἤδη βεβληκότος εἰς τὴν καρδίαν.

Unlike Luke, the author shows no tendency to imitate the Septuagint; several concepts and phrases, however, certainly come from the Greek translation of the O.T.; see also the O.T. quotations.

The Qumran texts often illustrate Johannine usage;[13] theological affinities will be discussed later (under ch. vii). The following list does not claim to be complete:

The double ἀμήν (25 times; cf. also 1 Ezra 9:47 LXX, codex B) is found in *1 QS*, 1:20; 2:10, 18;

3:19; 7:7 ἔργα πονηρά, *1 QS*, 2:5; cf. synonyms, in combination with "darkness" *1 QS*, 2:7; *1 QM*, 15:9;

3:21 ποιεῖν τὴν ἀλήθειαν *1 QS*, 1:5; 5:3; 8:2 (but also Is 26:10 LXX; Tob 4:6; 13:6);

3:36b ἡ ὀργὴ τοῦ θεοῦ μένει ἐπ' αὐτόν cf. *1 QS*, 4:12; but the concept was widespread in Judaism, especially in apocalyptic;

4:14 πηγὴ ὕδατος κτλ., cf. *Dam.*, 3:16; 19:34;

5:33; 18:37 μαρτυρεῖν τῇ ἀληθείᾳ, cf. *1 QS*, 8:6; *Dam.*, 20:31;

8:12; 12:35 περιπατεῖν ἐν τῇ σκοτίᾳ, cf. *1 QS*, 3:21; 4:11; 11:10; *1 QM*, 13:12;

8:12 τὸ φῶς τῆς ζωῆς, *1 QS*, 3:7; cf. *1 QM*, 17:6; *1 QH*, 12:15; 18:29;

on 8:44 cf. *1 QS*, 10:21; *1 QM*, 13:11 f.; *1 QH*, 2:16 f.; 4:10, 13 f.; 5:26 f.; 6:21 f.;

12:31; 14:30; 16:11 ὁ ἄρχων τοῦ κόσμου (τούτου), cf. *1 QS*, 3:21 (angel of darkness); 3:23 (his hostile rule); *1 QM*, 13:11 (Belial, angel of hostility); 17:5 f. (prince of the kingdom of wickedness);

12:36 υἱοὶ φωτός *1 QS*, 1:29; 2:16; 3:13 etc.; *1 QM*, *passim;*

14:17; 15:26; 16:13 τὸ πνεῦμα τῆς ἀληθείας, cf. *1 QS*, 4:21; also 3:18 f.; 4:23; *1 QM*, 13:10 (plural);

on 17:3 cf. *Dam.*, 3:20; *1 QS*, 2:3; 4:22; 11:6 f.; *1 QM*, 17:8; *1 QH*, 10:27; 11:28; 14:25;

17:12 ὁ υἱὸς τῆς ἀπωλείας, cf. *Dam.*, 6:15; 13:14 (children of destruction); *1 QS*, 9:16,22 (men of destruction); 10:19 f.;

17:19 ἁγιάζειν ἐν ἀληθείᾳ cf. *1 QS*, 4:20.

In the syntax, we can recognize—contrary to Bonsirven—a greater amount of Semitic influence, predominantly Hebrew according to Beyer. We have a Semitic construction, as Lagrange had already recognized,[14] where a phrase with πᾶν is put first *(casus pendens)* and then referred back to by means of a personal pronoun:

---

[13] The list is the author's; but see also H. Braun, "Qumran und das Neue Testament".

[14] *Évangile selon St Jean*, p. cxi.

6:39 ἵνα πᾶν ὃ δέδωκέν μοι μὴ ἀπολέσω ἐξ αὐτοῦ;
15:2 πᾶν κλῆμα ἐν ἐμοί . . . αἴρει αὐτό, καὶ πᾶν . . . καθαίρει αὐτό;
17:2 ἵνα πᾶν ὃ δέδωκας αὐτῷ δώσῃ αὐτοῖς ζωὴν αἰώνιον.

According to Beyer (pp. 215 f.), the much-debated text 7:38 could be of this type; ὁ πιστεύων εἰς ἐμέ, καθώς . . . would then mean: for him who believes, streams of living water will flow from him (Jesus). The ὃ γέγονεν of 1:3 could be explained in the same way, if it were to be taken with the words which come after it ("for that which was made, life was in him"); but see the commentary *ad loc.*

Another Semitic idiom would be the partitive ἐκ with omission of τίς, τίνες as in 3:25; 7:40; 16:17, and certainly also 1:24 (see *ad loc.*). According to Funk, *Greek Grammar*, para. 164, 2, this occurs at times in classical Greek, but is quite usual in Semitic, and frequent in the Septuagint.

The minute investigations of Beyer, who indicates the degree of probability in each case, are also valuable with regard to Semitic (Hebrew) influence on the conditional clauses, which often appear as parataxis or participles in John. We note the following cases. The construction πᾶν with a conditional participle followed by the principle clause in the negative: 3:16; 11:26; 12:46; cf. 1 Jn 2:23a; 3:6a,b, 9,10,15b; 5:18; 2 Jn 9 (Beyer, pp. 190 f., with notes). Very often the conditional participle is the grammatical subject of the principle clause: Jn 3:6a,b, 18a, 21, 31a,c, 33, 36a,b; 5:24; 6:35b,c, 47, 54, 56, 57, 58b; 7:18a,b; 8:12; 10:2; 11:25; 12:25a,b, 35b, 44, 45, 48; 13:10, 20a,b; 14:9b, 12, 21b; 15:5, 23 (Beyer, p. 211), again frequent in the Johannine epistles.[15] The probability of Semitic influence is increased when a πᾶς is put before the conditional participle: Jn 3:8, 15, 16, 20; 4:13; 6:40, 45; 8:34; 11:26; 12:46; 15:2b; 16:2; 19:12 (Beyer, p. 212). Thus the "monotonous" style which is typical of John, and which may also be observed in the Johannine epistles, is recognizably Semitic. Along with this way of expressing a condition by a participle, which according to Beyer occurs in John six times as frequently as the conditional relative (p. 211), grammatical parataxis for logical subordination is another important Semitic idiom: 1:10,11; 7:21, 22, 26, 34, 36; 8:52, 57; 9:34; 10:12; 11:8; 14:9a; 16:22 (Beyer, p. 280). Subordinate clauses also provide many instances of conditional parataxis: Jn 3:12a; 5:24; 6:26, 30, 36, 40, 50, 57, 58a; 9:30; 12:47; 15:10b; 20:29b (Beyer, p. 269). Finally, the construction: imperative with καί and the future is also characteristic: 1:39; 2:19; 14:8; 15:4a,7; 16:24; 20:15; 21:6, as is the imperative with a second imperative (ἴδε): 1:46; 7:52; 11:34 (Beyer, pp. 252 f.). These texts are given the *siglum* "S 1" by Beyer, to indicate that they are much more common in Semitic

[15] Schnackenburg, *The Letters of St John*, Introduction, ch. ii.

than in Greek, and there can be little doubt that the Semitic idiom is at work here.

Much more reserve is called for with regard to the supposed "mistranslations from Aramaic". Most of the emendations proposed by Burney and Torrey are rejected as unnecessary by other scholars. The major element here is the Aramaic particle דִּי or דְּ, which can be either the introduction to a relative clause or a conjunction.

The texts in question in John include one which M. Black[16] considers of some interest, 5:39, where the text usually given by editors reads: ἐρευνᾶτε (ἐραυνᾶτε) τὰς γραφάς, ὅτι ὑμεῖς δοκεῖτε ἐν αὐταῖς ζωὴν αἰώνιον ἔχειν, while P. Egerton 2 reads ἐν αἷς δο[κεῖτε] ζωὴν ἔχειν. This reading is supported, though not word for word, by the text of some Old Latin MSS (a, b, e, ff^2, q),[17] sy^c, arm. But even here there is no strict proof. The reading with ὅτι makes the sentence stronger, forces us to take ἐρευνᾶτε as an indicative, and not as an imperative, as in some of the Old Latin MSS, gives the reason for the indicative clause, and comes back to the Scriptures with καὶ ἐκεῖναι (καί is missing in P. Egerton 2).[18] Thus here too this reading could be the original, and the others secondary variants.

There is no real necessity to suppose any mistranslations from the Aramaic, and hence no ground for postulating an originally Aramaic text. John was written in Greek from the start, even though the language displays many Semitisms or Semitic colouring.

As regards the Greek itself, scholars have often noted its simplicity, the absence of long periods, of the compound words and the attributive adjectives favoured elsewhere, the laboured progress, the preference for parataxis and asyndeton and so on. This need not indicate poverty of resources or pedantry. It may be intentional, to recount the sacred events in a grave and simple manner, and to present the discourses of Jesus in the solemn "style of revelation" (on which, see below).

What conclusions can be drawn about the author of the fourth Gospel from these remarks on the language? The Semitic colouring will make one hesitate to question his Jewish origin, while the correct Greek, which is impressive in its own way, forces one to suppose that he lived for a long time in a Hellenistic environment. He may have lived in the Jewish diaspora, but the most recent investigations have also shown that he probably had some knowledge of Hebrew. The associations with the Qumran texts, however, leave many possibilities open: acquaintance with the texts themselves, or only contacts with Essene circles, either directly or through converts to Christianity; but the linguistic data would also be accounted for by a Jewish training, if it were not too narrow—the author

---

[16] *An Aramaic Approach*, p. 54; cf. p. 208.

[17] On the precise situation of the manuscript tradition, cf. the edition of Jülicher, Matzkow and Aland, pp. 50 f.

[18] See Barrett, *St. John*, p. 223.

had some acquaintance with rabbinical lore. Hence the language allows of no certain judgment with regard to his origin, and provides no information as to who the author was. He could have been a native of Palestine, but must surely have lived a long time in Hellenistic surroundings. The opinion of Bonsirven, that John the son of Zebedee, meditating on the words of Jesus (hence the Aramaisms in the vocabulary), wrote the Gospel in simple Greek, is certainly not impossible. But it is also possible that a Jewish disciple of John gave the Gospel its literary form, while retaining much of the vocabulary of his master. This disciple must have spoken Aramaic and some Hebrew in his youth, but was a Jew of the Diaspora, whether he was born there or moved there. In any case, the thesis put forward above (in ch. v) is not rendered invalid by an examination of the language.

2. Style, rhythm, types of discourse

The special style of John has been long noted and investigated. At the beginning of the century E. A. Abbott made a minute examination of Johannine vocabulary and grammar, comparing them with the Synoptics and looking for special peculiarities.[19] We can see from his lists that the author has a very personal way of expressing himself, but it seems as if the English scholar was often too subtle in finding nuances of meaning, where in fact the expressions were really synonymous and only changed for the sake of variation, as is the case of the different verbs for "seeing" (ὁρᾶν, θεωρεῖν, θεᾶσθαι). In Johannine usage, many words may be closely allied to each other, and still have their own special fields of application, as can be seen from the relationship between πιστεύειν and γινώσκειν, which has often been studied.[20] But one thing is certain: there is an unmistakable "Johannine" style, which shows itself as clearly in the epistles as in the Gospel. Many good observations on the style may also be found in the second part of Wellhausen's work on John,[21] though few will agree with him when he compares it to the priestly document in the Pentateuch, while his comments about "slow-moving pomposity", "pedantry" or "melodramatics" are certainly out of place.[22] The solemn and monotonous diction is rather due to the meditative and long-pondered theology of John, which gave rise to stereotyped expressions which may

[19] Abbott, *Johannine Vocabulary*; id., *Johannine Grammar*.

[20] See Schnackenburg, *Der Glaube im vierten Evangelium;* Bultmann, "γινώσκω", pp. 711–13; "πιστεύω", pp. 228–30; Willocx, *La notion de foi dans le quatrième évangile*, pp. 152–73.

[21] *Das Evangelium Johannis*, pp. 133–46.

[22] *Ibid.*, p. 146.

be abstract and colourless, but remain impressive and memorable; hence too the emphatic way of putting things by means of a positive statement and its negative counterpart and vice versa. A theological commentary should pay particular attention to this.[23]

The uniformity of language has also been appealed to to prove the unity of John.[24] The personal characteristics which work unconsciously on the style and have no theological significance, and hence are all the more revealing for the individual language of an author, were first pointed out by E. Schweizer in his book "*Ego eimi* . . .", and used by him to test the oneness of authorship in John.[25] The method was taken up by other scholars (J. Jeremias, Ph.-H. Menoud) and carried on in particular by E. Ruckstuhl, who ended up with a list of fifty criteria of Johannine style.[26] It needs to be tested and completed by further researches, but has already performed useful services to literary criticism. We have discussed it already (see above, ch. iii). It will always have to be taken into account in future, but its effectiveness must not be overestimated.[27]

New light is thrown on Johannine style when its poetic rhythms are considered. Scholars began by comparing the strophes and metres of the O.T.[28] and tried to show that the discourses in John were composed in a "hymnic" type of prose. The resulting analysis varies, of course, according to the way one determines the rhythm of thought and stress (two, three or four accents or ictuses to a line), and groups the units of thought into "strophes". The situation this was designed to meet *(Sitz im Leben)* was seen by W. H. Raney as the Christian liturgy,[29] while P. Gächter invoked oral tradition with its efforts to help the memory by rhythm and strophe, technical aids such as "inclusio" and concatenation, and constant repetition.[30] Gächter concluded that the farewell discourses could only be the reproduction of teaching which John had been giving for years with substantially the same content and in substantially the same form.[31] This is undoubtedly true to some extent, though it does not explain the special tone and language by which the discourses were shaped. Gächter's actual division into strophes will also raise many

---

[23] Little research has been done into the "formulae of immanence" in John; but see Borig, *Der wahre Weinstock*.

[24] Bromboszcz, *Die Einheit des Johannesevangeliums*, pp. 76–106.

[25] *Ego eimi*, pp. 87–111.

[26] *Die literarische Einheit*, pp. 180–219.

[27] See Schulz, *Untersuchungen*, pp. 51–59.

[28] *Ibid.*, p. 68, with some older work on Jn 1:1–18; also Burney, *The Poetry of Our Lord*, and Raney, *The Relation of the Fourth Gospel to the Christian Cultus*.

[29] Raney, esp. pp. 71, 80.

[30] Gächter, "Der formale Aufbau der Abschiedsrede Jesu", esp. pp. 199–203.

[31] *Ibid.*, p. 203.

doubts.[32] S. Schulz holds that rhythmic analysis is only one method among many,[33] and E. Haenchen has recently given a warning against supposing two or three-lined strophes in the prologue, which is undoubtedly the most proper field for such investigations, holding that it is rather a matter of "free rhythms".[34] It can hardly be denied that the style is lofty in the discourses, melodious in its way and even perhaps poetic, but this too seems to be due to the well-tempered and mature theology of John. It may be doubted that this style implies that the author was very old, and that it can be proved to be typical of advanced age,[35] since such psychological considerations are doubtful anyway, and out of place with regard to the N.T. in particular (as for instance on the Pastoral Epistles). And our author, even if he was in fact an old man when his Gospel was committed to writing, must have been led much earlier to work out his theological language to suit his subject and his aims.

There are so many unknown quantities in the problem (author, origins, environment, public) that a definite explanation of the peculiar style of John can hardly be given, since it can depend on various factors, and offers little that is apt or adequate to determine these factors. Hence we are justified in asking whether the greatest influence on the style of the discourses may not have been exercised by their larger environment, either directly through the use or incorporation of a source, or indirectly by their being adapted to a certain type of discourse. R. Bultmann opened up new perspectives when he asserted that the discourses were derived from a source containing Gnostic revelation,[36] a thesis which his pupil H. Becker sought to buttress by comparisons with revelation discourses in Gnostic literature.[37] The type of literary criticism which necessarily ensued, the re-arrangement of the text by splitting up existing units and re-building them into a mosaic of new units, has already been criticized above (ch. iii). But the question still remained open, as to whether the fourth evangelist had not adapted himself to a type of discourse then current, which he found it possible to use for his revelation of Christ. This possibility cannot be excluded, though it is scarcely possible to prove "dependence" on given texts and types such as the *Hermetica*, the *Odes of Solomon* or the Mandaean writings, both on account of the uncertainty of their dating and their historical coordinates, and on account of the

---

[32] See also his "Die Form der Eucharistischen Rede Jesu"; "Strophen im Johannesevangelium".

[33] Schulz, *Untersuchungen*, pp. 68–72; id., *Komposition*, pp. 18–24 (on the prologue), pp. 130 f. (in general).

[34] Haenchen, "Probleme des johanneischen Prologs", esp. pp. 333 f.

[35] See Hoffmann, *Johannesevangelium*.

[36] *Das Evangelium des Johannes*, see index under "Quellen: Offenbarungsreden" (p. 559).

[37] Becker, *Die Reden des Johannesevangeliums*.

difference and peculiarities of the discourses of Christ in John. We can only note a formal adaptation and a general recourse to a "soteriological type of discourse"[38] which must have been already in existence, and which the evangelist had in mind when composing the discourses of revelation and salvation spoken by Christ in his Gospel. In this connection, style and language probably matter less than considerations on the religions which formed the historical background to the Johannine theology (see below, ch. vii).

3. *Movement of thought*

Investigation of the structure and characteristics of Johannine thought has not been frequent. If we look beyond the studies of style and language mentioned above for special work on the movement of thought and the "technique" of John we find only the work of E. Stange,[39] now old but still useful in many ways, dealing chiefly with the discourses, and the essay of H. Windisch, which examined the Johannine narrative style and illustrated it by selected instances.[40] We can in fact make a distinction in the Johannine material between discourse and narrative matter, as the form-critical method has shown can be done for the Synoptics, though one of the peculiarities of the fourth Gospel is that it often links long discourses with brief stories.

If we begin with the narrative matter, the structure of the Gospel as a whole displays a notably dramatic element (see above, ch. i), which makes it different from the Synoptics in the way the action develops and reaches its climax. The skilfulness of the presentation is, however, also apparent in the longer individual episodes, of which the most notable examples have been treated by Windisch, the Samaritan episode (4:1–42), the cure of the blind man (ch. 9) and the raising of Lazarus (cf. 11).[41] But there are other parts which deserve to be mentioned here, such as the complex of narrative in ch. 6, introduced by the multiplication of the loaves, and the Resurrection narrative (ch. 20). Here too the reader is brought stage by stage and with ever growing certainty to the full self-revelation of Jesus, as in the three episodes mentioned above. The great

---

[38] Cf. Norden, *Agnostos Theos*, pp. 177–239. The views of the author on the history of religion (the Johannine discourses, the "product of a powerful theosophist, Gnostic, mystical movement") need revision.

[39] Stange, *Eigenart der johanneischen Produktion*. The lists showing the writer's peculiarities are useful, but the "psychological" explanations are unsatisfactory.

[40] Windisch, "Der Johanneische Erzählungsstil". See also Schmid, "Die Komposition der Samaria-Szene, Joh 4:1–42"; Connick, "The Dramatic Character of the Fourth Gospel". [41] *Ibid.*, pp. 178–86.

sixth chapter, on Galilee, begins with the sign of the multiplication of the loaves, continues with the disciples' seeing Jesus walk on the waters and rises to a dramatic climax through the dialogue between Jesus and the Jews in the synagogue of Capernaum, which is resolved partly by the apostasy of a great number of Jesus's followers, and partly by Peter's profession of faith made in the name of the Twelve. The Resurrection narratives are also so disposed that the reader shares the feelings of the women, the two disciples hurrying to the tomb, Mary Magdalene and the Twelve. With them he comes to an ever increasing certainty in his faith, or with Thomas, first sceptical and then conquered by the risen Lord and moved to a supreme expression of faith, he finds himself challenged to make his own act of faith. From this point of view, 1:19–51 is also a unity, which starts with the Baptist's deprecatory testimony about himself, continues with his positive testimony to Jesus and the coming of the first disciples, and rises to a climax with the confession of Nathanael and Jesus's word of revelation 1:51.

These complexes of narrative include displays of doubt and unbelief, as in chs. 6 and 9, and the reaction at the end of ch. 11, where unbelief leads to the Sanhedrin's decision on Jesus's death. For the receptive reader, all this is only a further stimulus to faith. In other groups of narrative, as in chs. 7 and 8, and 10:22–39, the visage of unbelief is shown as it stiffens and hardens. Ch. 7 uses the technique of brief, changing scenes to illustrate the conflict of opinions, the antagonism between belief and unbelief. At the same time, these episodes serve to present the great drama in which, seen from outside, the powers of darkness and unbelief are gaining the upper hand.

Even the short pericopes of the marriage at Cana, the cleansing of the temple and the healing of the official's son do not entirely escape the law of dramatic presentation, since they also contain a moment of suspense before the liberating vision is given to faith. The brevity of these pieces is due, no doubt, to the fact that this opening part is in the nature of an enunciation of themes (chs. 1–4; cf. commentary). The Nicodemus pericope also fits in with the narrative style of the "beginning", if it is limited to 3:1–12; so too the section on Jesus's baptizing in Judea (3:22–30). Only the Samaria episode is developed more fully, for other reasons. The linking up of the end of this episode (4:46–54) with the beginning in Cana (2:1–11) is also an artistic touch. One can say that the author chose and arranged and shaped his matter with no little artistic skill, which can have a gripping effect.

The technique of the discourses uses a number of effects which have already been noted in the epistles:[42] antithesis, verbal links through

[42] See above, note 15.

key-words, concatenation of ideas by means of recourse to earlier ones, *inclusio* whereby the thought is brought back to its starting-point, parallelism and variation—on the whole, the instruments of Semitic rather than Greek rhetoric. We are reminded most strongly of the technique of 1 Jn in Jn 3:13–31, 31–36; but we can also see the same means being used in the revelation discourses of chs. 5, 6, 8 and 12, and in the farewell discourses. It will be well to illustrate this by some examples.

8:12–20 begins in the evangelist's own characteristic way with a word of revelation introduced by ἐγώ εἰμι; a discourse about μαρτυρία and κρίνειν follows. The objection of the Pharisees, v. 13, is taken up by Jesus and opposed by the contrary thesis. Then the sequence of thought is evolved in a series of links:

v. 14 ὅτι οἶδα . . . — ὑμεῖς οὐκ οἴδατε
v. 15 ὑμεῖς . . . κρίνετε — ἐγὼ οὐ κρίνω οὐδένα.

In these two verses the opposition between Jesus and the Pharisees is displayed by antithesis; then the evangelist continues with an "illogical" contrast:

v. 16 καὶ ἐὰν κρίνω δὲ ἐγώ (so too 1:11 and 12; 3:32 and 33). He has recourse at the same time to v. 13, but varies ἀληθής by ἀληθινή. The explanatory ὅτι-clause (cf. v. 14) leads once more to the key-word μαρτυρία.

v. 17 then has the key-word μαρτυρία, and uses the law to explain the need for two witnesses.

v. 18 shows that two witnesses are present, and names the πατήρ emphatically at the end (cf. the end of v. 16).

v. 19 shows the interlocutors taking up the question of the πατήρ; Jesus again reproaches them with their "ignorance" (cf. v. 14c). This statement is then justified in positive terms.

The subject is a difficult one, but the means used to explain it are simple. On the one hand, the self-testimony of Jesus is sufficient (because he "knows"), while on the other hand he can produce a two-fold testimony (his own and the Father's), which is again, however, only one testimony (the testimony of the Father is contained in Jesus's self-testimony). As regards the movement of thought, the argumentation "circles" round the concepts of μαρτυρία and κρίσις; but still it moves forward, while remaining within a closed circle. The Johannine movement of thought is best compared to a spiral: the thoughts circle and return and still move onward.

14:21–24 offers a short example from the farewell discourses. The thought, "He who loves me keeps my commandments" had already been intoned in v. 15. It is taken up again, in inverse order, in v. 21a, and the assurance is given (21b) that he who loves in this way will be loved by the Father, and that Jesus will also love him and reveal himself to him.

v. 22 Judas's question takes up the key-word ἐμφανίσω, understands it of an external manifestation (Johannine "misunderstanding") and provides Jesus with the opportunity of explaining this "revelation" more precisely.

v. 23 The thought of v. 21 (and 15) is repeated and developed. Father and Son will come to one who loves in this way and keeps Jesus's words (τὸν λόγον μου variation for τὰς ἐντολάς μου), and take up their abode with him. Then the inverse is put in the negative: "He who does not love me, does not keep my words"—where the singular is a variation for the previous plural.

v. 24 Linking up with τοὺς λόγους μου, Jesus assures his disciples that his λόγος (in a comprehensive sense) is from the Father who sent him. This both closes and rounds off the whole discourse.

Here too we can see clearly how the thought "circles", repeating and insisting, and at the same time moving forward, explaining and going on to a higher level. This way of developing the thought can only be seen precisely in the analysis of the individual sections.

This way of studying the Johannine thought and methods of exposition is rewarded by many fruitful insights into exegesis, of which some indications at least may be given apropos of the two great "parabolic discourses" in John, the shepherd and the flock 10:1–18, the vine and the branches 15:1–10. The two groups of discourse are built up on similar lines: first a presentation of the matter, which has often been described as a parable, on account of its narrative character; it is clearly rounded off in 10:1–5, and expressly designated as παροιμία, v. 6; this element can be recognized only in a "stunted" form in 15:1–2. The strictly Johannine development only follows later, when some details of the imagery are taken up, illustrated and given their application, especially by restatement with ἐγώ εἰμι (used several times in ch. 10). The process can also involve shifts in the perspective and purpose, because the author uses traits of the imagery to exemplify and develop several ideas in succession, though preserving a unity by means of the blend of the various motifs. The technique of the "parabolic discourses" also displays the method of concentric thinking[43] which progresses in new circles: a meditative way of thought which uses few arguments but goes deeper and deeper into its subject to gain better and higher understanding of it.

This is, as we have said, the strictly and unmistakably "Johannine" movement of thought, which seems to have no direct parallels. Any impression it might give of "mysticism" disappears as soon as it is compared with the self-intoxication of the "ego-utterances" of, say, the Odes of Solomon; the "Gnostic" character of the Hermetic literature is again

[43] See Borig, *Der wahre Weinstock*, p. 95, note 3.

different, while the Hodayoth of Qumran, with an imagery nourished by the O.T., displays once more different features. It is a personal style, achieved by meditation on the revelation of Jesus Christ and used to clarify this revelation.

CHAPTER VII

Spiritual Setting and Origin

The spiritual background, the world of thought in which it is situated, is of supreme importance for the whole understanding of John. Since historical criticism does not tell us enough about its actual origins, we cannot draw on them to describe the setting of the Gospel. We must, on the contrary, try to deduce from the views put forward in the Gospel itself what are its coordinates in the history of religions and what surroundings might have given it birth. But here again our investigations are hampered by the shortcomings of our historical knowledge, the difficulty of reaching an apt verdict and the changing perspectives presented to us by the history of religions. But here too science has made progress, steadily if not always in a straight line. The earlier alternative of Judaism or non-Jewish Hellenism seems now to have been left behind, since careful study of the Johannine thought has revealed many connections with both "worlds" and it has been proved that Judaism and Hellenism were more strongly interwoven than had been thought. Not only was the Judaism of the diaspora Hellenized, but even the Judaism of Palestine seems to have been open, especially in non-Pharisaic circles, to a mysticism and a Gnosis which led to a syncretist approach to the surrounding world.[1] Our chief task today is to determine what were the most insistent, effective and dominating influences to which the fourth evangelist was subject. Very

[1] Cf. Liebermann, *Hellenism in Jewish Palestine;* Goppelt, *Christentum und Judentum im ersten und zweiten Jahrhundert*, pp. 131–6; Marcus, "Pharisees, Essenes and Gnostics"; Schubert, *Die Religion des nachbiblischen Judentums*, pp. 13–25, 80–97; Schoeps, *Urgemeinde, Judenchristentum, Gnosis*, pp. 44–61; Simon, *Les sectes juives au temps de Jésus*, pp. 74–93; Davies, *Christian Origins and Judaism*, pp. 19–30. Many scholars now suppose that there was a Jewish element in the origin of Gnosis, cf. for instance Quispel, *Gnosis als Weltreligion;* Haenchen, "Gab es eine vorchristliche Gnosis?"; Kretschmar, "Zur religionsgeschichtlichen Einordnung der Gnosis"; Quispel, "Jüdische Gnosis und jüdische Heterodoxie"; Daniélou, *Théologie du Judéo-Christianisme*, pp. 82–98, E. T.: *Theology of Jewish Christianity*, pp. 69–85; Scholem, *Jewish Gnosticism, Merkabah Mysticism and Talmudic Tradition;* van Unnik, "Die jüdische Komponente in der Entstehung der Gnosis".

different answers are still being given, and must be constantly revised in the light of new discoveries of texts (Qumran writings, Coptic Gnostic literature from Nag-Hammadi etc.)[2] and further researches into comparative religion (on the Mandaeans, Gnosticism, Jewish mysticism[3]). But the last word must always lie with one's verdict on the text of John itself, with the analysis of its thought and language.

How swiftly opinions can change may be seen at once from the studies of recent years which were preoccupied with comparative religion as applied to John. Ph.-H. Menoud, who published an account of such work shortly after the Second World War, still devoted his attention in the first place to "Hellenistic syncretism", which was "long considered to be the setting where the Johannine theology took its rise",[4] and then took up in particular "oriental Gnosticism",[5] to which W. Bauer and R. Bultmann had recourse in their commentaries. Somewhat later C. H. Dodd discussed, in the following order, the setting in early Christianity, the "higher religion of Hellenism: the Hermetic literature", Hellenistic Judaism (Philo of Alexandria), rabbinic Judaism, Gnosticism and Mandaeanism.[6] So too C. K. Barrett looks for most light on the Gospel from the background of Hellenistic Judaism, but pays great attention to apocalyptic and rabbinic literature.[7] The two English scholars leave Gnosticism, or as Barrett calls it, "the religions of salvation", to the end, and allow it no great influence on John. On the Catholic side, F.-M. Braun studied the various relationships between John and other religions in a series of essays which took in the Qumran literature.[8] The obvious affinities with the concepts and mentality of Qumran then gave rise, in the fifties, to a spate of studies,[9] which has, however, subsided somewhat in the meantime. In recent years, French-speaking Catholics have devoted

---

[2] On Qumran, see below; on Coptic Gnostic writings see Doresse, *Les livres secrets des gnostiques d'Égypte*, E. T.: *The Secret Books of the Egyptian Gnostics;* van Unnik, *Evangelien aus dem Nilsand*, E. T.: *Newly Discovered Gnostic Writings;* Leipoldt and Schenke, *Koptisch-gnostische Schriften aus den Papyrus-Codices von Nag-Hamadi;* Haenchen, "Literatur zum Kodex-Jung".

[3] On research into Mandaeanism, see Rudolf, *Die Mandäer*, vol. I; an account of research into the importance of the new finds of Gnostic writings is given by Schulz, "Die Bedeutung neuer Gnosisfunde für die neutestamentliche Wissenschaft"; on Jewish mysticism see Scholem, *Die jüdische Mystik in ihren Hauptströmungen*, E. T.: *Major Trends in Jewish Mysticism;* id., *Jewish Gnosticism.*

[4] *L'Évangile de Jean*, pp. 31 ff.; quotation from p. 31.

[5] *Ibid.*, pp. 33–42.

[6] *Interpretation*, pp. 10–130.

[7] *The Gospel according to St John*, pp. 25–33.

[8] "Essénisme et Hermétisme"; "Hermétisme et Johannisme"; "L'arrière-fond judaïque du quatrième évangile et la Communauté de l'Alliance"; "L'arrière-fond du Quatrième Évangile".

[9] Mowry, "The Dead Sea Scrolls and the Background for the Gospel of St John"; Schmitt, "Les écrits du Nouveau Testament et les textes de Qumran"; Cullmann, "The Significance

more attention than hitherto to the "great traditions of Israel", which, as they claim, were behind the Johannine theology, and need to be brought out more clearly on the basis of express or implicit allusions to O.T. texts, interests (Exodus and Sinai traditions), typological figures and speculations (Wisdom).[10] One could speak of a reaction, except that the other patterns derived from comparative religion are still being invoked, especially the Gnostic influences, while the research into the "typological" motifs seeks to portray new traits which point to a Judaism which has made progress in developing further the ancient traditions. We should rather speak of a forward-looking research and investigation which is trying to launch into new activity the studies of comparative religion which seemed to have run aground.

With research in this unclear and uncertain state, it seems best to keep all possible relationships in mind, as we did with the Epistles of St John;[11] here we shall only give an orientation, to justify the standpoint taken in the commentary.

1. The Old Testament and its influence in John

Old Testament quotations are not very numerous, as we have already noted (see above pp. 38 ff.), but raise many questions.[12] The nineteen quotations given as such are distributed fairly evenly over the Gospel, with four close together in ch. 19 (the Passion), and seem to have been chosen arbitrarily. The evangelist is not concerned with detailed proof of the fulfilment of Scripture, like Matthew; he is often content with a general allusion (1:45; 2:22; 5:39,46; 17:12; 20:9). His choice of Scripture texts was, as we have seen, dictated to some extent by primitive Christian tradition, in so far as he used the same parts of the O.T. as came to the fore in the rest of the N.T., even though he did not quote

---

of the Qumran Texts for Research into the Beginnings of Christianity"; Brown, "The Qumran Scrolls and the Johannine Gospel and Epistles"; Albright, "Recent Discoveries in Palestine and the Gospel of St John"; Baumbach, *Qumran und das Johannes-Evangelium*; Cross, *The Ancient Library of Qumran and Modern Biblical Studies*, pp. 153–62; Gryglewicz, "Der Evangelist Johannes und die Sekte von Qumran"; Teeple, "Qumran and the Origin of the Fourth Gospel"; Kuhn, "Johannesevangelium und Qumrantexte".

[10] See Boismard, *Le Prologue de Saint Jean*; id., *Du baptême à Cana;* Feuillet, *Études johanniques;* Braun, *Jean le Théologien*, vol. II.

[11] *The Letters of St John*, Introduction, ch. v.

[12] On the problem of the Old Testament quotations in John see, along with the commentaries, Barrett, "The Old Testament in the Fourth Gospel"; Smits, *Oud-testamentische Citaten in het Nieuwe Testament;* Tasker, *The Old Testament in the New Testament;* Lindars, *New Testament Apologetic;* Braun, *Jean le Théologien*, vol. II, pp. 3–21.

the same verses. He shows a lively interest in the fact that Jesus is the Messiah promised in Scripture (1:45; 5:39, 46; cf. 7:42; 12:13,15), and adduces Scripture to show that the decree of God lies behind such obscure and difficult facts as the betrayal of Judas (13:18; 17:12), the enigma of unbelief (12:38, 40) and the inexplicable hatred of the Jews (15:25).

At times the evangelist made deliberate changes in the text of Scripture. This seems clear in the quotation used at the cleansing of the temple (2:17), where the past tense of Ps 69 (68):9 is replaced by the future καταφάγεται,[13] to point forward to the death of Jesus. And the text quoted in 6:31 about the manna is not exactly that of Ps 78 (77):24. Here he uses ἄρτον ἐκ τοῦ οὐρανοῦ instead of ἄρτον οὐρανοῦ, and adds a φαγεῖν at the end, probably from the first part of the verse. He finds the "coming down from heaven" important, on account of its application to Christ (vv. 33, 38, 41f., 50f., 58), so too the "eating", especially with reference to the Eucharist (vv. 49ff., 53–58). Elsewhere, no particular purpose can be recognized in the alterations; it seems that the evangelist quoted freely, from memory.[14]

The decisive element in the choice and formulation is how useful and significant the texts may be in Christology. This is clear from 19:36, where there is a definite recall of the Paschal lamb, of which the bones were not to be broken by the Israelites, Exod 12:10,46; Num 9:12; but the verbal form συντριβήσεται recalls Ps 34 (33):21 (the suffering of the just man), so that this text too seems to be prophecy of Jesus. The following quotation, in 19:37, takes up the oracle of Zech 12:10, following neither the Masoretes nor the Septuagint but agreeing with Aquila and Theodotion, who have "him whom they pierced" (3rd person) for the Masoretes's "they will look upon me" (where the Hebrew is probably corrupt). This text may have been suggested by the primitive Christian tradition (cf. Mt 24:30; Rev 1:7).

Thus the evangelist goes his own way both in choice and formulation of texts. He also adduces Ps 82(81):6 in 10:34, in a way not paralleled elsewhere, to defend Jesus's claim to be Son of God against the charge of blasphemy. The most enigmatic quotation, however, is given in 7:38, where modern research suspects the presence of an Aramaic source (for ἐκ τῆς κοιλίας αὐτοῦ), and also sees the influence of thoughts suggested by the feast of Tabernacles: allusions to the source in the future temple (Ezek 47:2 ff.), to the purifying and fertilizing eschatological source of water in Jerusalem (Zech 13:1; 14:8) and to water flowing from the

---

[13] In LXX Ps 68:10 the reading of B and א is also καταφάγεται; but this was the Christian copyist's reminiscence of Jn 2:17, since the whole context contains only aorists.

[14] Goodwin, "How Did John Treat His Sources?"

rock in the desert (Ps 78:16,20).[15] His main interest is the typological fulfilment in Christ, a procedure seen to be at work elsewhere in the early Church (cf. 1 Cor 10:1–11) but developed further by him. The prophecy of the hardening of the heart in Is 6:9,[16] a text much exploited also in other parts of the N.T., is adduced at a turning-point of the presentation, again in a form proper to the evangelist (12:40), who then adds a Christological interpretation: the prophet Isaiah saw his (Jesus's) glory and spoke of him (v. 41). Obviously, he feels himself to be completely free to use the O.T. as he wills for his preaching of Christ. He seems to have drawn his material from various stocks, either the primitive Christian teaching tradition, Jewish traditions used by him in a Christian way, or his own reading of Scripture. Though his quotations are relatively few, they are enough to prove that his knowledge of Scripture was wide.

Further observations show still more clearly how deeply rooted the fourth evangelist was in the O.T. and biblical theology. His diction is also enriched by turns of phrase which suggest indirect quotations. Here are some examples:

1:47 ἐν ᾧ δόλος οὐκ ἔστιν cf. Ps 32 (31):2;
1:51 "the angels of God ascending and descending", cf. Gen 28:12;
3:12 "earthly" and "heavenly", cf. Wis 9:16;
4:48 σημεῖα καὶ τέρατα, very frequent in the O.T. (LXX), especially for the miracles of the Exodus;
5:27 "and he gave him power to pass judgment, because he is the Son of Man", cf. Dan 7:14,22;
7:34 "you shall seek me and shall not find me", cf. Prov. 1:28;
9:24 "give glory to God", a phrase frequent in the O.T.
9:31 "God does not hear sinners", cf. Prov 15:29;
9:34 "you were wholly born in sin", cf. Ps 51(50):7;
11:52 "gather the scattered", cf. Ezek 20:34; 37:21.

The two parabolic discourses, the shepherd and the flock, ch. 10, the vine and the branches, 15:1–8, are full of imagery drawn from the O.T. But the O.T. figures and themes which recur in John are more important than echoes of language and similarities of imagery. The Patriarchs are named with respect, and brought into relationship with Jesus as the Messiah: Abraham rejoiced to see Jesus's day (8:56), and his sacrifice

[15] See esp. Boismard, "De son ventre couleront des fleuves d'eau"; Grelot, "Jean VII, 38, eau du rocher ou source du Temple?"

[16] Mk 4:12; Mt 13:14 f.; Lk 8:10; Acts 28:26 f. We may suspect that the quotation from Isaiah also influenced the notion of "hardening" (πωρόω, πώρωσις); elsewehre cf. Mk 3:5; 6:52; 8:57; Rom 11:7, 25; 2 Cor 3:14. See Dodd, *According to the Scriptures*, pp. 36–39; Gnilka, *Die Verstockung Israels, Isaias 6:9–10 in der Theologie der Synoptiker;* Lindars, *New Testament Apologetic*, pp. 159–67.

of his only son is perhaps alluded to in 3:16; the instructive dialogue with the Samaritan woman takes place at Jacob's well, and the logion of 1:51 links up with Jacob's ladder; Joseph too is mentioned in 4:5. But the superiority of Jesus over the Patriarchs is constantly brought out: he is greater than the patriarch Jacob (4:12), and already existed before Abraham (8:58). So too Moses is claimed as witness to Jesus (5:45f.; cf. 1:45), his promise of the Messianic prophet is taken up (Deut 18:15, 18; cf. Jn 6:14; 7:40 and 1:21, 25) and his work used several times as a typological allusion to the greater event which was to take place in Christ (3:14 the lifting up of the brazen serpent; 6:32 the gift of the manna); but he is clearly subordinated to Jesus (1:17; cf. 7:19), even with a pointed contrast (cf. 9:28f.). The presentation in 1:14–18 may have been influenced by the Mosaic Sinai tradition, in ch. 6 by the typology of the Exodus.

The O.T. history of salvation, however, is never unfolded. The O.T. is already a sort of fixed quantity, which the evangelist ponders and exploits, using it as one of the bases of his Christology and as a source from which to enrich it. This may be seen in the peculiar Christological title of "lamb of God" (1:29, 36), behind which may be both the "servant of the Lord" of Is 53 and the Paschal lamb. But the Wisdom literature undoubtedly provided him with his strongest links. It is only the Wisdom speculation which throws full light on the Logos hymn with its concept of pre-existence, the incomprehensible rejection of the Logos by the world of men and the gracious dwelling of the incarnate Logos among his own. Looking on Jesus's "signs" as the miracles of N.T. revelation, the evangelist may have regarded them in the same light as the book of Wisdom (ch. 10f.) did the ancient miracles of the Exodus.[17] Many words of Christ sound like utterances of Wisdom,[18] so that he is made to appear in the role of Wisdom. But even this is not the final step. For in the characteristic formula of self-revelation, ἐγώ εἰμι, the Johannine Christ takes on the voice of God himself, who often proclaimed himself in the O.T. with these words as the one and unique God of Israel, holy and exigent but also merciful and giver of salvation.[19] Thus many thoughts and images of the O.T., mostly taken further in theological meditation and development, come together in John and are made to serve Johannine theology. This Gospel would be unthinkable without the O.T. basis which supports it.

---

[17] Cf. Ziener, "Weisheitsbuch und Johannesevangelium" (undoubtedly goes too far); id., "Johannesevangelium und urchristliche Passafeier".

[18] See Feuillet, *Études johanniques*, pp. 72–88.

[19] See Zimmermann, "Das absolute 'Εγώ εἰμι als die neutestamentliche Offenbarungsformel".

2. *Relations with contemporary Judaism*

(a) Hellenistic Judaism

In its use and grasp of the O.T., John stands very close to Hellenistic Judaism, whose reading and interpretation of the sacred Scriptures can be studied above all in Philo of Alexandria, though here much must be laid to the charge of his personal attitude, his philosophical formation and his training in allegorical exegesis.[20] There is a great gulf between the more typological use which John makes of the O.T., with a constant reference to Christ, and the allegorical and philosophical interpretation of Philo. But the Logos concept forms a strong bond of union, and it remains noteworthy, in spite of all differences of content, even as a stereotyped expression. It is certainly no accident that John avoids the more obvious concept of σοφία (this and the words associated with it are completely absent in John); the evangelist, or the early Christian circle whence he drew the Logos hymn, deliberately tried to link up with the term familiar to Hellenistic tradition, to give the Gospel message resonance and appeal. This was all the easier, as the term was also anchored in the biblical tradition by means of the notion of creation—God created the world by his word.[21]

Along with this admitted contact, other concepts may be referred to such as light, life, truth, knowledge, faith, contemplation and images like "source of life", "way" and "shepherd and flock"—indeed, "symbolism" in general;[22] but when these are examined more closely, considerable differences appear. On the other hand, such leading concepts of Hellenistic Judaism as ἀθανασία, ἀφθαρσία, εὐδαιμονία, εὐσέβεια, ἀρετή, εἰκών etc. are lacking; other basic concepts are given precisely a "non-Greek" meaning. The "mysticism" of union with God, which is supposed to be a link between John and Philo,[23] remains problematic in John, where the effort to achieve fellowship with Christ and God is something different from the Hellenistic desire for the union of the soul and God. The evangelist cannot have had very much contact with the diaspora Jews who had had philosophical training and been subject to Hellenistic

[20] See Stein, *Die Allegorische Exegese des Philo aus Alexandreia;* Heinemann, *Philons griechische und jüdische Bildung;* Völker, *Fortschritt und Vollendung bei Philo von Alexandrien*, pp. 1–47; Wolfson, *Philo*, pp. 3–86.

[21] See Procksch, "Wort Gottes im Alten Testament", p. 99; Kittel, "Wort und Reden im Neuen Testament", pp. 135 f.; Robert, "Logos"; Starcky, "Logos", cols. 490 ff. See also excursus i.

[22] See Dodd, *Interpretation*, pp. 55 ff.

[23] This conviction is the basis of Goodenough, *By Light, Light*, cf. pp. 1–10. See also Streeter, *The Four Gospels*, pp. 365–92.

influences. We note here only one trait in common, which is often overlooked: the notion of God. This Jewish heritage, which the diaspora Jews displayed proudly and contentedly in their missionary writings,[24] was also very precious to the evangelist. A pure and elevated worship of God who is "spirit" (4:23f.), an ethical service of God because he is pure "light" (1 Jn 1:5), knowledge of "the one true God" (17:3), the incomprehensibility of God whom "no one has ever seen" (1:18; 5:37; 6:46; 1 Jn 4:12,20): all this, though given a new accent within the revelation of Christ, is also a call to the Jewish diaspora, to which 7:35 looks and from which representatives come to seek Jesus according to 12:20f.; and through these "Hellenists" it is also a call to the world around them.

(b) Pharisaic and rabbinic Judaism

The contribution of Pharisaic and rabbinic ways of thinking and arguing is greater in John than might have been expected. P. Billerbeck and A. Schlatter have gathered much relevant material in their books;[25] we confine ourselves here to some notable points. The term ὁ νόμος is used in the wider sense of "Scripture" (cf. 1:45; 8:17; 10:34; 12:34; 15:25), as well as in the stricter sense of "law" (1:17; 7:19, 23, 49, 51; 18:31; 19:7), and in the second case its Mosaic origin is emphasized (1:17; 7:19,23).[26] The expression in 7:49, "this rabble which knows nothing of the law" corresponds to the ʻam ha- ʼarets used in the schools. Several individual precepts are mentioned, not only in the basic form given in the O.T. (cf. 8:17; 19:7), but also according to the rabbinical interpretation: so for circumcision on the Sabbath, 7:24,[27] the hearing of the accused, 7:51,[28] the prohibition of carrying burdens on the Sabbath (cf. 5:10) or of manual work in healing (cf. 9:14 ff., though these last two were already known from the Synoptics). The interrogation of the man born blind, with exact determination of the circumstances (cf. 9:15,19,26) is also part of Jewish practice; the argument of 9:16b,31f. is used in Jewish discussions.[29] In the same context the Pharisees boast of being "disciples of Moses", which was later a title of honour for the doctors of

---

[24] See Dalberg, *Die Theologie der hellenistisch-jüdischen Missionsliteratur*, pp. 124–30.

[25] Billerbeck, *Kommentar*, vol. II; Schlatter, *Der Evangelist Johannes*.

[26] We cannot speak of an antinomian attitude in John (see commentary on 1:17). On the attribution of the law to Moses cf. Kümmel, "Jesus und der jüdische Traditionsgedanke". On John's attitude to Moses see also Jeremias, "Μωυσῆς", pp. 876 f; Braun, *Jean le Théologien*, vol. II, pp. 187–206.

[27] Cf. Billerbeck, *Kommentar*, vol. II, pp. 487 f.

[28] Cf. Schlatter, *Der Evangelist Johannes*, p. 205 *ad loc.*

[29] Cf. Billerbeck, vol. II, pp. 534 f.

the law.[30] It is a Jewish boast to claim to be descended from Abraham and to have been no man's slave (8:33), not to have been born from adultery (idolatry) and to have only God for Father (8:41).

We also meet certain Messianic concepts which first saw light in Judaism, such as the Messiah's coming forward from hiding (7:27), his miracles (cf. 7:31), his remaining for ever (12:34). It was not surprising to the Jews that a rabbi should work miracles (as answers to prayer) (cf. 3:2). But they were struck by the fact that Jesus had had no training in the schools (7:15). The dialogue with Nicodemus recalls the rabbinic technique of disputation, as does the controversy in ch. 8. In 10:34 ff. Jesus presents a rabbinic type of Scripture proof "a minori ad maius", and the same procedure of the schools is behind 7:23. Skilful interpretation of Scripture, employed in a Christian sense, appears in 6:31 ff.; 8:56; 12:41. The saying of 5:39 fits in exactly with Jewish thought; and in 1:51; 3:14; 7:38 there even seem to be signs of acquaintance with midrashic interpretation.[31]

More astonishing still is the familiarity with the mentality and practice of official Judaism. That such Judaism is often merely termed οἱ Ἰουδαῖοι in general does not mean that the writer was unaware of the distribution of functions between different groups. "The high priests and Pharisees" are made responsible for deciding the death of Jesus, in a secret sitting of the Sanhedrin (11:47–53), and the "counsel" given by the high priest, which the evangelist treats as a prophecy (also a Jewish notion), is inspired by the political opportunism which is typical of the Sadducees (not named as such in John). The Pharisees appear as the influential group among the people (cf. 7:32, 47f.; 9:13,16; 11:46; 12:19,42), and though no explicit distinction is made between their "doctors of the law" and the ordinary "members" *(haberim)*, it is quite clear that the former are their spokesmen in 1:24; 3:1; 7:45–52; 8:13 ff.; ch. 9. The measures taken against Jesus are also credible: expulsion from the synagogue (9:22), decision on his death (11:53), summons to inform on him (11:57); only the expression ἀποσυνάγωγος calls for special consideration. The compound word does not indicate major or minor excommunication, but exclusion from the religious community of the Jews (cf. 16:2), a practice with regard to Christians which only became usual after A.D. 90.[32]

---

[30] Only the Pharisaic doctors are termed "disciples of Moses" in *Joma*, 4a Bar.; see Billerbeck, vol. II, p. 535.

[31] The unusual ἐκ τῆς κοιλίας αὐτοῦ could correspond to an Aramaic מִן גַּוָּהּ, cf. Boismard, "De son ventre", pp. 542 ff.; Grelot, "Jean 7:38", pp. 43 f., for the background of the quotation see the works mentioned above, n. 15.

[32] See Billerbeck, vol. IV, pp. 329–33; Carroll, "The Fourth Gospel and the Exclusion of Christians from the Synagogue".

But this opens up perspectives which are very important with regard to the fourth evangelist's knowledge of Pharisaic and rabbinic Judaism and his attitude towards it. The evangelist seems to be aiming above all at the Judaism of his day, which was dominated by Pharisaic legalists and was bitterly opposed to Christianity. He rejects it constantly, by implication, and tries to some extent to defeat it with its own weapons.[33] When the Gospel is read from this point of view, the "Judaeo-rabbinic stratum" is satisfactorily explained, though this does not necessarily obscure the historical level (the time of Jesus). The evangelist has shown how Jesus's conflicts with his opponents are relevant to his own times. No far-reaching conclusions may be drawn from this, however, with regard to the origins and formation of the author.

(c) Heterodox Judaism; Qumran

In spite of the Johannine eschatology, which re-models the language of the old apocalyptic and applies it to the immediate present, John is said to have been influenced by the apocalyptic trend, which, according to recent researches, was not confined to isolated groups but embraced wide circles of Judaism.[34] C. K. Barrett calls attention to the revelation of "heavenly" mysteries (cf. 3:12f.), which, like the "eschatological", form part of apocalyptic literature.[35] Other scholars are rather inclined to see here a reference to Jewish mysticism.[36] They do not exclude one another, since the "mystic" and the "apocalyptic seer" were very closely allied. But John displays little interest in future "eschatological" events, and he is likewise hardly interested in hidden "heavenly" mysteries. He even denies energetically that any man can contemplate them, since his one interest is to uphold the unique revelation given by his Christ (1:18; 5:37; 6:46; 14:8ff.). At the most one could suppose some knowledge of this type of thinking and its immediate rejection. But in any case the contact remains vague.

One of the Johannine titles of Christ, "Son of Man", is, however, most probably of "apocalyptic" origin, and the logia connected with it stand

---

[33] See Allen, "The Jewish Christian Church in the Fourth Gospel"; Dodd, "A l'arrière-plan d'un dialogue johannique" (on 8:33–58); Schnackenburg, "Die Messiasfrage im Johannesevangelium", pp. 249–52.

[34] See Bloch, *On the Apocalyptic in Judaism;* Plöger, *Theokratie und Eschatologie;* Reicke, "Official and Pietistic Elements of Jewish Apocalypticism"; Schubert, "Die Entwicklung der Auferstehungslehre von der nachexilischen bis zur frührabbinischen Zeit"; id., "Die jüdischen Religionsparteien", pp. 29–49; Vielhauer, "Apocalyptic", pp. 408–21.

[35] *St. John*, p. 26. See also Rössler, *Gesetz und Geschichte*, pp. 55–70.

[36] See Odeberg, *The Fourth Gospel*, esp. on 1:51 (pp. 33–42) and 3:13 (pp. 72–98); also Fischel, "Jewish Gnosticism in the Fourth Gospel" (on the expectation of "the Prophet").

out by their relative consistency and continuity. S. Schulz, who has studied the history of their transmission, holds that most of them (1:51; 3:13 ff.; 5:27 ff.; 6:27, 53; 13:31 f.) belonged to a pre-Johannine "tradition of a theme" and were given their form on the native soil of late Jewish apocalyptic, but then, of course, re-interpreted christologically.[37] But is it not possible that John simply took this whole traditional theme from Christian sources, exploiting and re-modelling it in his own way?[38] Whether he found the logia in a form which represented a development of the "Son of Man theology" known from the Synoptics, and whether they ultimately go back to certain Judaeo-Christian circles, is another question; but it is scarcely necessary to suppose immediate contact with Jewish circles or any great knowledge of apocalyptic.[39]

The problem has been given a new complexion by the discoveries at Qumran. The Johannine writings have certainly more affinities with these texts, which have been touched on above (see pp. 107 f.) from the linguistic standpoint, than with "apocalyptic literature" as previously known, and yet there is no doubt that the Qumran sect belonged to the "apocalyptic" trend. Most of its writings are now known, but the title "Son of Man" has not (yet) been met with. And it is not the sect's future hopes which recur or are reflected in John (unless perhaps "the prophet", cf. on 1:21), but above all its "dualistic" way of thinking and speaking (especially in *1 QS* and *1 QM)*, and its way of expressing its consciousness of election, divine revelation and proximity to God (especially in *1 QH)*. The frequently recurring concepts of "truth", "reveal" and "know", the importance of the divine Spirit, the longing for the heavenly world and also the close brotherly union seem to establish a close affinity between the Qumran community and the circle which one must envisage behind the Johannine writings, from their mentality and diction. But we must compare them more in detail to reach any sort of certainty.

The Essenes of Qumran and elsewhere were not the only groups who took a lively interest in purification, conversion and baptism. There was a widespread baptist movement in Judaism, studied well before the discovery of the Qumran texts by J. Thomas, whose work provided a survey of the extent and activity of the movement.[40] The fourth evangelist takes a palpable interest in John the Baptist and the question of baptism, not merely because of debates with later disciples of John, who were still active in the time of the evangelist and offering some competition to

---

[37] *Untersuchungen*, p. 123, cf. p. 180.

[38] Cf. Iber, *Überlieferungsgeschichtliche Untersuchungen zum Begriff des Menschensohnes im Neuen Testament;* Hahn, *Christologische Hoheitstitel*, pp. 39–41; Schnackenburg, "Der Menschensohn im Johannesevangelium".

[39] See Schulz, *Untersuchungen*, p. 124.

[40] Thomas, *Le mouvement baptiste.*

Christianity (see below, pp. 167 ff.), but also because of the type of thinking which was being done in these circles. Pointers in this direction are the contrast between baptism in water and in spirit (cf. 1:26, 33, though this is already in the Synoptics), the repeated allusions to "purification" (cf. 2:6; 3:25; 13:10f.; 15:3), the healings in chs. 5 and 9, to which must be added the themes of the "living water" (4:10–14; 7:38) and of Jesus as the life-giving source (cf. 6:35; 7:38f.; 19:34). These may even provide contacts with the "proto-Mandaeans", probably western in origin, according to recent researches.[41] In the light of these religious movements, it is understandable that S. Schulz's recent work should envisage the community from which the Johannine tradition arose—a sort of "habura" —as the melting-pot of the various heterodox groups of the Judaism of the time: "Qumranites, proto-Mandaeans, apocalyptic groups and baptist circles". The core of the Johannine habura is said to have been composed of Christians who came from the sectarian centres of late Palestinian Judaism—a syncretist and Gnosticizing Judaeo-Christianity.[42] But this view hardly does justice either to the undeniably close links with the synoptic tradition or to the "openness" to the Hellenistic world. It is highly doubtful that Johannine Christianity developed in such esoteric haburoth: it also contained a missionary component which made it turn towards the world (cf. 4:38; 10:16; 11:52; 12:20, 24,32; 17:18; 20:21; 21:11). We should not look for its *Sitz im Leben* in a narrowly-circumscribed Jewish Christianity, withdrawn from outside contacts.[43]

To look for surer ground, we shall try to explore more closely the contacts with the mentality of Qumran. The commentary will note particular points of parallelism in the texts; here we shall confine ourselves to some major points which have already been widely discussed, to illustrate the relationship. The most notable feature is the "dualism", the way of seeing things in black and white, which uses characteristic concepts to contrast opposing realms, the divine and its enemies, and derives therefrom theological assertions. But there are many forms of "dualism", and in the Hellenistic era it pervaded all forms of thinking of the world and existence.[44] Each particular form must be examined on its merits. G. Baumbach and H. W. Huppenbauer have studied the dualism of

---

[41] Cf. Macuch, "Alter und Heimat des Mandäismus nach neuerschlossenen Quellen"; Rudolf, *Die Mandäer*, vol. I, pp. 59–255; Colpe, "Mandäer", cols. 711 f.; Schmid, "Mandäismus", cols. 1345 ff.

[42] *Komposition*, pp. 182–7.

[43] See Teeple, "Qumran and the Origin of the Fourth Gospel", who concludes after a wide-ranging comparison that the author of the fourth Gospel was not a Jewish but a Gentile Christian, p. 24.

[44] See Pétrement, *Le dualisme chez Platon, les Gnostiques et les Manichéens;* Bianchi, *Il dualismo religioso;* Dörrie and Guillemin, "Dualismus", cols. 341–50.

Qumran.[45] Baumbach confines himself to the Rule of the Community *(1 QS)* but draws on late Jewish apocalyptic and uses his material to make a comparison with John. He finds that it is not possible to affirm a direct influence of the Rule of the Community on John, the terminology of which is closer to the late Jewish apocalypses, especially the older writings. Agreement with John is due to the common mentality of late Judaism.[46] Huppenbauer tries to give an exact picture of the dualism of the Qumran texts, which he studies one by one, and finally characterizes as a relative and ethical cosmic dualism. He compares it briefly with other forms of dualism and concludes that the attitude of Gnosis to the world is different from that of the Qumran texts.[47]

If we now compare the pairs of opposites which are most notable in John and the Qumran texts, we arrive at the following conclusion: some expressions are closer to one another than anywhere else in late Jewish literature—light-darkness,[48] truth-lie (deceit etc.), spirit-flesh. Here too we find the most Qumran-like passages in the Johannine literature; for light—darkness, cf. 1:5; 3:19 ff.; 8:12; 12:35 f., 46; 1 Jn 1:5 f.; 2:8–11; for truth-lie (deceit), cf. 8:44 f.; 1 Jn 1:6; 2:21,27; 4:6 ("spirit of truth and spirit of deceit"); for spirit-flesh cf. 3:6; 6:63 and 1:13. It is noteworthy, however, that the positive use of ἡ ἀλήθεια is much more extensive, though something of the same type of thing may be observed in Qumran—an outward sign of belief in the sovereignty of God and his power. In the contrast between spirit and flesh we must also bear in mind the considerable differences which stem from the concept of spirit at Qumran (see below).

The important contrast between life and death, however, which dominates Johannine thinking, has no parallel at Qumran. In John, ζωή (αἰώνιος) is the essence of the salvation revealed and mediated by Christ. A mere count shows that it occurs forty-nine times in John and the epistles, being deliberately contrasted with death or the realm of death (5:24; 8:51 f.; 6:49 f., 58; 11:25 f.; 1 Jn 3:14). In the Qumran texts, life means predominantly "human life", and the O.T. way of speaking is retained practically unchanged. This is perhaps the strongest argument to show that Johannine "dualism" cannot have been taken over from Qumran.[49]

---

45 Baumbach, *Qumran und das Johannesevangelium;* Huppenbauer, *Der Mensch zwischen zwei Welten;* see also Nötscher, *Zur theologischen Terminologie der Qumran-Texte*, pp. 79–92.

46 Baumbach, p. 53.

47 Huppenbauer, p. 118.

48 See Aalen, *Die Begriffe "Licht" und "Finsternis" im Alten Testament, im Spätjudentum und im Rabbinismus;* on the Qumran texts (not considered by Aalen) see Nötscher, *Terminologie*, pp. 92–133

49 See also Braun, "Qumran und das Neue Testament", pp. 194 and 219.

The other Johannine opposites, "above-below" (8:23; cf. 3:13, 31), "heavenly-earthly" (3:12; cf. 3:31), or in general, God—(this) world (cf.3:16f.; 8:23; 13:1; 16:28; 17:15f., 25; 1 Jn 2:16f.; 4:4; 5:4,19), do not stand out more strongly in Qumran than in the rest of late Jewish literature, especially apocalyptic. No parallel can be provided for the contrast of "freedom—slavery" in 8:32–36, but we are closer to Qumran once more when John speaks of "the ruler of this world" as the adversary of God and his plans (cf. 12:31; 14:30; 16:11; 1 Jn 5:19), or of the "devil" as the origin of evil and the "father" of those who belong to him (cf. 8:41,44; 1 Jn 3:8 ff., 15). His counterpart in Qumran is the "angel of darkness", who is master of the "children of darkness" and also misleads the "children of light" (cf. *1 QS*, 3:20 ff.), called "Belial" in other texts.[50] But the Qumran doctrine of the two spirits[51] is also only a more strongly emphasized form of the general Jewish doctrine of angels and demons, which is in any case subordinated to and incorporated into Jewish faith in God as the creator. One can hardly say more than that the Johannine "dualism", based on Jewish thought, has in many respects its closest parallels in Qumran, especially with regard to "light—darkness". But then there are profound differences which stem from the Christian faith and its doctrine of salvation.

The dualistic terminology is also responsible for the impression that both Qumran and John contain a doctrine of predestination. There are certain theological parallels, though the way of expressing them is different and the thought has other motivations in John. Several texts of Qumran (especially *1 QS* 3:15–21; 4:15–19; *1 QH*, 15:12–17) seem to say that the children of light and of darkness have been placed on their separate ways by the irrevocable decree of God, and the frequency with which the texts speak of the "lot" assigned to each man serves to strengthen this impression. But on closer examination it appears that the spirits struggle in the hearts of men, and that men retain their freedom and responsibility.[52] We have a strictly Johannine way of speaking when we read of those who "are of God" (8:47; 1 Jn 3:10; 4:1–3, 4, 6, 7; 5:19; 3 Jn 11) or who "are of the truth" (18:37; 1 Jn 2:21; 3:19), with their counterpart in those who "are of the world" (8:23; 15:19; 17:14, 16; 1 Jn

---

[50] See Huppenbauer, "Belial in den Qumrantexten".

[51] See Seitz, "Two Spirits in Man"; Wernberg-Möller, "A Reconsideration of the Two Spirits in the Rule of the Community"; May, "Cosmological Reference in the Qumran Doctrine of the Two Spirits and in Old Testament Imagery".

[52] See Nötscher, *Terminologie*, pp. 173–82; Braun, *Spätjüdisch-häretischer und frühchristlicher Radikalismus*, p. 42; Huppenbauer, *Der Mensch zwischen zwei Welten*, pp. 32 ff.; Wernberg-Möller, "A Reconsideration of the Two Spirits in the Rule of the Community"; Wibbing, *Die Tugend- und Lasterkataloge im Neuen Testament*, pp. 61–68; Nötscher, "Schicksalsglaube in Qumran und Umwelt".

2:16; 4:5), "of the earth", or, "from below" (3:31; 8:23) or even "of the devil" (8:44; 1 Jn 3:8; cf. 12). But the "children of the devil" (1 Jn 3:10) have not the same real relationship of origin to their "father" (8:44) as the "children of God" have to God from whom they "are born" (1:13; 1 Jn 2:29; 3:9; 4:7; 5:1, 4, 18). They only became what they are by their wicked desires and deeds (8:44; 1 Jn 3:8, 10, 12). The mystery of why they belong to the realm of evil is not explained; along with the "predestinationist" line, there is also a moral explanation of their hostility to God (3:19 ff.; cf. 7:7; 8:44), or rather, of their refusal to believe in Jesus, the revealer sent by God (cf. 5:40–44; 9:41; 12:43; 15:22f.). Here we have in fact the main difference between John and Qumran. The unbelief of the Jews is the heart of the problem in John: the divine revealer discloses the roots of their enmity in their rejection of his person. In Qumran, on the contrary, judgment is passed on the "children of light and of darkness" in terms of the purity and strict observance of the law demanded by the community, and a corresponding catalogue of virtues and vices (*1 QS*, 4:2–11). The similarity of theological structure, the juxtaposition of ethics and predestination, is not due to direct assimilation or influence, but to a formally similar pattern of thought which is a heritage of the O.T. and of Judaism. The similarity proves to be a parallel phenomenon.

This is also true of the doctrine of the Spirit, in which there are strong contacts between the Qumran and the Johannine literature: being filled with divine Spirit, and that at the present moment, access to God "in spirit and truth", the Spirit having the same functions in the men on whom it is bestowed. But on closer examination, the doctrine of the Spirit in Qumran[53] is seen to be essentially different from that of John: in Qumran, where the notion of the divine Spirit is still dominated by that of the O.T., the Spirit belongs to man from birth, but has then been weakened, but is reinforced again at the "purification" of man, his "conversion" from his evil ways (when he enters the community) and is strengthened again and again (by study of the Torah, observance of the law and rites of purification), till at the eschatological fulfilment it quenches the whole spirit of evil in man, purifies him fully and leads him to perfect glory (cf. *1 QS*, 4:20–23). In John, the Christian as a believer is already "born of the Spirit" (3:3, 5, 8) and this wonderful event (cf. 3:8)

---

[53] See Betz, "Die Geburt der Gemeinde durch den Lehrer", pp. 324 ff.; Nötscher, "Geist und Geister in den Texten von Qumran"; id., "Heiligkeit in den Qumran-Schriften", pp. 333–44; Coppens, "Le don de l'Esprit d'après les textes de Qumran"; Johnston, "Spirit and Holy Spirit in the Qumran Literature"; Foerster, "Der heilige Geist im Spätjudentum"; Betz, *Offenbarung und Schriftforschung in der Qumransekte*, pp. 119–42; Schweizer, "πνεῦμα", pp. 387–90.

can only be the eschatological gift of the Spirit, since it comes through the glorified Christ (7:39; cf. 20:22). The real work of the Spirit along with purification and the forgiveness of sin, which is only lightly touched on (cf. 15:3; 20:22f.), is to fill Christians with divine life (6:63a; 7:38) which leads to immediate fellowship with God (1 Jn 3:24; 4:13). In the activity of the Spirit in revelation there are also essential differences. In Qumran the Spirit gives a new understanding of Scripture, reveals the divine mysteries contained in Scripture,[54] while in John the "Spirit of truth" (the Paraclete) "teaches", "recalls" and discloses the words of Christ (14:26; 16:13), and performs the function of a witness (1 Jn 5:6), serving Christ's work of salvation within the Church (1 Jn 5:7) and in face of the world (15:26). These profound differences, which have merely been indicated here, show sufficiently that once more the resemblances are only formal, with certain common roots, but that the Johannine doctrine of the Spirit has become something quite new and independent under the influence of the Christian faith.

It is also instructive to observe how the Paraclete appears, a figure entirely rooted in Qumran thought according to a recent monograph of O. Betz.[55] There are five Paraclete sayings in John, where the figure appears unannounced but with a very distinctive character. It has been made an important point of research in the history of religions, and one can only agree with Betz and other scholars before him, that efforts to assign it a syncretist and Gnostic origin have been a failure, and that the Johannine Paraclete belongs to the Jewish thinking on the "intercessor".[56] But Betz's efforts are also unconvincing when he tries to trace it back directly and uniquely to Qumran conceptions, and asserts that the fourth evangelist had the image of the Archangel Michael before his eyes when he composed the promises about the Paraclete.[57] The texts may throw light on various functions of the Johannine Paraclete: his original judicial function, his "intercession" in a wide and comprehensive sense, his help and guidance—but direct borrowing from the Qumran texts (where neither the term nor a similar one is found) is extremely unlikely. Once more it is only the general Jewish background, now disclosed in clearer detail by the Qumran writings, which associates John with the community of the Essenes.

These examples should suffice to justify the verdict that though there are close contacts between John and Qumran on important points, it

---

[54] Betz, pp. 73–88, 135–40. [55] Betz, *Der Paraklet*.

[56] See Mowinckel, "Die Vorstellungen des Spätjudentums vom heiligen Geist als Fürsprecher und der johanneische Paraklet"; Johansson, *Parakletoi. Vorstellungen von Fürsprechern für die Menschen vor Gott in der alttestamentlichen Religion, im Spätjudentum und im Urchristentum* (1940).

[57] Betz, *Der Paraklet*, p. 207.

can scarcely be proved that the evangelist took over Qumran concepts directly. But that there were some associations must be seriously considered, however they were set up: by means of the disciples who came to Jesus from the school of John the Baptist (cf. 1:35–51), or by Qumran Essenes who later entered Christian, Johannine communities, or through the author's meeting such circles, which influenced his theological thinking.[58]

3. *Hermetism and Gnosticism*

The deep roots which John has in Jewish ground must not make us overlook the fact that it opens out to the Hellenistic world of syncretism. Recent research has no doubt shifted the balance much more towards Palestinian and Hellenistic Judaism, but it would be an exaggeration to deny all contacts in language, debate and mentality with the syncretist religions of paganism which were so much influenced by the East.[59] The historian, who must rely on the comparison of texts, finds himself faced with special difficulties here, because the age and origin of the literature in question are difficult to determine. There are no contacts between John and Greco-Roman philosophy, and mystery religions need hardly be considered, except possibly for the concept of "re-birth" (cf. 3:3, 5) which was widespread in many forms and occurred in the cults in question.[60] But the context alone in Jn 3 is enough to show (cf. commentary) that the presuppositions of the Johannine notion of "birth from on high" or "from God" (1:13; 1 Jn) are rather Jewish and early Christian. A more precise comparison is imperative only for the spiritual trend which we can recognize in various forms in the Hermetic, Mandaean and other "Gnostic" literature, and which has often been designated by the general concept of "Gnosis" in recent years. The term is

---

[58] Braun, "Hermétisme et Johannisme", p. 298, affirms that John must have already made contacts with groups connected with Qumran even before his stay in Ephesus. He describes in his essay "L'arrière-fond judaïque", pp. 43 f., the stages: John's first contacts were through John the Baptist, then through Christianized Essenes in Palestine and finally through Qumranites who had emigrated, in Antioch or Ephesus. But none of this is certain, cf. Mayer and Reuss, *Die Qumranfunde und die Bibel*, pp. 127–40.

[59] For the development of these "oriental" elements in Hellenistic piety the work of the students of comparative religion is important, in spite of its ill-considered judgment on many points. We may mention Reitzenstein, *Poimandres;* id., *Die hellenistischen Mysterienreligionen;* Dietrich, *Eine Mithrasliturgie;* Norden, *Agnostos Theos*, esp. pp. 220–23; Cumont, *Les Religions orientales dans le paganisme romain*, E. T.: *The Oriental Religions in Roman Paganism*; see also Nilsson, *Geschichte der griechischen Religion*, vol. II, pp. 581–701.

[60] Cf. *Letters of St John*, excursus viii.

problematical and controversial, it is made to cover many different phenomena and systems, it is applied to a movement of which the origin and progress, especially in relation to Christianity, is bristling with questions: still, it must be allowed to stand as the term which characterizes an understanding of the world and of existence, and a desire for salvation, which were then active and effective.[61] Once more we restrict ourselves to some typical comparisons, such as seem in fact to be suggested by John.

(a) The Hermetic literature

The literature comprised in the *Corpus Hermeticum*, study of which has advanced considerably both as regards the textual tradition[62] and the analysis of the thought,[63] shows many affinities with John. The allied traits are concentrated in the "dualistic" treatises, and in particular in Treatise I (Poimandres) and the esoteric dialogue "*De Regeneratione*" (Treatise XIII). The points of contact with the Johannine literature have been investigated by C. H. Dodd and F.-M. Braun in particular.[64] Both scholars provide lists of comparable phrases,[65] but judge the parallels differently. Dodd holds that John and the *Hermetica* merely share the same environment, that of "the higher religion of Hellenism", and rejects (with Reitzenstein and Scott) all Christian influence on the Hermetic literature.[66] Braun, however, having investigated the "history of tradition" of the treatises in question, does not hesitate to maintain (along with M.-J. Lagrange) that they underwent a secondary revision dictated by anti-Christian apologetics[67]—a problem which recurs in another form with regard to the Odes of Solomon (see below). The possibilities to which

[61] See esp. Jonas, *Gnosis und spätantiker Geist;* id., *The Gnostic Religion;* Quispel, *Gnosis als Weltreligion;* Wilson, *The Gnostic Problem*, cf. p. 261: "Gnosticism is an atmosphere, not a system; it is the general atmosphere of the period and affects to some extent all the religions and philosophies of the time"; Grant, *Gnosticism and Early Christianity*, cf. p. 10: "It is a religion of saving knowledge, and the knowledge is essentially self-knowledge, a recognition of the divine element which constitutes the true self."

[62] Scott's *Hermetica* in four volumes is valuable for the materials gathered and the commentary (vols. II–III) but the frequently arbitrary emendation of the text made it unsatisfactory. It is now replaced by Nock and Festugière, *Corpus Hermeticum.*

[63] Here we must mention first of all the important work of Festugière, *La révélation d'Hermès Trismégiste;* also Prümm, *Religionsgeschichtliches Handbuch für den Raum der altchristlichen Umwelt;* Nilsson, *Geschichte der griechischen Religion*, pp. 582–612; Zuntz, "On the Hymns in Corpus Hermeticum XIII"; Haenchen, "Aufbau und Theologie des Poimandres".

[64] Dodd, *Interpretation*, pp. 10–53; Braun, "Hermétisme et Johannisme".

[65] Dodd, pp. 34 f. and 50. f.; Braun, pp. 263 ff. and 275 ff.

[66] Dodd, p. 33.

[67] Braun, pp. 32, 266, 277 f.

Braun has pointed—the early circulation of John in Egypt, counter-polemics by the pagan Porphyrius, their adoption by his imitator Asclepius, to whom we owe part of the Hermetic literature, development of the Hermetic thought from Treatise I to Treatise XIII—can hardly be contested.[68] But it remains questionable whether such local contacts are sufficient to prove a secondary Christian influence. We may leave this problem aside, to concentrate on the main linguistic and conceptual contacts.

The Johannine concept of the Logos has a certain parallel in the Hermetic cosmogony (I, 5f.): from the realm of light "a holy Logos" descends upon nature; the earth, still mixed with and covered by water, is set in motion by the πνευματικὸς λόγος which passes over it; light is identified with Nous (here, the highest God), the Logos who proceeds from the Nous is lightsome (φωτεινός) and "Son of God" (I,6). Thus the Hermetic Logos has a function in creation, is of divine nature, and is a mediator between the realm of the divine and spiritual and the realm of the worldly and material. But similarity with the Johannine Logos stops there. Behind both there is a reminiscence of Gen 1,[69] but otherwise Treatise I,5f. is dominated by Stoic ideas about the separation of the four elements by the λόγος σπερματικός.[70] Further, the cosmic Logos has its counterpart in the Logos within the soul of man (cf. I,6 ad fin.), here too the instrument of the Nous to which it is united,[71] a concept entirely lacking in John. The same idea recurs in the passage dealing with the Logos in *Corpus Hermeticum*, Treatise XIII, para. 21, where the initiate who has been mystically "re-born" is to offer his sacrifice of prayer to the Father of the All διὰ τοῦ Λόγου, which presumably means that the divine Logos who has entered into him is to praise the Father (cf. XIII,18: ὁ σὸς Λόγος δι' ἐμοῦ ὑμνεῖ σε).[72]

The mystery of re-birth (Treatise XIII) takes place in a salvific revelation which is absorbed by the initiate in a vision which brings knowledge and redemption. He becomes one born of God, a "child of God", "the All in all, made up of all powers" (§ 2), who has "gone out of himself into an immortal body", and is "no longer what he was before, but born in mind" (§ 3), "deified" (cf. §§ 7,10)—a total transformation has occurred, in the Gnostic sense of the renewal of the "essential" (οὐσιώδης) man within the soul. This is very far from the Christian faith in

[68] On the relationships between Asclepius and John, cf. Braun, pp. 259 ff.

[69] Jewish influence on the Poimandres was worked out above all by Dodd, *The Bible and the Greeks*, on our passage, esp. pp. 115–32; but see also Haenchen, "Aufbau und Theologie des Poimandres", pp. 157 f.

[70] See Scott, vol. II, pp. 28–31, 122–26; Haenchen, pp. 156 ff.

[71] See Haenchen, pp. 158–61.

[72] See Scott, vol. II, p. 407.

revelation and redemption, as preached by John. The desire for "redemption" and "deification" is common to both, but the way is totally different.

The Greek of this Hermetic treatise undoubtedly provides many reminiscences of John, especially the pair of concepts "light—life", which is used in both to characterize the divine sphere distinct from the material, the concept of ἀλήθεια and the group of words associated with "knowing" and "seeing". It is easy to understand that the language of John could evoke echoes in the pagan Hellenistic world and so have an appeal which was probably intended by the evangelist. But one has only to read the Hermetic treatises attentively to gauge once more the distance from John, since we are constantly meeting typical Hellenistic concepts which are lacking in John, such as ἀθανασία, αἴσθησις, δημιουργέω, εἰκών, ἰδέα, νοῦς etc.; and the omission of the substantive γνῶσις is probably intentional in John. It may be said that the evangelist tries to make his message penetrate to the type of pagan Hellenistic reader who is revealed to us in the Hermetic literature, but that is the only link between John and these writings.

(b) Mandaean literature

Since R. Bultmann published in 1925 his programmatic essay on the "significance of the newly-discovered Mandaean and Manichean sources for the understanding of John",[73] Johannine studies have had to face the "Mandaean problem". Can the rich but difficult and disordered literature of this Gnostic baptismal sect throw light on the religious background of John and render essential services in the understanding of it? Is the oldest (pre-Christian) stage of its tradition to be considered one of the spiritual bases, if not one of the immediate historical sources, of the evangelist, or has research gone astray here? Is there any reason at all for using these texts to explain or at least illustrate the specifically Johannine thought? The decisive point in the comparison between Mandaean and Johannine literature was recognized clearly at once by Bultmann: the notion of the "myth of the redeemer", that is, a uniform pattern of thought which in spite of basic differences in interpretation as between "Gnostics" and "Christians" hinges on the descent and return of a redeemer and revealer from on high, and provides within this framework a great similarity of language—a dualistic form of expression, the leading concepts of "light" and "life", "truth" and "lie", the union of the redeemer with "his own" and his contrast with "the world" etc. The conclusion,

[73] "Die Bedeutung der neuerschlossenen mandäischen und manichäischen Quellen für das Verständnis des Johannesevangeliums".

that these texts should be used for the interpretation of John, was already drawn by W. Bauer in his commentary (3rd ed., 1933) and then by R. Bultmann himself who provided rich material for comparison in his great commentary on John, and gave an existentialist interpretation of the notion of revelation which John presented in "mythological" terms.

The sharpest attack on the "Mandaean"-Gnostic background was made by E. Percy in his studies of the origins of Johannine theology.[74] He went to the heart of the problem by comparing the "dualism", the "redeemer" and "redemption" in the two sets of writings. He finds that the pairs of opposites, "light—darkness", "truth—lie", the two "worlds" and "classes of men" in John have a different meaning, and can be adequately explained by late Jewish and early Christian presuppositions (pp. 13–143). The Christian figure of the "redeemer" did not exist in this form in an earlier Gnosis, and had in fact to be adapted to its purposes by Gnosticism (pp. 290 ff.); the notion of redemption as "life" and the Christian "knowledge" in faith are also independent (pp. 305–46). Bultmann's reaction to this position, so diametrically opposed to his own, was given in a long review of the book.[75]

What was needed above all in this controversy was an answer to the question of how far these late Mandaean writings contained ancient concepts already at work in pre-Christian times. Here new texts published by Lady E. S. Drower, analysis of the various strata of Mandaean material and comparison with other religious texts have enabled research to make notable progress.[76] We are not, however, in a position to pass definite judgments of the relationships between John and the ancient Mandaeans, though it may be admitted that the basic views of Mandaeanism go back to pre-Christian times and represent an early stage of "Gnosis". Hence the Mandaean texts cannot be neglected as at least material for comparison with John. Since the parallels have been collected in sufficient quantity by Bauer and Bultmann, it has not been thought necessary to display the whole range of the material in this commentary. A critical examination of the supposedly similar views seemed more revelant. Here opinions differ very widely, and we shall mention briefly the most important points in order to illustrate the viewpoint we have taken.

First of all we note some central theological concepts which give the Mandaean writings the same tone as the Johannine. "Light and life"

---

[74] *Untersuchungen über den Ursprung der johanneischen Theologie* (1939).

[75] "Johanneische Schriften und Gnosis".

[76] On the significance of the sources recently made available by Lady Drower (esp. *The Haran Gawaitha* and *The Canonical Prayerbook)* see Schulz, "Die Bedeutung neuer Gnosisfunde", pp. 306–11; on the history of research, *ibid.*, pp. 312–29; and earlier, Baumgartner, "Der heutige Stand der Mandäerfrage"; now very fully, Rudolf, *Die Mandäer*, vol. I.

are more strongly linked than in Jewish literature. Along with the contrasting terms "light and darkness", which also play a large part at Qumran, the other pair "life and death" are given the same importance. God, the "Lord of greatness" is constantly praised as the "high King of Light" and "the great Life". "He is the light in which there is no darkness, the living one in whom there is no death, the good one in whom there is no wickedness" (*Ginza*, 6:26f.). "The world where he is does not pass away: it is a world of brightness and light without darkness . . . a world of life for ever without dissolution and death, a world of living water, at the fragrance of which the kings (or the angels) rejoice" (*Ginza*, 10:34 ff.; cf. 32:9 ff.). The two "worlds", the upper world of the heavenly and the lower world of the material, are characterized by these two pairs of terms: "You saw that they left the house of life and turned their face to the place of darkness . . . They left the place of brightness and light, departed and loved the worthless dwelling" (*Ginza*, 69:8 ff.). But Mandaean dualism[77] is more radical and more basic than that of John. The oldest writings speak of two original principles (two "kings" and two "natures", *Book of John*, 55), the earth is wholly a "place of darkness" (cf. *Book of John*, 235f.) and hence everything corporeal and material is treated as utterly valueless (cf. *Ginza*, 430:13–21; 432: 26 ff.; 433: 33 ff.).

Another leading concept in Mandaeanism is "truth" *(kushta)*, a comprehensive concept with many aspects, which means primarily (as in Semitic thinking in general) "reliability, loyalty", and became for the Mandaeans "the essence of their religion, truth and rectitude in the relationship of the believers to the supreme being and to one another"[78] and then also "the personified power of salvation and redemption".[79] God sends "messengers of *kushta*" (*Ginza*, 56:31) and fills hearts with it (*Ginza*, 60:8). In a great hymn to *kushta* we read: "Come in goodness, *kushta*, light, the light which you bring to the house of your friends . . . You are the way of the perfect, the path which ascends to the place of light" (*Ginza* 271:20–26). This recalls Jn 14:6; but while the Johannine ἀλήθεια has similar functions in salvation, it is linked quite differently with the personal bringer of revelation and salvation, Christ,[80] and does

---

[77] See Percy, *Untersuchungen*, pp. 13–143; Rudolf, *Mandäer*, vol. I, pp. 143 ff. Rudolf thinks that Mandaeanism unites the "Iranian" and "Judaeo-Syrian" types, but with the Syrian form of Gnosis predominant, that is, its cosmology is determined by the motif of guilt; the positive evaluation of the world is clearly an echo of Jewish belief in creation (p. 145).

[78] Lidzbarsky, *Das Johannesbuch der Mandäer*, p. xvii; cf. the monograph of Sundberg, *Kushta I*.

[79] Rudolf, *Mandäer*, vol. II, p. 140.

[80] See Blank, "Der johanneische Wahrheitsbegriff".

not attain the same central importance as in the Gnostic community. The Mandaeans also know the *kushta* as a ritual handclasp with "salvific meaning" which brings them into union with "life" and with each other.[81] Thus the Mandaean *kushta* is deeply rooted in Gnostic thought and is its most concentrated expression; the Johannine ἀλήθεια is more like that of Qumran (see above), even though when Christ speaks precisely as revealer, the language often approximates formally to that of the Mandaeans. In the brotherly union of believers, it is not ἀλήθεια but ἀγάπη which is the dominant thought.[82]

Formal similarities along with profound differences of content can also be observed in the imagery. When writing his dissertation, E. Schweizer believed that the ἐγώ εἰμι sayings were to be explained in terms of a Mandaean background, but has since partly abandoned this thesis.[83] S. Schulz, in his investigation of the Johannine discourses, comes to the conclusion that only the parabolic discourses on the shepherd and the vine (with the characteristic addition of καλός or ἀληθινός) contain a polemic against the redeemer-figures of Hellenistic Gnosis, while the others are meant to show Jesus as the fulfilment of Old Testament and late Jewish hopes of salvation.[84] It is noteworthy that he finds that the Mandaean texts are significant only for the parabolic discourses on the shepherd and the vine, but his attitude towards this remnant is surprising. Do not these two long discourses in particular owe their imagery and their conceptual background to the O.T.? Is not this the readiest explanation of "shepherd and flock", from the Messianic point of view (cf. Ezek 34), and could not then the (primary) orientation be a Jewish one (cf. the role of the Pharisees in ch. 9)? For "vine and branches" the Mandaean parallels appear at first sight to be more impressive, but on closer inspection[85] lose their force. When they have lost their fascination, the O.T. thought of Israel as Yahweh's vineyard, as the noble vine etc., takes on a new impressiveness: in the understanding of the primitive Church, in Johannine theology, Jesus is the true eschatological vine, as he unites to himself a new community.

There remains the most difficult problem which Bultmann posed at the start: is not the basic Johannine concept of the heavenly envoy, the revealer, who as revealer brings redemption, only fully intelligible in the light of the Gnostic "myth of the redeemer", and is not this myth impres-

---

[81] Rudolf, *Mandäer*, vol. II, p. 146.

[82] On the concept of truth in John see also the dissertation of Lozano, *El concepto de verdad en S. Juan;* comparison with Mandaean literature, pp. 67–77.

[83] Contrast *Gemeinde undGemeindeordnung*, pp. 106 f., esp. n. 447, with *Ego eimi.*

[84] *Komposition und Herkunft*, pp. 90–131. It is precisely on the parables of the shepherd and the vine that Schweizer has changed his view.

[85] See Borig, *Der wahre Weinstock.*

sively displayed by the Mandaean texts? This question goes beyond the relations of John to Mandaean literature and will be treated fully in excursus vi. It is most improbable that the fourth evangelist was inspired by the Mandaeans in particular to take up the pattern of a saviour and revealer sent into the world, descending from the upper world and ascending there again. The confusing relays of mythological figures which merge into each other in Mandaean literature, and whose mythological contours point to their belonging to the oldest strata, can hardly have provided any special impulse to the development of so purified a notion as we meet in John, linked to the historical person of Jesus Christ. Manda d'Hayye himself ("knowledge of life"), the supreme Uthra (helper) and noblest "envoy", the embodiment of Mandaean faith in redemption,[86] shows the real meaning of the Gnostic "doctrine of envoys". It is the thought of redemption by Gnosis. The souls ("sparks from the light"), fallen from on high since the beginning of time and imprisoned in the lower world, are gathered by Manda d'Hayye, wakened from their abandonment to the world and forgetfulness of their true selves, and led back to the heavenly world of light. This process of self-redemption by Gnosis is described in the myth of the redeemer: the destiny and the way of the soul become graphic and certain through him. As Rudolf notes, the centre of the Mandaean act of revelation is the primitive revelation, "an idea utterly foreign to Christianity, but typical of Gnosticism".[87] When the various redeemer-figures come in each age of the world, it is always simply to renew the primitive revelation, and hence always a present event. The goal of human existence is known in its origin, and knowledge of the true self, the core of the person, becomes liberation from the oppression of destiny (the "planets", the lower powers).[88] Mandaeanism is, therefore, an example of the Gnostic faith in redemption, with its own type of ideas about "envoys", and, if its origins are really ancient, offers valuable material for a pre-Christian and non-Christian Gnosis (it always remained anti-Christian). But it can hardly be regarded as the immediate background of John, since the many designations of the envoys from the heavenly world do not include the specific title which occurs in the Johannine statements about the descent and ascent of the revealer and redeemer, the "Son of Man". Attempts to

---

[86] See Rudolf, *Mandäer*, vol. I, pp. 142 f., 164 f.

[87] *Ibid.*, p. 102.

[88] These basic concepts of Gnosis are well presented by Jonas, *Gnosis und spätantiker Geist*, vol. I, pp. 94–110; to bring out the "logos of Gnosis", that is, to show the consistency of its understanding of existence and salvation throughout all its bewildering mythological forms of expression, he takes the Mandaean literature as an "excellent source" (p. 94). See also Schlier, "Der Mensch im Gnostizismus"; Foerster, "Das Wesen der Gnosis"; Wilson, *The Gnostic Problem*, pp. 207–18.

find him behind the figure of Anosh or Enosh have broken down, because the parts of Mandaean literature which come in question have been recognized as late.[89]

(c) Christian-Gnostic literature

The rest of the Gnostic material which comes up for comparison comes from the Christian world, with the result that we must always ask ourselves whether similarities with John are not due to Gnostic acquaintance with this Gospel, which they so quickly made their own and interpreted in their own sense. If so, they make no immediate contribution to the description of the background of the Gospel, though their really Gnostic elements may throw light on notions and questions which the fourth evangelist had envisaged and used his Christian faith to deal with. The material has been greatly increased in recent years by the Coptic Gnostic texts from Nag-Hammadi. But we must first consider the *Odes of Solomon*, a work which has been known much longer, with resemblances to John which merit attention.

This distinctive collection of forty-two songs, full of symbolic imagery and mystical overtones, has been much discussed again recently, though scholars are still far from a unanimous verdict. The old position of A. von Harnack, which was vigorously combatted in its day, that the Odes were of Jewish origin (with a Christian revision) was given new force by the comparison with the *Hodayoth* of Qumran, especially since Ode 11, which was found in Greek in a papyrus from the Bodmer collection,[90] showed particularly strong affinities with the Thanksgiving Hymns.[91] J. Daniélou is convinced that the Odes are of Jewish-Christian origin,[92] and in spite of their "mythological structure" denies their "Gnostic" character, which, however, most scholars maintain. And when one observes how easily the redeemer merges with the redeemed (how the "Son" becomes "the sons"),[93] and notes the central thought in general,[94] one must agree with the ordinary view. It is not yet quite clear what the original language was. Many hold that these Odes, mostly preserved in Syriac, were originally written in Greek (a view encouraged by the recent discovery of Ode 11 in Greek); but A. Adam has tried to prove, in a noteworthy essay, that they were written in an Aramaic very like the Syriac of Edessa.[95] Their Syrian origin is also suggested by their affinities with Syrian hymnody, as represented later by Ephraim. F.-M. Braun risks a definite hypothesis, that they were written by Bardesan, who

[89] On the hypotheses of Reitzenstein and Schaeder see Colpe, *Die Religionsgeschichtliche Schule*, pp. 39 f. and 50 f.; on the Mandaean texts see Rudolf, *Mandäer*, vol. I, pp. 103 ff.

[90] Papyrus Bodmer XI in the edition of Testuz.

[91] See Carmignac, "Les affinités qumraniennes de la onzième Ode de Salomon".

[92] Daniélou, "Odes de Salomon", esp. col. 678; id., "Bulletin d'Histoire des Origines Chrétiennes II", pp. 576–9.

[93] See Abramowski, "Der Christus der Salomo-Oden", where the basic ideas are very well brought out.

[94] See Schulz, "Salomo-Oden", cols. 1340 f.

[95] "Die ursprüngliche Sprache der Salomo-Oden".

joined the Christian Church after an early familiarity with the system of Valentinus, but without fully dominating his Gnostic past, which still made itself felt in the Odes.[96] The Valentinian connection has now become clear from the striking parallels in the *Gospel of Truth*, and S. Schulz is ready to assign the *Odes of Solomon* to the same Gnostic circles of Egypt which produced the *Gospel of Truth*.[97] But the switch from Syria to Egypt can hardly be made so swiftly. Men in quest of the truth, including Valentinus himself, undertook many journeys in those days. Even without Braun's hypothesis, a Syrian could have become acquainted with Egyptian Gnosis. It is best, therefore, to continue to look to Syria for their origin,[98] a matter of some importance for John on account of its other relationships (with Qumran, Mandaeanism etc.). At the present state of research definite judgments are not possible.

The closeness of the *Odes of Solomon* to John is shown first by their preference for certain concepts: light, life, truth, living water, holy Spirit, knowledge, faith, joy and particularly love. Another link is the elevated language for a joyous and intimate fellowship with God, which the Odes also speak of, however, in sexual imagery, which is entirely absent from John.[99] Other images which likewise do not occur in John also stem from the symbolic, esoteric language which is typical of Gnosis. Hence the imagery of milk (4:10; 8:16; 19:1–4; 35:5), of the letter (23:5–22), of the garment of light (11:10f.; 15:8; 21:3; 25:8; 33:12), of the ascent of the soul to heaven (35:7; 38:1 ff.). Many of the images which are superficially similar are used in a different sense, as for instance that of the source of water, Ode 11, 6ff.: "And speaking waters touched my lips from the fountain of the Lord plenteously: and I drank and was inebriated with the living water that doth not die; and my inebriation was not one without knowledge . . ."[100] The image occurs in a different sense again in Ode 30:1f.: "Fill ye waters for yourselves from the living fountain of the Lord, for it is opened to you; and come all ye thirsty, and take the draught; and rest by the fountain of the Lord." In spite of the similarity with Jn 7:37f., it means the source of Gnosis, which is the repose and happiness of the restless, questing soul (cf. 30:3 and 7).

It is questionable, therefore, that John has been affected by the Gnostic imagery which is attested by the Odes of Solomon, and one should rather ask whether the author of the Odes has not been inspired in many ways by John. Many texts tell in favour of acquaintance with John:[101]

Ode 6:11f.; 30:1f.	(thirst-assuaging source) cf. Jn 4:14; 7:37
7:4 ff.	(he appeared like me . . . he is my grace) cf. Jn 1:14, 16

---

[96] *Jean le Théologien*, pp. 238–42.

[97] "Salomo-Oden", col. 1341.

[98] See Schmid, "Oden Salomons", col. 1095.

[99] See Schnackenburg, *Letters of St John*, excursus ii.

[100] Translations from Bernard.

[101] See Braun, *Jean le Théologien*, pp. 242 ff. The above list is that of the present writer.

8:14	(mine, whom I know) cf. Jn 10:14
8:22	(pray . . . abide in the love of the Lord) cf. Jn 15:7, 10
10:5	(the scattered gentiles gathered) cf. Jn 11:52
11:16	(coming from darkness to light) cf. Jn 8:12
12:7, 12	(the Word is light to the mind, its dwelling-place is man) cf. Jn 1:4
15:2; 18:6	(his light has driven all darkness from before my face; the enlightened shall not be conquered by darkness) cf. Jn 1:5; 12:35
16:19	(the worlds were made through his Word) cf. Jn 1:3
28:17f.	(they aimed at my death but did not succeed, because I was older than their memory) cf. Jn 8:57f.
31:4	(he lifted up his voice to the Most High, and offered him the sons that were in his hands) cf. Jn 17:11–16
31:5	(his person was justified, as his holy Father had granted him) cf. Jn 17:1, 5; 12:28
31:7	(they accused me . . . who was guiltless) cf. Jn 8:46
33:4	(he drew to himself all who heard him) cf. Jn 12:32
39:11 ff.	(the footsteps of our Lord as bridge and way) cf. Jn 14:2–6
41:13	(the Son of the Most High has appeared in the perfection of his Father) cf. Jn 1:14
41:15	(the anointed . . . was known before the foundation of the world) cf. Jn 1:1; 17:5,24.

These echoes, taking in isolation, do not prove that the author of the Odes knew John. But Ode 31:3–5 could also be a reminiscence of Jn 17 in content and order of thought, and likewise Ode 39:11 ff. of Jn 14:2–6. In other ways too the Odes reveal strong Christian influences; compare Ode 10:3f.; 22:1 with Eph 4:8f.; Ode 19:6–11 (virgin birth); Odes 27 and 42:1f. (allusion to the Cross); 41:12 (humiliation and exaltation); 42:11–20 (descent into the underworld). But all such "Christian" passages teem with Gnostic interpretations. Thus "the Word" occurs frequently, but in a way which departs from the Johannine usage (cf. especially Ode 12), and the same is true of "the way" (cf. Ode 22:7–12; 33:7–13; 39:5–13). We may conclude that the *Odes of Solomon* are a valuable example of Gnostic themes and imagery, but scarcely come in question as the concrete background of John; the dependence is rather the other way round.

The Coptic Gnostic writings from Nag-Hammadi published so far, which seem to come mostly from the second century A.D., clearly show knowledge (and use) of the N.T. literature, in varying degrees. But they are so deeply rooted in Gnostic thought that this trend must be regarded as something settled and presupposed, and hence certainly pre-Christian and non-Christian. A long established system of thought, differentiated no doubt in its various forms, has been given a Christian varnish only at a secondary stage, and the N.T. texts are pressed into service for the Gnostic mentality. Since the Christian writers only present the systems of the Christian Gnostic schools, and do so in the perspective of Church orthodoxy, it will be well to devote special attention to these new and original texts, in order to grasp the main lines and the basic structure of Gnostic thought. The question is whether John shows knowledge of it, takes cognizance of its questionings and adopts some of its expressions—and if so, how the evangelist reacts to it.

The clearest representatives of this typically Gnostic thought seem to be the *Gospel of Truth*[102] and the *Apocryphon of John*.[103] In these two works, where the influence of the N.T. is very superficial, the great Gnostic question is raised as to the whence and whither of human existence. Its briefest and most trenchant expression was found hitherto in the "Excerpts from Theodotus" given by Clement of Alexandria: "Knowledge of who we were, what we became; where we were, whither we were cast; whither we go, wherefrom we are freed; what (is) birth, what re-birth".[104] The same question occurs in the *Gospel of Truth:* "He who has learned this, knows whence he is come and whither he goes" (22:13 ff.). Another text explains where this origin and this goal lie: "But this is the Father, from whom the beginning proceeded, to whom all who proceeded from him shall return" (37:38–38:4). At the very beginning of the *Apocryphon of John*, a Pharisee asks John where his master has gone and he answers: "He has returned again to the place from which he came" (19:15f.). Here, then, the way of the redeemer is envisaged at

[102] Editions: Malinine, Puech and Quispel, *Evangelium Veritatis;* and for folia xvii–xviii, which were only found later, id., *Evangelium Veritatis, xvii–xviii* in collaboration with W. Till. The translations in the text follow that of Till, "Das Evangelium der Wahrheit, Neue Übersetzung des vollständigen Textes". The translation back into Greek attempted by Ménard, *L'Évangile de Vérité*, is also helpful. See further the translation into English by Grobel.

[103] There are a number of versions of the work, which was obviously highly esteemed in Gnostic circles: in Papyrus Berolinensis 8502 (ed. Till); and in three codices of the library of Nag-Hammadi (Krause and Labib). The version of Codex II from Old Cairo has been published with translation, introduction and commentary by Giversen, *Apocryphon Johannis*. The translations in the text follow that of Till. For further literature, see Giversen, "Nag-Hammadi Bibliography".

[104] Clement of Alexandria, *Exc. ex Theod.*, 78, 2 (Sagnard, p. 202).

once, which is, however, for the Gnostic his own way also, which he is enabled to walk by means of the knowledge imparted by the redeemer and revealer. The connection is displayed as follows in the *Gospel of Truth:* "For this reason has he brought him forth (the Son), that he might speak of the place and of his (the Father's) place of repose, whence he (the Son) has come . . . He (the Son) will speak of the place, whence every single one (each man) has proceeded, and he (each man) will hasten to return to the place from where he received his origin, and to be brought away from that place, the place where he has stood, since he has tasted of that place (the divine world of light) and received nourishment and growth from it." (40:30–41:12) Thus in the place where he "stands" (this world), the Gnostic learns from the revealer and redeemer his true home, the heavenly world of light (the pleroma), and he can "ascend" there again by means of this Gnosis.

Several texts in John seem to show clearly that the evangelist was familiar with this quest. In 7:27 f., 35; 8:14; 9:29 f.; 19:9, as also in 3:8; 4:11, we hear the mysterious "whence?" and "whither?" as queries about the origin and goal of Jesus. And there are also other texts in which men or the disciples are included in the question of where their way leads: 7:34, 36; 8:21f.; 12:26; 13:33, 36; 14:3 ff.; 17:24. The great Johannine kerygma of 3:31–36, 13–21 (see commentary) contains the fundamental assertion that the revealer and life-bringer who descended from heaven (and he alone) has ascended there again, to throw open to all who believe in him the way to light and life. The Christian answer to the Gnostic question about salvation is faith in the Son of God who has appeared in history, the Logos who came in the flesh. It is not by (self-redeeming) Gnosis, graphically represented by the myth of the heavenly redeemer, that the Christian attains the heavenly world and the goal of his existence, but by being united in faith to Christ, the true mediator of salvation. But the shaping of the question and the pattern of thought seem to have been stimulated and influenced by Gnosis.

The contrast noted earlier between the "higher" and the "lower" world also has remarkable parallels in these Gnostic texts, and cannot be thought of as a borrowing from John. The parallels are rather part of the language to which these basic Gnostic views are linked.[105] For the Johannine expressions "to be from above" (8:23) or "to come from above" (3:31; cf. 3:3,7; 19:11) there are no really cognate texts in Jewish literature, but the *Gospel of Truth*, 22:4; 35:1; 42:13 may now be cited. Even the Johannine "to be of God" can be verified in the *Gospel of Truth*, 33:32; for "in God" we can compare the *Gospel of Truth*

[105] See Barrett, "The Theological Vocabulary of the Fourth Gospel and the Gospel of Truth".

42:27f., "And the Father is in them, and they are in the Father" (cf. also 43:9 ff.), although the Johannine immanence (in the Father through the Son) is conceived quite differently. The term "return", with regard to the heavenly world of light, is met with constantly.

There could be a secondary influence of John on other concepts, especially for the terms "Word" and "redeemer", as the very beginning of the *Gospel of Truth* shows: "... to know him (the Father of truth), by virtue of the Word which proceeded from the πλήρωμα (and) which was in the thought and in the intellect (νοῦς) of the Father, that (the Word) is he who is spoken of as the Saviour (σωτήρ)" (16:33–37). But one can see how easily Gnostic speculation could adopt such expressions and insert them into its system. To judge from the context of the section, the image of the "way" seems also to have been derived from John: "Where none could know he (Jesus Christ, cf. line 16) has shone forth (and) has given (them) a way. But this way is the truth which he taught them" (*Gospel of Truth*, 18:19 ff., cf. Jn 14:6). The influence is slighter in the *Apocryphon of John*; many parallels should rather be explained by a common vocabulary, as for "light and life". In the *Apocryphon of John*, 25:13 ff., God is praised as "the eternal, the giver of eternity, the light, the giver of light, the life, the giver of life ..."; "he who comprehends himself in his own light which surrounds him, who is indeed the source of life, the light completely pure. The spring of the Spirit streamed from the living water of the light ..." (26:15–21). In particular cases in these texts it is often hardly possible to decide where authentically Gnostic language leaves off and Christian influence begins.

In the *Gospel of Thomas*,[106] where the relationship to the synoptic tradition is important, echoes of John are rare and doubtful. It speaks of Jesus's having appeared in the flesh (σάρξ) in logion 28, and says that the day will come when "you seek me (and) do not find me" (logion 38, cf. Jn 7:34), and that a vine not well established will be uprooted (logion 40, cf. Jn 15:6). Whatever problems the *Gospel of Thomas* may raise about the history of the synoptic tradition, the basic Gnostic question is again audible: "You shall find the Kingdom; because you come from it, (and) you shall go there again (πάλιν) (logion 49); "If they say to you: 'From where have you originated?', say to them: 'We have come from the Light, where the Light has originated through itself'" (logion 50).

In the recently published Gospel of Philip,[107] Gnostic thinking also prevails, but more use is made of John. Christ, the perfect man, "has

[106] Text and translation by Guillaumont and others. A translation back into Greek with theological commentary is given by Kasser. A survey of research is given by Haenchen, "Literatur zum Thomasevangelium"; see also Brown, "The Gospel of Thomas and St John's Gospel".

[107] Text and German translation by Till; introduction and German translation by Schenke

brought bread from heaven" (logion 15, cf. Jn 6:31f.); Jn 6:53 is quoted in logion 23, and given a peculiar interpretation to help with the question of the Resurrection: "His flesh (σάρξ) is the λόγος, and his blood is the Holy Spirit (πνεῦμα)", and this is the flesh in which men must rise. "His own" (logion 9) and the "lamb" (logion 27) also recall texts of John. Further quotations are: "What the Father possesses belongs also to the Son" (logion 37, cf. Jn 16:15; 17:10); "he who has knowledge (γνῶσις) of the truth (ἀλήθεια) is free (ἐλεύθερος), but he who is free does not sin" (logion 110, cf. Jn 8:32,34), and, "if you know the truth, the truth will set you free" (logion 123). The Gnostics were very ready to exploit the text about the "free men" and "slaves", but they did so again in a peculiar way. We need not follow up these Gnostic interpretations, which are difficult and have not yet been much studied. But they contain many traits (frequent allusions to sacraments, no hostility to marriage, the Saviour as bridegroom of the lower Sophia etc.) which point to Valentinian influence.[108] We have reached, at any rate, with the Gospel of Philip, the literature which deliberately exploited John for Gnostic speculations, a process which can be traced further.[109]

One thing should be clear now from our investigations. Christian Gnostic literature cannot be used to explain the imagery and thought of John. But the oldest writings, still little affected by Christianity, reveal a Gnostic frame of mind which was not wholly unknown to the fourth evangelist and of which he took silent cognizance, to oppose to it the Christian message. It remains only to ask where he became acquainted with it, and what conclusions it allows as to the environment and birthplace of John.

4. Place of composition suggested by the history of religions

Our review of the various possible influences of the surrounding world on John has resulted in no definite picture. Various relationships came to light, some of them, however, standing out more strongly than others. We noted the use of a primitive Christian tradition for O.T. quotations, and the interest of the evangelist in a developed biblical theology of a Jewish-Christian type, nurtured on the O.T. (see above, 1). There were contacts with contemporary Judaism, especially "heterodox"

in Leipoldt and Schenke, *Koptisch-gnostische Schriften*, pp. 31–65; English translation and commentary by Wilson. See also Schenke, "Die Arbeit am Philippusevangelium".

[108] See introduction by Schenke and Wilson's commentary (previous note).

[109] See von Loewenich, *Das Johannes-Verständnis im zweiten Jahrhundert*, pp. 60-115; Sanders, *The Fourth Gospel in the Early Church*, pp. 47–66; Wiles, *The Spiritual Gospel*, pp. 96–111. On the relationship of John to Gnosis, see Quispel, "L'Évangile de Jean et la Gnose".

Judaism, and parallels with the Qumran texts showing kinship with the mentality of Qumran, though hardly direct dependence on it (see above, 2). There was also a certain readiness to accept the questions put by Gnosticism and to adopt its terminology, though here again closer contacts with an early stage of Gnosis influenced by Judaism (see above, 3). All this suggests that we should not look too far away from Palestine.

When dealing with the question of Mandaeanism, our attention was called to Trans-Jordania, which may have been the meeting-place of various baptist sects—and perhaps the homeland of the "proto-Mandaeans". This site has also been supported by observations drawn from John itself: that it took an interest in southern Galilee (Cana, Tiberias, Aenon near Salim), Samaria and the country east of Jordan (1:28; 10:40), which could have been connected with the flight of the Jerusalem community to Pella, east of the Jordan, as far north as the border between Galilee and Samaria.[110] In all such considerations, however, one must remember the possible history of the Gospel, which could be based on older traditions which the evangelist incorporated into his work later on, in other surroundings. Such local traditions, which re-inforce the "baptist" background,[111] need have played no part in the main composition of the Gospel, for which the evangelist was responsible, or in the theology which he built up for his readers.

More recent research thinks of Syria, on account of the Gnostic associations in John.[112] One of the main arguments is the affinity with the *Odes of Solomon*, and it retains a certain force, although it is difficult to situate the Odes with certainty. Then there is the spiritual kinship between John and the letters of St Ignatius which, in spite of their untarnished Church orthodoxy, show themselves receptive to Gnostic ideas.[113] But the relationship between John and the letters of Ignatius of Antioch is still debated. There are many points which suggest that the Gospel was known to Ignatius,[114] but the theology of the Bishop remains his own and enables us to use his letters as a source of information about a mentality prevalent in Syria. A comparison of the theologies of the

[110] So Edwards, *The Disciple*, pp. 113–32.

[111] See Schulz, *Komposition*, pp. 150–87.

[112] Burney, *Aramaic Origin*, pp. 129 ff.; Jülicher and Fascher, *Einleitung*, p. 419; Bauer, *Johannesevangelium*, pp. 243 f.; Hirsch, *Das vierte Evangelium*, p. 71; Kümmel, *Einleitung*, p. 173.

[113] Schlier, *Religionsgeschichtliche Untersuchungen zu den Ignatiusbriefen.*

[114] So Maurer, *Ignatius von Antiochien und das Johannesevangelium*, pp. 11–43; Braun, *Jean le Théologien*, pp. 270–82. The opposite position, that Ignatius of Antioch (and other Apostolic Fathers) did not know John, was still defended by Sanders, *The Fourth Gospel*, pp. 11–19, who spoke of "the existence of a common Christian tradition, to which they both had access".

two writers, such as was undertaken by H. Köster,[115] shows that they have different perspectives in spite of the close affinities of the concepts which they use: two "theologies" which could have sprung up in the same place. On the other hand, one should not be too downright in affirming that the "Gnosis" with which John came in contact was "Syrian". The newly discovered Coptic Gnostic writings from Egypt, among which the *Gospel of Truth* shows close kinship with the *Odes of Solomon*, display the same basic Gnostic concepts, which alone are relevant with regard to "Gnostic" influence on John. This, of cource, does not exclude Syria, where Gnosis likewise flourished at an early date,[116] as the site of John; but it means that it is hard to situate definitely the Gnosis which John came upon (as defined also by the epistles).

John was early known in Egypt, and this has led some to think that the Gospel may have originated in this country, where the early history of Christianity is obscure.[117] The early circulation of John in Egypt is attested by P^{52} and Papyrus Egerton 2, and this seems to be confirmed by the texts from Nag-Hammadi, though clear proof hitherto is confined to the *Gospel of Philip* which can hardly be earlier than the second half of the second century, in view of its developed (Valentinian) system. But it is improbable that John was written in Alexandria and that the tradition was transferred to Asia Minor;[118] a movement in the opposite direction is just as conceivable. As for the "baptist theological traditions" and the "baptist communities" which have been supposed to be centred on Alexandria,[119] these are not sufficient reason for transposing John there. As against Alexandria, there is the traditional material collected in John, which suggests a Palestinian source and apostolic authority.

---

115 Köster, "Geschichte und Kultus im Johannesevangelium und bei Ignatius von Antiochien"; see also Maurer, *Ignatius* von *Antiochien*, pp. 44–99. But the "opposition" in the theological perspective of the two authors should not be exaggerated; both base themselves on common theological principles in vogue at the end of the first century in Syria and Asia Minor.

116 See Goppelt, *Christentum und Judentum*, pp. 176–209.

117 Bauer, *Rechtgläubigkeit und Ketzerei im ältesten Christentum*, put forward the thesis that the first representatives of Christianity in Egypt were heretics (pp. 53–57, cf. pp. 60–64). But one would need to know more about Christian origins in Egypt to be able to affirm this; it cannot be denied that a leaning towards Gnosticism showed itself early, to judge by the remains of the *Gospel of the Hebrews* (probably meant for Jewish-Christians) and the *Gospel of the Egyptians* (for the gentile Christians); see Schneemelcher, "The Gospel of the Egyptians".

118 So, as a hypothesis, Sanders, *The Fourth Gospel*, pp. 85 f.; Snape, "The Fourth Gospel, Ephesus and Alexandria".

119 See Stauffer, "Probleme der Priestertradition", pp. 145 ff., who understands John as a programme "meant primarily for the Baptist communities in Ephesus and Alexandria". It was composed in Ephesus but ("in a missionary counter-attack") circulated at once in Egypt also.

And it is precisely such things that do not seem to have been available to early Christianity in Egypt.

From the point of view of the history of religion, Asia Minor is on the same footing as Syria and Egypt. Religious syncretism soon flourished in Asia Minor, which provided favourable conditions for the Jewish-Gnostic heresies denounced in the Epistle to the Colossians and the Pastoral Epistles, for the Nicolaitans of Rev 2:6,15, for the docetes rejected by Ignatius of Antioch, for the Jewish-Christian Gnostic Cerinthus, and also for the heretics of the Johannine Epistles.[120] There are, therefore, no fundamental objections to the ancient tradition of the Church which places the composition of John in Ephesus. The controversies with contemporary Judaism reflected in John (see below, pp. 166f.) also favour Asia as the place where John took (final) shape.

But when one considers all the pointers to Syria, a more nuanced hypothesis is suggested, which has gained support recently.[121] It is that the Johannine tradition, originating in Palestine, was subjected to Syrian influences before it reached Asia Minor (Ephesus), where it was fixed and edited. In Syria, with its ancient gentile Christian metropolis of Antioch, where the spiritual currents of Judaism and Hellenism also met, the tradition absorbed the elements which display proximity to Qumran, the baptist sects and early Gnosticism. When this hypothesis, based on considerations of theology and history of religion, is linked with the question of authorship, many possibilities are still open. Did the Apostle John, whom we have assumed to be the first bearer of the tradition, leave Palestine for Syria and then Asia Minor? Or was it the disciple to whom we suggest the final responsibility for the Gospel should be assigned, who absorbed these spiritual impulses, and if so, where was his homeland? Here certainty is even harder to attain. It may have been only in Asia Minor that the evangelist came into contact with the influences coming from Syria. In spite of the uncertainty of the result, the investigation of the relationships of John to the spiritual trends of its time and environment cannot be said to be fruitless. Its cultural background has been focussed a little more sharply, its spiritual and also its geographical situation has been made more precise, and its *Sitz im Leben* clarified. An investigation of its theological and topical interests may enable us to make further progress.

---

120 See Schnackenburg, *Letters of St John*, Introduction, ch. iv.

121 See Manson, "The Fourth Gospel"; followed by Lightfoot, *St. John's Gospel*, pp. 5 f.; see also Robert and Feuillet, *Introduction à la Bible*, vol. II, p. 662.

CHAPTER VIII

Theological and Topical Interests

The fourth Gospel cannot be considered simply as the product of a certain milieu and of particular impulses, as a piece of writing composed for a definite historical purpose. It is a literary work which matured in a long process of meditation and preaching, embodying many interests and traditions, and it is, therefore, all the more urgent to determine its really central object. Questions and influences coming from the surrounding world, and its historical and cultural setting, may then have had a considerable effect on the presentation and the language, but cannot have robbed the work of its own special character. The first thing must be to define the "main interest" of John, which can hardly be any but theological, and then to consider the "subordinate interests" in the light of its times and surroundings. To determine its central theological interest calls for a certain decision: one must answer, so to speak, the question of the "heart" of this Gospel and hence perhaps of "the heart of the Gospel" as a whole in the Johannine perspective. But this decision on what is the core of Johannine theology must be tested by the rest of the theological affirmations of the evangelist. It must be shown that they can be grouped effortlessly round the supposed centre, are intelligible in the light of this principle and combine to give a comprehensive view. This is not, of course, the place to investigate and expound the whole of Johannine theology. We must confine ourselves to the most striking lines of its structure, with particular attention to the critical questions which are discussed by scholars. Our procedure will be directed by these considerations. We shall go from the main theological purpose to the other theological traits which are built on to and around the central one, and then take up the contemporary interests, whose link is more extrinsic, but which are still embraced by the theology and thus ordained to the whole.

Introduction

1. Theological interests

(a) The basic Christological interest

Every question about the central theological interest of John must start with the author's own assertion about the purpose of his book: "This has been written that you may believe that Jesus is the Christ, the Son of God, and that through (this) faith you may have life in his name" (20:31). It cannot, therefore, be doubted that what the evangelist has at heart is faith in the person of Jesus Christ and his salvific power; but this Christological and soteriological motive needs to be determined more closely. An analysis of the statement already helps us to gain more clarity: a) As the foundation of the faith which is then defined more precisely, the evangelist appeals to what has "been written", that is, to his own presentation, which he describes as a deliberate choice from among the "many other signs" which Jesus performed before his disciples (v. 30). Even if the evangelist took over v. 30 from a σημεῖα-source, his statement points back to his account of the work of Jesus, which confirms the proposition that his book is meant to be a "Gospel" (cf. ch. i above). b) The presentation of the "signs" which Jesus wrought and of the words whereby he revealed himself—which are inseparable from the signs, as the Gospel itself shows—is to make men believe that Jesus is "the Christ, the Son of God". The primary sense of the first epithet is of course "the Messiah", that is, the bringer of salvation promised in Scripture and expected by the Jews; but this hardly means that the Gospel was intended as a convincing "historical" proof that Jesus was the promised and expected Saviour, to break down the obstinate scepticism of Jews (in the Hellenistic diaspora.)[1] We must rather give full value to the second epithet, which implies the full Christian profession of faith, proclaiming the Messiahship of Jesus in a sense which surpasses all Jewish expectations, the unique dignity of the incarnate Logos as the "only-begotten of the Father" (1:14), the mystery of Jesus as "the Son" absolutely, a mystery grasped by faith (cf. also 1 Jn 1:3; 3:8, 23; 4:9, 15; 5:5, 13, 20). What is involved, therefore, is the foundation and justification of the primordial confession of faith in Christ by the early Church. c) But the expression "that you may believe" also tells us more about the intention of the evangelist. It need not be understood as the statement of a missionary aim, the winning of new converts,[2] but can also imply the confirmation and strengthening of faith

[1] So van Unnik, "The Purpose of St John's Gospel"; Robinson, "The Destination and Purpose of St John's Gospel". But see Schnackenburg, "Die Messiasfrage", pp. 240–64.
[2] See the commentaries and Schnackenburg, "Die Messiasfrage", pp. 257 f.

in those who already believe, so that, like the disciples in the Gospel, they may attain to a more profound and stable faith. The Gospel uses the witnesses to the great event (cf. 3:11; 15:27; 19:35; 21:24) to speak directly to the present, and to make the earthly Jesus as the present Christ, as is also demonstrated by the revelatory style of Jesus's discourses and the character of "sign" in his miracles. Faith is ordained to testimony, and the testimony is given in the form of an account of the earthly work of Jesus; but the faith is directed to the living and glorified Christ preached by the Church, who effects salvation as the glorified Lord (cf. 17:2) and who is none other than the Jesus of whom the Gospel speaks. d) The faith thus founded, and produced or strengthened by the words of the preacher, has power to impart salvation or "life"—"in his name". The final addition is not superfluous. It emphasizes once more what is already clear in the context, that faith in Jesus as the Christ and the Son of God has its salvific power through the person of Christ. As regards Jesus Christ, this means that his Messianic and divine dignity was brought out only to disclose his function as Saviour. The Johannine Christology is essentially ordained to soteriology. Everything that the Johannine Jesus says and does, all that he reveals and all that he accomplishes as "signs", takes place in view of man's attaining salvation, in view of his gaining divine life. And since this salvation is inextricably linked with himself, since he reveals himself in word and in deed, all his work is interpreted "Christologically" by the evangelist. Thus the concluding statement really provides us with the key to understanding the presentation according to the mind of the evangelist. We shall take a brief look at the Gospel to see whether we have grasped correctly the main intention of the evangelist.

In the Johannine presentation, the only task of John the Baptist is to bear witness to Jesus. The sentence in the prologue which certainly comes from the evangelist is enough to prove it: "He came to bear witness, to give testimony to the light, so that all should come to believe through him" (1:7). John attests that Jesus is "the light", as Jesus later affirms of himself (8:12). His testimony is meant to awaken faith; "faith" here, used absolutely, without further qualification, can only mean faith in Jesus as the light, and what that means is explained by the word of Jesus, "he shall have the light of life" (8:12). The prologue then goes on to display clearly the soteriological function of the Logos incarnate (cf. vv. 12f.; also v. 16 taken with v. 14), as does the Baptist in his testimony when he points out "the Lamb of God who takes away the sin of the world" (1:29, 36).

The significance of the σημεῖα is given at once by the evangelist with the first "sign": they reveal the δόξα of Jesus, but should also lead to faith (2:11). They only have their full significance for those who believe (cf. 6:26,36; 11:40; 12:37). What this is, is said most clearly at the last two great miracles, in a word of revelation spoken by Jesus. The cure of blindness reveals him as the "light of the world" (9:5, cf. 39), the raising of Lazarus as the "resurrection and the life" (11:25f.), for those, that is, who see him with the eyes of faith. But the Resurrection of Jesus himself is the event in which this life, the Holy Spirit, is imparted to the faithful (7:39; cf. 20:22).

In the words of revelation spoken by Jesus the central significance of the person of Jesus, both as regards Christological and soteriological assertion, is established with final certainty. The ἐγώ εἰμι sayings, round which the revelation discourses are crystallized, have as their component parts the revealer's description of himself, an invitation or a call to decision and a promise to those who respond.[3] The self-presentation always reveals something of the divine dignity and power of Jesus, taking up as it probably also does—especially in the absolute use, 8:24, 28; 13:19; cf. 8:58—the formula used in the O.T. theophanies.[4] The two other elements, which are not always brought out formally, and are partly given already by the character of the parabolic discourse (cf. 6:48; 10:7,11,14), express the significance of the revealer for the salvation of those who hear his voice. This soteriological function of the Son of God in the world is brought out explicitly and emphatically in the kerygmatic discourse 3:13–21 (especially v. 17), and again in 12:44–50 (especially v. 47b). At the same time, there can be no doubt that the salvation of the believer is only possible because he in whom he believes is "the only-begotten Son of God" (3:18), the "Son of Man" who came down from heaven (3:13; cf. 31). This should be enough to confirm the view of "the basic Christological (and soteriological) interest" of the evangelist as seen in 20:30f.

(b) The doctrine of salvation

Thus the Johannine theology also poses the question of the salvation of man and of the whole world, the latter, as in Paul, with great emphasis. Jesus is the "Saviour of the world" (4:42), a universalist viewpoint which is deeply rooted in the basic structure of the Johannine concept of the "world". John no longer asks like Paul about the ways of salvation of Jew and Gentile, but confronts all mankind with God, seeing it estranged from God and doomed to death, outside the divine realm of light and

---

[3] See Kundziņš, "Charakter und Ursprung der johanneischen Reden", pp. 221–24; Becker, *Die Reden des Johannesevangeliums*, p. 54; Schulz, *Komposition*, pp. 86 ff.

[4] See Zimmermann, "Das absolute Ἐγώ εἰμι als die neutestamentliche Offenbarungsformel".

life, till the revealer and Saviour sent by God shows it its way to the heavenly world (cf. 1:4; 3:13,16,19,31 f.; 5:24; 6:33; 8:23f.; 12:31 f., 46). This dualistic view of the world, coloured by the trends of the time, this disjunction between the lower world of darkness, where man is imprisoned in his historical situation, and the higher world of God, to which man undoubtedly belongs according to his original call (cf. 1:4,11), is overcome through and in Christ. In his way of salvation he unites the two worlds with each other once more by "descending" from heaven, indeed, by becoming man in the nothingness of the "flesh", and ascending once more to the heavenly world (6:62), to make the same way possible for all men who believe in him and follow him, becoming thus himself "the way" (cf. 14:2–6). The Christology breaks through the dualistic framework, its soteriology eliminates the predestined constraint (of sin) which detains man in slavery (cf. 8:32–36). By God's loving act of salvation, the sending of his Son (3:16), the light penetrates as the unconquerable power of love (cf. 1 Jn 2:8), goodness prevails over evil in spite of the deeper darkness of unbelief (cf. 3:19f.; 9:39), and the power of the forces hostile to God is broken on the Cross (cf. 12:31 f.). The "world" which murmurs and rebels against God is conquered (cf. 16: 33; 1 Jn 5:4), and this victory is final, though the "world" which rejects Christ and persecutes his disciples (cf. 15:18 ff.) may still struggle against it. God is greater than the power of evil (cf. 1 Jn 4:4), Christ remains the Saviour of the world (1 Jn 4:14).

But in this cosmic and universal redemption, is not the Cross of Christ given a different meaning than in the previous theology of early Christianity? Is it still the place of vicarious expiation? It might seem that the general Christian interpretation of the death of Jesus as a sacrifice of expiation had ceased to determine the Johannine view.[5] It is true that the emphasis has been put elsewhere, but the ancient thought has been retained and incorporated. The traditional formula with ὑπέρ has been expanded to take in the cosmos, and linked with the guiding Johannine concept of "life": ὑπὲρ τῆς τοῦ κόσμου ζωῆς (6:51c, cf. 33); and in the same text it is attached to ἡ σάρξ μου, so that the σάρξ of the incarnate Logos (1:14) is integrated into the soteriology. The Incarnation does not only mean the nuptials of the heavenly and eternal world with the earthly and transitory, it also means that the sacrifice of the Cross has been made possible. It is not merely the entry of the Logos into mankind and the sphere of its "flesh" (3:6a), it is also the assumption of the body of flesh which is sacrificed on the Cross "for the life of the world". It is possible that we have here a received formula of the Eucharist, another form of the words of

[5] See Bultmann, *Theologie des Neuen Testaments*, pp. 400 ff., E. T.: *Theology of the New Testament*, vol. II, pp. 54 ff.

institution (surviving in Ignatius of Antioch)[6]—though it was accepted by John and completely assimilated into its theology. But in any case 1:29 (the Lamb of God who takes away the sin of the world) shows that the thought of the expiatory sacrifice was genuinely part of the Johannine theology. There can be no other way of understanding the strange metaphor, which still goes directly to the heart of the matter.[7] But it is also probable that the thought of the paschal Lamb is to be evoked, and that a line goes from here to the scene at the Cross (19:33f.), which the evangelist links symbolically with the paschal sacrifice (19:36). The emphasis, it is true, is on the whole way of redemption from the Incarnation to the "lifting up" as a redemptive happening, as the fetching home of man to the divine world. But the redemption through the expiatory sacrifice of the Cross is integrated into the Johannine thought. 1 Jn did not just re-introduce the thought in the traditional sense, it merely accentuated it more strongly (ἱλασμός 2:2; 4:10; τὸ αἷμα Ἰησοῦ 1:7; cf. 5:6).

This observation is important for the understanding of the person of Jesus, which is not confined to his revelation and to a way of redemption which could be understood merely as a prototype. His person is important in the attainment of salvation. If we now turn to the "subjective" way of salvation, that is, to the call which goes forth to men and how they are to participate in salvation, the question of how John understands Jesus as revealer gains in urgency. The ordinary demand is to believe in him, and the soteriological offer is summed up in the formula (which can vary slightly): "He who believes in the Son has eternal life" (3:16, 36; 5:24; 6:40,47; 11:25; 20:31). The same thought is also expressed in many other places (cf. 3:15, 18; 6:35; 7:38; 8:12, 51; 12:36, 46; 1 Jn 5:12,13). What do "believe" and "believe in the Son" mean here?

The Johannine "faith" (cf. excursus vii) is so close to "knowing" (γινώσκειν) and "confessing" (ὁμολογεῖν) that the emphasis is on the acknowledgment of what the revealer says and what can also be expressed in articulate formulas (of confession of faith).[8] But the content of these statements is always concerned with the person of Christ, so that one could term it briefly a "Christological faith in the form of a confession", not indeed in a theoretical, doctrinal sense, but to emphasize its link

---

[6] See esp. Jeremias, *Abendmahlsworte*, pp. 101 f., 191–4, E. T.: *Eucharistic Words*, pp. 141 f., 156; also Bernard, *St. John*, vol. I, pp. clxx f.; Lohmeyer, "Vom urchristlichen Abendmahl", p. 308; Schürmann, "Joh. 6:51c", who, however, opposes the notion that a different formula of institution has been used (p. 247, n. 14).

[7] On the other interpretations see commentary *ad loc.*

[8] See the construction with a ὅτι-clause 6:69; 8:24; 11:27, 42; 13:19; 14:10, 11; 16:27, 30; 17:8, 21; 20:31. All these are Christological in character and ultimately refer to the person of the Revealer. There is a special theme only in 4:21, after πιστεύειν with dative ("believe me").

with the person of God's envoy—as the phrase most often used, πιστεύειν εἰς (36 times), also suggests. Thus faith too, as what is demanded of man for salvation (cf. 6:29), is completely Christological in its orientation. This confirms the "basic Christological interest" of the evangelist, but in addition, it reveals the situation of the Johannine communities, whose faith demanded confessional formulas for their worship (cf. the many titles and attributes of Christ) and for their struggle against heresy (cf. 1 John). Finally, the detailed interpretation (which must be reserved for the commentary) shows that this faith does not merely mean an existential decision at the summons of the revealer, but also and above all union with him as the bringer of salvation, following of him as the guide to and mediator of salvation (cf. 8:12). One may also suspect that there is an antithesis to the way of salvation of "Gnosis", as appears more clearly in 1 John.[9]

(c) The realized eschatology

We can see in the basic soteriological formula, "he who believes in the Son has eternal life", a further characteristic of Johannine theology: the actualization of eschatology. In its original meaning, and outside the Johannine writings, "eternal life" is an eschatological concept referring to the future world. But in John it is understood in the sense that the blessings of salvation are already present, as the essence of the salvation already attained in faith in Christ.[10] The same process by which eschatological assertions are transformed and re-interpreted to signify that the salvation made possible by Christ and linked to him has been attained in the present, can also be observed in the case of other concepts and expressions. This is true of the corresponding negative group of words about "judgment" (as "verdict of death"),[11] and also of "that day" (14:20; 16:23, 26—beginning with the Resurrection of Jesus), "joy (fulfilled)" (15:11; 16:20, 22, 24), "victory" (16:33; cf. 1 Jn 5:4), "peace" (14:27; 16:33), cf. also "kingdom of God" (3:3, 5) and indeed "Son of Man".[12]

The question is, what has led to this realization and actualization of the eschatology? For we are not prepared to deny that the evangelist retained an "eschatological outlook" with regard to the future eschatological events (cf. "last day", 6:39, 40, 44, 54; 12:48; bodily resurrection and judgment according to works, 5:28f.; but also "eternal life" in a futurist

---

[9] See Schnackenburg, *Letters of St John*, excursus iii; Bultmann, "πιστεύω", pp. 227 f. ("in fact, John's concept of faith has an anti--Gnostic orientation", p. 228).

[10] See Mussner, *Die Anschauung vom Leben im vierten Evangelium*, esp. pp. 144–58, who speaks of "the mystique of life" in John.

[11] See Blank, *Krisis*.

[12] See Schnackenburg, "Der Menschensohn im Johannesevangelium".

sense, 12:25; perhaps also 3:36b; 4:14, 36). According to our discussion of Johannine Christology, the main ground would seem to be the concentration of the theology on the *Christus praesens*, though the actual situation of the evangelist may also have played its part. There may be an opposition to the Gnostic attitude and an effort to encourage Christians in their stand against their anti-Christian surroundings (cf. 1 Jn 2:12ff., 27; 4:4ff.; 5:18ff.). It is undoubtedly the expression of a special ("eschatological") Christian understanding of existence, but it is neither "Gnostic" nor "existentialist": it does not do away with the whole of the old ("dramatic") eschatology in favour of each present moment of decision. Given the primitive Christian eschatological consciousness of living between salvation accomplished and fulfilment yet to come, the process was almost inevitable and was furthered by the recession of an imminent expectation of the end. This can also be seen in the theology of Paul, in spite of its being more strongly orientated to the end. He too sees eschatological life in the *pneuma Christi* as already present in us (Gal 2:20; 5:25; Rom 6:11; 8:2, 6, 10; 2 Cor 2:16; 4:12), and our life as hidden with Christ in God, to be revealed at last in glory (Col 3:3f.). In John, however, the strongest motive is the Christology, which shows the glory of the Logos still dwelling in the earthly Jesus, and the power of the exalted and glorified Lord already present in his word and work of salvation. In John, Christ is really the "eschatological present".

(d) The meaning of the sacraments; "mysticism" and ethics

Since John sees the saving power of Christ as present in the faith and life of Christians, one also expects some comment on the sacraments which the other N.T. writings show to have played an important part in the primitive Church. But the question is highly controversial with regard to John. The answers range from the assertion of an anti-sacramental tendency (R. Bultmann) to the view that the whole presentation, with its many symbolical allusions, makes the Christian liturgy show through with its fundamental sacraments of baptism and the Eucharist (O. Cullmann).[13] But it is less important to reach agreement about the extent of sacramental symbolism than to note how baptism and the Eucharist

---

[13] Cullmann, *Urchristentum*, p. 56, E. T.: *Early Christian Worship*, p. 54: "The Gospel silently presupposes that the historical event, as there presented contains along with what can be perceived by the senses the indication of further saving facts, with which these unique basic data are connected." But this "connection" needs to be envisaged more precisely; the sacraments are hardly to be considered as "further saving facts", but rather as signs and means whereby the unique event of salvation on the cross is re-presented and its strength and the fruits of its salvation applied to the recipient; cf. Schürmann, "Die Eucharistie als Representation und Applikation des Heilsgeschehens nach Joh 6:53–58".

are basically understood, the two sacraments to which the evangelist refers at least in chs. 3 and 6, perhaps also in some way at the washing of the feet, and certainly in 19:34f.[14] This last text in particular could show that for John these sacraments originate in the death of Jesus, and (if 1 Jn 5:6f. may be adduced) continue to attest and represent this salvific event and to make it fruitful in the effective application of salvation. Though we cannot undertake to justify this view here,[15] it may be admitted that it fits in well into the perspective of the *Christus praesens.* The sacraments would then be means, viewed Christologically, of importing into the present time the work of our salvation accomplished by Jesus which they recall as they bring his power into play.

The so-called Johannine mysticism, the assertions about "being in" and "abiding in" Christ and through him in God, also take on a special meaning in the light of the theological interests of John as we have tried to present them here. The living and fruitful union in grace between the believer and Christ is then not a timeless mysticism detached from history, but the full realization of Jesus's fellowship with his disciples, which first became possible for them—and for all who believe in Christ—after his glorification. That this presupposes the glorified mode of being of the risen Christ who has returned home to the glory of his Father needs no proof. But it is expressly said in 14:19f.: "But you see me, because I live and you also shall live. In those days you shall know that I am in my Father and you in me and I in you"—which is precisely an explicit "immanence formula". But it is also made clear—and this should not be overlooked—that this is really the fulfilment of the fellowship which the disciples had in an imperfect manner with their Lord while he was on earth (cf. for instance 14:7–11; 15:7–10; 16:22–28, 29–33). The fellowship with God disclosed and made possible in the earthly Jesus (cf. 14:7–11) is only given its full reality through the glorified Christ; but now it is open to all who accept the apostolic testimony to the Logos who appeared on earth and believe in Christ as the Son of God and the way to the Father (cf. 1 Jn 1:1–4). Thus the series of profound religious utterances which have been termed, somewhat misleadingly, the "Johannine mysticism" of union with Christ and God, remains intrinsically linked to the Johannine picture of Jesus, the Christ, to the self-revelation of the earthly Jesus as well as to the glorification of the Christ. This does not mean that one should deny that the "mystical" desires and language of the time and milieu in which the evangelist lived have been taken into account. But he

[14] See the most recent discussions: Lohse, "Wort und Sakrament im Johannesevangelium"; Macgregor, "The Eucharist in the Fourth Gospel"; Brooks, "The Johannine Eucharist". The older literature is given in the article cited in the next note.

[15] See Schnackenburg, "Die Sakramente im Johannesevangelium" (with lit.); see also the commentary *ad loc.*

produces an unmistakably Christian answer from his profound meditation on Christ, whence he also drew his specific formulations.

The Johannine "mysticism" of fellowship with Christ is inseparable from ethics. "Bringing forth fruit" is the goal of "abiding" in the vine, 15:4–8; "abiding in the love of Christ" presupposes the keeping of his commandments, 15:9f. And it is easy to see that this concentration of ethics on love is again due to the Johannine concept of Christ. The "new" commandment of brotherly love, in which moral exhortation is summed up and crowned, is outlined in its novelty and uniqueness in view of Christ: "that you love one another, as I have loved you" (13:34). And once more it is the earthly Jesus who exemplifies and makes possible the brotherly love of his disciples (cf. 13:14f.), as he gives the supreme proof of his love, his death on the Cross, on the threshold of his way to the glory which makes his love eternal and fruitful (cf. 13:1; 17:26). The divine love in the ultimate self-sacrifice became reality in him, obliging his own to love in the same way, and to prolong the movement of love which went forth from God (cf. 1 Jn 2:7f.; 3:16, 23; 4:9ff.). Ethics too forms part of the Christological perspective of John.

(e) Church and mission

Like the sacraments, the place of the Church in the theological thinking of the fourth evangelist is a subject of debate. The view is put forward in many forms that John does not reflect the official ecclesiastical Christianity of his times, but comes from a special group where Christians relied on the "Spirit" alone and even perhaps felt a certain tension towards "offices" in the Church. It has been pointed out that the term "Church" is lacking, that the ideal disciple "whom Jesus loved" is in competition with Peter who embodies the "office", that the commandment of charity is "restricted" to "brotherly love" and so on.[16] E. Käsemann goes furthest in this direction with his thesis that the "Presbyter", whom he regards as the author of the Johannine writings, was a "Christian Gnostic", "who with quite incredible daring, wrote a Gospel of the Christ of his own experience who addressed himself to the world of Gnosis".[17] Käsemann thinks that the Presbyter was opposed at once by the Church of the monarchical episcopate (in the person of Diotrephes, cf. 3 Jn 9f.) and

[16] See Kragerud, *Der Lieblingsjünger* (an inspired prophet, unattached, in contrast to holders of office in the Church;); Moule, "The Individualism of the Fourth Gospel" (individualist, mystical piety); see also Barrett, *St. John*, p. 113: "Comparison with the 1, 2 and 3 John shows at once that the evangelist stood apart from the busy and quarrelsome ecclesiastical life of the age. Probably he was not popular . . ."; on 2 and 3 John see also von Campenhausen, *Kirchliches Amt*, pp. 132 ff.

[17] "Ketzer und Zeuge", p. 302.

affirms that "the Johannine writings point to an *ecclesiola in ecclesia* as the constituent form of fellowship".[18] Older critics, on the contrary, did not go so far as to challenge the orthodoxy of the fourth evangelist or deny him his place in the missionary activity of the Great Church,[19] and in recent times more and more attention has been paid to the evangelist's sense of the Church and to his theology of the Church.[20]

It is in fact impossible to deny that John is deeply rooted in the thinking of the Great Church, or that the Church is present in the theology of John. The disciples in the Gospel are representative of the later Church, and they are brought into relationship with it more than once (cf. 4:38; 17:18, 20f.; 20:21). They appear as the flock of believers whom the Father has entrusted to the Son (cf. 10:1–18, 26–29; also 6:37, 39; 17:6–11), and under the image of the vine and the branches (15:1–8). And this is done in such a way that all, including later believers, are comprised under these metaphors. Further, Jesus speaks explicitly of "other sheep who are not of this fold" whom he must also lead (10:16), and of the "scattered children of God" whom he must "gather" (11:52). He prays for the unity of all who come to believe in him through the words of the disciples (17:20f.). When one notes that the Church is the responsible agent for the sacraments and the liturgy, one can see that the Church is still more deeply rooted in Johannine thought; for then the words about "adoration in spirit and truth" (4:23f.) refer to the cultic life of the Church, and the deeper doctrine of baptism and the Eucharist (see above) is meant to perform a theological service for the communities in their sacramental practice. The thought of the Church is also behind the sayings about the work of the Paraclete. It is in the Church that the Holy Spirit teaches through the apostolic word and brings to mind all that Jesus said (cf. 14:26; 16:13f.), and it is through the Church that he "convinces" the unbelieving world (16:8–11; cf. 15:26f.). The Church can finally be recognized in its missionary charge (cf. 17:18; 20:21), especially with regard to non-Jews (cf. 10:16; 11:52; 12:20–24) and in its missionary practice (cf. 4:38), and there is no indication that the evangelist isolates himself and the group to which he belongs from the apostolic missions of the universal Church.

---

[18] *Ibid.*, p. 303.

[19] See for instance Holtzmann, *Lehrbuch der neutestamentlichen Theologie*, pp. 432–37; Jülicher and Fascher, *Einleitung*, pp. 414–18.

[20] See Gaugler, "Die Bedeutung der Kirche in den johanneischen Schriften"; Faulhaber, *Das Johannesevangelium und die Kirche;* Allen, "The Jewish-Christian Church in the Fourth Gospel"; Corell, *Consummatum est*; Schweizer, "Der Kirchenbegriff im Evangelium und den Briefen des Johannes"; Schnackenburg, *Die Kirche im Neuen Testament*, pp. 93–106, E. T.: *The Church in the New Testament*, pp. 103–17; d'Aragon, *L'Église dans la Bible*, pp. 53–66; Feuillet, "Études Johanniques", pp. 152–74.

But what is the relationship of ecclesiology to the great Christological interests of John? Here too one may note the theological concentration on Christ. The flock and the vine as images of the Church point above all to the unity of Jesus with his disciples or the faithful, making him leader and head of those united to him and also the centre of their life and bond of union. It is to him and no one else that God has given the flock; he leads them to the pastures of life and is the true and faithful shepherd who risks and gives his life for his sheep (ch. 10). But he and his own are united by a deep and close bond of mutual "knowledge", trust and love (cf. 10:14, 27). The scene with Peter recounted in the epilogue, ch. 21, is not only important for the polity of the Church on account of the Petrine office. It is also theologically important because the risen Christ affirms once more that it is his sheep that he hands over to the chief of the Apostles. He remains the real shepherd charged by God, and continues to be united to his own. In the discourse on the vine, ch. 15, Christ is shown even more clearly as the source of life for those who are united to him, and of all fruitfulness. He is the true vine, representing the eschatological plantation of God (probably, however, as antitype of the ancient Israel, which appears often enough under such images in the O.T.), but he takes in all who are joined to him in faith and gives them life and fruitfulness—a concentration of ecclesiology on Christ such as is attained elsewhere only in the Pauline concept of the Body of Christ. This is also true of worship, because the new and perfect worship of God "in spirit and truth" is made possible by Christ. In him the hour for it has come (4:23), and indeed, for the evangelist, the body of the risen Christ himself is the eschatological temple of which Jesus spoke in the logion on the temple (2:21). We have already seen that it is probable that the Johannine meditation sees the sacraments in the water and blood which flowed from the side of the Crucified (19:34). The Eucharist is the sacrament which brings about union with Christ in a special way, and the fact that the immanence formula first occurs here is not without significance (6:56). Even the missionary work is included in a profound Christological perspective: the grain of wheat which falls to the ground and dies brings forth a rich harvest; Jesus, when he is "lifted up", will draw all to himself (12:24, 32).

Thus the Christological principle of interpretation is also confirmed for this group of concepts. The evangelist found in the person of Christ, as he grasped it in faith, the theological principle which enabled him to re-think the revelation of Christ proclaimed by the primitive Church and to disclose its depths. It is, therefore, correct to attribute to him the title of "the theologian" by which he was honoured later, and the concentration of his theology on Christology must be considered the dominant factor, the "major interest" of his presentation.

2. Topical interests

Along with and throughout the theological presentation of the fourth evangelist, we find a number of practical interests at work, arising from the historical situation of the evangelist and of Johannine Christianity. They are never spoken of explicitly, being woven into the presentation, but the exegete can recognize them from certain emphases and turns of phrase, and from assertions which point beyond the "historical" level, while the historian can compare other documents of the time of the evangelist and draw on his knowledge of the history of those later times in general. Since it is a matter of drawing conclusions from the narrative of the Gospel and of trying to fit it into the historical situation when the Gospel was composed, a measure of uncertainty must be allowed for in all judgments on the matter.

(a) Attitude to Judaism

It is immediately noticeable that "the Jews" are spoken of very frequently (71 times in John), with a special shade of meaning, but that often no distinction is made between the various groups in Judaism in the time of Jesus, particularly with regard to the leading circles, whom in fact the evangelist prefers to speak of simply as "the Jews".[21] In the synoptic Gospels the expression οἱ Ἰουδαῖοι is used much less often as a collective term (5 times in Matthew, 6 times in Mark, 5 times in Luke). They mention instead all the more frequently the Pharisees (Matthew 29 times, Mark 12 times, Luke 27 times, John 19 times), doctors of the law or scribes (Matthew 22 times, Mark 21 times, Luke 14 times, John never), Sadducees (Matthew 7 times, Mark once, Luke once, John never), "ancients" (the lay nobility in the Sanhedrin—Matthew 11 times, Mark 5 times, Luke 4 times, John never) and then the Herodians (Matthew once, Mark twice, Luke and John never). John does indeed also use the term οἱ ἄρχοντες for the members of the Sanhedrin (7:26,48; 12:42; 3:1 in the singular). But the generalizing description of the leaders as οἱ Ἰουδαῖοι is remarkable, as is the relatively frequent mention of the Pharisees. The reason can hardly be lack of "historical" knowledge of the situation. But another suspicion springs to the mind: that the evangelist is guided by a certain judgment he has formed on Judaism. Historically speaking, the leaders are made responsible for the unbelief of the Jewish people and Jesus's failure among them (cf. 11:47–53); but at the same

[21] See Lütgert, "Die Juden im Johannesevangelium"; Bauer, *Johannesevangelium*, excursus after 1:19; Gutbrod, "Ἰουδαῖος", pp. 378–81; J. Jocz, "Die Juden im Johannesevangelium".

time this circle is to appear, theologically, as the representatives of the unbelief and hatred of the "world" hostile to God (cf. 15:18ff.). They continue to live as contemporaries of the evangelist in the unbelieving Judaism of his day which persecutes the disciples of Christ (cf. 16:1–4) and which is led by the rabbinate of the Pharisees. The influential role of the Pharisees, who had a considerable following among the people (cf. 7:32, 47f.; 9:13, 15, 40; 11:46; 12:19), corresponds in fact to the historical situation in the time of Jesus, but can be still more strongly underlined after the catastrophe of A.D. 70 on account of their strengthened claim to continued leadership (cf. 12:42).

This view is definitely confirmed by the term ἀποσυνάγωγος in 9:22; 12:42; 16:2. Etymologically (it occurs only in these texts of the N.T.) it means "excluded from the synagogue"; but complete exclusion from the religious fellowship of the Jews hardly existed as yet in the time of Jesus.[22] There was only the "ban", a temporary excommunication—which may be intended in 9:22. After A.D. 70, however, the exclusion of Christians was practised, as may be deduced from the insertion of the "cursing of the heretics" *(birkat ha-minim)*, about A. D. 90, into the Shemone Esre.[23] This is clearly the practice which is envisaged in 16:2, and the measures of 9:22; 12:42 are seen in the light of this. That the evangelist's attitude towards the Jews is reserved can also be seen from the aloof way in which he speaks of the feasts and customs of "the Jews" (cf. 2:6, 13; 4:9; 5:1; 6:4; 7:2; 11:55; 18:20; 19:40, 42), though he does not deny the link with the Jews in the history of salvation (4:22, cf. *ad loc.*) and "Israel" remains for him the ancient title of honour (1:31, 49; 3:10; 12:13). Then the debates about Jesus's Messiahship must also partly reflect objections and attacks made by contemporary Judaism against faith in Jesus as the Messiah, especially 7:27, 41f.; 12:34.[24] Other matters are debatable, since they can be explained by the situation of the time of Jesus. One may, however, suspect that when the evangelist is dealing with Jesus's debates with "the Jews" (cf. ch. 8), which do not yet appear in the Synoptics as so sharp and continuous, he is also thinking of his own day, and hence making them more "transparent" and topical for his readers. We can also note a polemical interest in the interpretation

---

[22] Schürer, *Geschichte des jüdischen Volkes*, vol. II, pp. 507 ff. E. T.: *History of the Jewish People*, vol. II, pp. 60 ff., accepts it in the light of the New Testament texts; but see Billerbeck, *Kommentar*, vol. IV, pp. 329 ff. Real exclusion from the community is prescribed in Ezra 10:8 (for returned exiles who do not notify the authorities within three days of their arrival); but the rabbinic literature does not appeal to this text for the practice of excommunication.

[23] See Schürer, pp. 543 f., E. T.: pp. 85 ff.; Billerbeck, vol. IV, pp. 212 f., 218 f.; see also Doskocil, *Der Bann in der Urkirche*, pp. 40–43.

[24] See Schnackenburg, "Die Messiasfrage", pp. 249–52.

of Scripture, in contrast to the more positive and Christological attitude of the Synoptics. The Scriptures which "the Jews" search so zealously, testify precisely to Jesus (5:39); "the Jews" seek their own honour and not that of God (5:42ff.); the Moses in whom they hope will be their accuser (5:45). Christ is far superior to Moses (1:17; 6:32ff.); but they do not even keep the law of Moses (7:19), and use their own rules of interpretation to condemn Jesus unjustly (cf. 7:22f.). Though the Pharisees pride themselves on being disciples of Moses, they are blind and unreceptive to the open testimony of God for Jesus (cf. 9:28–34, 41). In all this, there must have been a polemical intention against the Pharisee rabbinate of the time of the evangelist. Judaism, especially in the towns of the diaspora possessing large Jewish colonies, had soon grown strong again and was a threat to the Christian communities (cf. also Rev 2:9; 3:9: "synagogue of Satan"). Thus the presence of an anti-Jewish tendency in John, occasioned by the contemporary situation, can hardly be doubted.[25] This does not exclude a missionary intention with regard to Jews of the Hellenistic diaspora who were men of good will, but this can hardly be one of the principle aims of the Gospel.[26]

(b) Disciples of John the Baptist and baptist groups

Since Baldensperger[27] emphasized forcibly, but too one-sidedly, that John had the polemical and apologetical intention of combatting the disciples of John the Baptist, who still existed and competed with Christianity in the time of the evangelist, the existence of this tendency has always been recognized, but the extent and bearings of the polemics have been a subject of controversy. It is certainly not the main interest of the Gospel, but it is definitely there.[28] Where and how does it make itself felt?

An apologetic point is unmistakable in the two insertions into the Logos hymn of the prologue which deal with the Baptist (vv. 6–8 and 15). The assertion: "He was not the light, but only to give testimony to the light" (v. 8) rejects an over-estimation of the Baptist, on which very

[25] See Jülicher and Fascher, *Einleitung*, pp. 416 ff. ("the most determined marshalling of the gospel story, to refute Jewish objections, or at least objections inspired by Jewish unbelief, against the gospel as hitherto known", p. 480); Grant, "Origin of the Fourth Gospel", p. 320; Goppelt, *Christentum und Judentum*, pp. 253–8; Wikenhauser, *Einleitung*, pp. 221 f., E. T.: pp. 306 f.; Kümmel, *Einleitung*, pp. 158 f.; Grässer, "Die antijüdische Polemik im Johannesevangelium".

[26] See above note 1; also Kümmel, *Einleitung*, p. 157 ("but the missionary character is entirely lacking in John"); Barrett, *St John*, pp. 114 f.

[27] *Der Prolog des vierten Evangeliums.*

[28] So too the recent Introductions; the question is examined closely in Schnackenburg, "Das vierte Evangelium und die Johannesjünger".

different judgments are passed. Was he held to be the Redeemer in the circles opposed by the evangelist, was the Logos hymn originally composed with him in view and are the allied views Gnostic? Or was he merely to be denied the same role as Jesus, that of Messiah (whatever that meant exactly)? The meaning of v. 15, the attestation of the pre-existence of Jesus by his precursor, which is taken up again in 1:30, seems to be correctly given by O. Cullmann: the words are directed against the argument of the later disciples of John (in the Pseudo-Clementine writings), that John is superior to Jesus because he appeared before him. To counter this argument, the evangelist makes John himself attest solemnly that Jesus really "existed before" him.[29]

Apologetics are also clearly present in John's answers to the envoys from Jerusalem (1:19–28, especially v. 20). He denies firmly that he has any Messianic claims. We get the same picture again from the last testimony of the Baptist before his disciples in 3:27–30; v. 28 is obviously addressed to disciples of John, to those of the present as well as the past: "You yourselves must bear me witness that I said, 'I am not the Messiah, but only sent before him'." Now it can be proved historically (from the Pseudo-Clementine writings) that at the beginning of the second century the disciples of John revered their master as the Messiah,[30] and this shows us what must have been the contemporary background to the insistence of the fourth evangelist. All further speculations about Gnostic views held by the sect, a Gnostic hymn to the Logos produced by them and connections with the Mandaeans lack solid foundation.[31]

It may be asked whether other passages in the Gospel also aim at the disciples of John and seek to counteract a too high esteem for the Baptist from the Jordan, as for instance 3:31f. ("he who comes from the earth" etc.; but see *ad loc.*), or 10:8 ("thieves and robbers" who "came before

---

[29] Cullmann, "Ὁ ὀπίσω μου ἐρχόμενος".

[30] *Pseudo-Clementine Recognitions*, I, 54 (*PG*, 1, cols. 1237 f.) and I, 60 (col. 1240); further discussion in Schnackenburg, "Johannesjünger", pp. 24 ff.; on the question of sources see Strecker, *Das Judenchristentum in den Pseudoclementinen*.

[31] On the Mandaeans and their attitude to the Baptist, see Rudolf, *Mandäer*, vol. I, pp. 66–80, who writes: "John is in no way a constitutive element in the Mandaean religion" (p. 73); "the baptism of John and the figure of John must once and for all be envisaged completely apart from Mandaeanism" (p. 76). He is also reserved in his judgment about later anti-Christian Baptist sects: they have no apparent connection with the Mandaeans (pp. 76–80); but he thinks (relying on Bultmann) that the prologue of the gospel contains a hymn from a Baptist community (p. 77) at the centre of whose faith John stood, as a Gnostic redeemer-figure (p. 79). The "Baptist" origin of the Logos Hymn is also maintained by Schulz, *Komposition*, pp. 66 f.; but his reconstruction of the development of the disciples of John (pp. 167–70) arouses misgivings; and when he affirms that "the existence of the original prologue is further proof of the thesis of syncretist influences within the Baptist communities of Palestine", he assumes what is not proved, that the original prologue came from Baptist circles (p. 168).

Jesus"). But this is highly uncertain, especially as John is not totally rejected but actually claimed as a God-given witness to Jesus (1:6f.; cf. 5:33 ff.). One must, however, earnestly consider whether other baptist groups, devoted to repeated baths and washings (a practice of which we have no evidence for the disciples of John), are not given a lesson incidentally in the scene of the washing of the feet (13:10, "He who has bathed, does not need to be washed . . ."), or in 15:3 ("You are already pure through the word which I have spoken to you"). There was a great baptist movement at the time of the evangelist.[32] But this would be really only a secondary interest, since the true (theological) meaning of the washing of the feet is different, and 15:3 also is only an incidental remark. Other brief sorties or allusions of the same type, occasioned by contemporary conditions, cannot be excluded in John; cf. 4:38 (who are the ἄλλοι?); 5:43b (ἄλλος, here suspected to be a historical personage, but probably wrongly); 8:31 (Jews who became believers[33]); 10:8 (thieves and robbers before Jesus); 14:22 (a question put on apologetical grounds); 21:20–23 (the death of the disciple whom Jesus loved). But to prove the various hypotheses, we should have to know more about the historical conditions in which John originated.

(c) Anti-Gnostic tendencies

Very different answers are also given to the question as to how far John is competing directly against Gnostic heresies or trends in his surroundings. This is due to the problems raised by the "Gnostic" background of its thought, which has been discussed above (see ch. vii, 3). Certain contacts with Gnostic questionings and concepts seem to be joined to a fundamentally anti-Gnostic attitude of faith. Here it is only a matter of noting anti-Gnostic utterances of the evangelist and determining them exactly.

There are testimonies in tradition to the effect that the fourth evangelist wished to combat a Gnostic heretic of his day, Cerinthus.[34] The oldest testimony is that of Irenaeus: "Johannes Domini discipulus

[32] See Thomas, *Le mouvement baptiste.*

[33] See Dodd, "A l'arrière-plan d'un dialogue johannique", who holds that Jn 8:33–58 reflects controversy with Jewish Christians inside the Church. It is true that v. 31 might envisage "Jewish converts to Christianity" (p. 7), but the sharp attacks need not be directed against Jewish-Christians; they could well be directed against apostates (cf. ἐάν . . . μείνητε) or Jews in general.

[34] Cf. Cladder, "Cerinth und unsere Evangelien"; Bardy, "Cérinthe"; Bludau, *Die ersten Gegner der Johannesschriften*, pp. 131–36; Grant, "The Origin of the Fourth Gospel", pp. 308–16 (who rejects the testimony of Irenaeus and holds that he wished perhaps to oppose Gaius, who ascribed John to Cerinthus, with the thesis that it was written against this heretic); H. Rahner, "Kerinthos".

volens per Evangelii annuntiationem auferre eum, qui a Cerintho inseminatus erat hominibus errorem, et multo prius ab his, qui dicuntur Nicolaitae . . .".[35] The context is concerned with the creation of the world, for which they taught that it was not God but a demiurge who was responsible; John emphasizes against them that God created the world through the Logos and bestowed redemption and salvation on men through the same Logos, his Son. Irenaeus goes on to mention Marcion and others of the same type who held that the world was not made through him (the Logos) and that he did not come to his own domain, but, on the contrary, to an alien place.[36] It is questionable, therefore, that Irenaeus wished to present here Cerinthus as the sole or actual Gnostic opposed by the evangelist; and the legend about the Apostle John's meeting Cerinthus in the baths[37] does not decide the question. The scholars who suppose that John contains polemics directed specifically against Cerinthus[38] mostly appeal to 1 Jn, which seems to attack the heresy of Cerinthus, particularly in 5:6f. But apart from the question whether the Gospel has the same orientation as the Epistle, an examination of the Epistle shows that its assertions do not exactly suit the heretical doctrines of Cerinthus, described in detail by Irenaeus, *Adv. Haer.*, I, 21, and are probably directed against other variants of a Gnostic (docetic) Christology.[39] And the virgin birth of Jesus which Cerinthus denied is not mentioned at all in 1:13 (on the reading with the singular; see *ad loc.*).

Though the names of early Christian Gnostics opposed by the evangelist cannot be given, there can be little doubt of the anti-Gnostic intention contained in the assertion of the Incarnation (1:14). The expression σάρξ ἐγένετο links up with the Christological professions of faith in 1 Jn 4:2; 2 Jn 7, and must be directed against a docetic watering down of primitive Christology in the Church, such as is typical of Gnosticism while taking many forms. The historicity of the divinely-sent Redeemer, and still more his entry into material σάρξ, which was likewise the presupposition for the bloody sacrifice of the Cross, was used as a declaration of war on the Gnostic myth of the Redeemer. Perhaps 19:34f. is also meant to hinder a docetic interpretation of the Crucifixion; for the fact that the evangelist may regard it as a symbolical reference to the sacraments of baptism and the Eucharist (the situation suggesting "blood" being put first), does not exclude an interest in the reality of the event.

---

[35] *Adv. haer.*, III, 11, 7 (Harvey, vol. II, p. 40).

[36] *Ibid.*

[37] *Adv. haer.*, III, 3, 4 (Harvey, vol. II, p. 13).

[38] Lagrange, *Saint Jean*, pp. lxxii f.; Wikenhauser, *Einleitung*, pp. 222 f., E. T.: *Introduction*, p. 307; contrast: Grant, "The Origin of the Fourth Gospel", pp. 308–16; Michaelis, *Einleitung*, pp. 121; Kümmel, *Einleitung*, p. 158.

[39] Schnackenburg, *Letters of St John*, Introduction, ch. iv.

It is true that no such stress is laid on the "blood" as in 1 Jn 5:6 (the water is the unexpected thing); but if one takes the scene as a whole, 19:34f. could also contain the thought that is uppermost in the Epistle, just as 1 Jn 5:7 reverses the priority and has a sacramental interest which is secondary to the anti-Gnostic polemic. For as John understands the sacraments, their function is to maintain and attest the historical act of redemption on the Cross (see commentary).

It is also difficult to make up one's mind about the remark that occurs in some places in the Gospel, that no one has ever seen God (1:18; 5:37; 6:46). The point of this pregnant and repeated assertion is certainly polemical, as is confirmed by other sayings of a similar emphasis: "No one has ascended to heaven except him who descended from heaven" (3:13); in the supper room, Philip expresses the wish that Jesus would "show" them the Father (14:8), that is, enable them to have direct contact with God (whatever way this is thought of), and Jesus answers him emphatically: "He who has seen me has seen the Father" (v. 9). It might be thought that these statements of the Gospel are due to an anti-Jewish tendency, to bring home to the Jews their estrangement from God, their ignorance of God (cf. 7:28; 8:19, 55) in spite of the revelation accorded to them on Sinai. Jesus seems to allude to this in 5:37: "You have not heard his voice or seen his form . . .", and 1:17 contrasts the law given through Moses with the grace and truth which came through Jesus Christ. But the polemic is almost too vigorous to allow us to confine ourselves to this Jewish background, which the evangelist certainly had in mind. For the official Judaism of the time refused to admit the possibility of an immediate vision of God in this aeon: one would in fact have to think of esoteric circles of Jewish mysticism or apocalyptic. But the same assertion is made in 1 Jn 4:12 (cf. 20), and given the actual setting of the Epistle, a refutation of Gnostic pretensions suggests itself. It is not, therefore, impossible that the Gospel, while seemingly addressing merely the Jews (5:37; 6:46), also rejects Gnostic claims. The positive Christian concept of revelation, "seeing" the Father in the Son (14:9; cf. 12:45), "hearing" his voice in the words of this heavenly revealer (cf. 1:18; 3:32 ff.; 5:38), is directed in different ways both against the Jewish claim to have free access to God, and the Gnostic idea of attaining immediate fellowship with God by knowledge and vision. But these texts of the Gospel cannot be used with certainty to prove an anti-Gnostic tendency.

Finally, it is questionable whether and how the brief statements on the role of the Logos in creation (1:3f., 10b) are directed against Gnostic heresies. Irenaeus, as we saw, was convinced of it. But it remains uncertain whether the Logos hymn is directed against ideas which were only developed in Christian Gnosticism, since it is primarily a positive application of the attributes of Wisdom to the Logos (see commentary). The sharp negative of 1:3b could indeed be intended polemically, but it is also explicable from the poetic style and the wish to underline the universal role of the Logos in creation. We know too little about the Gnostic concepts and systems which flourished in the neighbourhood of the evangelist or the Christianity which he represents.

This seems to have exhausted the list of possible anti-Gnostic trends in John. The yield is not very rich; but if it were only the Christology of the Incarnation which could be shown to have an anti-Gnostic character, the result is of great importance. It means that faith's aptest answer and strongest barrier has been set up by John against the growing menace of Gnosticism, which was to be a mortal danger to the Church of the second century. If, on the other hand, the evangelist perhaps threw open the door to Gnostic questioning, and attracted Christian Gnostic heretics by his language and approach, so that they could make use of the Gospel in their own sense, his profession of faith in the *Christus incarnatus* was enough to expose Gnosis and its myth and the error of its way of salvation.

CHAPTER IX

Textual Tradition and Textual Criticism

Since the attack on the Johannine writings in the second century (see below, ch. x) had no great result, except for Revelation, and the Church tradition about the authorship of the Apostle John the son of Zebedee was firmly established about 180 (cf. ch. v above), the text of John is as well attested as that of the Synoptics, and indeed better and more anciently since the happy discovery of two papyrus codices of the third century (P^{66} and P^{75}). Our ideas of the various forms of texts and of the course of their history have been considerably altered by these new acquisitions from the Bodmer collection, as well as by general progress in textual criticism.[1] It may be said that research has received a new impulse and is heading for new frontiers.[2] We cannot of course go into this discussion here, but only give an orientation.

1. Textual tradition and history of the text

We give the main witnesses for the textual tradition of John, omitting any grouping according to the chief forms of text, at least for the papyri, since the character of this, the oldest form of text attainable, is still debated (see under b on P^{66} and P^{75}) and cannot be easily assigned to any of the usual groups. It may no longer be possible to start from the "recensions" of the beginning of the fourth century, and perhaps a new approach must be made to the history of the text in the second and

[1] See Metzger, *Annotated Bibliography of the Textual Criticism of the New Testament 1914–1939;* also the survey of research given by Duplacy, "Où en est la critique textuelle du Nouveau Testament?" (on Jn, pp. 48–56); id., "Bulletin de Critique textuelle du Nouveau Testament"; Metzger, *The Text of the New Testament*, pp. 156–85.

[2] See Clark, "The Effect of Recent Textual Criticism upon New Testament Studies"; Colwell, "The Significance of Grouping of New Testament Manuscripts"; Aland, "Neue neutestamentliche Papyri II", pp. 304f. See further below on P^{66} and P^{75}.

third century (see below, c). This would include consideration and assessment of the quotations in the Fathers of the Church, as has been called for in particular by M.-É. Boismard (see below, d).

(a) The main witnesses for the text[3]

(I) Greek papyri:

P[5] (3rd cent., Oxyrhynchus) fragments from Jn 1; 16; 20
P[22] (3rd cent., Oxyrhynchus) Jn 15:25—16:2, 21–32
P[28] (3rd cent., Oxyrhynchus) Jn 6:8–12, 17–22
P[39] (3rd. cent., Oxyrhynchus) Jn 8:14–22
P[45] (3rd cent., Chester Beatty collection) parts of Jn 10–11
P[52] (about 130; John Rylands Library, Manchester) the oldest of all N.T. papyri: Jn 18:31–33, 37–38[4]
P[55] (6th–7th cent., Fayum) Jn 1:31–33, 35–38
P[59] (7th cent., southern Palestine) parts of Jn 1; 2; 11; 12; 17; 18; 21
P[60] (7th cent., southern Palestine) Jn 16:29—19:26 with large gaps
P[63] (c. 500) Jn 3:14–18; 4:9–10[5]
P[66] (beginning of the 3rd cent.; P. Bodmer II) Jn 1–14 fairly complete
P[75] (c. 200; P. Bodmer XV) Jn 1–12 almost complete, fragments of ch. 13 with 14:9–30; 15:7f.

(II) Greek parchments:

According to the usual grouping, the uncials B ℵ (from ch. 8 on) C L T W Δ Ψ belong to the Egyptian or Alexandrian type.

D represents a special group, akin to the Vetus Latina and the Vetus Syra, which was once given the siglum 𝔚 ("western text"), which has now been abandoned (in Nestle-Aland) on account of the problems of this type of text. The MSS with the "Caesarean text" must also be regarded as a special group. It includes Θ (codex Koridethi) and the two groups of minuscules φ (Ferrar group, fam. 13) and λ (Lake group, fam. 1); but this "Caesarean text" has only been collated and established for Mark.[6]

---

[3] On details see Aland, *Kurzgefasste Liste der griechischen Handschriften des Neuen Testaments*. On the papyri see further Aland, "Neue neutestamentliche Papyri II", pp. 306ff.; Metzger, *The Text of the New Testament*, pp. 247–55.

[4] First published by the discoverer, Roberts, *An Unpublished Fragment of the Fourth Gospel in the John Rylands Library*. Here we must also mention Egerton 2 (a little later, before 150), with fragments of an "Unknown Gospel", which cites Jn 5:39 and 45 in fragment 1, and contains other allusions to John. See Mayeda, *Das Leben-Jesu-Fragment Papyrus Egerton 2*; Jeremias, "An unknown Gospel with Johannine Elements: Papyrus Egerton 2" (with lit.); Braun, *Jean le Théologien*, pp. 87–94.

[5] See Aland, "Zur Liste der griechischen neutestamentlichen Handschriften", p. 468.

[6] On the problems and research into this form of text see Geerlings, *Family 13 —The Ferrar Group: The Text acc. to John;* Metzger, *Chapters in the History of New Testament Textual Criticism*, pp. 42–72, esp. 67.

The Koine text is to be found in A (for the Gospels) E F G H S V Y Ω.

Of special importance are the minuscules which have the Egyptian type of text: 33 579 892 1241, and the Ferrar group (fam. 13), 13 69 124 346 etc. and the Lake group (fam. 1), 1 118 131 209 mentioned above.

(III) Versions:

For the Vetus Latina we now have the edition of Jülicher-Matzkow-Aland[7], prepared from the collation of 18 MSS. Here too the quotations in the early Latin Fathers would have been important; but for this we must wait for the great Beuron edition. The chief MSS are:

a Vercellensis (4th–5th cent.)
b Veronensis (5th cent.)
c Colbertinus (12th cent.)
d Bezae, Cantabrigiensis (6th cent.)
e Palatinus (5th cent., "Afra" text)
f Brixianus (6th cent.)
ff^2 Corbeiensis (5th–6th cent.)

The Vulgate is cited according to the edition of J. Wordsworth and H. J. White.[8]

The Syriac versions are those generally indicated in the editions of the text:

sy^s Syrus Sinaiticus (4th–5th cent.)
sy^c Syrus Curetonianus (5th cent.)
sy^p Peshitto
sy^h Harclensis; sy^{hmg} indicates important marginal readings
sy^{pal} Syro-Palestinian translation (6th cent.)
sy^{ph} Philoxenian

For the reconstruction of the Diatesseron in Syriac we now have also the Syriac text from the commentary of St Ephraim in a MS of the Chester Beatty collection.[9]

The Coptic translations, of which the Sahidic (sa) and the Bohairic (bo) are important for the form and development of the Egyptian text, have been enriched by a find in the Bodmer collection, Papyrus Bodmer III, a papyrus codex in the Bohairic dialect from the 4th cent., comprising John and Gen 1–4:2.[10] The opinion of É. Massaux, that the translation shows Gnostic influences,[11] needs further investigation. A papyrus codex of John from the 4th cent. with a Fayum text, from the Michigan

[7] *Itala*, vol. IV.
[8] *Novum Testamentum Latine*, vol. I.
[9] Leloir, *Saint Éphrem, Commentaire de l'Évangile concordant, texte syriaque.*
[10] Kasser, *Papyrus Bodmer III: Évangile de Jean et Genèse I-IV, 2.*
[11] Massaux, "Quelques variantes importantes de Bodmer III et leur accointance avec la gnose".

collection, has also been published and is likewise important for the history of the Egyptian text.[12]

The other ancient versions, especially the Armenian and Georgian, are of only secondary importance, but are not to be overlooked.[13]

(IV) On the importance of the Fathers of the Church for the textual tradition see below (c). Origen's text of John is remarkably close to codex Vaticanus and codex Sinaiticus, but also shows that a text very like the "Caesarean" must have existed in Egypt.[14] But this is no longer surprising after the discovery of P^{66} and P^{75}.

An investigation of twenty-five lectionaries for John showed a text fairly close to the "Caesarean".[15]

(b) The importance of P^{66} and P^{75} for the tradition and history of the text

The two recently discovered papyrus codices from the beginning of the 3rd cent., of which P^{75} is perhaps somewhat older than P^{66}, are of an importance that can hardly be overestimated, on account of their age and the text which they provide. A number of collations and investigations were undertaken after the publication of P^{66}, which led, however, to different conclusions about the history of the text.[16] Meanwhile a new situation has been created by the publication of P^{75} five years later (1961), characterized by the proximity (to put it simply) of this papyrus to the Egyptian type of text represented above all by B.[17] This warns us to be cautious about many conclusions drawn from P^{66}.

As regards P^{66} it should be noted that the main portion of the codex (Jn 1–14) was published in Greek transcription without a photocopy of the MS (1956); the fragmentary text of Jn 14:29–21:9 was published in the same way in 1958, as a supplementary volume. A second, enlarged and amended edition of the "supplement"

---

[12] Husselman, *The Gospel of John in Fayumic Coptic;* see the review by K. H. Kuhn, *Journal of Theological Studies* 14 (1963), pp. 470ff.

[13] See Vööbus, *Early Versions of the New Testament*, pp. 133–209; Molitor, "Die Armenische Bibelübersetzung".

[14] See Tasker, "The Text of the Fourth Gospel used by Origen in his Commentary on John"; id., "The Chester Beatty Papyrus and the Caesarean Text of John".

[15] Buck, *The Johannine Lessons in the Greek Gospel Lectionary:* "a connecting link between the Caesarean text-type and the Byzantine recension", p. 76.

[16] Main studies: Aland, "Papyrus Bodmer II, Ein erster Bericht"; de la Potterie, "Papyrus Bodmer II"; Klijn, "Papyrus Bodmer II"; Boismard, "Le papyrus Bodmer II"; Zimmermann, "Papyrus Bodmer II und seine Bedeutung für die Textgeschichte"; Metzger, "Recent Developments in the Study of the Text of the Bible"; Birdsall, *The Bodmer Papyrus of the Gospel of John;* Clark, "The Text of the Gospel of John in Third Century Egypt" (on P^{66} and P^{75}); Aland, "Neue neutestamentliche Papyri II", *NTS* 10, pp. 62–79.

[17] See now the exact collation by Aland, *NTS* 11, pp. 14–21.

was published in 1962, with a photographic reproduction of the whole MS. An examination of the first edition against the photocopies, by M.-É. Boismard and G. Roux, resulted in a long list of corrections, which are to be preferred to the printed text.[18] Hence the photocopies (and Boismard's list of corrections) always have to be noted, though the first printed text, which was published so quickly and is on the whole reliable remains a laudable achievement. These necessary corrections must also be taken into account for the first collations of the printed text.

The surprise of the publication of P^{66} was that it showed fewer influences of "western" and "Caesarean" readings than the Chester Beatty P^{45}, of perhaps a half-century later.[19] It had been supposed by most scholars hitherto that there had been a gradual change from a more "western" type of text to the "Egyptian" type (B ℵ), as minor fragments of papyri had also suggested. But P^{66} showed that the two types of text had equally ancient rights in Egypt.[20] Closer collation[21] resulted in more or less the following picture: P^{66} agrees with ℵ B about 50 times against other witnesses, with B against ℵ and others almost 60 times, with ℵ against B and others over 90 times, but with D against ℵ B only 50 times all told. Even this superficial statistical survey shows the strong affinity with the Egyptian text, especially with B. The picture changes somewhat if a more thorough comparison is made, as was done by Boismard, with Tatian, the older versions and the quotations in the Fathers. Boismard can point to 49 readings, some quite important, which were not known from Greek MSS, but now appear as common to P^{66} and the witnesses just mentioned.[22]

The conclusion usually drawn from these findings is that the scribe of P^{66} proceeded eclectically. He must have had both the Egyptian and a form of the "western" text before him and created his own text by the choice and combination of readings which he thought best. Corrections to the text, which are clearly later, were more in the direction of the Egyptian text. Differences of opinion occurred mainly with regard to the origin and precise form of the "western" text. H. Zimmermann supposes that "there is an intrinsic connection between the papyrus and the Latin tradition" and that a Latin translation of the Gospels began to have no slight influence on the Greek text in north Africa.[23] Boismard takes a very different view. He thinks that there were two forms of the "western" text, one represented by ℵ D, the other by Tatian, the latter with

---

[18] Boismard, "Review of Papyrus Bodmer II, Supplément"; see also J. W. B. Barns, *Muséon* 75 (1962), pp. 327–9.

[19] Klijn, pp. 329f.

[20] *Ibid.*, p. 334.

[21] On the following, see the lists given by Zimmermann, pp. 226–43.

[22] See pp. 391 ff.

[23] See p. 225.

more influence on the ancient versions. P[66] used both B and ℵ D, but also adopted readings of the other "western" group (see above).[24] But a new element has been brought into the discussion by É. Massaux's careful analysis of previous explanations. He points out that the history of the text in the second and third century is usually depicted with reference to the four (or five, according to Boismard) types of text recognized hitherto in the *later* MSS. Should one not rather start with the recently discovered witnesses which are of an earlier date and then proceed to question the whole of the accepted picture?[25] Before we deal further with this question, which has also been raised by other scholars, we must turn to P[75].

The affinities between P[75] (dated by its editors between 175 and 225) and codex B (middle of the 4th cent.) have already been examined in an American dissertation, the main results of which have been made accessible by the author, C. L. Porter, in an article.[26] He gives a list of 205 variants in the papyrus compared with B, but notes that the number is small compared to the variants which he noted with regard to ℵ (702 variants), W (Freer MS, 506 variants) and P[66] (512 variants, in spite of a smaller basis of comparison). The list shows that a corrector often restored in B the same text as offered by P[75] and that vice versa a corrector of P[75] often preferred the same text as B. This provides us with an Egyptian text older by some 150 years and fairly close to B. K.W.Clark considers that P[75] gives us the best type of third century text, approximating most closely to that of B, and hence the key to the true history of the text.[27] This verdict must be tested by further collations; but the remarkable phenomenon of this good early text in Egypt cannot be gainsaid.[28]

(c) A new concept of the history of the text

The importance, and also the difficulty, of grouping NT. manuscripts has been emphasized by E. C. Colwell,[29] and if his principles are applied to the Egyptian material as enlarged by P[66] and P[75], it seems possible to speak of an "Egyptian type of text", but not of one of which the purest representative is the codex Vaticanus. It is rather a type which developed slowly and still must be distinguished from other types of text. But if so

[24] See pp. 389 ff.

[25] "Le Papyrus Bodmer II (P[66]) et la critique néotestamentaire", esp. p. 201.

[26] Porter, "Papyrus Bodmer XV (P 75) and the text of Codex Vaticanus".

[27] "The Text of the Gospel of John", p. 24.

[28] See also Metzger, "The Bodmer Papyrus of Luke and John".

[29] See "The Significance of Grouping of New Testament Manuscripts"; also id., "Method in Locating a Newly-Discovered Manuscript within the MS Tradition of the Greek New Testament" (attends to "multiple" and "distinctive readings").

it becomes important, as has been said, to start not from a later form of the text such as codex B, but from the earliest witnesses. J. N. Birdsall has worked on P^{66} in the light of this demand, and having sharply criticized the previous way of judging P^{66} with reference to the later texts, calls for an examination of the text of P^{66}, which began to fluctuate early, according to grammatical and exegetical criteria, demonstrating the method by some examples.[30] B. M. Metzger also remarks apropos of the two papyrus codices Bodmer XIV (Luke) and XV (John) comprised under the siglum P^{75}, that they prove that the text represented by the Vaticanus and the Sinaiticus was not created by the scribes or editors of these great parchment codices but merely transmitted by them.[31]

This calls in question a view defended for many years, that the great MSS of the fourth and fifth centuries with an "Alexandrine" text go back to a recension made at the beginning of the fourth century, which Jerome attributed to a certain Hesychius.[32] It seems to some[33] that the problem has been posed in all desirable clarity by C. L. Porter. Is the text which appears in codex Vaticanus a deliberate revision (recension), or does it represent a natural development? In other words, is the present Egyptian text a "mixed" one which was afterwards purified by a recension, or is it an originally Egyptian text which underwent constant evolution? Porter has no hesitation in affirming the latter,[34] and so too K. W. Clark,[35] who illustrates the importance of P^{66} and P^{75} from a number of significant readings. Thus the two new papyrus codices are of outstanding importance not merely because of their age, but because of their place in the history of the text, though of course their readings cannot be adopted without question.

(d) The work of M.-É. Boismard

The value of the "Egyptian" text may, therefore, be said to have been further enhanced. But for many readings at least, its value has been questioned by M.-É. Boismard, in his new theses on the history and criticism of the text, which he strives to demonstrate above all from John.

---

[30] See p. 11; he then speaks of "intrinsic criteria of style and language".

[31] "The Bodmer Papyrus of Luke and John", p. 203.

[32] See the latest work, Jellicoe, "The Hesychian Recension Reconsidered". He tries to restore credibility to the testimony of Jerome; but this does not alter the findings of textual criticism. Hesychius could have played a much more modest role in the improving of the Egyptian text.

[33] See Klijn, p. 328; Zimmermann, p. 225; Massaux, p. 201.

[34] See pp. 364, 366, 376; see also Birdsall, p. 10: "We must emphasize, however, that in fact the papyrus texts are not contaminated varieties of the later texts which we know already or mixed texts made up as it were of later texts . . .".

[35] See pp. 18 f.; see also Aland, "Neue neutestamentliche Papyri II", pp. 304 f.

He has presented his views in a number of articles in the *Revue Biblique*,[36] where he maintains that more importance must be attached to the quotations in the Church Fathers, since they represent an ancient textual tradition going back to the third and second century, and often have better (shorter) readings than the "Alexandrian" text which has taken their place.[37] This early text is also attested (often in agreement with the Fathers) by what has been hitherto called the "western" text, though here a distinction is said to be necessary. One form is represented particularly ℵ D, the other by the *Diatessaron* of Tatian and the ancient versions, which were influenced by it. Boismard examines many passages in John, adducing a large amount of comparative material, and often gives preference to a reading which is attested only—or practically only—by "western" witnesses and patristic quotations (see below, 2). The readings in question must be examined on their merits in each case; but one also wonders whether the principles of textual criticism behind them are well enough assured.

The publication of P^{66} with a text some 150 years older than B, which still remains very close to this main representative of the Egyptian text, did not appear to be very favourable to these views. But Boismard pointed out, in one of his longer studies, that P^{66} also contained many "western" readings in agreement with ℵ (especially up to the middle of Jn 8) and with D. He claimed to be able to demonstrate that the scribe had at his disposal both the "Egyptian" (B) text and the "western" (ℵ D or Tatian etc.), and was constantly choosing between them. In the light of what has been said above, one may doubt that this is the proper explanation. Boismard has not yet commented on the new situation created by P^{75}, but his further investigations, which always start from individual texts, will be awaited with great interest.

2. Textual criticism in John

Important as are the fundamental questions of the history of the text, textual criticism has to deal with the individual passages which offer variant readings and prove itself there. Critics of the text now generally

---

[36] "A propos de Jean, 5:39"; "Critique textuelle et citations patristiques"; "Lectio brevior, potior"; "Dans le sein du Père, Jo. 1:18"; "Problèmes de critique textuelle concernant le Quatrième Évangile".

[37] See also Suggs, "The Use of Patristic Evidence in the Search for a Primitive New Testament Text" (with further bibliographical indications, more reserved in judgment); criticism by Klijn, "A Survey of the Researches into the Western Text of the Gospels and Acts", esp. p. 165; Kümmel, *Einleitung*, p. 397. Good methodological principles in Metzger, *The Text of the New Testament*, pp. 86–92.

agree that in the present state of research no general theory can be laid down and that no group of MSS can be given an absolute preference. Each item must be investigated on its own merits—though here again one's idea of the history of the text and one's principles of textual criticism will, no doubt, influence one's decision.[38] All we shall try to do here is to show how much textual criticism is still to be done on John, what important variants there are which must be assessed. Detailed discussion of the individual texts must be reserved for the commentary.

(a) Passages not originally part of John

Textual criticism proves that the pericope of the adulterous woman, which is given in present-day editions (sometimes only in the critical apparatus) between 7:52 and 8:12, did not form part of the original Gospel of John. After the long exposition of the state of the text by H. von Soden,[39] we now have the monograph of U. Becker, giving a detailed investigation of the history of the text and its tradition.[40] The following points may be noted here. The most ancient Greek witnesses do not contain the pericope: P^{66} P^{75} B ℵ A C W T N Z, so too other MSS close to the Egyptian (and Caesarean) type: L Δ Θ Ψ 33 565 892 1241 etc. But the section is attested by D, and by the whole Koine group, though in many cases with a reference to the uncertainty of the tradition. Some MSS give the pericope elsewhere: minuscule 1 after Jn 21:24, representatives of the Ferrar group (φ) after Lk 21:38.[41] Among the versions, the section is missing in sy (except in more recent forms of later translations), sa, bo in Papyrus Bodmer III (but not in the late bohairic MSS) arm georg. The Vetus Latina is divided; it is not in a f l q, but is given in b c d e and the rest. Jerome defended his adoption of it into the Vulgate, and Augustine also championed it. The passage was unknown at first to the Greek Fathers as part of John. The case of Tatian is interesting. The

---

[38] See for instance Vogels, *Handbuch der Textkritik des Neuen Testaments;* Massaux, "État actuel de la critique textuelle du Nouveau Testament"; Aland, "The Present Position of New Testament Textual Criticism"; Schäfer, "Der Ertrag der textkritischen Arbeit seit der Jahrhundertwende"; Kenyon, *The Text of the Greek Bible;* esp. Metzger, *The Text of the New Testament*, pp. 175–9, 181.

[39] Von Soden, *Die Schriften des Neuen Testaments in ihrer ältesten erreichbaren Textgestalt hergestellt auf Grund ihrer Textgeschichte*, pp. 486–524, on which see Lietzmann, "H. von Soden's Ausgabe des Neuen Testaments. Die Perikope von der Ehebrecherin" and (after von Soden's reply) "Bemerkungen zu H. von Soden's Antikritik".

[40] Becker, *Jesus und die Ehebrecherin;* see also Metzger, *The Text of the New Testament*, pp. 223f.

[41] Probably due to the influence of the Byzantine lectionary, which uses Lk 21:12–19 on 7 October and the adultery pericope on 8 October; see Colwell and Riddle, *Prolegomena to the Study of the Lectionary Text of the Gospels*, p. 19 (reference due to J. Schmid).

pericope is not known to the Eastern tradition, except the late Persian translation, while it is given by the Western.

Becker is convinced that the pericope was accepted as canonical by the Eastern Church about A.D. 400, and also that Jerome was not the first to introduce the passage into the Latin translations.[42] He deduces from certain traces in the history of the tradition that it comes from Jewish-Christian circles of the second century and was adopted into the canon of the four Gospels only at the beginning of the third century.[43] But we need not pursue the question; from the point of view of textual criticism it is certain that the pericope does not belong to the original form of John.

This is also true of a second passage, namely the explanatory remark inserted into the scene at Bethzatha (or Bethesda), ch. 5, to the effect that the sick waited for the movement of the water because from time to time an angel of the Lord descended to the pool and stirred the water; then the first to enter the water was healed of whatever illness he suffered (v. 3 after ξηρῶν till the end of v. 4). The oldest Greek MSS, including P^{66} and P^{75}, do not give this popular explanation, and are supported by part of the rest of the textual tradition. V. 4 is missing in D 0125 33 f l q vg^{codd} sy^{c} (sy^{s} has a lacuna here); it is found (with various variants) in A L Θ, the Koine group, the rest of the Vetus Latina, many Vulgate MSS (and Vg^{cl}), $sy^{p.pal.\,h}$, bo (but not in Papyrus Bodmer III), and in a number of Church Fathers—Tertullian, Didymus, Cyrill of Alexandria, Chrysostom; there is some attestation for Tatian: in the Syriac (Ephraim), Arabic, Italian and Dutch translations. The last part of v. 3 has better attestation, which includes D f l, but this is readily explained as providing a basis for v. 7. The explanation added in v. 4 is probably an early gloss which penetrated the textual tradition on account of v. 7 and was later willingly accepted.[44]

The "epilogue", however, ch. 21 is solidly established by textual criticism, as is borne out by the fragments of P^{66}.

(b) Important variants

To give an impression of the need for textual criticism on John, we list here important variants, with a view to calling attention to some problems.[45] We give only a brief selection of witnesses (chiefly after Nestle-

---

42 See pp. 29f., 37f. 43 See pp. 150–64.

44 The authenticity was again defended by Bover, "Autenticidad de Jn 5, 3b–4"; on the reasons for its insertion see Fascher, *Textgeschichte als hermeneutisches Problem*, pp. 66f. (different features according to the MSS: the angel descends into the pool or he bathes in the pool). The item is still given in the text in the editions of Vogels and Merk.

45 The edition of Bover is useful, giving a copious apparatus along with the variants which are adopted into the text by the other editions. But there are quite important

Aland), paying special attention to P^{66} and P^{75}; for an exact account of the variants we refer to the critical editions, and for further discussion to the commentary. Proposed amendments, suggested according to the views taken by some scholars on the history of the text, will be discussed apart, under (c).

1:3 οὐδὲ ἕν] οὐδέν P^{66} ℵ* D pc. It is remarkable that P^{66}, unlike P^{75}, has οὐδέν here, though elsewhere it prefers the stronger form οὐδὲ ἕν (3:27; 5:19, 30; 8:28).

1:3f. The division of the phrase is uncertain. Does ὃ γέγονεν belong to οὐδὲ ἕν, or does it begin a new sentence? This is hard to decide, on account of the fewness of punctuation marks in the most ancient MSS, but it is important for the interpretation. There is no punctuation here in P^{66}, but the omission of ἐν in v. 4 may perhaps tell in favour of linking ὃ γέγονεν with αὐτῷ ζωὴ ἦν.[46] In P^{75}, the break is clearly made after οὐδὲ ἕν. Is this original or a sign of an early anti-Gnostic trend?

1:4 ἦν] ἐστίν ℵ D it sy^c ; Tischendorf.

1:13 The singular reading *(qui) non . . . natus est*, b Ir^{lat} Tert, has Christological consequences (see below under c). P^{75} has ἐγενήθησαν.

1:18 μονογενὴς θεός P^{66} 𝔖 sy^p Ir Or and other Fathers] ὁ μονογενὴς θεός P^{75} $ℵ^3$ 33 Cl] ὁ μονογενὴς υἱός 𝔎 Θ pl latt sy^c. The question still under discussion today, as to whether one should read θεός or υἱός, is of Christological interest; θεός is confirmed by $P^{66\,75}$.

1:34 ὁ υἱός] ὁ ἐκλεκτός P^5 ℵ* pc e sy^{sc}] *electus filius* a (b ff^2). The peculiar reading ὁ ἐκλεκτός merits consideration in spite of the slender attestation, and could be important for the "voice from heaven" at the baptism.

1:41 πρῶτον] πρῶτος ℵ* 𝔎 al] *mane* (πρωΐ) b e sy^s. The reading πρῶτον is confirmed by $P^{66\,75}$.

3:13 ὁ υἱὸς τ. ἀνθρώπου has an added ὁ ὢν ἐν τῷ οὐρανῷ in 𝔎 Θ pl lat $sy^{(c)p}$] ὁ ὢν ἐκ τ. οὐρανοῦ 80 88 sy^s, not in $P^{66\,75}$.

3:15 ἐν αὐτῷ] εἰς αὐτόν ℵ 𝔎 Θ pm] ἐπ'αὐτῷ P^{66} L] ἐπ' αὐτόν A. P^{75} now supports ἐν αὐτῷ (against P^{66}).

3:18 ὁ μή] ὁ δὲ μή $P^{66\,75}$ C 𝔎 W pl.

3:31c ἐπάνω πάντων ἐστίν 2° omit P^{75} ℵ* D λ it sy^c.

3:34 τὸ πνεῦμα $P^{66\,75}$ pl] omit B* sy^s.

variants which all editors put in the apparatus and which therefore do not appear at all in Bover. Further, this edition could not take P^{66} and P^{75} into account.

[46] See de la Potterie, "Een nieuwe papyrus van het vierde Evangelie, Pap. Bodmer II", esp. p. 122; id., "De punctuatie en de exegese van Joh. 1:3–4 in de traditie", and "De interpunctione et interpretatione versuum Joh. 1:3–4". Further literature in commentary.

4:6 ἐπὶ τῇ πηγῇ] ἐπὶ τῇ γῇ P^{66} (a singular reading which has been amended by a corrector).

4:25 οἶδα] οἴδαμεν $P^{66c\,75}$ G L φ 33 al sy^{hmg}.

4:35 ἔτι omit P^{75} D L pm sy^{c}. This is important for the question of whether it is a proverb or gives an exact date.

4:35f. ἤδη] Where does the punctuation mark come, before or after? P^{75} puts a full stop after it, like many later MSS and Origen, thus joining ἤδη to the previous sentence.

4:37 The whole verse is missing in P^{75}, but this is probably an oversight on the part of the copyist (both v. 36 and 37 end with ὁ θερίζων).

4:54 The δέ bracketed in the Nestle text is now also attested by $P^{66\,75}$.

5:1 ἑορτή] ἡ ἑορτή ℵ C ℜ λ pm. The reading without the article is supported by the new papyri; this is important for determining the feast in question.

5:2 The textual tradition about the pool with the five porticoes is very complicated. The text chosen by Nestle-Aland is now attested by $P^{66\,75}$, except for the Hebrew name, which both give, along with B W (Ψ) 0125 sa bo c vg sy^{h} Tert as "Bethsaida". This is certainly a secondary reading due to the well-known Bethsaida. "Bethesda" should probably be read in preference to the "Bethzatha" of Nestle-Aland. There seem to be no objections against J. Jeremias's reconstruction of the text:[47] "In Jerusalem, at the Sheep-pool, there is the place with five porticoes called Bethesda"; but the commas put before and after κολυμβηθρα by P^{66} might be meant to indicate that the word is not to be joined with προβατικη as the scribe understood things.

5:39 ὅτι . . . ἐκεῖναι] ἐν αἷς ὑμεῖς δοκεῖτε ζωὴν ἔχειν· ἐκεῖναι P. Egerton 2 a (b) e ff^{2} q sy^{c} arm. This way of taking the subordinate clause as a relative clause might be original; the clause comes up in the discussion of a possible Aramaic basis.[48]

5:45 κατηγορήσω] ἦλθον κατηγορῆσαι P. Egerton 2

6:22f. many variants; see under (c)

6:23 εὐχαριστήσαντος τοῦ κυρίου] omit D 69 pc a e sy^{sc}. This appended phrase is suspect, but the question should perhaps be solved not as a matter of textual but of literary criticism—a redactional interpolation.

---

[47] Jeremias, *Die Wiederentdeckung von Bethesda*, pp. 5–8.

[48] On the textual criticism see Boismard, "A propos de Jean 5:39", with copious collection and discussion of witnesses; on the Aramaic basis cf. Black, *An Aramaic Approach*, pp. 54f.; see also above, ch. vi, p. 110.

6:27 ὑμῖν δώσει] δίδωσιν ὑμῖν ℵ D e ff² j sy^c. A "western" reading which is preferred by Tischendorf, Lagrange and Bover.

6:36 με P^66 75vid. 𝔖 𝔎 D Θ pl; om. ℵ A pc it sy^sc; put in brackets by Nestle-Aland; omit Tischendorf, read by the other editors.

7:8 οὐκ] οὔπω P^66 75 𝔖 𝔎 Θ pm f g q. In spite of support from the Egyptian witnesses, οὔπω should probably be rejected as the easier reading; the editors are divided.

7:38 The question of whether ὁ πιστεύων εἰς ἐμέ goes with the preceding or the following clause is much debated. As far as can be judged from the MSS, c d e Cypr are for the former, P^66 Orig for the latter. It cannot be decided by textual criticism.

7:39 πνεῦμα P^66c 75 ℵ 𝔎 Θ Ψ pc] πνεῦμα δεδομένον lat sy Eus] πνεῦμα ἅγιον P^66* L 𝔎 W pm] πνεῦμα ἅγιον δεδομένον B e q.[49]

7:52 προφήτης] ὁ προφήτης P^66; the gap in P^75 also seems to suggest the article. If "the prophet" is original a particular Messianic figure is meant (cf. 1:21, 25; 6:14; 7:40).

8:25 τὴν ἀρχὴν ὅ τι] here the versions show that the scribes did not understand the Greek text and made their own efforts to produce a theological statement: ὅτι = quia b d vg^codd; qui vg^cl; "since I have begun (to talk to you, I have still more to say and judge before you)" P. Bodmer III (Bohairic, 4th cent.).

8:57 ἑώρακας] ἑώρακέν σε (P^75) ℵ* 0124 sy^s sa P. Bodmer III. In spite of the antiquity of the variants (P^75: εορακεν σε) it is certainly a secondary reflection (cf. v. 56).

9:4 ἡμᾶς] ἐμέ C 𝔎 Θ pl lat sy. The plural is given by P^66 75 along with other Egyptian witnesses, which also keep it after πέμψαντος (so too ℵ* L W bo 850). The question is also important for the plural in 3:11.

9:27 οὐκ] omit P^66 22 lat sy^s. But the negative is found in P^75.

9:35 τ. υἱὸν τ. ἀνθρώπου] τὸν υἱὸν τοῦ θεοῦ 𝔎 Θ pl latt. The title "Son of Man" is replaced by "Son of God" in the Latin versions (cf. 5:28) but retained in the Egyptian text (also in P^66 75).

9:38–39 ὁ δὲ . . . ὁ Ἰησοῦς] omit P^75 ℵ* W b (l).

10:7 ἡ θύρα] ὁ ποιμήν P^75 sa. The hitherto singular reading of the Sahidic is now reinforced by the early papyrus; it is exegetically important, but is it original?

10:8 πρὸ ἐμοῦ P^66 𝔖 D Θ φ pm] omit P^45 75 ℵ* al lat sy

10:29 ὃ δέδωκέν μοι πάντων μεῖζον] this reading, adopted by Nestle-Aland, has a number of variants; the text was in disorder at an early time and was corrected in various ways. The text with ὅς is now supported by P^66 75, but they leave the question of

[49] More details of the attestation in Metzger, *Text of the New Testament*, p. 225.

μείζων or μεῖζον unsolved. P^{66} has μιζων (like 𝔎 sy); P^{75} has a lacuna, into which, however, it seems that only μει[ζο]ν will fit (?). The question needs further discussion.[50]

12:7 ἵνα εἰς . . . τηρήσῃ] εἰς . . . τετήρηκεν 𝔎 pm, clearly the easier reading; the new papyri have the same reading as the other Egyptian witnesses.

12:31 ἐκβληθήσεται ἔξω] βληθήσεται κάτω Θ 1093 it sy^s Chrys; this reading is not given any new support, P^{66} reads like D βληθήσεται ἔξω, P^{75} as above.

12:32 πάντας] πάντα P^{66} ℵ* (D) latt.

12:41 ὅτι $P^{66\ 75}$ 𝔖 Θ al e] ὅτε 𝔎 D pm lat sy.

12:47 μή] omit $P^{66c\ 75}$ D Θ 1241. Dogmatic considerations could be responsible for the omission (done in P^{66} by a corrector).

13:10 εἰ μὴ τοὺς πόδας] among the variant readings of the verse, it is of particular interest to know whether this phrase is original or not; it is hard to decide by textual criticism. P^{66} has the longer text (+ μόνον); P^{75} unfortunately shows a gap (but for this text, see also under c).

13:32 εἰ ὁ θεὸς ἐδοξάσθη ἐν αὐτῷ] omit P^{66} 𝔖 D al it sy^s. Here (as elsewhere) the Egyptian text, and the "western" in part, was probably misled early on by a slip (homoioteleuton).

14:2 ὅτι] omit P^{66*} 𝔎 Θ al it, probably with a sign to show that the text is not in order (see commentary *ad loc.*).

14:7 εἰ ἐγνώκειτέ με B C* 565 al] εἰ ἐγνώκατε ἐμέ (με) (P^{66}) ℵ D* pc it, and ἂν ᾔδειτε B C* (L) al 33 565 al] γνώσεσθε P^{66} ℵ W D* pc it. The second reading seems to be preferable (so Tischendorf, Lagrange, Bover), since γνώσεσθε then corresponds better to (καὶ) ἀπ' ἄρτι γινώσκετε.

14:17 ἔσται] ἐστίν B W D* al it sy^{cp}.

16:13 εἰς τὴν ἀλήθειαν πᾶσαν] ἐν τῇ ἀληθείᾳ πάσῃ ℵ L W Θ D 33 565 it arm

18:13–24 The Syro-Sinaitic has the verses in the order: 13, 24, 14, 15, 19–23, 16–18; the minuscule 225 gives: 13a, 24, 13b, 14–23. But these changes are certainly due to the same awkwardness which makes modern interpreters hesitate.

18:15 ἄλλος P^{66} B ℵ* pc] ὁ ἄλλος C 𝔎 Θ pl, a variant to be considered in the identification of the enigmatic "other disciple"; the article probably presupposes his identification with "the disciple whom Jesus loved" (cf. 20:2).

---

[50] See Barrett, *St John, ad. loc.*, who pronounces in favour of ὅς . . . μεῖζον; contrast Birdsall, "John 10:29", who gives serious reasons for ὅ . . . μείζων ("My Father in regard to what He has given me is greater than all"). An auditive error regarding μείζων and μεῖζον could have led to the interchange, as many other variants show.

20:31 πιστεύητε B ℵ* Θ] πιστεύσητε rell. No conclusions of an exegetical order, such as a missionary intention, may be drawn from the aorist subjunctive; the change from present to aorist subjunctive often occurs elsewhere in the MSS.

(c) Some modern emendations

Exegesis has, of course, to work on critically established texts, but textual criticism cannot perform its task without exegetical considerations (internal criticism). And since it must often ask what were the factors and tendencies in the history of the text which gave rise to changes[51] and what was the probable genesis of the text, textual criticism often goes beyond the collection and sifting of material, collating texts and divining their history, to take in problems of theology and its history. And thus it takes on a new importance for exegesis. Here too many problems arise with regard to John, which was so quickly adopted by the Gnostics in the second century, and also played no small part in dogmatic development in the Church. Hence hypotheses put forward by textual criticism and new emendations proposed for individual texts are also of great interest for the theological exposition. We give here some examples from modern research, which are, however, only a selection and can only indicate the problems. Proposed conjectures are not considered here.

1:3f. This text, mentioned above, is also interesting because the division (after οὐδὲ ἕν [οὐδέν] or after ὃ γέγονεν) could have been based on doctrinal reasons, apologetical or dogmatic. It is also relevant to the question of a "hymn to the Logos" (see commentary).

1:12f. A. von Harnack concluded from the overcharged style of the two verses, and from some noteworthy variant readings in v. 13 (the singular, the absence of the relative), that the clause οὐκ ... ἐγεν[ν]ήθη was originally a marginal gloss on v. 14, which later made its way into the text.[52] M.-É. Boismard approaches it differently. Comparing these readings with quotations from the Fathers, he suspects that the original text was shorter, first circulating in a Semitizing form (with αἷμα and σάρξ), and then being Hellenized ("from the desire of man"). He thus takes parts of the different readings and reconstructs a text which is nowhere completely attested as such. Since he is also convinced that the reading with the singular is original, his reconstructed

[51] See Fascher, *Textgeschichte;* Wright, *Alterations to the Words of Jesus as Quoted in the Literature of the Second Century.*

[52] Von Harnack, *Zur neutestamentlichen Textkritik*, pp. 115–27.

text reads: ὅσοι ἐπίστευσαν εἰς αὐτόν, ἔδωκεν αὐτοῖς ἐξουσίαν τέκνα θεοῦ κληθῆναι. ὃς οὐκ ἐξ αἵματος οὐδὲ ἐκ σαρκός, ἀλλ' ἐκ θεοῦ ἐγεννήθη.[53] The procedure is difficult to justify, especially as we are not certain that the Fathers always cite their texts fully and correctly.[54] As regards the reading with the singular, it must still be asked whether the change to the plural is more easily explained than from the plural to the singular.[55]

1:18 Here again Boismard arrives at a new text, by choosing parts of readings and using patristic quotations. He also arrives at a new meaning by using a different punctuation and taking ἐξηγήσατο in a different sense: θεὸν οὐδεὶς ἑώρακεν πώποτε, εἰ μὴ ὁ μονογενής· εἰς τὸν κόλπον τοῦ πατρός, ἐκεῖνος ἐξηγήσατο, that is, "No one has ever seen God except the only-begotten (Fils Unique); he alone has led the way to the bosom of the Father".[56] This reconstruction seems extremely daring.

1:41 The various readings have been studied by Boismard in his *Du Baptême à Cana* (1956), where he pleaded for πρωΐ as the original reading.[57] In a more recent literary analysis he suggests that 1:43 should be excised as a redactional addition and that Philip is the second, unnamed, disciple (cf. 1:37,40). He thus comes to accept πρῶτον or πρῶτος as the original reading.[58] This is an example of how textual criticism can be influenced by other considerations.

2:4 A number of scholars are now ready to put a question-mark after ἡ ὥρα μου like several of the Fathers.[59] This involves far-reaching conclusions for exegesis (see commentary). Each such case must be examined on its merits, to see whether the change in the text resulting from such decisions, which are in themselves unobjectionable, really remove the difficulty or are merely skilful manipulation.

4:51 ὁ παῖς] ὁ υἱός P[66c] D L N U Y 33 al. G. D. Kilpatrick[60] has sug-

---

[53] Boismard, "Critique textuelle et citations patristiques", pp. 401–8 (reconstruction, p. 407); on the discussion about the singular reading see commentary.

[54] See Lamarche, "Prologue de Jean", pp. 498–506.

[55] The question was examined by Houssiau, "Le milieu théologique de la leçon εγεννηθη", who came to the conclusion that the singular comes from an anti-Ebionite milieu; no Gnostic tendency to pass from the singular to the plural can be noted.

[56] Boismard, "Dans le sein du Père, Joh. 1:18" (reconstruction p. 31).

[57] Boismard, *Du baptême à Cana*, pp. 82 ff.

[58] Id., "Les traditions johanniques concernant le Baptiste", pp. 39–42, esp. p. 41.

[59] See esp. Michl, "Bemerkungen zu Joh. 2:4" (noting Patristic exegesis); the same opinion is maintained e.g. by Seemann, "Aufgehellte Bibelworte", p. 231; Kurfess, "Zu Joh. 2:4"; Boismard, *Du baptême à Cana*, pp. 156 f.

[60] Kilpatrick, "John 4:51 παῖς or υἱός?"

gested that the true reading is ὁ υἱός, one reason being that this would be the only occurrence of ὁ παῖς in John—due to assimilation with Mt 8:6, 8, 13; Lk 8:7. The question is interesting, because then the Johannine episode was being read along with the synoptic narrative of the centurion of Capernaum as early as P^{75}.

5:39 The different text tradition in P. Egerton 2, Vetus Latina etc. and in quotations in the Fathers has led to certain conclusions about the tradition of the sayings of the Lord: here we would have a form of the logion independent of John, perhaps going back to an Aramaic type.[61] But the conclusion is hardly imperative.[62] The problem is as difficult as that of the relationship between many logia of the Thomas Gospel and the synoptic tradition.

6:22–24 This elaborate and somewhat obscure description, containing several textual variants, is explained by Boismard on a theory of his own, of which the most noteworthy result is that the multiplication of the loaves did not take place on the eastern shore (not far from Bethsaida) but near Tiberias on the western shore. The text is again arrived at by the combination of various witnesses, chiefly Tatian and Chrysostom, and interpreted in such a way that in Boismard's view it agrees with Mk.[63] But many misgivings arise both as regards the reconstruction of the text and the other conclusions.

6:63 P. Bodmer III (Coptic [Bohairic], 4th cent.) has the plural for πνεῦμα which É. Massaux thinks is a sign of Gnostic influence.[64]

7:37f. The difficulty of how to divide the sentence, and other questions raised by this important passage (source of the quotation, meaning of κοιλία, typology etc.), have led to various interpretations in the history of exegesis,[65] in which problems of the text have played an important part.

11:48–50 Boismard calls attention to notable variants in Chrysostom, Augustine and other Fathers; the words πάντες πιστεύσουσιν εἰς αὐτὸν καί are missing in v. 48, ὑπὲρ τοῦ λαοῦ in v. 50. Boismard thinks that they were also missing, with ἄνθρωπος, from the

---

[61] See Mayeda, *Das Leben-Jesu-Fragment Papyrus Egerton 2*, pp. 21, 71–74. Black, *Aramaic Approach*, p. 55, raises the question but leaves it open.

[62] See Barrett, *St John, ad loc.* Michaelis, *Einleitung*, pp. 108f.; Jeremias, *Unbekannte Jesusworte*, pp. 42 ff., E.T.: *Unknown Sayings of Jesus*, pp. 39 ff.

[63] Boismard, "Problèmes de critique textuelle du Quatrième Évangile", pp. 359–71.

[64] Massaux, "Quelques variantes importantes de Papyrus Bodmer III".

[65] See the copious material in H. Rahner, "Flumina de ventre Christi. Die Patristische Auslegung von Joh. 7:37–38"; further Ménard, "L'interprétation patristique de Joh. 7:38".

original text, with important bearings on the thought of the expiatory death, which would not then have been spoken of by Caiphas.[66]

12:31 f. Boismard appeals to several patristic quotations (and minuscule 317) for the excision of ἐκ τῆς γῆς in v. 32, and thinks of the reading βληθήσεται κάτω for v. 31.[67] This would in fact make things clearer; but the text of our editions, which is strongly attested, is the *lectio difficilior*, and κάτω seems to be the result of reflection.

13:10 The shorter text (without εἰ μὴ τοὺς πόδας) affects the explanation of the passage and also our idea of what the evangelist meant the washing of the feet to convey. There seem to be two disparate meanings side by side, one symbolical and theological (eventually sacramental) in 13:6–11, and the other an ethical exhortation. The question is how to explain this tension.[68]

13:24 By comparing and re-assembling the witnesses, Boismard[69] tries to show that the original text was νεύει οὖν αὐτῷ Σίμων Πέτρος, to which accretions were constantly added. Again the shorter text is supposed to be found in Chrysostom; but it is doubtful whether this conclusion can be drawn from his silence with regard to the rest of the text, and whether the genesis of the longer text can be traced at all on these grounds.

14:2a On the basis of many patristic quotations, Boismard suggests as the oldest text: πολλαὶ μοναὶ παρὰ τῷ πατρί.[70]

14:23 On similar grounds, Boismard here too proposes a shorter form for the original text: "He who loves me will keep my commandments, and my Father and I will come and take up our abode with him."[71]

17:5 The text given by Jerome in *Ep.*, 106, 30 (Hilberg, p. 262), πάτερ, δόξασόν με τῇ δόξῃ ᾗ εἶχον παρὰ σοὶ πρὸ τοῦ τὸν κόσμον γενέσθαι is held to be the original by Boismard.[72] This would include the omission of the καὶ νῦν, an interesting formula to which A. Laurentin has consecrated a study.[73]

---

[66] Boismard, "Problèmes de critique textuelle", pp. 350–3.

[67] Id., "Critique textuelle et citations patristiques", pp. 391 f.

[68] See Menoud, *L'Évangile de Jean*, pp. 54 ff. (on older works; in favour of the short text); Haring, "Historical Notes on the Interpretation of John 13:10"; Boismard, "Problèmes", pp. 353–6 (for the short text); Michl, "Der Sinn der Fußwaschung" (short text: given only exhortation and example); Boismard, "Le lavement des pieds" (short text; analysed into two literary strands with different meanings).

[69] Boismard, "Problèmes", pp. 356–9. [70] Id., "Critique textuelle"; pp. 388–91.

[71] *Ibid.*, pp. 392–4. [72] *Ibid.*, pp. 394–6.

[73] Laurentin, "*We 'attah—Kai nun.* Formule caractéristique des textes juridiques et

17:21 Following Origen and others, Boismard reconstructs the oldest text as follows: ὡς ἐγὼ καὶ σὺ ἕν ἐσμεν, ἵνα καὶ αὐτοὶ ἐν ἡμῖν ἓν ὦσιν.[74] But the text derived from the MSS gives such a good Johannine style that one will hesitate about following the patristic quotations. The Fathers may have made the text shorter and smoother in keeping with Greek idiom.

19:34 Here it is a question of the order of the words, "blood and water", given in this way by the overwhelming majority of the MSS and versions. The order is reversed in 579 e bo (though not in P. Bodmer III), and in the Fathers quoted by Boismard,[75] who pleads for the order corresponding to that of 1 Jn 5:6, "water and blood". He argues that the order, as taken over by the author of 1 Jn from the Gospel, was then felt to be "unnatural" in Jn 19:34 and was therefore changed. But this is not convincing, since the whole process is presented as something extraordinary or significant. Would not the Fathers have preferred to write "water and blood", with conscious reference to 1 Jn 5:6 and the sacramental order of baptism and the Eucharist in mind?

On the whole it may be said that Boismard's method and type of argument are not solidly enough established.

---

liturgiques (à propos de Jean 17:5)". The author questions Boismard's decision on the textual criticism (pp. 168, 432).

[74] Boismard, "Critique textuelle", pp. 396f.

[75] Id., "Problèmes", pp. 348–50.

CHAPTER X

The Fourth Gospel in History

When one attempts to trace the influence of the Gospel of John in the life and history of the Church, one is hindered by the lack of monographs which might cast light on particular points; but it is still possible to recognize certain turning-points. One of these occurred in the second century, as the Gospel began to exercise its influence, but here in particular these initial stages are full of obscurities. Was it mainly adopted by Gnostics to start with and made to serve their opinions, or was it quickly acknowledged by the whole Church? Did the Apostolic Fathers know and use the fourth Gospel, and in particular Ignatius of Antioch? How does the Logos doctrine of the early Christian apologists (Justin, Theophilus of Antioch) stand to that of John? One thing is certain, that Irenaeus saw the value of the fourth Gospel in the struggle against Gnosticism and that it is due to him above all that John was launched on its triumphal march in the Church. There is more obscurity about the little group of adversaries of the Johannine writings (Anti-montanists and Alogoi) within the Church.

Another turning-point may be observed in the third to fifth centuries, when leading Fathers of the Church began to exploit the "spiritual Gospel" for their theology. Its value in the struggle against Arianism and other Christological heresies was recognized, and it was drawn on positively in the construction of various theologies. But here new questions occur, those of the basic approaches to its interpretation. The "Alexandrine" school is opposed to the "Antiochene", and the "allegorical" method vies with the historical effort to find the true literal sense, with John in particular as a testing-ground.

The place of John in the great currents of exegesis and theology was then unquestioned. It had the same historical standing as the Synoptics, though the discrepancies were soon remarked (Augustine, *De consensu evangelistarum*), but was chiefly used as a source of profound theological interpretation and speculation (Augustine, Thomas Aquinas), on account of the way it appeared as a statement of revelation. The use of John by the speculative and mystical theology of the Middle Ages has, unfortunately, been little studied, but the growing number of writings on the study of the Bible in the Middle Ages[1] show that there can be no doubt of the important role played by the last of the canonical Gospels. The Reformation took the Pauline doctrine of justification as its starting-point, as indeed it made the "Pauline Gospel" its great interest, but the theologians of all confessions remained at one in their high estimation of John.

A change came over the situation only with the Enlightenment. It was inevitable that historical criticism should question John, underline the contrasts with the Synoptics, raise the question of authorship and try to clarify the character of the last Gospel. Thus John was drawn into all the movements and debates of modern theology. New impetus was given to the study of John by the problems raised by the study of comparative religions, and the discussion, so far from losing interest, has only been given new directions by the discovery of new sources and the broadening of our historical knowledge. Then, in recent years, basic questions have been raised with regard to interpretation, the hermeneutic principle, the relevant theological understanding, so that today one must pay greater attention to the various tendencies at work in the interpretation of John.

These reflections on the "turning-points" of the influence which John has exercised in the course of history, are merely to justify the divisions made in the following, which cannot purport to be more than a sketch. And one can only hope that further research will be done on this question, which has more than a merely historical interest.[2]

1. The fourth Gospel in the second century

Before we take up the much-discussed problem of the use of John by the ecclesiastical writers of the second century, we must first examine the Gnostics, who undoubtedly came very soon to regard John as their own domain.

(a) Gnostic use of John

The Gnostic appropriation of John is most noticeable in the Valentinian school, for which we can now draw on the texts from Nag-Hammadi. We

[1] See Spicq, *Esquisse d'une histoire de l'exégèse latin au Moyen Age*; Smalley, *The Study of the Bible in the Middle Ages;* de Lubac, *Exégèse médiévale*; Stegmüller, *Repertorium biblicum medii aevi;* Survey of research: H. Karpp, "Die Bibel in der mittelalterlichen Kirche".

[2] See Reuss, *Die Geschichte der heiligen Schriften des Neuen Testaments*, pp. 613–79; Grant, *The Bible in the Church;* Allen, *The Early Church and the New Testament;* on the more recent period see Kümmel, *Das Neue Testament. Geschichte und Erforschung seiner Probleme;* Neill, *The Interpretation of the New Testament 1861–1961.*

have already referred to the relationship between the *Gospel of Truth* (c. A.D. 150?) and John (see ch. vii, 3, c), but only with regard to how far this Gnostic book contributed to the background of John. If, on the contrary, one asks what the Gospel of Truth has in common with John and has perhaps derived from it, the result is by no means slender.[3] It may be illustrated by the following list:

Jn 1:1–4	cf. *Gospel of Truth*	18:1–4
1:3f.	cf.	27:34–28:1
1:4f.	cf.	18:16ff.; 24:37–25:1
1:9,11,14	cf.	26:4–15; also 19:34; 20:23f.; 37:8f. (Coming or appearance of the *Logos*)
1:16	cf.	16:31–35 ("Grace" received through *Logos*)
1:18	cf.	20:39–21:2; 24:9ff.; 27:8 (Revelation through the *Logos*)
3:13	cf.	19:2
3:19	cf.	25:36–26:1 *(Krisis)*
3:31; 8:23	cf.	22:4; 35:1 ("from above")
6:44; 12:32	cf.	21:13f.; 32:12; 33:9 etc. ("draw")
ch. 9; 11:37	cf.	30:15f. (open eyes)
13:32; 17:1	cf.	23:26f. (glory)
14:6	cf.	18:19ff.; 31:29 (the "way")
14:10f.; 17:21	cf.	42:27f. (the Father in them, they in the Father)
15:24f.	cf.	19:25 (Hatred of the envoys)
17:11f.	cf.	38:7–40:29 (the Father gave the "name")[4]
20:22	cf.	20:34 (breathing Spirit into).

Not all these allusions are equally certain; many may merely show that Gnostic language resembles that of the fourth Gospel. But these very affinities may have been one of the reasons why the Gnostics were so quick to take up John. One notes the strong Gnostic interest in the origin of the world, this lower world separated from the pleroma, in the "way"

---

[3] See van Unnik, "The Gospel of Truth and the New Testament", esp. pp. 115–21; Barrett, "The Theological Vocabulary of the Fourth Gospel and of the Gospel of Truth"; Braun, *Jean le Théologien*, pp. 113–33.

[4] On the speculation on "names" see Quispel, "L'Évangile de Jean et la gnose", esp. pp. 204–7. He considers that such speculation comes from esoteric Jewish traditions which have influenced the *Gospel of Truth*. In this case (to which others may be added) John is not simply the source of the expression in the *Gospel of Truth*.

which leads back to the upper world, and in the figure of the Saviour who "appears" on earth and opens up the way back. Hence the first verses of the prologue of John are interpreted in the Gnostic sense (see the developed cosmogony of the *Apocryphon of John*), the coming of the Logos is taken as the "appearance" of the Saviour, his revelations are understood as "*Krisis*", and the return to the pleroma is conceived, as in John, as an "ascension", where the Father or the Saviour "draws" those who hear. It is legitimate to ask whether many Gnostic expressions had not already been forged and were not taken over by John; but knowledge of John by the Gnostics and the assimilation of his assertions into their understanding of existence and salvation cannot be doubted.

There are instructive examples in the *Gospel of Philip* of how sayings from John influenced directly Gnostic "Gospels" (see above, pp. 148f.). Even the term σάρξ, so repugnant to Gnosticism, was pressed into service and explained as the Logos, that is, the spiritual element (Logion 23). The attention paid to the three women (Mary the mother of Jesus, her sister and Mary Magdalene), and the Gnostic significance attached to them, in Logion 32, also probably go back to John (cf. 19:25). The same is perhaps true of some speculation on the Holy Spirit (cf. Logia 23, 26, 33, 34, 36, 40, 74, 100). But in the case of the symbolism of the bridegroom and the nuptial chamber and other typically Gnostic symbols, we cannot be sure of a link with John. It need hardly be said that the content of Gnostic thought is completely different, with an understanding of existence and a doctrine of salvation utterly alien to the fourth Gospel.

It was probably a Gnostic who wrote the first commentary on John — Heracleon, whom we know from the vigorous refutation of him in Origen's commentary on John.[5] The fragments preserved in quotations give further proof that the commentary of this follower of Valentinus was typically Gnostic and alien to the thought of John. We need not discuss other Gnostics and the other schools;[6] it is certain that especially in Egypt, the Gnostic took over John. The origins of Christianity in Egypt are wrapped in obscurity, and it has been suggested that they were Gnostic and heretical.[7] It is therefore an urgent question to know whether here and elsewhere John, was also in early use in "Church" circles.

[5] The fragments in Origen are marked by spaced lettering in the edition of the *Commentarius in Johannem* by Preuschen ; also collected in Völker, *Quellen zur Geschichte der christlichen Gnosis*, pp. 63–86. See Foerster, *Von Valentin zu Herakleon*, pp. 3–44; Sagnard, *La Gnose Valentinienne et le témoignage de saint Irénée*, pp. 480–520; Janssens, "Héracléon. Commentaire sur l'Évangile selon saint Jean".

[6] See Foerster, *Von Valentin zu Herakleon*, pp. 3–44; von Loewenich, *Das Johannes-Verständnis*, pp. 60–115; Sanders, *Fourth Gospel*, pp. 47–66; Sagnard, *Gnose Valentinienne*, pp. 112–39; Wiles, *The Spiritual Gospel*, pp. 96–111.

[7] Bauer, *Rechtgläubigkeit*, pp. 49–64; Braun, *Jean le Théologien*, p. 80, points to the

(b) The use of John in the Church

We are less concerned here with the existence and circulation of John (attested at an early date by P^{52} and P. Egerton 2) than with its being used by admittedly orthodox "ecclesiastical" writers. The question of quotations or allusions in the Apostolic Fathers and the Apologists has been long debated.[8] The recent work of F.-M. Braun investigates systematically the extent of the influence of John in the ancient Church. Three regions are examined, Egypt, Rome (including the pictures from the catacombs) and Asia Minor and the neighbouring countries.[9] His very favourable verdict on John is, in fact, based on a positive approach to possible allusions, which will not commend itself to all critics. Since we cannot discuss the texts again here, we must confine ourselves to some observations and examples.

The *Epistle of Barnabas* (c. 130) would be important as regards Egypt, if this were certainly its place of origin, as there are good but not compelling reasons to believe.[10] The use of the O.T. in this pseudonymous work has now been examined in the light of a possible use of "Testimonia"[11] and is the main subject of interest, in view of its typological exegesis and anti-Jewish theology. Allusions to N.T. texts are mostly vague and general (except 4:14; 5:9), so that the difficulty of forming a judgment can be well illustrated from this work. The following expressions seem most likely to show the influence of John:

the frequent use of the phrase "to appear in the flesh" (φανεροῦσθαι) 5:6; 6:7, 9, 14; 12:10, to which is added in 6:14 ἐν ἡμῖν κατοικεῖν; cf. Jn 1:14, or, "he came in the flesh", 5:10, 11;

Jesus "revealed himself as Son of God" 5:9;

---

testimony of Julius Africanus who lists ten bishops of Alexandria before Demetrius (c. 189). Bauer wrote: "But this list, which he (Eusebius) owes to Julius Africanus, can ultimately do no more than make the deep obscurity, in which the beginnings are wrapped, even more uncanny. . . . The first ten names (after Mark, the disciple of the Apostles) mean nothing to us, and it is doubtful if they ever meant anything to anybody." But this is probably going too far.

[8] See *The New Testament in the Apostolic Fathers*, by a Committee of the Oxford Society of Historical Theology; Bousset, *Die Evangelienzitate Justins des Märtyrers in ihrem Wert für die Evangelienkritik;* the New Testament Introductions; von Loewenich, *Das Johannes-Verständnis;* Sanders, *Fourth Gospel*, pp. 47–66; Hoskyns, *Fourth Gospel*, pp. 96–106 (esp. on Ignatius of Antioch); also the literature mentioned in the following.

[9] *Jean le Théologien*, pp. 69–296.

[10] The Egyptian origin is maintained for instance by Altaner, *Patrologie*, pp. 66, E.T.: *Patrology*, p. 81; Kraft, "Barnabasbrief"; Braun, *Jean le Théologien*, pp. 81–86; with more reserves, Windisch, *Der Barnabasbrief*, p. 413; the question is left open by Schmid, "Barnabas", esp. col. 1217.

[11] Prigent, *L'Épître de Barnabé I-XVI et ses sources;* on which see Audet, "L'Hypothèse des testimonia".

Abraham "looked forward in the Spirit to Jesus" 9:7 (cf. Jn 8:56, but may also be due to typological thinking);

the brazen serpent as type of the Cross 12:7 (cf. Jn 3:14, but could also go back to a standard element of instruction independent of Jn[12]).

Apart from these points, the themes and the attitude of the *Epistle* have little in common with John. One would have to suppose indirect literary influence, but it is not certain that the echoes justify this, since the thoughts and phrases in question could have been derived from the general preaching of the Church. This is the case with most of the so-called "Apostolic Fathers". They have little interest in exact quotation, especially from the N.T., but reflect the living tradition of the N.T., particularly as regards the sayings of the Lord.[13] They make "free" use of them, in their orthodox way, exactly as the Gnostics used them to travesty them. That they attest an older, pre-canonical tradition cannot be proved, and is unlikely, to judge by the way they use Scripture, where their allusions are vague and hard to trace.

Much, therefore, depends on the method used in making comparisons and the critical attitude of the scholar. If we use the method of merely verbal association, we can find allusions to John even in the first epistle of Clement, from Rome; but the points adduced (43:6 cf. Jn 17:3;—47:4 "lesser sin" cf. Jn 19:11; 1 Jn 5:16;—49:5; 50:1–3 "perfected in love") can be explained without the help of the Johannine writings. Chronological reasons alone would suggest that this is the only true explanation. The position is much the same as regards the "Shepherd of Hermas". The imagery in the Similitudes (the vine climbing up the elm 2:3; the vine run wild 9:26, 4; the old rock and the new door 9:12, 1–3) has nothing specific in common with that of John; in the same way, the allusion to Jn 3:5 in *Sim.*, 16:2–7, or *Mand.*, 11:8, is too vague to be of use.

Literature from Syria is generally held to be more promising. Speaking of the *Didache*, the date of which is still debated,[14] W. von Loewenich says: "The contacts between John and the Didache [in the "Eucharistic" language of ch. 9–10] are far too striking to be accidental." With Ignatius of Antioch also in mind, he thinks that they "go back to a common local

---

[12] See Prigent, pp. 120 f. ("Christian midrash"); he explicitly rejects a borrowing from Jn 3:14 f.

[13] There is an interesting contrast between the opinions of Massaux, *Influence de l'Évangile de s. Matthieu sur la littérature chrétienne avant s. Irénée*, who sees a direct literary dependence, and of Köster, *Synoptische Überlieferung bei den Apostolischen Vätern*, who denies it.

[14] Earlier, it was mostly attributed to the first half of the second century but now the early dating, to the first century, seems to be prevailing. Audet, *La Didaché*, puts it as early as 50–70; for the end of the first century, Adam, "Erwägungen zur Herkunft der Didache"; Daniélou, "Bulletin I", pp. 66–73; see also Camelot, "Didache".

and then spiritual tradition".[15] But even this is contested by J.-P. Audet: "There is nothing here [in the Eucharistic sections] which obliges us to have recourse to 'Johannine circles' . . . On this point, the Didache is merely the heir to the Wisdom-Messianism, of which there are other witnesses to show that it was common to the milieu and era of the Didache. Direct literary dependence on John of any sort cannot be suggested."[16] There are undoubtedly formal similarities of language (e.g., between *Did.* 9:4, and Jn 11:52[17]), but whether they are enough to prove direct knowledge of John remains questionable.

The endless controversy about the relationship of John to the *Epistles of Ignatius* is much more important. Ch. Maurer has re-inforced the position that Ignatius knew John.[18] He finds that three quotations have the force of proofs:

Ign. Phld., 7:1	cf. Jn 8:14; 3:8
Ign. Phld., 9:1	cf. Jn 10:7, 9; 14:6
Ign. Rom., 7:3	cf. Jn 6:26–59.

More emphasis could also be laid (with F.-M. Braun[19]) on *Ign. Magn.*, 8:2, which speaks of the Logos "who did the good pleasure of him who sent him, in all things" (cf. Jn 8:29). To judge Ignatius properly, one has to remember that it made little difference to him whether the doctrine came in oral or written form. He was only interested in the content, and it is hard to tell whether his sources for a given point were oral or written.[20]

Thus various possibilities are open: Ignatius could have known John itself or an early form of the Gospel or a Johannine kerygma in oral form; or he may simply be in a similar tradition with regard to doctrine (cf. σάρξ [for σῶμα] and αἷμα in the language of the Eucharist).

In Asia Minor, Papias, Bishop of Hierapolis, perhaps knew the Gospel of John;[21] but he himself affirms that he was more interested in the living voice of tradition than in written books.[22] Polycarp of Smyrna certainly refers to 1 Jn 4:2f.; cf. 2 Jn 7, in his epistle (7:1), though not

---

15 *Das Johannes-Verständnis*, pp. 20 and 22.

16 *La Didaché*, p. 175.

17 See Braun, *Jean le Théologien*, pp. 251–62, esp. p. 256. He thinks it probable that the *Didache* knew John, which is very questionable in the light of recent research and the early dating of the *Didache*.

18 Maurer, *Ignatius und das Johannesevangelium*; he also gives a brief account of earlier research (pp. 7 ff.).

19 *Jean le Théologien*, pp. 274 f.

20 Grant, "Scripture and Tradition in St. Ignatius of Antioch", p. 327.

21 See Heard, "Papias' Quotations from the New Testament", p. 131.

22 See the quotation in Eusebius, *Hist. eccles.*, III, 39, 4.

giving an exact quotation; it is remarkable that no allusion to the Gospel can be discovered.[23]

We are on firmer ground when we come to the middle of the second century. Knowledge of John may be affirmed more confidently of Justin. The content of his Logos doctrine may owe more to philosophical (Stoic) impulses, but it undoubtedly links up with the text of the incarnation in John; so *Apol.*, 32 καὶ ὁ υἱὸς ὁ λόγος ἐστίν· ὃς τίνα τρόπον σαρκοποιηθεὶς ἄνθρωπος γέγονεν. *Apol.*, 61:4f. also provides a clear reference to Jn 3:3f.: "For Christ has also said: If you are not born again (ἀναγεννηθῆτε) you shall not enter the kingdom of heaven. But it is obvious to everybody that those who have been born cannot enter the womb of their mother." Justin, like Ignatius of Antioch, is also in the tradition which prefers σάρξ in the terminology of the Eucharist (cf. *Apol.*, 66:2 and 3). The treatment of John the Baptist in the *Dialogue with the Jew Trypho* is interesting: people thought he was the Messiah, but he himself cried out, "I am not the Messiah but only the voice of one who calls out" (88:7). The echo of Jn 1:20, 23 is unmistakable, and may perhaps also display acquaintance with contemporary disciples of the Baptist. The use of the typology of the brazen serpent for the Crucifixion (cf. Jn 3:14f.) occurs once more, as in the *Epistle of Barnabas*, but now more closely linked to the text of John (*Dial.*, 91:4).

We have certain proof of the high estimation in which John was held from the *Diatessaron of Tatian*, though it cannot be established that the work was composed before Tatian left Rome (about 170). This highly influential harmony of the Gospels puts the fourth Gospel on the same level as the Synoptics and accords it considerable space. The apologist Theophilus, Bishop of Antioch in Syria, c. 170–183, whose Logos doctrine is again much wider than that of John, appeals explicitly to "the sacred Scriptures and all the inspired men, including John", and then quotes the opening words of John;[24] this is apparently the first formal quotation from the Gospel. Another valuable witness is the *Epistula Apostolorum* (before 180), which makes great use of John in the struggle with the Gnostics.[25]

---

23 See von Loewenich, *Das Johannes-Verständnis*, pp. 22–25. But he points out that the *Martyrium Polycarpi* has traits which recall specifically the Passion story in John, from which he concludes that John was known at the time of the *Martyrium*.

24 Theophilus of Antioch, *Ad Autolycum*, II, 22 (*PG* 6, col. 1088; Bardy, p. 154).

25 C. Schmidt, *Gespräche Jesu*, pp. 224 ff.; cf. pp. 294–304; Duensing, "Epistula Apostolorum" (English translation with references to John in the apparatus). We read in ch. 3 (14), "We believe that *the Word*, which *became flesh* through the holy virgin Mary, was carried (conceived) in her womb by the Holy Spirit"; in ch. 5 (16) the marriage at Cana is related; there are constant allusions to Jn 13–20; the "new commandment" is cited in ch. 18 (29), and so on. Then a warning against Cerinthus and Simon is given in ch. 7 (18), since they "have come to go through the world. But they are the enemies of our Lord Jesus Christ".

Finally, we may mention Melito of Sardes whose Easter Homily (now re-discovered in its entirety) speaks of the Lamb whose bones were not broken (cf. Jn 19:36).[26] During the Quartodeciman controversy (about 190) Polycrates of Ephesus makes a fervent and emphatic appeal to John, who leaned on the breast of the Lord and was one of the great lights of the Church of Asia.[27]

This proves that it was not Irenaeus who discovered John in his refutation of Gnosticism and caused it to be adopted by the Church. It had already been held in high theological esteem. It is true that there are no irrefutable proofs for the use of John in the Church in the first decades of the second century, but there are still enough traces to enable us to recognize its growing influence. Along with the literary evidence from the second century, the pictures in the catacombs bear eloquent and reliable testimony to how the fourth Gospel, with its language and imagery, made its way into the life and piety of the Church.[28]

(c) Opposition to the Johannine writings at the end of the second century

As well as in Gnosticism, the Johannine writings gained considerable importance in the course of the second century in the movement of religious enthusiasm called Montanism. The Montanists are known to have appealed in particular to Revelation, with the result that this book had to struggle for recognition for many centuries in the East. The Gospel also suffered from their misguided appeal to the Johannine doctrine of the Spirit. According to the testimony of Irenaeus, opponents of Montanism who were clearly within the pale of the Church went so far as to reject not only Revelation but John: "illam speciem non admittunt, quae est secundum Johannem Evangelium, in qua Paracletum se missurum Dominus promisit; sed simul et Evangelium, et propheticum repellunt Spiritum." In doing so, these "unfortunate" people, according to Irenaeus, also denied the presence of the prophetic Spirit in the Church.[29]

---

[26] The homily, previously known only through fragments, was discovered in a fairly complete state in a papyrus codex, published by Bonner and by Lohse. A still better text has now been found in one of the Bodmer papyri (xiii, edition by Testuz). The saying about the lamb is found in para. 4; but there also seem to be other traces of Johannine influence in the homily; see Barrett, *St. John*, p. 94; Blank, *Meliton von Sardes, Vom Passa.*

[27] See Eusebius, *Hist. eccles.*, V, 24, 3; Melito follows in the same series (V, 24, 5).

[28] See Braun, *Jean le théologien*, pp. 149–60. According to Wilpert, *Die Malereien der Katakomben Roms*, pictures of the Samaritan woman and of Lazarus are as early as the second half of the second century (vol. I, p. 149).

[29] Irenaeus, *Adv. Haer.*, III, II, 12 (Harvey, vol. II, p. 51). Detailed discussion in Bludau, *Die ersten Gegner der Johannesschriften*. The expression "qui pseudoprophetae quidem esse volunt" causes difficulty; Bludau conjectures "nolunt" (pp. 31 ff.).

But he mentions them only incidentally when defending the canon of the four Gospels, and they do not seem to have gained much influence.

Irenaeus does not tell us where these anti-Montanists were to be found, but one may think of Gaul or Rome, since the Montanist "prophets" had penetrated as far as these regions. We learn from other sources, especially from fragments of a work of Hippolytus of Rome,[30] that under Pope Zephyrinus (199–217) there was a learned man in Rome called Gaius who rejected John (as well as Revelation) and even ascribed it to Cerinthus.[31] He too was mainly interested in refuting the Montanists. His effort to decry and eliminate John by pointing out the contrast with the Synoptics was obviously meant to deprive the Montanists of a weapon.[32]

We learn, finally, from another source, Epiphanius, that there was a group of "Alogoi" who rejected the fourth Gospel and Revelation, and ascribed them to Cerinthus, but were otherwise of the same mind as Catholics.[33] The deliberately ambiguous term used of them by Epiphanius ("deniers of the Logos" or "unreasonable") probably indicates only that they rejected John, where this title of Christ occurs, and not that they were heretics in Christology. A. Bludau came to the conclusion, after a painstaking study of them, that they showed no trace of anti-Gnostic interests, adoptianist Christology or opposition to the doctrine of the divinity of Christ and the Holy Spirit. They were an insignificant and nameless group, as the fact that Epiphanius styles them the "feeble serpent" (*Pan.*, 51, 1, 1) already suggests. Gaius supported them in his struggle against the Montanists by maintaining that Cerinthus was the author of John and Revelation; they themselves had not come to this view out of hostility to Montanism, but by internal criticism of John, based on its contrast to the synoptic presentation, and of Revelation, on account of its fantastic language and images.[34] One may differ from Bludau on details of his interpretation, but he seems to be right in saying that they were a restricted group without any great influence. Possibly the *Muratorian Canon* is directed against such depreciation of the

---

[30] The fragments are contained in a commentary of the Jacobite bishop, Dionysius bar Salibi (d. 1171) on Revelation (ed. by Sedlaček); they are also collected by Achelis, pp. 241–7.

[31] "Hippolytus Romanus dixit: Apparuit vir nomine Caius, qui asserebat Evangelium non esse Johannis, nec apocalypsim, sed Cerinthi haeretici ea esse" (Sedlaček, vol. LX, pp. 1 f.).

[32] See Bludau, *Die ersten Gegner*, pp. 69 f.

[33] Epiphanius of Salamis, *Pan.*, 51 (Holl, vol. II, pp. 248–311). His account has given rise to various interpretations. But they were not "heretics" in the ordinary sense, as appears from *Pan.*, 51, 4, 3 (Holl, vol. II, p. 251): "They appear, however, to believe what we believe." See further Bludau, pp. 137–50.

[34] Bludau, pp. 149, 199, 229 f.

fourth Gospel in its defence of John (lines 16–26).[35] But on the whole, such views as those of the Alogoi made no headway in the Church, and John soon became, along with Matthew, the most highly treasured of the Gospels.

2. John in patristic exegesis

It was Gnosticism which occasioned the first ecclesiastical interpretation of John. The first commentary which we have from patristic times is that of Origen, who was moved to write it by his controversy with Heracleon (see above). The great Alexandrian was asked to write a refutation by a nobleman called Ambrosius whom he had led from Valentinianism to the Church. This he did in a commentary which he began about 225 and continued to work on for many years, probably without ever finishing it. His aim was to oppose the false Gnostic interpretation by the genuine ecclesiastical one.[36] He was at one with his opponent in prizing an exegesis which went beyond the literal sense, but his method was strictly limited by his refusal to read fantasies into the text which were in accord neither with the Bible nor ecclesiastical tradition. This is not the place to evaluate the much debated exegesis of Origen;[37] we confine ourselves to the following remarks on the subject:

a) Origen is determined to start from the literal sense, and reproaches Heracleon with an exegesis which does violence to and falsifies the text (*Comm. in Jo.*, II, 14; XIII, 10, 17, 46 etc.).

b) Since he holds verbal inspiration, he sees the difficulties of a purely historical explanation (X, 3f.), and tries to find the "spiritual" sense. He makes use of allegory to a great extent when doing so, in keeping with Greek and Jewish tradition.

c) But he founds the spiritual sense more deeply on the nature of revelation and the word of God, which is still found in images and shadows in the Old Testament, under the veil of the letter (cf. e.g. X, 23 ff., on the cleansing of the temple), and continues to abase itself in the New, in the person of the Logos (cf. XXXII, 4, on the washing of the feet), and clothes itself in earthly garments. Origen does not wish to disregard the literal sense, but to go beyond it: "I believe that all the Scriptures,

---

[35] See Wikenhauser, *Einleitung*, p. 205, E. T., p. 284; Grillmeier, "Aloger". Bludau holds, however, that the author of the *Muratorian Canon* knew nothing of a "serious challenge to the Johannine writings" (p. 203).

[36] Edition by Preuschen.

[37] Daniélou, *Origène*, esp. pp. 145–74; de Lubac, *Histoire et Esprit. L'intelligence de l'Écriture d'après Origène;* Gögler, *Zur Theologie des biblischen Wortes bei Origenes*, a full study including further literature, including his translation of the Commentary on John.

even when fully and exactly known, are only a brief introduction to the most simple fundamentals of the whole knowledge of faith. Think of Jacob's well, from which the patriarch once drank. He no longer drinks from it. And his children drank of it, but now they have a better drink than he had, since the water given by Jesus is 'more than what is written' " (XIII,5).

d) For Origen, the guarantee of the true interpretation which goes beyond the words is the holy Church of Christ (V, 8), the apostolic understanding of Scripture (X,18). The great reproach which Origen makes against the Gnostics is that they put forward arbitrary, "private" interpretations of Scripture, which are, therefore, devoid of "testimony" (cf. II, 14; XIII, 17).

e) The content of this interpretation is Christological and eschatological. "The scriptures [of the Old Testament] are introductions—which we now call Jacob's well—which if properly thought out must lead to Jesus, so that he may give us the source which wells up to eternal life" (XIII,6). But Christ himself uses his word in this age to lead us to eternity, the "third Passover" (the Jewish Pasch being the first, and the one in which he himself was the slaughtered Lamb the second), "which is celebrated in the festal assembly of countless angels at the perfect and most blissful exodus" (X, 18). The allegorical method of such exegesis is undoubtedly strange to us; but if we prescind from the method and see what is behind it, we find a deep understanding of the word of God as incarnate in the Logos and the words of Scripture, and yet so concealed that it is never fully exhausted in any interpretation of it.

The following centuries were dominated by the doctrinal controversies on the Trinity and Incarnation and produced no notable commentaries (on the catenae, see below). John was, of course, much used in these debates (see for instance Tertullian, *Adv. Praxeas*, 21–25) and played an important part in the Arian controversy.[38] But for a positive interpretation, less marked by polemical zeal, we have to wait till the end of the fourth and the beginning of the fifth century. But the next positive commentaries after Origen do not come from his school at Alexandria but from its rival school at Antioch.[39] This tradition, which emphasized the literal sense, had no intention of merely letting the "bare letters" speak, but used its hermeneutic principle of θεωρία to offer an exegesis orientated to Christ (which is very clear for the O.T.).

---

[38] See Wiles, *The Spiritual Gospel*, pp. 112–28.

[39] See Guillet, "Les exégèses d'Alexandrie et d'Antioche"; Quasten, *Patrology*, vol. II, pp. 121 f.; H. Rahner, "Antiochenische Schule". Unfortunately, Diodorus of Tarsus, "On the Difference between Theoria and Allegory" is lost, as is Theodore of Mopsuestia's "Against the Allegorists" (see Quasten, vol. III, pp. 333, 414).

It did in fact contribute much to Christology, according to recent research. During the Nestorian controversy, however, it came under the ban of the Church, so that many of its productions are unfortunately lost or only preserved in fragments (in the *catenae*).

Here we must first mention, in chronological order, the homilies of John Chrysostom on John, which are much shorter than those on Matthew but make up for it by being less polemical in tone. Their pastoral intention is palpable, the exegesis not always convincing, but theologically clear and ardent. In refuting the Arians, who pointed to the human limitations and weaknesses even in the Johannine Christ, Chrysostom stresses the "condescension" (συγκατάβασις) of God, who embodied his word in the Bible in human form and language.[40] This is the same theology of revelation and a similar understanding of the word of Scripture as we find in Origen, though Chrysostom does not try to explore the "spiritual" sense like the latter.

In view of the suppression of the "Nestorian" writings such as the "Three Chapters", it must be considered a happy chance that we have once more at our disposal the full commentary of the greatest exegete of the Antiochene school, Theodore of Mopsuestia, in a Syriac translation.[41] The many extracts in Greek *catenae* are also accessible in critical editions.[42] The commentary itself displays the sound principles of the school, with its concern for the literal sense, but its theological contribution, especially in Christology, is also noteworthy. Theodore refuses to concede any inferiority on the part of the Son with regard to the Father, distinguishing constantly between the divine and human nature, though creating thereby many problems for exegetes.[43]

Somewhat later the Alexandrian school produced another important and extensive commentary on John, by the great Cyril of Alexandria.[44] It is more preoccupied with dogmatic theology and polemics, but does not mention Nestorius and hence must be dated before the outbreak of the controversy (429). An interesting comparison may be made between the Christological exegesis of Cyril and that of Theodore, as is done by M. F. Wiles.[45] His verdict is that both writers are in a straitjacket of dogmatic presuppositions from which the message of the Gospel itself was free. Theodore proceeds with a more rigid logic, while Cyril recognizes the inability of human speech to render the fullness of divine truth

---

[40] See Fabbi, "La condiscendenza divina nell'ispirazione biblica".

[41] Edition of text and French translation by Vosté.

[42] Edited by Devreesse.

[43] See Grillmeier, "Die theologische und sprachliche Vorbereitung der christologischen Formel von Chalkedon", pp. 144–55; Wiles, *The Spiritual Gospel*, pp. 133 ff.

[44] *PG* 73 and 74; see also edition by Pusey.

[45] See Wiles, *The Spiritual Gospel*, pp. 129–47, 136.

and does more justice to the divine condescension of the word in the Scripture.[46]

Augustine, however, has left us a commentary which goes beyond dogmatic quarrels (which are still echoed in many polemical disquisitions) and reaches a high level of theological maturity.[47] The 124 tractates are not a commentary in the modern sense, frequently paying little attention to the literal sense to press on at once to meditation and speculation. But they practise the theological exposition which is the strict characteristic of the patristic age, linking theology to the text of Scripture and applying it to Christian life. These homilies were actually delivered as sermons (between 414 and 416)[48] and still have a privileged place in the liturgy of the Church.

Many other commentaries were also produced which survive today only in excerpts in the *catenae*. Earlier editions were very unreliable in marking the beginning and end of the passages quoted and had also other defects;[49] the first edition to present the material in a compact and manageable fashion is that of J. Reuss.[50] He gives the preliminary results of his researches as follows: the *catenae* provide us with samples of the exegesis of the following Greek Fathers: Apollinaris of Laodicaea, Theodore of Heraclaea, Didymus ("the Blind"), Cyril of Alexandria (from Books 7 and 8 of his commentary, not preserved elsewhere), Ammonius of Alexandria and Photius of Constantinople.[51] He finds the homilies of Photius (who can be no other than the Patriarch) to be "the most valuable and independent exegetical achievement on John in Byzantine times".[52] Nonnus of Panopolis composed a rambling and exegetically insignificant paraphrase on John in hexameters about 450.[53] But the commentary of the Nestorian bishop, Ish'odad of Merv (about 850) is valuable.[54] In the ninth century we have an exposition of John by an anonymous author of the school of Theodore of Studios[55]—but here we are already in the Middle Ages.

[46] *Ibid.*, p. 136.

[47] *S. Aurelii Augustini in Johannis evangelium tractatus cxxiv;* Comeau, *S. Augustin exégète du quatrième évangile;* Pontet, *L'exégèse de S. Augustin prédicateur*, esp. pp. 555–80; Strauss, *Schriftgebrauch, Schriftauslegung und Schriftbeweis bei Augustin.*

[48] Altaner, *Patrologie*, p. 394, E. T.: p. 512; Pontet, p. 555 (dates the sermons to A.D. 418).

[49] On the *catenae*, see Devreesse, "Chaînes exégétiques grecques" (on John cols. 1194–1205); Reuss, *Matthäus-, Markus- und Johannes-Katenen;* Staab, "Katenen".

[50] *Johannes-Kommentare aus der griechischen Kirche.*

[51] See Schnackenburg, *Biblische Zeitschrift* 5 (1961), p. 316.

[52] J. Reuss, "Die Erklärung des Johannesevangeliums durch den Patriarchen Photius von Konstantinopel", p. 282.

[53] Edited by Janssen; see Altaner, *Patrologie*, pp. 252 f., E. T.: pp. 327 f.; J. Reuss, "Non(n)os von Panopolis".

[54] Edited by Gibson, *The Commentaries of Isho'dad of Merw.*

[55] Hansmann, *Ein neuentdeckter Kommentar zum Johannesevangelium.*

3. *From the Middle Ages to Modern Times*

Patristic exegesis remained authoritative in setting the trend in the early Middle Ages. There seemed to be no nobler task than to cherish and hand on the heritage of the Fathers. John Chrysostom was the great model in the East, as may be seen from the commentary of Theophylactus (c. 1100), though it cannot be denied that he preserves a certain amount of independence.[56] The tractates of Augustine on John were highly esteemed in the West, as is shown by the commentary long ascribed to the Venerable Bede, the great English Benedictine who did so much for biblical studies († 735). It is not cited in the list of his works which covers the years down to 732 and cannot be regarded as authentic.[57] The influence of Augustine may also be noted in the school of Alcuin († 804),[58] through whose disciple Raban Maurus († 856)[59] it came into Germany (cf. Wilfred Strabo [† 849]).[60] Commentators preferred "glosses", collections of scholia of which the material was mostly taken from the works of the Fathers. The most important of these productions, the so-called *glossa ordinaria*, comes, according to the most recent research, from Anselm of Laon († 1117), though it covered originally only the psalms and the Pauline epistles.[61]

If we prescind from John Scotus Eriugena († c. 877), who wrote a commentary on Jn 1:1–14 and some brief *Annotationes in Johannem*,[62] and from Christian of Stablo (later also known as Druthmar, † after 880), whose authorship of a short commentary on John is uncertain,[63] the most important commentators of John are Bruno of Segni († 1123)

---

[56] This is also true of Nicetas, Archbishop of Heraclea in Thrace (a contemporary of Theophylactus), whose *catena* on John is printed in part among the works of Cyril of Alexandria (*PG* 74, cols. 9–104), and of Euthymius of Zigabene, who is somewhat later (*PG* 129, cols. 1105–1502), noted for his grammatical precision.

[57] According to Stegmüller, *Repertorium*, vol. II, no. 1680, chs. 1–12 of this commentary are identical with Alcuin, *Johannes*, pars I, and chs. 13–21 are excerpts from Augustine.

[58] See Stegmüller, vol. II, no. 1096 (Jn 1–12, mostly excerpts from the Fathers).

[59] According to Stegmüller, vol. V, no. 7062, the Commentary on John, which has been ascribed to Maurus, comes from Ercanbert, Bishop of Freising (d. 854); on Ercanbert, see Stegmüller, vol. II, no. 2246.

[60] According to Stegmüller, vol. V, no. 9330, a commentary on John has also been wrongly attributed to him, which is also found among the works of the pseudo-Jerome (id., vol. III, no. 3427).

[61] On the *Glossa Ordinaria* see B. Smalley, *Study of the Bible in the Middle Ages*, pp. 46–66; this popular work of study and doctrine grew up gradually from many sources which can now hardly be determined in detail.

[62] The commentary is printed in *PL* 122, cols. 283–348; *Annotationes in Johannem*, ed. by Willis.

[63] Printed in *PL* 106, cols. 1515–20; see Stegmüller, vol. II, no. 1928.

who expounded all four Gospels,[64] Rupert of Deutz (†1129) who composed a special commentary on John, preferring the mystical and allegorical sense,[65] and then the great Scholastics, Albertus Magnus († 1280),[66] Thomas Aquinas († 1274)[67] and Bonaventure († 1274).[68] The exegesis of these leading theologians shows the influence of the scholastic method (clear arrangement, logical and theological analysis), but they feel themselves strictly bound by the literal sense, which is the only one that has force of proof for them. They are also in the main stream of patristic tradition and make use chiefly of John Chyrsostom and Augustine. Hence Thomas Aquinas is today rightly esteemed more highly as an exegete, and his clear theological developments retain their value for a profounder interpretation. Along with these giants of Scholasticism we must also mention Nicolaus of Gorran, O.P. († c. 1295) who wrote commentaries on all four Gospels.[69] But the most competent and influential exegete of the Middle Ages was undoubtedly the Franciscan Nicolaus of Lyra, O.F.M. († 1349), whose great *Postillae* on the Old and New Testament became the exegetical handbook of the later Middle Ages. He aimed chiefly at the literal sense, avoided all digressions and made use of Jewish commentators; the Reformers also owed much to him.[70] Towards the close of Scholasticism comes the very copious writer Denis the Carthusian († 1471), who also wrote commentaries on the whole of Scripture.[71] Finally we may mention the many unprinted commentaries on John, which are at least catalogued in F. Stegmüller's great reference book.

With Humanism came a greater interest in the languages of the Bible and more effort to produce a theology founded on the Bible and the Fathers. Erasmus was inspired to produce paraphrases of the N.T., including the Gospels (1522–23), which found a ready welcome in the following years. In the controversial theology of the Reformation John played no special part. Historical interest attaches to the experiences of the Franciscan John Wild (Ferus) with his expositions of John, first given orally in Mainz and then re-printed again and again. They were banned by the

[64] Printed in *PL* 165, cols. 451–604; see Stegmüller, vol. II, no. 1860.

[65] The commentary on John (c. 1119) is printed in *PL* 169, cols. 202–826; see Stegmüller, vol. V, no. 7580.

[66] See Stegmüller, vol. II, no 1001.

[67] "Postilla super Johannes", see Stegmüller, vol. V, no. 8050; new ed. by Cai; see also *Catena aurea in quattuor evangelia*, ed. by Guarienti.

[68] See Stegmüller, vol. II, no. 1778.

[69] See Stegmüller, vol. IV, no. 5781. Many MSS give the Commentary on John by Bonaventure (wrongly) under his name (previous note).

[70] The postils have often been printed since 1491/92; on the commentary on John, see Stegmüller, vol. IV, no. 5900.

[71] *Dionysii Carthusi opera omnia*, vol. XII, pp. 265–620.

Sorbonne, defended by M. de Medina, and were put on the Roman Index in 1590 (from which they have disappeared since 1900).[72] Among the Reformers who wrote commentaries on John were Philip Melanchthon (1523),[73] the Lutheran John Brenz and J. Oecolampadius of Basle,[74] but the most highly esteemed was that of John Calvin (1553). Among Catholics, the "golden age" of biblical studies began with the sixteenth century (1500–1630). The exegetical principles of Cardinal Cajetan were already remarkable (1469–1534). He tried to grasp above all the literal sense and give as exact a translation as possible, without coming into conflict with Church teaching; his N.T. commentary is from the years 1527–29. From the following years, which produced a rich exegetical literature, we may mention C. Jansen the Elder (Louvain, 1577), F. de Toledo S.J. (Cologne, 1588, often re-printed), F. de Ribera S.J. († 1591, whose commentary was published posthumously, Lyons 1623), J. Maldonatus, S.J. (Pont-à-Mousson 1597), whose penetrating observations on the Gospels are still prized today,[75] F. Lucas Brugensis (Antwerp 1616), J. Tirinus, S.J. (Antwerp, 1632) and Cornelius a Lapide, S.J. (Antwerp 1670), whose commentaries have frequently been re-printed in spite of their longwindedness. It was about these and other commentators that the great Oratorian Richard Simon, the founder of modern "Introductions to the Bible", wrote his work: *Histoire critique des principaux commentateurs du Nouveau Testament* (Rotterdam, 1693). A. Calmet, O.S.B. (Paris, 1707 ff.) and Alexander Natalis, O.P. (Paris, 1743) already belong to another era.

In those days, Lutheran orthodoxy with its adherence to verbal inspiration was not very fruitful. But at times philological interests led scholars to compare the N.T. with classical literature (J. Camerarius, H. Grotius) or to illustrate it from Jewish writings (J. Lightfoot), and this also benefited Johannine studies, though only by parallels and explanations for individual texts.[76] The great two-volume work of J. J. Wettstein[77] is an admirable achievement, even from the point of view of textual criticism, and the "Gnomon" of J. A. Bengel is still prized for its exegesis.[78] The Enlightenment then stimulated N.T. criticism (J. S. Semler, D. F. Michaelis), which furthered the historical understanding

---

[72] See Hurter, *Nomenclator*, vol. II, cols. 1486 ff.; Mercier, "Wild, Jean".

[73] *Enarratio in Evangelium Joannis.*

[74] See also Luther, *Das Johannesevangelium.*

[75] One of the last editions, Maldonatus, *Commentarius*, vol. II: *In Lucam et Johannem*, ed. by Raich.

[76] Camerarius, *Commentarius in Novum Foedus;* Grotius, *Annotationes in libros evangeliorum;* Lightfoot, *Horae Hebraicae et Talmudicae in quattuor Evangelistas.*

[77] *Novum Testamentum Graecum editionis receptae cum lectionibus variantibus.*

[78] *Gnomon Novi Testamenti.*

of the N.T. writings but was less fruitful as regards interpretation. Attention was turned to more general questions of religion, criticism of the N.T. narratives and literary criticism. The authorship of the Apostle John was soon questioned (see above, ch. i), and the "Johannine question" continued to be debated all through the nineteenth century. The fourth Gospel became, as H. J. Holtzmann wrote in 1892, "the σημεῖον ἀντιλεγόμενον for all N.T. criticism in modern times".[79] D.F. Strauss, as early as his "Life of Jesus" (1835–36), had declared that John was valueless as a historical source, being composed of myths and certainly not written by a contemporary or intimate disciple of Jesus.[80] In the course of his "critique of tendencies" F. Chr. Baur gave this view firmer contours: the fourth evangelist has no special historical tradition to offer in contrast to the Synoptics, but re-moulds the historical material with the idea of the divine grandeur and majesty of Jesus in mind.[81] In spite of many reserves as regards the Hegelian picture of history provided by Baur, his evaluation of John (often accompanied by a dating which put it well into the second century) held its ground in the critical research of the following period.[82] But there was always an intermediate position, which tried to save a basic element of John for the history of Jesus, and at the beginning of the twentieth century came the heyday of literary criticism, sorting out sources and trying to bring to light an "older stratum" or "basic document".[83] It has been succeeded at the present day by the study of the history of tradition, which has, however, different presuppositions.

It is all the more remarkable, therefore, that the nineteenth century produced, along with historical criticism, a growing number of interpretative commentaries of the Gospels. H. A. W. Meyer founded his *Kritischer und exegetischer Kommentar* in 1829, and was himself responsible for the commentary on John in the series (1834). This work, constantly reprinted and revised up to the present day, provides an interesting sample of the history of interpretation. The commentary of the founder went through five editions (till 1869), which was followed by four editions of the commentary of the more conservative B. Weiss (1880–1902), till R. Bultmann published (from 1941 on) his new commentary on totally different lines. But there were also other commentaries on John in which the various theological trends of the nineteenth century found

[79] Holtzmann, *Lehrbuch der historisch-kritischen Einleitung in das Neue Testament*, p. 434.

[80] See Schweitzer, *Geschichte der Leben-Jesu-Forschung*, pp. 86–9, E. T.: *The Quest of the Historical Jesus*, pp. 86–88.

[81] Baur, "Die Komposition und der Charakter des Johannesevangeliums"; id., *Kritische Untersuchungen über die kanonischen Evangelien;* see also Kümmel, *Einleitung*, p. 169.

[82] There is a survey in Holtzmann, *Lehrbuch*, pp. 433–8; among Anglicans, the critical standpoint was represented by Bacon, *The Gospel of the Hellenists*.

[83] See above, ch. iii; a survey in Howard, *Fourth Gospel in Recent Criticism*, pp. 53–68.

expression, which need not be mentioned in detail here. Catholic exegesis also began to take a greater interest in the work of commentating, partly with strong apologetical tendencies in face of the negative criticism, partly in a positive effort to carry on the Catholic tradition by linking up with the Fathers and later theologians. One of the best Catholic commentaries of the nineteenth century is that of the Tübingen professor P. Schanz, which gave considerable attention to patristic exegesis as well as to contemporary interpretation and took up a moderately critical standpoint.[84] The method of historical criticism was also adopted, gradually, by Catholic exegesis, a process in which the French Dominican M.-J. Lagrange, founder of the *École Biblique* in Jerusalem, played an especially meritorious part.[85] The school won a high reputation by means of its organ, the *Revue Biblique* (1892) and the commentaries and studies in the series *Études Bibliques*, in which M.-J. Lagrange also published a commentary on John (1925, often re-printed), an outstanding achievement in its fullness, judgment and maturity. Another crisis ensued with the modernist controversy, in which A. Loisy produced his commentary (1903); his standpoint in the second, revised edition (1921) is characteristic: the Johannine writings were put into circulation in Asia Minor by a group of the faithful who wished to claim the patronage of the Apostle John, who had nothing to do with the composition of these writings; not only is ch. 21 an editorial addition, but even the Epistles are not from one single pen; the Gospel is, in the main, "a sort of mystical and symbolical vision of the earthly manifestation of the Logos in Jesus Christ to save the children of God"; this is the mysticism developed and enlarged upon in the mysticism of Paul, which is still closer to pagan mysticism and Gnosis.[86] Lagrange's commentary was, so to speak, the Catholic answer to Loisy.

Still another trend in N.T. research must be mentioned, which was particularly important for John: the school of comparative religion. Scholars in the nineteenth century had already begun to note possible influences from the surrounding world, in order to explain John in terms of the language and mentality of its times. Affinities with Gnosticism had been noted early on; but it was rather the Christian Gnosticism of the second century that was envisaged, and efforts were made to situate John in the Hellenistic syncretism of that age.[87] The precise questions

---

[84] Schanz, *Commentar über das Evangelium des heiligen Johannes.*

[85] See his controversial work, *La méthode historique* (1903; 2nd ed., 1904).

[86] Loisy, *Le Quatrième Évangile.*

[87] The standpoint of Pfleiderer, of the Tübingen school, is characteristic. See his *Urchristentum*, vol. II, p. 451. The Johannine theology is to be understood in the light of "the connection with and opposition to the Gnosticism of the time of Hadrian, when the mystery-wisdom of the Orient had penetrated Hellenistic idealism and Pauline Christianity so

which were to be posed with regard to John could only be formulated after the concrete studies of the "school of comparative religion". Here a great impulse was provided by R. Reitzenstein, who first called attention to Egyptian Gnosis (Hermetism[88]) and then to Mandaeanism and the "Iranian redemption mystery" (of the "redeemed Redeemer").[89] He was followed in turn by R. Bultmann, who recognized early "the significance of the newly discovered Mandaean and Manichean texts for the understanding of John."[90] But there was also a movement in the contrary sense, which stressed how deeply rooted John was in Palestinian Judaism.[91] Since then, the question has never been allowed to rest, and the discussion about the "historical religious background" to John, stimulated by the discovery of important new texts, is continued vigorously to the present day (see above, ch. vii).

Instead of naming the many modern commentaries, we shall try to depict some characteristic tendencies in modern exegesis.

4. Tendencies in present-day exegesis

Present-day interpretation of John, at least in Germany, is still marked by the impression made by the mighty work of R. Bultmann,[92] which was in fact a turning-point. Though in many ways it gathers up and carries on the heritage of previous research, especially on the history of religions and source-criticism, it is, nonetheless, from the hermeneutic and systematic point of view, a daring theological advance which is new and astonishing in the history of exegesis. It is easy to trace the links which bind it to critical historical research. W. Bauer preceded him (stimulated, however, by Bultmann's writings) in adducing and evaluating the Gnostic sources, especially the Mandaean literature;[93] and Bultmann's complicated distribution of sources arouses in fact a sense of uneasiness which has been nourished by long and unhappy experience in this field, where he has found few followers, except his pupil H. Becker. With its richness of comparative material and its discussion of many individual points of

---

thoroughly that this syncretistic religion was as attractive as it was dangerous for the Churches".

[88] Reitzenstein, *Poimandres.*

[89] Id., *Das Mandäische Buch des Herrn der Grösse und die Evangelienüberlieferung;* id., *Das iranische Erlösungsmysterium.*

[90] Bultmann, "Die Bedeutung der neuerschlossenen mandäischen und manichäischen Quellen für das Verständnis des Johannesevangeliums".

[91] See above, ch. vi, 1 (linguistic character) and vii; Neill, *Interpretation*, pp. 315–8.

[92] *Das Evangelium des Johannes.*

[93] Bauer, *Johannesevangelium*, pp. 3f.

controversy, including textual criticism, his commentary does indeed also represent a summa of the work done in critical research. But all this, highly as it is everywhere prized, is not the real characteristic of his interpretation. The impact and the excitement come from his propounding the Johannine kerygma in terms of an existential theology, from his displaying it consistently as the call of the Redeemer whereby man is faced with decision here and now, as, according to Bultmann, it was intended by the evangelist. The assertions are clad in the language of myth (that of the "heavenly envoy", that of the "Son of Man" who came down from heaven, etc.), which is to be explained by the use of a source consisting of "Gnostic revelation discourses". But they are really concerned with the summons which since that event is always and ultimately valid, and reaches each man in the preaching of the Gospel, calling on him to question his previous understanding of existence and gain a new one.

This "existential" interpretation of Bultmann appears in all desirable clarity as early as his exposition of the prologue. It is enough to quote some sentences: "For just as 'life' implies the definitive self-understanding which allows of no more questions, no more riddles, so too the 'light' which man yearns for as this definitive illumination implies freedom from death, the fate which makes existence simply unintelligible. But the more consistently the φῶς is considered as an eschatological good, the more strongly the conviction is formed that the definitive illumination of existence does not lie within the potentialities of man, but can only be a divine gift. Hence φῶς takes on the meaning of revelation. And if a revealer is spoken of, he can be designated as the 'light' or as bringer of light. In John, Jesus is the light in this eschatological sense, as the revealer who bestows on men the understanding of themselves in which they have 'life'" (on 1:4; pp. 24f.). "The terms are those of *mythology*. Just as antiquity and the East told of gods and divine beings who appeared in human form, so too the Gnostic myth of the redeemer, of which the main element in fact is that a divine being, the son of the most high, took on human form, clothed himself in flesh and blood, in order to bring revelation and salvation. This is the mythology in which the notion of revelation is expressed; it means, 1) that revelation is an event from the beyond, 2) that this event, if it is to mean anything to man, must take place in the human sphere. And in fact: man knows what revelation *means*, just as well as he knows what light means, just as well as he can speak of the bread or the water of life. That is why the evangelist can take over the mythological language of Gnosis. In his *concept* of revelation man has foreknowledge of revelation, which consists of a questioning knowledge of his own situation. In such foreknowledge he does not at all possess revelation—the ἀληθινόν; indeed, his foreknowledge can be his ruin, if he tries to derive from it the criteria by which he judges how God must meet him, how revelation is to become a reality. For it becomes reality only as incomprehensible event . . . The event of revelation is questionable, scandalous. This is precisely what is meant by ὁ λόγος σὰρξ ἐγένετο" (on 1:14; pp. 38f.).

This theology is extracted from the Gospel by means of a conscious hermeneutical principle, and pervades the whole commentary. Its implications were not perhaps recognized at once, till Bultmann's lecture "New Testament and Mythology" opened people's eyes and started the avalanche. It was clear that Bultmann's programme of demythologizing had been carried out in the commentary on John. And still more, it was also clear that he saw in the fourth evangelist the supreme example of a process of demythologizing which had already begun in the N.T. itself, by which the old "dramatic" eschatology was eliminated in favour of the true "eschatology" in terms of the historical existence of man, and that he wished to disentangle the authentic and perpetually valid message from the trappings of a language of an older day. Thus Bultmann's interpretation of John stands or falls with his passionately contested theology (which cannot be discussed here[94]). Though the material from the history of religions and the detailed interpretation (analysis of the text, philological explanation, significance of the context, etc.) retain their value, Bultmann's real intention is missed—and, to his mind, the true interpretation—if this theological significance is not also grasped, if this claim of the text on the hearer is not recognized. This procedure takes exegesis beyond its task of historical criticism and analysis of text and directs its effort towards theology, as Bultmann has stated even more clearly in his *Theology of the New Testament*, especially in the Epilogue.[95]

Another interpretation, independent and distinctive, is to be found in the works of the English writers E. C. Hoskyns and C. H. Dodd. Anglican exegesis of John has a tradition of its own to which it has been faithful to the present day.[96] In the last century the commentary of B. F. Westcott, rich in theological content, marked an epoch.[97] Westcott, an exponent of the conservative view as regards authorship, was thoroughly scholarly, discussed the problems of the text and, though retaining the usual "word by word" method of English scholarship, was also alert to the Johannine theology, taking up once more the patristic exegesis and seeking for new insights by close attention to the text (cf., e.g., his commentary on Jn 14:28b with excursus, pp. 213 ff.). The same tendency is pursued in the commentary which E. C. Hoskyns worked on for many years, and which was published only after his death.[98] Many problems are seen more clearly, as for instance the relation of John to history;[99] certain theological aspects, especially the Christological and soteriological, are developed

---

[94] Bultmann's theology and his notion of Johannine eschatology have been examined in many books; on his commentary on John, see Blank, *Krisis*.

[95] Bultmann, *Theologie*, pp. 349–439; see also "Epilegomena", pp. 577–91; E. T.: vol. II, pp. 3–92 and 237–51.

[96] See Howard, *Fourth Gospel*, pp. 19–52, 243–67 (by the editor, Barrett); Schnackenburg, "Neuere englische Literatur zum Johannesevangelium".

[97] *The Gospel according to St. John*.

[98] *The Fourth Gospel*.

[99] See the chapter of the introduction, pp. 107-28, written by the editor Davey on the basis of notes left by the author.

positively; the O.T. and Jewish traditions behind John are assessed and emphasized; but no attention is paid to the "Gnostic" background. The problems of comparative religion were first taken up by C. H. Dodd, whose work is not precisely a commentary, but throws great light on the Gospel.[100] He avoids all one-sided emphasis, sees the evangelist as linked by many ties to the spiritual milieu, with a certain preference for the Hermetic literature, leans towards a Platonizing view, but succeeds impressively in bringing out the "leading ideas" and the main lines of the structure of the Gospel. English scholars do not care much for dissecting the Gospel by means of literary criticism. The two-volume commentary of Archbishop J. H. Bernard in the series "The International Critical Commentary on the Holy Scriptures" (1928) made some concessions ("displacement of pages"). But a commentary published after the work of Bultmann, that of C. K. Barrett (1955), attractively balanced in its judgments, simply notes such efforts without according them much attention; so too the "Gnostic" thesis. Finally, many shorter commentaries published in England and America, often by noted theologians, show how great the interest is in a theological interpretation.

German Protestants, who were formerly also represented by important "conservative" commentaries (T. Zahn, A. Schlatter; F. Büchsel for wider circles), have fallen rather silent, apart from R. Bultmann. Only the not very copious commentary of H. Strathmann (*NT Deutsch*, first published 1951) deserves mention, on account of its very definite orientation. He finds that John is "nothing but preacher and interpreter"; "the historical has become for him a mere means of presentation by which he tries to give vivid and plastic form to his knowledge of the essential Christ, which he has gained from personal contact and from long and constantly developing recollection, meditation and inner experience" (p. 5). This is true of both the miracles and the discourses: "the discourses uttered by the Johannine Christ are discourses of John about Christ" (p. 22). John accepts throughout "the principle of kerygmatic stylization"; "he shapes the material with the freedom of the artist, to make it completely subservient to this task" (p. 23). There is an element of truth in this ("John does not pay homage to historicism in his presentation", p. 22), but it is pushed too far, and the proper value is not accorded to all the data of the Gospel. Above all Strathmann seems to have failed to grasp the fact that the author was, after all, intent on writing a "Gospel" (see above, ch. i). But this new type of "symbolical" interpretation of the fourth Gospel, treating it as Christology crystallized into the form of history, seems to be a widespread tendency.

---

[100] *The Interpretation of the Fourth Gospel.*

This brings us to the various forms which symbolical explanation has taken. It cannot be doubted that many levels of thought lie under the surface of the Johannine language and presentation. They were intended by the evangelist, who gave hints of them to the believing and attentive reader. But the question is where exactly this well-known "symbolism" of John is to be taken into account and how strongly the interpretation is to be directed towards it. It is now generally agreed that we cannot return to the allegorization which often flourished so luxuriantly in patristic and medieval times; still, various tendencies may be seen to be at work as scholars try to depict the deeper levels of thought and present them as the result of objective exegesis, faithful to the mind of the evangelist. One need only think of "the disciple whom Jesus loved", whom even "critically-minded" scholars readily take to be a symbolic figure—which is, however, explained in very different ways. There is even an inclination to go further and take all the "persons" of the Gospel as "types".[101] The numbers given in the Gospel are, of course, fair game. Must there not be a deeper meaning behind all the numbers, and not just the mysterious hundred and fifty-three big fishes of 21:11? It has been suggested that if the days given in 1:19–2:11 are counted, they make up a "week", which corresponds to the week of creation and leads up deliberately to the day of the miracle of the wine. And since this takes place on the "third day", it is said to be an allusion to the resurrection of Jesus.[102] But is this not rather a thought transferred to the text than indicated by it? This inclination to discover symbolic connections goes right through the ranks of the exegetes, independently of their confessional allegiance. On the basis of an exegesis tied to the literal sense, soundness of method demands that the evangelist may be supposed to have profounder levels of thought and interest only where such intentions can be proved from the text, from parallels, or from the procedure of the evangelist.

A special form of this interpretation is to be found in the sacramental symbolism said to be contained in the Gospel. This line of approach was opened up by O. Cullmann,[103] taken up by Catholics like B. Vawter and P. Niewalda, and retained by L. Bouyer in his commentary as a guiding line.[104] Since it is hard to deny that the evangelist has a certain interest in the cult and the sacraments, this question becomes a test-case for recognizing allusions of the evangelist, as for instance at the miracle of the wine, at the mention of the pool of Bethesda and Siloam, at the washing

---

[101] See Kraft, "Die Personen des Johannesevangeliums".

[102] See Boismard, *Du baptême à Cana*, who marks off each day; on the symbolism of the seventh day, esp. p. 136.

[103] Cullmann, *Urchristentum und Gottesdienst*, E. T.: *Early Christian Worship*.

[104] Vawter, "The Johannine Sacramentary"; Niewalda, *Sakramentssymbolik im Johannesevangelium?* Bouyer, *Le quatrième Évangile*, p. 30.

of the feet, etc. A new type of effort to explain the form and structure of John on "cultic" grounds is the thesis put forward by A. Guilding, which has evidently made an impression in England. It is that John follows the old Jewish "lectionary system", that is, a certain order of the pericopes as read at divine worship,[105] but again, such investigation of "patterns" can only be carried out with great caution and circumspection. Another field of research, for Catholic writers this time, are the two scenes where Mary the mother of the Lord appears, first at the beginning of Jesus's ministry at Cana and then at the end, under the Cross (19:26f.); does the Evangelist here intend to make deeper "Mariological" statements or at least provide the basis for them?[106] Here too one should aim at soberness and circumspection, even though it seems to be a "minimizing" exegesis. But if we wish to avoid the errors of the past, the exegete intent on the literal sense will prefer to wring "too little" rather than "too much" out of the text.

In this connection we must mention another tendency in interpretation which has also gained a certain popularity. This is the question of typology. There are in fact certain indications in John that the evangelist himself favoured such perspectives where O.T. and N.T. are compared and contrasted, either in longer sections (cf. ch. 6: Moses, the manna) or in shorter logia (cf. 1:51; 3:14; 7:37f.; 19:36). But how strongly is this typological thinking at work? The Swedish scholar H. Sahlin tried to trace a continuous Exodus typology in John.[107] This did violence to the text and found, therefore, little support. Some Catholic exegetes, especially from Spanish-speaking countries, go very far indeed in the search for typology. It may be conceded that there is a memory of the events of Sinai behind the verses of the prologue, 1:14–18, but one will have misgivings when a whole theology of the "New Covenant" is deduced from it.[108]

Finally, one may note that these and other exegetes are striving to depict more clearly the "scriptural background", to show the influence of the O.T. and the "great traditions of Israel". Good work has been done in this line by F.-M. Braun in his last great work.[109] But even in these endeavours some scholars seem to use too powerful lenses, so that one can doubt whether the evangelist really thought of what present-day exegesis finds in the text.[110] The effort at a deeper understanding of Johannine

---

105 Guilding, *The Fourth Gospel and Jewish Worship.*

106 See for instance Braun, *La Mère des Fidèles;* Gaechter, *Maria im Erdenleben;* Galot, *Marie dans l'Évangile;* Feuillet, "L'Heure de Jésus et le Signe de Cana".

107 Sahlin, *Typologie.* 108 See Boismard, *Prologue*, pp. 165–75.

109 Braun, *Jean le Théologien*, vol. II.

110 Boismard, for instance, holds that Mary's words in 2:5 ("Do whatever he tells you") echo Pharaoh's words to the Egyptians, Gen 41:55 (Du baptême à Cana, p. 154); Feuillet,

theology, which is being carried on in a growing number of weighty monographs as well as in commentaries, can only be welcomed. But one must be careful of a theological over-evaluation which cannot be justified by the text of John itself.

This enumeration of some tendencies at work in exegesis today, and the critical comments on them, also serve to indicate the way which the present commentary tries to follow. It tries to keep strictly to the text, advancing cautiously and soberly rather than boldly and unwarily. It aims at discovering the theological content, though without neglecting the many individual problems which present themselves. Only an exegesis intent on the literal sense, investigating the text and listening carefully to it, can also bring out the deeper treasures which are contained within the fourth Gospel.

"Les adieux du Christ à sa Mère", using typological symbolism and "allusive" theology (e.g. γύναι a reminder of Gen 3:15) finds no fewer than six deeper theological perspectives.

COMMENTARY

CHAPTER I

The Prologue

Before we enter upon the exegesis of the famous "prologue", with its many exegetical and theological problems,[1] we must first consider why this section is pre-fixed to the Gospel narrative proper, what is its relation to it, what is its point and what theological background comes to light in it.

1. Prologue and Gospel

The "prologue", as the section Jn 1:1–18 is ordinarily called, is not a literary preface like Lk 1:1–4. It is also somewhat different from the proem of 1 Jn 1:1–4 (see *ad loc.*), in spite of its many contacts with it in language and theology. In its present form, it is indissolubly linked with the Gospel itself, and it only remains to ask what is its point as the opening section. Should it be read apart from the body of the Gospel as a section with its own significance, or should it be taken as intrinsically connected with the Gospel? Is it a sort of overture which precedes the Gospel, to prepare for and intone the thought, an introduction to Christ or a hymn of praise, after which the Gospel narrative proper begins, or is it to be read as an integral part of the Gospel, as the "beginning" of the message—because the evangelist does not wish to begin only with the public ministry of Jesus or even with his birth, but deliberately takes the existence and the way of the Redeemer back to the beginning before creation, to his eternal being "with God"? From the literary point of view the question may also be put this way: was the "prologue" added subsequently, as a fitting "introduction", to a fully thought out Gospel, or had it always been foreseen as part of the structure of the Gospel?[2]

---

[1] The most important literature is mentioned below. We cannot discuss the new interpretation put forward by Lamarche, "Le Prologue de Jean", which appeared after this volume was finished.

[2] The alternative was put as early as von Harnack, "Über das Verhältnis des Prologs des

Reasons can be adduced for both views. Let us take the first case, that the prologue is only more or less loosely linked with the Gospel. Apart from verses 1:6–8 (and 15), there is no direct connection with what follows (as, for instance, through a time of youth and hiddenness). The pre-existence and incarnation of the Logos (at least in this or similar form) is scarcely reflected or recapitulated in the Gospel (apart from 1:30; 8:58; 17:5). The "concluding remarks" of 20:30f. do not refer to them, and seem to restrict the Gospel to the time of Jesus's work in the world (the time of the "signs"). It has, therefore, been suggested that the Gospel originally began with the verses about John the Baptist (vv. 6ff.), which are continued in 1:19ff., and that the rest of the prologue is a later accretion to the Gospel from another pen.[3] But 1:6–8 are closely linked to the surrounding verses (testimony to the "light"),[4] while the thought and even the style (in many verses) are closely akin to that of the evangelist. On the whole, the prologue is more than a summary of the thought of the Gospel (which is the form a "preface" usually takes when composed subsequently). But it is also different from a later meditation on the Gospel, or from an introduction meant for another milieu and another circle of readers.

There is also much in favour of the other view. When we compare Luke with Mark, we see that Luke provided his Gospel with a "history of the infancy". Matthew was led by other reasons, of a dogmatic and apologetical nature, to begin his Gospel with a genealogy and then narratives in support of the Davidic origin of Jesus.[5] It is, therefore, understandable that John should have been impelled by his image of Christ to pursue the "history" of Jesus back into his pre-existence, to transpose the "opening narrative" into the ultimate origins and to proclaim them in a confession

vierten Evangeliums zum ganzen Werk": "Does the Gospel begin where the prologue stops, or is the prologue as it were the essence of the Gospel signalled in advance?" (p. 191.) He decided that the prologue was meant to prepare Hellenistic readers for the Gospel (p. 230). Since then the answers vary; when one thinks of a hymn which the evangelist has worked into the prologue new possibilities ensue and solutions have become more nuanced; see the works mentioned below.

[3] So Robinson, "The Relation of the Prologue to the Gospel of St. John", esp. p. 127.

[4] Hirsch, *Studien*, p. 45, put vv. 6–8 immediately before v. 19 in his "original Gospel", while keeping the prologue as such (without the "redactional" additions). He saw correctly that the Baptist narrative, as he had reconstructed it, presupposed the prologue with its affirmations about the Logos as "light". To explain the transposition of vv. 6–8 to their present place, he suggested that the redactor wished to ensure that 1:9–13 was not applied to the "Logos asarkos" *(ibid.)*. But what Hirsch attributes to the redactor may also be understood as the intention of the evangelist, if he was using an existing hymn to the Logos. Boismard, "Les traditions johanniques concernant le Baptiste", pp. 18 f. also considers vv. 6–8 as the introduction to vv. 19ff. in an earlier stage of the literary genesis.

[5] See Vögtle, "Die Genealogie Mt 1:2–16 und die matthäische Kindheitsgeschichte" (with the earlier literature).

of praise. If so, the prologue is not an afterthought, it has not been grafted on to the Gospel incidentally, so to speak. It is a considered theological composition, placed at the beginning for Christological reasons, and the "bracket" between the confession of faith in the prologue and the Gospel story of Jesus Christ is formed by the testimony of the Baptist, which is explicitly taken up (v. 15) and indeed taken into the hymnic "account" (vv. 6–8).

But perhaps there is a middle way, which does justice to these contrasting observations. Following the traditional form of the written Gospel, the author certainly wished to give an account of Jesus's work on earth, as he saw it in faith (20:30f.). But in keeping with his faith in Christ, he also wished to change the ordinary frame of reference and reveal to his readers from the very beginning the mystery of Jesus's origin (glimpses of which occur often enough in the Gospel). Such was his intention, but it was not easy to carry it out. He must have used—as we may assume for the moment without further proof (see below, 2)—a primitive Christian hymn which celebrated the pre-existence and incarnation of Christ, added his own comments and forged links between it and the Gospel narrative.

These links (the verses referring to John the Baptist) call for special attention. Verses 6–8 cannot be simply an apologetical interpolation, since v. 6 begins in the style of sacred narrative (cf. commentary). And v. 7 belongs to the same literary genre, an apologetical note occurring first at v. 8. An "outrunner" like 1:6f. is practically indispensable for the Gospel narrative which begins in 1:19. On the other hand, these verses cannot have been mechanically transplanted from, say, before 1:19 and put into the middle of the prologue, since both the "giving testimony to the light" (v. 7b) and the second ἵνα-clause with the intransitive πιστεύειν (v. 7c) presuppose the preceding verses of the prologue. We are, therefore, dealing with a deliberate piece of redaction which, as is also suggested by the presence of criteria of Johannine style, can be attributed only to the evangelist himself.[6] Even more obviously, the testimony of the Baptist (v. 15) given between the closely-knit verses 14–16 is an insertion. Its aim is probably apologetical (see commentary) as well as positively theological: the contemplation of the δόξα of the Logos incarnate remains possible even for later believers through the "testimony" of those who have experienced the event of his historical coming. And at this point the testimony of the Baptist is also valuable because it confirms the pre-

---

[6] Against Haenchen, "Probleme des johanneischen Prologs", esp. pp. 325–33, who thinks that the writer who added vv. 6–8, 12–13, 15 was perhaps "the same man who added ch. 21 to the Gospel" (p. 334). But why should not the evangelist himself have seen "the work of the incarnate described from v. 5 on" (p. 329) and have added "the testimony of John to that of the community"? Haenchen makes no use of stylistic criteria.

existence of the Logos, which had been proclaimed as a hymnic confession. The two passages which deal with the testimony of the Baptist are then taken up by καὶ αὕτη in v. 19, for the narrative then gives the testimony for the Messiahship of Jesus (vv. 20f., 27) and then repeats word for word the testimony to his pre-existence (v. 30), though the evangelist probably derives it from the words of the Baptist, v. 27 (see commentary). One can see that the prologue and the first section of the Gospel are inseparably linked by this procedure, which is clearly deliberate.

Finally, there is another important observation to be made on the way the prologue is orientated to the Gospel narrative which follows. Whether or not one considers that v. 18 is part of the "hymn", it leads precisely to the point where the Gospel can start with its message: the work of revelation done by the incarnate Logos. S. de Ausejo has correctly observed that all other primitive "hymns to Christ" contain the three modes of being of Christ (and three corresponding strophes): pre-existence, earthly life and exaltation, and tries to find them again in the hymn to Christ in the prologue.[7] But the return to the glory of heaven, the exaltation to the right hand of the Father, is not explicitly mentioned in the last part of the prologue, though it is presupposed (cf. v. 16), as it is throughout the Gospel. The prologue concludes with a pointed statement of the one historical (aorist) revelation brought by the unique Son of God.[8] Here we can recognize once more the Christological interest which made the evangelist put the prologue before the Gospel narrative proper: only the demonstration of the divine origin of the revealer can throw proper light on his unique significance for salvation, as it is later displayed in the words and works of the earthly Jesus. Hence the "prologue" has rather the character of a theological "opening narrative", the believer's telling of the "pre-history" which becomes the "history of Jesus" at the historical turning-point of the Incarnation.

2. Prologue and Logos-hymn

The conviction has prevailed in recent research that the prologue is based on a song or hymn which was taken up by the evangelist and used for the

[7] "Es un Himno a Cristo el Prólogo de San Juan?", esp. pp. 407f., 425f. He understands ὁ ὢν κτλ. in v. 18 of the sitting at the right hand of God and makes it still part of the hymn. But both the interpretation and the allocation are dubious (see *ad loc.*). The general reconstruction of the hymn as of three strophes, corresponding to the other Christological hymns (pp. 414ff.), with the division between the second and third strophe coming between v. 14b and 14c (before καὶ ἐθεασάμεθα) is not convincing.

[8] Boismard's effort in his essay "Dans le sein du Père" to understand the verse differently (see *ad loc.*) is hardly acceptable.

beginning of his Gospel. Discussion is confined to asking what verses belong to this poem, what was its original form, where it originated and what occasioned it.[9] Since the present writer has treated of the matter elsewhere,[10] there is no need to discuss all attempted reconstructions here and justify the standpoint here taken. We shall merely present some widely accepted findings and take up certain points with which previous discussion has been more strongly concerned. This will provide a basis for the commentary.

a) The main reasons for thinking that the prologue makes use of a Logos-hymn are as follows. (i) Literary criticism can point to poetical and rhythmical sentences, verses and perhaps strophes (though not exactly definable by metre, stress etc.)., and distinguish them from prose elements or additions, as in vv. 6–8, and also in 12 (in its entirety or perhaps only c), 13, 15, 17 (?). The "rhythm" of the hymn is, indeed, debatable. Some find a regular succession of groups of two or three lines,[11] others "free rhythms".[12] But the fact itself can hardly be doubted. (ii) The structure and the movement of thought, hence the content exegetically examined, also reveal breaks and sudden switches. These are again particularly clear in the two interpolations about John the Baptist (vv. 6–8, 15); but the difficulty and indefiniteness of v. 9, the pleonasms of vv. 12–13, and the unexpected nature of the last two verses (17–18), the impression they give of being attached loosely or merely by external association, reinforce the idea that a well-constructed and finished poem has been worked over and added to. (iii) Analysis of the style is also important. Using the methods of E. Schweizer and E. Ruckstuhl, one can note in several verses or portions of verses the absence of typical criteria of Johannine style, and their frequent presence elsewhere. These observations agree very well with the analysis of rhythm and content.[13] (iv) Analysis of the style is supported by observations on the terminology and concepts used in the re-discovered Logos-hymn. It is remarkable that the title of Logos is used only here (1:1, 14) and in the phrase ὁ λόγος τῆς ζωῆς in the proem of 1 Jn (see *ad loc.*). Other theological concepts confined to the prologue are the "dwelling" of the Logos ("in a tent")

---

[9] See Schaeder, "Der Mensch im Prolog des vierten Evangeliums"; Gaechter, "Strophen im Johannesevangelium", ZKT 60 (1936), pp. 99–120; Kahlefeld, *Der Hymnus vom Wort*, pp. 5–30; Green, "The Composition of St John's Prologue"; de Ausejo, "Es un Himno"; Schlier, "Im Anfang war das Wort"; Schnackenburg, "Logos-Hymnus und johanneischer Prolog"; Käsemann, "Aufbau und Anliegen"; Schulz, *Komposition*, pp. 7–69; Haenchen, "Probleme des Prologs".

[10] "Logos-Hymnus".

[11] So esp. Gaechter, "Strophen", and most others.

[12] So, emphatically, Haenchen, "Probleme des Prologs", pp. 308f., 333f.

[13] See Schnackenburg, "Logos-Hymnus", pp. 77–82.

among men (v. 14), his "fullness" and his communication of "grace" (v. 16)—very important theological expressions which are, however, missing from the characteristic vocabulary of the fourth evangelist. The meaning of οἱ ἴδιοι in the prologue (1:11) is different from that found later in the Gospel (13:1). The simplest explanation is that the evangelist took up a hymn whose theology and outlook was close to his own, and made this poem, once an independent entity, the opening of his Gospel.

b) The detailed reconstruction of the hymn depends to some extent on one's chosen methods and approaches. A purely rhythmical division (Gaechter) gives a different result from that which ensues when one looks for a structure of themes such as is found in other primitive hymns to Christ;[14] the balance may be swayed in a different direction when one also uses stylistic criteria or when one attends to the historical religious background.[15] A one-sided view can only be avoided, it seems, when all methods are combined. But to sift and assess the methods statistically according to the results reached by their various users, to try to make an approximate estimate of the original form of the Logos-hymn on the basis of a "multiplicity of approaches", as is done by S. Schulz,[16] is likewise problematical, since the statistics include uncertain results and the various methods have not all the same value. The decision will have to be personal, with the element of uncertainty noted. The solution here offered makes no other claims. The result to which the present writer earlier came in reconstructing the Logos-hymn was as follows:

1. (v. 1) Ἐν ἀρχῇ ἦν ὁ λόγος
καὶ ὁ λόγος ἦν πρὸς τὸν θεόν,
καὶ θεὸς ἦν ὁ λόγος.
(v. 3) πάντα δι' αὐτοῦ ἐγένετο
καὶ χωρὶς αὐτοῦ ἐγένετο
οὐδὲ ἕν, ὃ γέγονεν.

2. (v. 4) Ἐν αὐτῷ ζωὴ ἦν
καὶ ἡ ζωὴ ἦν τὸ φῶς τῶν ἀνθρώπων

(v. 9) Ἦν τὸ φῶς τὸ ἀληθινόν,
ὃ φωτίζει πάντα ἄνθρωπον.

3. (v. 10) Ἐν τῷ κόσμῳ ἦν
καὶ ὁ κόσμος αὐτὸν οὐκ ἔγνω.
(v. 11) Εἰς τὰ ἴδια ἦλθεν
καὶ οἱ ἴδιοι αὐτὸν οὐ παρέλαβον.

4. (v. 14) καὶ ὁ λόγος σὰρξ ἐγένετο
καὶ ἐσκήνωσεν ἐν ἡμῖν,
πλήρης χάριτος καὶ ἀληθείας.
(v. 16) Ὅτι (Καὶ) ἐκ τοῦ πληρώματος αὐτοῦ
ἡμεῖς πάντες ἐλάβομεν
καὶ χάριν ἀντὶ χάριτος.

The cultic hymn thus reconstructed consists of four strophes. The first proclaims the primordial and divine being of the Logos and his role in

[14] So de Ausejo, "Es un Himno", in keeping with the three modes of being of Christ, before the incarnation, in his earthly work and after his exaltation.

[15] See esp. Bultmann, "Der religionsgeschichtliche Hintergrund des Prologs"; id., *Das Evangelium des Johannes*, pp. 1–5.

[16] *Komposition und Herkunft*, pp. 10–28 (literary analysis); pp. 28–56 (religious background).

creation, the second describes his significance for the world of men (life and light), the third laments the rejection of his work in humanity before the Incarnation, and the fourth finally praises the joyful event of the Incarnation which brings salvation to those who believe. Whatever variations may be made in dividing and defining the strophes, the general movement of thought can hardly be disputed. According to the hypothesis which we then put forward, the procedure used by the evangelist as he adapted this hymn to his purposes at the beginning of the Gospel was that he expounded it more strictly in terms of the Incarnation and of the reception of the Logos among men (belief and unbelief).

In the light of the present structure of the prologue, one should rather distinguish three sections: vv. 1–5, the pre-existent being of the Logos; vv. 6–13, the coming of the Logos to the world of men, the Incarnation being already hinted at, and his incomprehensible rejection; vv. 14–16 or 18, the event of the Incarnation and its meaning for the salvation of believers. The main theological change, therefore, is that the evangelist always has the incarnate Logos in mind, and this new perspective, introduced for the sake of the Gospel, is attained by the insertion of vv. 6–8. The introduction of John the Baptist here, in narrative style, already suggests the time of the historical coming of Christ, the Incarnation of the Logos, which is then resoundingly proclaimed in v. 14. This seems also to be the point of the phrase ἐρχόμενον εἰς τὸν κόσμον in v. 9, which was attributed, therefore, to the evangelist. So too, on grounds of style and content, were v. 2, as a repetition and reinforcement of v. 1b (cf. also v. 10b with v. 3), v. 5 with the favourite Johannine term ἡ σκοτία, the remarkable present of φαίνει and the contrast of light and darkness, and also the explanatory remarks of vv. 12–13—the evangelist being preoccupied and oppressed by the unbelief which greeted the coming of the "light" into the world (cf. 3:19ff.; 9:39; 12:46). It seemed that the Logos-hymn ended with v. 16; the two following verses were considered as further reflection on the part of the evangelist and a theological confession. The middle part of v. 14 (καὶ ἐθεασάμεθα... πατρός), very much in the style and thought of John, seemed likewise to be an addition of the evangelist, whose interest in preaching led him to insert it here. It is, of course, also possible to maintain that some of these verses (especially vv. 5,[17] 14c–d, 17) belonged to the original hymn. This is not of decisive importance, as long as one admits in principle that an independent Logos-hymn has been transformed into the introduction to the Gospel.

This is the view which we should still maintain, adding only some remarks apropos of questions then discussed. Was a primitive Christian

[17] See Kahlefeld, Schlier ("Im Anfang", p. 279) and others; according to the statistical method of Schulz, most scholars take vv. 1–5 as part of the original prologue (*Komposition*, p. 27).

hymn ever concerned so closely with the time before the Incarnation as is presupposed here? Apart from some faint traces (cf. 1 Cor 10:4) no proofs can be adduced. But it must not be forgotten that this Logos-hymn has its own special character which marks it off from others which have been preserved (cf. 1 Tim 3:16) or deduced (Phil 2:6–11; Col 1:15–20; Heb 1:2f.). The stage consisting of Christ's exaltation is not described—or was it perhaps contained in another strophe which the evangelist has omitted? But above all, nowhere else do we read of the rejection of the Redeemer by the world (contrast 1 Tim 3:16c). On this point the Logos-hymn has something special to say, due no doubt to the fact that it had its own particular setting in real life and that it was conceived along the lines of Wisdom speculation. It is a recurrent theme in the Wisdom literature that Wisdom met with rejection when it came among men. In the same literature, which forms the main background of the Logos-hymn (see next section), the pre-existence of Wisdom and its role in creation are also strongly emphasized. Hence it is quite possible and intelligible that the Christian community should also give more place to the activity of the pre-existent Logos who takes the place of Wisdom. The author of the hymn may also have had the Incarnation in mind. But then the statements about the activity (and rejection) of the pre-existent Logos take on a special value: after the failure of all redemptive efforts among pre-Christian mankind—in the concrete, among Israel—the Incarnation appears as the new and undreamt-of act of grace, as is also brought out by the paradoxical formulation, that the Logos became σάρξ. "In spite of this rejection, the Logos did not give up. He has now taken the supreme step, the last step still possible. To gain entry among men, he himself became man."[18] Hence it is quite possible that the original hymn envisaged in strophes 2 and 3 the activity of the λόγος ἄσαρκος and that it was only the evangelist who saw everything in the perspective of the λόγος ἔνσαρκος, because in his Gospel all the interest is centred on the acceptance or rejection of the incarnate Son of God, on faith or refusal with regard to Jesus Christ.

M.-É. Boismard's book on the prologue contains many profound insights and blazes new trails. Some ideas the exegete will find too daring, but it is well worth considering whether the events of Sinai do not form the background of verses 14–18, as Boismard suggests. If, up to this point, the author of the hymn drew his inspiration for the Logos from "Wisdom", why should he not have used another theological "pattern" for the event of the Incarnation, to which the Wisdom literature did not offer a clear analogy? The "dwelling" of Yahweh among his people in the holy tent, the revelation given to Moses, the bestowal of grace by the

---

[18] Haenchen, "Probleme des Prologs", p. 322.

God of the covenant, "abounding in steadfast love and faithfulness" (Exod 34:6, Hebrew; cf. πλήρης χάριτος καὶ ἀληθείας, Jn 1:14), the "sight" of Yahweh accorded to Moses and the elders: all this can form the scriptural background of Jn 1:14–18. Is it not then better to continue the last strophe of the hymn to v. 18, that is, take vv. 17–18 as part of the hymn and not the work of the evangelist? However, one must also consider the possibility that the evangelist recognized clearly the allusions to Sinai in the hymn (v. 14 ἐσκήνωσεν, πλήρης . . .), pondered them further on his own account and added two comments (v. 17 and v. 18), including the phrase χάριτος καὶ ἀληθείας (v. 17). This solution should be preferred, because the hymn made *positive* (typological) use of these theological concepts, while v. 17 announces a sort of antithesis, though not a total one; and v. 18 is still more sharply polemical. Since the hymn is written in the style of sacred poetry for well-informed believers, it could very well have spoken of the Logos up to this point in a veiled, anonymous way, and only have mentioned his name explicitly at the end. But the sharpness of the contrast with Moses does not seem to tell very much in favour of v. 17 as the conclusion of the hymn, and the mention of "Jesus Christ" could also be easily ascribed to the evangelist (cf. 17:3).[19] If v. 17 still has some claim to be considered part of the Logos-hymn, the same can hardly be said of v. 18, which begins without any link with the foregoing—especially as the same polemical thought occurs twice more in the Gospel (5:37; 6:46); v. 18b also, from style and content, could very well be a composition of the evangelist.

We keep, therefore, to the hypothesis which we put forward earlier. It must be the task of the actual exegesis to show how far the supposition of this Logos-hymn is justified.

3. Origin and background of the hymn to the Logos

As early as 1923 R. Bultmann put forward the thesis that the Logos-hymn was originally a Gnostic composition, from Baptist circles, which the fourth evangelist appropriated to sing the praises of his Christ.[20] The basic notion of a Gnostic hymn was taken up by H. H. Schaeder, who

[19] The two ὅτι at the start of v. 16 and v. 17 do not prove that v. 17 must belong to the hymn as well as v. 16. On the contrary, they are a pointer to the work of the evangelist. The hymn contains no other particles but moves in parataxis joined by "ands". Possibly v. 16 also began with "and" originally (so many MSS), which the evangelist changed into ὅτι on account of the insertion of v. 15. As the continuation of v. 14 "and" is, at any rate, more suitable than ὅτι. See the commentary. Haenchen, "Probleme des Prologs" takes a particularly personal view of v. 17 (pp. 323f.).

[20] See "Der religionsgeschichtliche Hintergrund".

gave, however, a different reconstruction and interpretation of it. Following C. F. Burney, he affirmed that the original was in Aramaic, and suggested that it had been a hymn to Enosh (the god "Man").[21] The statement of v. 6a, according to Schaeder ("Enosh was sent by God"), was not merely part of the original hymn but the key to its interpretation. But this is the fatal weakness of the hypothesis, quite apart from the questionableness of the re-translation back into Aramaic. The statement can be understood of John the Baptist without any difficulty, and the secondary nature of vv. 6–8 can hardly be doubted. Bultmann's thesis of a "hymn from Gnostic Baptist circles", which he retained in his commentary on John, has remained influential. According to S. Schulz, "in the field of comparative religion, the origin of the constitutive elements of the prologue of John is to be sought in the Hellenistic Gnostic use of the term Logos, in the Wisdom tradition of late Hellenistic Judaism and in the Old Testament concept of theophany".[22] He follows Schaeder, Bultmann and Stauffer in maintaining that the hymn actually originated in a pre-Christian Baptist group.[23]

But there are considerable difficulties against this view, above all the affirmation of the Incarnation in Jn 1:14, which can hardly be understood except as a strictly original Christian confession. This made Bultmann hesitate in his first work; he envisaged the possibility "that a source was used only in vv. 1–13 and the evangelist's own work began in v. 14", but decided in favour of the view that the whole prologue 1:1–18 (except the additions) was taken over from a Baptist composition.[24] In fact, to excise the part beginning with v. 14 would be to deprive the hymn of its triumphant conclusion; but if it is part of the original Logos-hymn, it is much more probable that the whole originated in Christian circles. This consideration has impressed critical scholars like E. Haenchen[25] and E. Käsemann, who writes: "The pre-Christian character of the hymn is more than problematical, an Aramaic original incredible, the supposed hymn to the Baptist a pure hypothesis."[26] Since it can be shown that

[21] "Der Mensch im Prolog", with reconstruction of the hymn and translation back into Aramaic, pp. 339ff.

[22] *Komposition und Herkunft*, p. 51; cf. pp. 56f.

[23] *Ibid.*, pp. 66f.

[24] "Der religionsgeschichtliche Hintergrund", pp. 24 and 26.

[25] "Probleme", p. 334. He sees three stages of development; originally a pagan myth full of lament for this wayward world which has no place for Wisdom, then a Jewish hymn to the Torah or Wisdom, which found a resting-place in Israel, and finally a Christian hymn which gave the Logos (= Wisdom) a new goal: the Logos became man and found a community of believers.

[26] "Aufbau und Anliegen", p. 86. Surprisingly, he ends the basic hymn at v. 13 (or v. 12, since v. 13 is said to be a comment) and ascribes vv. 14–18 to the evangelist (p. 97); but he understands vv. 5–13 of the "historical epiphany of the revealer" (i.e. the incarnate Logos) and thinks that it was never meant to refer to anything else (p. 86).

similar hymns to Christ existed in the primitive Church (see above and cf. Eph 5:19), there is no real objection to the supposition of a genuinely Christian hymn to the Logos. On the other hand, it is problematical in the extreme that the disciples of John (in competition with Christians) should have applied the Gnostic myth of the heavenly envoy to their master at an early date, and have considered the son of Zechariah as the pre-existent revealer and redeemer who became flesh.[27]

It may then be asked what Christian circles produced the Logos-hymn. They were certainly Christian "Hellenists", as is shown by the use of the title "Logos" without any qualification (see excursus i). They may be identified more closely as converts from Hellenistic Judaism, since there are strong echoes of the O.T. and speculations on Wisdom and the Torah (the events of Sinai, see above) from the same source. It is difficult to decide whether the author of the hymn also knew the Gnostic doctrine of salvation and countered it with a profession of faith in the incarnate Saviour of Christianity. As regards the evangelist, we left this possibility open (see Introduction, ch. vii, 3); as regards the hymn which he incorporated, the question is whether the use of the title "Logos" (instead of ἡ σοφία) and the affirmation of the Incarnation (as an anti-Gnostic interpretation) are enough to justify this supposition. The preference for the theology of the "Word" instead of that of "Wisdom" could be due to the notion of revelation; the choice of σάρξ for the Incarnation is at first sight rather normal, in view of 1 Tim 3:16a; cf. Rom 1:3; Heb 5:7; 10:20; 1 Pet 3:18. Nonetheless, in the Logos-hymn the word has a special emphasis. It does not contrast the earthly mode of being with the later "pneumatic" one, as is done in the older σάρξ—πνεῦμα Christology. All the emphasis is on the entry of the Logos into the realm of earth and matter, and hence we are in the atmosphere of the anti-Gnostic confessional formulae of 1 Jn 4:2 (cf. 5:6b; 2 Jn 7) or of the anti-docetic teaching of the epistles of Ignatius (*Smyrn.*, 3:1; 5:2; 7:1 etc.). One may suspect that the evangelist or the author of 1 John were not the first to have to challenge the perverted teaching of the Gnostics. The Christian community which produced the Logos-hymn may have already had to do so. But we cannot be certain.

The theological background of the hymn, however, is definitely determined by the Wisdom speculation of Hellenistic Judaism, though hardly to such an extent that the author drew directly on the model and structure supplied by the book of Sirach.[28] But he was constantly influenced by these texts. This is clear from the list of parallels given by S. Schulz[29] and will be demonstrated in the course of the commentary. This

---

[27] See Schnackenburg, "Johannesjünger".

[28] So Spicq, "Le Siracide et la structure littéraire du Prologue de S. Jean".

[29] *Komposition und Herkunft*, pp. 32–34.

also confirms the supposition that an authentic hymn from the Christian liturgy was taken over, since the other primitive Christian hymns to Christ (especially Col 1:15–20; Heb 1:2f.) also display the same influence. But the revelation on Sinai and the tent of the sanctuary, which we must also invoke for the affirmations of Jn 1:14 (cf. 17), also occur frequently in early Christian theology—as the background of the eschatological revelation in Jesus Christ (cf. 2 Cor 3), of the new covenant (cf. Heb 8:5; 9:19 ff.) and of the "dwelling" of God among his people (cf. Rev 21:3)—so that similar ideas, in a Christological dress, could also appear in a cultic hymn. By incorporating a community hymn, the fourth evangelist shows that he is tributary to the primitive Christian tradition, whose Christological insights he was to enrich and develop in his Gospel and his own theology.

1:1	Ἐν ἀρχῇ ἦν ὁ λόγος καὶ ὁ λόγος ἦν πρὸς τὸν θεόν καὶ θεὸς ἦν ὁ λόγος.	In the beginning was the Word, and the Word was with God, and the Word was God.

Three fundamental statements describe the pre-existing Logos (Word) in his eternal divine being. The phrase "in the beginning" contains no reflection on the concept and problem of time.[30] It is chosen deliberately with reference to Gen 1:1, since the Logos proclaimed by the hymn is the "Word" by which God created all things (v. 2). But this "Word" is more than the "utterance" of God at the dawn of creation. It is the personal "Word" which became "flesh" at a given time of history, Jesus Christ, whose existence is here traced back to before the world, to the divine eternity. So too the words "in the beginning" mean more than in the account of creation. The phrase does not mark the coming into existence of the created world. It expresses the being of the Logos as it was before the world. That which already existed "in the beginning" has precedence over all creation. The rabbis also taught that seven things "were created before the world";[31] but the Logos was not created, he simply "was", that is, he already existed, absolutely, timeless and eternal. It is a real, personal pre-existence (cf. 1 Jn 1:1; 2:13a), a thought only found with this clarity in the professions of faith in Christ pronounced by the Christian community (cf. excursus ii), of which the Johannine prologue is not the first instance, since there were earlier formulations of it in other hymns and Christological affirmations (Phil 2:6; Col 1:15; Heb 1:3).

---

[30] Philo, *De opif.*, 26, speaking of creation and time, says: "Time there was not before there was a world . . . It is either coeval with or born later than the world."

[31] *Pes.*, 54a (Billerbeck, vol. II, p. 353; Epstein, p. 265).

The ἦν expresses from the standpoint of the Christian believer what Christ said of himself 8:58 in the timeless present: "Before Abraham existed, I am."[32] "The words 'in the beginning' designate simply eternal and infinite being."[33] The prologue (or the Logos-hymn) is orientated from the start to the incarnate Logos and makes the unheard-of statement in praise of the Word made flesh that he already existed without a body of flesh "in the beginning", before the existence of creation. Vv. 1–3 are not a cosmological meditation put forward for its own sake, but the first strophe of a Christian hymn of praise to the Redeemer. This explains the definiteness with which the author speaks of the "Word" as a person: he simply "was", as a person exists in and of himself; he "was with God", as one person is with another; he "was God", which defines the being of the persons. The personal character of the Logos forms a definite contrast to the Wisdom speculation of Hellenistic Judaism, to the doctrine of the Logos in Philo and above all to Gnostic notions of creative powers proceeding from God and emanating from one another. By looking back to the beginning of creation, the evangelist is enabled to disclose the divine and eternal origin of the revealer and redeemer who was "with the Father" (cf. 17:5), and since he came "from above", could impart the full and authoritative truth of revelation and salvation (cf. 3:31 f.), out of his eternal knowledge and immediate vision (cf. 8:14). In this "pre-history" of the earthly Christ, his nature is revealed in his origin, and his authority in his nature.

Hence the second affirmation also speaks at once of the personal union of the Logos with God, which is what is meant by the statement, "and the Word was with God". The opening of 1 John, which renders freely the thought of the prologue, and may be read as the oldest commentary on it, states that "the eternal life (= the Logos of life) was with the Father (πρὸς τὸν πατέρα)" (v. 2), and that the faithful too are called through this Logos to "fellowship with the Father and his Son Jesus Christ". This strict union with the Father in thought, will and action, a total oneness (10:30; 17:10), is also proclaimed constantly by the incarnate Son of

[32] The ἦν is stressed by the Fathers, cf. Alexander of Alexandria in Theodoretus, *Hist. eccles.*, I, 4, 19 (Parmentier, p. 13); Athanasius, *Or. II c. Arian.* 58 (*PG* 26, col. 270); Cyril of Alexandria, *In Jo.*, I, 1 (*PG* 73, col. 25); Basil, *De Spir. sancto*, 14 (*PG* 32, col. 90); Theodore of Mopsuestia, *In Jo.*, I, 1 (Devreesse, pp. 307 ff. Gr. fragment 2); Augustine, *In Jo.*, I, 12 (*Corpus Christianorum*, p. 7).

[33] Chrysostom, *Hom. in Jo.*, II, 4 (*PG* 59, col. 34). The Fathers also used one meaning of ἀρχή to understand it as the principle from which the Logos is generated, e.g. Basil, *Hom.*, 23, 4 (*PG* 31, col. 597). This was applied to the Trinity, but meant a departure from the thought of the text. The Gnostics also used this meaning to make the Logos which proceeded from the First Principle become then the source of further emanations of aeons, cf. the Valentinians in Irenaeus, *Adv. haer.*, I, 1, 18 (Harvey, vol. I, pp. 75 ff.). Further details in Bultmann on Jn. 15:4.

God. The preposition πρός certainly does not here mean movement towards a goal, an immanent process of life in the godhead. It is, according to the usage of the Koine, the equivalent of παρὰ τῷ θεῷ.[34] When the earthly Jesus, in the high priestly prayer, looks back to the glory which he had "with the Father" before the existence of the cosmos (17:5), the same idea is expressed; the "glory" which he then possessed is his closeness to God, his communion in the divine life, which was given him by his Father's love (cf. 17:24). Thus the prologue affirms that the primordial, eternal being of the Logos (v. 1 a) is an existence which proceeds from God and his love, is filled with the life of God (cf. 5:26) and shares in his glory. The first statement receives thereby a fuller and more vivid content, though it remains a metaphorical expression, which says much more, however, than the comparable descriptions of the closeness of Wisdom to God and its presence at creation.[35] Wisdom (Sophia, *ḥokmâh*) is pictured as God's companion and partner in the creation of all things,[36] but the Logos is really there before creation, in personal fellowship with God, living in God and from God. The active partnership is also a personal union, and the proximity also implies reciprocal indwelling (cf. 14:11f., 20 etc.). The Logos is "with God", in terms of space, so to speak, when considered from the point of view of the distance between the world and God; he is "in God (in the Father)", when the union of the Son with the Father on earth is considered in its transcendent depth and closeness, which is always based on his pre-existence "with God". When the evangelist is passing from the prologue to the Gospel proper, he has a formula which comprises both aspects: "he who is in the bosom of the Father" (1:18).

The third statement about the pre-existent Logos forms the climax: "and the Word was God". It takes up the last word of v. 1 b ("God"), stresses it, and attributes godhead to the Logos. The θεός before the copula is predicate, but does not simply identify the Logos with the ὁ θεός mentioned just before. The Logos is God as truly as he with whom he exists in the closest union of being and life. Hence θεός is not a genus, but signifies the nature proper to God and the Logos in common. It is only the fullness of divine being which the Son receives from the Father's love which guarantees his absolute power as revealer and redeemer (cf. 3:35). Like the whole hymn to the Logos, this assertion is made in view of the

[34] See Mt 26:18; Mk 6:3; 9:19; 14:49; Lk 22:56; Acts 12:20; 1 Cor 16:6f.; 2 Cor 11:9; Gal 1:18; 4:18, 20; 1 Thess 3:4; 2 Thess 2:5; 3:1, 10. Funk, *Greek Grammar*, para. 239, 1; Zerwick, *Graecitas*, p. 74; see also the interchange of πρός τινα and πρός τινι in the papyri: Mayser, *Grammatik*, vol. II, 2, p. 371.

[35] Prov 8:27 συμπαρήμην αὐτῷ; 8:30 ἤμην παρ' αὐτῷ . . ἐν προσώπῳ αὐτοῦ.

[36] See van Imschoot, "Sagesse et l'Esprit dans l'Ancien Testament", esp. pp. 37–40; Ziener, *Die theologische Begriffssprache im Buche der Weisheit*, esp. pp. 109–13.

activity of the Logos in the world, his function of life and light for men (v. 4) and his giving of grace after the Incarnation (vv. 14,16); but his divine being is what makes this possible, and hence θεός does not merely designate a function.[37] The predicate θεός is in fact the beginning of a Christology which embraces function and being, though it never loses sight of its soteriological purpose (cf. 20:28, "*my* God"; 1 Jn 5:20, "the true God and eternal life").

Lofty epithets are also used of Wisdom: she is "a breath of the power of God, and a pure emanation of the glory of the Almighty; . . . the radiance of eternal light, a spotless mirror of the power of God and an image of his goodness" (Wis 7:25f.). But these sublime metaphors, on which N.T. Christology drew (cf. 2 Cor 4:4; Col 1:15; Heb 1:3), never became in the Wisdom literature such direct affirmations as we have in the Logos-hymn, which leaves the metaphorical behind to attribute divine being directly to the Logos. In the theology of late Judaism, the Torah is also called the "daughter of God", but this again is only figurative and metaphorical.[38] In Philo, the Logos is the second being after God,[39] even though "above all the world, and eldest and most all-embracing of created things".[40]

Philo gives the Logos divine attributes only in an improper sense, as he himself explains at one place,[41] and never in fact arrived at a clear determination of the relationship between God and the Logos.[42] Hence when he calls the Logos "divine", the meaning is not the same.[43] The Logos doctrine of the "Poimandres" is also different.[44] The Johannine prologue developes the statement "the Word was with God" into a confession of his godhead, that is, of his true divinity, to which correspond Thomas's profession of faith in the risen Lord at the end of the Gospel, and the attestation that Jesus Christ is "the true God and eternal life" at the end of 1 John (5:20).[45]

---

[37] Against Cullmann, *Christologie*, pp. 272f., 316f. 336; E. T.: pp. 265f., 306f., 330. Boismard, to whom Cullmann (p. 273, n. 2) appeals (and to Dupont), notes correctly that "the function which Christ fulfils is based on his nature, his being" *(Prologue*, p. 123*)*.

[38] *Midrash Rabbah, Song of Songs*, 8, 11, para. 2 (Freedman and Simon, pp. 320f.; Billerbeck, vol. II, pp. 355f.).

[39] *Leg. all.*, II, 86. [40] *Ibid.*, III, 175.

[41] *De somn.*, I, 228f.: the "chief Word of God" is called "God", without the article (on Gen 31:13 LXX); see also *De conf. linq.*, 146.

[42] See Bréhier, *Les idées philosophiques et religieuses de Philon d'Alexandrie*, pp. 98ff.

[43] *De opif.*, 20; 31; 146; *Leg. all.*, III, 171; *De sacr. Cain*, 66 etc.

[44] *C. Herm.*, I, 6: ὁ δὲ ἐκ Νοὸς φωτεινὸς Λόγος υἱὸς θεοῦ . . . τὸ ἐν σοὶ βλέπον καὶ ἀκοῦον, λόγος κυρίου, ὁ δὲ νοῦς πατὴρ θεός. The text is difficult and also the situation of the thought in the history of religion; see Nock and Festugière, n. 16 (p. 18); Dodd, *Interpretation*, pp. 39ff.: "λόγος here takes the place which in other dialogues is occupied by such mediating entities as αἰών, or the cosmic νοῦς, which is not cut off from the essence of God but evolved out of it like the light of the sun" (*C. Herm.*, XII, 1). On the relationship God—world in Hermetic Gnosis, see Festugière, *Révélation*, vol. II, pp. 55–71; on the cosmogony, *ibid.*, vol. IV, pp. 40–43. See also Haenchen, "Aufbau und Theologie des Poimandres", esp. pp. 158–61; Braun, "Hermétisme et Johannisme", esp. pp. 265f.

[45] On the antecedent of οὗτος (Jesus Christ), see Schnackenburg, *Letters of St John, ad loc.*; Cullmann, *Christologie*, p. 318; another view in Scheidweiler, "Paradoxie in der neutestamentlichen Christologie", pp. 263f.

1:2	οὗτος ἦν ἐν ἀρχῇ πρὸς τὸν θεόν	He was in the beginning with God.

Having defined the nature of the Logos in these terms, the evangelist returns to his opening statement. The οὗτος at the beginning of the sentence is a mark of his own style.[46] His intention is undoubtedly to underline the starting-point of the way of Jesus the Redeemer: he was with the Father (cf. 1 Jn 1:2), and came forth from the Father (8:42; 13:3; 16:27f., 30; 17:8), to return there after his work on earth (17:24). The eschatological envoy of God had his origin in God before all time, and this determines his nature, his dignity and his authority. This verse probably did not belong to the original Logos-hymn.

1:3	πάντα δι' αὐτοῦ ἐγένετο καὶ χωρὶς αὐτοῦ ἐγένετο οὐδὲ ἕν, ὃ γέγονεν.	All things were made through him, and without him was made nothing that was made.

The Logos-hymn is now taken up again. The Logos participates in creation. But no exact description of how he does so is given. Only the fact is stressed: "all things were made through him". The activity indicated by the preposition διά leaves several possible interpretations open. He could have been a helper charged by God and equipped with his creative power, a demiurge, or the exemplary cause, the prototype according to which the actual world was created in all its multiplicity, or finally the Creator himself through whose action "all things" came to be.[47] One is first of all reminded of the biblical account of creation, according to which God created the world by his word, a thought which is only given emphasis in some poetic passages of the O.T.[48] But this does not take us much further, because the Logos-hymn only starts with this and its affirmations about the personal and absolute nature of the Logos transcend any thing in the O.T. When Wisdom is described as sharing in creation as spectator and master workman (Prov 8:27–30; Wis 9:9), as counsellor (Wis 8:4), as artisan (Wis 8:6) and even as creator (Wis 7:12; cf. Prov 3:19; Ecclus 24:3), we are already in the realm of reflective thought, but it remains metaphorical. When the Fathers identify "Wisdom" with the Logos, they are in fact interpreting these assertions in the light of the Christian notion of the Logos.[49] Philo constantly uses the preposition διά of

[46] Cf. 1:7; 3:2; 4:47; 6:50, 58, 71; 7:40, 41; 9:8; 12:21; 21:24; also Schlatter, *Der Evangelist Johannes, ad loc.*

[47] On διά as indicating exemplary cause see the texts from Philo in the following notes; on its indicating the efficient cause see Funk, *Greek Grammar*, para. 223, 2; Mayser, *Grammatik*, vol. II, 2, pp. 421 ff.

[48] Ps 33:6, 9; 147:15–18; 148:5; Is 40:26; 48:3; Wis 9:1; Ecclus 42:15; 43:5, 10.

[49] Justin, *Dial.*, 129, 3; Athenagoras, *Supplic.*, 10, 3 (cf. 2); Clement of Alexandria, *Strom.*,

the activity of the Logos as demiurge, but understands the Logos as the instrumental cause used by God to fashion the material world.[50] The Logos in Philo is both the κόσμος νοητός in the Platonic sense of the ideal world of "forms" which was the pre-existent prototype of the visible world,[51] and the organ and instrument of the creation of the world.[52] Philo makes the Logos inferior to God and uses the notion to bridge the gulf between the pure spirituality of God and the material world. The Latin Fathers took up the notion of exemplary cause, but still described the Logos in terms of his relationship within the Trinity.[53] To interpret the διά of v. 3 correctly, we must take as our starting-point, as the Fathers did,[54] the other Christological assertions of primitive Christianity. The formula used by Paul in 1 Cor 8:6 is probably ancient; it makes a distinction between God the Father, *from* whom are all things (ἐξ οὗ τὰ πάντα) and the one Lord Jesus Christ, *through* whom are all things and we also (δι' οὗ τὰ πάντα καὶ ἡμεῖς δι'αὐτοῦ). But the title of κύριος, which expresses the divine dignity of the exalted Lord (cf. Phil 2:11 with 6), excludes the notion of a dependent instrumental cause. The difference in the prepositions merely indicates the different relationships in which we and the world stand to God and to Christ. They are different aspects in each case, and in Rom 11:36 even occur together in the praise of God himself (ἐξ αὐτοῦ καὶ δι' αὐτοῦ καὶ εἰς αὐτὸν τὰ πάντα). The hymn of Col 1:16 uses the same

---

VI, 16, para. 138 (Stählin, vol. II, p. 502); VII, 2, para. 7 (Stählin, vol. III, p. 7); Origen, *Comm. in Jo.*, I, 34 (Preuschen, p. 39); Cyprian, *Lib. testim.*, II, 1f. (Hartel, vol. III, pp. 62ff.) etc. Cf. Hudal, *Die religiösen und sittlichen Ideen des Spruchbuches*, pp. 108ff. (Patristic explanation of Prov 8:22; in the Arian controversy the meaning of ἔκτισεν played an important part).

[50] See *Spec. leg.*, I, 81: "And the image of God is the Word through whom the whole universe was framed (ἐδημιουργεῖτο)"; *Leg. all.*, III, 96: "But God's shadow is his Word, which he made use of like an instrument, and so made the world. But this shadow, and what we may describe as the representation, is the archetype for further creations." See also the following notes.

[51] *De opif.*, 20; 24; 139; *De sacrif. Cain*, 83; *De somn.* I, 75.

[52] In *De cherub.*, 125ff. Philo goes into this point. God is the first cause of the world (ὑφ' οὗ); the matter from which it was produced (ἐξ ὧν) is the four elements; the instrument by which they were formed (δι' οὗ) is the Logos. See also *De sacrif. Cain*, 8; *De immutabil.*, 57; *De fuga*, 95; *De somn.*, I, 241f. Here διά with genitive varies with the instrumenta dative.

[53] So in particular Augustine, cf. *In Jo.*, I, 17 (*Corpus Christianorum*, 10); *De Gen. ad litt.*, II, 12 (*PL* 34, cols. 267f.); V, 29ff. (*ibid.*, col. 331); *De vera relig.*, 66 (*ibid.*, *cols.* 151f.); *De trin.* IV, 3 (*PL* 42, col. 888); VI, 11 (*ibid.*, col. 931). In this last text, the second divine person is called "ars quaedam omnipotentis atque sapientis Dei, plena omnium rationum viventium incommutabilium". See Schmaus, *Die psychologische Trinitätslehre des hl. Augustinus*, pp. 356ff.; Perler, *Der Nous bei Platon und das Verbum bei Augustinus als vorbildliche Ursache der Welt*, esp. pp. 57ff.; 106ff.; Polman, *Het Woord Gods bij Augustinus*, pp. 14f., 25ff.

[54] Chrysostom, *Hom. in Jo.*, V (*PG* 59, cols. 55–58); Basil, *De Spir. Sancto*, 4, 10 (*PG* 32, cols. 73, 84).

prepositions (διά and εἰς) to praise Christ as cause and end of all things; only the preposition ἐκ is reserved for God the Father, since the notion of the origin of all being is attached to him alone. According to Heb 1:2, God created the aeons through his Son, and a series of scriptural quotations is adduced to prove the divine dignity of the Son, including Ps 101:26ff. (LXX) where the κύριος addressed to God is applied to Christ. The exordium of Hebrews, whose Christology is so closely allied to that of the prologue of John, is decisive in excluding all doubt that the Logos, who according to v. 1b (and 2) is most intimately united to God, is characterized in v. 3 as his active collaborator. "He (the evangelist) shows clearly that the words 'all things were made through him' were used not to denote service, but cooperation".[55] The Logos-hymn, like Heb 1:10ff., transfers God's creative activity to the pre-existing Christ, but the use of the concept of Logos safeguards the truth that God is the Creator, who called all things into being through his "Word".

The Jewish way of thinking and speaking in this verse is also illustrated by the Qumran texts, which contain comparable sayings. *1 QS*, 11:11, " ... and through his knowledge everything came to be. He establishes everything that is according to his plan, and without him nothing comes to pass"; *1 QH*, 10:2, "and without thy will nothing comes to pass"; *ibid.*, 10:9, "Without thee nothing is done, and nothing is known except through thy will". The similarity of these passages is only formal; God's creative activity is only implicit, the thought of his action in history or the history of salvation is paramount. His "knowledge" or "will" (or "good pleasure") are not hypostasized in any way. But the sharp, antithetical mode of expression ("all things"—"nothing") is comparable; in Jn 1:3 it is applied to the Logos.

"All things" were made by the Logos, all created things, and hence "the all" (though τὰ πάντα is not found in John). The affirmation cannot be restricted to the world of man. Humanity is envisaged only in v. 4, where the Logos as the (divine) fullness of life is said to be its "light". All realms of creation owe their existence to the Logos, as the negative repetition in v. 3b stresses still more emphatically. The πάντα has as its counterpart οὐδὲ ἕν,[56] which is unmistakably stressed; is it to be explained merely on rhetorical or poetical grounds? The distich undoubtedly intends to bring out the universal significance of the Logos: in the work of redemption he alone is the eschatological revealer and giver of life, and in the work of creation everything owes its existence to him. But we must also ask whether there may not also be polemical (anti-Gnostic) overtones. It is unlikely that the Logos-hymn envisages, like Col 1:16, speculation on the role of angels or aeons which cast doubt on the exclusive role of

[55] Theodore of Mopsuestia, *In Jo.*, 1, 3 (Devreesse, p. 312, Gk. frg. 3, cf. Vosté); cf. also Chrysostom, *Hom. in Jo.*, V, 2 (*PG* 59, col. 56).

[56] P[66] ℵ* D 1 1582 139 71 Theodot, sometimes Or and Euseb read οὐδέν. P[75] has οὐδὲ ἕν, which is probably the better text.

Christ. But there could be an attack on Gnostic views, which can be shown to be current in the second century, according to which the material world proceeded from an inferior principle, such as a demiurge.[57] Then the hymn, maintaining the universal role of the divine Logos in creation, would be defending indirectly the goodness of all created things.

There has been much discussion as to whether ὃ γέγονεν belongs to οὐδὲ ἕν (or οὐδέν), or is to be attached to the following (the beginning of v. 4). Historically, the second alternative is preferable. The Gnostics of the second century base their interpretation on the reading: "Et sine ipso factum est nihil. Quod factum est in ipso, vita erat."[58] And the full stop after "nihil" is found in many early Fathers, like Theophilus of Antioch, Clement of Alexandria, Origen, Tertullian and Irenaeus, and down to the Greek and Latin Fathers of the fourth century, even though they divide the phrase differently: "Quod factum est, in ipso vita erat."[59] As far as palaeography allows of a conclusion, the reading is also found in the manuscripts $P^{66\ 75}$ C* D L W G Θ,[60] in some Old Latin MSS (e a b q f ff^2) and in sy^c and sa. The first witness for the break between v. 3 and 4 is Adamantius (about 300).[61] Hence the "new" reading of the text was not first produced in the Arian controversy, though it became an important weapon in the debate. Chrysostom and Theodore of Mopsuestia also used it in the struggle against the Pneumatomachi.[62] It is quite possible that the early Fathers were influenced by the division of the text given by the Gnostics; in this case, the earliest reading need not be the original.[63]

---

[57] Heracleon, for instance, according to Origen, *Comm. in Jo.*, II, 14, interpreted the text to mean that the Logos left it to the Demiurge to be cause of the world's coming to be; the Logos was not the ἀφ' οὗ or the ὑφ' οὗ, but merely the δι'οὗ, that is, he had only the role of an intermediary; cf. v. Loewenich, *Das Johannes-Verständnis*, pp. 83f.; Haenchen, "Probleme des Prologs", p. 317; on the explanation see Janssens, "Héracléon", pp. 278ff.; on Gnostic interpretation in general, see Orbe, "*En los orígenes de la exégesis juanea, Joh 1-3*".

[58] The Valentinians explained ὃ γέγονεν ἐν αὐτῷ as an aeon called Ζωή, a syzygy of the Logos: Irenaeus, *Adv. haer.*, I, 1, 18 (Harvey, vol. I, p. 77); Clement of Alexandria, *Exc. ex Theod.*, 6, 4; for the Peratae, it was "Eve"; Hippolytus, *Ref.*, V, 16, 12–14 (Wendland, p. 113). The Naassenes explained it as the race of the "perfect men": Hippolytus, *Ref.*, V, 8, 5 (Wendland, pp. 89f.).

[59] See Zahn, *Johannes*, excursus i (pp. 708–11); de la Potterie, "De punctuatie en de exegese van Joh 1:3, 4 in de traditie"; Lamarche, "Le Prologue de Jean", pp. 514–23 (very copious material). On Jerome, see J. Mehlmann, "De mente S. Hieronymi circa divisionem versuum Joh. I: 35"; de la Potterie, "De interpunctione", pp. 193–99; H. Langkammer, "Die Zugehörigkeit des Satzteiles ὃ γέγονεν ἐν αὐτῷ in Joh. I: 3–4 bei Hieronymus".

[60] On P^{66}, where there is no stop, but where the first scribe omitted the ἐν before αὐτῷ, see Teeple and Walker, "Notes on the Plates in Papyrus Bodmer II"; de la Potterie, "Een nieuwe papyrus", p. 122 (the haplography— ἐν falling out because of the preceding γέγονεν —suggests that there was no break after γέγονεν). P^{75} has a stop after οὐδὲ ἕν.

[61] Adamantius IV, 15 (van de Sande Bakhuyzen, p. 172), discovered by Mehlmann, "A Note on John 1:3". But Alexander of Alexandria, in Theodoretus, *Hist. eccles.*, 1, 4 (Parmantier, p. 12) is to be omitted, since it is not the original reading.

[62] Chrysostom, *Hom.*, V, 2 (*PG* 59, col. 55); Theodore of Mopsuestia on 1:3 (Devreesse, pp. 312f., Gr. frg. 4).

[63] So too Haenchen, "Probleme des Prologs", pp. 319f.

Grammatically, neither of the ways of linking ὃ γέγονεν with its context gives good Greek. Attached to οὐδὲ ἕν it should rather be ὧν γέγονεν (or, after οὐδέν: ὅ τι γέγονεν); if taken with the following, difficulties also arise (unless ἐν αὐτῷ is referred to the relative clause — which is excluded by the context). The rhythm and structure of the verse likewise allow of no firm decision. If ὁ γέγονεν is attached to v. 4 (or omitted), v. 3 is a good distich, ending effectively with οὐδὲ ἕν (or οὐδέν). But even with the questionable addition, the rhythm is good: a tristich with each line ending in a similar way.[64]

Exegetically, great difficulties arise if ὃ γέγονεν is attached to the following, as patristic interpretation already proves.[65] Ἐν αὐτῷ can only refer to the Logos: in him was "life"; but what ζωή would this be? Since the anaphora of the article (cf. Funk, *Greek Grammar*, para. 252) in the next phrase takes up this ζωή and affirms that it is the light of men, it can only be the divine, spiritual life with which the Logos is filled, and which is imparted by him to men; and the Johannine writings constantly speak of this eternal, divine ζωή.[66] If then ὃ γέγονεν is attached to v. 4, the Logos would be the principle of life for "what was made", that is, for all realms of creation.[67] But then one would have to settle for a fluid notion of life. On this supposition, it matters little whether the comma is put before or after ἐν αὐτῷ.[68] "What was made in him" could only mean: "what came into existence through him (as cause)". In keeping with the previous verse, this would still have to be referred to all created things, since the thought moves on to the world of man only in the next statement.

If ὃ γέγονεν is attached to the preceding, the exegesis of v. 4 is also freed from other unnecessary complications. After the view of all creation in v. 3, v. 4 clearly envisages the world of men, and introduces the allied concepts of light and life which are so important for it. V. 4 may then be considered as the beginning of the second strophe of the original Logos-hymn, and the strophe starts at once with an affirmation about the Logos: in him was life.[69] We keep, therefore, ὃ γέγονεν with οὐδὲ ἕν. Its early attachment to the following is due perhaps to the Gnostics (see above) and the Greeks may have felt οὐδὲ ἕν to be the natural ending of a sentence.

With this affirmation about the creative Logos, all notions of a demiurge or a go-between between God and the world are left behind and everything mythical is excluded. The Logos is not an emanation who

---

[64] See Gaechter, "Strophen", 60 pp. 99ff., esp. 102.

[65] See for instance Ambrose, *De fide*, III, 6 (*PL* 16, col. 598); *Expl. Ps. 36: 35–37* (Petschenig, pp. 98ff.). These difficulties probably led to a change in the text in v. 4: for ἦν *(primo loco)* ἐστίν is read by ℵ D a b e f ff² z vg^{codd} sy^{c} ; Tat. (codex leodiens.), Theodotus, Clement, Irenaeus^{Gk}, Augustine; for ἦν *(secundo loco)* also by b sy^{cp} sa Tat. The reading with the present is preferred by Boismard, *Prologue*, pp. 24f.

[66] See Mussner, ΖΩΗ, pp. 80f.

[67] The Fathers thought mostly of natural life and all the realms of creation, cf. Gennaro, *Exegetica in prologum*, pp. 107–19. Boismard; *Prologue*, pp. 31f., adopts this meaning for ὃ γέγονεν. But most of the modern exegetes who put ὃ γέγονεν as the beginning of v. 4, apply it to men, for whom the Logos was source of divine life, see the commentaries of Calmes, Loisy, Bultmann, Wikenhauser, Hoskyns; Dupont, *Essais*, p. 217; de la Potterie, "De interpunctione", p. 208. But ὃ γέγονεν must refer back to v. 3 and v. 4a–b is not a synonymous parallel; v. 4b takes the assertion of 4a further, and men are mentioned only here.

[68] Vawter argues for "what came to be in him was life".

[69] See Schnackenburg, "Logos-Hymnus", pp. 82f.

leads on to the world of matter through further emanations (cf. *Corp. Herm.*, 1:1–6), and he is not merely a way of speaking of the creative power of God or of the forms according to which God created the world. Since he is fully divine, he cannot be reduced to an intermediate stage; since he is a person, he cannot be dissolved into an idea. It must again be emphasized that the statements of v. 3 are not made for their own sake, but to bring out the unique greatness of the incarnate Logos and to praise him.

1:4	Ἐν αὐτῷ ζωὴ ἦν καὶ ἡ ζωὴ ἦν τὸ φῶς τῶν ἀν- θρώπων.	In him was life and the life was the light of men.

Here begins a new strophe of the hymn. It describes the relationship of the Logos to the world of men. As he was the giver of existence to all creation, so too for men he is the vehicle of everything that gives their particular existence its fullness and sense: light and life. The two concepts form a closely-allied pair, life being the more basic and light a closer determination of it, which shows that life under a particular aspect for men: the life which was in the Logos means light for men. If we may link v. 9a–b with this, its importance is brought out even more strongly: he was the true light which enlightens every man. In the same sense, the Johannine Jesus says: "He who follows me . . . shall have the light of life" (8:12), life that becomes light, light that is a vital force. To illustrate this use of the symbol "light" for the work of the Logos in man, the Wisdom literature again suggests itself, with its development of certain themes already hinted at in the O.T.[70] Wisdom too is described as the primordial light,[71] the "radiance of eternal light" (Wis 7:26), a light which surpasses

[70] "Light of life" means primarily physical life on earth which man enjoys in the light of the sun, cf. Ps 56:14; Job 3:20; 33:28, 30; but since this life is given by God and lived out before God, it has also a deeper religious meaning, which is expressed for instance in Ps 27:1, "The Lord is my light and my salvation, of whom shall I be afraid? The Lord is the protector of my life, whom shall I fear?" or in Ps 36:10, "With thee is the fountain of life; in thy light we shall see light"; cf. the analysis in Aalen, *Licht und Finsternis*, pp. 64f. In late Judaism, knowledge, coming from God, is praised as "light", cf. Hos 10:12 LXX; "Harvest the fruit of life, enlighten yourselves with the light of knowledge" (φωτίσατε ἑαυτοῖς φῶς γνώσεως); *Test. Lev.*, 4:3, "The light of knowledge shalt thou light up in Jacob, and as the sun thou shalt be to all the seed of Israel", cf. *Test. Gad*, 5:7; *Test. Benj.*, 5:3. The thought is also to be found at Qumran, cf. *1 QS*, 4:2, "to enlighten the heart of man and to smooth before him all the paths of true righteousness"; 11:3, "For from the source of his knowledge he has opened his light"; 11:5, "Light is in my heart from his marvellous mysteries"; *1 QH*, 4:5, "I shall praise thee, O Lord, because thou hast enlightened my face for thy covenant". See further above, in text.

[71] See Aalen, *Licht und Finsternis*, pp. 175–8.

all created light: "I chose to have her (Wisdom) rather than the light, because her radiance never ceases" (Wis 7:10). It is an effective force in man, giving him a divinely spiritual life which is holy and blessed: "While remaining in herself, she renews all things; in every generation she passes into holy souls and makes them friends of God and prophets" (Wis 7:27).[72] Two thoughts are important here: the power of Wisdom to create anew (to give life), and its work in souls from generation to generation. The Logos too, in our hymn, is to fill men with the divinely spiritual life which is in keeping with their being, the life which distinguishes them from the rest of creation (non-rational) and consists both of knowledge of their godlike nature and of a blessed union with God in holiness of conduct. This divine life-giving force was fully present in the Logos, as in an inexhaustible source, fed from the depths of the divine life (cf. Jn 5:26), and he is charged with imparting this life to men. He is for them the source of life and the giver of divine light. He had taken over this saving function for man since creation, and was to exercise it for all generations (cf. v. 9). Thus v. 4 still looks to creation's dawn, but not to describe just the time of paradise, for instance, but the order of creation as a whole, according to which this task belongs to the Logos (cf. the present φωτίζει, v. 9). Just as divine life "was" in him without any restriction of time, so too he "was",[73] in the divine plan, always "the light of men". Whether and how long since the work of creation this task of the Logos, to give light to men, was actually performed is not specifically considered here; and the revealing and redeeming activity of the incarnate Logos is likewise omitted or at least kept in the background. The fall of man is not described, but it is presupposed, though only in v. 10 (at the beginning of the third strophe), where it comes in unheralded.

The two concepts of life and light occur still more frequently and still more closely allied in Hellenistic mysticism and Gnosis. The question, therefore, arises whether the Logos-hymn is also influenced by this current of thought. In the Poimandres, the Nous is united to the Logos by the "life"; but the Nous is also the "light" and the Logos is the "lightsome Logos" who is Son of God (*Corp. Herm.*, I, 6). The Nous is "life and light" (I, 9, 12, 21) and hence the Logos derives its quality of life and light from its union with the Nous. The two concepts of light and life then also recur in anthropological contexts. The "primal Man" is born of the "Father of all", the Nous, which is life and light (I, 12); from being life and light he became "soul and

---

[72] See also Ecclus 50:29; Hos 10:12 LXX; *Syriac Apoc Baruch*, 54:12–14, where life, light, reason, wisdom and law are closely connected. In the Old Testament but esp. in Judaism, the law is praised as light, e.g. Ps 119:105; Is 26:9; Bar 4:2 LXX; Prov 6:23; Wis 18:4; Ecclus 24:23, cf. 27; 32:16 LXX; *Syriac Apoc Baruch*, 59:2; 77:16; 4 *Esdr.*, 14:20f.; *Test. Lev.*, 14:4. For the rabbis, the law was the light of the world, a lamp for Israel but also a giver of light for the individual; cf. Billerbeck, vol. II, pp. 357f.; Aalen, *Licht und Finsternis*, pp. 186ff., 227ff.

[73] On the reading with the present, see previous note 65.

reason (once more: νοῦς)", from being life he became soul and from being light he became reason (I, 17). Hence the object of the Hermetic Gnosis is to lead present (empirical) man, through knowledge and vision, back to "light and life". This goal is attained by the aspirant at the end of the vision which is transmitted to him: "I attain (at this very moment) to life and light" (I, 32).[74] This tractate combines various currents of thought; the direct influence of Christianity can hardly be proved.[75] Hence it must be considered as an example of a syncretist trend and a mentality which the Christian Logos-hymn also had in mind. In still another way, the Jewish writer Philo turned his attention to this mystical world of thought. He deduces from the creation narrative that spirit and light existed first, which he also interprets as "life" and "light".[76] But in Philo God is distinct from these; he is more than life, since he is the source of life (*Fuga*, 198), more than light, since he is the prototype of all light (*Somn.*, I, 75). The Logos (who comes between God and the world) transmits to (spiritual) creatures the light which they need for their spiritual existence: "For what could be brighter or more far-shining than the divine word, by communion with which even other things dispel their mist and gloom, eagerly desiring to become sharers in the light of the soul?"[77] The Logos is not merely the prototype of human reason (νοῦς), which was created in his image and is rendered akin to God by him,[78] he also dwells in the spirit of man[79] and is the divine teacher of their souls.[80] Here too the same concepts are used to describe the religious experience whereby "enlightenment" comes to man from God for his salvation. Hence the Logos of Philo also takes over the same task fundamentally as the personal Logos who is God in our hymn. In Gnosis, the "envoy", that is, "Gnosis" itself personified, appears in the same role. There is a difference in content—the act of "knowledge" itself becomes the real agent of salvation—but the terminology, characterized by an abundant use of the expressions "light" and "life", is obviously very close. In the non-Christian Gnosis of the Mandaeans, God is called the "great (first) Life", which dwells in the "light-worlds", towards which the Mandaeans strive, with the help of Manda d'Hayye ("Knowledge of Life"). The verbose hymns, the multiplicity of personages and their changing names, the farrago of mythical images, all go to express the same thought: ascent to the world of life and light.[81] The poetic language of the Odes of Solomon,

---

[74] See also the texts in the allied tractate XIII (on rebirth) paras. 9, 18, 19, and the final prayer of the Λόγος τέλειος (Pap. Mimaut, col. XVIII) according to Reitzenstein's restoration, *Die hellenistischen Mysterienreligionen*, p. 286, para. 2, and Scott, vol. I, p. 376 (Latin *Asclepius*, 41; but see Nock and Festugière, pp. 353f., who reconstruct differently, with Preisendanz).

[75] See Haenchen, "Aufbau und Theologie des Poimandres", pp. 188–91; Braun, "Hermétisme et Johannisme", pp. 270, 294.

[76] *De opif.*, 30: "Special distinction is accorded by Moses to life-breath and to light. The one he entitles the 'breath' of God, because breath is most life-giving, and of life God is the author, while of light he says that it is beautiful pre-eminently." Dodd, *Bible and Greeks*, pp. 135f. concludes correctly that Philo found "light and life" as a ready-made combination.

[77] *Leg. all.*, III, 171.

[78] *De praemiis et poenis*, 163; *Spec. leg.*, III, 207; IV, 14; *Abr.*, 41.

[79] *De post. Cain*, 122; *Leg. all.*, III, 169; *Immut.*, 134; *Quod deter.*, 146.

[80] *Migr.*, 174; *Immut.*, 138; *De post. Cain*, 78; *Mutat.*, 18; *De somn.*, I, 68.

[81] The notion is found everywhere. Typical examples: *Mand. Lit.*, pp. 8f. (Lidzbarski): "The light shone, the light shone, the light of the great first life shone. Wisdom and illumination shone forth, insight and praise of the first man, who had come out of his place." *Ibid.*, p. 75:

which show Christian influences, is also permeated by the motif of "light and life".[82] We must conclude from all this that the concepts were already current and possessed great appeal, though we cannot determine the exact extent of the dependency. The content resulted in each case from the doctrine which made use of these magic words.

The same power is ascribed to the Logos in the Christian hymn as in the non-Christian literature: he can give men divine light and life. But he is not a heavenly power or a mythical figure: he is a divine person, who then became man in Jesus Christ, to do his work for fallen and benighted man. The parallelism between creation and redemption which is recognizable in the non-Christian texts here becomes totally clear. What the Logos should have been for men according to the plan of creation, he became in fact for believers in his historical mission. Thus the assertion of v. 4 is illuminated still more clearly by the self-revelation of the Johannine Jesus. Jesus is the "light of the world" (8:12; 9:5; 12:35f., 46), in so far as he makes it possible to possess the "light of life" (8:12). Hence the "light" also evokes the notion of the eschatological salvation, which is another link with the Jewish world of the O.T.[83] The activity of the Logos as "light" begins with creation and extends by means of the Incarnation to the eschatological fulfilment. Indeed, from the very beginning, it is aimed at bringing men home to God's world of light. Everything that is necessary for this end, the giving of revelation and life, the banishment of the darkness of sin and guilt, the moral behaviour which conquers evil works (cf. 3:19ff.) and lusts (1 Jn 2:16f.), is part of the light which the Logos radiates.

"Great repose and supports of life, which shines through its light and whose light gives light." *Ibid.*, pp. 192f.: "The man of tested righteousness sprang forth and shone in the world. He spoke by virtue of the mighty life and revealed hidden mysteries. He clad his friends in brightness; but all the worlds persecuted him." *Ginza*, p. 91, 11ff. (Lidzbarski): "A beloved son comes, who was formed from the bosom of brightness . . . He comes with the enlightenment of life, with the command which his Father gives." *Ibid.*, p. 312, 23f.: "I give thee the garment of brightness, that you may brighten the darkness of the perishing house." *Ibid.*, p. 327, 33f.: "The heart in which I came to dwell was given light and brightness immeasurable by me." In the *Book of the Dead ("left" Ginza)*, the "helper" says to the soul (463, 7ff.): "Go out and dwell in the world, till thy measure is full. . . . Then I shall come to thee with great brightness and light without end." Cf. also *Mand. Lit.*, p. 77 (Lidzbarski): "Thou dost fetch us from death and link us with life; thou dost fetch us from darkness and link us with life."

[82] Cf. *Odes of Solomon*, 10:1f., "The Lord hath directed my mouth by his word: and he hath opened my heart by his light: and he hath caused to dwell in me his deathless light"; cf. v. 6. The symbolism of light (which gives knowledge and life) is strongly stressed, cf. 7:14; 11:11–14, 19; 12:3; 15:1f.; 21:3, 6; 25:7; 29:7; 38:1; 41:4, 6, 14.

[83] Light as eschatological salvation, Amos 5:18, 20; Mic 7:8; Hab 3:4; Is 2:5; 9:1; 51:5 LXX; 58:8, 10; 60:1ff., 19f.; 61:1; Bar 5:9.

1:5	καὶ τὸ φῶς ἐν τῇ σκοτίᾳ φαίνει καὶ ἡ σκοτία αὐτὸ οὐ κατέλαβεν.	And the light shines in the darkness, but the darkness did not grasp it.

The difficulties of this verse—the present φαίνει and the aorist κατέλαβεν, which envisage a different level of time than the ἦν of v. 4—are most readily solved if one takes v. 5 as a digression of the evangelist, who continues to meditate on the light coming to mankind from the Logos. His hand may also be seen in the use of one of his favourite words, σκοτία (instead of σκότος).[84] The hymn is resumed only in v. 9a–b, where it is explained that the Logos was the *true* light for every man.

In the original hymn, the "was" of v. 9a probably looked back at the order of creation, like v. 4; but the evangelist thinks at once (after vv. 6–8) of the activity of the incarnate Logos and adds in explanation ἐρχόμενον εἰς τὸν κόσμον. The painful fact that the "world" did not know the Logos, that his "own" did not accept him, was also recognized by the hymn (vv. 10–11), but here it probably still means the time before the Incarnation. The evangelist, however, has the eschatological revelation of the incarnate Logos constantly before his mind, when "the light came into the world" as a unique historical event, offering the final possibility of salvation; but "men loved darkness more than the light" (3:19). Hence his meditation in v. 5 extends to take in the present time (φαίνει). The assertion is then concerned both with the historical coming of the Logos into the world and the time of the evangelist, in which the power of the divine light brought into the darkness of the world by the incarnate Logos still continues to work. In 1 Jn 2:8 a similar present is used to speak of the perceptible effects of the light and love already realized in Christ and his community (see *ad loc.*). Hence φαίνει is neither the equivalent of a past tense (cf. Bauer, *ad loc.*), nor is it timeless or outside time: it brings the shining of the light down to the present time. But at the historical coming of the Logos it became apparent that "the darkness did not grasp" the light. "Darkness" in John means primarily the world estranged from God, the place of man's existence not yet (or no longer, if the dawn of creation is considered) illuminated by divine light (cf. 8:12 "to walk in darkness"; also 12:46; 1 Jn 2:11a–b—described as a sinister power in 11c). Then it comes to mean men themselves, as they yield to this darkness and are oppressed and blinded by it (cf. 9:39; 12:40; 1 Jn 2:11c). It is of this blinded world of men ensnared by evil that the σκοτία of 1:5 is to be understood. It is the same as the "children of darkness", though this ex-

---

[84] Σκοτία 6:17; 8:12; 12:35a,b, 46; 20:1; 1 Jn 1:5; 2:8, 9 ,11a,b,c in contrast to σκότος Jn 3:19; 1 Jn 1:6. In the rest of the New Testament σκοτία occurs twice (or 3 times); σκότος 26 (27) times. We can therefore treat σκοτία as a Johannine characteristic (Ruckstuhl, *Die literarische Einheit des Johannesevangeliums*, no. 22).

pression is never found in John (cf., however, the passages just cited, and also 8:44; 1 Jn 3:10: "children of the devil").

Here the Johannine concept of "darkness" comes very close indeed to the Qumran texts, where, however, the notion of the "light" being offered to the "children of darkness" is missing. They appear as doomed to darkness from the start, but—as in Jn 3:19–21—because of their evil works (cf. *1 QS*, 3:21; 4:9–14)[85]. The opposition of light and darkness is primarily on a cosmic scale, but it makes itself felt particularly in the world of man, where it is revealed in the moral attitude of man. "Children of darkness" is the usual term, especially in the "War"; but there is one passage which says that God wills to "bring (the) darkness low and to strengthen (the) light" (*1 QM*, 13:15). Hence the enemies of God do not merely walk in darkness (cf. *1 QM*, 13:12; 15:9f.), they are themselves "darkness".

If the evangelist is thinking in v. 5 of the encounter of the Logos, the light, with the world of men—as can hardly be doubted after v. 4—then of the two possible meanings of καταλαμβάνειν, "master" (= overwhelm) and "grasp" (= embrace with mind and will), only the second can be considered. The metaphor expresses clearly that man is called on to make his own active decision (of faith), but that he did not "lay hold" of it when it was within his grasp.[86]

Commentators have been divided from the earliest times as to the meaning of καταλαμβάνειν. Origen,[87] and after him most of the Greek Fathers took it in the sense of "overwhelm"; so too many moderns.[88] According to the metaphor used elsewhere in John (6:17; 12:35), the word can mean the sudden irruption of darkness, the "quenching" of the light by the darkness of night; but this metaphorical character is not present in 1:5.[89] The expression here is the equivalent of οὐκ ἔγνω, v. 10, and οὐ παρέλαβον, v. 11, and according to the mind of the evangelist can hardly mean anything except "believe in the light" (12:36). As παραλαμβάνειν means to welcome something that arrives, so too καταλαμβάνειν means to lay hold of something that is present. In the N.T., the meaning "understand", which, however, is weaker than the active "grasp", occurs frequently in the middle voice (Acts 4:13; 10:34; 25:25; Eph 3:18); but in Greek literature there are examples enough of the active voice in the same sense.[90]

---

[85] On the Qumran texts, see Nötscher, *Terminologie*, pp. 175f.; id., *Gotteswege und Menschenwege in der Bibel und Qumran*, pp. 91–6.

[86] See *Odes of Solomon*, 42:3, "And I became of no account . . . to those who did not *take hold* of me."

[87] *Comm. in Jo.*, II, 27 (Preuschen, p. 84).

[88] See commentaries of Zahn and Schlatter; Delling, "καταλαμβάνω", p. 10; Strachan, *Fourth Gospel*; Dodd, *Interpretation*, pp. 36, 107 and other English scholars, cf. Revised Version; W. Nagel, "Die Finsternis hat's nicht begriffen".

[89] John does not use the image for the attacks of Jesus's enemies and the demonic powers behind them (cf. the "prince of this world" 12:31; 14:30; 16:11; at most, he understands the "night" of the Judas episode symbolically. The passage from the Acts of Thomas adduced by Delling, "καταλαμβάνω", p. 13: φῶς τὸ μὴ καταλαμβανόμενον proves that the meaning "overwhelm" is possible, but there it is in a different context (speaking of the eternal, inviolable light of heaven).

[90] See Bauer, *Johannesevangelium, ad loc.*; Arndt and Gingrich, *Lexicon, sub voce* 1, a; Liddel and Scott, *Lexicon, sub voce* 1, 3.

Hence the notion of conflict is to be avoided. A reminiscence of the mythical struggle between light and darkness at the beginning of the cosmos[91] is excluded by the fact that humanity is already envisaged in v. 4. Even a metaphorical recourse to the myths of primitive times would be very strange, since mythical language and cosmogony are entirely absent. But it is also hardly possible to think of the darkness having failed to quench the light of Christ in the world: John is so convinced of the victory of Christ (cf. 12:31; 16:11, 33) that even the possibility of defeat is not suggested (cf. at the most, 13:30; 14:30). Hence too the recent proposal, that the expression was deliberately kept ambiguous (Omodeo, Hoskyn, Barrett), should be rejected. There seems to be no need to have recourse to an Aramaic אַקְבֵּן, "darken",[92] or אַחֵד, "seize".[93]

Hence the tenses of the verbs were chosen deliberately by the evangelist. He recognizes that the Logos illuminates unceasingly, and that the light endures down to his own day (φαίνει) and after. But he is also aware of the incomprehension and refusal of men, who have closed their hearts to the redemptive work of the Logos (οὐ κατέλαβεν). The coming of the incarnate word is in the foreground, but he prolongs the perspective down to the present by φαίνει. The way men acted then becomes a warning to the reader not to close out the redemptive revelation of Christ, and an exhortation to embrace the light which still streams from the Logos, to become a child of God by faith (v. 12) and to allow the light to penetrate further into the darkened world, by the exercise of charity (cf. 1 Jn 2:8).

This is the first occurrence in John of the contrast "light" and "darkness", which appears again in 3:19; 8:12; 12:35, 46; cf. 9:4; 11:9f. (day and night), also in 1 Jn 1:6f.; 2:8, 9–11, and is important for the question of Johannine "dualism". The statements are metaphorical, but not similes: they use the image to speak directly of the thing itself. These metaphorical expressions present the divine realm of light as fundamentally opposed to the darkness which is the enemy of God (1:5a; 1 Jn 1:7; 2:9). Jesus, the "light of the world", brings the divine power of light and life once more into the darkened cosmos (1:9; 3:19; 12:46). It is a way of looking at things which brings out the dynamic movement of the history of salvation, since in the earthly realm only a certain amount of time is allowed for the work of the divine bringer of light (9:4; 11:9f.; 12:35). Thence comes the urgent call to faith (12:35f.), which, however, in the mind of the evangelist, is directed not only to the men of that time, but to all hearers of the Christian message (8:12; 12:46). Finally, the metaphor is used of the moral conduct of men, which is disclosed for what it is by the divine bringer of light (3:19 ff.; cf. 1 Jn 1:6f.; 2:9 ff.). All these aspects are evoked and combined by the coming of Christ as the "light": the triumphant irruption of the divine light into the darkness of the cosmos to bring salvation, the summons to mankind to decide here and now for the light, the division of mankind according to whether it belongs to the light or the dark, and the irresistible advance of the divine light (cf. 1 Jn 2:8).

---

[91] See Dodd, *Interpretation*, p. 36, n. 1: "reduced survival . . . of the primitive myth of the conflict of the Light-God with the monster of darkness."

[92] Burney, *Aramaic Origin*, pp. 29f.

[93] Schaeder, "Der Mensch im Prolog", pp. 312f.

These points must be kept in mind, if one is to make a fruitful comparison with other texts which are dominated by the contrast of light and darkness. For the O.T. and late Judaism, the material has been collected and carefully discussed by S. Aalen.[94] The Johannine imagery seems to be a development, the Christological application and eschatological fulfilment of the thoughts given there. Gnostic dualism, on the other hand, is of a different structure, as may be seen from the Mandaean literature in particular,[95] where the dualism is based on cosmology and exploited to enunciate the doctrine of salvation in corresponding mythical terms. The dynamism of a history of salvation is entirely lacking, and the moral aspect recedes into the background, though it is not quite missing; but moral exhortations are mostly based on the thought of the examination of the soul and the judgment of the dead as they ascend to the heavenly world of light.[96] The Gnosticism of the *Odes of Solomon* uses the imagery of light and darkness for the mystic union of the soul with God and for estrangement from God; the light is the Gnosis which comes from God and unites with God.[97]

Turning to Jewish literature, we find that the *Testaments of the Twelve Patriarchs*, which also speak often of the contrast of light and darkness, do not go beyond ethical exhortation and can hardly be said to think in terms of cosmic principles.[98] The closest and most striking parallels are in the texts from Qumran, where there is a sort of cosmic dualism,[99] since "the prince of light holds sway over all the children of righteousness, and they walk on the paths of light, but the angel of darkness holds sway over all the children of wickedness, and they walk on the paths of

---

[94] *Die Begriffe Licht und Finsternis im Alten Testament, im Spätjudentum und im Rabbinismus.*

[95] Percy, *Untersuchungen*, pp. 23–50. The "wicked" only sink deeper into the darkness from which they come, when the Gnostic envoy calls out, cf. *Book of John* (Lidzbarski, p. 203): "I am the treasure, the treasure of life. The wicked are blind and do not see. I call them to light, but they bury themselves in the darkness. 'O, ye wicked', I call to them, 'who are sinking into the darkness, rouse up and do not fall into the depths.' I call to them, but the wicked do not hear and they sink into the great sea of the Sûf."

[96] See e.g. *Book of John* (Lidzbarski), pp. 169ff., 173ff., 178ff., 225f. In these texts, "light" and "darkness" are only the other-worldly places of reward or punishment. "Let your hands do righteous deeds, that you may ascend and see the place of light" (Lidzbarski, p. 172); "The wicked and the liars shall be cast down into darkness" (id., p. 175).

[97] See *Odes of Solomon*, 10:6, "And the footprints of the light were set upon their heart and they walked in my life and were saved"; 15:2, "Because he (the Lord) is my sun and his rays have made me rise up and his light hath dispelled all darkness from my face." See also above n. 82.

[98] See *Test. Lev.*, 19:1, "Choose, therefore, for yourselves either the light or the darkness, either the law of the Lord or the works of Beliar"; *Test. Benj.*, 5:3, "Where there is reverence for good works and light in the mind, even darkness fleeth away from him"; *Test. Gad*, 5:7, "For true repentance after a godly sort (destroyeth ignorance and) driveth away the darkness and enlighteneth the eyes and giveth knowledge to the soul and leadeth the mind to salvation." It is said only of the coming Priest-Messiah, *Test. Lev.*, 18:3f. "His star shall arise in heaven as of a king, lighting up the light of knowledge as the sun the day. ... He shall shine forth as the sun on the earth and shall remove all darkness from under heaven"; see also *Test. Lev.*, 4:3.

[99] See Otzen, "Die neugefundenen hebräischen Sektenschriften und die Testamente der zwölf Patriarchen", pp. 135–42; Huppenbauer, *Der Mensch zwischen zwei Welten*, pp. 103–15.

darkness" (*1 QS*, 3:20f.). But unlike Gnosticism, this is not a contrast between two ultimate principles, since God is over the good and evil spirits: "He created the spirits of light and darkness, and upon them he founded every work" (*1 QS*, 3:25). The conflict in which the spirits and the men led by them are engaged takes place on the moral level (*1 QS*, 4:2–12). In so far as the elect sin, their misdeeds likewise belong to the darkness (cf. *1 QS*, 11:9f.), but God sends them help and light. Sayings occur which remind us of the work of illumination done by the Logos. "From the source of his knowledge he has let his light shine forth: my eyes saw his marvels and my heart was enlightened by the mysteries of what was and what will be for ever" (*1 QS*, 11:3f.). "My heart is enlightened by his wonderful mysteries. My eyes have seen what will be for ever, a wisdom hidden from men" (*ibid.*, 5f.). "I will praise thee, o Lord, for thou hast illumined my face unto thy covenant" (*1 QH*, 4:5). "For thou art to me an eternal light, thou hast set my feet on [level ground]" (*1 QH*, 7:25). "Through thy glory, my light has shone, for with light out of darkness thou hast illumined me" (*1 QH*, 9:26f.).

But there are fundamental differences with regard to John. There is no question of the conversion of the "children of darkness", who are to be annihilated in the eschatological war (*1 QM*). The "children of light" find safety in strict observance of the law and separation from the rest of the world. Above all, the figure of the divine bringer of light is missing. Though the speaker in many of the hymns *(Hodayoth)* may be the "Teacher of Righteousness",[100] he affirms that his "illumination" is a grace from God, which gives him a new understanding of Scripture, insight into the wonderful ways of God and grasp of his holy will in the law, so that he can then "illuminate" others, the members of his community. Hence he can say: "Thou didst appear to me in thy strength, in perfect light . . . Through me thou hast illumined the face of many, and displayed thy might times without number, for thou didst instruct me in thy marvellous secrets" (*1 QH*, 4:23, 27). But the very same language is used in a blessing called down upon all: "May he make you holy among his people, and a . . . light [to illumine] the earth in knowledge, and to illumine the face of many" *(1QSb*, 4:27). This is something quite different from the communication of divine life and light by the Logos. The enlightened teacher, who also feels the weight of the "fragile flesh", is completely of the human sphere. Where in John it is the Logos who gives enlightenment, revelation, life and salvation, in Qumran it is God himself or the Torah. In the eschatological war, God sends the "prince of light" or Michael *(1QM*, 17:6f.); but a heavenly envoy whose coming in the flesh is a historical event and who is himself the "light of the world", is unknown to Qumran. It is only the spiritual trend, the dualistic but theocentric thought, the hope of divine light in the darkness of this world, and the thankful acceptance of God's gracious revelation and help that brings the texts of Qumran into line to some extent with the thought of John.

The Mission and Significance of John the Baptist 1:6–8

1:6	Ἐγένετο ἄνθρωπος ἀπεσταλμένος παρὰ θεοῦ, ὄνομα αὐτῷ Ἰωάννης·	A man appeared, sent by God, whose name was John.

It is not difficult to see that vv. 6–8 are an interpolation of the evangelist. Here he is clearly on historical ground. His plan is certainly to begin his account of the earthly work of the Logos with the coming of John the

[100] See Jeremias, *Der Lehrer der Gerechtigkeit*, pp. 168–267.

Baptist, as was the practice in the primitive kerygma (cf. Acts 1:22; 10:37; 13:24) and the oldest Gospel writing (Mk 1:1 ff.). The reason why he does so here is the key-word "light", which is his favourite image for the work of the incarnate Son of God (cf. commentary on v. 5). To judge by v. 8, it is probable that the disciples of John outside the Christian Church claimed this title for their master (cf. also 5:35); still, this insertion of vv. 6–8, which is also proved to be secondary by its rhythm, its prosaic style in contrast to the hymnic verses of the prologue, cannot simply be the result of apologetical tendencies. Extravagant views of the Baptist are not refuted till v. 8, while v. 6 speaks of his divine mission as the O.T. does of the prophets.[101] Hence the evangelist must have seen here an occasion for introducing his historical narrative. And hence, too, the construction cannot be improved by transferring vv. 6–8 to before v. 19.[102] The evangelist put them here deliberately.

The coming of the man who is to point out the Messiah to Israel (1:26, 31) and to bear witness to the incarnate Logos (1:30), the redeemer of the world (1:29, 36), is the work of God. He is hardly called "man" in deliberate contrast to the "divine" Logos (v. 1); it is the usual Hebrew equivalent of "someone". In contrast to ἦν, however, ἐγένετο implies an appearance at a given moment of history (cf. Mk 1:4; Lk 1:5). It should not be taken with ἀπεσταλμένος (as Chrysostom points out). On the contrary, the divine mission is the subject of a new and significant assertion, from which it also appears that the evangelist did not denigrate the Baptist like the late Jewish-Christian pseudo-Clementine writings in their attack on the disciples of John.[103] He lays claim, in fact, to the great baptizer and preacher of penance, as a witness for Jesus, the light of the world. The name of the man sent by God to take over the greatest of all prophetic roles is added solemnly and reverently (likewise in a Hebrew turn of phrase, which is, however, also possible in Greek[104])—though the reader must have known at once who was meant.

1:7	οὗτος ἦλθεν εἰς μαρτυρίαν, ἵνα μαρτυρήσῃ περὶ τοῦ φωτός, ἵνα πάντες πιστεύσωσιν δι' αὐτοῦ.	He came to bear witness, to give testimony to the light, so that all should come to believe through him.

[101] Exod 3:10ff.; 4:13, 28; 5:22; 7:16; 1 Sam 12:8; 15:1; 16:1; 2 Sam 12:1; 2 Kgs 2:2, 4, 6; Is 6:8; Jer 14:14; 19:14; 23:21; Ezek 2:4; 13:6; Zech 2:13, 15; 6:15; Mal 4:5 (3:23).

[102] So Hirsch, *Studien zum vierten Evangelium*, pp. 44f.

[103] *Hom.*, II, 16f.; *Recogn.*, III, 61 hold that in each syzygy the first is the evil member, so too John with regard to Jesus; cf. Cullmann, "Ὁ ὀπίσω μου ἐρχόμενος".

[104] See Bauer, *Johannesevangelium, ad loc.* The MSS א* D* W insert an ἦν before ὄνομα.

In contrast to the Synoptics, (Mk 1:2; Mt 11:10 par.), there is little emphasis on his function of "precursor" and "preparer of the way", in fulfilment of the prophecy of Mal 3:1,[105] though he continues to proclaim him "who comes after" him (1:15,27,30; 3:28). In the fourth Gospel he is the great "witness", who gives weighty testimony before official Judaism (1:19–28), before all Israel (cf. 1:31) and before his own disciples (1:35 ff.). This is acknowledged by Jesus, but only as human testimony which must be of less value than the divine (5:34 ff.). This evaluation of the Baptist must be due to the fact that the evangelist wished to deprive contemporary Baptist circles of their master, at least as a competitor of Jesus, and to keep (or win) the great herald of God for the Christian community, as champion of the Messiahship of Jesus. There was less advantage in the evangelist's emphasizing the precursorship of John at the time, because Baptist circles were trying to argue to their master's superiority to Jesus from the fact that he came before him in time (see on v. 15). Hence this envoy of God "came"—human "coming" corresponding to divine "sending"—with only one mission (εἰς, final) that of giving testimony. But the evangelist also had intrinsic theological reasons for being interested in the Baptist's role as witness. He sees all faith as a response to testimony, which provides support and impulse without lessening the need for personal decision. Nowhere do the concepts of μαρτυρεῖν and μαρτυρία stand out so strongly as in the fourth Gospel,[106] and there they occur in the service of Johannine faith. The nature of this faith already appears in 1:7, where the object attested is called the "light", that is, the Logos who is life and light of men (v. 4). The transition to historical narrative (v. 6) shows beyond doubt that the evangelist understands the "light" here as the incarnate Logos, that is, the "light" insofar as it came into the world at a given time (cf. v. 9). The object of faith is indicated in John practically exclusively as the person of Jesus, and in particular, as the evangelist clearly affirms, that he is "the Christ, the Son of God" (20:31). It is a Christological faith, concentrated on the person of the divine revealer and redeemer, as even the vocabulary shows.[107] The witnesses or testimonies mostly appear in the dative (cf. commentary on

---

[105] Cf. Mal 4:5 (3:23); Mt 11:14; Mk 9:11 ff. parr.; Lk 1:17; Kraeling, *John the Baptist*, pp. 141–5, 180f.; Trilling, "Die Täufertradition im Matthäusevangelium", esp. pp. 279 ff. On Elijah in John, see on 1:21.

[106] Μαρτυρεῖν 33 times in John, 6 times in First Letter of John, 4 times in Third Letter of John (though not in the typical Johannine sense); 32 times in the rest of the New Testament but closely connected with faith only Acts 10:43; cf. 23:11; 1 Cor 15:15; also Rev 1:2. Μαρτυρία 14 times in John, 6 times in First Letter of John once in Third Letter of John; also frequent in Revelation (9 times) but in a special sense; 7 times in the rest of the New Testament. Μαρτυρεῖν περί is characteristic of John (Ruckstuhl, *Die literarische Einheit*, no. 30), while μαρτύρομαι, μάρτυς and μαρτύριον are missing.

[107] See Schnackenburg, *Der Glaube im vierten Evangelium*, pp. 4–11.

5:31 ff.). Where πιστεύειν is used absolutely, it is clear from the context or for other reasons that faith in Jesus, the Son of God and bringer of salvation, is meant;[108] so too here in the second appended[109] ἵνα-clause. "Through" John, the witness, faith is only aroused and helped, a faith which in the context is directed to the "light". Πάντες is not emphasized, but it shows the universal salvific will of God (cf. 3:15–17); John first performs his task of witnessing before the ancient community of salvation, Israel, to whom he presents the Messiah (1:31), but to the mind of the evangelist his testimony persists as a clarion call (cf. 1:15a) for all time, for the whole world, to which he announces its saviour (cf. 1:29).

1:8	οὐκ ἦν ἐκεῖνος τὸ φῶς, ἀλλ' ἵνα μαρτυρήσῃ περὶ τοῦ φωτός.	He was not the light, but only to give testimony to the light.

Only now is the apologetical interest of the evangelist apparent: he combats the view that John was the "light". The verse, which displays characteristics of Johannine style,[110] is directed against an over-estimation of the Baptist, of which we are informed by later and indeed meagre sources. In the second century there were still Baptist circles competing with Christianity, and they considered John himself as the Messiah.[111] That is all that we can legitimately deduce from the polemic; to conclude from the designation of "light" that the followers of the Baptist ascribed to him pre-existence and cosmic functions (in a Gnostic sense), is certainly going too far. The argument of v. 15 would break down if the disciples of John for their part attributed pre-existence and the other prerogatives of the Logos to the Baptist. That the controversy between Christians and disciples of John at the time of the evangelist was concerned with the question of Messiahship, and only no doubt with this, may be seen from 1:20 (see there). V. 8 is concerned only with the relationship of John to the Logos-Light who has appeared in the flesh, even though his testimony, according to the evangelist, also embraces the pre-existence of Jesus (1:15,30). If the later devotees of John did in fact designate their master as "light" (cf. also 5:35), this was probably only a figure of speech for the

---

[108] 30 times in all; the object can often be deduced from the context (as Jesus Christ), see previous note and excursus vii.

[109] For this construction see 16:1f., 21, 23, 24; in parataxis καὶ ἵνα 20:31.

[110] The ἐκεῖνος is characteristic (Ruckstuhl no. 17), also the elliptic ἀλλ' ἵνα (*ibid.*, no. 13), though the ellipsis can be found elsewhere in Greek (Funk, *Greek Grammar*, para. 448, 7; Radermacher, *Grammatik*, p. 170). But it is so remarkable in John (also 1:31; 9:3; 13:18; 14:31; 15:25; 1 Jn 2:19), in contrast to the rest of the New Testament (only Mk 14:49) that it must be considered a personal characteristic, probably due to a Semitic way of thinking, cf. Schlatter, *Sprache und Heimat*, *ad loc.*

[111] Pseudo-Clementine, *Recogn.*, I, 54, 60; Ephraim, *Ev. concordantis expositio* (Moesinger, p. 288). See Schnackenburg, "Johannesjünger", pp. 24f.

"sun of righteousness" (cf. Mal 3:20); but the expression negatived in v. 8 may also have been chosen merely on account of the context, to stress the distance between John and Jesus.[112]

1:9	Ἦν τὸ φῶς τὸ ἀληθινόν, ὃ φωτίζει πάντα ἄνθρωπον, ἐρχόμενον εἰς τὸν κόσμον.	He (the Word) was the true light which enlightens every man, (the light) that came into the world.

The verse links up once more with v. 4, and must have been originally (in the Logos-hymn) its continuation. The statement, "He was the true light which enlightens every man", explicitates the "light of men", v. 4, just as v. 3b emphasizes the creation of all things by the Logos alone (v. 3a). The power of the Logos to give light and life is universal, and indispensable to every man. In him, and in him alone, was the divine life for the true spiritual being of men, and he, and he alone (note the continuation of the ἦν-sayings) was the true divine life for all. In the original hymn this statement (like v. 4) certainly referred to the order of creation, that is, to the Logos before his incarnation. It transfers to the Logos the functions ascribed in Jewish literature to Wisdom or the Torah, which took on later in Jewish thought the role of giver of light which Wisdom had played since creation (see on v. 4).[113] Hence the "illumination"[114] given by the Logos must have primarily envisaged the knowledge and the choice of good conduct in keeping with man's situation and the will of God—"walking in the light", which leads finally to the full light and salvation of God. But the Christian hymn insists that Christ, the Logos, possessed this power before his earthly existence and merely exercises it anew in his mission of salvation, because it essentially belongs to him (φωτίζει), and because he is the "true" light. This attribute (ἀληθινόν) can indicate

[112] See Schnackenburg, "Johannesjünger", pp. 33–35.

[113] Cf. Ps 119:105; Is 26:9; Bar 4:2 LXX; Prov. 6:23; Wis 18:4; Ecclus 24:27 cf. 23; 32:16 LXX; *Syriac Apoc Baruch*, 59:2; 77:16; *4 Esdr.*, 14:20f. etc. Also Billerbeck, vol. II, pp. 357f.; Aalen, *Licht und Finsternis*, pp. 186ff., 277ff. The most noteworthy parallel to our present text is *Test. Lev.* 14:4, τὸ φῶς τοῦ νόμου τὸ δοθὲν εἰς φωτισμὸν παντὸς ἀνθρώπου (β: τὸ δοθὲν ὑμῖν).

[114] For the linguistic usage cf. esp. Ecclus 24:32, "I will again make instruction shine forth (φωτίω) like the dawn, and I will make it shine (ἐκφανῶ) afar." 34:17 LXX, "(The Lord) lifts up the soul, enlightens the eye, gives healing, life and blessing." See also the Qumran usage (see above, n. 70) esp. *1 QS*, 4:2, "to enlighten the heart of man . . . for all the paths of true righteousness." In these texts (esp. *1 QH*, 4:5) the "enlightenment" is a grace for the "children of light", enabling them to choose and go the true way (of the commandments). It is this *salutary* enlightenment which is intended in Jn 1:9, just as in v. 4. Hence it is not to be taken with the φαίνει of v. 5, as if the "light" shone "regardless of whether and how far men are receptive to its revelation", indeed, as if it blinded unbelievers (Bultmann, *Johannes*, pp. 32f.; see also Barrett, *St John*). On the texts from Ecclesiasticus see also Spicq, "Le Siracide et la structure littéraire du Prologue de S. Jean", pp. 186–8.

the "genuineness" of a thing or person in contrast to the "false, improper". But even in the confession of the "living, one and true" God,[115] it does not merely note the formal contrast to the "false, worthless" idols; it is used to express the fullness of being and reality in God. It can mean then in Hellenism simply the divine being as qualitatively unique in its incomparable excellence.[116] Thus the Logos has a transcendent power of illumination, which comes from his godhead (v. 1c) and which can and must be displayed in every man who desires to reach his goal. How far this came about in fact, how far men allowed themselves to be illumined and guided by this divine light of life—this is something of which the verse speaks as little as v. 4; the subject is reserved for the next strophe (vv. 10–11). In the present context, however, after the insertion of vv. 6–8 by the evangelist, it can hardly be doubted that the reader is meant to think at once of the incarnate Logos whose "illumination", active since creation and always remaining (present) active, has been bestowed in a special manner since the Incarnation on men, that is, on those who believe in him (v. 7). The historical coming of the Logos-Light into the world (cf. 3:19) has reduced the previous spiritual illumination to something unessential in the eyes of the evangelist, and he has absorbed the second strophe of the original hymn directly into this historical perspective. After the precautionary remark of v. 8, the adjective ἀληθινόν must also have had for him the significance of the "true, genuine light" in contrast to all other ostensible bringers of light.

There is disagreement about the parsing of ἐρχόμενον at the end of the verse. Is it to be joined with ἦν as a periphrastic conjugation, or is it acc. masc. agreeing with ἄνθρωπον (as in Vg)? There are reasons in support of both views. The periphrastic conjugation is not foreign to the style of John;[117] the separation of ἐρχόμενον from ἦν is not impossible, though the insertion of a relative clause makes it unique. A serious objection is that the expression would be an imperfect, whereas elsewhere it indicates a custom or a state, hence not the occurrence of a new event.[118] But obviously the author does not wish to speak here of the continual coming of the true light. In support of the second view, the rabbinic periphrasis of "one who comes into the world" for

---

[115] Cf. Is 65:16 LXX; *3 Macc.*, 6:18; 1 Thess 1:9; Jn 7:28; 17:3; 1 Jn 5:20; Philo, *Congress.*, 159; *Spec. leg.*, I, 332; *Legat.*, 366; Josephus, *Ant.*, VIII, 343; *Sib. Or.*, I, 20; III, 46 (Geffcken).

[116] Cf. Philo, *Leg. all.*, I, 32, 35 (God breathed δύναμιν ἀληθινῆς ζωῆς into the νοῦς); III, 52; *Magical Papyrus*, VII, 634f.: πέμψον μοι τὸν ἀληθινὸν Ἀσκληπιὸν δίχα τινὸς ἀντιθέου πλανοδαίμονος (in Arndt and Gingrich, *Lexicon*, sub voce, 3); Christian amulet (6th cent.): ὁ φῶς ἐκ φωτός, θ(εὸ)ς ἀληθινὸς χάρισον ἐμέ . . . (in Moulton and Milligan, *Vocabulary*, p. 22); see also Bultmann "ἀληθινός", p. 251. On the Johannine usage of ἀληθινός see also Schweizer, *Ego eimi*, pp. 133f.; Ruckstuhl, *Die literarische Einheit*, pp. 235ff.

[117] See 1:28; 2:6; 3:23; 10:40; 11:1; 13:23; 18:18, 25.

[118] Funk, *Greek Grammar*, para. 353, 1 cites Jn 1:9; but Zerwick, *Graecitas*, no. 255, holds that the construction is doubtful here.

"man" could be adduced[119]—if it were not for the presence of ἄνθρωπον. To excise the word as a clue to the interpretation[120] is arbitrary. And it does not make sense to refer the "enlightenment" to the moment of birth in particular.[121] There is a third possibility: to read the last phrase as an afterthought, qualifying φῶς (equivalent to a relative clause), "(a light) that came into the world", though according to the rules of grammar the article should have been repeated.[122] Every interpretation presents difficulties. The phrase is perhaps best understood as an addition made by the evangelist to the original hymn, which continued to speak of the function of the Logos as bringer of light (cf. v. 4). The subject of ἦν is the Logos, as again in vv. 10f., but the evangelist, having once turned to history in vv. 6–8, decided to mention himself the historical coming of the light after the testimony of John. He then added the final remark, rather awkwardly and incorrectly put, which does betray his own style (3:19; 6:14; 9:39; 11:27; 12:46; 16:28; 18:37).

With the vague phrase "coming into the world", the evangelist prepares for the incarnation of the light (v. 14) and also places the following strophe (vv. 10f.) in the same context. How precisely the light comes into the world remains unsaid; not till v. 14 will it be made clear that it took place in an undreamt-of manner: the Logos became flesh.

1:10	Ἐν τῷ κόσμῳ ἦν,	He was in the world,
	καὶ ὁ κόσμος δι' αὐτοῦ ἐγένετο,	and the world was made through him,
	καὶ ὁ κόσμος αὐτὸν οὐκ ἔγνω.	but the world did not know him.

Vv. 10–11 form a new strophe in the original hymn. After the divine being and creative activity of the Logos (vv. 1 and 3), and his relationship of life and light for the world of men (vv. 4 and 9), we have a new thought: the rejection of the Logos by the κόσμος. With this the process of history comes into view, the conduct of men. The κόσμος in v. 10 is the world as the dwelling-place of man, and then takes on the meaning of "the world of man" or "humanity".[123] The Logos was not just the fundamental and universal principle of light in the divine plan: he also illumined the existence and way of man from within the historical reality of man's environment or "world". "He was in the world", so close to men that they could reach him and cleave to him for their salvation; but the "world", that is, humanity installed in its earthly, historical home, "did not know him". This is the brutal and shattering fact which the hymn signals in a few short words, and re-iterates more poignantly in the fol-

[119] See the examples in Billerbeck, vol. II, p. 358; Schlatter, *Johannes*, *ad loc.*

[120] So Bultmann, *Johannes*, pp. 31f. with n. 6; Schaeder, "Der Mensch im Prolog", pp. 327f. gives his reconstructed Enosh Hymn as follows: "He was the light of the Kushta, which enlightens all, Enosh, who comes into the world."

[121] Glasson, "John 1:9 and a Rabbinic Tradition", suggests that the rabbis thought of prenatal instruction.

[122] See Funk, *Greek Grammar*, para. 412, 4, for Jn 6:14; 11:27.

[123] See Sasse, "κόσμος", pp. 887ff.

lowing verse (v. 11). Thus the hymn pursues, of set purpose, the thought of the second strophe, the relationship of the Logos to mankind, but depicts the tragic breach in the historical course of the relationship. The term κόσμος, which appears unheralded here (on 9c, see above) was certainly not chosen at random: it signals the transition from creation and the order of creation to "history". But "history" is not the general development of created things, the natural process. It is essentially human history, the action and reaction of man in triumph and disaster and the resulting chain of consequences. This gives the same meaning to κόσμος in 10a and c; but the intervening clause, "and the world was made through him" uses κόσμος in a different sense, that of the sum of created things. V. 10b thus clearly echoes v. 3: "all things (πάντα) were made through him", and forms an incidental remark which interrupts the flow of thought from v. 10a to 10c. It should probably be taken as a comment by the evangelist.

It is also possible, on the supposition that the evangelist is responsible for all three phrases, that he moved swiftly from one meaning of "world" to another, using it first spatially (vv. 9c and 10a), then in the sense of creation (v. 10b), and finally, with a brusque change of meaning, for mankind rejecting the Logos (v. 10c). But then the thought would be unclear and inconsequential. Why repeat that the Logos was in the world, after saying that he came into the world? Would it be to indicate a consequence ("hence, he was in the world")?[124] Or perhaps a sort of reminder ("he was, indeed, already in the world")?[125] Both are unsatisfactory. The connection would be better if in v. 9 ἐρχόμενον εἰς τὸν κόσμον were referred to πάντα ἄνθρωπον: the Logos was in the world into which each man comes (as he is born). But v. 10 is not concerned with the encounter between the Logos and the individual, but with his historical involvement with mankind as a whole. If one notes that though v. 10 and v. 11 are parallel in structure there is a line too many in v. 10, and that the "superfluous" v. 10b uses "world" in a somewhat different sense, it is hard to escape the conclusion that the evangelist added a comment to the original verse, adapting it to context which he had created (v. 9c, referring to the coming of the light).

Of what period of time is the presence of the Logos "in the world" to be understood? If our demarcation of the hymn has been correct, it must have been thinking of the time before the Incarnation. This is indicated by the ἦν, which echoes the ἦν of vv. 4 and 9; the Incarnation is only announced in v. 14, and then as a new event (καί . . . ἐγένετο). An activity of the Logos in pre-Christian times is not foreign to primitive Christian thought, which was open to the Wisdom speculation and notions of pre-existence current among Jews (see below). In a quite different context, Paul identifies the mobile rock from which the Israelites received "spiritual drink" in their desert wanderings, with the pre-existing Christ (1 Cor 10:4). This train of thought could be linked with Hellenistic

---

[124] See commentaries of Zahn, Lagrange, Hoskyns.

[125] So Ruckstuhl, *Die literarische Einheit*, p. 92.

notions of the Logos, as was done not so much later by Justin in his doctrine of the λόγος σπερματικός.[126] The Fathers of the Church were almost unanimous in applying v. 10 to the λόγος ἄσαρκος, trying to lead men to the worship of God and to salvation by the light of natural reason—an interpretation which held the field till modern times.[127] But the hymn does not describe the partial success of the work of the Logos among mankind. It concentrates on the sad fact that the world "did not know him", his own "did not accept him". The same experience is ascribed to Wisdom in Jewish writings. "They did not know the way of wisdom (οὐκ ἔγνωσαν), or understand her paths. And their children did not reach her; they strayed far from her way" (Bar 3:20f.; cf. 31). Even Israel, among whom Wisdom had appeared (3:37), in the form of the Torah (4:1), had to be urged to repent: "Turn, O Jacob, and take her (ἐπιλαβοῦ αὐτῆς); walk in the radiance of her light" (4:2; cf. Prov 1:20–33). According to *Enoch*, 42:1f., Wisdom could find nowhere to dwell and was given a home in heaven. Whether or not the Wisdom speculation was here using an ancient myth and adapting it to its purposes need not be discussed here.[128] The affinities of our hymn with these texts may also be seen from the concept of "knowledge", which is nowhere a theoretical attitude, a rational apprehension, but the willing acceptance of instruction from God (cf. v. 11, "did not accept him"), and the following out in practice of the precepts given by Wisdom or the Torah or the Logos. Thus we read in Bar 3:9, "Hear the commandments of life, O Israel; give ear and learn wisdom (γνῶναι φρόνησιν)"! This notion of Wisdom coming from God, knowing his mind and instructing man in the right paths is developed in Wis 9:9–18, "With thee is wisdom, who knows thy works and was present when thou didst make the world, and who understands what is pleasing in thy sight and what is right according to thy commandments. Send her forth from the holy heavens, and from the throne of thy glory send her, that she may be with me in my toil and that I may learn what is pleasing to thee . . ."[129] Thus the "world" has deliberately and culpably closed its heart to the enlightening and salvific

[126] Main texts, *Apol.*, 5:2–4; 63:10, 16; *Append.*, 8:1–3; 10:1–8; 13:1–6. See R. Holte, "Logos Spermatikos. Christianity and Ancient Philosophy according to St Justin's Apologies".

[127] According to Schanz, *Johannes*, *ad loc.*, Maldonatus was the first to propose to explain it of the Logos incarnate, with only Gaudentius to appeal to among the Fathers, cf. *Tr.*, XII, 8f. (Glück, p. 112). Even after Maldonatus the older view prevailed, and it was only in more modern times that everything after v. 6 came to be applied to the work of the incarnate Logos (correctly, as we think, to the evangelist's mind).

[128] So Bultmann, "Der religionsgeschichtliche Hintergrund", esp. pp. 19ff. on the myth.

[129] For this concept of "knowing" see also Bar 3:10–14, 23, 31f.; 4:13; Prov. 1:2; 4:1; 9:10; 13:15; 30:3; Eccles 1:16–18; 7:25; 8:16; Wis 5:7; 10:8; Ecclus 6:27; 18:28 (all according to LXX).

work of the Logos and in doing so has rejected God himself. The ignorance is a disastrous refusal, by which men cut themselves off from God and from the realm of life.

The evangelist, however, undoubtedly referred the verse to the incarnate Logos. He signalled his historical coming at the end of v. 9, and now he sees in the refusal the unbelief which Jesus met with among his people. The leading circles of the Jews represent the κόσμος; they remain impervious, without understanding (cf. 8:14, 19; 9:29; also 8:28, 43) and indeed blind (9:39) when confronted with the "light of the world". It is a culpable attitude, and the ignorance is an obstinate refusal to believe (cf. 3:12; 5:38; 6:36; 8:24, 45; 12:37). If one reads the prologue continuously, this interpretation forces itself upon one: vv. 10f. must be understood of the Logos incarnate, as the history of modern exegesis (since Maldonatus) shows.

The interjection in v. 10b, which we have ascribed to the evangelist, may have been meant to refute the notion that the "world" owed its origin to an evil principle (cf. Gnosticism). This strophe of the hymn does in fact treat the "world" as something negative, which approximates to the notion of cosmos which we find in the Judaism of the day, in Hellenism and especially in Gnosis, though with all the different shades of meaning proper to each of these currents of thought and religious life. The "world" is a realm of evil which encompasses and influences man. Possibly the evangelist wished to obviate false conclusions as to the origin of the "world". Otherwise the interjection could be explained as stressing the Logos's claim on the "world" by reason of his having created it and its belonging to him (cf. τὰ ἴδια, v. 11)—or simply the identity of the pre-existent and incarnate Logos.

1:11	εἰς τὰ ἴδια ἦλθεν	He came to his domain,
	καὶ οἱ ἴδιοι αὐτὸν οὐ παρέλαβον.	but his own did not accept him.

The enigmatic and painful fact, that the Logos met with rejection in the world, is expressed still more pointedly, almost paradoxically, in v. 11: he came into his own realm, but his own, those who belonged to him, did not accept him. This does not mean that the hymn itself—as the Fathers often thought, on the basis of ἦλθεν—here spoke of the mission of the Logos incarnate and mourned his rejection. It is much more likely that the hymn followed its usual style (cf. v. 3a with 3b, v. 4b with 9a–b) and repeated the thought of v. 10 and intensified it. Originally v. 11 also continued to speak of the spiritual coming of the Logos to the world of human darkness, which closed its door, as it were, to the Logos who was so intimately akin to it. The aorist ἦλθεν does not stand in the way of this interpretation; the aorist οὐκ ἔγνω had already been used in the counterpart to "He was in the world". These aorists merely reflect the fact that the encounter between the Logos and the world took place in the reality of history. The Logos "was" in the world as a force constantly at work and permeating it, and still he "came" to it, insofar as it existed historically and was constantly made new offers. The "coming" of the Logos has a mythological ring, as in the Gnostic texts which speak of the "coming" of the heavenly envoy, meaning "Gnosis", as "redeemer".[130] But the Wisdom literature already used this type of imagery, in a non-mythological sense. In Wis 7:7 Solomon says: "Therefore I prayed, and understanding was given me; I called upon God, and the spirit of wisdom came to me (ἦλθέν μοι πνεῦμα σοφίας)." In Ecclus 24:6f. Wisdom says: "In the waves of the sea, in the whole earth, and in every people and nation I sought to reign.[131] Among all these I sought a resting place and someone in whose inheritance I could dwell." Wisdom, therefore, it is implied, found a welcome nowhere. V. 8 goes on to describe how Wisdom, at the command of her creator, pitched her tent in Israel. There is a remarkable parallel of thought and imagery in Jn 1:11 and 14: the Logos who was not accepted by the world of men pitched his tent, when he became incarnate, "among us", that is, among believers, who take the place of the ancient Israel.[132] The whole train of thought seems to be transposed on the Christian level, Wisdom replaced by the Logos, the pitching of the tent fully realized by the Incarnation. But there other symbols and typologies may also be involved (see commentary on v. 14).

That the Logos came εἰς τὰ ἴδια can mean: to his homeland or to his domain or property.[133] But the second alternative should be chosen, since the true homeland of the Logos is with God (cf. v. 1b). The world is called the domain (cf. Ezra 5:47 LXX; Lk 18:28; Jn 8:44) of the Logos, because it belongs to him by his creating it and is ordained to him as the world of man. Hence it is all the more saddening that "his own" did not accept him. The expression, which can indicate various types of association, is used above all of "those belonging to" someone, in the strict sense.[134] In the religious language of mysticism and Gnosis, the ἴδιοι are

[130] See *Odes of Solomon*, 6:10; 7:12ff., 21; 23:11, 16; 30:6; 33:1; 37:2; very frequent (with varying names) in Mandaean literature, cf. Jonas, *Gnosis*, vol. I, pp. 122–6; Bultmann, *Johannes*, pp. 462, 482; Manichean texts in Widengren, *The Great Vohu Manah*, *passim*. According to *Ascensio Is.*, 10–11, the redeemer Jesus Christ (a Gnostic figure) takes on all possible forms in a series of changes as he descends from the highest heaven. On the Gnostic concept see further Schlier, *Religionsgeschichtliche Untersuchungen*, pp. 35ff. See further excursus vi.

[131] LXX ἐκτησάμην. (א corr ηγησαμην); sy Vg "to reign".

[132] Spicq, "Le Siracide", holds that the prologue depends directly on Ecclesiasticus. He adduces Ecclus 17:11ff. as well as 24:7ff. (pp. 188f. and the tables p. 191).

[133] Arndt and Gingrich, *Lexicon*, s. v. 3 b; Bauer, *Johannesevangelium*, favours the first meaning; Jervell, "Er kam in sein Eigentum. Zu Joh. 1:11", esp. p. 21 also favours "homeland".

[134] Arndt and Gingrich, *Lexicon*, s. v. 3a with the texts there cited.

the favoured and elect who have received divine revelation and attained the goal of union with God.[135] Such a notion can hardly be intended here, since all men are envisaged and it is precisely their estrangement from the revealer that is stressed. Otherwise one would have to assume that the hymn was contesting the claim of those who called themselves ἴδιοι, on the grounds that they had closed their hearts to the true envoy, the real divine "light". It is to be noted that the evangelist does use the word in the strict sense, to express actual union (13:1; cf. 10:3f., and "mine" in 10:14, 27, "thine" in 17:6, 9f.). The Logos who comes to his "domain" lays claim to all men, because for all he is the "light" (vv. 4 and 9). "Receive" is probably from the metaphor of welcoming to a house[136] or has perhaps the more general sense of accepting as partner.[137]

The evangelist once more certainly understood the verse of the historical coming (ἦλθεν, cf. ἐρχόμενον, v. 9c) of the Logos and saw in the non-acceptance the mysterious fact of Jewish unbelief. It is then quite possible that at τὰ ἴδια he thought of the people who were God's "own possession"[138] and at οἱ ἴδιοι of the Jews of the day who as members of this people incomprehensibly rejected the eschatological saviour.[139] He could thus link up still more closely with the texts which spoke of Wisdom's dwelling in Israel (cf. Bar 3:37f.; Ecclus 24:8 ff.). "Israel" is still an honoured name for him (cf. 1:31, 49; 3:10; 12:13) and it is only disbelief with regard to Jesus that makes him see the people of God as "the Jews", who become the representatives of the godless "world". However, since no such polemic is audible in the rest of the prologue, even where it is certainly the work of the evangelist, there is no compelling reason to believe that he had Israel in mind.[140] He too could have thought of men in general as the ἴδιοι, insofar as they had opposed and still opposed the acceptance of the Logos in the flesh. In this case his

---

[135] *C. Herm.*, I, 31: Ἅγιος ὁ θεός, ὃς γνωσθῆναι βούλεται καὶ γινώσκεται τοῖς ἰδίοις; *Odes of Solomon*, 7:12 (14): "He hath given Him(self?) to be seen of them that are his" 42:20 (26): "For they are free men and they are mine"; also 7:16, 8:14, 20; 10:6; 17:11 24:6; 26:1. Texts from Christian Gnosis in Bultmann, *Johannes*, pp. 34f., n. 7; see further Jervell, "Er kam in sein Eigentum", pp. 16–20.

[136] Cf. Jud 6:21; Song 8:2 LXX; Mt 1:20, 24; (2 Jn 10); Josephus, *Ant.*, I, 302; XVII, 9. According to Schlatter, *Johannes*, *ad loc.*, the Semitic had no way of expressing what παρέλαβον added to ἔλαβον; is this a sign that the hymn was composed in Greek?

[137] Cf. Liddell and Scott, vol. II, col. 1315; Arndt and Gingrich, *Lexicon*, s. v. 3, translates "accepted".

[138] But Exod 19:5; 23:22; Deut 7:6; 14:2; 26:18 have λαὸς περιούσιος; Is 43:21 λαόν μου, ὃν περιεποιησάμην; cf. 31:5; Ezek 13:18f.; Mal 3:17; Acts 20:28; Eph 1:14; 1 Pet 2:9.

[139] So the commentaries of Schanz, Knabenbauer, Tillmann, Pölzl and Innitzer, Lagrange, Strachan, Hoskyns, Barrett (who allows also the wider sense); Dodd, *Interpretation*, p. 402.

[140] Cf. commentaries of Thomas Aquinas (Cai), Loisy, Bauer, Schlatter, Bultmann, Wikenhauser.

presentation would also be an urgent appeal to join the number of believers (cf. 1:12f.; 20:31).

1:12	ὅσοι δὲ ἔλαβον αὐτόν, ἔδωκεν αὐτοῖς ἐξουσίαν τέκνα θεοῦ γενέσθαι, τοῖς πιστεύουσιν εἰς τὸ ὄνομα αὐτοῦ,	But to all who received him he gave power to become children of God, to those who believe in his name,

The depressing fact, that the Logos met with misunderstanding and rejection from men when he came into the world, is now contrasted with the truth that there were still some who "received" him. This dialectical procedure and the expression λαμβάνειν τινά show clearly the hand of the evangelist. When looking back on the public ministry of Jesus (12:37–43), he likewise first states categorically that Jesus's hearers did not believe in him in spite of the great signs (v. 37), and uses Scripture to explain this enigmatic hardening of their hearts (vv. 38–41); but then he goes on: "Nonetheless, even among the rulers there were many who believed in him" (v. 42). The same movement of thought is found in 3:32f., and it is in keeping with his way of seeing things in black and white, and contrasting negative and positive statements.[141] The expression λαμβάνειν τινά is a characteristic of Johannine style, to speak of the acceptance of faith,[142] of the reception of the divine envoy and his words[143] (cf. 5: 43; 13:20); in the logion 13:20 the Synoptics use δέχεσθαι instead (Mt 10:40 par.).[144] Just as in Gnosis the envoy from the heavenly world is in a strange land where he finds his own, who listen to his "revelation" and learn Gnosis, too in John the Son of God made man meets men who belong to him. But on closer inspection there are important differences: in John (1) it is the Father who leads believers to Jesus and entrusts them to him (cf. 6:37 ff., 44, 65; 10:29; 17:6, 9); (2) it is the personal decision of faith which brings about union with Jesus; (3) there is no basic exclusion of non-Gnostics, those who are not "pneumatics" by nature. The contrast with Gnosticism becomes even clearer as the verse goes on: to those who received him in faith, the Logos gave power to *become* children of God. Hence they are not yet his children and do not become so by knowledge

---

[141] Cf. 3:18 ff., 35f.; 5:29; 6:36 ff., 64f.; 8:23 ff.; 9:39; 10:13f., 26f.; 12:44 ff.; 15:18 ff.; 17:6 ff., 14 ff.

[142] Cf. *Odes of Solomon*, 9:7, "that those who have known him may not perish, and that those who receive [him] (נְסַב) may not be ashamed"; also 42:3(4), "that I might be hidden to those that were not holding me" (אָחִיד).

[143] Cf. λαμβάνειν τὴν μαρτυρίαν 3:11, 32f.; τὰ ῥήματα 12:48; also 17:8.

[144] A stylistic criterion, Ruckstuhl, *Die literarische Einheit*, no. 23 (on which see p. 196); on Jn 13:20 cf. Noack, *Zur johanneischen Tradition*, pp. 68 and 98. Ἔρχεσθαι πρός can have the same sense, cf. 5:40; 6:35, 37, 44f., 65; also 3:20f.; 7:37.

of their pneumatic quality. They must first receive from the Logos the real capacity[145] to be children of God. In fact, ἐξουσίαν could have been omitted (cf. Bultmann, *ad loc.*), because in John διδόναι alone (with infinitive) can indicate God's bestowal of grace (cf. 3:27; 5:26; 6:31, 65; 19:11); but it can also be added as a mark of emphasis (cf. 5:27; with ἔχειν, 10:18), to lay stress on the power conferred by God. Men of themselves cannot attain to sonship of God (cf. 1 Jn 3:1); sonship only becomes a real possibility when the capacity thereto conferred by divine power is revealed by the mediator. How it comes about, we are not told for the moment; but the evangelist makes it clear shortly after (v. 13), in terms which the Christian reader can understand, that he means baptism.

Divine sonship is a gift of God according to the Johannine writings, bestowed gratuitously by God's love on the baptized (cf. 1 Jn 3:1).[146] It brings with it the moral duty of proving oneself to be child of God, especially in the exercise of brotherly love. But it is most unlikely that "becoming children of God" in v. 12 expresses directly this ethical consequence of being born of God by grace (v. 13)—the sequence would also be strange. It speaks of the supernatural process which takes place in baptism. Thus the relative clause in v. 13 adds a fuller explanation of how one becomes a child of God. John never speaks of "becoming" in the moral sense.[147] The basic Johannine (and Pauline) precept of Christian morality is not "become what you are", but "be and be known for what you have become".[148]

But before illustrating the supernatural process of birth from God, the evangelist explains further what is required of man. The reception of the Logos and redeemer from God takes place in faith. The dative participle after αὐτοῖς takes up the relative clause at the beginning of the sentence (a similar construction in 1 Jn 5:13). Faith is the basic prerequisite for salvation, and in Johannine theology the one condition which contains all others (cf. 6:29). The expression "believe in his name" is typically and

---

[145] To give or to have ἐξουσίαν is a phrase which plays a certain part in Gnosticism, cf. *Odes of Solomon*, 22:4, "He who gave me authority over my bonds that I might loose them" (the Coptic has ἐξουσία "power"); 23:9(8), "because it was not permitted them to loose its seal"; also *C. Herm.*, I, 13, 14, 32. The translation "to be entitled to" (cf. Foerster, "ἐξουσία", p. 566) is too weak.

[146] Cf. 1 Jn 3:10 ff.; 4:7 ff.; 5:1 ff.; see Schnackenburg, *Letters of St John*, excursus viii.

[147] When John is urging the children of God to prove themselves such, he either invokes directly the commandment of brotherly love (13:34; 15:12f.; 1 Jn 2:7 ff.; 3:11, 23; 4:21) or points out that such love is an indelible sign of sonship of God (1 Jn 3:10; 4:7, 12, 20; 5:2). The moral behaviour of the children of God, of which Chrysostom, Theophylactus, Bede, Maldonatus, Calmes and Schanz think, and which is also considered by Thomas Aquinas, is foreign to the context, since it deals with accepting the Logos, the faith required for this and the power of acquiring salvation which is bestowed on believers.

[148] See Kirchgässner, *Erlösung und Sünde im Neuen Testament*, p. 153.

exclusively Johannine (cf. 2:23; 3:18; 1 Jn 3:23; 5:13) and implies the acceptance of Jesus to the full extent of his self-revelation. Such an act of faith is possible only in the encounter with a historical bringer of salvation, a person who is the mediator of salvation (cf. excursus vii).

1:13	οἳ οὐκ ἐξ αἱμάτων οὐδὲ ἐκ θελή- ματος σαρκὸς οὐδὲ ἐκ θελήματος ἀνδρὸς ἀλλ' ἐκ θεοῦ ἐγεννήθησαν.	who are born not of blood, nor of the desire of the flesh, nor of the desire of man, but of God.

Just as "to those who believe in his name" is added to explain "those who received him", so too v. 13 explains how to "become children of God". Natural birth does not make one child of God, nor any other natural process. It is a strictly supernatural event, wrought by God alone. The three negatives excluding all natural factors are, however, so striking that one may well suspect "vehement polemics" behind the verse (von Harnack). But the first question is whether the tripartite division is original. Two MSS (B, 17) and many patristic quotations[149] omit the third phrase οὐδὲ ἐκ θελήματος ἀνδρός.

There are still more variants in the patristic quotations. For the plural αἱμάτων, which is strange—and hence probably original—some have a singular; elsewhere οὐδὲ ἐκ θελήματος σαρκός appears as οὐδὲ ἐκ σαρκός, so that we have a phrase with the two terms "blood and flesh", which is a Semitic way of saying "man" (for the inversion of the customary "flesh and blood", cf. Eph 6:12; Heb 2:14). Boismard suggests[150] that the reading "not through blood and not through flesh" competed with οὐκ ἐκ θελήματος ἀνδρός originally, and that the two readings were later combined to give the three-membered reading of most of our MSS. (The reading with the singular is discussed below). This is possible, but not certain, since it involves a number of hypotheses.

The sharp antithesis is probably to be explained by the positive theological interests of the evangelist, who presents the birth from God as the incomprehensible work of the divine Spirit, utterly beyond man's reach (cf. 3:6). He stresses the supernatural origin of the children of God, to show their contrast to the "world" (v. 10) and their kinship with the Logos, the mediator of divine grace and truth (v. 16). The consciousness of belonging to God and being born of God characterizes "Johannine" Christianity and gives it the certainty of being superior to the "world" (cf. 1 Jn 4:4; 5:4).

The "birth from God" itself remains a mystery (cf. 3:8), and it appears as such by the contrast to the natural birth of man. This is described by three phrases which are designed to bring out the earthly character of the

149 Listed by Boismard, "Critique textuelle et citations patristiques", pp. 403f.

150 Boismard, pp. 407f.

event. It is linked with the blood,[151] sexual desire in general and the urge of the man in particular, as God says in the *Book of Enoch* to the "watchers of heaven" (the "sons of God" of Gen 6): "Though you were holy, spiritual and living the eternal life, you have defiled yourselves with the blood of women and have begotten children with the blood of flesh, and as the children of men, have lusted after flesh and blood as those also do who die and perish" (*Enoch*, 15:4); see further Wis 7:1f. The birth from God is an act (note the aorist) of divine and heavenly origin (cf. 3:3, ἄνωθεν; 3:6, 8, ἐκ τοῦ πνεύματος). The Christian reader cannot but think of baptism (cf. 3:5), whereby sonship of God is *acquired*, which it is important to emphasize in contrast to the Gnostic position—cf. *Odes of Solomon*, 41:1, 8ff.: "All the Lord's children will praise him . . . All will be astonished that see me. For from another race am I: for the Father of truth remembered me: He who possessed me from the beginning: for his bounty begot me and the thought of His heart."

V. 13 appears in a completely different light if one accepts the reading in the singular (ὅς . . . ἐγεννήθη) as the original. It may have been read this way as early as Justin,[152] and then by Hippolytus;[153] it was certainly in Irenaeus[154] and the *Epistula Apostolorum*.[155] It is formally attested by the Old Latin *Codex Veronensis* (b), the *Liber comicus* (Toledo lectionary),[156] some MSS of the Syriac versions[157] and above all by Tertullian in North Africa. He reproaches the Valentinians with using the plural to support their doctrine of "the secret seed of the elect and pneumatic".[158] But he overlooks the point that the plural ascribes birth from God to all believers, so that the Valentinians would be deforming their own doctrine with this reading. Tertullian is therefore an indirect witness to the antiquity of the plural in Africa, and hence the text

---

151 The plural αἵματα occurs in the Old Testament for shedding the blood of a number of people, cf. 2 Sam 16:8; 1 Kgs 2:33; 2 Kgs 9:7, 26; 1 Chr 22:8; Ps 9:13 etc. (LXX); *Letter of Aristeas*, 88, 90; cf. Behm, "αἷμα", p. 172; Funk, *Greek Grammar*, para. 141, 6. It is found only in classical Greek for birth, cf. Cadbury, "The Ancient Physiological Notions Underlying Joh 1:13a; Heb 11:11". Augustine, *Sermo* 121, 4 (*PL* 38, col. 679); cf. *Tr. in Jo.*, II, 14 also spoke of the *mixtis sanguinibus* of the two parents.

152 See esp. *Dial.*, 63, 2, but also *Apol.*, 22, 2; 32, 9; *Dial.*, 54, 2; 61, 1, 76, 2. But it is controverted that Justin is alluding to Jn 1:13 in these passages.

153 *Ref.*, VI, 9, 2 (Wendland, p. 136); but it is very questionable that it is a quotation.

154 *Adv. haer.*, III, 17, 1; 20, 2 (cf. 26, 1; 27) V, 1, 3.

155 "The Word, which became flesh through the holy virgin Mary, was carried (conceived) in her womb by the Holy Spirit and was born not by the lust of the flesh but by the will of God" (Duensing, "Epistula Apostolorum", p. 192).

156 Ed. Morin, p. 60: "qui non ex sanguinibus neque ex voluptate viri, sed ex deo natus est."

157 Sy^{c} and six Peshitto MSS have the relative in the plural and the verb in the singular. But Lagrange, *Saint Jean*, p. 18, is certainly correct in saying that the loss of the *vau* in the verb means little, since it often happens in Syriac; Zahn, *Johannes*, p. 714, takes a different view, and explains the Syriac *'ilein d^{e}* by the influence of Greek MSS.

158 *De carne Christi*, 19 (*Corpus Christianorum* 2, p. 907a).

given by all Greek MSS cannot be a late innovation.[159] According to internal criteria, the plural reading is to be preferred. It is easy to understand that an attestation of the virgin birth was sought in the fourth Gospel at an early date, but it is hard to imagine the opposite case, that such a testimony would have been later eliminated.[160] And it is only the change from the plural to the singular that explains the awkwardness of the expression with regard to the birth of Jesus: it seems to exclude not merely a human father, but any type of human cooperation. The virgin birth of Christ, finally, which was deduced from the text by the *Epistula Apostolorum* 3, and then by Tertullian (*De carne Christi*, 24, 2, against the Ebionites), does not fit into the context, since ἐγεννήθη would anticipate the subsequent affirmation of the Incarnation (v. 14). Or is it not the virgin birth that is emphasized, but the fact that the Logos, "born of God" in the sublimest way, enables those who receive him to be born of God?[161] But it is questionable whether 1 Jn 5:18 may be adduced for this (see there); the aorist indicative would be strange and the grammatical connection bad. Both readings may be ancient, but the plural must be considered original,[162] in spite of the suspicion that this text (v. 12c and 13) was added to the first draft (v. 12a–b) at some stage. Since v. 12a–b, on account of its Johannine style, may be regarded, as we have said, as the evangelist's expansion of the hymn, and since vv. 12c–13 also display characteristics of Johannine style and thought, possibly the disciples, in the course of the redaction, added in some more explanatory comments of their master—but rather awkwardly, from the grammatical point of view, and not called for by the movement of the thought.[163]

1:14	καὶ ὁ λόγος σὰρξ ἐγένετο	And the Word was made flesh
	καὶ ἐσκήνωσεν ἐν ἡμῖν,	and dwelt among us,
	καὶ ἐθεασάμεθα τὴν δόξαν αὐτοῦ,	and we saw his glory,
	δόξαν ὡς μονογενοῦς παρὰ πατρός,	the glory, such as belongs to the only-begotten from the Father,
	πλήρης χάριτος καὶ ἀληθείας.	full of grace and truth.

[159] The textual problem is discussed more fully in Resch, *Ausserkanonische Paralleltexte zu den Evangelien*, pp. 57–60; Zahn, *Johannes*, pp. 711–4; Harnack, *Zur neutestamentlichen Textkritik*, pp. 115–27; Lagrange, *Saint Jean*, pp. 16–18; Braun, "Qui ex Deo natus est, Joh 1:13"; Boismard, "Citations patristiques", pp. 406f; id., *Prologue*, pp. 56f.; Castellini, "De Jo 1:13 in quibusdam citationibus patristicis" (Apollinaris of Laodicea and Procopius of Gaza not witnesses for the singular); J. Schmid, "Joh 1, 13", esp. pp. 119f.

[160] Cf. Houssiau, "Le milieu théologique de la leçon ἐγεννήθη, Jo 1:13".

[161] So Boismard, "Citations patristiques", p. 407; id., *Prologue*, p. 56.

[162] The singular reading is favoured by Resch, Loisy, Zahn, Harnack, Büchsel, Braun, Boismard; but most modern commentators prefer the plural, as also J. Schmid, "Joh 1:13" and Williams, *Alterations to the Text of the Synoptic Gospels and Acts*, pp. 30f.; Lamarche, "Le Prologue", pp. 506–10.

[163] Harnack, *Textkritik*, pp. 124f., proposed the following explanation: a marginal gloss (in the singular) on v. 14 originally, was later taken into the text of v. 13. For an answer in the sense given above see Bernard, *St John*, vol. I, pp. CXLV and 15 ("comment to avoid misunderstanding of v. 11"); see further Schmid, "Joh 1:13", p. 124, though he makes v. 12a–b part of the original hymn to the Logos.

The hymn to the Logos now reaches its climax. The fact that the Logos is again mentioned explicitly is already a link with v. 1; but the thought itself swoops back. It expresses the unmistakable paradox that the Logos who dwelt with God, clothed in the full majesty of the divinity and possessing the fullness of the divine life, entered the sphere of the earthly and human, the material and perishable, by becoming flesh.[164] This is something new (καί . . .) and unique, which took place only once, a real event (ἐγένετο). The καί indicates in the original hymn to the Logos a stage of historical progress (it is, therefore, a καί which really marks an advance). The Logos had already been spiritually present and active in the world, even though he met with rejection from men (vv. 10f., 3rd strophe); but now the incomprehensible takes place: he comes into the flesh, becomes man and pitches his tent among men. In the present construction of the prologue, as worked over by the evangelist, this special coming of the Logos once in history is probably presupposed since v. 9; now its full reality is made explicit. On this supposition the καί must be understood as confirmative ("and indeed, truly").[165] A profound theological truth is contained in the interpretation of Chrysostom and Augustine, who understand the καί as explanatory: through the Incarnation, the Logos enabled us to be partakers of the divine sonship.[166] But this does not do justice to the context, and displaces the centre of gravity from v. 14 back to vv. 12f. But the main interest is centred on the Logos, and it is only at the end of this last strophe of the hymn (v. 16) that we are told how this unique event affects our salvation: through the coming of the Logos we have all received grace upon grace from his fullness.

That the marvellous process of the Incarnation is in the nature of a historical event, is brought out by the ἐγένετο which follows the series of ἦν (vv. 1, 4, 9, 10). It is a different γίνεσθαι from the "appearance" of John the Baptist (v. 6) and the "coming to be" of creation (vv. 3, 10b); the context alone provides the key. The affirmation, which is fundamental for Christology, cannot mean: "The Logos was changed into flesh", since the Logos remains the subject in the following affirmation ("and dwelt among us") and made his divine glory visible—in the flesh—to believers. And it cannot mean that the Logos merely appeared in a fleshly disguise; this would not do justice to the verb γίνεσθαι. Athanasius is on good Johannine ground when he explains the σὰρξ ἐγένετο as εἰς σάρκα παραγέγονεν;[167]

---

[164] The Fathers already linked v. 14 with v. 1, esp. Athanasius, cf. Gennaro, *Exegetica*, pp. 145 ff.

[165] The καί can be taken as consecutive ("and so"), Funk, *Greek Grammar*, p. 442, 2, or as καὶ νῦν ("and now"), *ibid.*, 442, 15; cf. the καί in v. 16; Lagrange, *ad loc.*

[166] Chrysostom, *Hom. in Jo.*, XI, 1 (*PG* 59, col. 79); Augustine, *Tr. in Jo.*, II, 15 (*Corpus christianorum* 36, pp. 18f.).

[167] Athanasius, *Sermo maior de fide*, 1 (*PG* 26, col. 1265); on his interpretation, see Gennaro, *Exegetica*, pp. 157f.

the Johannine profession of faith Ἰησοῦν Χριστὸν ἐν σαρκὶ ἐληλυθότα (1 Jn 4:2; cf. 2 Jn 7) has the same meaning. The ἐγένετο announces a change in the mode of being of the Logos: hitherto he was in glory with his Father (cf. 17:5, 24), now he takes on the lowliness of human, earthly existence; formerly he was "with God" (1:1b), now he pitches his tent among men, and in human form, in the full reality of the σάρξ, to attain once more the glory of his heavenly mode of being after his return to the Father (17:5). This is a history-centred view of salvation, which also finds expression in terms of the descent and ascent of the Son of Man (3:13, 31; 6:62). He who descends and ascends is the one heavenly Son of Man who even on earth remains in constant union with heaven (1:51). The Incarnation, the "coming in the flesh", takes place so that mankind on earth may be brought heavenly revelation and divine life (cf. 3:31–36). Hence the Logos's "becoming flesh" marks a turning-point in the history of salvation; it provides a final ("eschatological") possibility of salvation for men. The way of the Redeemer down into the flesh, and the way upwards through the flesh to heavenly glory also becomes a way for all who attach themselves to him in faith (cf. 14:2f., 6). In this perspective the two "natures" of Christ, the divine and human, do not stand out; it is rather a sequence of events in the history of salvation which is depicted (Geiselmann[168])—as in Phil 2:6–11. But the doctrine of the two natures is comprised therein, in germ, and can be developed legitimately from 1:14 in the metaphysical thinking of the Greek Fathers.[169] "The Word became flesh ... and did not cease to be what he was before".[170]

Why does the hymn speak of becoming flesh and not simply of becoming man? When it stands by itself, σάρξ is not just another way of saying "man" (as πᾶσα σάρξ, 17:2). In Johannine terms, it expresses that which is earth-bound (3:6), transient and perishable (6:63), the typically human mode of being, as it were, in contrast to all that is divine and spiritual.[171] In the mind of the evangelist, it is linked up with the cosmic dualism of "above–below" (cf. 3:3; 8:23) and "earth–heaven" (3:31); in the incarnate Logos heaven sinks to earth. On the other hand, the notion of flesh as sinful, inclined to sin or fettered by sin (1 Jn 2:16), is

---

[168] Geiselmann, *Jesus der Christus*, p. 146.

[169] See Grillmeier, "Die theologische und sprachliche Vorbereitung der christologischen Formel von Chalkedon", esp. pp. 25–28.

[170] Jerome, *Adv. Jovinianum*, II, 29 (*PL* 23, col. 326), quoted by Gennaro, *Exegetica*, p. 169, with wrong reference.

[171] Cf. the Old Testament opposition between "weak flesh" and "God", e.g. Gen 6:3; Is 31:3; Jer 17:5; Ps 78:39; Job 10:4f.; Ecclus 14:17f. So too *1 QH*, 4:29, "But how can flesh be equal to his, and how can a thing of clay do such wonders?" This is not the same as the strongly dualistic tendency to contrast "(sinful) flesh" and "spirit", which is apparent at Qumran and comes to dominate Pauline thinking.

not included here. For John, Christ in the flesh is not the representative of Adamite man, as in Paul (cf. Rom 8:3), but the leader who brings earth-bound man home to the heavenly world of life and glory (cf. 6:62f.; 14:6; 17:24). It may also be doubted that the Logos-hymn contains the thought of the expiatory sacrifice, of the "flesh for the life of the world" (6:51c). But it is probably already in the mind of the evangelist, who then brings it out clearly in the discourse on the bread of life; the flesh assumed by the Logos in the Incarnation is the presupposition of the death on the Cross (cf. 19:34; 1 Jn 5:6). Σάρξ indicates full human reality; the Fathers were right in claiming this for Christ against all efforts to diminish it (e.g. Apollinaris).[172] But they also felt that docetism was attacked, and the Logos hymn undoubtedly envisaged Gnostic falsifications of the Christian faith, which were already giving the communities some trouble, and which they parried by professions of faith (cf. 1 Jn 2:22; 4:2f.; 5:1, 5f.). We cannot say for certain whether the false doctrine attributed only an apparent body to the Redeemer (cf. also 19:34f.), or denied the identity of the man Jesus with the divine Logos or held in general that redemption by a man of flesh and blood was superfluous; but in any case, the anti-Gnostic tone is unmistakable. The Johannine mode of expression is not fully explained if it is taken merely as a profession of faith or as a liturgical utterance (cf. Rom 1:31; 1 Tim 3:16—where, however, there is a contrast between the "fleshly" and "pneumatic" modes of Christ's being).

But if there is an anti-Gnostic point, all the ostensible parallels which have been adduced from Hellenism, and in particular from Gnosticism,[173] become very dubious. The idea of a divine being appearing—but doing no more than that, *appearing*—on earth in human form was widespread at the time and could take on various forms. But after the affirmation of the Incarnation in 1:14 the Christian teaching on the Son of God made man cannot be reduced to one variety among others: it can only be understood as a protest against all other religions of redemption in Hellenism and Gnosticism. It is a new and profoundly original way of confessing the Saviour who has come "palpably" (1 Jn 1:1) in history as a unique, personal human being, who has manifested himself in the reality of the "flesh". And the "language of mythology" (Bultmann) is not retained in Jn 1:14; for such language takes the utmost pains to avoid the term σάρξ,[174] and it never speaks of "becoming flesh".

---

[172] Esp. Gregory of Nazianzus; cf. Gennaro, *Exegetica*, pp. 148.ff.

[173] Cf. Bauer, *ad loc.*; Bultmann, "Mandäische und manichäische Quellen", pp. 104ff.; id., *Johannes*, *ad loc.*; see also the material in Schlier, *Religionsgeschichtliche Untersuchungen*, pp. 6ff.; Widengren, *The Great Vohu Manah*, *passim*; further, excursus vi.

[174] Arndt and Gingrich, *Lexicon*, s. v. σάρξ 3, quotes Artemidorus 2:35, ἐὰν σάρκινοι οἱ θεοὶ φαίνωνται; but it is significant that this text says "*appear* in fleshly form"; φαίνεσθαι does

The fundamental affirmation of the Incarnation must also be borne in mind in the next phrase, which speaks metaphorically of the Logos "pitching his tent" or "dwelling" among us (both translations are possible[175]). The image, for which a genuine parallel can hardly be found in pagan Hellenism, recalls primarily the Wisdom speculation, where there are clear affinities in Ecclus 24:8 (κατασκήνωσον), cf. also v. 4 and v. 10 (see commentary above on Jn 1:11). According to *Enoch* 42:1, heaven is assigned to Wisdom as its dwelling-place, after it has sought one in vain among men. But the Christian message is that the Logos, in spite of rejection by men (vv. 10f.), set up his tent among us in a new and unique way. This mode of presence surpasses everything that could have been said of Wisdom, as a comparison with Bar 3:38 shows: "Afterwards she (Wisdom) appeared (ὤφθη) on earth and lived with men." But the Logos stayed among us as a real man. But since the earthly presence of the Logos is the vehicle of grace and salvation ("full of grace and truth"), the theme of God's dwelling among the people of Israel must also have been envisaged, and applied here to the Logos.

The sacred tent, which was originally the "place of meeting" where Yahweh gave Moses and the people instructions and precepts from time to time, is not (at least originally) a symbol of the perpetual dwelling of God in Israel. But the ark of the covenant was regarded as Yahweh's throne, and passages like Num 35:34; Jos 22:19; 1 Kg 6:13; 1 Chr 23:25; 2 Chr 6:1f.; 2 Ezra 6:12; 7:15; 11:9 (LXX), where κατασκηνοῦν stands for שָׁכַן, show how natural the thought of Yahweh's "dwelling" in the sanctuary had become. Here perhaps originally disparate notions[176] have been combined. And the "glory of Yahweh" (כָּבוֹד, δόξα), which first appears in the "cloud" (cf. Exod 16:10), is afterwards linked to the sacred tent and the temple, cf. especially Exod 40:34f., "The cloud covered the tent of meeting, and the glory of the Lord filled the tabernacle"; for the temple, cf. 1 Kg 8:11. This could also explain the mention of the δόξα of the Logos in 1:14. But there is reason to believe (see below) that this theological association was not yet present in the original hymn. The clause v. 14 b has probably been inserted by the evangelist, while the hymn telling of the Logos staying among us went on to say at once: πλήρης χάριτος καὶ ἀληθείας. The hymn is intent on the presence of the Logos with all his blessings (cf. v. 16); the vision of the δόξα of Jesus is referred specifically in the Gospel to the believer's comprehension of the miraculous signs (cf. 2:11; 11:40).[177] The late Jewish term *Shekina*, which is not met with before the destruction of the temple, is merely a substitute for the divine name. It expresses, for instance, the gracious presence of God among the pious when gathered

---

not occur in the New Testament in Christological contexts (only φανεροῦσθαι). The *Gospel of Philip* 23 shows how the Gnostics could travesty the sense of σάρξ.

[175] Cf. Arndt and Gingrich, *Lexicon*, s. v. σκηνή and σκηνόω; Liddell and Scott, vol. II, pp. 1608f.

[176] Cf. Nötscher, *Biblische Altertumskunde*, pp. 270–9; von Rad, "Kabhod im Alten Testament", p. 243; id., *Theologie des Alten Testaments*, vol. I, pp. 233–40, E.T.: pp. 234–41; Eichrodt, *Theologie des Alten Testaments*, vol. I, pp. 59–63, E.T.: pp. 109–12.

[177] The Old Testament typological background is certainly overestimated by Goppelt, *Typos*, pp. 218f.; Boismard, *Prologue*, pp. 169f.

for prayer or for study of the law[178]—a type of thought and language confined to the Jews, which can hardly have influenced Jn 1:14.

"Among us", in the context of the hymn and according to the parallels from the Wisdom literature, means no more than "among human beings" —though the community chanting the hymn must also have been aware that the coming of the incarnate Logos is only apprehended by believers. But there is no suggestion of a restricted circle of the elect: the Logos, the light for every man (v. 9) also came in the flesh to all men. Hence the next statement, "and we saw his glory", creates a certain difficulty. The speakers ("we"—though this is not emphasized) are not simply representatives of the human race, nor even believers as a whole (cf. v. 16, ἡμεῖς πάντες), but those who saw the glory of the incarnate Logos—the witnesses, in fact, of his work on earth and particularly of the "signs" whereby he revealed his glory (cf. 1:50f.; 2:11; 11:40). The evangelist undoubtedly voices here—as in 1 Jn 1:1–3—his own experience as a believer, based on immediate fellowship with the incarnate Logos. He and a group of similar witnesses apprehended the divine glory of the eternal Logos, in and in spite of the flesh (cf. 1 Jn 1:1), by means of the "signs" which were at once so clear and so mysterious.[179] He was hardly thinking of any particular manifestation of the divine radiance, such as the transfiguration of Jesus, which is not recounted in John;[180] he and his fellow-witnesses experienced the divine majesty of Jesus in his works. Hence this clause must be considered as an addition made by the evangelist to the hymn, especially as the continuation, "the glory, such as belongs to the only-begotten, from the Father" also shows traces of his hand.

The Logos hymn had spoken only of "God", not of the "Father";[181] and μονογενής as an epithet for Christ, the Son of God, is also a term proper to the evangelist (1:18; 3:16, 18; cf. 1 Jn 4:9). Since δόξα as such is a propriety of all heavenly beings, the evangelist wished to stress the unique δόξα of the Son of God; hence the ὡς does not mark a restriction ("as though", "as it were") or make a comparison, but defines the glory precisely and indicates its exact nature.[182] The μονογενής is probably

---

[178] Cf. *Aboth*, III, 2b: "R. Chananiah ben Teradion said ... 'But if two sit together and study the words of the Torah, the *shekina* is in the midst of them"; see further Billerbeck, vol. II, pp. 314f.; Marmorstein, "Iranische und jüdische Religion", pp. 239f., who says: "Wherever Israel goes into exile, to Babylon, Media, Greece or Rome, the spiritual temple, the living *shekina* goes with it."

[179] The verb θεᾶσθαι, which also occurs 1 Jn 1:1 does not allow us to conclude to a metaphorical sense of "spiritual", much less "mystical" seeing, cf. the further occurrences 1:32, 38; 4:35; 6:5; 11:45. On the question of who the "we" are, see Schnackenburg, *Letters of St John*, excursus i.

[180] Against Dupont, *Essais*, p. 279; Boismard, *Prologue*, p. 71.

[181] Cf. esp. 1:1 πρὸς τὸν θεόν with 1 Jn 1:2 πρὸς τὸν πατέρα.

[182] This is often the function of ὡς, cf. Arndt and Gingrich, *Lexicon*, s. v. III, 1; so too

based on the Hebrew יָחִיד, which can mean both "unique, only-begotten" and "beloved".[183] The preposition παρά need mean no more than a genitive[184] and should be taken with μονογενοῦς rather than with the remoter word δόξαν. Then the phrase would simply mean "the only-begotten Son of God" (3:18; cf. 3:16; 1 Jn 4:9). But it is also possible that it is a short way of saying "the only-begotten (Son), coming from the Father"—a thought that recurs constantly in the context.[185] All the passages which have been cited since the Fathers to prove the "procession" of the Son within the Trinity refer, in the mind of the evangelist, to the temporal mission in the world (8:42; 13:3; 16:27f.; 17:8). If, however, one joins παρὰ πατρός to δόξαν, it is also possible to understand: a glory which befits him as the uniquely-loved Son, coming from the Father, that is, given by the Father (cf. 17:5, 24), just as his life is given him by his Father (5:26). The Son would then participate in the divine life and glory by virtue of the eternal love which the Father had for him even before the creation of the world (17:24), and the patristic interpretation, which finds the immanent Trinity attested here,[186] would be supported—not by the being "born of the Father", for which the preposition παρά would in any case be too weak—but by the primal, eternal communication of the divine glory to the Son by the Father. However, it is undoubtedly better to take παρὰ πατρός with μονογενοῦς.

According to the Greek, the notion of origin cannot be excluded from μονογενής;[187] but in view of the Hebrew sub-stratum, it cannot be certainly affirmed. It might have been part of the Son of God Christology of the evangelist; but once more he appears to remain for the moment within the tradition of the voice from heaven at the baptism (cf. the variant ὁ ἐκλεκτός in 1:34).

---

already Chrysostom, *Hom.*, XII, 1, *PG* 59, 82; see further Lagrange, Schlatter, Bultmann *ad loc.*; Boismard, *Prologue*, pp. 72f.

[183] LXX translates יָחִיד both by μονογενής and ἀγαπητός, cf. Jg 11:34 where both are combined; μονογενής: Ps 21:21; 24:16; 34:17; ἀγαπητός Gen 22:2 (Aquila: μονογενής); 22:12 (Symmachus: μονογενής); 22:16; Amos 8:10; Zech 12:10; Jer 6:26 (Aq., Symm., μονογενής); cf. Prov 4:3, ἀγαπώμενος. Cf. further the synoptic ἀγαπητός Mk 1:11 parr.; 9:7 parr.; 12:6 parr.; the word is found in Mt 12:18 in the quotation from Is 42:1 instead of LXX ἐκλεκτός; cf. also Lk 9:35 and Jn 1:34 *var. lect.* See Büchsel "μονογενής"; pp. 746f.;

[184] Cf. Mayser, *Grammatik*, vol. II, 2, p. 487; "often used instead of the genitive or the personal pronoun".

[185] So Boismard, *Prologue*, pp. 73f.

[186] So for instance Origen, Cyril of Alexandria, Bede, Euthymius, Schanz, Knabenbauer, Tillmann; Lagrange is against it.

[187] This can hardly be questioned for the Greek compound, cf. Büchsel, "μονογενής", pp. 745f.; the underlying Hebrew need not exclude the element of origin, which the evangelist certainly combines with this attribute of the Son; cf. Büchsel, p. 749, 7–11. Hence the demand of Moody, "God's only Son", that the word should only be translated as "unique, uniquely beloved" is not quite justified.

Since μονογενής in John undoubtedly goes back to the Hebrew, there is no point in looking for a Hellenistic background, especially as the cosmological meaning which the term sometimes has in Hellenism[188] is completely foreign to John. In the Gnostic systems some emanations (aeons—whose place and rank in the series is not always the same—are called Μονογενής.[189] The Gnostics probably took the title from John and inserted it into their speculations, perhaps along with older traditions from mythology and philosophy. If we should in fact ascribe the part of 1:14 in question to the evangelist, there is no reason to think that μονογενής comes from a Gnostic "source" and that it should be taken otherwise than in the other passages in John.[190]

The last phrase, "full of grace and truth", speaks once more of the Logos. According to our analysis of the original hymn, it was in the nominative there, in apposition to ἐσκήνωσεν. In the present text, it should be taken with the genitive μονογενοῦς,[191] not with δόξαν, since the δόξα, as that of the only-begotten Son, needs no further description. The incarnate Logos bears in himself the fullness of grace, for which all believers are jubilantly thankful (v. 16). The association of χάρις καὶ ἀλήθεια is not a Greek idiom, but is well rooted in the O.T. God's graciousness and fidelity (to the covenant), חֶסֶד וֶאֱמֶת, are often spoken of together, as for instance at the giving of the covenant itself (Exod 34:6) and in other places.[192] Though the Septuagint usually translates חֶסֶד by ἔλεος, in later times χάρις comes to the fore.[193] Philo lays much stress on the free, gracious action of God in creating and saving, and his favourite word for it is χάρις; according to his doctrine of the virtues, χάρις is not only God's gracious attitude, but also the communication of divine

---

[188] The word is used of being in Parmenides (*frg.*, 8, 4), of heaven in Plato (*Tim.*, 31b; 92b), of the cosmos in Basilides; so Clement of Alexandria, *Strom.*, V, 74, 3 (Stählin vol. II, p. 376); see further Bultmann, *Johannes*, p. 48.

[189] Cf. Clement of Alexandria, *Exc. ex Theod.*, 6; 7; 10; Irenaeus, *Adv. haer.*, I, 1, 1; Hippolytus, *Ref.*, VI, 30, 4; 38, 6 (cf. VIII, 9, 3; 10, 5; 9); "Unbekanntes altgnostisches Werk" ed. by Schmidt and Till, pp. 335ff., cf. index; also Bultmann, pp. 48f.

[190] Against Bultmann, p. 47, n. 2.

[191] πλήρης is treated as indeclinable, cf. Funk, *Greek Grammar*, para. 137, 1; Zerwick, *Graecitas*, no. 6; but this is a vulgarism, which offended some copyists (D reads πλήρη here). Schlatter defends πλήρης as a nominative; Bultmann, 49, n. 1, considers the possibility (with Burney) that v. 14e was an independent clause ("He was full of grace and truth"), forming a distich with v. 16. The combination of χάρις and δόξα in Ecclus 24:16 to which Spicq, "Siracide", p. 189 refers, means something else, more or less "charm and honour", cf. Ecclus 4:21; Prov 26:11; Ps 83:12 (LXX), according to the general sense of χάρις and δόξα in Ecclesiasticus.

[192] 2 Sam 2:6; Ps 25:10; 40:12; 61:8; 85:11; 89:15; 115:1; 138:2; Prov 3:3; 14:22 etc. For the concept cf. also *1 QH*, 1:32, "For thou, in thy mercy and in thy great graciousness (חֶסֶד) hast strengthened the spirit of man in face of [tribulation]"; 2:23, "Thou dost help my soul by thy grace"; 2:25, "Through thy grace do I stand."

[193] Septuagint translates חֶסֶד by χάρις, Est 2:9 (cf. 17); Ecclus 7:33; 40:17; so too Symmachus, 2 Sam 2:6; 10:2; Ps 30:8; 39:11; 88:25; in the *Quinta*, Ps 32:5; in the *Sexta*, Ps 30:17; 32:18. See also Dodd, *Interpretation*, p. 175.

gifts and power, so that he can also speak of the χάριτες as the streams of God's grace.[194] When the O.T. phrase is applied to the Logos, it takes on a new depth of meaning. Since χάρις is not adopted into the Johannine world of concepts (except in 1:17), the context only allows us to affirm that χάρις is both the riches of grace and the liberality of the Logos (v. 14) and the gift of grace itself which men receive from him (v. 16). To the mind of the evangelist it certainly does not differ essentially from πνεῦμα and ζωή. In this grouping, ἀλήθεια is the subordinate term, as may be seen from the fact that only χάρις is taken up again in v. 16. Hence "truth" need not have here the special Johannine colouring, in particular that of "divine revelation" (cf. 8:32, 45; 17:17; 18:37c). It is possible that in the hymn ἀλήθεια kept its O.T. sense of "steadfastness, fidelity"; but the evangelist probably took it to mean "divine reality" in a more strongly ontological sense (cf. v. 17), as he understands ἀλήθεια in 4:23f.; 8:44; 14:6; 17:17; 18:37d. The hymn sees in the bodily presence of the Logos among men the eschatological fulfilment of God's dwelling among his people. But the evangelist understands this advance as the replacement of the O.T. revelation of law by the higher revelation of salvation and the gift of life in the N.T. (v. 17).

1:15	Ἰωάννης μαρτυρεῖ περὶ αὐτοῦ καὶ κέκραγεν λέγων· οὗτος ἦν ὃν εἶπον, Ὁ ὀπίσω μου ἐρχόμενος ἔμπροσθέν μου γέγονεν, ὅτι πρῶτός μου ἦν.	John gives testimony to him, crying out: "This was he of whom I said, 'He who comes after me ranks before me, for he was before me.'"

V. 15 stands out from the context even more sharply than vv. 6–8. Though v. 16 is the direct continuation of v. 14, the evangelist inserts a statement of the Baptist which testifies to the precedence of the incarnate Logos and bases it on his pre-existence. It is not meant to be a continuation of the historical account begun in v. 6; but it shows the same polemical interest as v. 8. The present μαρτυρεῖ and the perfect κέκραγεν in the sense of a present[195] are hardly intended as historical narrative (historical present):[196] they make the voice of the precursor audible in the present time, just as the disciple who guarantees the Johannine tradition trans-

[194] In Philo, χάρις is far more frequent than ἔλεος (cf. Leisegang's index in ed. Cohn and Wendland). In *Immut.*, 104ff., he discusses the frequent Old Testament phrase "to find grace"; see also *Cher.*, 122f. For the plural, cf. *De opif.*, 23; 168; *Leg. all.*, II, 80; III, 163f. etc. The Logos is also πλήρης χαρίτων; *De somn.*, II, 223, cf. 183.

[195] On κεκραγέναι understood as a present, cf. Funk, *Greek Grammar*, para. 341; Grundmann, "κράζω", p. 898, 34–37.

[196] So Funk, para. 321, n.; but it is not "vivid narrative, at the events of which the narrator imagines himself to be present"; the evangelist sees the Baptist as a present witness.

mits his testimony (21:24; cf. 19:35), or as Spirit, water and blood have become perpetual witnesses (1 Jn 5:7f.). The strange οὗτος ἦν (instead of ἐστίν)[197] is only intelligible on these terms. John's clarion call, which never ceases to ring out,[198] testifies for all time that the incarnate Logos was the greater. This interjection of the evangelist is determined by his polemic against disciples of John who were challenging Christianity in his day. They ranked the Baptist higher than Jesus, appealing to Mt 11:9, 11,[199] but certainly also to the fact that their master had been there before Jesus and hence took precedence.[200] The evangelist answers by citing John himself to prove that Jesus, though coming later, ranks higher than him (ἔμπροσθέν μου)[201] because in reality he existed before him (πρῶτός μου).[202] The verse is very revealing for the evangelist's theological procedure and his way of presenting his Gospel.

The saying of the Baptist does not occur in the narrative till 1:30, but there too it is supposed to be known (εἶπον), probably referring to 1:27, which, however, does not agree with it word for word, since it is closer to the synoptic logion, Mt 3:11 par. The fourth evangelist no doubt supposes that this saying of the Baptist given in the Synoptics is generally known ("he who comes after me is stronger than I"), but interprets it in his own way. He explains the "stronger", whose laces the Baptist does not consider himself worthy to undo (Mt: whose shoes he is not worthy to carry), as the pre-existent who is higher in rank. John does not write his Gospel as a completely new account, nor as a "supplement" to the Synoptics, but as a presentation standing in its own right, using his own special knowledge to explain known events, sometimes adding new traits, and trying to bring his readers to a deeper understanding of the faith. In his attitude to the Baptist he is notably different from the pseudo-Clementine writings, which attack the disciples of John in a much more hostile way. Using the principle of "syzygy"—conjunction and opposition—they see the great Baptist as the evil figure associated with Jesus, since on this principle the representative of the good is always preceded by an embodiment of evil.[203] But the fourth evangelist claims John as a witness sent by God to give testimony to Jesus (1:6) and thus, like the Synoptics, draws him into the ambit of Christianity. This is one more way in

---

[197] For the ἦν cf. 5:35, where Jesus speaks in this way of the Baptist, looking back on his whole work and testimony. Another antecedent, the Baptist, is given by the reading: οὗτος ἦν ὁ εἰπών B* C* ℵ³ Orig, which arose, no doubt, from the desire to avoid the difficulty created by the ἦν of the text; ὃν εἶπον is good Greek for ὑπὲρ οὗ ἐγὼ εἶπον (1:30); the omission in ℵ* is unwarranted (it makes up for it by inserting ὅς before ἔμπροσθεν.

[198] The κέκραγεν shows that the discourse is prophetic, cf. Josephus, *Ant.*, X, 117; Rom 9:27; so too in rabbinic literature, cf. Grundmann, "κράζω", p. 900. This is a solemn proclamation by divine command; used of Jesus himself in Jn 7:28, 37; 12:44.

[199] Cf. on v. 8 above note 111.

[200] Cf. Cullmann, "Ὁ ὀπίσω μου ἐρχόμενος".

[201] "Ἔμπροσθεν" can have this meaning, which is necessary here according to the context; cf. Arndt and Gingrich, *Lexicon*, s. v. 2,f (with examples from classical literature). Bultmann, *Johannes*, p. 50 adduces the rabbinical "to precede", that is, to have the greater dignity (cf. Gen 48:20).

[202] Πρῶτος=πρότερος, see Funk, para. 62; Radermacher, *Grammatik*, p. 70.

[203] Cf. *Pseudo-Clementine Hom.*, II, 16–17 (Rehm, pp. 41f.); *Recog.*, III, 61 (*PG* 1, col. 1308).

which he shows his solidarity with the Christianity of the Great Church, in complete contrast to the Jewish-Christian particularism of the pseudo-Clementine writings.

1:16	ὅτι ἐκ τοῦ πληρώματος αὐτοῦ ἡμεῖς πάντες ἐλάβομεν, καὶ χάριν ἀντὶ χάριτος.	For from his fullness we have all received, grace upon grace.

Contrary to the opinion of many Fathers,[204] this verse is not part of the Baptist's words. It describes the outpouring of grace on believers from the riches of the Logos (v. 14e). The movement of thought suggests that the verse should rather begin with καί, which is in fact read by many MSS; but ὅτι is to be preferred, as in the main Alexandrian witnesses and as the *lectio difficilior*.[205] The evangelist probably put it in on the same principle as in v. 17, intending to illustrate the glory of the Logos from the fullness of the gifts given by him. But the original hymn may have had καί, which is used in fact to introduce the strophe (v. 14a). Πλήρωμα takes up πλήρης and has certainly nothing to do with Gnostic speculation on the pleroma.[206] The term has no cosmological connotations here; the Logos is not the supreme divine realm which encompasses the worlds, nor a primal divine unity prior to the emanations, but the bearer of the fullness of divine salvation, which he personally imparts to believers (cf. 3:34; 5:26; 6:57; 7:38f.). One is rather reminded of the quite ordinary expression in the O.T., "the fullness"—of God's grace, Ps 5:8, of his graces, Ps 106:45, of his mercy, Ps 51:3; 69:17; so too *1QS*, 4:4, "the fullness of his grace". John, however, is not just thinking of the superabundant mercy of God. He also means the riches of divine life which the Logos receives from the Father (5:26) and from which he enriches his own (10:10). The hymn adds in explanation (καί):[207] "(that is to say) grace upon grace". The ἀντί, according to most modern commentators, indicates the ceaseless stream of graces which succeed one another.[208] Perhaps the preposition

[204] Heracleon, Origen, who also maintains against Heracleon that v. 18 is part of the Baptist's discourse, *Comm. in Jo.*, VI, 3, 13f. (Preuschen, pp. 108f.), Theodore of Mopsuestia (Vosté, trans. p. 26) and many other Fathers. But Chrysostom, *Hom.*, XIV, 1 (*PG* 59, col. 92), recognized that the evangelist is again speaking in v. 16; so too Cyril of Alexandria (*PG* 73, col. Ꝁ 169c).

[205] Καί A W Θ lat sy; ὅτι P[66 75] B C* D L 33 sa bo al.

[206] Contrast *Odes of Solomon*, 7:11 (13), "He it is that is incorrupt, the fullness of the ages (aeons) and their father"; see further Lightfoot, *St. Paul's Epistle to the Colossians and to Philemon*, pp. 255–71; Dupont, *Gnosis*, pp. 453–76; Delling, "πλήρωμα", pp. 297–304 (with further lit.) who comments correctly on Jn 1:16, that it is neither Gnostic nor cosmological (p. 301, n. 37); Schlier, *Der Brief an die Epheser*, pp. 96–99.

[207] The most direct object of ἐλάβομεν is ἐκ τοῦ πλ. (Funk, para. 169, 2); the καί is then explanatory (Funk, para. 442, 9).

[208] Mostly on the basis of Philo, *De post.*, 145, where God is said to give constantly new graces in the place of earlier ones; cf. also *Leg. all.*, III, 82.

also indicates the correspondence between the grace possessed by the Logos and that of those who receive him: what they possess, they have received from him, and it corresponds to what he bears within himself in supreme fullness.[209] The greater fullness of grace under the new covenant, in contrast to the old, is not envisaged.[210] "We have *all* received . . ."—this is the jubilant confession of all who have received Christ in faith (cf. v. 12), including Christians of a later date who did not see him during his life on earth. The original Logos hymn probably ended with this word of thanksgiving.

There is a similar thanksgiving in the final prayer of the Λόγος τέλειος (the Latin *Asclepius* or the Greek papyrus Mimaut[211]), one of the products of Hermetic mysticism. But it shows clearly the difference between the Gnostic way of salvation and the Christian faith. The Gnostic says: "Through thy grace alone we have attained the light of knowledge . . . Thou hast given us intellect (νοῦς), reason (λόγος) and knowledge (γνῶσις): intellect to grasp thee, reason to search for thee, knowledge that we may rejoice to know thee." The Christian's thanksgiving is not for a knowledge which is ultimately concerned with the divinity of their own nature, an immanent experience of God in their own being, but because they have received superabundant gifts of salvation from the incarnate Logos or from the Lord who has returned to his glory (cf. 6:62), through the Holy Spirit (cf. 7:38f.).

1:17 ὅτι ὁ νόμος διὰ Μωϋσέως ἐδόθη, ἡ χάρις καὶ ἡ ἀλήθεια διὰ Ἰησοῦ Χριστοῦ ἐγένετο.

For the law was given through Moses, but grace and truth came through Jesus Christ.

This verse and the next are probably additions of the evangelist, as both style and content suggest. The asyndeton in v. 17b is noticeable, where one would have expected a δέ[212]—a characteristic of Johannine style[213] not confined to the narrative; so too the mention of "Jesus Christ" without previous introduction, as in 17:3; 1 Jn 1:3; cf. also 1 Jn 2:1; 3:23; 4:2, 15; 5:6, 20. V. 17 also contains a new thought of which there

[209] So Bover, "Χάριν ἀντὶ χάριτος, Joh 1:16", esp. p. 458; P. Joüon in *RSR* 22 (1932), p. 206, finds an Aramaic basis for the expression.

[210] So Chrysostom, *Hom.*, XIV, 2 (*PG* 59, col. 94); Theodore of Mopsuestia, *ad loc.*; so too Frangipane "Et gratiam pro gratia, Jo 1:16". But all graces come from the incarnate Logos, and v. 17 also tells against this explanation. Only the law was given through Moses, grace only came through Jesus Christ.

[211] The Latin text is confirmed by the Greek of the "Papyrus Mimaut" (Preisendanz, vol. II, pp. 591–609), which is, however, not very well preserved; cf. Reitzenstein, *Mysterienreligionen*, pp. 285–7; Scott, *Hermetica*, vol. I, pp. 374 ff.; vol. III, pp. 284ff.; Nock and Festugière, vol. II, pp. 353ff. Festugière's notes give further parallels from the Hermetic writings.

[212] P[66] W vet lat do in fact read δέ.

[213] The asyndeton epicum is characteristic of John (Ruckstuhl no. 6). On the absence of δέ cf. 1 Jn 3:2 (growing emphasis); 3:8a (contrast).

was no hint throughout the hymn. The evangelist takes up the "grace and truth" of v. 14 and ponders how the reality of divine grace only came upon earth with the incarnate Logos—the ἐγένετο being also characteristic of John.[214] Hence the first part of the verse, dealing with the law of Moses, must be interpreted in terms of Johannine thought, which is not dominated by the same problems and sharp antitheses as the Pauline. John does not oppose the "law" as way of salvation; he speaks without misgivings of "keeping the commandments"[215] or the "new commandment" (13:34; 1 Jn 2:7f.), not in such a way as to contradict Paul, but still showing clearly that Jewish nomism is not a live issue for him. As a rule, he uses the term ὁ νόμος to designate Scripture as source of revelation (1:45; 8:17; 10:34; 12:34; 15:25). Moses is not merely the lawgiver (7:19, 22f.), he is also an authority who speaks in Scripture (1:45; 5:45–47; cf. 9:29). In this capacity, Moses is a witness for Jesus, like John (5:45 ff.), and as leader of the exodus he has a certain typological role (cf. 3:14; 6:32). Thus John sees no absolute contradiction between Moses who gave the law (at God's command), and Jesus Christ who brought grace and truth. The evangelist only disassociates himself from the law in the same way that he finds the Jewish cult (4:21–24), purifications (2:6; 3:25; cf. 11:55; 19:40, 42) and feasts "of the Jews" (2:13; 5:1; 6:4; 7:2; 11:55) obsolete and no longer important. In view of 9:28f., one may indeed suspect polemics against the Judaism of his day; if so the "Torah" would represent "a code-name for the perverted Jewish way of life, in opposition to Christ, the Messiah of Christian faith".[216] But such a definite polemical point is not recognizable, since the verse rather aims at showing the previous legal system has been surpassed by the reality of the grace of Jesus Christ. The law was only "given" by Moses (cf. the old Hebrew formula נָתַן תּוֹרָה), while grace and truth "came" through Jesus Christ. This brings out the eschatological character of the event of salvation. Behind both facts is the will of God.[217]

1:18	Θεὸν οὐδεὶς ἑώρακεν πώποτε· μονογενὴς υἱὸς ὁ ὢν εἰς τὸν	No one has ever seen God. The only-begotten Son, who is in

[214] Γίνεσθαι in the sense of "come", 1:6 (15, 30?); 6:19, 21, 25; 10:35; 12:30; 1 Jn 2:18; 2 Jn 12. But this is also frequent outside John, cf. Arndt and Gingrich, *Lexicon*, s. v. 4, c.

[215] Cf. Jn 14:15, 21; 15:10, 12; 1 Jn 2:3f.; 3:4, 22, 24; 4:21; 5:2f.; 2 Jn 6.

[216] Grässer, "Die antijüdische Polemik im Johannesevangelium", esp. pp. 81f. Grässer notes correctly the contemporary polemics of the evangelist, but exaggerates their import, which affects his explanation of 1:17 (pp. 78–82).

[217] Moses is not merely a "negative witness" to Jesus in John (Hoskyns), but also plays a positive role (5:46). Jeremias, "Μωϋσῆς", pp. 877, 9ff., is correct in seeing in Jn 1:17 a synthetic, not an antithetic parallelism.

κόλπον τοῦ Πατρός, ἐκεῖνος ἐξηγήσατο.	the bosom of the Father, he has brought tidings.

This verse is also recognizable as an addition of the evangelist. The disclaimer in 18a is a point which he stresses elsewhere (5:37; 6:46; cf. 1 Jn 4:12,20), and in 18b μονογενής and the additional ἐκεῖνος are features of his style.[218] Not only is the N. T. revelation superior to the old, it is absolutely unique, because it was brought by the only-begotten Son of God who had direct knowledge of his Father. He alone, coming down from heaven to earth, could speak of heavenly things from his own experience (cf. 3:31f.). The absolute claim of the Christian revelation could not be put more definitely.

Who are aimed at by the assertion of v. 18a that no one has ever seen God? Is it a reminder that Moses, on Sinai, desired to see the "glory of the Lord" (Exod 33:18)? And does it condemn such desires, which were still felt by pious Jews (cf. Jn 14:8)? This is conceivable, in view of the polemics of 5:37, which is obviously directed against the Jews. If so, the evangelist is affirming that after the revelation of the Son there is only one means of access to the Father, which is Christ (cf. 14:9). But the Judaism of the day was fully convinced that no man could see God with his bodily eyes while on earth (cf. Exod 33:20; 19:21; Is 6:5 for an earlier period), and that the immediate vision of God was reserved for the age to come.[219] Heavenly raptures and mystical visions were viewed with distrust by official Judaism, though some particular groups were favourably inclined.[220] If one recalls the sharp polemics of 1 Jn 4:12, 20 and the anti-Gnostic attitude of this work, there is no difficulty in admitting that there is a latent rejection of such trends in the Gospel also. Hellenistic mysticism and Gnosis tried to attain, even on earth, perfect knowledge of God and total union by means of self-recollection and ecstasy.[221]

---

[218] A characteristic of Johannine style (Ruckstuhl, no. 17).

[219] Cf. Baudissin, "Gott schauen in der alttestamentlichen Religion"; Nötscher, *Das Angesicht Gottes schauen*, pp. 170ff.; R. Bultmann, "Untersuchungen", pp. 176–88; Michaelis, "ὁράω", pp. 339f.; Aalen, *Licht und Finsternis*, pp. 259f., 317. The later midrash explained that "to see God", as was granted to the people during the Exodus, was a special grace for the generation which was thus rescued, and probably as a prefiguration of the eschatological fulfilment; cf. *Pesiqta*, 108a: "R. Levi (c. 300) said: They (the Israelites on Sinai) saw the face of God, and whoever sees the face of the King, does not die"; *Ex. Rabba*, 29 (88d): "R. Levi said: The Israelites asked two things of God, to see his glory and to hear his voice; and they saw his glory and they heard his voice" (Billerbeck, vol. IV, pp. 939f., with more instances).

[220] Cf. the story of the four rabbis who "entered paradise" during their life on earth and "saw" it (in ecstasy): *j. Chagigah*, 77a (Bonsirven, no. 1104). On the age and origin of Jewish mysticism, see Scholem, *Jüdische Mystik*, pp. 43–52; this passage discussed on pp. 56f.

[221] For the Gnostic vision of God the *Hermetica* are instructive, cf. *Tr.* I and XIII, 13; also *Exc. ex Stob.*, VI, 18 (Nock and Festugière, vol. III, p. 39): ὁ ταῦτα μὴ ἀγνοήσας ἀκριβῶς δύναται νοῆσαι τὸν θεόν, εἰ δὲ καὶ τολμήσαντα δεῖ εἰπεῖν, καὶ αὐτόπτης γενόμενος θεάσασθαι καὶ θεασάμενος μακάριος γενέσθαι. Frequent in magic, cf. Nock and Festugière, vol. III, p. 43, n. 33. On Philo see Völker, *Fortschritt und Vollendung bei Philo von*

The action of Jesus Christ as the revealer is here designated as ἐξηγεῖσθαι. The usage of the term varies according to the cultural setting: in pagan Hellenism it is used of the disclosures made by gods in prophecy,[222] in Josephus it is "the technical term for interpretation of the law as practised by the rabbinate" (A. Schlatter on Jn 1:18). Here, where there is no object, but where it is a question of "seeing God", it must mean speaking of things hidden in God, tidings of the divine glory. There is a similar question in Ecclus 43:31, "Who has seen him (God) and can describe (ἐκδιηγήσεται) him?". Here, however, the question is concerned with the greatness of the creator, and the pious sage must confess that he has seen only a few of his works (v. 32). Jn 1:18 is concerned with salvific revelation.

A different picture emerges if one reconstructs the original somewhat differently, with M.-É. Boismard[223] (inserting εἰ μὴ ὁ before μονογενής, with W it arm aeth Tat(?), omitting ὁ ὢν before εἰς τὸν κόλπον), and translates: "No one has ever seen God except the only-begotten: to the bosom of the Father, he has led the way." The thought is authentically Johannine (cf. 14:2f., 6; 17:24; 1 Jn 3:1 and, as we understand it, 3:13–15). However, Boismard's textual criticism rests on insecure foundations, and none of the witnesses which he cites can be shown to have understood the text in this way. Further, though his translation is defensible on purely linguistic grounds, it is impossible to explain the aorist ἐξηγήσατο satisfactorily (contrast the perfect ἀναβέβηκεν in 3:13).

The bringer of revelation, drawing upon his immediate experience of God and appearing at a given time upon earth (aorist ἐξηγήσατο) is described as "(the) only-begotten, God" or, according to another reading, "the only-begotten Son", "who is in the bosom of the Father". This is a profound Johannine view, in harmony with the image of Christ depicted in our Gospel. Whether one reads θεός or υἱός after (ὁ) μονογενής makes no essential difference.

The data for textual criticism are as follows:

μονογενὴς θεός	P^{66} ℵ* B C* L 850 bo $sy^{p.hmg}$ Tat Gnostics (Valentinus, Heracleon, Ptolemy, Theodotus) Iren Clem Al., al.
ὁ μονογενὴς θεός	P^{75} $ℵ^{3}$ C^{3} 33
ὁ μονογενὴς υἱός	A Θ 𝔎 it (q: unigenitus filius Dei) vg sy^{c} Latin Fathers and Antiochians
ὁ μονογενής	Ephr Aphr Cyr (of Jerusalem) Vict Ambr Old arm.[224]

Alexandrien, pp. 279–314; Jonas, *Gnosis*, vol. II, 1, pp. 70–121; Thyen, "Probleme der neueren Philo-Forschung", pp. 244f.; on the whole question see also Bultmann, "Untersuchungen", pp. 173–5; id., *Johannes*, pp. 54f.

[222] Mostly said of the priests explaining the oracles, but also of the Delphic Apollo himself (Plato, *Rep.*, IV, 427c); other examples of the usage in Büchsel, "ἡγέομαι"; Moulton and Milligan, *Vocabulary*, p. 223. Philo also sees the divine Logos as ἑρμηνεύς in the sense of προφήτης, cf. *Leg. all.*, III, 207; *Mut. nom.*, 208; *Immut.*, 138; *Quod deter.*, 40; *Migr. Abr.*, 81 etc. On Philo see Dodd, *Interpretation*, p. 72.

[223] "Dans le sein du Père, Jo 1:18", pp. 23–39; id., *Prologue*, pp. 91f.

[224] On the Syrian, and the old Armenian deduced from a later quotation, see Boismard, "Dans le sein du Père", p. 25.

Further variants:

ὁ ὤν	om. ℵ a Tat Novat Iren (?) Tert (?)
ἐξηγήσατο	add. ἡμῖν W c Tat $sy^{c.pal}$

The weight of the testimonies is in favour of θεός; it was, in any case, an early Alexandrian text, as is shown by $P^{66\ 75}$. But many commentators postulate υἱός, to correspond with πατρός, for the original text. But the same motives may have been at work to displace θεός from the original. Another possibility is (ὁ) μονογενής by itself (cf. v. 14), to which θεός or υἱός was added early on, by way of explanation. The question cannot be decided with certainty.[225] If (ὁ) μονογενὴς θεός is taken as the original reading, on account of the strong external evidence, θεός is probably in apposition to (ὁ) μονογενής: the only-begotten, whose being is divine. But ὁ μονογενὴς υἱός seems preferable.

The revealer can speak with authority, because he is the only-begotten, and remains most intimately united to his Father, even in his earthly life, at one with him in nature and action. Jesus's unique relation of sonship with the Father is propounded by John in the revelation discourses of his Gospel: he who speaks on earth is identical with the Logos of whom the hymn sang, so that the affirmations of the prologue with regard to the eternity of the Logos with God and as God (1:1) are continued in the self-attestation of Jesus. The incarnate Logos retains the direct, divine knowledge of his pre-existence, he who descended from heaven remains fully conscious of his heavenly experience (cf. 3:32). If one bears in mind how the language of the hymn is combined with Jesus's testimony to himself, the reading "(the) only-begotten, God, who is in the bosom of the Father" gains in probability. At the end of his prologue, the evangelist affirms once more the full divine dignity of the Son of God on earth, and also his unique capacity as revealer. In doing so, he prepares the ground for his subsequent account of the revelation discourses of Jesus. Hence this verse forms a link between the hymn to the Logos and the presentation of the Gospel.

"In the bosom of the Father" is a metaphorical expression of the evangelist (cf. 13:23), which renders the "with God" of v. 1 in another way. In the O.T. the metaphor is used of married life (Gen 16:5; Deut 13:7; 28:54, 56 etc.), of the infant at the side of (1 Kg 3:20) or in the lap of (1 Kg 17:19) its mother, and of God's care for Israel (Num 11:12). In the N.T. the metaphorical sense is found in Lk 16:22f. (Abraham's bosom); see further Clement of Alexandria, *Paed.*, II, 10, 105, 1 (Stählin, vol. I, p. 220, 5): ἐν κόλποις τοῦ πατρός. The image is used of fellowship with Jesus in *2 Clem*, 4:5 (Funk and Bihlmeyer, p. 188): Ἐὰν ἦτε μετ' ἐμοῦ συνηγμένοι ἐν τῷ κόλπῳ μου

[225] On the textual witnesses, see Zahn, *Johannes*, pp. 714–9; Lagrange, pp. 26f.; Boismard, pp. 23–29. Westcott and Hort, B. Weiss, Vogels, Merk decide in favour of υἱός, Tischendorf, von Soden, Bover in favour of θεός. Among modern exegetes θεός is chosen by Zahn, Bernard, Bauer, Tillmann, Lagrange, υἱός by Hoskyns, Schlatter, Bultmann, pp. 55, 4, cf. also Wikenhauser, Barrett. Burney, *Aramaic Origin*, pp. 39f. conjectures μονογενὴς θεοῦ, which cannot be correct; the Old Latin "unigenitus filius dei" (q) is clearly a secondary development.

καὶ μὴ ποιῆτε τὰς ἐντολάς μου, ἀποβαλῶ ὑμᾶς (probably a spurious agraphon). The image is also frequent in rabbinical literature.[226] As often in the Koine, εἰς with acc. is certainly the equivalent of ἐν with dat.[227]

It is of secondary importance to establish which precise mode of Christ's existence the evangelist envisaged with ὁ ὤν (omitted by some witnesses to the text, see above)—his pre-existence, his life on earth or the time after his exaltation. If the evangelist is thinking of Christ's previous existence with the Father, ὁ ὢν κτλ. explains the subsequent historical revelation; if he is thinking of Christ who has returned to the Father, he is looking back from his own period of history to the revelation which has already taken place.[228] It is improbable, however, that the meaning is: while the only-begotten still remained in the bosom of the Father, he also brought us revelation as the incarnate Son. This would not be in keeping with the presentation of the evangelist elsewhere, which is to distinguish the descent of the Son of Man from his return to on high as successive acts (cf. 3:13, 31; 6:62; 13:1; 16:28).[229]

Verses 14–18 could be based on a consistent theological conception, exploiting typologically the themes of Moses and the exodus. The holy tent and "God dwelling" among Israel, the glory and vision of God, the giving of the law through Moses and the leading of the people home to the promised land: these themes are said to re-appear in the thought and language of Jn 1:14–18, typologically fulfilled and surpassed in the incarnation and salvific activity of the Logos.[230] But this view goes too far. Though the echoes are not to be ignored, one should speak of the presence of individual themes rather than of a continuous typological connection. A uniform theological interpretation is ruled out by the structure, the various interests displayed by the additions (contrast v. 15 and v. 18), and by the different theological perspectives of the evangelist (vv. 17, 18). His aim was to formulate pregnantly, in conjunction with the Logos-hymn, some thoughts which he considered important, and to provide the transition to the following presentation. — *See excursus i.*

---

[226] See Schlatter, *ad loc.;* on the usage in Hellenism see Bauer, *ad loc.;* see in general Meyer, "προφήτης".

[227] See Funk, *Greek Grammar*, para. 205, 218; according to Mayser, *Grammatik*, vol. II, 2, p. 373, rare in the papyri. Schlatter thinks that εἰς and ἐν mean the same thing here.

[228] So Bernard, Lagrange, against Zahn, Tillmann.

[229] See Windisch, "In Joh. 1:51", pp. 221–3, against Odeberg. The view rejected above is also held by Dodd, *Interpretation*, pp. 258 ff.; see further, commentary on 1:51 and 3:13.

[230] So Boismard, *Prologue*, pp. 165–75; cf. Sahlin, *Typologie*, pp. 60 f. (contrast between the mission of Moses and that of Jesus).

CHAPTER II

John's Testimony and the First Disciples (1:19–51)

Within the first great division of John (chs. 1–12), the section 1:19–4:54 represents the beginnings of Jesus's ministry, which it presents in the form of a continuous narrative with a large number of chronological details.[1] The reader first meets Jesus at the Jordan where John is baptizing (1:29), follows him to Galilee (1:43), where he performs his first "sign" at a marriage in Cana (2:1–11), and then to Capernaum for a brief stay (2:12), after which Jesus goes to Jerusalem for the Passover (2:13). After the feast, Jesus goes to the countryside of Judea, where he spends some time baptizing, along with his disciples (3:22). We are not told how long this lasted, but the impression is that it was not for long (cf. 4:1). He then goes back to Galilee with his disciples, passing rapidly through Samaria, where, however, he stays at Sychar for two days at the invitation of the inhabitants (4:40). Soon after his return to Galilee he meets the royal official from Capernaum. The encounter takes place in Cana, where he had changed the water into wine, as the evangelist notes expressly (4:46). In contrast to this continuous narrative, the following sections mostly begin with a vague μετὰ ταῦτα and a reference to a feast which suggests that the evangelist meant to give only a selection of the episodes which appeared most important to him. The first section also differs in content and structure from the following, in so far as the element of discourse is far shorter and less frequent, and the whole treatment is more in the narrative style.

For these reasons, it seems correct to end the first section at 4:54. It raises, of course, many points which are taken up later (baptism 3:5—Eucharist 6:53 ff.; living water 4:14—bread of life 6:35; healing of mortal illness 4:46–54—raising of Lazarus, ch. 11, and so on); the forces at work (belief and unbelief) and the various circles (disciples, people, rulers;

[1] 1:29, 35, 43; 2:1, 12, 13; 3:24; 4:40, 43. These numbers cannot have a purely symbolic meaning; see commentary.

Galilee, Jerusalem) are already recognizable. But the section seems to be in the nature of an enunciation of themes before their detailed presentation, or the setting of the stage for the drama that is to be played out. At any rate, the division after ch. 4 is certainly justified, and one can work back from this to define the first section.[2] But there is a difficulty about where it begins, because it is not certain whether it includes the ministry of John and the calling of the first disciples or not. Many exegetes, in fact, begin the section on Jesus's ministry only with ch. 2.[3] This is not a minor point, if full value is to be given to the verdict of the evangelist on the coming of John the Baptist. The following reasons suggest that 1:19–51 should be included as a relevant element of the revelation of Jesus: a) In the fourth Gospel, the Baptist appears in close connection with Jesus, merely as a witness to him, and with no significance apart from him. He does not, for instance, preach penance (cf. 1:6–8, 19–23; 3:23–30; 5:33–35). He does not merely go before Jesus, as in the Synoptics, he works beside him and for him (cf. 1:29–34, 35f.; 3:29f.). b) All his testimony bears on Christ. When rejecting Messiahship for himself (1:20; 3:28), he proclaims Jesus as the Messiah. When he speaks of him "who comes after him", his words have the character of genuine, God-given revelation (cf. 1:15, 26f., 30, 33), and the titles he gives Jesus ("the lamb of God", 1:29, 36; "the Son of God" or "the elect of God", 1:34) announce him as Saviour. c) By leading the first disciples to Jesus (1:35 ff.), John lays the foundations of the believing community (cf. also 3:29) which gathers round Jesus and receives his revelation fruitfully. Thus the gathering of the flock of believers, which is part of Jesus's task (cf. 6:37 ff.; 10:27f.; 11:52), and the forming of the front to oppose the quickly growing ranks of unbelief (cf. 2:13–22) are already beginning in 1:35–51. The repeated emphasis on "the disciples" in chs. 2–4 is intentional; but their "coming to Jesus" is already narrated in 1:35–51. d) The self-revelation of Jesus has already begun in this section, indirectly at first in the statements of the disciples whom he gains (1:41, 45), and then directly in his own marvellous knowledge, as revealed with regard to Nathanael (1:48; cf. the earlier statement to Simon, v. 42) and in the important word of revelation 1:51. This particular Son of Man saying is highly important for the whole of Jesus's work on earth; it is a key to all his words and actions. e) Finally, the beginning of ch. 2 is linked so closely with the foregoing that it is hardly possible to make a division here. Even

[2] Some exegetes do, in fact, put no major break after 4:54. Bernard makes part 1 go to the end of ch. 6 (ch. 5 is put after this as the opening of part 2); Bultmann closes part 1 ("the encounter with the revealer", from 2, 3) with 4:42; Lightfoot takes 2:12–12:50 together.

[3] Pölzl and Innitzer, Tillmann, Bultmann, Wikenhauser, Dodd, *Interpretation*, p. 297, who begins here the "Book of the Signs", van den Bussche, *Het vierde evangelie*, vol. I, p. 68.

if "the third day" is to be taken symbolically (see *ad loc.*), it is included in the numbering of the days (cf. 1:29,35,43), and it links the activity of the Baptist with that of Jesus. The aim of the evangelist seems to be to show Jesus coming forth from concealment, with the help of the divinely inspired testimony of John (cf. 1:31), then introducing himself to his first disciples as the promised Messiah, surpassing and intensifying their hopes (1:50f.) and finally beginning the revelation of his glory with the first "sign" (2:11).

The section contains a considerable amount of matter not known from the Synoptics, and an independent treatment of the matter where it coincides with them (the work of the Baptist and the call of the disciples; cf. also the purging of the temple and the healing of the son of the royal official). All that is recounted of the Baptist is his testimony to Jesus (before the envoys from Jerusalem, before the people, before the disciples). The winning of the first disciples does not square with the stylized account of vocation in Mk 1:16–20 par. The Marcan account of the public ministry of Jesus only begins after the arrest of the Baptist (Mk 1:14), while in Jn 3:22ff. the Baptist continues his activity. Historically speaking, we should insert Jn 1:19–4:54 (or at least 1:29–4:1), between Mk 1:13 and 14. But a strictly historical viewpoint is hardly relevant, since kerygmatic interests have determined the presentation both in the Synoptics and John. Compare Mark's programme of Jesus's preaching and call of the disciples (Mk 1:14–20), followed by the Capernaum episodes (Mk 1:21–39), with Luke's outline: appearance and rejection in Nazareth (Lk 4:16–30), Capernaum episodes (Lk 4:31–44) and the draught of fishes and call of the disciples (Lk 5:1–11). The same lack of historical interest accounts for the obscurity of many questions which arise: when and how did Jesus begin his work? Did he start to baptize and preach while John was still active, or did he begin with his special message only after John was imprisoned? When and where did he begin to announce the kingdom of God? Even the pericopes which allow of a closer comparison between John and the Synoptics present major difficulties. When did the purging of the temple take place? Does Jn 4:46–54 refer to the same event as Mt 8:5–13 and Lk 7:1–10, and if so, what are we to make of the details of time and place? This much, at any rate, seems certain: Jn 1:19–4:54 provides material which is instructive for the beginnings of Jesus's work, even from the historical point of view.

The object of the evangelist in this opening section is first to describe the beginnings of the self-revelation of Jesus, where his words (to Nicodemus and the Samaritan woman) are preceded and followed by his signs (first and second miracle at Cana); and then, to show how this revelation was received, with the opposing fronts of belief and unbelief already adumbrated, according to persons (disciples, people and rulers) and scenes (Galilee and Jerusalem), with a further glimpse of the winning of non-Jews (ch. 4, in Samaria). Thus the section outlines the themes and poses the problems which are continued and developed in the rest of the presentation.

The testimony of John the Baptist is given by the evangelist according to a clear plan: first he acts as witness (cf. 1:6–8) before official Judaism (the envoys from Jerusalem 1:19–28), in a rather indirect and negative way; then before "Israel", the people of God, in a positive way (1:29–34); finally he urges his own disciples to go to Jesus (1:35f.). Hence his testimony is (juridically) valid, public and effective. It is also consistent: Jesus is the Messiah in the full sense of the Christian faith, he has the attribute of pre-existence (1:30, cf. 15) and as 'lamb of God' he brings salvation to the whole world through the expiatory sacrifice of his death (1:29,36).

Hence the division of the section is clear: the testimony of the Baptist before official Judaism and Israel (1:19–34), and the success of this testimony, the winning of the first disciples to Jesus (1:35–51). The first part does not read smoothly, especially in vv. 26f. and 31–33, which has given rise to various suggestions for "improving" it on the basis of distribution of sources or later redaction.[4] But none of the proposals are quite satisfactory, and the present order of the text, with its uniform if somewhat prolix style, may be safely attributed to the evangelist, if we bear in mind the object of his narrative: the answer to the embassy from Jerusalem (vv. 19–28), and the Baptist's announcement to Israel of the Messiah revealed to him by God and designated by the Spirit (vv. 29–34, with v. 32 making a fresh start, in order to justify the testimony).

The numerous Messianic titles which occur in the section show the kerygmatic and perhaps also the liturgical interests of the evangelist. At the same time, his account contains a number of concrete details (cf. vv. 28, 39, 44, 48), and particulars about the first disciples, which are based on trustworthy tradition. Here too attention to objective facts is combined with profound insights of faith. But the evangelist presupposes throughout a general knowledge of the work of the Baptist and of the baptism of Jesus.

---

[4] Bultmann, p. 58, reconstructs as follows: vv. 19–21, 25–26 (except ἐγὼ βαπτίζω ἐν ὕδατι) 31 (except ἐν ὕδατι), 33 (from ἀλλ' to ἐστίν inclusively), 34, 28, 29–30. But what could have induced the redactor to have put the concluding remark, v. 28, in its present place? In any case, the reconstruction is based on a definite notion of the original gospel and the "ecclesiastical redaction", which lacks proof. Boismard, "Les traditions johanniques concernant le Baptiste", esp. pp. 5–25, proposes a new solution: two texts, one being the "relecture" of the other, have been woven together.

The testimony of John before the envoys from Jerusalem (1:19–28)

The passage is divided into two parts: 1) the Baptist interrogated by priests and Levites as to the Messianic significance of his person (vv. 19–23); 2) the question as to the meaning of his baptism, put by Pharisees (vv. 24–27)—presuming that the present text of v. 24 is the original and that our interpretation of it is correct (see below). Then there is a final remark (v. 28) establishing the place of the hearing. The whole passage is given a deliberately "official" tone.

1:19	καὶ αὕτη ἐστὶν ἡ μαρτυρία τοῦ Ἰωάννου, ὅτε ἀπέστειλαν πρὸς αὐτὸν οἱ Ἰουδαῖοι ἐξ Ἱεροσολύμων ἱερεῖς καὶ Λευίτας ἵνα ἐρωτήσωσιν αὐτόν· σὺ τίς εἶ;	And this is the testimony given by John, when the Jews of Jerusalem sent priests and Levites to ask him, "Who are you?"

The evangelist had already presented John as witness for Christ in the prologue (1:6–8,15). Now he develops this testimony (καὶ αὕτη ἐστίν) by explaining the occasion on which it was given, whom it was addressed to and what form it took. It is entirely and consistently testimony to Christ.[5] "Witnessing" is indispensable in the Johannine notion of faith, because the incarnate Logos and Son of God does not, as such, display openly his nature and his dignity, but must be attested by "witnesses" or "testimonies" (5:31–47; see *ad loc.*). Hence the Johannine "testimony" has a supremely religious function, even when it is combined with juridical notions (cf. 5:31f.; 8:14, 17f.), for even such adjuncts are only there to confirm the reliability of the testimony offered, to provide a surer ground for faith. Here too ἡ μαρτυρία has these juridical overtones, because it is given in an official interrogation. The envoys come from the "Jews" of Jerusalem, that is, from the central authority of the Jews, the Sanhedrin. The priests and Levites do the bidding of the ruling party of the "high priests", who formed a special group in the Sanhedrin, composed of the acting high priest, former holders of this office who had been deposed and other priests of high rank.[6] The fact that they are spoken of simply as "the Jews" is due to the fourth Gospel's way of using "the Jews"—no doubt deliberately—with varying accent, and for various groups indifferently, as appears on closer inspection.

---

[5] See Strathmann, "μαρτυρία", pp. 502f.; de la Potterie, "La notion johannique de témoignage", esp. pp. 199f. (with further lit. p. 193).

[6] See Jeremias, *Jerusalem zur Zeit Jesu*, vol. II B, pp. 33–40, correcting also the older view (E. Schürer) that they mean members of the high priestly families.

This phenomenon was noted long ago, and has given copious matter for discussion, especially for the problem of "John and Judaism".[7] That the evangelist stands aloof from Judaism cannot be doubted, particularly in the light of the addition "of the Jews" when feasts are spoken of (2:13; 5:1; 6:4; 7:2; 11:55). But it displays various degrees of detachment, from a perfectly neutral and dispassionate mention to a comment which is an emphatic accusation, when "the Jews" appear as the representatives of the obstinate hostility of unbelief, as the actual embodiment of "the world" in the worst (dualistic) sense of the term. We may distinguish: a) "Jew" or "Jews" as an ethnic term used by non-Jews, 4:9; 18:33, 35, 39; 19:3; cf. 19:19, 21; b) "Jews" in the historical sense or straightforward narrative, 3:25; 4:22; 11:19, 31, 33, 36; 18:20; 19:20; c) in the same sense, but with the writer clearly disassociating himself from them, 2:6, 13; 3:1; 5:1; 6:4; 7:2; 11:55; 19:21, 40, 42; d) in the same sense, but with the overtone of "unbelieving" (especially of groups of the people who are undecided, wavering or fickle), 6:41, 52; 7:11, 15, 35; 8:22, 31; 10:19; 11:45, 54; 12:9, 11; 13:33; e) "Jews" as a designation for certain hostile circles of unbelievers among the influential classes (Pharisees) and the responsible authorities (high priests), 5:10, 15, 16, 18; 7:1, 13; 8:48, 52, 57; 9:18, 22; 10:24, 31, 33; 11:8; 18:12, 14, 31, 36, 38; 19:7, 12, 14, 31, 38; 20:19. This is the circle envisaged in 1:19, though it is not necessary to suppose that "Jews" here already has a negative sense.[8] But they already appear in an unfavourable light in 2:18, 20, and the reader can suspect that they are to be Jesus's opponents. The same type of expression is to be found in the *Gospel of Peter* 1:1; 6:23; 7:25; 12:50, 52.[9] This terminology cannot be satisfactorily explained either by the general anti-Semitism of antiquity or the destruction of the Jewish State in A.D. 70. The evangelist knows that Jesus was a Jew (4:9; 18:35), and this leads him to make a positive affirmation about the Jews (4:22; see *ad loc.*). The real explanation is in the evangelist's experience and faith: the Jewish people as a whole did not find its way to faith in Jesus, the Messiah and Son of God, was responsible through its leading representatives for the death of Jesus and thus erected a wall of partition between itself and the Christian community. Nonetheless, the absence of the missionary spirit—in contrast to the early parts of Acts—may well seem strange; if the Gospel had been meant to convert Israel, it would have had to be written in a different tone.[10] But after 70, Judaism became openly hostile to Christianity, threatened Christians with exclusion from the synagogue (cf. 9:22; 12:42; 16:2) and used its influence in Asia Minor (cf. Rev 2:9; 3:9) and other parts of the diaspora to start persecutions.[11] These facts of contemporary history undoubtedly contributed to the Jews being regarded finally as representatives of the godless "world" in general (cf. 15:18–16:4; 16:8–11; 19:11b).

---

[7] Cf. Lütgert, "Die Juden im Johannesevangelium"; Bauer, excursus after 1:19; Jocz, "Die Juden im Johannesevangelium" (on the vocabulary, pp. 139ff.); Grässer, "Die antijüdische Polemik im Johannesevangelium".

[8] See Gutbrod, "'Ιουδαῖος", p. 379, 20–28.

[9] In the fragment from Akhmîm (Klostermann, pp. 4ff.). The theme of fear of the Jews is particularly characteristic (12:50 and 52).

[10] The thesis that John is a missionary gospel intended for Israel, put forward by Bornhäuser, *Das Johannesevangelium, eine Missionsschrift für Israel*, has been taken up again in a modified form by van Unnik, "The Purpose of St John's Gospel" and by Robinson, "The Destination and Purpose of St John's Gospel". See *Introduction*, VIII, 1.

[11] The insertion of the curse against the "Nazarenes" in the twelfth prayer of the *Shemone 'Esre'*, on the initiative of R. Gamaliel II (c. 90) is significant (Billerbeck, vol. IV, pp. 212f. and 218). Measures against Christians included, as well as exclusion from the synagogue,

The Synoptics tell us nothing of such an official interrogation of the great preacher of penance by the Jordan, but it is quite in keeping with the mentality and practice of the authorities of the Jewish theocracy that they should have watched and investigated every religious movement among the people. That there were doubts in Jerusalem about John's mission may also be deduced from Mk 11:29–33 parr.

1:20	καὶ ὡμολόγησεν καὶ οὐκ ἠρνήσατο, καὶ ὡμολόγησεν ὅτι Ἐγὼ οὐκ εἰμὶ ὁ Χριστός.	And he confessed and did not deny; and he confessed, "I am not the Messiah".

The question as to his person (cf. the question put to Jesus 8:25; and see 10:24) is answered by John with the confession that he is not the Messiah. At a time when Messianic hopes were lively, and Messianic movements often gave rise to political complications,[12] the envoys' question probably had also some political motivations (cf. 11:48). The preacher of penance, to be sure, brought Israel a strictly religious message, and it must have been known in Jerusalem that his only object was to prepare the people for the imminent wrath of judgment and the immediate coming of the Messiah (cf. Mt 3:7 ff. and Lk 3:7 ff.); but once this mighty personality had appeared in the desert, the people were also asking whether he himself might not be the Messiah (Lk 3:15). Thus the interrogation of the Baptist is historically intelligible; but the evangelist's interest is not confined to the past, as may be seen from his way of reporting, with its pleonastic and emphatic "he confessed and did not deny; and he confessed . . ." The expressions cannot be fully explained as a peculiarity of style.[13] According to 1:8 (see there) there can be no doubt that the unambiguous confession of John was meant by the evangelist to have bearing also on contemporary disciples of John, who were proclaiming their master as Messiah.[14] The emphatic ἐγώ implies: "It is not I, but another already in your midst who is the Messiah" (cf. v. 26).

1:21	καὶ ἠρώτησαν αὐτόν· Τί οὖν; Ἠλίας εἶ σύ; καὶ λέγει· Οὐκ εἰμί.	And they asked him, "What then? Are you Elijah?" And he

burning of the gospels (*Tos. Sabb.*, 13, 5), economic and social boycott (Billerbeck, vol. IV, pp. 331–3). On this contemporary background see also Goppelt, *Christentum und Judentum*, pp. 153 ff.; Allen, "The Jewish Christian Church in the Fourth Gospel".

[12] Cf. the Zealot movement, e.g. Farmer, *Maccabees, Zealots and Josephus*, and the clashes of which Josephus speaks: the Samaritan pseudo-prophet (*Ant.*, XVIII, 85 ff.); Theudas (*Ant.*, XX, 97 ff.); the Egyptian (*Ant.*, XX, 167 ff.).

[13] The parallels adduced by Bauer, *ad loc.*, from Aelian *Nat. an.*, II, 43 and Josephus *Ant.*, VI, 7, 4 contain only rhetorical antitheses; in Jn 1:20 the expressions are not even logically suitable. On ἀρνεῖσθαι see my commentary on 1 Jn 2:22 in *The Letters of St. John*.

[14] See above, Prologue, n. 111.

ὁ προφήτης εἶ σύ; καὶ ἀπεκρίθη· Οὔ.

said, "I am not". "Are you the prophet?" And he answered, "No".

Having refused the title of Messiah, John then disassociates himself from other Messianic figures with a clear "no". As these are distinguished from the Messiah, they are either precursors or attendants of the Messiah, or, more probably, Messianic figures promising salvation according to another set of hopes; otherwise the Baptist could hardly have answered with a flat "no".[15] The expectation of Elijah's return was based on Mal 3:1, 23, cf. Ecclus 48:10f., and was very lively in the time of Jesus.[16] Opinions were divided on what functions he would exercise after his return; only one thing seemed certain, that his return would signal the immediate coming of the day of salvation.[17]

The refusal of the Baptist to accept the title of Elijah raises a problem with regard to the synoptic tradition, where Jesus says to his three disciples as they are coming down from the hill of the transfiguration, "Elijah has come, and they have done to him what pleased them" (Mk 9:13, cf. Mt 17:12). The same view of John, that he should be regarded as Elijah returned to earth, is also expressed in the logion Mt 11:14.[18] Luke, however, who did not adopt these views in his Gospel, transmits a saying in the infancy narrative according to which John was merely to act "in the spirit and force of Elijah" (Lk 1:17). Hence the figure of the Baptist could be viewed from various angles. Here as elsewhere John is closer to the Lucan tradition.

It is more difficult to trace exactly the expectation of "the prophet", at least with regard to a clear and definite figure, to which the article points (also in 1:25; 6:14; 7:40,52 [P[66]]). There were in fact various ideas current among the people about the coming of a prophet in the days of salvation (cf. Mk 6:15; 8:28 parr.); but they were not consistent, and the Jewish sources likewise fail to provide a clear picture.[19]

Hitherto the best documentation was provided by 1 Macc 4:46; 14:41 ("a trustworthy prophet" προφήτης πιστός), cf. 9:27 and Ps 74:9, which, however, rather expresses the cheerlessness of an age without prophets; see also Philo, *Spec. leg.*, I,

---

[15] See Bultmann, *Johannes*, p. 62 with n. 4; Richter, "Bist du Elias? Joh 1:21".

[16] Cf. Billerbeck, vol. IV, pp. 779–98; Volz, *Eschatologie*, pp. 195–7; Jeremias, "Ἠλ(ε)ίας" (lit.).

[17] One of the most important functions of Elias on his return will be to "restore all things" (Mal 4:6 LXX; Ecclus 48:10), cf. Mk 9:12; Mt 17:11. The rabbinical interpretation built largely on it, cf. Billerbeck, vol. IV, pp. 792ff.; Jeremias, "Ἠλ(ε)ίας", pp. 935f.

[18] Cf. Trilling, "Die Täufertradition im Matthäusevangelium", p. 281.

[19] The literature is copious, e.g. Fascher, ΠΡΟΦΗΤΗΣ, pp. 142–64; 173–82; Michel, "Spätjüdisches Prophetentum"; Giblet, "Prophétisme et attente d'un Messie-Prophète dans le Judaïsme"; Cullmann, *Christologie*, pp. 11–49, E.T.: pp. 13–50; Schnackenburg, "Die Erwartung des Propheten nach dem Neuen Testament und den Qumran-Texten"; Teeple, *The Mosaic Eschatological Prophet;* Meyer, "προφήτης" (late Judaism); Friedrich, "προφήτης" (John the Baptist).

65, which, however, need not necessarily refer to a particular eschatological prophet; and Josephus, *Ant.*, XX, 97, 169 (*Bellum*, II, 261), where it is related that Messianic pretenders called themselves "prophets"; *Testament of Benjamin*, 9:2, "till the Most High sends his salvation by the rule of a unique prophet" (ἐν ἐπισκοπῇ μονογενοῦς προφήτου according to the reading of β–b [Charles]).[20] The Samaritans also expected "a prophet like Moses" (according to Deut 18:15,18) who had royal as well as prophetical traits.[21]

The texts from Qumran now add valuable information. The *Rule of the Community* reads (9:11), "till the coming of a prophet and the Messiahs of Aaron and Israel". The second part of the phrase certainly refers to the sect's expectation of two Messiahs, and hence the "prophet" must accompany them, whatever be the precise nature of his role.[22] The expectation is based on Deut 18:18, as may be seen from a fragment from Cave IV which contains a number of "Testimonia" which the community found important: Deut 18:18f. (combined with 5:28–29), Num 24:15–17 (the oracle of Balaam on the star from Jacob) and Deut 33:8–11 (Jacob's blessing of Levi).[23] This now clearly perceptible expectation of "the prophet" of Deut 18:15,18 as a Messianic saviour-figure is also behind the third question put to John. It does not prove that the evangelist had direct knowledge of the Qumran texts or that he depended on them (contrast their doctrine of the two Messiahs, where Elijah again appears to have no role). But it shows that he was very well acquainted with the views of the Jews of those days.

---

[20] The text varies considerably in the MSS; but 9:2 with the reading quoted probably belongs to the ancient Jewish substratum of the *Testament*, since the notion of the future glorious temple to which the twelve tribes, and only after them the gentiles, gather, is part of Jewish (and Essene) hopes, cf. the Qumran texts; so too even de Jonge, *The Testaments of the Twelve Patriarchs* who considers that the work is essentially a Christian product. But Philonenko, *Testament des Douze Patriarches*, goes too far, when he identifies the "unique teacher" with the "Teacher of Righteousness".

[21] Cf. Jeremias, "Μωυσῆς", p. 863, n. 126; Teeple, *Prophet*, pp. 63–65, 114; MacDonald, *The Theology of the Samaritans*, pp. 197f., 363ff., 443.

[22] Brownlee, *The Dead Sea Manual of Discipline*, App. D (p. 50) tried to identify the "prophet" of 9:11 with the Messiah, by whom those named next were to be anointed, i.e. the "holy remnant"; but contrast K.G. Kuhn in *NTS* 1 (1954/55), pp. 178f. For further discussions see esp. van der Woude, *Die messianischen Vorstellungen der Gemeinde von Qumran*, pp. 75–89. The identification of the expected "prophet" with the "Teacher of Righteousness" is a much-debated question; but it cannot be proved that he was expected to return, cf. Carmignac, "Le retour du Docteur de Justice à la fin des jours?" G. Jeremias, *Der Lehrer der Gerechtigkeit*, pp. 268–307, esp. 295–8.

[23] Text with notes by Allegro, "Further Messianic References in Qumran Literature". The quotation from Jos 6:26 which follows in the same document seems to be taken from an apocryphal work *(The Psalms of Joshua)*, according to another fragment from Cave 4 (*ibid.*, p. 186). See also Milik in Barthélemy and Milik, *Qumran Cave I*, pp. 121f.

1:22	εἶπαν οὖν αὐτῷ· Τίς εἶ; ἵνα ἀπόκρισιν δῶμεν τοῖς πέμψασιν ἡμᾶς· τί λέγεις περὶ σεαυτοῦ;	So they said to him, "Who are you?—so that we can give an answer to those who sent us. What do you say about yourself?"
1:23	ἔφη· Ἐγὼ φωνὴ βοῶντος ἐν τῇ ἐρήμῳ· εὐθύνατε τὴν ὁδὸν κυρίου, καθὼς εἶπεν Ἠσαΐας ὁ προφήτης.	He said, "I am the voice of one crying in the wilderness: 'Prepare the way of the Lord!', as the prophet Isaiah said."

After the three negatives, the envoys press John for a positive statement about his position, to enable them to satisfy their principals—another sign of the official character of the interrogation. John answers with a quotation from Is 40:3, which in the Synoptics is not found on the lips of the Baptist but in the narrative of the evangelist (Mk 1:3 parr.). The common quotation is not due to literary influences, because the text in John differs from that of the Synoptics (and Septuagint) by giving εὐθύνατε instead of ἑτοιμάσατε. The Johannine text is probably influenced by the next part of Is 40:3, εὐθείας ποιεῖτε κτλ. and offers a "compressed" form of the quotation.[24] The Baptist's one desire is to be "the voice of one calling", which in John means the witness for him who comes after; "in the desert" goes with this, as in the Synoptics, Septuagint, Vulgate, Targum and Peshitta of Is 40:3, and not with the next words of Isaiah, as in the Masoretes (and also *1 QIsa*; *1 QS*, 8:14). John calls out "in the desert", the place in which he chose to come forward on account of its theological importance in the history of salvation.[25]

As *1 QS*, 8:13f., shows, the quotation from Isaiah also played a part in the Qumran community. But it would be overbold to rely on this to link John to the settlement by the Dead Sea. The "desert" was part of the general picture in the religious and Messianic ideas of Israel, and the Baptist's understanding of the text of Isaiah differs substantially from that of the Essenes. He sees the desert as the place where he is to carry out his Messianic task, while they consider it the appropriate place for withdrawal from the "people of the lie" and for "clearing the way of God" (*1 QS*, 8:13), meaning in fact to study and live by the Torah (8:15), cf. 9:19f. This does not exclude an eschatological perspective; according to *1 QM*, 1:2f., they considered themselves the "exiles of the desert", a community preparing itself for the holy war; cf. also *Dam.*, 1:15.

The second part of the quotation, "Prepare (make straight) the way of the Lord", is not exploited in John from the point of view of its content.

---

[24] Cf. Goodwin, "How did John treat his sources?", esp. p. 64; Noack, *Zur johanneischen Tradition*, pp. 72f.

[25] Cf. G. Kittel, "ἐρημός"; Schmauch, "In der Wüste"; Funk, "The Wilderness"; Steinmann, *S. Jean-Baptiste et la spiritualité du désert*.

The important thing in this testimony of the Baptist to himself is not his preaching of penance, but the voice he raises on behalf of Christ (v. 26).

1:24 καὶ ἀπεσταλμένοι ἦσαν ἐκ τῶν Φαρισαίων.

And the envoys included some of the Pharisees.

This verse causes difficulties when compared with v. 19, and some exegetes have tried to remove them by literary criticism.

Wellhausen, Spitta, Goguel and Boismard consider vv. 19–21 and vv. 22–24 as doublets or a parallel tradition.[26] Hirsch and Bultmann take vv. 22 or vv. 22–24 as interpolations of the redactors.[27] But such explanations should only be adopted if the present text proves impossible to deal with.

The verse can also be understood as a comment inserted by the evangelist. It is not new envoys, but members of the same embassy who belong to the Pharisees, who put further questions about the meaning of John's baptizing. The partitive ἐκ, sometimes without τίς or the like, is part of the Johannine style, due no doubt to Semitic idiom.[28] According to the less well-attested reading, with the definite article,[29] the whole embassy consisted of Pharisees or was sent by the Pharisees (ἐκ of origin), which would in fact give an unacceptable picture of them.[30] But the evangelist's actual use of the term "Pharisee" appears justifiable when one recalls that it also includes for him the (Pharisaic) "doctors of the law" in the Sanhedrin (7:32,45; 11:47,57; 18:3; cf. also 8:13; 9:13,15,16,28,40).[31] He calls attention to this group, deliberately no doubt, since in the time of

---

[26] Wellhausen, *Das Evangelium Johannis*, p. 9; Spitta, *Das Johannesevangelium als Quelle der Geschichte Jesu*, pp. 21–24; Goguel, *Jean-Baptiste*, p. 80; Boismard, *Du baptême à Cana*, pp. 18–21, 34.

[27] Hirsch, *Studien*, pp. 51f. (v. 24 redactor's addition); Bultmann, *Johannes*, pp. 57f.; 62, 6 (vv. 22–24 redactional).

[28] Cf. (without the addition) 7:40; 16:17; 18:17, 25; 2 Jn 4; also in the Semitizing language of Rev, 2:10; 3:9; 11:9; 18:4. See Schlatter *ad loc.*; Funk, *Greek Grammar*, para. 164, 2.

[29] W Θ 33 892 pl. 𝔎 lat sy$^{p\ pal\ h}$ arm. But the article is absent from the main witnesses for the Egyptian text (also from P$^{66\ 75}$). Only Vogels puts it in the text, in brackets; the reading with the article is preferred by Loisy, *Le quatrième Évangile*, and Boismard, *Du baptême à Cana*, pp. 33f.

[30] The messengers are from the Sanhedrin, in which the Pharisee doctors of the law only formed one group; though there were many priests in the Pharisee party, it remains improbable that the whole embassy was composed only of Pharisees. Only when the reading with the article is accepted is the criticism made by Bauer and Barrett *(ad loc.)* justified. The best general account of the Pharisees is in Jeremias, *Jerusalem zur Zeit Jesu*, vol. II B, pp. 115–40.

[31] The expression οἱ γραμματεῖς is not found in John, except in the pericope of the woman taken in adultery (8:3), which is also a sign that the passage was not originally part of the gospel.

Jesus it was influential in the Sanhedrin and controlled public opinion,[32] while after 70, with the end of the temple liturgy and the re-modelling of religious life on the basis of the law and the synagogue, it remained in sole command. Their alliance with their opponents, the Sadducees, on certain questions, is also attested by the Synoptics (cf. Mk 11:18,27; 14:1,43,53 parr.). In John the Pharisees are the ever-watchful and suspicious adversaries of Jesus, who keep the people under surveillance and influence it with their propaganda (cf. 4:1; 7:32a,47f.; 11:46; 12:19,42). The Pharisee envoys were probably doctors of the law (cf. v. 19, since the doctors of the law formed a group in the Sanhedrin), and since it is precisely these who ask about John's baptism, they show that they recognized that the rite, administered only once, had a special religious significance. Elsewhere in the Gospel the Pharisees are also the experts in religious matters (cf. 3:1f., 10; 7:47–49; 8:13; 9:16,28f., 40f.).

1:25	καὶ ἠρώτησαν αὐτὸν καὶ εἶπαν αὐτῷ· Τί οὖν βαπτίζεις εἰ σὺ οὐκ εἶ ὁ Χριστὸς οὐδὲ Ἠλίας οὐδὲ ὁ προφήτης;	And they asked him, "Why then do you baptize, if you are not the Messiah or Elijah or the prophet?"

To the mind of the Pharisees, the baptism administered by John must have a Messianic meaning. The distinctive features of the rite were that it was done only once, in contrast to the purificatory baths of the Essenes; it was administered by another, the "Baptist"; and the whole people was called on to undergo it, in contrast to the baptism of proselytes—which like John's, was done only once. The Pharisees must also have been acquainted with the eschatological call to penance which accompanied the baptism (Mt 3:7–10 par.), and which is presupposed here. Hence the first thing that must have suggested itself to the questioners was "to consider the baptism of John as the symbolic action of the eschatological prophet".[33]

1:26	ἀπεκρίθη αὐτοῖς ὁ Ἰωάννης λέγων· Ἐγὼ βαπτίζω ἐν ὕδατι· μέσος ὑμῶν ἑστήκεν ὃν ὑμεῖς οὐκ οἴδατε,	John answered them with the words, "I baptize only with water. There is one among you whom you do not know,

---

[32] Cf. Josephus, *Ant.*, XIII, 288, which says that they had so much influence on the people that they were also trusted when they spoke against a king or a high priest; XVIII, 15: worship and piety were practised according to their rules; XVIII, 18: even the Sadducees followed their rules on account of public opinion; cf. XVII, 41f. (influence at court). More in Jeremias, *Jerusalem*, pp. 136–8.

[33] Friedrich, "προφήτης", p. 839, 26f.

Here too John's answer is calculated to shift attention from his own baptism to the action of him who comes after him. It clearly presupposes the synoptic logion which contrasts his baptism of water (and penance) with the baptism of the Spirit (and fire) to be administered by "the stronger", whom he proclaims, the Messiah (Mk 1:8; Mt 3:11 = Lk 3:16). The fourth evangelist has deliberately omitted the second part, which contrasts the baptism of the Messiah with that of John (cf. v. 33), in order to concentrate attention on the person of him to whom he gives testimony as "the voice of one calling". His baptism fades into insignificance beside his testimony, and appears merely as a rite into which water enters, but without any special significance.[34] Its symbolical character really disappears; the rite is carried out merely as a divine command (v. 33), to provide an opportunity of presenting to Israel the giver of baptism in the Spirit (v. 31). This is a consciously "christiana et christologica interpretatio". The Baptist's next words also point clearly to the synoptic logion about "the stronger" who follows (Mk 1:7 parr.). But it is attached to the present context by a phrase which is clearly Johannine in character: "There is one among you whom you do not know". Obviously, the Baptist already knows him; the emphatic ἐγώ (cf. Mk 1:8 parr.) already indicates his presence, and the ὑμεῖς also seems to be stressed: unlike them, John has recognized him, through divine revelation (v. 33). Thus the event to which he refers in the next part of his testimony (vv. 32f.) has already taken place. Before the envoys of the Sanhedrin, the Baptist does not mention the name of the person who is to be expected. His words "one whom you do not know" are heavy with foreboding: the divine revelation is not given them, and they also lack readiness to accept it. They are not just ignorant for the moment. They are profoundly estranged. In the same way, the Johannine Jesus reproaches his unbelieving interlocutors with not knowing his true origin and nature (8:14,19), even though they are well-informed about him on externals (6:42; 7:27f.). The Messiah's remaining a stranger to those who should know him reminds one of the relationship of the Gnostic revealer to the world.[35] With Jesus, however, it is not the metaphysical distance between the envoy from the heavenly light and the slaves to the material world, but the moral opposition between those blinded by malice (cf. 3:19–21) or estranged from the God whom they religiously affirm (cf. 7:28f.; 8:54f.), and the envoy sent by

---

[34] The enquiring Pharisees must have known that the Holy Spirit was part of the Messianic blessings (cf Ezek 36:25f.; 37:5f.; 39:29; Joel 3:1ff.; Is 32:15; 44:3; 59:21) and hence that a ritual merely of water fulfilled no Messianic function.

[35] Cf. Jonas, *Gnosis*, vol. I, pp. 96f., 122–6; Schlier, *Untersuchungen*, pp. 14ff.; R. Bultmann, "Mandäische und manichäische Quellen", pp. 119–23; id., *Johannes*, *ad loc.:* "This is probably a Judaizing form of the Gnostic theme of the hiddenness of the revealer" (p. 63,3).

God. It is through their own fault that the revealer and saviour remains unknown to them.

It is unlikely that the words of the Baptist allude to Jewish expectations, as for instance that the Messiah was to come forth from concealment (cf. 7:27),[36] or that he would be anointed and proclaimed by Elijah (Justin, *Dial.*, 8,4; 49,1; 110,1) or—as in apocalyptic—that the Messiah, hitherto in heaven, would appear at a certain time to men on earth (cf. *Enoch*, 69,26; *Apoc. Baruch Syr.*, 29,3; cf. *4 Esdr.*, 7:28; 13:32 etc.[37]). The phrase of 1:26 has a certain polemical sharpness, and does not sound as if it were making allowances for Jewish ideas, with a view to winning the Pharisees for Jesus or preparing the "Jews" for the Christian image of the Messiah.

1:27	ὁ ὀπίσω μου ἐρχόμενος, οὗ οὐκ εἰμὶ ἐγὼ ἄξιος ἵνα λύσω αὐτοῦ τὸν ἱμάντα τοῦ ὑποδήματος.	he who is coming after me, whose shoe-laces I am not worthy to undo."

While speaking to the Jewish envoys, John speaks only in a veiled and mysterious way of him who comes after him and whose shoe-laces he is unworthy to undo. It is the same logion as in the Synoptics (Mk 1:7 parr.), but does not sound so full of promise; for these Jews it is not kerygma but martyria, one that can easily become testimony against them (cf. 5:33–35). Immediate literary dependence on the Synoptics is excluded by the fact that instead of the characteristic ἱκανός found in all three Synoptics, John has ἄξιος (but see Acts 13:25), and he has ὑπόδημα in the singular.[38] The logion came through oral tradition, and is given a still more strongly Christological interpretation in 1:15,30.

1:28	Ταῦτα ἐν Βηθανίᾳ ἐγένετο πέραν τοῦ Ἰορδάνου, ὅπου ἦν ὁ Ἰωάννης βαπτίζων.	This took place in Bethany beyond the Jordan, where John used to baptize.

The concluding remark makes John's testimony read almost like an affidavit. The place-name, like Aenon near Salim, 3:23, comes from the special Johannine tradition and is a trustworthy piece of information.[39] The name has varied in the course of transmission, but textual criticism points to "Bethany" as the original reading.

---

[36] See Billerbeck, vol. II, pp. 488f.; vol. IV, p. 766; Sjöberg, *Der verborgene Menschensohn*, pp. 72–82.

[37] Cf. Volz, *Eschatologie*, pp. 208f.; Sjöberg, pp. 41–54 (apocalyptic); pp. 54–64 (rabbinism).

[38] Some MSS (N E F G) add, like Mt 3:11 par. Lk: "He will baptize you with Holy Spirit and fire"; such harmonizations are often found in MSS of John. On the comparison with the synoptics see also Gardner-Smith, *Saint John*, pp. 3f.; Noack, *Zur johanneischen Tradition*, pp. 92f.

[39] Against Kundziņš, *Topologische Überlieferungsstoffe im Johannesevangelium*, pp. 20f., who supposes that the point is to eliminate a cult of the Baptist which still persisted here in the time of the evangelist.

This is the reading of all the majuscules of the Egyptian text, of vet lat, vg sy^{p} bo and many minuscules, and also of Heracleon, according to Origen (Preuschen, p. 149). After visiting the region, Origen himself decided against "Bethany", because he found no place with this name there; he was followed by Eusebius and Jerome, who, however, let Bethany stand in the Vulgate—Βηθαβαρα which Origen championed, is found in ΚΠΨλ 33 al., sy^{sc} sa arm.—Βηθαραβα א^{3} sy^{hmg} and Βηθαρα in a Peshitto MS must be ruled out completely. The variants probably reflect later local traditions.

There is no agreement about the situation of the place. The Madaba mosaic shows a Bethabara on the west bank of the Jordan, with a boat to the north, drawn by a rope. This could suit Bethabara ("The place of the crossing"), but also Bethany (if from בֵּית אֳנִיָּה, "the place of the ship"). But the map also shows on the east bank, opposite the church of St John (the present Prodromos Monastery) Αἰνὼν ἔνθα νῦν ὁ Σαπσαφᾶς (pasture). This could be the locality containing springs in the wadi El-ḥarrar, somewhat off the Jordan (Bethany from בֵּית עֵינוֹן "the place of the springs"), where there was also a hill revered as the place where Elijah was taken up into heaven, and where John was supposed to have baptized, according to a later tradition which persisted for many centuries.[40] Should the "Bethany" of Jn 1:28 be sought here, or should we look for it further to the north, at Tell-el-Medesh, where the Wadi Nimrin joins the Jordan, north of the present-day King Hussein bridge (formerly Allenby bridge)?[41] It does not, of course, follow from 1:28 that the interrogation took place where Jesus was baptized. But the very ancient local tradition suggests that this "Bethany", which can hardly have been a mistake for the Bethany near Jerusalem,[42] was the centre where John baptized; and John himself may have wished to link up with the tradition about Elijah. If so, the fourth Gospel has preserved the name of the important place on the east bank of the Jordan, near to several fords, where John administered baptism[43]—(ἦν . . . βαπτίζων indicates a prolonged activity).

The testimony of the Baptist before Israel (1:29–34)

After the silent departure of the envoys of the Sanhedrin, a new situation arises, which the evangelist indicates by giving a date. This does not

[40] Cf. Dalman, *Orte und Wege Jesu*, pp. 97–102, E.T.: *Sacred Sites*, pp. 89–92; Kopp, *Die heiligen Stätten*, pp. 153–66, E.T.: *Holy Places*, pp. 110–29.

[41] So Féderlin, *Béthanie au delà du Jourdain;* Lagrange, *ad loc.;* id., "Le réalisme historique de l'Évangile selon saint Jean", p. 332; Barrois, "Béthanie"; cf. Abel, *Géographie de la Palestine*, vol. II, p. 267.

[42] Against Parker, "Bethany beyond Jordan".

[43] Cf. the final verdict of Kopp, *Die heiligen Stätten*, p. 166, E.T.: *Holy Places*, p. 128: "So far no signs of habitation in the time of Christ have been discovered. This is the serious archaeological difficulty. In spite of it, the conclusion is permissible, that here was the Baptist's base and consequently, the Bethany of Jn 1:28."

mean that he is bent on historical detail. He merely indicates a change of scene and at the same time that the testimony of the Baptist continues. Interest in the theological content prevails so much over the historical that it is not even clear whom John is now addressing. From v. 31 it appears that a circle is envisaged large enough to represent "Israel". And this is in fact the point of the second testimony: the Messiah, the "lamb of God", the "elect (or Son) of God" is to be presented to the people of God, and made known to them. This also explains why the same testimony is intoned twice (vv. 29 and 32) and why the baptism of Jesus is only alluded to. It is unlikely that it takes place at this precise moment, with the Baptist giving testimony to Jesus as he comes to be baptized.[44] His own words make it clear (vv. 31, 33) that he did not know Jesus as the Messiah before he was enlightened by God. And the tenses of the verbs in vv. 32 and 34 rather indicate an event in the past, of which the Baptist now speaks before Israel. The testimony itself, and the view taken of the divine manifestation at the baptism of Jesus, reflect mature Christian interpretation.

1:29	Τῇ ἐπαύριον βλέπει τὸν Ἰησοῦν ἐρχόμενον πρὸς αὐτόν, καὶ λέγει· Ἴδε ὁ ἀμνὸς τοῦ θεοῦ ὁ αἴρων τὴν ἁμαρτίαν τοῦ κόσμου.	The next day, he saw Jesus coming towards him and said: "There is the lamb of God, who takes away the sin of the world!

With the mention of "the next day", the evangelist begins an enumeration of the days which runs to the marriage at Cana (cf. 1:35, 43; 2:1) and embraces one week. Many exegetes consider that this has a symbolic meaning (the week of this world and the dawn of the new creation with the "first sign"—see commentary on 2:1); but τῇ ἐπαύριον serves primarily merely to link up with the foregoing. Pointing (ἴδε) and urging allegiance (cf. vv. 36f.), John says of Jesus as he draws near—so too Jesus later with Nathanael, v. 47—"Look, there is the lamb of God, he who bears away the (burden of the) sin of the world!" This stereotyped metaphor, which must have been familiar to the first readers, perhaps from liturgical usage or from traditional preaching, presents exegesis today with a double problem. First, one must try to establish the meaning of the evangelist and show if possible how it can be derived from Jewish and biblical or Christian concepts; and then there is the problem of whether and how the saying could occur on the lips of the Baptist, since the synoptic tradition says nothing of it. Opinions differ widely even on the

[44] Cf. Origen (Preuschen, p. 159), Theodore of Mopsuestia (Vosté, trans. pp. 29f.); Goguel, *Jean-Baptiste*, pp. 157–61; Boismard, *Du baptême à Cana*, pp. 42f.

first problem. But there is a sure starting-point in 1 Jn 3:5, a verse which echoes this text and provides a sort of commentary on it: "You know that he has appeared to take away sins (ἵνα τὰς ἁμαρτίας ἄρῃ) and there is no sin in him." This proves first of all that "the sin" of Jn 1:29 means the whole collective burden of sin which weighs on mankind. And then, in the light of other passages of the epistle (cf. ἱλασμός 2:2; 4:10; τὸ αἷμα of Jesus 1:7; 5:6), it cannot be doubted that the vicarious expiation of Jesus's death is meant (see commentary on 1 Jn 3:5).

The latter point is contested, indeed, by M.-É. Boismard,[45] who uses the context of this very text in the epistle to arrive at a different explanation of Jn 1:29. He thinks that Jesus is called the lamb of God who removes sins because he gives men power to cease sinning. This is to be deduced from 1 Jn 3:5, and is said to be in accord with the Baptist's testimony, once lamb of God is taken in its original sense of servant of God, that is, "the servant of the Lord" who being himself the possessor of the Spirit of God now fills ("baptizes") men with the Holy Spirit, so that they need sin no more. However, this explanation of "taking away the sin of the world" cannot well be based on 1 Jn 3:5. The first half of the verse must envisage the unique redemptive act of Christ, which makes it possible to avoid sin in the future (cf. v. 8b): the Christian, freed from his sins by Christ (5a), united with Christ the sinless (5b) and abiding in him, sins no more (v. 6) (see *ad loc.*). Hence the thought of Jesus's unique and universal expiation is at the base of the exposition in 1 Jn 3:5; still less can it be eliminated from Jn 1:29. The lamb of God does not remove the sin which is in the world (so Boismard, p. 51), but the sin of the world, that is, of all mankind, which is hardly thinkable except in view of the Cross.

The thought of vicarious expiation was linked in primitive Christianity with the prophecy of the suffering servant of the Lord (Is 52:13–53:12), and since the Messianic interpretation of the song is ancient[46] (though the application to a *suffering* Messiah is not proved), this seems the obvious place to look for the roots of the expression "lamb of God".

This has been done in two ways. Some scholars take up the comparison of the servant of the Lord with the sheep which is led to the slaughter and the lamb which does not open its mouth (Is 53:7) and point out that the servant of the Lord "bears our sins" (53:4). This "bearing" of sins (φέρειν LXX) is not the same as the "taking away" of sins in Jn 1:29; 1 Jn 3:5 (αἴρειν). This αἴρειν might be understood in the sense of taking upon oneself the punishment of sins[47] (cf. the αἴρειν of the Cross in Mk 8:34

---

[45] Boismard, pp. 47–60; Lagrange, *ad loc.* also seeks an explanation not involving the expiatory death.

[46] Cf. Jeremias, "παῖς θεοῦ", pp. 685–98; Hegermann, *Jesaja 53 in Hexapla, Targum und Peschitta.* Though the Messianic interpretation of the fourth Servant Song is certain for pre-Christian Judaism, grave objections to the notion of the expiatory sufferings of the Messiah must still be met, cf. Lohse, *Märtyrer und Gottesknecht*, pp. 108f.; Cullmann, *Christologie*, pp. 55f., E.T.: pp. 57ff.; Haag, "Ebed-Jahwe Forschung 1948–58", esp. p. 183 (with further lit.).

[47] So esp. Billerbeck, vol. II, pp. 363–70; cf. Tillmann, *ad loc.*, Wikenhauser (only registering and criticizing the position).

parr.), but this would fall short of the Christian notion, that Jesus's expiation blots out the guilt of man's sin, which is undoubtedly present in 1 Jn 3:5. (On the Baptist's understanding of it, see below). And since the simile of the lamb does not fully explain the pregnant expression "lamb of God", many moderns think that "lamb of God" is the same as "servant of God", both going back to the Aramaic טַלְיָא which can mean both "boy, servant" as well as "lamb".[48] There are good reasons for this view.[49] But the question remains as to how "servant" became "lamb" in Greek. Was it merely due to a mistake in translation? Were there not also theological reasons? The reminiscence of the simile of Is 53 is hardly a sufficient explanation.

Once due attention is paid to the symbolism of the *lamb*, the context of the paschal lamb cannot be excluded, since it played such a part in early Christianity[50] and was used in Jn 19:36 to bring out the significance of Jesus's death. The paschal lamb of the N.T. dies, according to the Johannine chronology, just when the paschal lambs of the Jews are being slaughtered in the temple, and none of his bones are broken. There are also other passages in John where the Passover could be a theological component,[51] of which the actual setting would be the primitive Christian "Passover" celebrations which took the place of the Jewish Passover and gave it a totally new content.[52]

As regards the expiatory character of the Passover sacrifice, it is true that the annual killing of the paschal lambs in Jerusalem was not considered an expiatory sacrifice; it seems, however, that this quality was attributed to the Passover of the exodus and to that of the last days.[53] But the question is not very important for the Christian inter-

---

[48] Cf. Burney, *Aramaic Origin*, pp. 104–8; Jeremias, "ἀμνός", p. 343, 6–19; id. "Ἀμνὸς τοῦ θεοῦ—παῖς θεοῦ", pp. 115–23; Cullmann, *Urchristentum und Gottesdienst*, p. 65, E.T.: *Early Christian Worship*, p. 65. Wolff, *Jesaja 53 im Urchristentum*, p. 81; Gärtner "טַלְיָא als Messiasbezeichnung"; Boismard, *Du baptême à Cana*, pp. 46f., 59. The view is criticized by Bultmann, *Johannes*, p. 67 with note, Dodd, *Interpretation*, p. 235, Barrett, *ad loc.*

[49] See the material in Jeremias, pp. 116f.; Gärtner, who makes great use of *Targ.* Ps 118:22–29, where טַלְיָא is also said to be a designation of the Messiah.

[50] The most important texts are 1 Cor 5:7 τὸ πάσχα ἡμῶν ἐτύθη Χριστός; 1 Pet 1:19, where Christ, in the context of an Exodus typology, is compared to a pure and stainless lamb; Lk 22:15–18, an "account of a paschal supper" of which the actual setting was probably the early Christian celebration of the Pasch; cf. Schürmann, *Der Paschamahlbericht Lk 22*; Rev 5:6, 9, 12; 12:11, where the "lamb" which was "slain" also recalls the paschal lamb. Cf. Walther, *Jesus, das Passalamm des Neuen Bundes*; Higgins, *The Lord's Supper in the New Testament*, p. 77; Jeremias, "πάσχα", pp. 899f.; Holtz, *Die Christologie der Apokalypse des Johannes*, pp. 39–47.

[51] Chiefly in ch. 6 (time of the passover, midrash of the manna, possibly a *Sitz im Leben* in an early Christian celebration of the Pasch), cf. Gärtner, *John 6 and the Jewish Passover;* Ziener, "Johannesevangelium und urchristliche Passahfeier" goes still further, holding that the Gospel itself, where the signs are presented within the framework of a *Passover Haggadah*, possibly originated from an early Christian Passover celebration.

[52] Cf. Casel, "Art und Sinn der ältesten christlichen Osterfeier"; Schürmann, "Die Anfänge der christlichen Osterfeier"; B. Lohse, *Das Passafest der Quartadecimaner;* Jeremias, "πάσχα", pp. 900–3.

[53] Cf. Jeremias, *Abendmahlsworte Jesu*, pp. 216f., E. T.: *Eucharistic Words*, pp. 146f.;

pretation. As soon as Jesus was regarded as the paschal lamb of the N. T., the thought of his expiatory death was necessarily involved: *this* lamb extinguishes the sins of the world. The triumphant lamb in Rev (τὸ ἀρνίον) still bears the indelible marks of slaughter upon him (5:6, 9, 12; 7:14; 13:8), so that the same typology is at work.[54]

Hence there is no need to think of other sacrificial lambs, such as the perpetual sacrifice in the temple, the *tamid*, at which every morning and evening a year-old lamb without blemish was offered. The scapegoat, which was laden symbolically with sins of the people on the day of expiation and then driven out into the desert (Lev 16:7 ff.) must also be excluded from consideration.

It has been proposed recently, on the basis of certain notions occurring in apocalyptic, to attribute the lamb of God not the function of expiation but the traits of a ruler.[55] The lamb in Rev, always designated as τὸ ἀρνίον (28 times), is the conqueror at the end of days. It is possible that the seer of Rev took up the image of the "lamb of God who takes away the sin of the world" and used apocalyptic traditions to develop the notion. But the opposite process is hardly possible—that "the lamb" (without further attribute) of Rev explains the pregnant expression of Jn 1:29, 36.[56]

In all probability, the metaphor of the "lamb of God" is not to be explained either by the "servant of the Lord" alone or the "paschal lamb" alone.[57] If a Christian Passover theology can be traced behind John (which cannot, however, be strictly proved), the reference to the paschal lamb seems likely; but the phrase "lamb *of God*", which does not occur elsewhere, must also contain a reference to the "servant of the Lord" of Is 53, a figure who played such an important part in the thought of early Christianity, as he had undoubtedly done in Jesus's own understanding of his Messiahship. John with the Passover in mind, and also perhaps the two meanings of טַלְיָא, has turned "servant of God" into "lamb of God", to arrive at a concept which contains the two typologies—not an uncharacteristic process, since Johannine thinking is done at many levels.[58]

The other problem, whether John the Baptist could actually have given such testimony to Jesus, is very difficult. According to the Synop-

---

formal testimony to the expiatory power of the eschatological Passover is found only late, in *Pirqe R. Elieser*, 29 (quoted by Jeremias, p. 217, n. 1; also by Billerbeck, vol. IV, p. 40); see also E. Lohse, *Märtyrer*, pp. 142f.

[54] Cf. Jeremias, "ἀμνός", p. 345; "πάσχα", pp. 899f.; Walther, *Passalamm*, pp. 68–73.

[55] So esp. Dodd, *Interpretation*, pp. 230–8; hints of this already in Lagrange, *ad loc.;* also Steinmann, *Jean-Baptiste*, pp. 84f.

[56] Criticism of Dodd's explanation in Barrett, "The Lamb of God"; id., *St. John, ad loc.*

[57] The Fathers always understood the expression of the expiatory death of Jesus; the Latins mostly started from the thought of the paschal lamb, while the Greeks derived the expression mostly from Is 53:7; see Boismard, *Du baptême à Cana*, p. 45, n. 7. Among modern exegetes, Schanz, Calmes, May (*Ecce Agnus Dei! A Philological and Exegetical Approach to John I: 29, 36)*, Braun, van den Bussche think exclusively of the Servant of the Lord of Is 53. Walther (*Passalamm*, p. 69) and Bultmann (pp. 66f.: "probably"), appeal only to the Passover typology.

[58] In a similar sense Bauer, Hoskyns, Wikenhauser, Barrett, Schick, Lightfoot, Jeremias ("παῖς θεοῦ", p. 700, 3ff., cf. "πάσχα", p. 899, 25), and others.

tics, he proclaims the imminent judgment of the unrepentant (Mt 3:10 par. Lk); the Messiah, the "stronger" (as also in Mk 1:7), has the shovel in his hand and is about to winnow his threshing-floor (Mt 3:12 par. Lk). Efforts to understand Jn 1:29 in this sense[59] have been unsatisfactory. If one accepts the fact that the saying alludes to Jesus's expiatory death, and that this again is viewed in the perspective of the "servant of the Lord" in Isaiah, one could think of the voice from heaven which almost certainly contains an allusion to this figure (cf. 42:1 and the reading "the elect of God" Jn 1:34).[60] But it could not have given the Baptist even the remotest inkling of the expiatory death (Is 53), and in any case his question from prison (Mt 11:2f., par. Lk) still remains very strange. The exclamation of 1:29, with its deep theological content, must be taken along with the equally profound theological utterance of 1:30 (cf. 1:15), which by attesting the real pre-existence of Jesus raises the same problem. The solution is to be sought in the genre chosen by the evangelist who starts with the Baptist's testimony to the Messiahship of Jesus to disclose to his readers the unique character of this Messiahship. This method of interweaving the *interpretatio christiana* into the historical narrative can already be observed in the Synoptics.[61] The evangelists were not interested in historicizing their narrative, they followed another literary genre in which the narrative was employed in the service of faith, by means of a presentation which developed more fully what was already contained in germ in the historical elements.

1:30	οὗτός ἐστιν ὑπὲρ οὗ ἐγὼ εἶπον· Ὀπίσω μου ἔρχεται ἀνὴρ ὃς ἔμπροσθέν μου γέγονεν, ὅτι πρῶτός μου ἦν.	This is he of whom I said, 'He who comes after me ranks before me, because he existed before me.'

The prophetic words with which John pointed out the "lamb of God" are followed by the affirmation that the person thus designated (on οὗτος cf. 1:6, 15) is the one whom he has already announced. This can only refer to the statement about him "who comes after" in v. 27, since the similar statement in v. 15 was still part of the prologue of the evan-

[59] Cf. Lagrange, *ad loc.;* Dodd, *Interpretation*, pp. 230–8 (see above nn. 55 and 56).

[60] Cf. Joüon, "L'Agneau de Dieu"; Cullmann, *Urchristentum*, pp. 64–66, E.T.: *Early Christian Worship*, pp. 63–66. Jeremias, "παῖς θεοῦ", p. 619, 20ff. But the voice at the baptism (Is 42:1) cannot be understood as the proclamation of Jesus as the suffering, expiating Servant of God, as if this was already the command to undergo the "baptism of death" (against Cullmann, *Die Tauflehre*, pp. 11–14, E.T.: *Baptism*, pp. 12–14, and others after him).

[61] The procedure of Matthew is very instructive on this point; a good example in Mt 14:32f., compared with Mk 6:51f. see Renié, "Une antilogie évangélique".

gelist, and was rather in the nature of an anticipation of v. 30. Thus having described the higher dignity of his successor in v. 27 by means of the (synoptic) metaphor of undoing the shoe-laces, the precursor now sums up the matter by saying: "he has taken precedence of me" (cf. on 1:15). The only modification with regard to v. 15 (cf. v. 27), that ὁ ὀπίσω μου ἐρχόμενος is now replaced by the clearer ἔρχεται ἀνήρ, is perhaps occasioned by the "human presence of Jesus" (Lagrange).[62] John's testimony is sharp and to the point, put trenchantly for the purposes of the kerygma, and has a paradoxical sound: "He existed before me" (on πρῶτός μου see 1:15). In the present situation (as in v. 15), this can only mean the real pre-existence of Jesus—which is as astounding as the indication of Jesus's expiatory death. The profound Christology of the primitive Church is already on the lips of the Baptist! The "Servant Songs" of Isaiah, which could be drawn on to explain the expression "lamb of God", contain nothing on which belief in the pre-existence of the Messiah could be based.[63] It is only in apocalyptic, especially in the "Parables of Enoch" and in *4 Esdras*,[64] that the real heavenly pre-existence of the Messiah (the "Son of Man") is taught in the time of Jesus,[65] and the demonstrably early faith of the primitive Church in the pre-existence of its Messiah probably goes back to some extent to apocalyptic (cf. excursus ii). John may contain overtones of the idea so characteristic of apocalyptic, that the Messiah comes forth from concealment (in heaven) and reveals himself. (Cf. v. 26, ὃν ὑμεῖς οὐκ οἴδατε, and v. 31, ἵνα φανερωθῇ—but see the commentary). In the light of the Logos-hymn, however, pre-existence here has a very special meaning of its own. If the Baptist was merely supposed to be taking up the apocalyptic notion of pre-existence, v. 30 would have had to be put differently; but he testifies to the pre-existence of Jesus in the Christian sense.[66] Since he cannot have derived the notion from the ordinary Jewish thinking on the Messiah, and since it is impossible to see how he could have derived it from the voice from heaven or the revelation given to him at the baptism (cf. v. 33), we must allow here, as in v. 29, for the contribution made by the evange-

[62] Possibly it is also meant figuratively: the man behind has become the man in front, cf. Zahn, *ad loc.* (p. 89).

[63] On Is 53 Gressmann, *Der Messias*, p. 311, notes that there is no mention of pre-existence.

[64] Cf. *Enoch*, 39:6f.; 40:5; 46:1; 48:6; 62:7; *4 Esdr.*, 13:26, 52; 14:9; also *Syriac Apoc. Baruch*, 30:1; *Apoc. Abraham*, 31; *Sib.*, V. 414f.; see further excursus ii.

[65] See esp. Sjöberg, *Der verborgene Menschensohn*, pp. 44–54 (apocalyptic); on the rabbinical writings he notes: "Clear proofs of belief in a pre-existent Messiah cannot be found for the Tannaite period" (pp. 57f.). For later occurrences of the thought (esp. in *Pesiqta rabbati*, a homily of the 7th cent. at the earliest) see there pp. 60–68.

[66] Hence there would not be much advantage in explaining the "lamb of God," as Dodd and others do, from apocalyptic literature. The texts adduced (*Enoch*, 89f.; *Test. Joseph*, 19:8; cf. also *Ps. Solomon*, 17:23–29, 41f.) do not teach the pre-existence of the Messiah.

list's interpretation. His procedure was based on and justified by the Baptist's testimony to the superiority of Jesus, which to the mind of the evangelist led ultimately to the thought of pre-existence. He was certainly convinced that the divine declaration in favour of Jesus had led John to understand his Messiahship in a higher sense than was possible for the Jews. — *See excursus ii.*

1:31	κἀγὼ οὐκ ᾔδειν αὐτόν, ἀλλ' ἵνα φανερωθῇ τῷ Ἰσραήλ, διὰ τοῦτο ἦλθον ἐγὼ ἐν ὕδατι βαπτίζων.	I too did not know him; but that he might be revealed to Israel, that is why I came, baptizing with water."

The Baptist put his testimony to Christ at the beginning. Now he turns to his own person and his own task, as compared to that allotted to the Greater. The statement, "I too did not know him", serves to stress the difference between them. Like all other men, he had no inkling of the mystery of Jesus; but he had received a charge and a mission from God (διὰ τοῦτο ἦλθον), to make the Messiah known to "Israel" the people of God. In contrast to οἱ Ἰουδαῖοι (see commentary on v. 19), "Israel" always has a good sense in John (cf. 1:50; 3:10; 12:13); it is the chosen people of God, to whom the revelation and the promises were given (cf. the title of honour "the teacher of Israel", 3:10), and over whom the Messiah is to be king (cf. 1:49; 12:13). The charge of "making him known" probably presupposes the Jewish notion that the Messiah is to dwell unknown at first among the people, till he is one day revealed (according to several texts, by Elijah).[67] This is John's mission as baptizer, though his baptism is only with water (cf. v. 26); it is his prerogative (as the ἐγώ emphasizes), but also his limitation.

1:32	Καὶ ἐμαρτύρησεν Ἰωάννης λέγων ὅτι Τεθέαμαι τὸ πνεῦμα καταβαῖνον ὡς περιστερὰν ἐξ οὐρανοῦ, καὶ ἔμεινεν ἐπ' αὐτόν.	And John gave testimony, saying, "I saw the Spirit like a dove, coming down from heaven, and resting upon him.

The preceding testimony is now explained. John saw the Holy Spirit descending like a dove upon Jesus and resting upon him. This takes up and adds to the synoptic narrative: we learn here explicitly for the first time that John was one of those who saw the descent of the dove, and only here is it affirmed that the Spirit remained upon Jesus (but see Lk 4:18). Full and permanent possession of the Spirit is the distinctive

[67] See above on v. 26 (n. 36). The situation in v. 31 is different. Here the positive object of the Baptist's mission is expressed, while in v. 26 the Pharisees are given an obscure, almost menacing intimation of it.

characteristic of the Messiah (cf. Is 9:2; 61:1).[68] The voice from heaven is not mentioned, but is probably presupposed in v. 34 (see there). No contrast to the synoptic narrative is intended, though there the voice from heaven was directed to Jesus in person (Mk 1:11; Lk 3:22) or was in the nature of a general proclamation (Mt 3:17). In the fourth Gospel, the Baptist does not comment on the event as such, but simply contents himself with declaring that he was then allotted his role of witness. It is only from the fourth Gospel, however, that we learn that the people needed such instruction, and that John was charged with transmitting it.

1:33	κἀγὼ οὐκ ᾔδειν αὐτόν, ἀλλ' ὁ πέμψας με βαπτίζειν ἐν ὕδατι ἐκεῖνός μοι εἶπεν, 'Εφ' ὃν ἂν ἴδῃς τὸ πνεῦμα καταβαῖνον καὶ μένον ἐπ'αὐτὸν, οὗτός ἐστιν ὁ βαπτίζων ἐν πνεύματι ἁγίῳ.	I too did not know him, but he who sent me to baptize with water, he it was who said to me, 'He on whom you see the Spirit coming down and resting there, this is he who baptizes with Holy Spirit'.

If it had stood alone, the supernatural event at the baptism of Jesus would have conveyed nothing to John. "And I did not know him" (cf. v. 31) now refers less to the person of Jesus than to his prerogative, of baptizing with the Spirit. To enable him to interpret properly the descent of the Spirit in the form of a dove, God first gives John a revelation: he who is designated and filled by the Holy Spirit (cf. 3:34; 7:37–39)[69] is the giver of baptism with the Spirit, that is, the coming Messiah. Since John here appeals to his personal mission from God, the divine communication is to be considered as an inward prophetical illumination. John was thus prepared for what happened at the baptism, since God himself had given him the correct understanding of it. But further, God himself is behind John's testimony in two ways: he authorizes his office as witness, and he guarantees the content of his testimony. John goes on to distinguish still more sharply between his own baptism and that of Jesus; his own is but a shadow of the Messianic baptism with the Spirit. The evangelist perhaps accentuates this in view of the challenge to Christianity offered by the disciples of John (cf. Acts 19:1–7).

---

[68] See Koch, *Geist und Messias;* M.-A. Chevallier, *L'Esprit et le Messie dans le Bas-Judaïsme et le Nouveau Testament;* Sjöberg, "Ruaḥ im palästinischen Judentum", p. 382 (with further lit., pp. 331f.).

[69] Cf. the Lucan tradition which underlines the anointing and the inspired Messianic work of Jesus: Lk 4:1, 14, 18; 10:21; Acts 10:38. Cf. Barrett, *The Holy Spirit and the Gospel Tradition*, esp. pp. 25–45; id., "The Holy Spirit in the Fourth Gospel"; Lampe, "The Holy Spirit in the Writings of St Luke"; Schweizer, "πνεῦμα", pp. 402f.; cf. p. 436, 19ff. (though he fails to do justice to Jn 1:33).

How John understood the "baptism with Holy Spirit", we are not told; he concentrates on the person of the giver of this baptism. Historically, he could well have been thinking of the purifying force of the Holy Spirit in the good, which the O.T. prophets foretold for Messianic times (cf. Is 32:15–18; 44:3–5; Ezek 36:25–27) and of which late Jewish texts also speak (*Jubilees*, 1:23; *4 Esdr.*, 6:26; *Testament of Judah*, 24:3; rabbinical texts in Billerbeck, vol. III, p. 240).

Valuable new documentation for this view is offered by *1 QS*, 4:20f. (a reminiscence of Ezek 36:25 ff.): "Then God will purify through his truth all the deeds of man, and cleanse for himself the body of man. He will take away completely the spirit of perversity from the midst of his flesh, and will cleanse him of all wicked deeds through holy spirit. He will sprinkle him with the spirit of truth like lustral water . . ."[70]

But the evangelist certainly has in mind the Christian notion that Jesus brings about "birth from water and Spirit" (cf. 3:5), as in the sacrament of baptism, which makes men children of God through the power of the Holy Spirit (cf. 1:12f.). Jesus (alone) is he who "comes from above" (3:31) and makes possible the birth "from above" (3:3), the heavenly birth in the Spirit (cf. 3:6–8). Thus the testimony to him who "baptizes with the Spirit" expands the Christological confession of the Baptist in vv. 29f.: the pre-existent divine Messiah from heaven, who takes away the sin of mankind by his expiatory death, is the only one who can bring men the true gift of salvation, the Holy Spirit, and hence eternal divine life (cf. 3:34; 6:63; 7:37–39).

1:34 κἀγὼ ἑώρακα, καὶ μεμαρτύρηκα ὅτι οὗτός ἐστιν ὁ ἐκλεκτός τοῦ θεοῦ. And I have seen it and given testimony: this is the elect (v. l. the Son) of God."

John's testimony to Jesus, which stems from what he has seen with his own eyes (ἑώρακα) and which remains always valid (μεμαρτύρηκα) is finally summed up in the words: "This is the elect of God"—or, according to another reading, "the Son of God".

The reading ὁ υἱὸς τ. θ. is given by the majority of MSS; but the reading ὁ ἐκλεκτὸς τ. θ. is undoubtedly to be preferred. It is found in P[5] (to judge by the length of the lacuna) ℵ* 77 218 e ff[2]* sy[sc] Ambr; and the *electus filius* of a (b ff[2c]) sa shows that an original *electus* was conflated with *filius*. Hence "the elect of God" is an early reading, found in the various regions where Greek, Latin or Syriac was spoken. For intrinsic reasons, it is undoubtedly to be preferred; the title occurs only here in John and elsewhere

[70] On the translation "and purify for himself the body of man", cf. Yadin, "A Note on DSD, IV, 20"; on "from the midst of his flesh", cf. Brownlee, *The Dead Sea Manual of Discipline*, p. 17, n. 40; Lambert, "Le Manuel de Discipline", p. 27, n. 55; Wernberg-Möller, *The Manual of Discipline*, p. 27 and nn. 71–72 (p. 86).

only in Lk 23:35 (cf. also Lk 9:35, ὁ ἐκλελεγμένος). It is easy to understand the alteration from this unusual and peculiar title to the ordinary "Son of God". J. Jeremias has suggested that the change was made in the 4th century to rebut Adoptianism;[71] but it is as old as P[66] [75]. Though the ordinary editions of the Greek text print ὁ υἱὸς τοῦ θεοῦ, on account of the stronger eternal evidence, an increasing number of scholars since Harnack have pronounced in favour of "the elect of God".[72]

This testimony probably echoes the voice from heaven; "the elect of God" is only a variant of "the beloved" (Mk 1:11; Mt 3:17; cf. Lk 9:35, the transfiguration) and is an even closer rendering of Is 42:1 (MT בְּחִירִי; LXX ὁ ἐκλεκτός μου) which confirms the fact that the voice from heaven contains an allusion to this text about the servant of the Lord, the elect of God, in whom he is well-pleased (cf. ἐν σοὶ [ᾧ] εὐδόκησα, Mk 1:11; cf. Mt 3:17), and on whom he lays his Spiri; and that the evangelist is conscious of the allusion. This is the assurance on which the Baptist's testimony to Christ is based, even though the evangelist has given it a deeper and more specifically Christian meaning. Even "Son of God" on the lips of the Baptist (as on the lips of Nathanael 1:49 and Martha 11:27) would have to be understood primarily in a Messianic sense, even though the evangelist meant it to be taken in the higher sense of "metaphysical" Sonship of God (cf. 20:31).

The gaining of the first disciples (1:35–51)

Through John Jesus also wins his first disciples, who represent the true Israel which answers the call of God's messenger and follows the Messiah (cf. 1:31, 47, 49), and who form the beginnings of the community which God himself gives to the Messiah (cf. 3:27, 29). This is an aspect which differentiates the following section from the call of the disciples in the Synoptics (Mk 1:16–20; 2:14 parr.), where men give up home and profession to follow Jesus as his disciples. Historically, the two presentations are not at all incompatible, since the synoptic account can presuppose earlier acquaintance with Jesus on the part of the disciples, while the Johannine does not exclude such conjunctures as the leaving of the nets to become "fishers of men". We only learn from the fourth Gospel that the first disciples came from the school of John the Baptist. According to Mk 2:18 parr. (cf. Mt 11:2 ff. = Lk 7:18 ff.; Lk 11:1), the disciples of

---

[71] "παῖς θεοῦ", p. 687, n. 260.

[72] So already Spitta, *Johannesevangelium*, p. 31 and Zahn, *ad loc.;* also von Harnack, "Zur Textkritik", pp. 552–6; Lagrange, Loisy, *ad loc.;* Windisch, "Angelophanien", p. 218; Cullmann, *Urchristentum*, p. 64, n. 33, E.T.: *Early Christian Worship*, p. 33 n. 2; Jeremias, see previous note; Mollat, van den Bussche; Boismard, *Du baptême à Cana*, pp. 47f.; cf. also Barrett, Lightfoot, *ad loc.*

John continued to form a group with religious practices of their own, distinct from the disciples of Jesus; but the fourth Gospel does not say that all the disciples of John followed out the indications of their master. The attitude of those who remained with John is not made very clear in the Gospels; but serious competition between the two groups, during the lifetime of John, cannot be demonstrated. It was different later, cf. on 1:15, 20; 3:26 ff. It would be groundless to assume that we have here in the Johannine account of the two disciples following Jesus a tendentious re-moulding of the story in Mt 11:2 ff. par. Lk of the messengers sent by John. And the suggestion that John the Baptist and perhaps the disciples whom he sent to Jesus had previously been associated to the Qumran community, and hence provide a link between Jesus and the Essenes,[73] remains a pure hypothesis; similarities are recognizable, but not such as prove dependence or the presence of direct influence.[74]

The section falls into several closely-linked scenes: the two disciples with Jesus, vv. 35–39; the meeting with Simon Peter, vv. 40–42; the winning of Philip and Nathanael, vv. 43–50. The last part is the climax; it leads, through Nathanael's confession (v. 49) to a final and yet forward-looking word of revelation (v. 51), which provides a good transition to the "signs" by which the glory of Jesus is revealed. There is no reason to doubt the literary unity of the passage;[75] v. 43, however, might be an addition of a redactor (see *ad loc.*).

The two disciples of John with Jesus, 1:35–39

1:35	Τῇ ἐπαύριον πάλιν εἱστήκει ὁ Ἰωάννης καὶ ἐκ τῶν μαθητῶν αὐτοῦ δύο,	The next day John was there again with two of his disciples,
1:36	καὶ ἐμβλέψας τῷ Ἰησοῦ περιπατοῦντι λέγει,	and he looked at Jesus going by and said,
1:37	Ἴδε ὁ ἀμνὸς τοῦ θεοῦ. καὶ ἤκουσαν οἱ δύο μαθηταὶ αὐτοῦ λαλοῦντος καὶ ἠκολούθησαν τῷ Ἰησοῦ.	"There is the lamb of God"! The two disciples heard him speak, and followed Jesus.

[73] Cf. Molin, *Die Söhne des Lichtes*, pp. 181–5, 222–4; Brownlee, "John the Baptist in the New Light of Ancient Scrolls"; Geyser, "The Youth of John the Baptist"; Steinmann, *Jean-Baptiste*, pp. 58–61.

[74] Cf. Braun, "L'arrière-fond judaïque", pp. 41f.; Burrows, *More Light on the Dead Sea Scrolls*, pp. 45–51; Schubert, *Die Gemeinde vom Toten Meer*, pp. 109–14; Cross, *The Ancient Library of Qumrân*, pp. 151f., n. 9; Rowley, "The Baptism of John and the Qumran Sect"; Gnilka, "Die essenischen Tauchbäder und die Johannestaufe"; Pryke, "John the Baptist and the Qumran Community".

[75] See the acute analysis of Bultmann, p. 68, which, however, makes demands on the narrative style of the evangelist which are far too modern.

The indication of the day (cf. v. 29) is meant to link the following scene very closely with the testimony of the Baptist. In a few short words, John points out the lamb of God (see commentary on v. 29) and urges the two disciples beside him to join Jesus. They understand and follow. Ἀκολουθεῖν, here understood for the moment literally, is used metaphorically in John for the dedication of faith (cf. 8:12 with 12:36; also 10:4f., 27).[76] Their "following" is the first step to faith on the part of the two disciples; it leads to "remaining" with Jesus, not just that day (v. 39) but in permanent fellowship with him.

1:38	στραφεὶς δὲ ὁ Ἰησοῦς καὶ θεασάμενος αὐτοὺς ἀκολουθοῦντας λέγει αὐτοῖς, Τί ζητεῖτε; οἱ δὲ εἶπαν αὐτῷ, Ῥαββί (ὃ λέγεται μεθερμηνευόμενον Διδάσκαλε), ποῦ μένεις;	But Jesus turned and saw them following and said to them, "What do you seek?". They said to him, "Rabbi (which is translated teacher), where do you stay?"

Jesus makes it easy for the two men to join him, by asking "What do you seek?"—a question which the reader of the Gospel is also perhaps to feel addressed to him (cf. 12:21). The disciples of John answer with another question which implies a request for an undisturbed conversation. "Rabbi" is the usual way for a disciple to address his master (said to John 3:26; to Jesus 4:31; 9:2; 11:8). The request probably indicates a desire to hear Jesus expounding the Scriptures, on the all-decisive question of the Messiah (cf. v. 45). The Baptist was probably more active in putting before his disciples Messianic "applications" of Scripture texts than our sources reveal (but cf. 1:23). We can now form an idea of such exposition of Scripture from the scrolls of the Qumran community, especially the *pesharim*,[77] though important differences may be noted in the various approaches to Messianism.[78] The members of "the covenant of God" were obliged to an intensive study of Scripture (cf. *1 QS*, 6:6f.; 8:12–15); but

---

[76] The thought brought out in the Synoptics, that the "follower" enters into fellowship of life and destiny with his master, is retained in the Johannine logia 12:26; 13:36f.; 21:19f., 22 (though characteristically modified to being "there where Jesus is"). More clearly than in the Synoptics, the concept of "following" in John is applicable to later believers.

[77] Cf. Brownlee, "Biblical Interpretation among the Sectaries of the Dead Sea Scrolls"; Elliger, *Studien zum Habakuk-Kommentar vom Toten Meer*, esp. pp. 118–64; Vermes, "A propos des Commentaires bibliques découverts à Qumran"; Betz, *Offenbarung und Schriftforschung in der Qumransekte;* Silbermann, "Unriddling the Riddle"; Carmignac, "Notes sur les Peshârîm".

[78] See for instance Schubert, "Die Messiaslehre in den Texten von Khirbet Qumran"; van der Woude, *Die messianischen Vorstellungen in der Gemeinde von Qumran;* id., "Le Maître de Justice et les deux Messies de la Communauté de Qumrân"; a different view (only one Messiah) Laurin, "The Problem of two Messiahs in the Qumran Scrolls".

their approach had been dictated to them by their great "searcher of the law" (*Dam.*, 6:7; 7:18), who was certainly the founder or the first great leader of the community (the "Teacher of Righteousness", cf. *Dam.*, 1:11; 20:32; *1 QpHab*, 1:13 etc.). The two former disciples of John find in Jesus more than a master of exegesis; they come to the conviction that he is the Messiah promised in Scripture (cf. v. 41).

1:39	λέγει αὐτοῖς, Ἔρχεσθε καὶ ὄψεσθε. ἦλθαν οὖν καὶ εἶδαν ποῦ μένει, καὶ παρ' αὐτῷ ἔμειναν τὴν ἡμέραν ἐκείνην· ὥρα ἦν ὡς δεκάτη.	He answered, "Come, and you shall see". So they came (with him) and saw where he was staying, and remained with him that day. It was about the tenth hour.

The brief report is meant to give the definite impression that the two seekers are won over by Jesus himself and that John was merely an intermediary. Jesus invites them to come with him. We are not told where he was staying, and it is not important. Though his invitation is couched in commonplace terms,[79] there is probably a deeper sense in ὄψεσθε. It sounds almost like a promise, like the words addressed to Nathanael (1:50) and then those to all the disciples (1:51). The evangelist draws the veil of silence over the subsequent conversation; in all these encounters, it is rather the majesty of Jesus's own person which is at work. The time mentioned (the tenth hour, four in the afternoon) can hardly have a symbolic meaning.[80] It serves to indicate the length and fruitfulness of the conversation, which went on all the evening —or does "that day" also mean the following day? It also suggests the importance of the hour for the disciples—the hour in which they enter into fellowship with Jesus.

The meeting with Simon Peter, vv. 40–42

In the three following scenes, more disciples find their way to Jesus. What is important to the narrator in these encounters is how Jesus behaves, what he says, how he judges and wins these men. It is taken for granted that the reader knows who Andrew and Simon Peter are. Otherwise the evangelist could not start by saying, "Andrew, the brother of Simon Peter, was one of them".[81] When Simon is brought to him, Jesus's

---

[79] Cf. Billerbeck, vol. II, p. 371, on 1:46; Schlatter, *ad loc.*

[80] On the significance of the number ten in Judaism and apocalyptic, see Hauck, "δέκα". Some commentators think that it means the hour of "fulfilment", the beginning of the "Christian era".

[81] This is the way that Mary of Bethany is introduced as "she who anointed" (11:2),

penetrating look takes him in, and he is told at once of the significant name which he will have in the future—"Rock". Jesus knows him and chooses him. We are not told of Simon's reactions, only of the joyful confession of Andrew, which shows what the effect of being together with Jesus has been, and is in the nature of an appeal. But it is of minor importance compared to the majestic word of Jesus. What matters in Andrew's words is that he has designated Jesus as "the Messiah". The first disciples find in Jesus the "king of Israel" (v. 49) of whom Scripture prophesied (cf. v. 45). But Jesus proves to be more than this. He is endowed with divine knowledge, he is in the most intimate and familiar union with God, a Messiah of an undreamt-of kind, who transcends all the expectations of the Jews (cf. 6:69, "the holy one of God").[82]

1:40	Ἦν Ἀνδρέας ὁ ἀδελφὸς Σίμωνος Πέτρου εἷς ἐκ τῶν δύο τῶν ἀκουσάντων παρὰ Ἰωάννου καὶ ἀκολουθησάντων αὐτῷ·	Andrew, the brother of Simon Peter, was one of the two who had heard the words of John and followed him.
1:41	εὑρίσκει οὗτος πρῶτον τὸν ἀδελφὸν τὸν ἴδιον Σίμωνα καὶ λέγει αὐτῷ, Εὑρήκαμεν τὸν Μεσσίαν (ὅ ἐστιν μεθερμηνευόμενον Χριστός).	He first found his brother Simon and said to him, "We have found the Messiah" (which is translated Christ).

The narration here poses some problems. Only one of the two disciples is named, Andrew; it has long been suspected that the other may be John the son of Zebedee, who may also have guarded his anonymity behind the title of "the disciple whom Jesus loved" (13:23; 19:26; 20:2; 21:7, 20; cf. the "other disciple" 18:15; 20:2 ff., 8). This is possible, but cannot be proved. It cannot be deduced from the πρῶτον that this disciple then (after Andrew) brought his brother James to Jesus (Zahn, Barrett and others). It could only be Philip, who does in fact, like Andrew, seek out another (Nathanael) and brings him to Jesus (v. 45), if one is ready to excise v. 43 for reasons of literary criticism (see *ad loc.*).

The πρῶτον of v. 41 has given rise to a number of hypotheses; the reading itself is not certain.[83]

Πρῶτον is in an excellent position, being found in P66 75 B ℵ3 Θ ℵ 083 33 φ λ a c ff l bo arm pm., and hence is preferred by all modern editors of the text except Tischendorf, who read πρῶτος after ℵ W L 𝔎. There is also the reading πρωΐ (mane), e b r (j) sy^{s}, which suits the text very well, but which most editors find suspect, as an attempt

---

before the anointing itself took place (12:1ff.). This shows that the matter has been frequently spoken of before Christian hearers.

[82] Cf. Schnackenburg, "Messiasfrage", pp. 240–64.

[83] On the following cf. Boismard, *Du baptême à Cana*, pp. 82–84.

to smooth away the difficulty. Πρῶτον or πρῶτος is the *lectio difficilior*, because nothing is said of any further action on the part of Andrew, which explains why the word is omitted in Tat sy[c] Aug Chrys. The undoubtedly ancient reading πρωΐ of the Old Latin and the Old Syriac could have been supplanted by πρῶτον (πρῶτος), if one presupposes an originally Aramaic tradition, since קדם can mean "to be early" or "to be earlier" (Jastrow, *Dictionary*, vol. II, col. 1316); or one could suppose a dittography of τόν (cf. Bernard, Boismard, Mollat). But this remains conjecture. If v. 43 is omitted, πρῶτον (better than πρῶτος) would refer to Philip—a hypothesis which merits consideration.[84]

Since ἴδιον in the Koine is often just a substitute for the possessive pronoun,[85] it cannot be used to prove that a second pair of brothers is envisaged. Hence all solutions are uncertain (but see commentary on v. 43).

1:42	ἤγαγεν αὐτὸν πρὸς τὸν Ἰησοῦν. ἐμβλέψας αὐτῷ ὁ Ἰησοῦς εἶπεν, Σὺ εἶ Σίμων ὁ υἱὸς Ἰωάννου· σὺ κληθήσῃ Κηφᾶς (ὃ ἑρμηνεύεται Πέτρος).	He brought him to Jesus. Jesus looked at him and said, "You are Simon, the son of John. You shall be called Cephas" (which is translated Peter, Rock).

The evangelist's main interest is the fact that Jesus announced that Simon will have the name Κηφᾶς. It appears from the scene with Nathanael that here too Jesus is meant to be seen as the possessor of divine knowledge: he "looks at" Simon and knows all about him, and at the same time reveals what his future name will be. It is this urgent, personal address (σύ—σύ; cf. v. 49b) which wins Simon. In contrast to Mt 16:17, Simon's father is here called "John", not Jonah, which suggests independent, perhaps original tradition.[86] The future κληθήσῃ can hardly mean that the name is given at once (Semitic future of volition); it is rather a prophecy, and Jesus speaks as revealer. The translation of Κηφᾶς (Aramaic כֵּיפָא, Rock, with final ς in Greek) is given, not just to

[84] Bultmann, 70, n. 8, who supposes a secondary change in v. 43, concludes from πρῶτον that Andrew was originally the subject of εὑρίσκει in v. 43, or from πρῶτος that it was then the other disciple. Boismard, "Les traditions johanniques", pp. 39–42, now identifies the latter with Philip.

[85] Cf. Funk, *Greek Grammar*, para. 286, 1; Bauer, *ad loc.*

[86] Apart from Jn 1:42; 21:15ff., the name of Simon's father is given in this form in the *Gospel of the Hebrews*, fr. 9. The variant reading Ἰωνᾶ is assimilation to Mt 16:17. Codex Θ in 1:42 has Ἰωαννα, in 21:15ff. Ἰωνα, which could also be a contraction for the first form. Jona is hardly a short form for Jochanan (not verified in Aramaic, but possible in Greek, cf. LXX); it is a different name, though not found after the prophet Jonah till the 4th cent. A.D. Either the father of Simon and Andrew had the unusual name of Jonah, which was then replaced by the common name of John, or the Greek contraction affected the Aramaic tradition (Mt 16:17). Cf. Jeremias, "Ἰωνᾶς", p. 410; Schmid, "Jona".

mention the well-known name of Peter for the benefit of Greek readers, but to explain it.[87] It is taken for granted, therefore, as in Mt 16:18, that Jesus designated Simon by a meaningful epithet, which only came into use later as a secondary name.[88] It is not made clear in John, any more than in the Synoptics, when the actual designation took place.

Hence 1:42 is not a parallel to Mt 16:17 ff.; Simon Peter's confession of faith in Jesus as the Messiah is given only at 6:69. And it does not come into conflict with Mk 3:16 parr., since it presupposes the same fact—which Mk 3:16 likewise does not fix chronologically. We have here a clear example of the Johannine narrative approach, which is to take facts known from tradition and place them in a certain light—above all Christological.

At the very first meeting, the Johannine Jesus foretells the future significance of this disciple. This is important for the evangelist, not just as part of his image of Christ, but on account of his ecclesiastical interests. He stresses the role of "the disciple whom Jesus loved" alongside of Peter (cf. 13:23 ff.; 19:26f.; 20:3–8; 21:20–23), but he does not pass over Peter's precedence as spokesman of the Twelve (6:67 ff.) and pastor of the flock of Christ (21:15 ff.), and pays special attention to his martyrdom (13:36; 21:18f.). The "competition" between the two disciples never hardens into conflict, and it is not exploited polemically against Peter. There is no question of Peter's being disparaged in the present text, either by the fact that he is not one of the first two disciples to follow Jesus, or that he only comes to Jesus through the mediation of another, his brother Andrew.[89] On the contrary, since the evangelist has passed over in silence Jesus's conversation with the first disciples, Peter is distinguished by the words addressed to him and the prediction of his future rank.

On the other hand, too much is read into the text if it is taken to mean (with Origen[90]) that Jesus, the "Rock" absolutely speaking, here calls

---

[87] Πέτρος in Greek is rather the (loose) block of stone; used of rock which has been rolled into place as a boundary-marker, Sophocles, *Oed. Col.*, 1595; metaphor for stability, id., *Oed. Tyr.*, 334; cf. Liddell and Scott, vol. II, p. 1398. Πέτρα, the solid rock, would have been better, but πέτρος was suggested as a masculine form, especially as the distinction was not always strictly observed even in Greek, cf. Cullmann, "πέτρα", p. 94; 100, 5–17. Against wrong conclusions drawn from the meaning "stone" by Dell, "Matthäus 16:17–19", esp. pp. 17ff., see Cullmann, *Petrus*, p. 20, E. T.: p. 19.

[88] Cf. Cullmann, *Petrus*, pp. 18–23, E. T.: pp. 17–21; Schmid, "Petrus, der Fels, und die Petrusgestalt in der Urgemeinde". The fourth evangelist preferred the two-fold designation of "Simon Peter" (17 times). He uses "Simon" alone where he refers to his parentage (1:42, 43; 21:15ff.), "Peter" alone, obviously for brevity, where the two names have been given just before (1:45; 13:8, 37; 18:11, 16ff., 26f.; 20:3f.; 21:7, 17, 20f.). He does not refer elsewhere to the meaning of the word "rock".

[89] Against Kragerud, *Der Lieblingsjünger*, pp. 19ff. On Kragerud's general thesis see the author's review in *Biblische Zeitschrift* 4 (1960), pp. 302–7.

[90] *Comm. in Jo.*, frg. 22.

Simon, the "Rock" of the Church.[91] Among the numerous Christological titles in John, that of "the stone" or "the rock" is never found; contrast the transfer of the "pastoral office" by Jesus, the true pastor of God's flock (10:11–16,27 ff.), to Simon Peter (21:15 ff.). All that can be said is that the Johannine Jesus already has the vision of the later Church before his eyes as he gathers his first disciples around him.

The Meeting with Philip and Nathanael, 1:43–50

1:43	Τῇ ἐπαύριον ἠθέλησεν ἐξελθεῖν εἰς τὴν Γαλιλαίαν, καὶ εὑρίσκει Φίλιππον καὶ λέγει αὐτῷ ὁ Ἰησοῦς, Ἀκολούθει μοι.	The next day he decided to set out for Galilee, and met Philip. Jesus said to him, "Follow me".

Jesus's summons, "Follow me!", makes the meeting with Philip most like the synoptic stories of the call of the disciples (cf. Mk 2:14 parr.; 10:21 parr.; Lk 9:59). The mention of another day (cf. vv. 29,35) and the remark that Jesus was about to set off for Galilee are not important for the context; they are so vague that they may have been deduced from 2:1. Other points (cf. "he [Jesus] met . . .", with v. 41 and v. 45; the mention of Jesus by name in the second part) suggest that v. 43 is an addition of the redaction.[92]

On this hypothesis some things are easier to understand: (1) the redactor had the "third day", 2:1, in mind, and wished to show Jesus setting out, to explain his presence at the marriage. (2) If v. 44 was originally intended to describe the doings of the second disciple, hitherto unnamed (vv. 37–39), the πρῶτον of v. 41 becomes intelligible. (3) The redactor, who did not grasp this, still had to recount the "call" of Philip. Or did he deliberately leave the second disciple in a mysterious obscurity? Did he remove from v. 44 an indication that Philip was the second disciple? The lack of such a very desirable indication, on the other hand, makes the whole hypothesis questionable.

1:44	ἦν δὲ ὁ Φίλιππος ἀπὸ Βηθσαϊδά, ἐκ τῆς πόλεως Ἀνδρέου καὶ Πέτρου.	Philip was from Bethsaida, the same town as Andrew and Peter.

Philip comes from the fishing-village of Bethsaida ("place of the fishery"), to the east of where the Jordan enters the lake (probably near the present-day Kirbet el-'araj); there was no other place also called "Bethsaida in Galilee" (cf. 12:21), which term the evangelist retains as

[91] Cf. Boismard, *Du baptême à Cana*, pp. 86ff. (adduces also 1:51, Jesus as the stone of Bethel). See also Betz, "Christus–petra–Petrus", who takes in more than John.

[92] So already Spitta, *Johannesevangelium*, pp. 56f.; further Wilkens, *Entstehungsgeschichte*, p. 35 and esp. Boismard, "Les traditions johanniques", pp. 39–42.

the popular designation (in spite of its belonging politically to the territory of the tetrarch, Herod Philip).[93] Philip's connection with Andrew and Peter is explained by the fact that all came from the same town. The Synoptics speak only of the brothers' living later in Capernaum (Mk 1:29). There is no reason to doubt the fact as given in John and it shows precise knowledge. Philip, whose name occurs in the Synoptics only in the catalogue of the Apostles, appears again several times in John (6:5,7; 12:21f.; 14:8f.), along with Andrew at 6:7 and 12:22.

1:45	εὑρίσκει Φίλιππος τὸν Ναθαναὴλ καὶ λέγει αὐτῷ, Ὃν ἔγραψεν Μωϋσῆς ἐν τῷ νόμῳ καὶ οἱ προφῆται εὑρήκαμεν, Ἰησοῦν υἱὸν τοῦ Ἰωσὴφ τὸν ἀπὸ Ναζαρέτ.	Philip met Nathanael and said to him, "We have found him of whom Moses in the law and the prophets wrote, Jesus the son of Joseph from Nazareth."

The last of the encounters, which is recounted more fully, represents the climax. Philip "meets" Nathanael, just as Andrew had found his brother (v. 41), probably still where John used to baptize. Nathanael is mentioned only in John; according to 21:2 he came from Cana in Galilee.

The subsequent first "sign" in Cana (2:1–11; cf. 4:46) and the remark about Nazareth (v. 46) strengthen the impression of an independent and reliable tradition.

Efforts have constantly been made to identify Nathanael ("God has given") with other disciples known from the Synoptics, but Augustine (*In Jo.*, VII, 17) and Chrysostom (*Hom.*, 20) already saw that this was a fruitless task. It is not strictly necessary, according to the Johannine narrative, that he should have belonged to the Twelve. Epiphanius proclaims his conviction that he was the unnamed disciple on the road to Emmaus.[94] The tradition that he was identical with Bartholomew can be traced back to Isho'dad in the East (c. 850), and to Rupert of Deutz in the West (d. 1129). It is pointed out that Philip and Bartholomew are mentioned together in the catalogue of the Apostles, Mk 3:18 (but not Acts 1:13), and that Bartholomew is a patronymic ("son of Tholmai"), which leaves open the possibility of another name. In the lists of the Apostles in the ancient *Epistula Apostolorum*, 13 (2) and the Apostolic Constitutions[95] Bartholomew is mentioned along with Nathanael. The Greek liturgical tradition identified him with Simon the Zealot. Hence the question must be left open.[96]

---

[93] On Bethsaida, see Dalman, *Orte und Wege Jesu*, pp. 173–80; Abel, *Géographie*, vol. II, pp. 279f.; Kopp, *Heilige Stätten*, pp. 230–43, E. T.: *Holy Places*, pp. 180–6.

[94] *Pan.*, 23, 6,5 (Holl p. 255).

[95] Schermann, *Die allgemeine Kirchenordnung*, p. 12; cf. Horner, *Statutes of the Apostles*, p. 9.

[96] Cf. Schmidt, *Gespräche Jesu*, pp. 229ff.; Bauer, excursus, p. 43; Holzmeister, "Nathanael fuitne idem ac S. Bartholomaeus Apostolus?"

Philip assures Nathanael that he and his companions have found in Jesus "him of whom Moses in the law and the prophets wrote"—a formula which embraces the whole scripture of the O.T.[97] Hence Nathanael also belonged to that circle of questing men, well-schooled in Scripture, who awaited the Messiah. The fact that Philip calls Jesus the son of Joseph does not prove that this is also the mind of the evangelist. It rather indicates the usual designation of Jesus's father on the lips of the people (cf. 6:42); the evangelist also records without commentary the objection of the people that the Messiah must be born in Bethlehem (7:41 f.)—he does not say what he knows.

1:46 καὶ εἶπεν αὐτῷ Ναθαναήλ, Ἐκ Ναζαρὲτ δύναταί τι ἀγαθὸν εἶναι; λέγει αὐτῷ Φίλιππος, Ἔρχου καὶ ἴδε.

Nathanael said to him, "From Nazareth—can there be anything good from there?" Philip said to him, "Come and see".

The mention of the town from which Jesus comes arouses at once the scepticism of Nathanael. His ironical question expresses a doubt that the Messiah can come from so unimportant a place as Nazareth. It is not inspired by study of the Scripture, as in the case of the members of the Sanhedrin, 7:52. Nazareth had, in fact, played no part on the political and religious scene, and is nowhere mentioned in the O.T. and early rabbinical writings.[98] Nathanael, who lived in near-by Cana, objects to the Messiah having so lowly an origin, as do the Jews, 6:42. It is the scandal given by the appearance of the Messiah in the flesh, as long as he has not been met with faith. It will be shown in the case of Nathanael that only faith overcomes all objections and recognizes the divine origin of Jesus in spite of his earthly lowliness—and it is Jesus himself who awakens this faith, by his words and by his majesty. Philip makes no effort to clear away Nathanael's misgivings, but leads him at once to Jesus, merely saying "come and see" (cf. commentary on v. 39), certain that he too will be won over by Jesus.

1:47 εἶδεν ὁ Ἰησοῦς τὸν Ναθαναὴλ ἐρχόμενον πρὸς αὐτὸν καὶ λέγει περὶ αὐτοῦ, Ἴδε ἀληθῶς Ἰσραηλίτης ἐν ᾧ δόλος οὐκ ἔστιν.

Jesus saw Nathanael coming towards him and said of him, "There is a true Israelite, a man with nothing false in him."

---

[97] Cf. (with mention of Moses) Lk 16:29, 31; 24:27; Acts 26:22; 28:23; ("the law and the prophets" only) Mt 5:17; 7:12; 11:13; 22:40; Lk 16:16; 24:44; Rom 3:21.

[98] On Nazareth see Dalman, *Orte und Wege*, pp. 61–88, esp. p. 87; Kopp, *Heilige Stätten*, pp. 86–92, E. T.: *Holy Places*, pp. 49–86; Schmitt, "Nazareth", esp. pp. 318–29.

Once more Jesus shows that he is possessed of supernatural knowledge. Though he has not yet met Nathanael, he sums him up as he is coming towards him, with the words, "There is a true Israelite, a man with nothing false in him." Superficially, this power to read hearts recalls the Hellenistic demi-gods (θεῖοι ἄνδρες);[99] but the fourth Gospel does not attribute Jesus's knowledge to miraculous powers with which he is endowed, but to the intimate union of Jesus with his Father (cf. 3:35; 11:42; 13:3). Just as he knows his own task and way (2:4; 6:6; 8:14; 13:1; 17:1; 18:4), he knows the men whom he meets, those who believe and those who refuse to believe (cf. 10:14f., 26ff.), the disciples whom he has chosen and the betrayer (6:61,64,70; 13:11,18,38; 17:12). He sees into the hearts of men (2:25; 5:42; cf. 6:15; 21:17), because he is united with the Father and his Messianic vocation makes him sharp-sighted. His verdict expresses a high esteem for Nathanael. The new arrival receives the honourable title of "Israelite" (cf. on 1:31), and a word of praise which probably alludes to Ps 32:2.[100] On account of the logion v. 51 (Jacob's dream), many commentators have seen here an allusion to Jacob, the patriarch Israel. But this is improbable. Nathanael is not called "a man with nothing false in him" in contrast to Jacob, the "deceiver" (cf. Gen 27:35f.), but because he is a genuine[101] Israelite, that is, a worthy representative of the people of God (cf. v. 49, "king of Israel"). "Falsehood" (δόλος) and "false" (δόλιος) speech can take on religious overtones in the language of the O.T. (cf. Ps 12; 17:1; 43:1; 52:5f.; Prov 12:6; denied in the servant of the Lord Is 53:9), and can even designate infidelity to God (cf. Hos 12:1; Zeph 3:13; Jer 9:5). Ps 32 praises the holy and upright mind which impels the worshipper to a sincere confession of guilt before God.

1:48	λέγει αὐτῷ Ναθαναήλ, Πόθεν με γιγνώσκεις; ἀπεκρίθη Ἰησοῦς καὶ εἶπεν αὐτῷ, Πρὸ τοῦ σε Φίλιππον φωνῆσαι ὄντα ὑπὸ τὴν συκῆν εἶδόν σε.	Nathanael said to him, "How is it that you know me?" Jesus answered him, "Before Philip called you, I saw you under the fig-tree".

---

[99] Cf. Wetter, *Der Sohn Gottes*, pp. 69–72; Reitzenstein, *Mysterienreligionen*, pp. 236–40; Bieler, ΘΕΙΟΣ ΑΝΗΡ, pp. 89–94; Bultmann, pp. 71f., n. 4.

[100] The quotation does not follow the Septuagint exactly, the reading of which is "In *his mouth* there is no guile" (31:2); cf. also Is 53:9. It is closer to the basic Hebrew text. "The Greek text predominates in Johannine usage, but the Hebrew also makes itself felt, as also happens with Mt, which indicates that both are from Palestine" (Schlatter, *ad loc.*).

[101] Ἀληθῶς is adverbial, almost the same as ἀληθινὸς Ἰσραηλίτης, cf. 4:42; 6:14; 7:40; 8:31 and 6:55 *var. lect.* The usage was classical, cf. Plato, *Phaedo*, 109E; *Laws*, 642C, D; Plutarch, *Isis et Osiris*, 3; see also Ruth 3:12; *4 Macc.*, 11:23; Josephus, *Ant.*, IX, 256; Ignatius, *Rom.*, 4:2.

Nathanael, who has heard the comment of Jesus, is deeply moved and asks how Jesus comes to know him. He is all the more touched at being praised because he has just belittled Jesus's native place. After Jesus's answer he has no doubt that Jesus disposes of miraculous knowledge. The proof which overwhelmed Nathanael is not so clear to us (contrast the case of the Samaritan woman, 4:17f.). Jesus reminds Nathanael of a certain situation: unobserved by others, he was under a fig-tree—but Jesus saw him. Is Jesus just giving palpable proof of his knowledge?[102] This would hardly justify his deep knowledge of Nathanael's heart. The usual explanation appeals to the rabbinical phrase "to sit under the fig-tree"[103] and the custom of the doctors of the law, of sitting under a tree to study Scripture.[104] Nathanael, then, hidden from the eyes of others under a sheltering fig-tree, would have been studying Scripture, especially the Messianic prophecies. If so, his reaction to Jesus's revelation, his acknowledging him as the Messiah, is still more understandable (v. 49). According to J. Jeremias, the fig-tree is an allusion to the tree of knowledge in paradise, which late Judaism thought was a fig-tree; Nathanael confessed his sins sincerely before God, and Jesus reminded him of this by the quotation from Ps 32, a thanksgiving for the pardon of sin.[105] The words are so brief that it is impossible to explain with certainty what they refer to; at any rate, Jesus's words corresponded to the "inner" situation of Nathanael.

1:49	ἀπεκρίθη αὐτῷ Ναθαναήλ, Ῥαββί, σὺ εἶ ὁ υἱὸς τοῦ θεοῦ, σὺ βασιλεὺς εἶ τοῦ Ἰσραήλ.	Nathanael answered, "Rabbi, you are the Son of God, you are king of Israel."

Nathanael is so overwhelmed by Jesus's knowledge and his power of reading hearts that he proclaims spontaneously his faith in Jesus as the Messiah, with a personal warmth of dedication (the two-fold σύ). After the usual address of "rabbi" (see commentary on v. 38), he gives him two significant titles, in the style of a confession of faith,[106] "Son of God" and

[102] So Moule, "A Note on 'Under the Figtree' in John 1:48, 50".

[103] In *Midr. Cant.*, 4, 4, R. Abba b. Cahanah (c. 300) speaks of the learned in general as "sitting under the olive tree and vine and fig-tree and studying the Torah" (see Billerbeck, vol. II, p. 371).

[104] See the examples in Billerbeck, vol. II, p. 371, and the instructive one from *Midr. Qoh.*, 5:11, in Billerbeck, vol. I, p. 858.

[105] Jeremias, "Die Berufung des Nathanael".

[106] On σὺ εἶ cf. Mt 11:3 (14:28); 16:16 parr.; Mk 3:11; Jn 4:19; 6:69 (8:53; 10:24); 11:27. Norden, *Agnostos Theos*, pp. 183ff. sees here an oriental form of address, characteristic esp. of invocations. Against this view, cf. Kundzinš, *Charakter*, pp. 215f., who stresses that the formula is in the nature of a confession, also recalling the profession of faith of the Christian community (p. 217).

"king of Israel". Taken together, they confirm Philip's announcement that Jesus is the Messiah promised in Scripture (v. 45), and also bring out the special nature of Jesus's Messiahship. Of itself, "king of Israel" could sum up the popular ideas of the Messianic liberator, the restorer of the kingship of God in Israel.[107] John recognizes this title as correct (cf. 12:13), since in his eyes it has been purified of political Messianic associations by the addition of "Israel" (cf. 6:15, only "king")—in contrast to "king of the Jews" (18:33,39; 19:3,19,21). The "Son of God" which precedes it is remarkable, since it cannot be proved to have then been a usual designation of the Messiah.[108]

Even if one assumes that "Son of God" did occur as a Messianic title[109] and was eliminated merely because of anti-Christian polemics,[110] it was certainly not a usual title, and the immediate use of it by Nathanael would remain striking. One could, of course, appeal to Ps 2:7,[111] where the Messianic king is declared to be son of God; but if Nathanael had this passage in mind, one would have expected the titles in the inverse order. The putting of "Son of God" first is clearly intended to convey the immediate impression which Jesus's knowledge made on Nathanael.

In the context, "the Son of God" is probably meant to express closeness to God, union with God, and perhaps even origin from God.[112] But then the derivation from Ps 2 is inadequate. It is much more likely that the evangelist wished to give first a title, which, like "the holy one of God", 6:69, expresses the purely religious meaning of the Messiahship. The same procedure is used at the confession of Martha (11:27) where the title of Messiah is followed by the words, "the Son of God, who is to come into the world", so that the reader is prepared for the full Christian confession

---

[107] See *Ps. Solomon*, 17:21, 42. Rabbinical writings often have "the King Messiah", cf. Moore, *Judaism*, vol. II, pp. 324ff.; Staerk, *Soter*, vol. I, pp. 48ff.; Volz, *Eschatologie*, p. 174, but mostly "Son of David".

[108] Cf. Dalman, *Worte Jesu*, pp. 219–23, E. T.: pp. 268–88; Gressmann, *Der Messias*, pp. 383f.; Mowinckel, *He That Cometh*, pp. 293f., 386. The verdict of Billerbeck, vol. III, pp. 15–20 and Volz, *Eschatologie*, p. 174 is more positive.

[109] This might be supported by the Messianic interpretation of Ps 2 in Judaism, cf. the ancient testimony in *Sukka*, 52 a *Bar.* (Billerbeck, vol. III, p. 19, and the further instances in Dalman and Billerbeck). See also Lagrange, *Le messianisme chez les Juifs*, pp. 104f.; Taylor, *The Names of Jesus*, pp. 53f.; Manson, *Jesus the Messiah*, p. 103; Cullmann, *Christologie*, pp. 279–81, E. T.: pp. 272–5; Howton, "Son of God in the Fourth Gospel". Further, the testimony of the Synoptics (esp. Mk 14:61 par.; Mt 27:40, 43; Mk 3:11; 5:7 par.) must not be underestimated. Against the thesis of the infiltration of the Hellenistic title "Son of God" into the synoptic tradition, see Bieneck, *Sohn Gottes als Christusbezeichnung bei den Synoptikern*; on the age and authenticity of the tradition see van Iersel, *"Der Sohn" in den synoptischen Jesusworten.*

[110] Dalman, *Worte Jesu*, p. 223, E. T.: p. 272; Billerbeck, vol. III, p. 20.

[111] Jeremias, "Die Berufung des Nathanael", p. 4; Boismard, *Du baptême à Cana*, p. 104.

[112] See Schlatter, *ad loc.*: "The second follows from the first; from the origin from God, which gives him unity with God, follow his royal rights."

(cf. 20:31).[113] Nonetheless, the evangelist did not mean to suggest that Nathanael recognized in Jesus the full dignity of (metaphysical) sonship of God; otherwise Jesus would not have promised a still fuller revelation of his nature (vv. 50,51). The titles used by Nathanael are meant as Messianic, but provide the reader with the possibility of a deeper understanding (cf. on 1:29).

1:50	ἀπεκρίθη Ἰησοῦς καὶ εἶπεν αὐτῷ, Ὅτι εἶπόν σοι ὅτι εἶδόν σε ὑποκάτω τῆς συκῆς πιστεύεις; μείζω τούτων ὄψῃ.	Jesus answered him with the words, "Do you believe, because I told you that I saw you under the fig-tree? You shall see greater things than this."

Whether it is a question or an affirmation, Jesus's answer to Nathanael is not to be taken as sceptical: it is a recognition and a promise, with no trace of doubt or reproach (as in 4:48; cf. 2:23; 6:2). How else could Nathanael have come to believe, except through Jesus's first words to him? The evangelist is interested in noting that all the misgivings of this critical mind disappear before the person of Jesus. But Jesus promises that he will see, that is, experience, still "greater things". The term is probably deliberately vague, but must refer to the revelation through the "signs", and primarily to the miracle of Cana, which Nathanael is to witness and which can reveal more magnificently the δόξα of Jesus than his marvellous knowledge (cf. 2:11). Once Nathanael has believed, he receives a still greater promise from Jesus; the initial faith which Jesus has brought about is to grow through further revelations of Jesus.

A Revelation for the Disciples, 1:51

1:51	καὶ λέγει αὐτῷ, Ἀμὴν ἀμὴν λέγω ὑμῖν, ὄψεσθε τὸν οὐρανὸν ἀνεῳγότα καὶ τοὺς ἀγγέλους τοῦ θεοῦ ἀναβαίνοντας καὶ καταβαίνοντας ἐπὶ τὸν υἱὸν τοῦ ἀνθρώπου.	And he said to them, "Truly, truly, I tell you, you shall see the heavens opened and the angels of God ascending and descending on the Son of Man."

A further logion of Jesus is addressed to all disciples in spite of the singular of the introduction (λέγει αὐτῷ) and thus forms the conclusion and the climax of the whole section. The link with the preceding is merely

---

[113] Cf. Lagrange, *Saint Jean*, p. CLV: "Dans tous ces cas, ce qui frappe surtout, c'est le dessein de ne pas laisser isolée l'expression de Messie, d'empêcher qu'on l'entendît dans un sens terrestre et national, surtout de préparer les esprits à mettre tout l'accent sur le titre de Fils de Dieu, qu'il fallait entendre dans le sens propre."

verbal (ὄψῃ—ὄψεσθε), and the logion may have circulated originally without any setting. Nonetheless, no better context can be found for it. Here it is clearly intended to describe or define the "greater things": the heavens opened and the angels of God ascending and descending over the Son of Man.[114] In the Johannine tradition, it was probably placed here from the start. It can be characterized as a "Johannine logion", as appears at once even in the introductory formula, "Truly, truly I tell you,"[115] which occurs 25 times in John. The use of "Amen" as a solemn asseveration at the start of an affirmation was peculiar to Jesus.[116] The doubling is typical of John, though it is also found in the Qumran texts (at the end of sentences, however), and is due, no doubt, to liturgical usage.[117]

As regards the content, the logion is unique in the fourth Gospel. Nowhere else is there mention of angels as intermediaries between the Son of Man on earth and God in heaven. If it is not an erratic block from another tradition which contained "angelophanies",[118] it must be taken as a metaphor. It can hardly refer to the synoptic story of the temptation (Mk 1:13 parr.), which is not mentioned in John, but has a fixed place in the synoptic tradition between the baptism of Jesus and the call of the disciples.[119] Since the temptation would have had to be placed before the events narrated here, the disciples would not have "seen" anything of the angels' ministrations. The relationship to the vision of Jacob's ladder cannot be denied, since the words of Gen 28:12, "the angels ascending and descending", recur in the same order.[120] But the allusion to the O.T. story need take in no more than this; the free use of one particular trait from an O.T. image is also found in Jn 3:14f., which is likewise a Son of Man logion.

But what is the teaching behind the imagery? The usual explanation is the closeness of the Son of Man on earth to heaven, his unceasing union with God. More definitely, it should be that the Son of Man is the "place" of the full revelation of God ("Bethel"), where God manifests his glory to the vision of faith (cf. 2:11; 11:40; 14:8ff.). According to the image of the "heavens opened", the angels should rather descend first and then ascend. The reverse order, here and in Gen 28:12, shows that the scene is viewed from the earth, in the case of Jacob or the "seeing" disciples. But

---

[114] See Noack, *Zur johanneischen Tradition*, p. 154.

[115] *Ibid.*, pp. 65–71.

[116] See Dalman, *Worte Jesu*, pp. 185ff., E. T.: pp. 226–9; Schlier, "ἀμήν"; Jeremias, "Kennzeichen der *ipsissima vox Jesu*".

[117] *1 QS*, 1:20; 2:10, 18 (after blessing and cursing); cf. *1 QS*, 10:1–17 (acrostic); In Ezra 9:47 (LXX 1 Esdr) the "amen" is also doubled in codex B, in Tob 8:8 LXX in codex S.

[118] So Windisch, "Angelophanien", esp. pp. 223ff.

[119] See Michaelis, "Joh 1:51, Gen 28:12 und das Menschensohn-Problem", esp. cols. 572f.

[120] Against Michaelis.

the Son of Man also can only be thought of as on earth, since the Son of Man, after his exaltation (cf. Mk 14:62 parr.; Acts 7:56) is at the right hand of God, and in John too has regained his earlier glory (cf. 3:13; 6:62; 12:32; 17:5,24).[121] From the Son of Man on earth, the angels go up to God with his desires and prayers, and come down to serve him. The same thought is expressed directly by Jesus when standing before the open tomb of Lazarus: "Father . . . I knew that you always hear me" (11:42), upon which the greatest miracle of the Johannine Jesus takes place, the raising of Lazarus, where the believer can "see the glory of God" (11:40). The opening of the heavens is an eschatological motif in Is 63:19, and at the baptism of Jesus it is seen by early Christian thought as a sign of the Messiah (Mk 1:10 parr.). The same thought underlies other passages as well: at the birth of the Messiah, the heavenly hosts appear on earth (Lk 2:13 ff.); at the transfiguration of Jesus, the heavenly figures of Elijah and Moses range themselves beside him (Mk 9:4 parr.). Above all, the Son of Man is to come in divine glory with the clouds of heaven (Mk 13:26 parr.; 14:62 parr.). But in Jn 1:51 the motif is made to serve Johannine Christology: heaven opens above the Son of Man, so that what is a vision of the future in the Synoptics is already present in John, and even the "angels" (cf. Mk 8:38 parr.) are already there, though their function is different. The perfect participle ἀνεῳγότα leaves the length of the vision undefined, but can hardly mean any one particular vision or a recurrent one. The disciples will experience ("see") in all Jesus's work the union with God which is his and his alone. Thus the Son of Man on earth is the "gate of heaven" (cf. Gen 28:17), the place of the presence of God's grace on earth, the tent of God among men (cf. 1:14).[122]

To look for further theological meanings is to ask too much of the logion. In particular, the speculations of later Jewish mysticism should not be read into it, making the Son of Man on earth communicate with his "heavenly image", while the disciples are taken up into heavenly glory and united with the Father, on account of their connection with the Son of Man.[123] It is urged that the Son of Man represents and embodies the people of God of the N.T., as Jacob did the ancient Israel, so that he leads men to God "in himself". This would explain the ἐπ' αὐτόν, without recurring to the Jewish mysticism which applied the בו (MT) to Jacob, instead of to the ladder, as in LXX.[124] But this sort of mysticism is in conflict with Johannine soteriology, which always calls for faith in Jesus and attachment to him as the unique personal mediator of divine life. Christ in John remains the distinctive figure of the revealer and redeemer, with

---

[121] Against Quispel, "Nathanael und der Menschensohn".

[122] See Jeremias, "Die Berufung des Nathanael", p. 5; Traub, "οὐρανός", p. 530, 4ff.

[123] So esp. Odeberg, *Fourth Gospel*, pp. 33ff.; Dodd, *Interpretation*, pp. 245f.; cf. also (with reserves) Bultmann, *Johannes*, p. 74, n. 4.

[124] See *Gen. Rabbah*, 68, 18, where R. Hiyya refers the בו to the ladder, R. Jannai to Jacob (appealing to Is 49:3); but these are Amoraeans of the third generation. Misgivings are expressed by Barrett, *ad loc.*, Boismard, *Du baptême à Cana*, pp. 124f.

exclusive demands, the one Son of Man who has descended from heaven and ascends there again (3:13,31f.; 6:62). The other Son of Man logia (cf. 3:14; 5:27; 6:27,53; 8:28; 9:35; 12:23,34; 13:31) are also incompatible with an "inclusive" interpretation.

Another point that can hardly be insisted on is that on the analogy with Gen 28 Nathanael now takes the place of Jacob (Israel) looking at the ladder, while the designation "Israelite" already suggests the interpretation "seer".[125] It is true that in Philo and the Fathers "Israel" is explained as the "seer" or "the man who sees God",[126] and that the "looking at" the Son of Man raised up from the earth has theological import in John (cf. 3:14f.; 19:37).[127] But there are a number of weaknesses in this view. In 1:51 it is not the "true Israelite", Nathanael, who is signalled as the visionary: the promise is directed to all the disciples (ὄψεσθε). The "look" of faith at the Son of Man "raised up" or "pierced" (3:14f.; 19:37) is not the same as "seeing" the "heavens opened" here. The trait taken from the story of Gen 28:10–19 is not Jacob's dream and his behaviour, but simply the image of the ladder with the ascending and descending angels.

Why does the Johannine Jesus here speak of the Son of Man? The word belongs to a series of Son of Man logia, which could have formed a special "traditional theme".[128] But it is unlikely that it was borrowed directly from apocalyptic and then merged with the theme of Jacob and Bethel. It is rather a Johannine development of the Son of Man theology of the early Church (cf. excursus v). As to its relationship with the synoptic logia on the Son of Man, the words of Jesus to the Sanhedrin spring to mind at once: "You shall see the Son of Man sitting at the right hand of the Almighty and coming with the clouds of heaven" (Mk 14:62). The vision of glory has been transposed into the present time in 1:51; the Johannine Son of Man has brought his glory to earth with him, though he reveals it only to believers—which is the "Messianic secret" in John. The ἀπ' ἄρτι of the future (Mt 26:64; cf. 23:39) becomes an ἀπ' ἄρτι of the present when Jesus speaks in John (14:7): the disciples already know and "see" the Father in Jesus.

This first logion on the Son of Man does not speak of his "exaltation" and "glorification",[129] but merely mentions this pregnant title in words full of mystery and promise, and puts it in a prominent position at the end of the logion. The logion itself emphasizes the Son of Man's close and continual intercourse with heaven, which already hints at his origin and his goal. Hence it is particularly suitable as the first words of revelation on the Son of Man, which are then followed by others which develop the theology of the Son of Man. — *See excursus iii.*

---

125 So Boismard, pp. 125f.

126 *Ibid.*, pp. 98–100.

127 *Ibid.*, pp. 112–8.

128 See Schulz, *Untersuchungen*, pp. 96–103.

129 See Thüsing, *Erhöhung*, pp. 226ff., 258f.

CHAPTER III

The Beginning of the "Signs": The Miracle at the Marriage-Feast in Cana (2:1—11)

The story of this first "sign" by which Jesus reveals his glory (v. 11) is both the climax of the foregoing, which pressed on towards a visible manifestation of the Messiah acclaimed but not fully known by his first disciples (cf. 1:50,51) and the starting-point for the whole self-revelation of Jesus which is given through "signs" (cf. 12:37; 20:30). This is indicated by the final remark of the evangelist, v. 11, particularly valuable after the brief narrative, since it points forward to other "signs" to come (11a) and rounds off at the same time the story of the winning of the first disciples (11c). If one keeps these two points of view in mind, the faith of the disciples which is brought to perfection by Jesus's self-revelation in "signs", and the "beginning of the signs", by which the peculiar nature of the Johannine portrayal of Jesus's earthly work is signalled, one should be able to appreciate properly the situation and significance of the (first) miracle of Cana.

The first impression given by the narrative is that of a simple miracle-story. But the mysterious words about the "hour" of Jesus, the lavish quantity of wine, the final remark of the evangelist and indeed the whole purport of the story make it clear that there is a deeper meaning behind the words of the narrative; and this level of thought forms the real problem. The evangelist mentions the miracle itself only in a subordinate clause (v. 9), and breaks off with the head-waiter's strange rule about serving wine, which sounds like a joke but still provides food for thought, with its mention of the "good wine" kept till the end by the bridegroom. Nothing is said of the effect of the miracle on the guests and the public; it appears from 4:45 that the Galileans were not impressed until Jesus's actions in Jerusalem. But there is no point in asking about the historical repercussions of a miracle. The interest of the evangelist is restricted to its "theological" impact, in Cana to the faith of the disciples, in which the revelation of Jesus's glory bears fruit (2:11), and in Galilee to the negative result of the many "signs" seen by the sensation-hungry crowd in Jerusalem (cf. 4:48). The self-disclosure of Jesus through "signs" can give rise to both effects. But since the miracle of Cana is signalled under the positive aspect, it is the positive significance of the story that must be looked for.

Stylistic and other criteria have suggested to some that the evangelist here makes use of an existing narrative, which sounds almost "synoptic" in its brevity. None of the usual criteria of Johannine style are to be found in it.[1] But the mention of Jesus's "hour" (v. 4) is enough to assure us that it has been given a Johannine shape, and its insertion into the train of Johannine thought is further guaranteed by the final comment (v. 11). It is hard to say whether the evangelist takes up a special "Cana tradition", to which the second "Cana" miracle, 4:46–54, could be a pointer. If he was following a written source,[2] he has certainly exploited it in his own way. There are similarities in the narrative style of the multiplication of the loaves, where the actual provision made for the crowd is likewise mentioned only in a subordinate clause (6:12). The curt allusion to the actual miracle is a feature which the present passage shares with the healing at the pool of Bethesda (5:8f.), the walking on the waters (6:19, 21), the cure of the man born blind (9:6f.) and even the resurrection of Lazarus (11:43f.). It is not necessarily a sign of the presence of "synoptic" narrative. What is really astonishing about the miracle at Cana is that Jesus himself makes no use of it to develop his revelation. But this is probably due to its introductory character. The "sign" allows only of a preliminary, though comprehensive, view of Jesus's "glory", and the possibility of a special symbolic meaning such as the bread of life, the light of the world, the resurrection and the life is reserved for the later "signs".

This in itself is enough to make us wary of a too narrow or one-sided determination of the deeper meaning. The only sound method is to weigh the text exactly and try to note where the evangelist has placed special emphasis, so that the underlying thought can be traced by comparison with the rest of the presentation. But the narrative is so brief and sparing of words that the analysis is difficult, and has in fact led to very different results. The points which cause particular difficulty are the exchange of words between Jesus and his mother, and Jesus's subsequent conduct, and the difficulty here is all the greater because some of the phrases may be taken in different ways ("my hour", v. 4b—statement or question?). Ultimate certainty is perhaps not attainable in the interpretation. With

---

[1] See Schweizer, *Ego eimi*, p. 100.

[2] A σημεῖα-source was already envisaged by Faure, "Die alttestamentlichen Zitate", pp. 107–12, who takes 20:30f. as the immediate sequel to 12:37, and is postulated by Bultmann, *Johannes*, p. 78 and *passim*, who holds that 2:11, at least in its primordial form, is from this source. See further Introduction, ch. iv, 3.

the proviso, therefore, that other explanations retain the probability that should be allotted to them, we give first a positive analysis of the text, with comment on details, and then try to assay the deeper meanings.[3]

Analysis of text

2:1	Καὶ τῇ ἡμέρᾳ τῇ τρίτῃ γάμος ἐγένετο ἐν Κανὰ τῆς Γαλιλαίας, καὶ ἦν ἡ μήτηρ τοῦ Ἰησοῦ ἐκεῖ·	And on the third day there was a marriage in Cana of Galilee, and Jesus's mother was there.

In all probability, no symbolical meaning should be attached to "the third day", which continues the series of dates given in 1:29,35,43. Since there is another day between 1:39 and 41, a week has passed since 1:19, if the days are added up. Is this meant to indicate the first week of Jesus's Messianic work?[4] But Jesus does not speak until 1:38 and only begins to perform his "signs" with the miracle of Cana at the end of the section (cf. 2:11). Or is the week of the new creation to be contrasted with the week of creation?[5] But the thought of creation only occurs in the prologue, where it is in any case not central (1:3, 10); the miracle of Cana can certainly be understood as the fulfilment of eschatological hopes (see below), but it is doubtful whether it can be regarded as the "Sabbath rest" or "consummation" of the world. More importance may be attached to the view which maintains that the "third day" alludes symbolically to the morning of the Resurrection,[6] especially if Jesus's "hour" is to be referred to his glorification and the "sign" of Cana is an anticipation and promise of this true disclosure of his "glory". But the only reference in the Gospel to the Resurrection of Jesus "in three days" (2:19f., cf. 21f.) is purely Christological (referring to Jesus's "body"), and the Johannine Resurrection narrative makes no mention of the "third day". All these interpretations go beyond what can be gathered from the narrative itself. The primary meaning of the date in 2:1 is probably that the promise made by Jesus in 1:50 or 51 was fulfilled very soon. On the other hand,

[3] From the copious literature on the point we may mention: Schmidt, "Der johanneische Charakter der Erzählung vom Hochzeitswunder in Kana"; Schulz, "Das Wunder zu Kana im Lichte des Alten Testaments"; Gaechter, "Maria in Kana"; id., *Maria im Erdenleben*, pp. 155–200; Braun, *La Mère des Fidèles*, pp. 47–74; Schnackenburg, *Das erste Wunder Jesu*; van den Bussche, "Het wijnwonder te Cana"; Michl, "Die Hochzeit zu Kana. Kritik einer Auslegung" (on Gaechter, Braun and others); Boismard, *Du baptême à Cana* 133–59; Ceroke, "Jesus and Mary at Cana: Separation or Association?"; Charlier, *Le signe de Cana*; Feuillet, "L'Heure de Jésus et le signe de Cana"; Dillon, "Wisdom, Tradition and Sacramental Retrospect in the Cana Account (Jn 2,1–11)"; Derrett, "Water into Wine".

[4] Cf. Boismard, *Le Prologue*, pp. 136–8 (appealing to É.-B. Allo).

[5] So Boismard, *Du baptême à Cana*, p. 15.

[6] Cf. Dodd, *Interpretation*, p. 300.

the evangelist was hardly thinking of reckoning the distance from the site of the baptism to Cana (cf. 1:43a); the "third day" is probably a round number (cf. Lk 12:32) which links up with the foregoing but still points forward. The mention of Cana in Galilee is certainly based on sound tradition (cf. 4:46; 21:2); Josephus also mentions a place with this name in Galilee.[7] Pilgrims are now shown Kafr Kenna, some 4 miles north-east of Nazareth; but it can be proved that the tradition has been erroneously transferred from the original Kirbet Qana, some 8 miles to the north of Nazareth, on the northern border of the plain of Battōf. Only some ruins mark the place, which is also attested by a more consistent pronunciation of the name (with ק), which is also associated with a good cistern (*birqana*).[8] The carpenter's family from Nazareth was probably personally acquainted with the families of the bride and bridegroom. The presence of Jesus's mother at the marriage is specially mentioned on account of the following scene.

2:2	ἐκλήθη δὲ καὶ ὁ Ἰησοῦς καὶ οἱ μαθηταὶ αὐτοῦ εἰς τὸν γάμον.	And Jesus and his disciples were also invited to the marriage.

Jesus may have been invited for family reasons; the disciples are those whom he has just gained. There is an interesting tradition in the *Epistula Apostolorum*, 5 (16), which speaks of Jesus's brothers instead of his disciples.[9] But we cannot say whether the source contained something of the sort (cf. v. 12). The evangelist is interested in the disciples as believing witnesses of the miracle (v. 11).

2:3	καὶ ὑστερήσαντος οἴνου λέγει ἡ μήτηρ τοῦ Ἰησοῦ πρὸς αὐτόν, Οἶνον οὐκ ἔχουσιν.	And as the wine gave out, Jesus's mother said to him, "They have no (more) wine."

The first scene, which prepares for the miracle, is played out between Jesus and his mother. The marriage festivities lasted for a week according

[7] *Life*, 86. *Ant.*, XIII, 391 deals with places outside of Galilee, so too *Ant.*, XV, 112 and *Bellum*, I, 334. Eusebius, *Onom.*, 116, 4–7 identifies the Cana of the miracle wrongly with the Cana of Jos 19:28, which is in the territory of Asher, c. 8 miles south-east of Tyre.

[8] Kafr Kenna was supported for instance by Meistermann, *Guide de la Terre Sainte*, pp. 524–31; Lagrange, *Saint Jean*, pp. 54f. On the authenticity of Khirbet Kana see Dalman, *Orte und Wege Jesu*, pp. 108–14, E. T.: *Sacred Sites*, pp. 101–106; Abel, *Géographie*, vol. II, pp. 412f.; Kopp, *Das Kana des Evangeliums*; id., *Heilige Stätten*, pp. 184–95, E. T.: *Holy Places*, pp. 143–54.

[9] "Then there was a marriage in Cana of Galilee. And he was invited with his mother and his brothers" (Duensing).

to Jewish custom, when the bride was married for the first time. Care was taken to provide enough wine, which was freely poured on such occasions.[10] Wedding presents were customary, and were in fact demanded by right of most of the guests.[11] The embarrassment of the hosts, as the wine ran short,[12] is understandable. The week of celebrations must have been nearly over, so not much time can have elapsed between Mary's words and the miraculous intervention of Jesus. It is not clear from the text that Mary is asking for a miracle from her son, as many Fathers and modern exegetes assume. On the face of it, she simply calls his attention to the shortage; she can hardly be urging him to depart. It has been suggested that the thought of a miracle was far from her mind, and that Jesus blames her for this very reason.[13] But this is ruled out by v. 5, which clearly intends to portray Mary as believing, the tranquil servant of her Son (cf. also 19:25). If we compare Martha's meeting Jesus before the raising of Lazarus (11:20–27), we see Martha making the same type of request (v. 22)—imprecise, inspired by hope and confidence in Jesus, not excluding a miracle, and indeed, in the mind of the evangelist, already hinting at it, while Jesus takes up her request, to turn her mind from earthly hopes to the deeper significance of his action (v. 25). Mary too asks for the alleviation of distress; as guests, Jesus and his disciples could be considered obliged to give presents. She leaves it to her Son to decide on the form of his aid. But Jesus cannot accede at once to her request.

2:4	λέγει αὐτῇ ὁ Ἰησοῦς, Τί ἐμοὶ καὶ σοί, γύναι; οὔπω ἥκει ἡ ὥρα μου.	Jesus said to her, "What would you have me do, madam? My hour is not yet come."

Jesus's answer is certainly highly significant to the evangelist, above all for his portrayal of Christ, but it is not easy to interpret.[14] Is Jesus refus-

---

[10] On Jewish marriage customs see Billerbeck, vol. I, pp. 500–17. The earliest testimony to a seven-day celebration is Tob 11:18 (even 14 days in Tob 8:19); rabbinical testimonies in Billerbeck, vol. I, p. 517. On the coming and going of the guests during the festal week see *Keth.*, 7b *Bar. (ibid.*, 514f. under *u); for* the wine-drinking *Tos. Sabb.*, 7, 9 *(ibid.*, 516 under *cc)*. Even rabbis made merry (*Ber.*, 30b) or even got drunk (*Ber.*, 9a).

[11] Cf. Derrett, "Water into Wine", pp. 81–89.

[12] The longer reading οἶνον οὐκ εἶχον, ὅτι συνετελέσθη ὁ οἶνος τοῦ γάμου· εἶτα א * a b ff r sy^{hmg}; *factum est per multam turbam vocatorum vinum consummari* e l, is secondary. A copyist was probably explaining ὑστερεῖν, which is only frequent in this sense in late Greek. א * then also changes the words of Mary: οἶνος οὐκ ἔστιν, as is also read by Tat sy$^{p\ pal\ h}$.

[13] So Boismard, *Du baptême à Cana*, pp. 157f.

[14] See also (along with the literature given above n. 3) van den Bussche, "De Betekenis van 'het Uur' in het vierde Evangelie"; Leal, "La hora de Jesús, la hora de su Madre"; Michl, "Bemerkungen zu Jo 2:4"; J. Cortés Quirant, "Las Bodas de Caná"; Ceroke, "The Problem of Ambiguity in John 2:4". See also n. 19.

ing Mary's silent request? Is he giving her to understand that she must not interfere in his Messianic tasks and calling? But we must always remember that in v. 5 Mary still helps to provide the miracle. Hence she cannot have understood Jesus's answer as a complete refusal. On the other hand, it is impossible to deny that Jesus holds himself aloof from his mother (and her request) to some extent. The first part of his answer is a widely-used phrase, which can be verified both in the Old Testament and Judaism, as well as in the Greek and Hellenistic world.[15] It never means, "What concern is that of yours and mine?" The καί must be understood as marking a certain contrast, which, however, can take on various nuances according to the context—and the tone of voice. It does not necessarily express disassociation or harsh rejection. It can be a much milder "Leave me in peace!" or "What would you have me do?".[16] But it connotes a certain aloofness, which is also expressed by addressing Mary as γύναι, which must be taken with the first clause (cf. Mk 1:24; 5:7; Mt 8:29; Lk 4:34; 8:28). The word "woman" is certainly not a disrespectful form of address, but when used towards one's mother, at least among the Semitic peoples, it is unusual and astonishing.[17] It is also found in the other place in John in which Jesus addresses his mother (19:26), and hence can contain no trace of disparagement, though it is not proved to be a mark of honour (by reason of the possible theological implications of the passage). The meaning of the question in 2:4a can only be discussed in conjunction with the following clause.

The mysterious saying about Jesus's "hour" has been much debated. To a great extent, the profounder interpretation of the miracle at Cana depends on the meaning given to these words. The explanation takes different forms, according to the way one answers two doubts raised by exegesis. Is the phrase a statement or a rhetorical question? Does the "hour" mean the immediate revelation of Jesus's glory in the sign at Cana, or is it the hour of Jesus's death and of the glorification which it brings with it?

Statement or question? Like Gregory of Nyssa, Theodore of Mopsuestia, perhaps Ephraim and Tatian in antiquity,[18] many modern exegetes, especially Catholic,

---

[15] Hebrew מַה־לִּי וָלָךְ : Jg 11:12; 2 Sam 16:10; 19:23; 1 Kgs 17:18; 2 Kgs 3:13; 2 Chr 35:21; Mk 1:24; 5:7; Mt 8:29; Lk 4:34; 8:28; in rabbinical writings only *Pesiq. R.*, 5 (in Billerbeck, vol. II, p. 401). For Hellenistic Greek see Epictetus, *Diss.*, I, 1, 16; 22, 15; 27, 13; II, 19, 16 (cited by Bauer, *ad loc.*); *C. Herm.*, XI, 21.

[16] See Langrange, *ad loc.*; Michl, "Bemerkungen zu Joh 2:4", pp. 493–8.

[17] Examples of "Woman" as a respectful form of address in Bauer, *ad loc.* and Michl, "Bemerkungen", pp. 498f., but only in the Hellenistic world. On the strangeness of such a way of speaking to one's mother among the Jews see Dalman, *Jesus-Jeshua*, E. T.: p. 202.

[18] Gregory of Nyssa, *Hom. on 1 Cor 15:28* (*PG* 44, col. 1308 D); Theodore of Mopsuestia, on Jn 2:4 (Vosté, *CSCO* 116, p. 39); Ephraim, *Comm.*, V (Leloir, *CSCO* 145, pp. 44f.; the

maintain with growing definiteness that it is a question.[19] This is grammatically possible.[20] The sense would then be: "What would you have me do? After all, my hour has already come!"—the hour, that is, of my Messianic work. This eliminates the difficulty which the rejection of Mary's request gives rise to, namely that Jesus then performs the miracle at once and that Mary prepares it tranquilly and carefully. But the rhetorical question contains a slight reproach: after all, you should have known this![21] Has Jesus already begun his Messianic work or told his mother of his intention of doing so? Is he reminding her of his leaving home? But these are matters of which there is not the slightest hint in John, and hence the rhetorical question poses its own difficulties. Even if it is a statement, to the effect that Jesus's hour has not yet come, it is possible to trace a satisfactory sequence of thought, if one pays attention to the narrative style of the evangelist. Jesus first makes a remark which brings home to his mother the distance between them, and then informs her that the law according to which he works is imposed on him by another. This is in keeping with the answers we hear in the Synoptics (Lk 2:49; Mk 3:33–35 parr.; Lk 11:28). Even his mother must yield place to his Messianic call and work. Jesus's hour, which has not yet come, is not so much a point of time, a fixed and calculable date, as a decree issued by the Father. If this is borne in mind, there is no difficulty, even on the supposition that the "hour" means the immediate revelation of Jesus's glory (in the miracle), in the fact that Jesus performs the miracle a little later. And neither does Mary disregard this teaching, when she gives the servants her prudent instructions and still leaves the action to be taken by her Son. For the style of narrative, one may compare 7:6–10. Here too the reader has the impression that Jesus acts differently from what his words in v. 8 would lead one to expect. But the evangelist sees no contradiction, since Jesus, following his appointed time, merely refuses to reveal himself publicly before the world (cf. v. 4). His going "secretly" to Jerusalem need not entail such revelation of himself. But all this does not yet tell us how Jesus really understands his "hour" in 2:4.

Once we have rejected the rhetorical question which would point to Jesus's present Messianic work, we are obliged to consider seriously whether when speaking of his "hour", he is not alluding mysteriously (in a way incomprehensible, of course, to Mary) to the full revelation of his glory after the Cross and Resurrection. His "hour" in 7:30 and 8:20 refers unmistakably to the moment of his death, but this perspective is very remote from 2:4, where Jesus can hardly fear that his action may hasten the hour of his death. But for John, the death of Jesus is also the hour in which the Son of Man is "glorified" (cf. 12:23, 27, 31 f.; 13:31 f.; 17:1 f.), when he passes from this world to the Father (13:1). It is

---

Latin translation of Leloir gives it as an assertion; a question according to Boismard, *Du baptême à Cana*, p. 157); Tatian according to the Arabic Diatessaron (see Michl, "Bemerkungen", p. 506, n. 2.).

[19] Knabenbauer, Durand, *ad loc.*; Seemann, "Aufgehellte Bibelworte", p. 231; Kurfess, "Zu Joh. 2:4"; Michl, "Bemerkungen zu Joh 2:4", pp. 505–9; Boismard, *Du Baptême à Cana*, pp. 156 f. and others.

[20] οὐ in questions is frequent in John, see 4:35; 6:70; 7:19, 25, 42; 8:48; 9:8; 10:34; 11:37, 40; 14:10; 18:26; 19:10. On οὔπω in questions cf. Mk 4:40; 8:17; Funk, *Greek Grammar*, para. 427, 2.

[21] Cf. Mk 4:40; 8:17. Michl's appeal to Mt 8:29 is irrelevant, since there it is a positive question ("Bemerkungen", p. 505).

impossible to doubt that this hour was of supreme theological importance for the evangelist and that it colours his language. But it is also plain enough that the Johannine Jesus recognizes that the whole of his earthly work is governed by the law established by his Father for its length and purpose. Along with the sayings about "completing his work(s)" (4:34; 5:36; 17:4) we should note in particular the metaphor of the twelve hours of the day in which the work is to be done (11:9; cf. 9:4). Could not Jesus also designate the beginning of this span of time allotted him by the Father for his work as "his hour", precisely in the qualitative sense of which we have spoken, namely that it can be dictated only by the Father? If so, Jesus's "hour" in the narrower sense would only be the concrete form of the law which is palpably at work throughout the whole of Jesus's work: the will of the Father determines the action of the Son (cf. 5:17, 19, 30; 10:18; 14:31)—because the will of the Father is particularly manifest with regard to the hour of Jesus's death (cf. 19:28, 30). Hence even when Jesus first speaks of it, this distant hour may be evoked, in the background; but first and foremost his "hour" here signifies the Father's sovereignty over Jesus, asserted precisely in view of Mary.

If one feels impelled by the theological usage of John[22] to interpret the "hour" of which Jesus speaks in 2:4 as referring directly to his exaltation and glorification, this will mean, more or less, that it is only the hour of his death which brings about the revelation of Jesus's glory, the fullness of his Messianic gifts. And the "sign" which Jesus nonetheless performs will be merely an indication of those higher gifts, perhaps of the Eucharist in particular, a "pre-figuration of the lavish bounty of the age of salvation after Jesus's death".[23] In this case, Mary could hardly have understood Jesus's answer (but cf. for a similar case 11:25f.), and one would have to deduce from her behaviour (v. 5) that she misunderstood him; but this is not the impression which the passage makes on the reader—in contrast to the other "misunderstandings" in John. The explanation is possibly correct, if one allows for the depths within John, where many words of Jesus only become intelligible later, ultimately only in the light of the Resurrection; but it cannot be said to be probable. It can hardly be right to reduce the present revelation of Jesus's glory to an anticipation of his future state. The eyes of faith see the δόξα of Jesus even in his earthly work; it is precisely the δόξα present in the incarnate Word which is spoken of in 1:14. It is not the primary or sole function of the "sign" to point on to the future. It rather discloses—though only to believers—the saving power present in the person of Jesus. The miracle of Cana, like

---

[22] See Thüsing, *Erhöhung*, pp. 92ff.; so too Barrett, *ad loc.*

[23] Van den Bussche, *Het wijnwonder*, p. 29.

the multiplication of the loaves, the curing of the man born blind and the raising of Lazarus, is undoubtedly meant to illustrate Jesus's character as the giver of God's eschatological gifts, here and now. As in the later signs, there is no need to mention Jesus's glorification as the presupposition for the full and effective bestowal of salvation, since it is the person of the Saviour as such which is the centre of interest. And in the miracle at Cana, everything in the story seems undoubtedly to be orientated to the present revelation of Jesus's glory.

Even less satisfactory is the interpretation of the "hour" as the death of Jesus, when propounded from a special Mariological viewpoint. It has been suggested that Jesus here promises his mother, after his death, what he now refuses—to respond to her petitions. Jn 19:26 is also invoked as proof. The meaning of Jesus's answer to Mary in 2:4 is then said to be: "Once this hour has dawned, Jesus will no longer answer his mother, 'What have I to do with you?' For then the relationship between Jesus and Mary, with all that it implies, will be fully restored, after being interrupted for a while."[24] But this reads too much into the answer. The "not yet" cannot have this meaning, any more than we are entitled to conclude from the answer of the risen Lord to Mary Magdalene (20:17) that she is to enter into a closer relationship to him later on. The time is mentioned to explain the aloofness as such, not to promise anything for the future. We must reserve discussion of the relationship between this first scene with Mary and the second, under the Cross, for the commentary on 19:26f. The evangelist, in depicting a scene involving Mary at the beginning and the end of his Gospel, was guided rather by his interest in her history than in theological propositions concerning her.

2:5	λέγει ἡ μήτηρ αὐτοῦ τοῖς διακόνοις, Ὅ τι ἂν λέγῃ ὑμῖν ποιήσατε.	His mother said to the servants, "Do whatever he tells you."

Mary has sensed that Jesus will act, even though his answer remains mysterious to her. Unassumingly she does her best to facilitate her Son—a delicate touch, which is in keeping with the biblical picture of Mary: faith from which the mysteries of the divine plans are ultimately concealed (cf. Lk 1:38, 45), readiness to help and serve (cf. Lk 1:39, 56), steadfast loyalty to her Son even when he has gone far from her. Her summons to the servants does not anticipate Jesus's action, since the conditional and generalized relative clause does not oblige Jesus to speak and does not determine what he may say.

We should reject as ill-advised the interpretation which says that Mary felt herself rejected by Jesus but turned to God himself and so gained her request. Nothing of the sort can be found in the text, and the whole Gospel represents the Father's dispositions as unalterable. On Jesus's "prayer of petition" cf. 11:41f.

---

[24] Gaechter, *Maria im Erdenleben*, p. 188.

2:6	ἦσαν δὲ ἐκεῖ λίθιναι ὑδρίαι ἓξ κατὰ τὸν καθαρισμὸν τῶν Ἰουδαίων κείμεναι, χωροῦσαι ἀνὰ μετρητὰς δύο ἢ τρεῖς.	Now there were six stone water-jars there, for the purifications in use among the Jews, each holding some twenty or thirty gallons.

The miracle is now prepared for. The narrator mentions the great stone water-jugs, each of which contained from two to three "metretes" ("measures"—1 "measure"=39.39 litres, about 9 gallons). There is archaelogical proof of the existence of such vessels, which were mostly embedded in the ground.[25] They were mostly of earthenware, but those made of stone were prized, since stone did not contract levitical impurity.[26] It would be idle to look for a symbolic value in the number six (six days of the week of creation, followed by the Sabbath age of the world or the like). The vessels holding so much water were used for the "purifications of the Jews" (cf. Mk 7:3f.), a remark which has suggested to many exegetes that there is an allusion to an outmoded Judaism with its ritual precepts. There is some justification in the Gospel for this further explanation, since the question of καθαρισμός comes up again in 3:25, and the reader has been prepared by 1:17 for the coming of the "grace and truth" of Jesus Christ which is to surpass the time of the law of Moses. But we shall examine the question more closely when we are discussing the deeper sense of the narrative (see below).

2:7	λέγει αὐτοῖς ὁ Ἰησοῦς, Γεμίσατε τὰς ὑδρίας ὕδατος. καὶ ἐγέμισαν αὐτὰς ἕως ἄνω.	Jesus said to them, "Fill the jars with water." And they filled them to the brim.

Jesus now intervenes, without further introduction; we are not told how much time has passed in the meantime. What is, on the other hand, important to the evangelist is the fact that the servants filled the great jars to the brim. This shows the greatness of the miracle, the lavishness of Jesus's gift. The servants, who are ready to obey since Mary spoke, follow Jesus's directions without more ado.

2:8	καὶ λέγει αὐτοῖς, Ἀντλήσατε νῦν καὶ φέρετε τῷ ἀρχιτρικλίνῳ· οἱ δὲ ἤνεγκαν.	And he said to them, "Now draw some off and bring it to the head-waiter." They did so,

[25] Galling, *Biblisches Reallexikon*, pp. 321f.: storage jars for oil, wine and corn, 60–120 cm. high, with a capacity of 20–50 litres. On the system of measures (1 Attic metretes = Hebrew bath) cf. Barrois, "La métrologie dans la Bible" esp. pp. 200f., 205, 212; id., *Manuel d'archéologie biblique*, vol. II, pp. 247–52; Scott, "Weights and Measures of the Bible", esp. pp. 30ff. [26] Cf. Lev 11:33; Billerbeck, vol. II, pp. 406f.

The fresh start and the νῦν mark the time it has taken to fill the jars. Even Jesus's new orders, to draw off some of the water and bring it to the head-waiter, that is, the organizer responsible for the banquet,[27] are carried out by the servants without question. Thus the timely warning uttered by the mother of Jesus was not superfluous; it helped the narrator to blunt the edge of many difficulties.

2:9	ὡς δὲ ἐγεύσατο ὁ ἀρχιτρίκλινος τὸ ὕδωρ οἶνον γεγενημένον, καὶ οὐκ ᾔδει πόθεν ἐστίν, οἱ δὲ διάκονοι ᾔδεισαν οἱ ἠντληκότες τὸ ὕδωρ, φωνεῖ τὸν νυμφίον ὁ ἀρχιτρίκλινος	but when the head-waiter had tasted the water, now turned into wine, not knowing where it came from—though the servants who had drawn the water knew—the head-waiter called out to the bridegroom

The miracle itself is not described, but merely verified—very vividly—by the conduct of the master of ceremonies. In the same way, the miracle of the loaves is established by the collection of the pieces left over (6:12f.). The narrator hurries on to the final scene between the head-waiter and the bridegroom; all the rest, in the line of explanation, is incorporated into a subordinate clause, to the effect that the head-waiter had tasted the water now turned into wine, that he did not know where the precious wine came from, but that the servants knew. The words from καὶ οὐκ to τὸ ὕδωρ should be taken as a parenthesis. The servants are mentioned because they can testify to the miracle (the interrogation of the man born blind in ch. 9 displays a similar interest). The πόθεν has a deeper meaning; the question of "where" Jesus's gifts come from (4:11) and "where" he himself comes from (7:27f.; 8:14; 9:29f.; 19:9) is raised again and again throughout the Gospel. The mention of the source also serves as an indication of the (heavenly and divine) nature of the gift, or of the reality to which it alludes symbolically; and the gift raises the question (as in 4:11f.) of the giver and his significance.

2:10	καὶ λέγει αὐτῷ, Πᾶς ἄνθρωπος πρῶτον τὸν καλὸν οἶνον τίθησιν, καὶ ὅταν μεθυσθῶσιν τὸν ἐλάσσω· σὺ τετήρηκας τὸν καλὸν οἶνον ἕως ἄρτι.	and said to him, "Everyone sets out the good wine first, and the poorer sort only when people are drunk. You have kept the good wine till now."

[27] This is not the "master of the revels" (chosen from among the guests) but the supervisor of the servants. Rabbinical writings supply hardly any relevant parallels (Billerbeck, vol. II, pp. 407ff.). Bauer, *ad loc.*, cites Heliodorus, *Aeth.*, VII, 27: ἀρχιτρίκλινοι καὶ οἰνοχόοι.

The remark of the connoisseur about the wine is probably meant humorously, as it is impossible to prove that a serious "rule" of the sort existed for serving wine.[28] But the final phrase must be accorded a deeper sense: the "good" wine, which has been kept "till now" is the wine which Jesus has given. The narrative is of masterly brevity and nonetheless vivid. It falls into three scenes, Mary and Jesus, Jesus and the servants, the head-waiter and the bridegroom. Everything unimportant and distracting has been pruned away. Mary's watchful care links the first and second scenes; the execution of Jesus's orders by the servants links the second and third. The story breaks off deliberately with the head-waiter's remark, to allow it to echo in the mind of the hearer and to draw attention to its deeper meaning.

2:11	Ταύτην ἐποίησεν ἀρχὴν τῶν σημείων ὁ Ἰησοῦς ἐν Κανὰ τῆς Γαλιλαίας καὶ ἐφανέρωσεν τὴν δόξαν αὐτοῦ, καὶ ἐπίστευσαν εἰς αὐτὸν οἱ μαθηταὶ αὐτοῦ.	Thus Jesus began his signs, in Cana of Galilee, and manifested his glory, and his disciples believed in him.

The final remark, which shows the hand of the evangelist at least in the last two clauses, throws still more light on the story. The three statements are closely linked: what happened in Cana is a sign, which reveals the glory of Jesus and leads those whose faith is ready (the disciples) to a deeper understanding of the person of Jesus. An important point is that this revelation of the glory of Jesus is not a timeless "epiphany" but has a fixed place at the "beginning" of a whole series of "signs" which Jesus performs in historical succession. This "epiphany" does not leave the ground of history, but remains attached to a given occasion (the marriage feast) and locality (Cana in Galilee). It also has its importance for the historical path of Jesus, since it ratifies, reinforces and deepens the faith of the disciples, and hence binds the faithful to him, in contrast to the counter-movement of hostile scepticism which is soon to set in (cf. 2:18 ff.). The exigent character of the self-revelation of Jesus, which challenges men to decision, is already visible in this first "sign".

The concept of "sign", which is applied to the great miracles of Jesus in John, has a deep theological significance for the evangelist, which we shall try to assess in excursus iv. The "sign" reveals the "glory" of Jesus, but only to those who look at it with believing eyes. As a means of Jesus's

---

[28] Windisch, "Die johanneische Weinregel, Joh. 2:10", tries to prove its existence, appealing particularly to an (inauthentic) fragment of Theopompus (pp. 253ff.). But this only rebukes the *bad* habit of the Spartans of first giving their guests good wine and inferior wine later.

self-revelation, it has the same force as his words, and as appears from the great miracles to come later (the multiplication of the loaves, the healing of the man born blind and the raising of Lazarus), Jesus's words of revelation do no more than disclose the real meaning of the sign more fully. The first "sign" is not followed by such a discourse; its Messianic and Christological meaning is to be gathered from the presentation itself, especially from the points stressed in v. 10 (the "good wine" which has been kept "till now"). Further light is thrown on the meaning by the final remark of the evangelist, that Jesus "revealed his glory" by the sign, and that his disciples "believed in him". The revelation given in the signs is ordained to faith, to which they are meant to lead by their grandeur and number. They failed of their effect with the great mass of the people (cf. 12:37), but their goal remains unchanged, and it is for this reason that the evangelist records them in his Gospel for later believers (cf. 20:30f.). Thus the three clauses of 2:11 are a programmatic statement of what the "signs" essentially are and should be: the unveiling of the "glory" of the Word made flesh (cf. 1:14), of the Son of Man who dwells on earth and remains linked with the heaven; it is a glory which can be grasped in faith and can thus lead to full faith "in Jesus", the Messiah and Son of God (20:31).

By noting that the miracle at Cana is the "first sign", the evangelist calls attention to the beginning of Jesus's self-revelation before the world, which is to be fully public (cf. 7:4). The Messiah introduced by the Baptist and presented to the people of Israel (cf. 1:31) begins the work given him by his Father (cf. 4:34; 5:19f., etc), and even the beginning of this work is determined only by the Father's call, which is the law of his "hour" (cf. on 2:4). The next miracle wrought in Cana, the healing of the son of the official in Capernaum from afar, is described expressly by the evangelist as the second (4:46–54) in spite of the "signs" done in the meantime in Jerusalem (2:23; cf. 3:2; 4:45). This may be due to the fact that he follows a σημεῖα-source (cf. Introduction, ch. iv, 3). If so, he has exploited the source in his own way, selectively (which explains why he does not continue the numeration) with emphasis on certain signs (contrast 6:2), and with a new and deeper insight. In his understanding of the "signs" he has also gone beyond that of his source (cf. excursus iv).

The *doxa* revealed by Jesus through the change of water into a munificent gift of wine, is primarily his divine and creative power, the δύναμις which is proper to him as God. The latter term, which plays such an important part in the Christology of Paul, does not occur in the Johannine Epistles and Gospel, though one would have expected it to be used to describe Jesus's work. This probably means that the notion of δύναμις is included or absorbed in that of δόξα, since Jesus's power (δύνασθαι) of performing "signs" is affirmed several times (3:2; 9:16; 10:21; 11:37;

cf. 5:19). But his power is so much part of his nature that the evangelist finds it more correct to adopt a term which expresses both the nature of God as it manifests itself and his mighty action, "radiant brightness" and "powerful activity", notions already combined in the O.T. כָּבוֹד which underlies the terminology.[29] And the fact that δόξα is combined with verbs of seeing[30] does not allow us to conclude at once that it always means the divine radiance, the heavenly "brightness", penetrating as it were the veil of the flesh. Nonetheless, the choice of "to see" to express the experience of faith is not without significance. There is no transfiguration, no temporary elevation of Jesus to a heavenly mode of being in John; even the walking on the waters (6:16–21) contains no such trait. This is no accident. John takes the Incarnation so seriously that the veil of the σάρξ is never removed, and the divine glory of Jesus is never displayed except to the eyes of faith (cf. 14:8–11). The direct view of Jesus's divine glory, that is, of his heavenly brightness, is reserved for the future, to the time when the believer himself is there where Jesus has preceded him (17:24). The glory which Jesus possesses and manifests on earth must be taken as the effect of his divine and heavenly glory, which he had before the creation of the world (17:5), since it is the glory of the only-begotten Son of God (1:14), though under the restrictions of fleshly existence and not yet in the freedom of the heavenly sphere (cf. 17:24). Hence the question as to whether δόξα in 2:11 means miraculous power *or* radiant brightness is wrongly put.[31] The term implies both elements and the glory is manifested in a different way in Christ's pre-existence, in his incarnation and in his glorification. Hence it would be wrong to restrict the revelation of the δόξα of Jesus at Cana to his divine and miraculous power. In the divinely-wrought event the believer experiences something of the divine being of Jesus, contemplates the majesty of the Son of God and also senses the brightness of the heavenly world which he cannot yet see with his bodily eyes. The φανεροῦν[32] is more than an

---

[29] Cf. Exod 16:6–10; Num 14:21f.; Ps 66:2f. etc. This may be connected with the fact that in the most ancient times the glory of God was experienced in the thunderstorm. See further Stein, *Der Begriff Kebod Jahwe und seine Bedeutung für die alttestamentliche Gotteserkenntnis*; von Rad, "Kabhod im Alten Testament", pp. 242f.; Eichrodt, *Theologie des Alten Testaments*, vol. II, pp. 11–15.

[30] Jn 1:14; 11:40; 12:41; 17:24; cf. 1:50.

[31] The notion of "the divine power of Jesus becoming visible" is brought out in particular by H. Kittel, *Die Herrlichkeit Gottes*, p. 241; see also Bauer, *ad loc.*, Bultmann, *Johannes*, p. 44, 1. Others recur with more emphasis to the brightness of God's glory, cf. Schneider, *Doxa*; G. Kittel, "Der Neutestamentliche Gebrauch von δόξα", pp. 251–2.

[32] Φανεροῦν is also used of the apparitions of the risen Lord, Jn 21:1, 14, of eschatological manifestation, 1 Jn 2:28; 3:2, but also of the incarnation, 1 Jn 1:2; 3:5, 8; 4:9). The expression in 2:4 can be understood either in the perspective of the incarnation or in that of (realized) eschatology.

external demonstration, such as the unbelieving brothers of Jesus ask for in 7:4; it is a manifestation (an "epiphany", when rightly understood) visible to the spiritually open eyes of the believer. It may, of course, be asked whether the disciples of Jesus have already attained the full insight of faith at the miracle of Cana, since they are still beset by misunderstandings in the supper room (cf. 14:5, 8; 16:12, 17f., 25, 29 ff.). But what the evangelist means is that their faith had received an essential impulse from the sign at Cana: their faith has grown stronger within them and richer in content. This is clear from the Christological formula "they believed in him".[33] This faith of the disciples which contains in principle (or at least potentially) the full Christological faith is also to be a headline to the readers of the Gospel.

The deeper meaning

What are the thoughts behind the narrative of the evangelist? The most important for the evangelist is the revelation of Jesus's glory (v. 11) and any interpretation which departs from this Christological perspective loses sight of the central issue. Revelation in John is the self-revelation of Jesus; all the rest stems from this. The question as to whether he is the hoped-for Messiah is a lively one (1:41, 45; 7:26f., 31, 41f.; 10:24f.; 11:27; 12:34). But he reveals himself as the Messiah in a special and unique sense, as the Son of Man come down from heaven, as the Son of God sent by the Father and united to him, bringing revelation and light. So too his gifts may not be separated from his person and made into independent symbols. At the marriage, it is not the wine in itself, or the wine in contrast to the water, which constitute the pregnant "signs"; the significance of the wine is that it is Jesus's gift, a sign which comes from him and points to him. This is indicated by the brief remark, apparently incidental, to the effect that the master of ceremonies did not know πόθεν ἐστίν (v. 9), which, as we have seen, recurs constantly in the Gospel and actually intones a central theme of Johannine theology: Jesus, who on the face of things comes from Galilee (1:45f.; 7:41f., 52) and has human parents (6:42), is in fact of a higher origin (7:28). He has come down "from above", (3:13, 31; 8:23), he has gone forth from his heavenly Father (8:42b; 16:27f.; 17:8; cf. 13:3), and his doctrine (3:32; 7:16; 8:26, 28; 12:44 ff.) and gifts (6:32, 57; 7:37f.) come from him who sent him. Hence men estranged from God do not "know" him (cf. 7:28f.; 8:19, 28) and his words are unintelligible to them (6:60; 8:43, 46f.). At the miracle of Cana, as at the other "signs" and "works", it is his origin

[33] πιστεύειν εἰς 36 times in John. See on 1:7, also Schnackenburg, *Der Glaube im vierten Evangelium*, pp. 6–11; Bultmann, "πιστεύω", pp. 211ff., 224f.

from God and his union with the Father that must be believed and recognized (cf. 5:17, 19; 9:31 ff.; 10:38; 11:40 ff.; 14:11 f.). The logion of 1:51 is already sufficient indication of the fact that in the miracle of the wine Jesus wishes to manifest himself as the Son of Man come down from heaven who remains in constant union with God.

As a gift of Jesus, however, the wine also is significant; it is given at the end, and it is so precious and copious that it is the eschatological gift of the Messiah. In the O.T. (Amos 9:13; Hos 2:24; Joel 4:18; Is 29:17; Jer 31:5) and in late Judaism (*Enoch*, 10:19; *Apoc Bar Syr*, 29:5; *Or Sib*, II, 317 f.; III, 620–4; 744 f.[34]) wine in abundance (along with oil or milk) is a sign of the age of salvation; in the ancient blessing of Jacob it is a characteristic of the Messiah from Judah (Gen 49:11 f.). The Synoptics retain the metaphor of the new wine which is not to go into old vessels (Mk 2:22 parr.), and the early Church certainly associated this with the thought of the new thing which came with Jesus's person and work. But John's understanding of it is even more strongly Christological, as appears from the way he explains the logion on the temple as referring to the body of Jesus (2:20 f.; cf. also 7:38). It may also be asked whether the evangelist is thinking in particular of the eucharistic wine, which would make Cana a parallel to the miracle of the loaves in ch. 6.[35] But the material on which the miracle is worked is water, and it is far-fetched to see in it an allusion to a sacramental usage in which water was taken instead of wine in the holy Eucharist.[36] Wine does not occur in John as symbol of the blood of Jesus, not even in 15:1–6; one could just as well think of baptism on account of the water (in opposition to Jewish baptisms or the baptism of the disciples of John). The sacramental interpretation restricts the scope unduly, even though the sacraments, as life-giving signs, are not to be excluded from the gifts of Jesus.[37] One would remain more definitely within the bounds of Christological interpretation if the wine were referred to the new doctrine which Christ brings as Wisdom in person, for which approach texts can be adduced

---

[34] See Zapletal, *Der Wein in der Bibel*; Busse, *Der Wein im Kult des Alten Testaments;* Volz, *Eschatologie*, pp. 387 ff.; Jeremias, *Jesus als Weltvollender*, pp. 27–31; Seesemann, "οἶνος", pp. 164 f.

[35] So already Fathers like Irenaeus, *Adv. haer.*, III, 17, 7 (Harvey, vol. II, p. 88); Cyprian *Ep.*, 63, 12 (Hartel, vol. II, pp. 710 f.); Cyril of Jerusalem, *Cat. myst.*, IV, 2 (Quasten, pp. 93 f.). More recently Craig, "Sacramental Interest in the Fourth Gospel"; Cullmann, *Urchristentum und Gottesdienst*, pp. 69 ff., E. T.: *Early Christian Worship*, pp. 68 ff. (main protagonist); Bouyer, *ad loc.*; Niewalda, *Sakramentssymbolik im Johannesevangelium*, p. 166.

[36] See Eisler, "Das Rätsel des Johannesevangeliums", pp. 487 f.; also Omodeo, *Saggio di Commentario al IV Evangelio, 1:1–3:21*, p. 58 (according to Bultmann, *Johannes*, p. 84, n. 1).

[37] Cf. Schnackenburg, *Die Sakramente im Johannesevangelium*, pp. 235–54, esp. pp. 251 ff.

from the Wisdom literature, from Philo (who calls the Logos "cupbearer" and "master of the revels"[38]), and from some Fathers of the Church.[39] But this is hard to reconcile with the fact that Jesus does not speak as revealer or teacher of Wisdom at Cana, and does not initiate his disciples into his doctrine, like O.T. Wisdom. One would be well-advised, therefore, not to look for any special symbolic meaning, and to see under the many images of water (cf. 4:10, 14; 7:37f.; 6:35b), bread, wine, of Christ as shepherd, vine etc., the comprehensive gift of divine life or the Holy Spirit, as promised constantly by the Johannine Jesus (3:16, 18, 36; 5:24; 6:40 etc.). Eschatological salvation is always present in Christ, whatever the form under which it is bestowed.

If this is the positive theological meaning of the miracle at Cana, if, therefore the main interest of the evangelist is concentrated on the Messianic and Christological self-revelation of Jesus, the polemical note grows fainter, but it need not disappear entirely. The text lends most support (cf. commentary on v. 6) to the frequently expressed view that the story represents Jesus's break with Judaism and the superiority of the New Testament to the Old. The precious wine of the Gospel is contrasted with the water of Jewish rites of purification, the order of grace with that of the law (cf. 1:17).[40] Commentators appeal to the intrinsic connection with the purging of the temple which follows (2:13–22) and even with the dialogue with Nicodemus (ch. 3), all of which constitute a clash with Judaism. But there are also some objections to be mentioned to this view (which should never obscure the positive Christological purpose). It is not certain that the evangelist is really so hostile to Jewish purifications (and not merely indifferent), since he also mentions ritual customs without disparagement (cf. 7:22; 11:55; 18:28; 19:40). The encounter with the "Jews" gives rise above all to the question of faith, as is particularly clear in the Nicodemus episode, where the representative of legalistic Judaism is displayed in no unsympathetic light. The cultic antithesis at the purging of the temple is overshadowed by the positive Christological interest, as also in 4:22f. Polemic against the disciples of the Baptist can only be seen in the passage (cf. 3:25), if

---

[38] *De somn.*, II, 249, cf. 183; also *Immut.*, 158; *Leg. alleg.*, vol. III, p. 82. Dodd, *Interpretation*, pp. 298f., lays stress on this.

[39] Origen, *Comm. in Jo.*, XIII, 62 (Preuschen, pp. 294f.); fragment 74 (*ibid.*, pp. 541f.); *In Cant. Cant.*, I (Baehrens, p. 95). Other Fathers in Boismard, *Du baptême à Cana*, p. 140, n. 6, who accepts this interpretation (pp. 139–42).

[40] See already the Monarchianist prologue to John: "debeat ac veteribus immutatis nova omnia, quae a Christo instituuntur, appareant" (Corssen, p. 13, lines 23f.). Also Ephraim, *Comm.* V, 7 (Leloir, *CSCO* 145, p. 46): "Christ changed by his doctrine all that the law and the prophets brought". Among the moderns, Schmidt, "Hochzeitswunder"; Bauer, Barrett, Lightfoot and others, *ad loc.*

it is assumed that such polemic is a dominant and pervasive trait of John. But it seems as though the evangelist only made polemical points now and then, as occasion offered.

We need not consider the elaborate allegorizations which are to be found in some of the Church Fathers.[41] Such interpretation runs the risk of obscuring the essential. But the explanation derived from the history of religions, which is still favoured in some quarters, calls for attention. Here it is taken for granted that an "element of the Dionysus legend" has been taken over in the story of Cana.[42] Stories of miraculous wine, like that of Cana, were narrated apropos of feasts of Dionysus.

A custom at Elis is of particular interest.[43] "It was the custom in Elis on the eve of the feast to put three empty jugs in the shrine of Dionysus, in the presence of some men of standing. The doors were then shut, and the next morning the jugs were found to be full of wine. We may suspect that we have here the origin of the miracle of Cana. The epiphany of the god Dionysus and its miracle were given their counterpart in the epiphany of the new god . . ." The writer, W. Bousset, points out that the date of the beginning of this festival of Dionysus was 5 January (to be more exact, probably the night of 5 to 6 January), the date, that is, of the ancient Christian feast of the Epiphany.[44]

The main point to be noticed here is the totally different character of the Epiphany in the Johannine narrative, which is concerned not with the godhead's coming to give assistance or to manifest himself in the cult, but with the revelation of the divine δόξα of Jesus, with its unquestionably O.T. traits, to the eyes of faith. Later, the miracle of Cana was associated with the feast of the Epiphany;[45] but this is irrelevant, since the association is secondary, based on the existing Johannine narrative. There is no other sign of any influence of the cult of Dionysus on the Gospel of John. The abundance of wine provided by Jesus is an element of the Jewish expectations, so that a borrowing from pagan Hellenism is also unnecessary from this point of view. — *See excursus iv.*

---

[41] But it must be remembered that the allegorization of the Fathers had a religious purpose and was rather application than exegesis.

[42] See Grill, *Untersuchungen*, vol. II, pp. 107–120; Carpenter, *The Johannine Writings*, pp. 379f.; Bousset, *Kyrios Christos*, pp. 62, 270–4; Bauer, p. 47; Bultmann, p. 83 with n. 3. For a criticism see Hoskyns, pp. 190ff.

[43] *Athenaeus*, I, 61, quoted in Bauer, p. 47.

[44] Bousset, *Kyrios Christos*, p. 62 with n. 1.

[45] The feast of the Epiphany probably began in Egypt, to replace the feast of the birth of the god Aeon from the virgin Kore; the custom of drawing water from the Nile, which the Egyptians believed would be turned into wine, could have linked the theme of Cana to the Epiphany. Cf. Holl, "Der Ursprung des Epiphaniefestes". But many of the circumstances of the origin of the feast remain obscure or uncertain, cf. Fendt, "Der heutige Stand der Forschung über das Geburtsfest Jesu am 25. Dezember und über Epiphanias"; Nagel, "Epiphaniasfest"; Frank, "Epiphania".

CHAPTER IV

The Beginnings in Jerusalem: Cleansing of the Temple Many Signs, Dialogue with Nicodemus (2:12–3:12)

In the course of his outline of the "history of Jesus" the evangelist brings his reader to Jerusalem. He had rounded off, so to speak, the call of the disciples and the first revelation of Jesus before them with 2:11, and now with 2:12, he leads up to the first appearance of Jesus in Jerusalem. The "historical" narrative would offer no difficulty, if it did not present here the cleansing of the temple, which according to the Synoptics only took place after Jesus's final entry into Jerusalem. But the Johannine presentation itself, in 2:12–3:12 (for the demarcation of the dialogue with Nicodemus, see commentary on ch. 3), provides indications that the evangelist is strongly influenced here by theological and narrative interests. The faith of the disciples (2:11; cf. 2:22) contrasts sharply with the sceptical and unbelieving attitude of the (leading) "Jews" (2:18). The scene of the first revelation of Jesus's glory in Galilee changes to the place where danger threatens (cf. 2:17), which is Jerusalem, and in fact the temple—an unmistakable signal of how the great drama will proceed. But even in Jerusalem there are still shades of difference with regard to belief and unbelief: there are the aggressively hostile "Jews" from the ruling classes; there are the crowds, eager for marvels but lacking in real faith (πολλοί, 2:23); and there is the councillor Nicodemus, a Pharisee schooled in the Scriptures, inclined to believe but inhibited by theological difficulties and failing to attain to true faith (3:1–12)—a summary picture which is fully confirmed in ch. 7 in particular. Possibly Jesus's own attitude begins to show a change. While he displays no notable reserve in Galilee, in Jerusalem he does not trust himself to the crowds (2:24f.) and expresses doubts about Nicodemus and his fellows ever coming to the faith (3:12).

When one realizes that certain interests have moulded the narrative, one will not attach too great importance to certain details which could raise awkward questions, especially the succinct and almost incidental remark that Jesus performed "signs" in Jerusalem. It is merely an occasion for characterizing the (inadequate) faith of the crowds (2:23) and for explaining Nicodemus's visit to Jesus by night (3:2). The interest which the evangelist takes in re-moulding his material may make us suspect that the cleansing of the temple is not in its historical place, but this does not force us to assume that the Johannine narrative of the first days of Jesus's public appearance in Jerusalem is wholly unhistorical and valueless. The meeting of Jesus with Nicodemus forms a special tradition, which is supported by further information about Nicodemus (7:50; 19:39). And there is no need to cast doubts on the "signs" (perhaps healings) done by Jesus during this visit to Jerusalem which is not recounted by the Synoptics. The evangelist is interested in showing the state of faith in the centre of Judaism during Jesus's first stay in the holy city and at his first appearance in public, in order to prepare the reader for the outcome.

These observations should also make us cautious about undertaking manipulations in the name of literary criticism. The presentation as it stands gives so good a picture from the point of view of "theological history-writing" that the sequence may well be attributed to the evangelist's plan and need not be reserved for the work of the final redaction. There are no unquestionable indications that the cleansing of the temple was only moved to its present position at a late stage of the literary production. It will not do to appeal to the "paschal framework"[1] nor to the supposedly secondary, "redactional" character of vv. 23–25, since stylistic criteria do not prove the point (see *ad loc.*). The section 3:13–21 (cf. 3:31–36) is in a different situation. Other considerations provide some grounds for separating it from the actual dialogue with Nicodemus, though it cannot be ascribed to another hand than that of the evangelist (see commentary on ch. 3).

2:12 μετὰ τοῦτο κατέβη εἰς Καφαρναοὺμ αὐτὸς καὶ ἡ μήτηρ αὐτοῦ καὶ οἱ ἀδελφοὶ καὶ οἱ μαθηταὶ αὐτοῦ, καὶ ἐκεῖ ἔμειναν οὐ πολλὰς ἡμέρας.

After that, he went down to Capernaum, he and his mother, his brothers and his disciples, and they stayed there, though not for long.

The statement about the short stay in Capernaum links the marriage feast of Cana with the cleansing of the temple. If the evangelist drew on a σημεῖα-source, he might have found v. 12 there, as the introduction to the second "sign" (in Capernaum, cf. 4:46b). If so, he has added οὐ πολλὰς

---

[1] Against the hypothesis of Wilkens, *Entstehungsgeschichte*, see my review in *Biblische Zeitschrift* 4 (1960), pp. 300ff.

ἡμέρας for his own purposes.[2] He regards the stay as merely temporary, and says nothing of Jesus's settling in Capernaum. According to the Synoptics, Jesus chose this place as his residence and the centre of his activity (Mt 4:13; cf. 9:1; 17:24–27; Mk 1:29–38; 3:20; 9:33). The mention of Jesus's mother is due to the Cana episode; but the brothers of Jesus are introduced for the first time (unless they were mentioned originally in v. 2, see *ad loc.*). They re-appear on the scene in 7:1–10, with no faith in Jesus. Nothing is said of any impression made on them by the miracle of Cana; they merely serve the description of Jesus's entourage.[3] As the phrase "though not for long" indicates, Jesus is eager to start his mighty work in Jerusalem also.[4] When in the fourth Gospel Jesus stays at a given place, or leaves it and avoids it, this is always something more than a merely historical record. It indicates a deliberate purpose on the part of Jesus, which is dictated by the will of the Father.[5] Hence 2:12 is also more than a stage in an itinerary, in the eyes of the evangelist. Jesus is not tied to home or family or friends, but presses on to the self-revelation which is to be made in the city of God.

The cleansing of the temple (2:13–22)

This story, like that of Cana, has some puzzling features. The presentation is similar, though covering very different ground. The narrative is remarkably succint, though containing several concrete details. Both stories break off rather suddenly, the former with the innocent but evocative words of the head-waiter, the latter with the unintelligent but thought-provoking question of the Jews, to which, however, the evangelist appends a commentary. Both stories aim at throwing light on the self-revelation of Jesus, the former in Galilee, the latter in Jerusalem, but mark a strong contrast: in Cana it is a joyous festival, in Jerusalem a serious conflict, full of menace. Among his countrymen, there is no danger; the incident in the holy city culminates in an interrogation which sounds

---

[2] See Schnackenburg, "Zur Traditionsgeschichte von Joh 4:46–54", pp. 63f.

[3] The words καὶ οἱ μαθηταὶ αὐτοῦ *om.* ℵ W 245 al. a b e ff[2] 1 arm, probably because the mention of Jesus's disciples appeared unwarranted. For ἔμειναν P^{66c} A Λ F G X^{b} 565 1241 λ al. b sy^{pal} bo arm read ἔμεινεν. Since the evangelist speaks only of Jesus' movements just before (κατέβη) and after (v. 13 ἀνέβη), this is probably a deliberate correction.

[4] The evangelist hardly means that the little convoy, which wished to avoid the short route through Samaria (why?), gathered in Capernaum (Lagrange). V. 13 makes a new start with the narrative, and no further mention is made of people travelling with Jesus. In view of the theological presentation of the evangelist, historical links should not be multiplied without necessity.

[5] Cf. 4:1–3, 4, 40, 43f.; 7:1, 10; 8:20; 10:23, 40ff.; 11:6–10, 54, 57; 12:1.

a note of warning. Along with the believing disciples, the "Jews" now appear on the scene and will prove to be relentless and unbelieving opponents of Jesus. The theme of the "signs" is also continued. The lordly action of Jesus in the court of the temple is not given this name, which is reserved for miraculous works; but the interrogators demand a "sign", and Jesus announces enigmatically a sign of a quite different type—and here too the gulf of misunderstanding and unbelief is seen to open up between Jesus and the "Jews" (cf. 6:30, 36). In the end, only the disciples show faith. But again, as at Cana, all this is rather hinted at than described. It is only the programme of the dramatic development which is to unfold later—a beginning only, but one which already prefigures the end.

In view of the synoptic narratives of the cleansing of the temple (Mk 11:15–19; Mt 21:10–17; Lk 19:45–48) certain questions arise with regard to the history of tradition and to the theological content. First there is the historical problem already mentioned, as to when the cleansing took place. It can, of course, have happened only once. The story in the form in which it is given by the evangelist is secondary, as often been established, sometimes by means of over-sharp criticism.[6] As in the rest of the chronology of the Passion, this need not prove lack of historical knowledge, but simply that the story has been re-told repeatedly, with a constant insistence on certain points.[7] The historical problem is linked, as we have noted, to the theological, that is, to the intentions of the evangelist in the narrative. Hence the question of why he placed the cleansing of the temple at the beginning of Jesus's work in Jerusalem is not unimportant, even for the deeper meaning of the scene. However, we shall take up these questions later, after a running commentary on the text.

The construction of the narrative is strikingly in the nature of a diptych: a) the action of Jesus, vv. 14–15; the words of Jesus, v. 16; the "remembering" on the part of the disciples, vv. 21–22; b) the action (or reaction) of the "Jews", v. 18; the enigmatic words of Jesus, v. 19; the misunderstanding on the part of the "Jews", v. 20; the commentary of the evangelist and the "remembering" on the part of the disciples, vv. 21–22. It does not necessarily follow that the evangelist has combined two originally independent episodes, though the possibility cannot be excluded.[8] The cleansing of the temple and the "saying on the temple",

---

[6] Hypercritical theories in Mendner, "Die Tempelreinigung"; but a secondary re-working is also admitted by Sigge, *Johannesevangelium*, pp. 143ff.; see further Haenchen, "Johanneische Probleme".

[7] See Haenchen, "Johanneische Probleme", on the cleansing of the temple, pp. 34–46, here esp. pp. 43f.

[8] See Bultmann, p. 86: "It is easy to understand that this saying (on the destruction and re-building of the temple) and the story of the cleansing of the temple should have gravitated together and been combined into an uneasy unity."

the action of Jesus and the reaction of the "Jews" form an admirable unity. Even when one considers the synoptic version, especially that of Mark, it seems that Jesus's action in the temple and the "question of authority", as it is termed in the Synoptics, form a historical unity. (Matthew and Luke present matters differently). The whole passage, that is, the two elements which have been combined, shows that the evangelist is well acquainted with Jewish views and historical facts, such as the building of the temple. But everything is made to serve his theological perspective.[9]

2:13	Καὶ ἐγγὺς ἦν τὸ πάσχα τῶν Ἰουδαίων, καὶ ἀνέβη εἰς Ἱεροσόλυμα ὁ Ἰησοῦς.	The Jewish Passover was not far away, and Jesus went up to Jerusalem.

Here we have the first item in the Johannine "Calendar of Feasts", which contains three Passovers: the "pre-synoptic Passover", 2:13, 23; the Passover of the multiplication of the loaves, 6:4; the Passover of the crucifixion, 11:55; 12:1. The unnamed feast of 5:1 should not be regarded as another Passover (see *ad loc.*). The resulting duration for the public ministry of Jesus, two years and some months, is perfectly credible.[10] The expression "the Passover of the Jews" proves only that the evangelist did not (or had ceased to) share in the Jewish Passover. The stereotyped phrase, "and (but) the Passover of the Jews was near" (2:13; 6:4; 11:55) is hardly a "formula indicating the paschal structure" of the Gospel,[11] since the evangelist also says, apropos of the feast of Tabernacles, that it "was near" (7:2). Jesus goes up to Jerusalem[12] with the other pilgrims for the great feast. His action in the court of the temple probably preceded the feast since the last days before the calm of the feast saw the vendors and money-changers doing brisk business in the courtyards (see also the synoptic chronology).

---

[9] Special literature on the cleansing of the temple according to John: Braun, "L'expulsion des vendeurs du Temple"; Dubarle, "Le signe du Temple"; Léon-Dufour, "Le signe du temple selon s. Jean"; Cooke, "The Cleansing of the Temple"; Scott, *The Crisis in the Life of Jesus. The Cleansing of the Temple and Its Significance, Jo 2:12–22;* Mendner, "Die Tempelreinigung", Sabbe, "Tempelreiniging en Tempellogion"; Buse, "The Cleansing of the Temple in the Synoptics and in John"; Haenchen, "Johanneische Probleme", pp. 34–46.

[10] See Schmid, *Das Evangelium nach Lukas*, pp. 95f.; Blinzler, "Chronologie", col. 423. But Holzmeister, *Chronologia Vitae Christi*, thinks it more likely that another Pasch occurs between 2:13 and 6:4.

[11] Against Wilkens, *Entstehungsgeschichte*, pp. 9–24.

[12] "To go up" is the usual term. The lake of Gennesaret is about 600 feet below sea level, Jerusalem more or less 2600 feet above.

2:14	καὶ εὗρεν ἐν τῷ ἱερῷ τοὺς πωλοῦντας βόας καὶ πρόβατα καὶ περιστερὰς καὶ τοὺς κερματιστὰς καθημένους,	He found in (the court of) the temple the sellers of oxen, sheep and doves, and the money-changers seated there.

These were busy days for the sellers of animals for sacrifice and for the money-changers,[13] who set up their stalls and tables in the "court of the gentiles"—a practice which could hardly be avoided, but which Jesus condemns, because it takes place "in the sanctuary" (or "temple"). Of set purpose, no distinction is made between the outer and the inner courtyards. In contrast to the Synoptics, John mentions, along with the doves, the sheep and oxen which were required for holocausts and peace-offerings.[14] But he describes Jesus as taking action only against the sellers, not against the buyers.

2:15	καὶ ποιήσας φραγέλλιον ἐκ σχοινίων πάντας ἐξέβαλεν ἐκ τοῦ ἱεροῦ, τά τε πρόβατα καὶ τοὺς βόας, καὶ τῶν κολλυβιστῶν ἐξέχεεν τὸ κέρμα καὶ τὰς τραπέζας ἀνέτρεψεν,	He made a whip of cords and drove them all out of the temple, with their sheep and oxen, scattered the coins of the money-changers and overturned their tables.

The making of a whip out of cords is also a feature noted only in John. Weapons were forbidden in the temple area, but did not include such whips (the Greek loan-word is from the Latin *flagellum*, which is also found as a loan-word in the Mishna). Jesus probably used it to drive out the beasts, though πάντας (masc.) refers primarily to the men. The evangelist, however, adds, "and the sheep and oxen".[15] Jesus scatters the coins of the money-changers and finally overturns their tables (so too the Synoptics).

---

[13] See Billerbeck, vol. I, pp. 850ff., 760ff. He can find no direct example of trading in the temple precincts, but certain hints (pp. 851f. under *e*). See further Jeremias, *Jerusalem zur Zeit Jesu*, vol. I, p. 55. The temple tax, to be paid by every Israelite of 20 years and over, and all other temple offerings had to be in the ancient ("Tyrian") coinage; in the time of Jesus, only Roman money was coined in Palestine, hence the need for money-changers. Cf. Schürer, *Geschichte*, vol. II, pp. 314f., E. T.: *History of the Jewish People*, vol II, p. 250.

[14] Cf. Lev 1 and 3; Nötscher, *Biblische Altertumskunde*, pp. 321ff.; de Vaux, *Institutions*, vol. II, 291f., E. T.: *Ancient Israel*, pp. 415f.

[15] τά τε πρόβατα καὶ τοὺς βόας can hardly be taken as in apposition to πάντας, because the gender is different and the evangelist only uses τε to make an advance on the previous assertion, cf. 4:42; 6:18. The meaning is given correctly by *oves quoque et boves* b c f vg. Bauer, *ad loc.*; Hirsch, *Studien zum vierten Evangelium*, p. 47, take the phrase as an early gloss.

2:16.	καὶ τοῖς τὰς περιστερὰς πωλοῦσιν εἶπεν, Ἄρατε ταῦτα ἐντεῦθεν, μὴ ποιεῖτε τὸν οἶκον τοῦ πατρός μου οἶκον ἐμπορίου.	And he said to the sellers of doves, "Take these things away! My Father's house is not to be turned into a market."

Jesus's reprimand is directed to the sellers of doves, who refuse to be dislodged by the whip. (According to the Synoptics, Jesus overturns their tables also.) In contrast to the Synoptics, this is not a subsequent piece of instruction and justification of Jesus's conduct drawn from the Scriptures (cf. Is 56:7; Jer 7:11), but a good Johannine logion:[16] "Do not turn my Father's house [cf. Lk 2:49] into a market-place!" This could also be understood in a Messianic sense (cf. Zech 14:21), but it arises out of the situation and contains no direct allusion to a text of Scripture. For John, the words of Jesus come from his consciousness of being the Son, which is to be still more clearly expressed later in the course of the Gospel (cf. 5:17, 19 etc.). The evangelist is less interested in the objective implications of the action than in its significance and its consequences for the person of Jesus. As in the Synoptics, the onslaught arouses no opposition. The sufferers probably complained to the temple authorities (cf. v. 18), but the narrative is silent on the point.

2:17	Ἐμνήσθησαν οἱ μαθηταὶ αὐτοῦ ὅτι γεγραμμένον ἐστίν, Ὁ ζῆλος τοῦ οἴκου σου καταφάγεταί με.	His disciples remembered the words of Scripture, "Zeal for thy house will destroy me."

According to the evangelist, the disciples grasp the dangerous consequences of Jesus's action: his zeal for the house of God "will cost him his life". This is the meaning of the quotation from Scripture (Ps 68:10 LXX), because the psalm too speaks of something more than an inwardly consuming zeal. The psalmist suffers contumely and provokes many to hate him. The early Church understood the psalm as Messianic.[17] The disciples are described as "remembering" it in the actual situation (unlike v. 22), but the reader is meant to think also of the mortal hatred of the "Jews" which is soon to be aroused (cf. 5:16, 18). This is why the evangelist has changed the κατέφαγεν με of the original text[18] into a future. There are

---

[16] Haenchen, "Johanneische Probleme", p. 44, finds here the trace of the tradition used by the evangelist. No doubt he could have taken over "my Father's house" from tradition, but if so he managed to fit it very well into his purposes. But the non-synoptic tradition may well go back to the evangelist himself.

[17] See Jn 15:25; 19:29; Mk 15:36 par.; Mt 27:34; Acts 1:20; Rom 11:9f.; 15:3; also Lindars, *New Testament Apologetic*, pp. 104ff.

[18] Rahlfs, *Septuaginta*, vol. II, in the apparatus, *ad loc.*, is right in thinking that καταφάγεται B א came in from Jn 2:17. At Jn 2:17 some witnesses read κατέφαγεν: Tat φ al. sy georg Euseb.

no convincing reasons for considering v. 17 as a later addition of the redaction.[19] The structure of the whole pericope (see above), the disciples' remembering a text of Scripture (cf. 12:16) and the insertion of such an "aside" (cf. 4:27, 33; 11:16; 12:16, 17f.; 13:28f.; 16:17f.) rather tell in favour of the narrative style of the evangelist himself.

2:18	ἀπεκρίθησαν οὖν οἱ Ἰουδαῖοι καὶ εἶπαν αὐτῷ, Τί σημεῖον δεικνύεις ἡμῖν, ὅτι ταῦτα ποιεῖς;	The Jews then challenged him, with the words, "What sign can you give us, to prove that you can do this?"

Without any further explanation, the "Jews" now appear on the scene. In the present situation, the authorities involved would be the "overseers of the temple" who had charge of good order in the temple and controlled the levitical temple police (cf. 7:32, 45f.)[20]. They call Jesus to account,[21] and demand from him a "sign" to prove his right to act as he did. The demand for a "sign" reminds us of the request of the unbelieving Jews for a "sign from heaven" if they are to believe him (cf. 6:30; also the passages in the Synoptics, Mk 8:11f.; Mt 12:38f.; 16:1; Lk 11:16, 29f.). In fact, however, as may be suggested by the variation in the formulation (with a ὅτι-clause and not with a ἵνα-clause),[22] they ask for proof that God has authorized his procedure in the temple area. He must be accredited by a miracle, as for instance the prophets. Thus their demand resembles very much that put forward in the "question of authority" which is narrated by the Synoptics soon after the cleansing of the temple (Mk 11:27–33 parr.), though not linked directly to it. It is only in Mark that it seems to refer to the cleansing of the temple, since nothing else relevant occurs in the interval. Matthew and Luke keep the question of authority more definitely apart, since it is preceded in their Gospel by a description of Jesus's teaching in the temple (Mt 21:23; Lk 20:1). When John makes the question of authority take the form of the demand for a sign, his

---

[19] Hirsch, *Studien*, p. 48; Haenchen, "Johanneische Probleme", p. 44; but then one would also have to affirm that τῇ γραφῇ καί is an interpolation in v. 22, which is very unlikely; ἡ γραφή in the singular (also for the whole of Scripture? See 20:9) is actually common in John (11 times).

[20] See Jeremias, *Jerusalem zur Zeit Jesu*, vol. II B, pp. 23–33, 38f., 72ff. The overseers of the temple are called στρατηγοί, Lk 22:4, 52; Jeremias identifies them with the אֲמַרְכְּלִין of the Jewish sources.

[21] ἀπεκρίθησαν καὶ εἶπαν without a previous question is a Hebrewism, see also Jn 5:17, 19; fairly frequent in the Synoptics, cf. Dalman, *Worte Jesu*, vol. I, pp. 19f.; Joüon, "Respondit et dixit"; Funk, *Greek Grammar*, para. 420, 1.

[22] On ὅτι, Lagrange compares 7:35; 8:22; 9:17; 11:47; 14:22; 16:9 and finds that it is Semitic in character; see also Schlatter, *ad loc.* It need not be taken consecutively, cf. Zerwick, *Graecitas*, no. 297.

intention is clearly to stigmatize the "Jews" as unbelievers. And in fact they do form a definite contrast to the disciples of Jesus (vv. 17, 22) who have his interests at heart and who, in spite of their immediate lack of understanding, will one day "believe the Scripture and the words which Jesus had spoken".

2:19	ἀπεκρίθη Ἰησοῦς καὶ εἶπεν αὐτοῖς, Λύσατε τὸν ναὸν τοῦτον καὶ ἐν τρισὶν ἡμέραις ἐγερῶ αὐτόν.	Jesus answered them by saying, "Tear down this temple, and in three days I will raise it up (again)."

Jesus apparently agrees to the demand of his interlocutors, but holds out a quite different type of "sign". He answers with an enigmatic saying, which cannot but remain obscure to them. Formally, it resembles the procedure of the O. T. prophets, who often used a cryptic "mashal" to give a "sign" (cf. especially Is 7:10–17). But it is also in keeping with the procedure of the Johannine Christ, who often utters words of revelation which almost inevitably lead his hearers to "misunderstand" him (cf. 3:3; 4:10, 32 etc.). We should not therefore first ask what is the meaning of the saying in the actual situation or how was it actually formulated. We should try to understand it in terms of the intention of the Johannine Jesus. The way the command is couched is a direct evocation of the sense which is elucidated by the evangelist in his commentary, v. 21: Jesus is speaking of the "temple" of his body. This explains the use of the expressions "tear down" (λύειν, cf. 1 Jn 4:3 *var. lect.*) and "build up" (ἐγείρειν) which can refer to a building as well as to the body of Jesus.[23] The second word, of course, is the usual term for "resurrection". Hence the addition of "this" (τοῦτον) to "temple" is not an obstacle, though in the actual situation (which, however, is not the limit of Jesus's horizon) it seems to focus attention on the temple of stone.[24] Then, "in three days", which is a conventional phrase to express a short period, is not exactly the same as the definite "on the third day" of the Resurrection narrative (1 Cor 15:4; Mt 16:21 etc.); but this Christological sense is already attached to it by the evangelist. We have throughout a clear example of the influence of the synoptic "saying on the temple", which we find in the tradition of the trial before the Sanhedrin on the lips of the false witnesses (Mk 14:58; Mt 26:61), and which is then echoed by the mockers under the Cross (Mk 15:29; Mt 27:40) and in the charge against Stephen (Acts 6:14).

[23] On λύειν for demolishing a building see Arndt and Gingrich, *Lexicon*, s. v. 3; on ἐγείρειν for putting up a building, *ibid.*, s. v. 1, a.

[24] It is wrong to suppose that Jesus pointed to his body; this would make the Jewish misunderstanding incredible.

The historicity of this saying is confirmed by the variety of the tradition, but the wording and meaning, on the other hand, are obscured, since there are notable differences in the formulation. The restoration of the *ipsissima verba* of Jesus can never succeed, because they appear on the lips of "false witnesses" from the start (Mt 26:60; Acts 6:13) or are branded as "false testimony" (Mk 14:57). Some of the variants in the Synoptics can be explained as deliberate distortions on the part of the Jews, to show Jesus as the destroyer of the temple (in the first person Mk 14:58; Mt 26:61; in the third, Mk 15:29; Mt 27:40; Acts 6:14—this last quotation without the further promise of rebuilding). Other variants are due to early Christian interpretation ("this temple built by hands"—"another not built by hands", Mk 14:58; modified to "I can ...", Mt 26:61). The explanatory addition in Mark comes closest perhaps to the original intention of Jesus, which was to speak of the eschatological community of salvation in metaphorical terms;[25] but this need not detain us here. Jn 2:19 also presupposes some such saying of Jesus, though the evangelist need not have known the synoptic tradition in its written form.[26] The τοῦτον is also found in Mk 14:58 (except in D sy[c]) and Acts 6:14 (τὸν τόπον τοῦτον), and the ἐν τρισὶν ἡμέραις also in Mk 15:29 (only the reading ἐν is uncertain) and Mt 27:40, in the same sense, undoubtedly, as the διὰ τριῶν ἡμερῶν of Mk 14:58; Mt 26:61. These elements show how the evangelist felt himself bound by his tradition; but he goes on at once to interpret the saying of Jesus in the Christological sense which he himself discovered in it.

The misunderstanding between Jesus and the "Jews" is total. Jesus means only his body, which he will "raise up" again in three days, if the Jews "demolish" it.[27] (This Christological interpretation will be further discussed at vv. 21 f.) As was only to be expected from the formulation, the "Jews" take Jesus's words at their face value, as always happens in the Johannine "misunderstandings",[28] and apply them literally to the visible temple of stone which rises before their eyes.

The same question arises here as later with Nicodemus in 3:4. Were the Jews not capable of giving it a different, metaphorical sense? The Messianic age was expected to bring with it a greater measure of glory for Jerusalem and also for the temple. It can be shown that after the destruction of Herod's temple in A.D. 70, a magnificent new sanctuary was hoped for, which, according to some texts, was to be built by the Messiah.[29] The use of "temple" in a transferred sense, especially to indicate the community, could not be verified formerly in Palestinian Judaism. It seemed that a spiritualization of cultic concepts could only be spoken of in Hellenistic Judaism.[30] Now,

---

[25] See Jeremias, *Jesus als Weltvollender*, pp. 37–40. Michel, "ναός", pp. 887–9; Schmid, *Das Evangelium nach Markus*, pp. 281–3. A different view (primarily referring to Jesus himself) in Simon, "Retour du Christ et reconstruction du Temple dans la pensée chrétienne primitive".

[26] See Noack, *Zur johanneischen Tradition*, pp. 103 f.

[27] The imperative in the preceding clause is conditional in character (Semitic parataxis); the main assertion is contained in the following clause; cf. Beyer, *Syntax*, vol. I/1, p. 252.

[28] See 3:3 f.; 4:15, 33; 6:34; 7:35; 8:52 f., 57; 14:8, 22; 16:7 f.

[29] On the expectation of the eschatological temple see Ezek 40–44; Hag 2:7 ff.; Zech 2:5–9; Tob 13:16 f.; 14:5; Ecclus 36:18 f.; on rabbinical and apocalyptic expectations see Billerbeck, vol. I, pp. 1003–5; vol. IV, pp. 884 f.; Volz, *Eschatologie*, p. 217.

[30] See Wenschkewitz, "Die Spiritualisierung der Kultusbegriffe Tempel, Priester und Opfer im NT".

however, the texts of Qumran show clearly the use of building or temple as metaphor for the community, cf. *1 QS*, 5:5f.; 8:7–10 (apropos of Is 28:16); *1 QH*, 6:25–28 (fortified city); cf. 7:7–9; *4 QpPs 37*, 2:16 ("to build him a community"). In the book of Enoch, in eschatological contexts, we also have the expression "the house of the community" (*Enoch*, 53:5) and the metaphor of the "new house" where the sheep are kept (90:28f.), Jerusalem, no doubt, or of a house to be "built for the Great King" (91:13). The notions of community, city and temple are closely associated.[31] Thus the metaphorical sense was not ruled out for the Jews. But in this instance, the words give little hint of it, and it was very far indeed from their minds.

2:20	εἶπαν οὖν οἱ Ἰουδαῖοι, Τεσσαράκοντα καὶ ἓξ ἔτεσιν οἰκοδομήθη ὁ ναὸς οὗτος, καὶ σὺ ἐν τρισὶν ἡμέραις ἐγερεῖς αὐτόν;	The Jews then said, "Forty-six years were spent in building this temple, and you will raise it up in three days?"

The objection made by the Jews, therefore, is concerned with "this temple", the one then in existence, the "second temple", built after the exile, but so magnificently extended and decorated by Herod the Great that it could be said to have been re-built. The figure of "forty-six years" seems to refer to the beginning of this work, which was completed in fact only shortly before the Jewish War.[32] Though we cannot be absolutely sure of the starting-point,[33] the most probable date is 20–19 B.C. (the eighteenth year of Herod according to Josephus, *Ant.*, 15, 380). This would bring us to A.D. 27–28 (the fifteenth year of Tiberius, cf. Lk 3:1) for the present debate, which would suit the chronology of the life of Jesus very well. The Passover of Jn 2:13 would then be that of A.D. 28, with the last Passover in 30. But even in antiquity a symbolic sense was looked for behind the number 46, in particular, a reference to Adam, since the gematria of the Greek *(sic)* 'ΑΔΑΜ gives 46, or again, to the four cardinal points, that is, to the cosmos, since 'ΑΔΑΜ contains the initials of the Greek words for these points.[34] But this can hardly have been the intention of the evangelist. If anything, there might be an allusion to

[31] See Hempel, "Der Symbolismus von Reich, Haus und Stadt in der biblischen Sprache"; on the Qumran texts see Maier, *Die Texte vom Toten Meer*, vol. II, pp. 93f.

[32] The work went on into the time of the governor Albinus, c. A. D. 63, cf. Josephus *Ant.*, XX, 219.

[33] In contrast to *Ant.*, XV, 380, Josephus in *Bell.*, I, 401 gives the fifteenth year of Herod the Great; possibly the beginning of the work had been delayed. The date in *Ant.* is probably correct, because it was the year in which Augustus went to Syria, which according to *Dio Cassius*, LIV was in the spring or summer of 20 B.C.; see Schürer, *Geschichte*, vol. I, p. 369, with n. 12, E. T.: vol. I, i, p. 438 with notes; Holzmeister, *Chronologia vitae Christi*, pp. 85–91; Hölscher, *Die Hohenpriesterlisten bei Josephus und die evangelische Chronologie*, p. 26.

[34] See Augustine, *In Jo.*, tr. X (*Corpus christianorum* 36, pp. 107f.), who appeals at the end (tr. X, 12) to the fact that this "ab anterioribus maioribus dicta sunt". See further Carpenter, *Johannine Writings*, pp. 370f.; Vogels, "Die Tempelreinigung und Golgotha".

Christ's age (cf. 8:57, not yet fifty years old).[35] But what is primarily intended is undoubtedly the time taken to build the temple, a precise detail which seems to support the date given by the evangelist for the cleansing of the temple, the beginning of the public ministry of Jesus.

2:21	ἐκεῖνος δὲ ἔλεγεν περὶ τοῦ ναοῦ τοῦ σώματος αὐτοῦ.	But he was speaking of the temple of his body.

The crude misunderstanding of the Jews is followed by the evangelist's own commentary: when speaking of the "temple", Jesus meant his own body (τοῦ σώματος, epexegetic gen.). Such explanatory remarks of the evangelist are not uncommon.[36] They show that he has meditated on the words of Jesus, and testify in particular to his Christological interests (cf. 2:25; 6:6, 64; 9:7; 11:51 f.). His image of Christ is also determined by the thought of the death and glorification of Jesus, which, however, he always sees as a unity (in the "exaltation", cf. 3:14 f.; 8:28; 12:23, 32 ff.; 13:31 f.; 17:1 f.). The explanation given in 2:21 gives the saying about the destruction and rebuilding of the temple a similar, supremely Christological significance. Jesus freely surrenders his body to destruction; but within three days he will deliver it again from death (cf. 10:18). Here, in contrast to the rest of the N.T., which speaks of the resurrection of Jesus as the work of God, we notice that this power is attributed to Jesus himself. Further, this explanation makes Jesus the "place" where God is to be adored, the true "house of God" (cf. 1:51). With him and in him the time of the worship of God "in spirit and truth" (4:23) has dawned. His body is the source of the waters of life (19:34; so too 7:38, see *ad loc.*), his person is the vine through whose vital force the disciples can work and bear fruit (15:4–8). In view of all this, it is impossible to doubt that we have here a specifically Johannine interpretation, which is unique in being linked up with the saying on the temple. The saying to be attributed historically to Jesus envisaged originally perhaps the eschatological community of salvation (see commentary on v. 19). But John sees this spiritual temple as coming about only through the death and resurrection of Jesus, and he sees it portrayed in the body of the risen Lord. His ecclesiology is based entirely on Christology, though he does not reflect further on the relationship between the glorified body of Christ and the "body" of the Church. This Pauline thought is not found in John, though the evangelist in his own way gives equally strong expression to the doctrine of the unity of the risen Lord with his Church.

---

[35] Vogels, p. 104 recalls that Irenaeus claimed to have heard from the πρεσβύτεροι that Jesus reached the age of between forty and fifty: *Adv. haer.*, II, 33, 3 (Harvey, vol. I, p. 331); see further Holzmeister, *Chronologia*, pp. 99–103.

[36] Cf. 2:24b–25; 6:6, 64, 71; 7:5, 39; 9:7; 11:13, 51 f.; 12:6, 33; 20:9.

2:22 ὅτε οὖν ἠγέρθη ἐκ νεκρῶν, ἐμνήσθησαν οἱ μαθηταὶ αὐτοῦ ὅτι τοῦτο ἔλεγεν, καὶ ἐπίστευσαν τῇ γραφῇ καὶ τῷ λόγῳ ὃν εἶπεν ὁ Ἰησοῦς.

When, therefore, he was raised from the dead, his disciples remembered that he had spoken in this way and they believed the Scripture and the words which Jesus had spoken.

The evangelist now notes that the meaning of Jesus's words only dawned on the disciples after the Resurrection. Their understanding of them was certainly helped by the fact that it was "on the third day" (or "after three days") that Jesus rose, and that the logion spoke of "within three days". Thus the original indication of a short space of time could be given a precise interpretation. The reference to the Scripture is probably also to be taken in the same way (cf. 20:9); but it is also possible that the τῇ γραφῇ is meant to refer back to the text quoted in v. 17. It "reminded" the disciples of the death in store for Jesus, and their master's own word (v. 19) then revealed to them that he was to rise again to life from the dead. The second mention of the disciples' "remembering" links v. 22 to v. 17, but it also shows that the evangelist is thinking in terms of his post-paschal experience and interpreting the past event. After the fulfilment, the disciples see Jesus's words, and hence his action in the temple, in a new light, which is also confirmed by the Scripture. Ultimately, therefore, the cleansing of the temple becomes a revelation of his glory (cf. 2:11) which is disclosed to those who believe.

The relationship to the synoptic narrative

There are strong reasons for thinking that the cleansing of the temple which is recounted in the Synoptics after Jesus's entry into Jerusalem is the same event which John places at the beginning of Jesus's public ministry. The discrepancies which have been noted in the commentary are not such as to demand different events, though they are enough to suggest that there is no literary dependence but that another channel of tradition is present. It is very doubtful that the fourth evangelist here used any written source at all.[37] One can easily imagine that he knew the oral tradition, which surely spoke of Jesus's criticism of abuses in Jewish worship, and that he inserted it into his own vision of Jesus as the new "temple" and the inaugurator of a new worship.

---

[37] So Bultmann, pp. 85f.; he supposes that this written source contained a short controversy after the cleansing of the temple and that here the logion on the temple had a different sense than that given it by the evangelist (cf. p. 91). Others suppose only the adoption of oral tradition (Haenchen, "Johanneische Probleme", p. 54: the evangelist heard a non-synoptic type of gospel in the liturgy of his community).

That the event took place only once is also accepted today by Catholic exegesis,[38] but opinions are divided as to whether the Johannine or the synoptic chronology is historically preferable. A number of Catholic scholars, and some few Protestants, prefer the Johannine dating,[39] and this appears logical, in so far as most exegetes today would prefer to follow John on the question of the date of Christ's death (14 or 15 Nisan). But the cleansing of the temple offers a more difficult problem, since reasons can be adduced for and against the Johannine placing of it.

The defenders of John invoke chiefly the following argument. The reason why the Synoptics place the cleansing of the temple so late is obvious. They bring Jesus to Jerusalem only shortly before his Passion and hence are compelled by the arrangement of their matter to insert here an event which occurred earlier. It need not necessarily be connected with the solemn entry of Jesus into Jerusalem, and their accounts hint of no such connection, which is in fact improbable, since such a major move (as Matthew would wish it to be seen) would have had to have greater repercussions. And in point of fact, neither the entry into Jerusalem nor the cleansing of the temple play a part in the trial of Jesus. The argument is supported by some others drawn from John. The connection between the cleansing of the temple and the demand for a sign or the question of authority seems reasonable and credible, and perhaps suggests historical knowledge which was less clear to the Synoptics (see above, commentary on v. 18). The saying on the temple, which appears without previous explanation at the trial of Jesus in Matthew and Luke, is likewise given a suitable setting in the life of Jesus in the Johannine version. And the fact that the witnesses cannot agree on the wording rather points to something said by Jesus in the remoter past. The reaction of the temple authorities sounds a note of warning, but does not go as far as the intention of "putting him to death" (cf. Mk 11:18). Hence the Johannine presentation claims more historical probability.

But this view is also open to grave objections. At the Sanhedrin's proceedings, Jesus's "attack on the temple" probably played a greater part than appears from the episode of the "false witnesses".[40] And in view

---

[38] See Lagrange, p. 64; Braun, "Expulsion", pp. 185–7; Sigge, *Johannesevangelium*, pp. 139–49; Buzy, *Évangile selon s. Matthieu*, pp. 273f.; Wikenhauser, *Johannes*, pp. 82f. and others.

[39] See, most recently, Braun, "Expulsion"; others, like Mollat, p. 42, van den Bussche, vol. I, p. 220, Wikenhauser, leave the question open. Lagrange, p. 65 tries to keep the cleansing of the temple where John puts it, with the dialogue with the Jews postponed till just before the Passion (hardly practicable). Among Protestants, Taylor, *The Gospel according to St Mark*, pp. 461f. expresses misgivings about the Marcan narrative; Stauffer, *Jesus, Gestalt und Geschichte* upholds the Johannine chronology.

[40] This is indicated by the fact that the blasphemers under the cross take up the saying about the temple and that it also plays a part in the accusations against Stephen. See also Goguel, *La vie de Jésus*.

of the weight laid on the exact investigation of details in Jewish legal procedure, it is not astonishing that the witnesses could no longer be certain about the exact words, even if the statement had been made only a short time before. This saying of Jesus was, after all, more important than his action in the court of the gentiles, masterful though it was, which, in any case, he had defended very competently, if this is what Mk 11:27–33 refers to. But above all, the cleansing of the temple rather belongs to a period when the tension between Jesus and the Sanhedrin had reached its height and the conflict was coming to a head. The saying on the temple also, on account of its content, must be assigned to the final period of Jesus's ministry. It has also been pointed out that the fact noted by Mk 11:16, that Jesus would not allow anyone to carry a vessel through the temple area, presupposes that he had followers to help him. But we should not delay over these attempted reconstructions. Reflections on John itself are more important. Here too it cannot but strike us as strange that Jesus's action has no recognizable after-effects and comes to nothing, as it were. An initial action on this impressive scale is incompatible with the general synoptic picture of Jesus's work—his studied and prolonged reserve, which in Mark is emphasized by the "Messianic secret"—while it does not jar in the Johannine presentation, which is on different lines. It is easy to see why John's narrative and theological purposes could have led him to place the event at the beginning of Jesus's self-revelation (see p. 344 above). Too little should not be made of these interests of John, especially as he points to another incident as bringing the conflict between Jesus and the authorities to a head—the raising of Lazarus, which gives the final impulse to the decision on Jesus's death (cf. 11:45–53, 57; 12:9 ff., 17 ff.).

It is not easy to decide between the Synoptics and John on historical grounds. Each of the narrators, including the synoptic authors, follows his own line;[41] only the fact itself, like the entry into Jerusalem, is not open to question. Forced to choose between the alternative dates (there is no third solution), we must allow for the basic attitudes of the observers, more historical in one case, more theological in the other. The Johannine narrative does not become worthless if one does not follow it for the dating of the cleansing of the temple. The profound insights which it communicates allow us to recognize the secret forces at work in unbelief, to see the gulf between Jesus and official Judaism and to sense the coming catastrophe from the very start. It also allows the reader to share at once the perspective of faith.

---

[41] See Schnackenburg, "Zum Verfahren der Urkirche bei ihrer Jesusüberlieferung", pp. 443–6.

The question of a deeper symbolism

Many exegetes are not content with the Johannine commentary on the words of Jesus on the temple, and look for a deeper meaning in the whole episode. And in fact an interpretation suggests itself, which is closely connected with the saying on the temple but also takes in the action of Jesus. The cleansing of the temple is meant to portray the abrogation of the Jewish cult by Jesus, and its replacement by himself and his community. It was taken in this way as early as Origen,[42] and many recent authors hold this view.[43] A number of points indicate that this might also have been the intention of the evangelist: the similar allusion to Jewish ritual customs at the marriage-feast of Cana (2:6, see *ad loc.*), the reference to the various animals for sacrifice in the episode itself (v. 14ff.), but above all Jesus's dialogue with the Samaritan woman about the place for the true worship of God (4:20–24). Here we find the same concentration on the person of Jesus, through whom the perfect, eschatological worship becomes possible, a worship which surpasses and abrogates even that of the Jews, which had been the legitimate one hitherto (4:22). This is a perspective which has already been opened up in 1:17. The Johannine Church sees itself as the worshipping community in which this eschatological "adoration in the Spirit and the truth" made possible by Jesus Christ, is realized, because the community is united with the person of Christ who is himself the true "temple". The blessings of salvation are present in Jesus (cf. the sign at Cana), and the true meeting with God takes place in him. The new element in our pericope is that the way there leads only through the death and resurrection of Jesus—unless one sees an initial allusion to this in the "hour" of Jesus, 2:4.

This view is confirmed when we recall the remark which goes beyond the actual situation to mention the faith of the disciples (v. 22). The disciples are representatives of the believing community of the future, which understands what the death and resurrection of Jesus mean for them, and recognizes that the eschatological turning-point of the history of salvation has come about in the person of Jesus. In this respect we can say—without calling in question the historicity of the narrative or the event that once took place, as though it were only the symbolic clothing of an idea—that the voice of the later Church can also be heard here and that it voices here its own self-understanding. But this view of the later Christian community, which has abandoned Jewish worship and learned to recognize its own independence, remains in the background. The primary meaning is the Christological one, in which the evangelist is, as we

---

[42] *Comm. in Jo.*, X, 24 (Preuschen, pp. 196f.).

[43] See Strathmann, p. 64; Dodd, *Interpretation*, p. 303; Barrett, p. 164, cf. p. 158; Lightfoot, p. 114; Haenchen, "Johanneische Probleme", p. 46.

have said, greatly interested, both in itself and for the sake of his further presentation of the "history of Jesus".

One is surely going too far, therefore, if one tries to find in the "body" of Christ a direct allusion to the community or its Eucharist. No doubt "the worship of the actual community is centred on the crucified and risen Lord", but that "the community is portrayed in the liturgy as the body of the crucified and risen Christ"[44] is a thought that cannot be derived from the fourth Gospel. It was reserved to Paul to consider the Church as the σῶμα Χριστοῦ, and even for the eucharistic interpretation it is to be noted that the eucharistic formula in John employs σάρξ and not σῶμα (cf. 6:51–56, 63). The only other use of σῶμα in John is for the dead body of Jesus (19:38, 40; 20:12). Hence a comprehensive interpretation, which takes the "body" of Christ as already including his Church, is unacceptable. While allowing for the unity between Christ and the Church, John lays very strong stress on union with his person (in faith), and the Church itself only comes into view in so far as Christ's saving gifts become efficacious in the Church and are communicated through its sacraments.

Many signs in Jerusalem (2:23–25)

Just as the miracle in Cana was followed by a statement in 2:12 which formed a transition to the cleansing of the temple, so too there is a short section here which links the temple episode to the dialogue with Nicodemus. This gives the impression of a continuous narrative. But we are dealing with matter which is not purely historical. It is also theological reflection.

The repeated efforts which have been made to prove that vv. 23–25 are not the work of the evangelist but of a redactor[45] remain unconvincing. They do, in fact, present certain difficulties. The swift conversion of a large number in Jerusalem is said to be as improbable as the "signs" which Jesus now performs, contrary to his attitude towards the "Jews" of 2:18f. who are demanding "signs". Jesus's knowledge of "all men" and his pessimistic verdict on "man" (which must originally have designated a definite person, like his betrayer) is said to be out of place, in view of the Jews who believed and of his revelation to Nicodemus. The "signs" in Jerusalem do not tally with the enumeration of the "signs" between 2:11 and 4:54. On closer inspection, however, most of the difficulties disappear. The belief of the crowds "in his name" (not

---

[44] Cullmann, *Urchristentum*, p. 75; see also Dodd, *Interpretation*, p. 302, who thinks that the Church of Ephesus must have been reminded of the Pauline doctrine of the "Body of Christ".

[45] See Wellhausen, p. 16; Hirsch, *Studien*, pp. 6, 48 (v. 25 probably inserted by redactor); esp. Mendner, "Johanneische Literarkritik", pp. 420–5; see also Wilkens, *Entstehungsgeschichte*, p. 127 (does not count 2:23ff. and the dialogue with Nicodemus as part of the "basic elements").

"in the name of the only-begotten Son of God" as in 3:18; cf. 1 Jn 3:23) is characterized as an inadequate belief attached to miracles, which Jesus deliberately rejects. The bestowal of such "signs" is not in contradiction with the refusal of a sign from heaven (cf. 6:30), and the reserves of the revealer with regard to the sensation-hungry crowds are explicitly justified. And the verses are actually a necessary presupposition (cf. 2:23 with 3:2) or a preparation for the dialogue with Nicodemus, since they enable the reader to follow more closely and understand more easily the encounter of a thinking, questing Jew with the revealer. Criteria of Johannine style are present in sufficient numbers (πιστεύειν εἰς, χρείαν ἔχειν ἵνα [found again only 16:30; 1 Jn 2:27 in the whole of the N.T.], μαρτυρεῖν περί) to entitle us to attribute the verses to the evangelist himself. The peculiar expression πιστεύειν αὐτόν τινι is to be explained by the effort to mark the contrast (αὐτὸς δέ) to the "faith" of the crowds.

2:23	Ὡς δὲ ἦν ἐν τοῖς Ἱεροσολύμοις ἐν τῷ πάσχα ἐν τῇ ἑορτῇ, πολλοὶ ἐπίστευσαν εἰς τὸ ὄνομα αὐτοῦ, θεωροῦντες αὐτοῦ τὰ σημεῖα ἃ ἐποίει·	But while he was in Jerusalem for the Passover during the festal days (or: in the festal crowds) many came to believe in his name, as they saw the signs which he performed.

The evangelist takes up the question of faith (cf. v. 22) and notes that during the feast of the Passover (ἐν τῷ πάσχα), while Jesus was surrounded by the festal crowds (ἐν τῇ ἑορτῇ[46]), or during the festival week (cf. 7:14), many came to believe in him, though only because of seeing the miraculous signs which he performed. Jesus's miracles in Jerusalem are mentioned here as incidentally and as summarily as those in Galilee, 6:2. They were also probably healings. The fourth evangelist is not interested in describing such works of the Saviour in detail, unless they attain such significance for his picture of Christ as in chs. 5–9. The synoptic narrative, which covers the great activities of Jesus in Galilee, is not a reason for casting doubt on the miracles performed during his brief pilgrimages to Jerusalem. The faith of the "numerous" believers remains, as in Galilee, over-attached to miracles (cf. 4:45, 48) and its deficiencies are clearly seen by Jesus. That the evangelist describes it as faith "in his name" (cf. 1:12; 3:18; 1 Jn 3:23; 5:13) does not imply that it is fully adequate, since he is speaking here only of the grounds of faith. Probably hopes of material succour and political liberation were aroused (cf. 6:14f.).

2:24	αὐτὸς δὲ Ἰησοῦς οὐκ ἐπίστευεν αὐτὸν αὐτοῖς διὰ τὸ αὐτὸν γινώσκειν πάντας,	But Jesus himself did not trust himself to them, because he knew all men

[46] For this meaning (also in 7:11) see Liddell and Scott, s. v. 4; Jeremias, *Abendmahlsworte*, pp. 66f.

Jesus, therefore, is cautious, and during his whole stay in the city trusts himself to nobody (cf. the imperfect). The use of πιστεύειν with the reflexive pronoun is singular, but well enough attested outside the N. T.[47] The phrase is aptly chosen to express Jesus's reaction to the confidence which the people reposed in him. The explanation is typically Johannine. Jesus knows everybody and sees into the hearts of all (cf. on 1:48), especially of those who do not believe in him (cf. 5:42).

2:25	καὶ ὅτι οὐ χρείαν εἶχεν ἵνα τις μαρτυρήσῃ περὶ τοῦ ἀνθρώπου· αὐτὸς γὰρ ἐγίνωσκεν τί ἦν ἐν τῷ ἀνθρώπῳ.	and because he had no need of anyone's testimony about man; for he himself knew what was in man.

He has not to rely on other men's testimony about "man", because his own knowledge of men (αὐτός) is unique and supreme. "Man", in the singular in the Greek, does not reflect a different original context which envisaged a specific individual (Judas, his betrayer). It is generic, and envisages human inadequacy as such, in face of which Jesus with his knowledge of the human heart is close to God, who is often described in the O. T. as searching and penetrating the heart.[48]

The texts from Qumran also speak frequently of God's supreme knowledge, the primary object of which is the thoughts and actions of man; cf. *1 QS*, 4:25, "He knows the fruit of their works always and ever"; *1 QS*, 1:7, "Before you created them, you knew their deeds for ever and always"; *ibid.*, 23f., "What can I say that has not been known, and what can I proclaim that has not been told? Everything has been inscribed before you by a pen which records it for all eternity";[49] cf. 7:13; 9:12. As in the text of John which is under discussion, the pessimistic trend set by Gen 6:5 comes to the fore. "Before they were established, he knew their works and abhorred the generations (as they arose?)", *Dam.*, 2:8f., cf. C. Rabin, *The Zadokite Documents* (2nd ed., 1958); "To the children of men belong the service of sin and the works of deceit", *1 QH*, 1:27.

It is, therefore, unnecessary and misleading to give Hellenistic parallels from the superhuman knowledge of "divine men". But the texts cited by Odeberg from Jewish mysticism[50] present objective affinities. Metatron, the heavenly consort of God, is given knowledge of all the secrets of Wisdom and the Torah, and learns the thoughts of all hearts. But there is no proof that the evangelist was tributary to this mystic line of thought. His conviction of Jesus's profound insight into hearts stems from his Christology, which makes him see the earthly Jesus as most intimately united with the heavenly Father (cf. on 1:51). The notion that Jesus remains unrecognized and

---

[47] Cf. *Epistle of Aristeas*, 270; Josephus, *Ant.*, XII, 396; Plutarch, *Mor.*, 181 D etc. (see Arndt and Gingrich, *Lexicon*, s. v. 3).

[48] See 1 Sam 16:7; 1 Kgs 8:39; Ps 7:10; 38:10; 44:22; 94:11; 139:1–4; Jer 11:20; 17:10 etc.

[49] See the discussion in Nötscher, *Theologische Terminologie*, pp. 91f.; 175f.; 180f.

[50] *Fourth Gospel*, pp. 43–7; 3 *Enoch*, II, pp. 30f., 168f.

misunderstood is also there, though hardly in the sense that he deliberately maintains an incognito,[51] since he wishes to reveal himself to true believers, and does in fact reveal himself.

John 3: Preliminary literary criticism

The conversation with Nicodemus, to which 2:23–25 forms a good introduction, terminates apparently in a monologue of Jesus, or is continued, as many modern exegetes think, by a set of reflections offered by the evangelist, though authors differ as to where the reflections begin.[52] Further, the developments from v. 13 or 16 on go beyond the theme and situation of the dialogue with Nicodemus, as is particularly clear in v. 19, which presupposes the whole public ministry of Jesus (like 1;10f. and 12:46ff.). But "a gradual transition from historical narrative to the presentation of the evangelist's own reflections on it", or "an imperceptible change from the words of Jesus to the words of Christians about Jesus"[53] cannot be shown to have taken place elsewhere. The Johannine Jesus constantly speaks in a lofty theological language which owes much to the evangelist, but the discourses of Christ are always clearly recognizable as such, mostly because they are in the first person (cf. 12:44 to 50) or return to it after some statements about the Son or the Son of Man (cf. 5:19–30). But the evangelist never interweaves them with reflections of his own. There is only one other passage in John which can be compared to the discourse ending at 3:21, and that is 3:31–36, which is not far away from it and is very like it in content. These verses are on the face of it a continuation of the discourse of John the Baptist, but an examination of their contents shows that they cannot possibly be attributed to him and that they are as "free-floating" as the last part of the Nicodemus episode. The question of literary criticism then arises, as to whether the two passages are really in their original place, or whether they are not rather passages which for one reason or another were incorporated into the Gospel at an early date. The latter hypothesis, which we have developed elsewhere,[54] we propose to propound briefly once more here, with certain modifications.

---

[51] Against Stauffer, "Agnostos Christos. Joh. 2:24 und die Eschatologie des vierten Evangeliums", esp. p. 292. On his far-reaching conclusions with regard to the eschatology preached by Jesus (cf. also his *Jesus, Gestalt und Geschichte*, pp. 117–20) see the criticism of Kümmel, "Futuristische und präsentische Eschatologie im ältesten Christentum", esp. pp. 115f.

[52] Calmes, Belser, Tillmann start the discourse of the evangelist with v. 13, Bernard, Lagrange, Braun, Lightfoot with v. 16.

[53] Quotations from Tillmann, p. 92 (cf. also Schick, p. 42), and Strathmann (p. 62) respectively.

[54] Schnackenburg, "Die 'situationsgelösten' Redestücke in Joh. 3".

1. The dialogue with Nicodemus, as the evangelist wished to present it, comprises only vv. 1–12. The Gospel narrative is resumed in 3:22–30. Immediate evidence of this is the fact that Jesus addresses Nicodemus and his fellows in the second person up to the end of v. 12, but not after that. The conversation ends with a question left hanging in the air by Jesus, as in 5:47. The evangelist does not need to give any further information about the visitor's attitude, since his scepticism is already made clear enough by the question. The evangelist also ends other conversations or disputes in the same way, cf., with 5:47, also 7:24, 36; 9:41; 13:38; 18:11; 20:23, 29.

2. Verses 13–21 do not form part of the Gospel narrative, but come from a kerygmatic exposition of the evangelist which was originally independent, very like the kerygmatic parts of 1 John (cf. especially 4:9 ff.; 5:10 ff.). It is easy to imagine that the evangelist composed a summary of the "message" of Jesus (cf. 1 Jn 1:5) in conjunction with the Nicodemus dialogue, and that this summary was incorporated into the Gospel itself by the disciples of the evangelist during the redaction (cf. 21:24). But, as the καί at the beginning suggests, 3:13–21 is probably not the beginning of this "kerygmatic discourse" (as we suggest this addition to the Gospel should be called, in keeping with its literary genre), but the displaced passage v. 31–36, which is totally foreign to the Baptist, but suits admirably the preacher who speaks in vv. 13–21.[55]

3. Verses 31–36 may be recognized as the first part of the "kerygmatic discourse" from the following traits. The passage begins by contrasting him "who comes from above" with him "who is from the earth", and affirming that he is "above all" (v. 31). It speaks of his heavenly "testimony", that is, his revelation, which is his divine mission (vv. 32–34), explained as an event which demands faith and brings salvation (vv. 35 ff.). A second section, which we think is to be sought in vv. 13–21, follows very suitably here. Having spoken of him who has come down from heaven, of the Son in fact, the preacher now envisages him as having ascended once more into heaven (v. 13) and in conjunction with his "exaltation" also designates him as Son of Man (vv. 13ff.), then taking up once more the meaning of the "Son" of God for salvation (vv. 16 ff.). In view of his historical experience, however, he recognizes that men "loved darkness more than the light" (v. 19), and looks for an explanation of this baffling fact (vv. 19c–21), while also summoning his hearers inexorably to decision. All this is unmistakably "Johannine" in style and content, and must come from the pen of the evangelist himself.

---

[55] Dodd, *Interpretation*, p. 311, cf. p. 309, also recognizes that 3:31–36 is an "Explanatory appendix to the dialogue with Nicodemus", but without drawing any further conclusions.

4. It was probably the dialogue with Nicodemus which in fact occasioned the composition of this "kerygmatic discourse". The contrast made in v. 31 may reflect the contrast between Jesus and Nicodemus (cf. ἐκ τῆς γῆς λαλεῖ with the answers of Nicodemus in vv. 4 and 9), though the contrast between "to be from above" and "to be from the earth" has been enlarged to affirm a fundamental principle: only one comes from on high and brings divine revelation, to which the earthly race of man must open its heart and submit. In any case, there are unmistakable echoes of the dialogue: v. 32 corresponds directly to v. 11, the ἄνωθεν of v. 31 to that of v. 3, and vv. 34f. are reflections on the words of revelation which have been given by Jesus in v. 12. In the last verse of the dialogue with Nicodemus, faith is said to be the prerequisite for the acceptance of revelation, and the "kerygmatic discourse" issues in the necessity of faith, forming as it does an urgent appeal to the hearers. It probably also throws light on what Jesus meant by the "heavenly things" to which he alluded in his final question (v. 12) without explaining them (which was also the way the evangelist understood the conclusion of the dialogue).

5. How are we to explain these insertions into the Gospel narrative, and also the division of the "kerygmatic discourse" into two parts and their present arrangement? It should not be too difficult to find a solution, if we recall the probable literary genesis of the Gospel (cf. Introduction, chs. III and IV). The disciples of the evangelist who published his work probably found some of his writing already in position after the dialogue with Nicodemus (possible on two leaves corresponding to vv. 13–21 and 31–36) and tried to fit them in "suitably", as may also be presumed for 7:15–24, whose "correct" place would be after 5:47. Their procedure was dictated by rather extrinsic reasons (cf. 7:15, which links up with the mention of Jesus's "doctrine" in v. 14). Hence vv. 13–21, which formed originally the second part, were attached to v. 12, on account of the echo of the ἐπουράνια in the "ascending to heaven". And vv. 31–36, originally the first part, were perhaps attached to the words of the Baptist because "he who is from earth" was interpreted of the humble speaker of v. 30. The procedure was deliberate, though not perfectly successful. The redactors seem to have made no alterations in the text.

6. If this hypothesis—which is all it can claim to be—is correct, the dialogue with Nicodemus is clearly demarcated and fits admirably into the structure of the first chapters. The difficulties which even a man of good will among the ruling classes experiences in coming to believe are presented clearly, and the forebodings about Jesus's prospects of winning their belief cannot be missed (v. 12). At the same time, an important theological theme is discussed, the "supernatural" presuppositions for attaining salvation, and further revelation, on the "heavenly things", is promised. If these "loftier" themes are not treated at once (as one would

have to assume they were if the discussion was continued in vv. 13–21), the dialogue with Nicodemus merely loses a burdensome appendage. After the doubts expressed in Jesus's question of v. 12, a continuation of the theme becomes at once improbable. And from the point of view of the contents (the mystery of the "exaltation of the Son of Man" and the survey of the whole work of Jesus), and of exegesis (see commentary on v. 13), the difficulties would be almost insuperable. But in our present hypothesis, the Gospel narrative proceeds rather briskly to the following scene, which takes place where John is baptizing (3:22–30), and Jesus's stay in Jerusalem retains its character of prelude and prefiguration, in keeping with this introductory part of the presentation, which prepares for further developments. Further, the evangelist is thereby freed from the suspicion of making his Jesus speak, without warning, as "the post-resurrectional, exalted Christ" (Strathmann), no matter how much he has re-moulded his words in terms of his own image of Christ. Finally, the Johannine Jesus need not be thought of as giving revelation in a mysterious, impersonal and merely allusive way (cf. Bultmann). On the contrary, the speaker here is the Christian preacher, summing up the essentials of the Christian message, whose voice (or that of one close to him) is also heard in 1 Jn as herald of the faith and pastor of souls.[56]

The dialogue with Nicodemus (3:1—12)

This meeting between Jesus and one of the leading Jews—elsewhere he is engaged only with "the Jews" or "the Pharisees"—is intended as a real dialogue, though Nicodemus's only contribution is to interpose twice (vv. 4 and 9) a perplexed question. Though Nicodemus is a member of the Sanhedrin, a Pharisee and a doctor of the law (v. 10), the conversation cannot be put down under the heading of "discussions with official Judaism". Nicodemus is a well-intentioned representative of the ruling classes, a man with religious questions, and one from whom Jesus does not remain totally aloof, in spite of the principle laid down in 2:25. Though the encounter leads to no positive result (but cf. 7:50f.; 19:39), and Jesus finally expresses his doubt that Nicodemus and his fellows will

---

[56] Mendner, "Nicodemus", supposes much more manipulation on the part of a late redactor (2nd cent.). The discussion took place only after the scene of 7:45–52 and contained only fragments from 3:2–13 and 3:31–36 in the original account (cf. the survey pp. 314f.). The transfer of the dialogue with Nicodemus into the first visit to Jerusalem is said to be connected with the story of the cleansing of the temple, which was also introduced later. All very ingenious, but quite unconvincing, in view of the highly complicated reconstruction which results.

come to believe (v. 12), this merely illustrates the difficulties with which Jesus sees himself faced on account of their attitude, and is no more than a hint of the coming conflicts (cf. chs. 5; 7–10). Nicodemus can hardly be considered as a "typical" case of the unbelieving Jew. At the most, he is typical of the doctors of the law, whose principles make it hard for them to submit to the new revelation "from above" and bow to this revealer of salvation who claims direct authority from God.

Jesus's attitude to official Judaism is of less interest to the evangelist in this section than the theological theme which is discussed by Jesus and the learned councillor: the basic question of what is necessary for salvation. The Synoptics also show how seriously the Judaism of the day was preoccupied with the question. The query of the rich man, "What must I do to attain eternal life?" (Mk 10:17 parr.) or that of the doctor of the law, "What is the gravest commandment of all?" (Mk 12:28) are significant. In contrast to this approach, Jesus informs his visitor, who may have put a similar question (cf. v. 3), that it is not primarily a matter of human effort and the accomplishment of the law, but of being "born from above". This answer was supremely important for primitive Christianity, particularly when dealing with Judaism, since it explained why Christian baptism was the beginning of salvation (cf. Acts 2:28; 1 Cor 6:11; Tit 3:5f.; Heb 6:1f.; 1 Pet 1:23). The evangelist's positive interest in this fundamental-doctrine also makes it unlikely that he meant to oppose the baptism of the disciples of John which was only "in water". This may have been a secondary motive of topical interest, but here the horizon is much wider. It takes in the fundamental revelation of salvation, though without saying everything about it (omitting, for instance, the "heavenly things" of v. 12).

There is no reason to doubt the historicity of the nocturnal scene. The fact that Jesus answers the captious questions of the scribe in terms which betray the influence of primitive Christian theology in their "kerygmatic stylization" presents no greater problem than the rest of the Johannine presentation. We must try to grasp the core of the thought and then decide whether we accept the doctrine that man must be "born from above" as the doctrine of Jesus—in the light of his resurrection and gift of the Spirit. Exegesis can only demonstrate the existence in Judaism of certain principles in the light of which the doctrine could have been possible and, as presented to Nicodemus, understandable. The figure of Nicodemus does not remain entirely in obscurity. He is mentioned twice again in the Gospel (7:50f.; 19:39), and in such a way that his ultimate conversion to Christianity may be deduced (see on 3:1). In spite of being made to some extent a typical figure, he also retains some quite personal traits.

3:1	Ἦν δὲ ἄνθρωπος ἐκ τῶν Φαρισαίων, Νικόδημος ὄνομα αὐτῷ, ἄρχων τῶν Ἰουδαίων·	There was one of the Pharisees, called Nicodemus, a councillor of the Jews

Nicodemus (a Greek name, also a loan-word in Aramaic) is presented to the reader as a Pharisee and a Jewish councillor, that is, a member of the Sanhedrin (cf. 7:50). In this assembly, which possessed supreme religious and civil jurisdiction, he was one of the group of doctors of the law, as is confirmed by v. 10, where Jesus addresses him as one of the acknowledged teachers of Israel. If he later became a Christian, as is perhaps also suggested by an ancient and somewhat confused passage of the Talmud,[57] the silence of Jewish sources about a scholar of this name is sufficiently well explained by the rabbinical tactics of never mentioning an outlaw. Possibly the two other mentions of Nicodemus (7:50f.; 19:39) are meant to indicate his gradual progress to the faith. The Pharisee, who began by meeting Jesus only in secret, then speaks out on his behalf in the Sanhedrin, and finally is not afraid, after Jesus's death on the Cross, of contributing lavish amounts of spices for his burial (Zahn). But the few hints we possess do not enable us to depict the development of his faith. He is not a representative of those whose faith is only superficial (3:23). He has thought much about Jesus and considers him a teacher (v. 2) to whom he can turn for light on serious matters.

3:2	οὗτος ἦλθεν πρὸς αὐτὸν νυκτὸς καὶ εἶπεν αὐτῷ, Ῥαββί, οἴδαμεν ὅτι ἀπὸ θεοῦ ἐλήλυθας διδάσκαλος· οὐδεὶς γὰρ δύναται ταῦτα τὰ σημεῖα ποιεῖν ἃ σὺ ποιεῖς, ἐὰν μὴ ᾖ ὁ θεὸς μετ' αὐτοῦ.	who came to Jesus by night and said to him, "Rabbi, we know that you have come from God as a teacher. For no one can do such signs as you do if God is not with him."

The statement that he came to Jesus "by night" also allows of no sure conclusions about his character. It may indicate his timidity, as many commentators think (cf. 19:38 on Joseph of Arimathaea), or—more probably—symbolize his coming from the darkness to the light which Jesus

---

[57] *Sanhedrin*, 43a *Bar.* names five disciples of Jesus: Mathai, Naqai, Nezer, Buni and Toda. According to Dalman, *Grammatik des jüdisch-palästinensischen Aramäisch*, p. 179, Naqai is the Aramaic form of Naqdemon, Nicodemus. Billerbeck, vol. II, p. 418 further thinks that Buni is a mistake for the Naqdemon ben Gorion of *Ta'an.*, 19b, formerly known as Buni, a man famous for his wealth, though not a rabbi. Klausner, *Jesus of Nazareth*, pp. 29f. holds, on the contrary, with Krauss, that Naqai is Luke and that Buni is a corruption from Juhanni, i.e. Johannes. It is certain that there was a noble family in Jerusalem in which the name Nicodemus (Naqdemon) was current. Josephus, *Ant.*, XIV, 37 names a Nicodemus as envoy of Aristobulus to Pompey; Schlatter, p. 84 thinks that he may have been the ancestor of the Jerusalem family.

is (cf. 3:21). But the night is also recommended for the study of the Torah, and rabbis are often found prolonging their discussions well into the night;[58] this type of information is given elsewhere in the Gospel.[59] It is not an unmistakably symbolic allusion, as in the case of Judas, whose departure when "it was night" (13:30) signals the coming of the hour of darkness and evil (cf. Lk 22:53).[60] The miracles of Jesus have also made an impression on Nicodemus; they prove to him that God is "with him".[61] The Jews held that God hears the prayers of the just (cf. 9:31 ff.), and famous rabbis were credited with all sorts of miracles which guaranteed their piety and confirmed their teaching.[62] Nicodemus concludes that Jesus must also be a divinely-enlightened teacher. It speaks well for the respected scholar that he seeks out someone who has not been formed in the schools (cf. 7:15), addresses him as "rabbi" and enquires about his doctrine. It is a polite exaggeration when he affirms that the other doctors also share his opinion (οἴδαμεν). It is unlikely that they sent him to Jesus. He came on his own initiative. But the affirmation gives the dialogue a more universal import (cf. v. 11), and the readers could feel themselves reminded of learned debates about the Scriptures between Jews and Christians in their own day (cf. the dialogue between Justin and the Jew Trypho).

3:3 ἀπεκρίθη Ἰησοῦς καὶ εἶπεν αὐτῷ, Ἀμὴν ἀμὴν λέγω σοι, ἐὰν μή τις γεννηθῇ ἄνωθεν, οὐ δύναται ἰδεῖν τὴν βασιλείαν τοῦ θεοῦ.

Jesus answered him with the words, "Truly, truly, I tell you, unless a man is born from above, he cannot see the kingdom of God."

Jesus understands Nicodemus as being moved by the question which preoccupied all Jews: "What must I do to share in the world to come?"—for which his own usual expression was, according to the Synoptics, "enter into the kingdom of God".[63] This has the same meaning as "see the kingdom of God" (cf. v. 5), though here the kingdom of God, in the Johannine perspective, should rather be considered as the heavenly

[58] Cf. Billerbeck, vol. II, pp. 419f.

[59] Cf. 1:39; 4:6; 6:4, 10, 17; 10:22b; 18:28; 19:14. The evangelist seems to attach some significance to the fact that Nicodemus came "by night", since he mentions it again in 19:39.

[60] See further Meinertz, "Die Nacht im Johannesevangelium".

[61] This is an Old Testament and Jewish expression, cf. Gen 21:20; 26:24; 28:15; 31:3; Deut 31:23; Jos 1:5; Jg 6:12 etc.; also Lk 1:28, 66; Acts 7:9; 10:38; 11:21; Josephus, *Ant.*, VI, 181, 231; XV, 138.

[62] See Fiebig, *Jüdische Wundergeschichten*, esp. pp. 19 ff. (healing through prayer).

[63] Mt 5:20; 7:21; 18:3 par.; 19:23f. par.; 21:31; 22:12; 23:13 par.; 25:10, 21, 23; Mk 9:47. "To see the kingdom of God" also Lk 9:27 (for Mark's "see coming"). Rabbinical

realm on high to which the divine envoy leads (cf. 14:3; 12:26; 17:24). The synoptic echo in the Johannine logion, which, with v. 5, is the only instance of "kingdom of God" in John, shows that it derives from fixed (oral) tradition. It is difficult to believe that it is based on Mt 18:3 (Mk 10:15),[64] since the evangelist would have had to modify the thought considerably: he would have turned "becoming (once more) as children (a child)" into a straight-forward "becoming a child", and then understood this very realistically as re-birth, new creation or "birth from above". The ὡς is an essential element of both forms of the synoptic logion, just as on the other hand the Johannine logion is not concerned with man's conversion, but with God's action upon man.[65] Since the thought of a new creation was not foreign to Judaism—it is presupposed in Jesus's words in v. 10, and now also attested by the texts of Qumran (see below)—the supposition is unnecessary, though not incompatible with the history of tradition.

The translation of γεννηθῆναι ἄνωθεν causes difficulty, because ἄνωθεν can mean: 1, from above; 2, from the beginning; 3, once more. Among the older versions, the Latin, Coptic and most of the Syriac (except sy^{pal}) take the third sense. Justin (*Apol.*, 61,4 ἀναγεννηθῆτε), Clement of Alexandria (*Protrept.*, IX, 82), Tertullian (*De bapt.*, XIII), Augustine, Jerome and many moderns take it in the same way. But Greek Fathers such as Origen, Cyril of Alexandria and Chrysostom preferred "from above", from God, as do the modern commentators Calmes, Tillmann, Lagrange, F.-M. Braun and others. Many are undecided, others suppose a deliberate ambiguity (Barrett). There is no Aramaic word which allows of the two meanings like the Greek; if there was a play upon words, it could only have been in Greek, and one would have to consider the dialogue as fictive. But there is no need to do so. According to the usage of ἄνωθεν elsewhere in John (3:31; 19:11,23), and his doctrine of "birth from God" (1:13; 1 Jn 2:29; 3:9; 4:7; 5:1), the only justifiable translation is "from above".[66] Above all, the ἄνωθεν of 3:31 undoubtedly takes up that of 3:3 (cf. the preliminary remarks on ch. 3), and establishes clearly the notion of an event which originates in heaven and is brought about by divine forces outside human control. There are two ostensible reasons for the other translation: 1, the misunderstanding on the part of Nicodemus in v. 4; 2, the widespread Hellenistic notion of "rebirth", which can be verified in the N. T. itself (1 Pet 1:3,23; Tit 3:5; see also Justin, *Apol.*, 66,1; *Dial.*, 138,2). Nonetheless, the

---

parallels *Sanh.*, 29c *Bar.* "to have a share in the world to come", see Dalman, *Worte Jesu*, p. 89, E. T.: p. 108; on the Jewish terminology in general, *ibid.*, pp. 79–113, esp. p. 110, E. T.: pp. 91–139, esp. p. 135: the term ἡ βασιλεία τοῦ θεοῦ on the lips of Jesus corresponds most closely to the rabbinical "world (age) to come" or "life of the world (age) to come".

[64] So esp. Jeremias, *Die Kindertaufe*, pp. 63ff.; de la Potterie, "Naître de l'eau et naître de l'Esprit"; Robinson, *The New Quest of the Historical Jesus*, p. 121.

[65] The form with ἀναγεννηθῆτε in Justin, Clement of Alexandria, *Pseudo-Clementine Hom.*, XI, 26, 2 and *Recog.*, VI, 9, even if it circulated independently, presupposes the logion of Jn 3:5. Clement, *Protr.*, IX, 82, 4 (Stählin, vol. I, p. 62) combines the synoptic and the Johannine logia: ἢν γὰρ μὴ αὖθις ὡς τὰ παιδία γένησθε καὶ ἀναγεννηθῆτε, ὥς φησιν ἡ γραφή . . . οὐδ'οὐ μὴ εἰσελεύσεσθέ ποτε εἰς τὴν βασιλείαν τῶν οὐρανῶν.

[66] See Mussner, ΖΩΗ, pp. 118ff.

misunderstanding is not necessarily due to the word ἄνωθεν (the δεύτερον occurs only in Nicodemus's second question, following up the thought expressed in the first question). The misunderstanding follows from the thought as such. It is enough for Nicodemus to hear of any sort of "birth" or "begetting" (both meanings are also possible for the Aramaic יְלַד) in order to fall into a crude misunderstanding. The other Johannine misunderstandings are of a similar type; the hearers reach wrong and stupid conclusions (cf. 4:15; 6:34,52; 8:57; 14:8), because they fail to listen properly to what Jesus says. The other question, as to whether John here takes up the Hellenistic notion of "rebirth", can only be decided by the exegesis of the whole dialogue. To think that he must have done so is the result of preconceptions. Even where the terminology is most closely allied, Tit 3:5, the Christian notion itself still differs considerably from the Hellenistic analogies (cf. v. 6).[67]

Hence ἄνωθεν designates the divine and heavenly world, by whose powers man must be renewed. The notion of the higher world as the dwelling-place of God and his angelic hosts, and as a way of indicating a region reserved to God and inaccessible to man, was familiar in Judaism.[68] Of itself, the expression was intelligible, and Nicodemus could have understood that Jesus was speaking of an event brought about by God's grace. Prior to all human effort to attain to the kingdom of God, God himself must create the basis of a new being in man, which will also make a new way of life possible.

3:4 λέγει πρὸς αὐτὸν Νικόδημος, Πῶς δύναται ἄνθρωπος γεννηθῆναι γέρων ὤν; μὴ δύναται εἰς τὴν κοιλίαν τῆς μητρὸς αὐτοῦ δεύτερον εἰσελθεῖν καὶ γεννηθῆναι;

Nicodemus said to him, "How can a man be born if he is old: can he enter his mother's womb a second time and be born?"

But Nicodemus concentrates on the demand for a "birth" and, as was usual in the scholastic exercises of the rabbis, raises objections which are couched as paradoxically as possible. His two questions are meant to bring out the senseless nature of the doctrine (cf. 6:52) and force Jesus to admit to an absurdity (cf. Mk 12:20–23 parr.). "Being born" is something that happens to man at the beginning of his life; unthinkable, if he is old. Nicodemus need not be thinking of himself; the extreme case of the aged makes flagrantly clear what is true of every age, that there is only one birth. The second question is even more sharply pointed, as the Pharisee follows up his thought: surely a man cannot return once more into his mother's womb and be born? If one notes that δεύτερον goes with εἰσελθεῖν and that the stress is only on γεννηθῆναι, one has additional proof

---

[67] See Dey, Παλιγγενεσία; Schnackenburg, *Das Heilsgeschehen bei der Taufe nach dem Apostel Paulus*, pp. 8–14.

[68] Cf. Odeberg, *Fourth Gospel*, pp. 48, 63; Bietenhard, *Die himmlische Welt im Urchristentum und Spätjudentum*, pp. 82ff.; see also on Jn 1:51.

that Nicodemus has only taken up and analyzed "being born"; he seems to have ignored completely the ἄνωθεν of Jesus.[69]

3:5	ἀπεκρίθη Ἰησοῦς, Ἀμὴν ἀμὴν λέγω σοι, ἐὰν μή τις γεννηθῇ ἐξ ὕδατος καὶ πνεύματος, οὐ δύναται εἰσελθεῖν εἰς τὴν βασιλείαν τοῦ θεοῦ.	Jesus answered, "Truly, truly, I tell you: unless a man is born of water and Spirit, he cannot enter the kingdom of God.

Jesus makes no direct answer to the objection, but goes on to define the ἄνωθεν. This allows the words of revelation (introduced again solemnly by ἀμήν, ἀμήν) to be intoned once more, with greater urgency and resonance, an effect deliberately intended by the evangelist (cf. 6:53 with 51; 7:36 with 34; 8:58 with 56; 14:9f. with 6f.; 16:16 with 17 and 19). The "birth" or "begetting" of which Jesus speaks is of a completely different nature. It comes about "from water and Spirit". Every Christian hearer or reader of the Gospel must have thought at once of baptism. The authenticity of the words ὕδατος καί has been often challenged, on the grounds of their being due to an "ecclesiastical" redaction, but without sufficient grounds. Textual criticism provides no reason for doubting that they belonged to the original constitution of the Gospel.[70] The "higher criticism" can point to the fact that only the πνεῦμα is spoken of in the following verses, but this is due to the standpoint and the purpose of the instruction, which is precisely to explain the supernatural character of the birth in question, which originates in the realm of the divine and heavenly. The only real hindrance to attributing the mention of baptism to the evangelist is the prejudice that he has no interest in the sacraments. But when one observes that the eucharistic section 6:53–58 grows as it were inevitably out of the discourse on the bread of life in ch. 6, one must also credit the evangelist with seeing the "birth from the Spirit" realized concretely in baptism. Each of the passages provides support for the other, but both together are also proved to be deliberate references on the part of the evangelist to baptism and the Eucharist by his latent interest in the sacraments (cf. 19:34f.).[71] But it remains true that baptism in water (as an external rite and requisite) is not the real focus of interest, but the "birth from the Spirit (of God)", the fundamental process of salvation

[69] The addition of ἄνωθεν in Nicodemus's first objection in some MSS (H 28 sa bo e a q z, sometimes in reverse order) must be a secondary insertion of the copyists.

[70] The words in question are missing only in the Vulgate codex Harleian 1023, probably through inadvertance. Efforts to understand ἐξ ὕδατος otherwise than of baptism with water (Odeberg, pp. 48–71, esp. p. 63, who makes it a metaphor like 1 Jn 3:9) have met, rightly, with no general acceptance.

[71] See Schnackenburg, *Die Sakramente im Johannesevangelium*, pp. 235–54.

which, for the early Church—according to the commandment of its Lord—was linked only with the sacrament of baptism. Hence Jesus's words to Nicodemus are not concerned directly with baptism, but with the new creation by the Spirit of God.[72]

Judaism had given much thought to the Holy Spirit and his eschatological functions. The Spirit was to bring about at the end an inward change of heart, which would make a ready and perfect fulfilment of the law of God possible (Ezek 11:19; 36:25 ff.; Is 44:3; Jer 31:33). The apocrypha and the rabbinical writings show that these ideas were very active in the time of Jesus.

In *Jub.*, 1:23 we read: "I will create in them a holy spirit, and I will cleanse them so that they shall not turn away from me from that day unto eternity." It is to be noted that the passage goes on to speak of the children of God, so that here too, as in Jn 1:12f. (and 1 John) the notion of new creation (through the Spirit) is associated with that of divine adoption. Cf. further *Jub.*, 1:16; 5:12; *Ps. Sol.*, 18:6; *Enoch*, 92:3 ff. 10:16; *Assumption of Moses*, 13; *Test. Lev.*, 18:11; *Test. Jud.*, 24:3; *Or. Sib.*, III, 373f.; 573 ff.; on which see Volz, *Eschatologie*, pp. 392f. It was also held at Qumran that entry into the community brought with it a complete purification and an inward transformation, cf. *1 QH*, 3:21, "Thou hast cleansed the perverted spirit from great transgression"; 11:10–14, "For the sake of thy glory thou hast cleansed man from sin, that he may consecrate himself to thee . . . to be renewed, with all that is to be." The Holy Spirit is the purifying force, cf. 7:6f.; 9:32; 12:12; 16:12; 17:26. "Here we have a new creation of man, which brings about a real change not only in his situation but in his being."[73]

In rabbinism, the notion of purification from sin was linked with penance (conversion), especially with that of the Day of Expiation; Rabbi Akiba, however, declared, on the authority of Ezek 36:25, "Blessed are you, the children of Israel. By whom are you purified, and who cleanses you? Your father in heaven" (*Mishna, Yomah*, VIII, 9). The text of Ezek (v. 26) which goes on to speak of the gift of the Spirit was mostly interpreted eschatologically, but sometimes also applied to some extent to the present.[74]

Hence Nicodemus could well have understood that Jesus affirmed the necessity of man's being cleansed and totally transformed by God, if he was to reach the kingdom of God. The notion that the Spirit was already

---

[72] De la Potterie, "Naître de l'eau et naître de l'Esprit", though not excluding baptism, refers the function of the Spirit primarily to faith ("infusion of faith" being of supreme importance for the reception of the sacraments, p. 440) and holds that the doctrine of the logion is "substantiellement la même que celle du logion synoptique, quoiqu'elle soit formulée d'un autre point de vue et dans un vocabulaire différent" (p. 438).

[73] Sjöberg, "Neuschöpfung in den Toten-Meer-Rollen", p. 136.

[74] The Day of Expiation is probably always envisaged here; further texts in Billerbeck, vol. I, p. 113. See also *Ex. Rabbah*, 15 (76c): "If the Israelites have fallen into sin on account of the evil urge within them, and repent and do penance, God forgives their sins every year (on the Day of Expiation) and renews their hearts so that they may fear him, as it is written: I will give you a new heart, Ezek 36:26" (quoted by Billerbeck, vol. IV, p. 474).

actually given may have been on the whole confined to some special groups (see above), and rabbinical circles may have expected it only in the future eschatological times,[75] but the learned Pharisee should have been alert enough to ask himself who could have dared to propound such doctrine. But he is completely at a loss (cf. v. 9).

Since Judaism, with its views on the Spirit and the new creation, provides sufficient basis for Jesus's statements to Nicodemus, there is no need to have recourse to Hellenistic concepts. No doubt, readers living in a Hellenistic milieu could also be reminded of "rebirth" in the mystery religions, of "birth in the spirit" (νοῦς!) in Hermetic Gnosis and so on,[76] but they must also have recognized the fundamental differences in the Christian doctrine.

3:6 τὸ γεγεννημένον ἐκ τῆς σαρκὸς σάρξ ἐστιν, καὶ τὸ γεγεννημένον ἐκ τοῦ πνεύματος πνεῦμά ἐστιν.

What is born of the flesh is flesh, and what is born of the Spirit is spirit.

The impossibility of man's attaining the kingdom of God by his own powers comes from the essential difference between the two realms of being, σάρξ and πνεῦμα. Man belongs, by virtue of his earthly birth,to the region of the σάρξ, and the divine and heavenly world of the πνεῦμα is beyond his reach. In Johannine thinking, the nature is determined by its origin, as appears from the frequent εἶναι ἐκ, which affirms both origin and type of being.[77] It is sometimes used simply to characterize moral attitudes (cf. 8:44; 1 Jn 3:8), but in the present passage it clearly designates two different orders of being. He who is born of the flesh is essentially merely "flesh", and only he who is born of the Spirit is of the nature of "spirit" and hence (as is implicitly said) able to enter the higher (vv. 3, 7), heavenly (cf. v. 13) and divine sphere (cf. εἰς τὴν βασιλείαν τοῦ θεοῦ v. 5).[78]

---

[75] Here *Midr. Ps.*, 14 is instructive, where the fulfilment of the promise of the outpouring of the Spirit in Ezek 36:26 and Joel 3:1 is expressly reserved for the world to come (see Billerbeck, vol. II, pp. 615f.); so too *Ex. Rabbah*, 41 (98a), according to which the evil urge incites men to idolatry in this world, while in the future God will expel the evil urge and give them a heart of flesh, according to Ezek 36:26 (Billerbeck, vol. IV, p. 847f.). It seems as if it were precisely this belief in the evil urge which hindered faith in a change of heart (by the Spirit) in the present, see Billerbeck, vol. IV, pp. 482f. and 913f. and the texts noted there.

[76] See Schnackenburg, *Letters of Saint John*, excursus viii; on the mystery cults, see also Wagner, *Das religionsgeschichtliche Problem von Römer 6, 1–11.*

[77] 3:31; 8:23, 44, 47; 15:19; 17:14, 16; 18:36f.; 1 Jn 2:16, 21; 3:8, 10, 12, 19; 4:1–3, 4–6; 5:19. On the connection between "to be born of God" and "to be of God" see Schnackenburg, *Letters of Saint John*, excursus viii, 1; xii.

[78] In the MSS the thought is explicitated by various additions. After σάρξ ἐστιν, 161 it^{codd} sy^{c} Tert add ὅτι ἐκ τῆς σαρκὸς ἐγεννήθη; after πνεῦμά ἐστιν, e a ff^{2} j m z (sy^{c}) add *quia Deus spiritus est*, and a j (sy^{c}) *et ex Deo natus est.* An early commentary, and a correct one.

Hence follows the necessity of the man "born of the flesh" being also "born from above" (v. 7). The reader has been prepared for this line of thought by 1:13, where human birth as a result of natural urges and desires is also contrasted with "birth from God".

What is the origin of this opposition between the realms of "flesh" and (divine) "Spirit"? It is not the (Platonic) dualism within man, which divides the bodily and sensual from the spiritual and mental, but the contrast between the transitory existence of the human creature on earth and the inviolable power of the absolute, spiritual life of God. The σάρξ in this sense is incapable of helping man to attain his true and eternal life; this can only be done by the divine πνεῦμα (6:63). The Johannine contrast between "flesh" and "spirit" differs from the Pauline, in so far as it does not envisage the propensity of the flesh to sin, but concentrates on its creaturely impotence.[79] At first sight, it seems to approximate to Gnostic thought,[80] but on closer inspection fundamental differences appear. Above all, the Gnostic believes that he is by nature possessor of the divine πνεῦμα, as the spark from the divine in the gloom of his earthly existence. It is the authentic kernel of his being, which he has to "know" in order to be divinized again.[81] In Christian teaching, however, the πνεῦμα is bestowed (sacramentally) on man and is superadded to his human, "fleshly" being. The Johannine contrast between the two realms has an initial counterpart in the O.T., as for instance when Gen 6:3 says, "Then the Lord said, 'My spirit shall not abide in man for ever, for he is flesh'", or when Is 31:3 says, "The Egyptians are men, and not God; and their horses are flesh, and not spirit"; cf. also Job 34:14f. Though "spirit" in Gen 6:3 and Job 34:14f. means the breath of natural life which comes from God (cf. Ps 104:29f.), the underlying thought is that permanent life is only with God, who is "spirit" in a pre-eminent sense (Is 31:3). The full reality of "spirit" is promised to man only in the last days (Ezek 11:19; 36:26; Joel 3:1f.). The weakness and unreliability of the "flesh", the human impotence and dependence on God implied in the "flesh", are often spoken of.[82] This way of contrasting the human and the divine spheres is expressed even more strongly in late Judaism and also appears in the texts of Qumran. The dwelling-place of the divine glory is hidden from all flesh (*1 QS*, 9:7); "flesh", the creature of clay, dare not compare itself to God and his deeds (*1 QH*, 4:29); there is no safety in the "flesh" but only in God (*ibid.*, 7:17); cf. also 8:31; 9:16; 10:23; 15:17; 18:21f. However, "flesh" is then also considered in its moral weakness, its sinfulness, and the formal contrast between "flesh" and (divine) "spirit" is hardly perceptible, since man continues to be considered as possessor of "spirit".[83] But the category of the heavenly and divine is more sharply

---

[79] On Paul, see Schauf, *Sarx.*, pp. 117–71; Schweizer, "σάρξ", pp. 131–4.

[80] See Reitzenstein, *Mysterienreligionen*, pp. 308ff.; Schlier, *Religionsgeschichtliche Untersuchungen*, pp. 130–5; id., "Der Mensch im Gnostizismus" esp. pp. 65f. Bultmann, p. 100, n. 4 says: "This is the understanding of σάρξ and πνεῦμα which is characteristic of Gnostic anthropology and has been adopted by John as well as by Paul." Schweizer, "πνεῦμα", pp. 393f., 414–9, 437f. is more critical.

[81] See Mussner, ΖΩΗ, pp. 123ff.; Schlier, "Der Mensch im Gnostizismus", pp. 75f.; Schweizer, "πνεῦμα", pp. 391ff., 437f.

[82] Cf. Ps 78:39; Job 6:12; 10:4; Is 40:6; Ecclus 14:17ff.; 17:30f.; 40:8f.; see also the texts cited by Ramón Díaz, "Palestinian Targum and New Testament", p. 79 from *Targum* Jerushalmi and Neofiti I on Gen 6:3, "I have given my spirit to the sons of man because they are flesh and their works are bad works."

[83] See Kuhn, "Die in Palästina gefundenen hebräischen Texte"; Nötscher, *Theologische*

opposed to that of the frail and earthly. John has gone a step further, inspired by his eschatological concept of πνεῦμα (cf. 7:39); here he approximates most closely to the primitive Christian contrast between σάρξ and πνεῦμα, as it appears in Rom 1:3f.; 1 Tim 3:16; 1 Pet 3:18b.[84]

3:7	μὴ θαυμάσῃς ὅτι εἶπόν σοι, Δεῖ ὑμᾶς γεννηθῆναι ἄνωθεν.	Do not wonder that I said to you, 'You must be born from above'.

After this consideration of the two spheres, it must be perfectly clear that earthly man must be born "from above", which means in fact being created anew out of the divine spirit of life; he cannot attain to God's heavenly world otherwise. Jesus finally returns to his thesis of v. 3 ("inclusio"), with an appeal to Nicodemus not to refuse the evidence of this truth, not to be astonished at it—a rhetorical phrase also used in 5:28; 1 Jn 3:13 and found in rabbinical and Hellenistic literature.[85]

3:8	τὸ πνεῦμα ὅπου θέλει πνεῖ, καὶ τὴν φωνὴν αὐτοῦ ἀκούεις, ἀλλ' οὐκ οἶδας πόθεν ἔρχεται καὶ ποῦ ὑπάγει· οὕτως ἐστὶν πᾶς ὁ γεγεννημένος ἐκ τοῦ πνεύματος.	The wind blows where it wills and you hear the noise but do not know where it comes from and where it goes. So it is with everyone who is born of the Spirit."

This does not mean, however, that the supernatural process has been explained or made comprehensible. It remains mysterious and impenetrable of its very nature. Jesus illustrates this for his hearer by means of an analogy which is based on the two meanings of רוּחַ and πνεῦμα, "spirit" and "wind". This is a short parable (as Chrysostom rightly saw, in contrast to other Fathers), as is proved by the following οὕτως. The central idea is that the wind is also a mystery as to its origin and goal, but it still remains a reality, perceptible by means of its sound ("voice"), recognizable through its effects. None of the elements which make up the picture should be interpreted on their own—the independence and unpredictability of the wind, its being perceived by the hearing, its origin or goal; the ὅπου θέλει is in fact taken up

---

Terminologie, pp. 85f.; Flusser, "The Dead Sea Scrolls and Pre-Pauline Christianity", pp. 252–63; Meyer, "σάρξ im Judentum", pp. 110–3.

[84] See Schweizer, "Röm. 1:3f. und der Gegensatz von Fleisch und Gesetz vor und bei Paulus"; id., "πνεῦμα", pp. 414f., 437.

[85] Rabbinical examples in Schlatter, *ad loc.*, Hellenistic in Bultmann, p. 109, n. 2 with supplementary fascicule; the aorist is more decisive than the present, cf. Funk, *Greek Grammar*, para. 337, 3: i.e. "Stop wondering" (cf. v. 4).

in the πόθεν and ποῦ, where it is explicitated and explained. The positive affirmation is that the wind blows of its own power, according to its own law. This is also true of the man born of the Spirit.[86] The origin and goal of the divine power bestowed on him, the nature and character of the process are divinely mysterious; but these powers are present, the divine Spirit is at work in him. And hence the Spirit is also recognizable through the effects which he produces in man. That the man born of God is recognizable as such is affirmed several times in 1 John. The children of God are identified by their freedom from sin, their holiness and their brotherly love (cf. 1 Jn 3:9f.; 4:7); in one place the divine Spirit himself is named as the sign of their union with God (1 Jn 4:13). Hence the phrase "the Pneuma blows where it wills" is not to be interpreted in terms of the freedom of God's election and call to grace and salvation, but as depicting, by means of the image of the wind, the supernatural process of salvation invisible to man which takes place at baptism and in which the Holy Spirit is at work. The allusion to the mysterious nature of the event implies that Nicodemus should abandon his probings and believe (v. 12).

Once we are satisfied that we are dealing with a parable, we can dispense with criticism of the imagery based on our superior knowledge of the wind, and we have not to look for a deeper meaning. No doubt the "whence" and "whither" recall the question which moved the Gnostics, where man comes from and where he goes, and the path of the "redeemer" who is conscious of his origin and his goal (cf. 8:14). But one has to do violence to the parable to bring it into line with Gnosticism. Must the verse really go back to "Gnostic tradition"? The image of the wind was already in use in Judaism to depict the incomprehensibility of God's providence, and the two meanings of רוּחַ were also played upon.[87]

3:9	ἀπεκρίθη Νικόδημος καὶ εἶπεν αὐτῷ, Πῶς δύναται ταῦτα γενέσθαι;	Nicodemus answered him with the words, "How can this be?"

Nicodemus, however, continues to brood on the matter, and asks for a definite explanation of the "how", or the possibility (πῶς in the Semitic sense[88]) of the miraculous event. He fails to see that in doing so he casts doubts on the power and wisdom of God and receives Jesus's words with incredulity, thereby reinforcing his own obtuseness (v. 4).

[86] Here ℵ it sy add (ἐκ) τοῦ ὕδατος καί, which is a supplement based on v. 5, but superfluous after the parable of the πνεῦμα.

[87] See Eccles 11:5, "As you do not know how the breath finds its way into the beings in the womb of the pregnant, so too you do not know the work of God who rules all things;" also the *Targum*: "You do not know how the wind blows" (Billerbeck, vol. II, p. 424). See also Prov. 30:4; *4 Esdr.*, 4:5, 9ff.; also Is 59:19; Ezek 1:4; 3:12.

[88] See J. Bauer, "Πῶς in der griechischen Bibel", esp. p. 84.

3:10	ἀπεκρίθη Ἰησοῦς καὶ εἶπεν αὐτῷ, Σὺ εἶ ὁ διδάσκαλος τοῦ Ἰσραὴλ καὶ ταῦτα οὐ γινώσκεις;	Jesus answered him with the words, "You are a (recognized) teacher in Israel and do not understand this?

Hence Jesus does not withold his reproof. Nicodemus, as an acknowledged[89] teacher of Israel, as an authority in scriptural scholarship, should, after all, have grasped what Jesus meant by birth from the Spirit (ταῦτα as in the preceding verse). He is obviously reminding him of the texts which speak of the action of the Holy Spirit in the last days (cf. commentary on v. 5). Jesus also appeals to the testimony of Scripture, or of Moses, in 5:39, 46f., without indicating particular texts. Scripture reveals its meaning only through Jesus's revelation; the promises are only seen clearly in the light of their fulfilment. This explains the ineffectiveness of the rabbinate; it needed and it lacked faith in the eschatological envoy of God.

3:11	ἀμὴν ἀμὴν λέγω σοι ὅτι ὃ οἴδαμεν λαλοῦμεν καὶ ὃ ἑωράκαμεν μαρτυροῦμεν, καὶ τὴν μαρτυρίαν ἡμῶν οὐ λαμβάνετε.	Truly, truly, I tell you, what we know, we speak, and what we have seen we bear witness to, but you do not accept our testimony.

With a solemn asseveration, Jesus, therefore, opposes to Nicodemus and his fellow doctors of the law (cf. v. 2, οἴδαμεν) the testimony of those whose knowledge is derived from immediate experience. This is the meaning of the two parallel expressions, both of which indicate progression, "what we know, we speak, and what we have seen, we give testimony to". It is first-hand and certain knowledge, which is derived from the immediacy of vision and when put into words becomes testimony addressed to others. The words and the style are typically Johannine (see commentary on 1:7 and 1 Jn 1:2); the only difficulty is the plural. Does Jesus mean only himself (cf. v. 32), or does he include his disciples (in which case the οἴδαμεν would correspond to that of v. 2) or—a possibility which must be weighed—is this an utterance of the later community, placed on the lips of Jesus for preference?

If one assigns the words only to Jesus, one can appeal to v. 32, which echoes v. 11 b–c almost word for word. Jesus would then be designating himself as the heavenly revealer in an absolute and exclusive sense, which would suit the context very well. He would be opposing his revealed knowledge to the defective knowledge of Scripture

[89] Examples of the use of the article stressing the subject as a well-known or representative personality, in Bauer, Schlatter, *ad loc.*; Funk, *Greek Grammar*, para. 273, 1: "the great (true) teacher".

possessed by the doctor of the law. But then how is the change to the plural to be explained? To vary the style? But an "editorial we", such as is usual in the epistolary style (see commentary on 3 Jn 9) would be out of place here. As a plural of majesty, to mark the speaker's consciousness of his high dignity?[90] But when the Johannine Jesus gives utterance to his full dignity he uses ἐγώ, and the only comparable text in the Gospel (9:4) is inapposite, because there Jesus is addressing the intimate circle of his disciples. In view of v. 2, one could consider the possibility of the disciples being included in Jesus's "we", as a counterpart to the collective "we" of Nicodemus. But then the assertion itself causes difficulties. The disciples are not primary bearers of revelation in the same sense as Jesus, and if one falls back on their experience of being "born of the Spirit", this is not true of Jesus in the same way. Thus a *pluralis ecclesiasticus* suggests itself,[91] either in the sense that a certain group of preachers speak (cf. 1 Jn 1:1–4; 4:14; see *The Letters of St John*, excursus i) or that the community as such joins in. Then one would have to suppose that the testimony bore above all on the experience of the "birth from the Spirit": what Nicodemus has not grasped or even suspected, in spite of his learning, has become a reality for the believing Christian community. However, it is highly questionable that the evangelist abandons so boldly the framework of the dialogue, especially as Jesus speaks at once again in the singular in the next verse.

The right way out of the difficulty may perhaps be found by taking bearings on 3:32 and 9:4. The first text gives the clue that 3:11 does not speak of the experience of the "birth from the Spirit", as shared by all later believers, but of the special revelation which Jesus, and Jesus alone, has brought from his direct "seeing" (and "hearing", v. 32) in heaven. The second text is important (9:4), because Jesus must primarily mean himself, but clearly takes in the disciples also: the "must" of the history of salvation—to work while it is day—affects his disciples as being inseparably linked to him and his work. When applied to 3:11 this means that the eschatological revelation which was only possible through Jesus is entrusted to the disciples to be carried on by them, so that when the earthly Jesus's lips are silenced, his disciples and messengers continue to proclaim the same revelation. In this sense, he can associate himself with them, and does in fact describe their work as the prolongation of his own (13:20; note the recurrence of λαμβάνειν; cf. also 15:20). This implies a certain departure from the framework of the dialogue, but a very slight one, more or less as in 4:38; 17:18. Jesus looks forward to the time when his disciples make his "testimony" their own, as part of their preaching.[92]

Thus Jesus confronts the representative of Jewish learning, with all the authority of the heavenly, eschatological revealer, whose revelation ("testimony") is also attested, and transmitted, by his disciples (along

---

[90] So von Harnack, "Das 'Wir' in den Johanneischen Schriften", pp. 106f.

[91] See von Campenhausen, *Die Idee des Martyriums in der alten Kirche*, p. 37, n. 2; Kragerud, *Lieblingsjünger*, pp. 101f. (on 1 Jn); Dodd, *Interpretation*, p. 328, n. 3: the testimony of Christ "mediated corporately by the Church".

[92] But the explanations of the "We" take many different forms. Some see it merely as an expression of the dignity of Jesus, cf. Schanz, Lagrange, Wikenhauser. Bultmann (p. 104) says it is to preserve the air of mystery, just as singular and plural vary in the Mandaean texts. Tillmann, Braun and Schick think it probable that the evangelist mingles his voice with that of the Master. The Fathers with their theological perspective saw the testimony of the Son as linked with that of the Father or the Holy Spirit or both. Later commentators (so too Hoskyns) heard therein the testimony of the prophets or John the Baptist; but then Jesus's unique claim would fail: Moses and John testify to him, but not with him.

with the Holy Spirit, cf. 15:26f.). But (καί *adversativum*, "and yet"),[93] this testimony is not accepted by Nicodemus and his fellows. Here the evangelist is passing judgment (cf. 1:10f.; 3:32; 5:43; 12:37); the cleavage is beginning to show itself (cf. 3:19; 9:39). Here in the dialogue, however, Jesus does not wish to condemn his interlocutor definitively, but merely to place him before a serious decision. A refusal would bar the way to further revelation (cf. v. 12).

3:12	εἰ τὰ ἐπίγεια εἶπον ὑμῖν καὶ οὐ πιστεύετε, πῶς ἐὰν εἴπω ὑμῖν τὰ ἐπουράνια πιστεύσετε;	If I speak of earthly things and you do not believe, how shall you believe if I speak to you of heavenly things?"

In what he has said hitherto, Jesus was merely putting before Nicodemus the initial elements of his revelation, or, as he now says, "speaking of earthly things". Since Nicodemus and the circle which he stands for already withhold their belief (the εἰ-clause is a real supposition), it is scarcely credible (πῶς) that they will believe if he speaks of "the heavenly things" (the ἐάν-clause is hypothetical). Before any attempt is made to define the meaning of the controversial τὰ ἐπίγεια and τὰ ἐπουράνια, it should be clearly understood that Jesus has already uttered "the earthly things" but that he envisages the revelation of "the heavenly things" as for the future, though still to come during his work as revealer on earth.[94] In the concrete, the teaching already given can only be the doctrine of the "birth from (water and) the Spirit", which must be taken in its entirety, and not just the parable of the "wind", for instance, which was used to exemplify the doctrine. This image is derived from "earthly" matters, and hence could be mistakenly identified with τὰ ἐπίγεια. But it is not proposed as an object of faith. What is meant is the whole fundamental doctrine that ("earthly") man must undergo a new creation by the divine Spirit if he is to take the first step towards salvation.

The content of the passage reminds us at once of the "degrees" in the knowledge of salvation which the N.T. speaks of elsewhere. Paul contrasts "milk" and "solid food" (1 Cor 3:2), and considers that the Corinthians are still "fleshly", immature and not yet capable of eating solid food, for which they would have to be "spiritual" (cf. 1 Cor 3:1f.). Still more significant is the contrast made in Heb 6:1f. between the "elementary doctrines" about Christ and "perfection", that is, the instruction given

---

[93] Cf. Funk, *Greek Grammar*, para., 442, 1; Zerwick, *Graecitas*, no. 314.

[94] Thüsing, *Erhöhung*, p. 257, understands by τὰ ἐπουράνια what Jesus utters through the Paraclete when he has ascended into heaven, "the revelation from heaven"; so too already Strathmann, *ad loc.* But apart from linguistic difficulties (the two expressions are, after all, the things spoken about) such a revelation, which merely discloses more fully the earthly revelation of Jesus, cf. 16:13, is promised only to the believing disciples.

to those whose faith is fully mature. The rudimentary truths comprise a number of things which are indispensable in Christian "initiation", including "instruction on immersions", which probably means the difference between Christian baptism and other rites of immersion. If the fourth evangelist had baptism and the necessity of baptism in mind at Jesus's answer to Nicodemus (see commentary on v. 5), must he not have comprised baptism and the rudimentary doctrines connected with it under the "earthly" things? No doubt he uses another terminology and this needs to be explained. But perhaps the comparison with Heb 6:1 enables us to pass a provisional verdict on the difficult expression τὰ ἐπουράνια; "perfection" in Heb is connected with Christian "fulfilment" (τελειοῦν), the definitive and effective entry into the heavenly world, to which Jesus has paved the way and which he has entered first (cf. Heb 2:10; 5:9; 7:28; 10:14; 12:23). Our attention is then drawn to the great discourse on the bread of life in John, where Jesus appears as the bread come down from heaven to impart his divine life to those who believe in him and partake of him in the Eucharist, whom he then leads to the heavenly world (cf. especially vv. 33, 51, 57, 62). The "heavenly" goal is at the very core of the Johannine doctrine of salvation (cf. 8:12; 12:32; 13:33; 14:2–6).

The general explanation of the terms "earthly" and "heavenly" is probably to be sought in the Johannine way of looking at things "vertically", which leads to the contrast between the earthly and the heavenly realms (cf. on ἄνωθεν, v. 3). But here it is not a matter of contrast but of degree. The "heavenly" surpasses and overshadows the "earthly", for which Jewish literature still remains the most likely source.

Wis 9:16 says: "We can hardly guess at what is on earth . . . but who has traced out what is in the heavens?" The contrast is brought out sharply in *4 Esdr.*, 4:21: "Those who dwell upon earth can understand only what is on the earth, and he who is above the heavens can understand what is above the height of the heavens"; so too *Sanhedrin* 39a: "You do not know what is on the earth. How should you know what is in heaven?"[95] These are merely formal parallels in terminology, since the texts in question only mean "natural" things when they speak of the "earthly" and are not thinking of truths of revelation. But (later) Jewish mysticism knew of earthly and heavenly mysteries which are revealed to Metatron. The *Hebrew Book of Enoch* (Odeberg, *Fourth Gospel*, pp. 29f.) says: "For the Prince of Wisdom and the Prince of Understanding have I committed to him, to instruct him in the wisdom of heavenly things and of earthly things, in the wisdom of this world and the world to come" (10, 5); "And there was nothing above on high nor below in the deep hidden from me" (11:3, *ibid.*, p. 31).[96] Among the rabbis too the antithesis "below—above" was equivalent to that of "this world—the world to come".[97]

No doubt the contrast "below—above" also played an important part in Gnosis. But the lower, earthly realm is deprived of all value, cf. *Odes of Solomon* 34, 4f.: "The likeness of what is below is that which is above; for everything is above; what is below is nothing but the imagination of those that are without knowledge" (see further, commentary on 3:31). There is no question of such an antithesis in Jn 3:12. For a similar notion Bultmann appeals to the "lesser" and "greater" mysteries in Gnosis, and other ways of expressing different degrees (*Johannes*, pp. 105f., n. 2).

---

[95] See Billerbeck, vol. II, pp. 424f.

[96] See further Odeberg, pp. 46f., 98ff.

[97] See Schweizer, *Erniedrigung und Erhöhung*, pp. 179f. See further excursus vi.

But then the terminology once more fails to correspond. For the passage from initial to advanced knowledge or degrees of enlightenment in faith, the passages from the N.T. cited above are much more apt than the Gnostic texts. This is not to deny the possibility of their having influenced each other in turn.

Thus no complete parallels to 3:12 have been found. The phrasing was probably invented by the evangelist for the occasion, and perhaps left vague deliberately. But we may still ask what exactly he meant by the "heavenly things" which were still to be revealed. Since they are a continuation of the theme of the "birth from the Spirit", the basic requisite for man's attaining salvation, he probably had in mind the mysteries involved in the fullness of salvation, the entry of man into the heavenly world. And in fact the Gospel still has essential matters to communicate on this point: Christ is the way to this goal (14:6), and it is only in union with him that the light of life can be attained (8:12). We meet again and again in various forms the same theme of the ascent of Christ (6:62; 20:17), of his return to the Father (13:1; 16:28), his "exaltation "(3:14; 8:28; 12:32) and glorification (12:23; 13:31f.; 17:1). But the theme is not only Christological. It is also soteriological, since in the same process salvation is conferred on us (12:31f.; 17:2), life and glory are bestowed on believers (6:62f.; 7:39; 17:24). It is essential to this revelation that the believer should be united to the heavenly envoy and guide to salvation and this point is also developed later, especially in the teaching on the "bread of life" which the believer must eat (6:32–58) and the "vine" in which he must abide (15:1–10). Thus, for the evangelist, the doctrine of the "birth from the Spirit", baptism, leads on to that of the Spirit-laden and life-giving gifts (cf. the Eucharist, 6:53–57), by which alone initiation into the mysteries of salvation is completed. The mystery of Christ and redemption, the way of Christ and our way to the heavenly world, Christ's action from heaven and his heavenly gifts—all this is indicated by the "heavenly things". It is not so much a question of any particular doctrine as of the whole way which Christ opened to the heavenly world. And this is the only key to the Johannine understanding of "entering the kingdom of God". But Nicodemus fails to understand even the first fundamentals. How then could he grasp the "heavenly things" which have not yet been disclosed?

The patristic interpretation (as the profounder mysteries of faith, the Trinity, Incarnation, divinity of Christ and so on) sees correctly that a progressive revelation must be implied, but does not keep it in line with the Johannine thought and the orientation of the dialogue with Nicodemus. The modern explanation, which sees the revelation of the "heavenly things" in the following verses (especially 13–15)[98] defines the content correctly in part, since the "exaltation of the Son of Man" is

---

[98] See Odeberg, pp. 72ff.; Bultmann, pp. 107f.

certainly included, but does not pay sufficient attention to the situation provided by the dialogue. It is also hard to imagine that Jesus would go on, after his sceptical question of v. 12, to disclose the "heavenly things" to the uncomprehending scribe. Our preliminary literary criticism (see above, pp. 361–3) has rather led us to assume that the dialogue ends with v. 12 and that vv. 13 ff. are part of a "supplement" of the evangelist, which must be treated in connection with the dialogue with Nicodemus.

The heavenly revealer and bringer of life: the Johannine kerygma—a supplement (3:31–36, 13–21)

Jesus's last words to Nicodemus (v. 12) are a question which suggest many lines of thought: the revelation brought by Jesus, the necessity of faith in this eschatological revealer and redeemer, and the actual behaviour of those who heard Jesus preaching his message and were challenged by it. The evangelist may well have followed up the dialogue with Nicodemus by a set of reflections or meditations which formed an answer to these urgent questions. His eye for the essential and his density of thought—not strictly logical but following meditatively the associations of words (cf. 1 John) could have produced such a connected and complete discourse as we think we can recognize in 3:31–36, 13–21. The Nicodemus episode was probably the occasion, as the many echoes in thought and language suggest (cf. before ch. 3), but the discourse—perhaps only a draft or summary of the thoughts to which it inspired him—ranges far beyond the situation of the nocturnal dialogue. The discourse may be said to be a condensation of the principal assertions of John and the Johannine theology. We have the central affirmation of the coming of the eschatological revealer—the sending of the Son by the Father for the salvation of the world which he loved; the "way" of this redeemer back to heavenly glory by the Cross; his summons to men to follow him in faith and the need for decision which is thereby imposed on men; and along with this "kerygma", a verdict on the actual behaviour of men, which is in effect a new summons, a warning and an appeal to the contemporary hearers of the message (cf. 1:10–13; 12:37–43). Thus the discourse contains in brief all that the evangelist had at heart in the composition of his Gospel (cf. 20:31): a retrospect of the great and singular event of which he tells, a clear vision of the men for whom he writes; interpretation of history and summons to his contemporaries, testimony and kerygma.

It may also be asked whether it is meant to be a "revelation discourse" of Jesus himself (cf. 12:44–50) or a kerygmatic discourse of the evangelist. The style in which it is couched does not rule out the possibility that the evangelist wishes the lapidary phrases to be understood as Jesus's own words, since affirmations in the third person occur at times when Christ is speaking elsewhere, especially of the "Son" or the "Son of Man" (cf. 5:19–29; 6:32f., 53; 12:23f., 35f.; 13:31f.). It is noteworthy, on the other hand, that in the present section, 3:31–36, 13–21, the first person does not occur, that there is no solemn asseveration ("truly, truly, I tell you" as in 5:19, 24, 25) and above all no ἐγώ εἰμι (as in all the other great discourses). The ἐγώ εἰμι is characteristic of the style of the Johannine "revelation discourses", and its absence here can hardly be explained by the mystery in which the whole is supposed to be shrouded—"the air of mystery" which it is said to have.[99] But perhaps the alternative, "revelation discourse of Christ" or "kerygmatic discourse of the evangelist" is falsely put. If our explanation of the "we" in 3:11 is correct, the evangelist has taken up the heavenly testimony of the eschatological revealer and transposed it into his testimony as preacher. For the contemporaries of the evangelist, it is the words of Jesus which are still audible in the words of the authorized witness enlightened by the Holy Spirit (cf. 15:26f.; 16:13f.), and from this point of view the "revelation discourse" of Jesus merges into the kerygmatic testimony of the evangelist. Thus the question whether Christ or the evangelist speaks becomes secondary. We have here the Johannine kerygma which to the mind of the evangelist is none other than the revelatory testimony of Jesus.

3:31	Ὁ ἄνωθεν ἐρχόμενος ἐπάνω πάντων ἐστίν· ὁ ὢν ἐκ τῆς γῆς ἐκ τῆς γῆς ἐστιν καὶ ἐκ τῆς γῆς λαλεῖ. ὁ ἐκ τοῦ οὐρανοῦ ἐρχόμενος ἐπάνω πάντων ἐστίν.	He who comes from above is above all men. He who comes from the earth is earthly and speaks earthly things. He who comes from heaven is above all men.

The discourse begins by contrasting him who "comes from above" with him who "comes from the earth". The former can only be Jesus, the heavenly witness and revealer (v. 32), the one beloved "Son" of the Father (v. 35, cf. vv. 16f.), the Son of Man who has come down from heaven (v. 13). He is "above all" others, that is, all the inhabitants of earth, who belong to the realm "below" (cf. v. 12) and hence are at the mercy of human weakness and deficiencies (cf. "flesh" v. 6). The ἐπάνω keeps to metaphor of ἄνωθεν, and πάντων must be a masculine, on account of the masculine which takes it up immediately. But the spatial category implies a judgment of rank and value. He who is "above all" others is superior to them, in principle, by virtue of origin, unrestrictedly and absolutely. Since the heavenly figure is in the singular, one might be

[99] Bultmann, p. 93.

inclined at first to take "him who is from the earth" also as an individual; but the emphasis is on the uniqueness of the heavenly revealer, and the πάντων brings in at once the whole of the human race on earth, so there is no difficulty in taking "him who is from the earth" generically. It means men in general, who are inferior to him and dependent on his revelation. Since they are of "earthly" origin, they are also earthly in nature, orientated and restricted in thought and language to earthly possibilities. The expression εἶναι ἐκ is not tautological, but brings out the two meanings of ἐκ, origin and type, with the origin determining the type (cf. v. 6). In nature and powers, "he who is from above" and "he who is from below" are sharply opposed, separate and mutually exclusive. Similar sharply dualistic terms are used later by Jesus when addressing the unresponsive Jews, and by the author of 1 Jn when speaking of heretics (4:5). Possibly ἐκ τῆς γῆς is not so negative as ἐκ τοῦ κόσμου (τούτου); but the distance is great enough. The dualism or contrast, however, is not metaphysical. The heavenly envoy comes to earth and gives all the earth-born the power to become "children of God" (1:12). By being "born from above," they can have access to the heavenly world (cf. 3:3, 5). The earthly realm is not treated as utterly valueless by nature, but merely in relation to the higher, heavenly realm, to which it is subordinated and ordained. It is fatal only for those who close their hearts to the revelation and offer of salvation "from above" and whose behaviour makes them prisoners of the realm "below" (see commentary on 8:23). This "dualism" is very far from being Gnostic, and remains in the line of Jewish thought, especially as it appears in the texts of Qumran.[100] The additional comment, "and he speaks earthly things", is remarkable,[101] and seems to refer to something definite. The deficiency of such unintelligent human discourse forms a contrast, no doubt, to the authoritative testimony of the revealer (v. 32) or his "speaking the words of God" (v. 34). But it is hardly there just to form a contrast which will point on to the next development. It is rather a reminiscence of a definite occasion on which such speech was heard, and from what we know of the passage, this must be the interventions of Nicodemus (3:4,9), which revealed an "earthly" way of thinking. If the whole kerygmatic discourse was conceived on the occasion of the dialogue with Nicodemus, the "reminiscence"

---

[100] See Huppenbauer, *Der Mensch zwischen zwei Welten*, esp. pp. 68f., 104f., who tries to present the sharp contrast between creator and creature as a "metaphysical dualism" (p. 10). But this way of speaking is better avoided, to eliminate the Gnostic negation of the earthly and material world, and to bring out the orientation of the whole man towards God in the Bible, his "openness" and receptivity for the divine being.

[101] Cf. Is 8:19 LXX where τοὺς ἀπὸ τῆς γῆς φωνοῦντας means ghosts—a merely verbal parallel.

is understandable, and Nicodemus is used to illustrate the principles now to be exposed (cf. also v. 12).

The older exegetes considered vv. 31–38 as the continuation of the words of the Baptist, vv. 27–30, a view which has been abandoned by most commentators (except Hoskyns), though an allusion to the Baptist is still often seen in the words "coming from the earth and speaking earthly things".[102] The redactors who put the passage here may have shared this view. And it would in fact have been a shrewd move in the contemporary struggle against the disciples of John to have placed these words on his lips, so that the humble precursor of the Messiah (v. 28), the friend of the bridegroom (v. 29) would himself have affirmed his inferiority to Jesus in the clearest possible terms. This, however, can hardly have been the intention of the evangelist. According to Jesus's statement in 5:33 ff., John was a witness to the truth, a burning and a shining light, and the evangelist was convinced that he was a man sent by God (1:6). The contrast in 3:31 would be too harsh for this. Further, the solution that the phrase "he who is from the earth" indicates in general all unauthorized propounders of revelation or all men, in so far as they are of earthly origin and nature,[103] is not satisfactory. Ultimately, no doubt, this is what is meant, but the marked contrast with one "who comes from above", without the immediate mention of "all", rather suggests a typical representative of such speakers.

The next sentence is typically Johannine in style, taking up a previous affirmation, varying it and elucidating it. "He who comes from heaven is above all" makes it perfectly clear that "from above" indicates a truly heavenly origin, by virtue of which the heavenly envoy's testimony is exclusively his own. And once more we hear that he is superior to all,[104] all others being obliged to submit to him. This kerygmatic summons (to faith) is what matters to the evangelist.

3:32	ὃ ἑώρακεν καὶ ἤκουσεν τοῦτο μαρτυρεῖ, καὶ τὴν μαρτυρίαν αὐτοῦ οὐδεὶς λαμβάνει.	He gives testimony to what he has seen and heard, and no one accepts his testimony.

The true revealer from heaven draws on direct knowledge and experience, described by the analogy of human "seeing" and "hearing", expressions used elsewhere by Jesus of the knowledge which he has gained with the Father and from the Father, though the terms only occur together here (cf. 1:18; 6:46; 8:26, 40; 15:15; the conjunction in 5:37 only refers indirectly to Jesus's knowledge). The words also indicate that Jesus is the recipient of revelation, though the Son's knowledge is

[102] See Bauer, Strachan, Barrett, Strathmann, Schick, *ad loc.*

[103] See Zahn, Lagrange, Braun, Bultmann, Wikenhauser, *ad loc.*

[104] ἐπάνω πάντων ἐστίν 2° *loco om.* ℵ* D 565 it sy^c sa arm; Tischendorf, Hort (marginal reading), Lagrange. Though the shorter reading gives a more forcible context, the longer is probably the original, since the repetition, which here plays the part of an *inclusio*, is Johannine in style.

not thereby restricted or his dignity lessened, since the Father, in his love for him, has placed "everything" at his disposal (v. 35). Behind such words we can sense the profound Christology of John and the mystery of the Trinity. The Johannine Jesus is conscious of his direct access to revelation. He knows that by virtue of his Sonship he is in primordial and assured possession of the truth which he proclaims. Hence he can affirm again and again that his doctrine is not his own, but that of "him who sent" him (7:16; cf. 8:26, 28; 12:49; 14:24). And since his revelation comes from immediate "perception", it takes the form of an act of testifying, an authentic and unwavering "testimony" (cf. 8:14). It is as reliable, therefore, as the testimony of eye-witnesses in earthly matters, more so indeed, since any possible error in sense-perception is excluded. What this heavenly witness discloses and attests is not only true, it is the divine truth itself (cf. 8:32, 40, 45; 17:17; 18:37), which is light (see commentary on 3:19), life (14:6) and the power that saves men. The function of Jesus's revelation as mediator of "truth" is indicated in this passage in v. 33: to accept his testimony is to confirm the "truthfulness" of God, in the twofold sense of the reliability of what is attested and what is promised, the truth of God's word, and God's fidelity to his word. When speaking of the heavenly testimony of the revealer, the evangelist deliberately puts his "seeing" first, because it expresses even more strongly than "hearing" the immediacy of the Son to the Father, and also because "hearing" leads on to the communication of the truth in words, an element which is always included in "testifying". This whole process of revelation, which stems from the intimate fellowship of the Son with the Father, and leads to the communication of saving knowledge to men by the Son who is sent into the world, is also expressed in another way, tersely and pregnantly, in 1:17. The difference of tenses, however ("to see" in the perfect, "to hear" in the aorist), is probably only to vary the style.[105] All this sounds very much like an exposition of theological principles, but the evangelist does not separate them in the least from historical experience. He always has concretely in mind the story he tells in the Gospel, looking back, of course, on the event as a whole: "But (καί *adversativum*) no one accepts his testimony." Even from this unique and supremely well qualified witness men have withheld and still withhold their faith. Jesus had said the same to Nicodemus, in such a way ("we" and "you") as to include the later preachers who accepted and handed on his testimony. The rejection of Christ's revelation has become for the evangelist a heart-rending fact, and one which has been constantly experienced since the days of Jesus (cf. 15:20; 1 Jn 4:5).

---

[105] Funk, *Greek Grammar*, para. 342, 2 take it differently; but see on 1 Jn 1:1.

3:33 ὁ λαβὼν αὐτοῦ τὴν μαρτυρίαν ἐσφράγισεν ὅτι ὁ θεὸς ἀληθής ἐστιν.

He who accepts his testimony, confirms that God is truthful.

But with an abrupt change of perspective, which is a characteristic of Johannine thought and style (cf. 1:11 with 12; 8:15 with 16; 12:37 with 42), the evangelist now speaks of those who accept the testimony of the heavenly revealer. Though the world is impervious to the message of God's eschatological envoy, there are still some who welcome his enlightening and saving words. They are the community of believers, which thus appears as a group attentive and obedient to God in the midst of the multitudes who are enslaved by the "earth" and the world (cf. 1:12f.; 10:14, 27; 11:52; 17:6, 20; 18:37d). This community is addressed, and each member of it is urged to remain steadfast in his acceptance of Jesus's revelation. By accepting the message, he confirms as it were with his "seal"[106] that God is behind it and that his words do not deceive or disappoint. God's truthfulness guarantees the truth of the testimony and the certainty of the promise of salvation. To accept revelation is to give God glory and to allow his word to be effective. The very similar passage in 1 Jn 5:9–12 shows that this "existential" understanding of the text is both possible and necessary. To believe in the Son of God is to make the divine testimony one's own, permanently and efficaciously, and thereby to attain eternal life. To refuse to accept the testimony which God gives on behalf of his Son, is to disbelieve God and to "make him a liar". This is the negative counterpart to the positive formulation in our present text. The notion of testimony differs, no doubt, in each case, since 1 Jn speaks of God's testimony to his Son, while Jn 3 speaks of the divine testimony in the Son's revelation. But ultimately these are only two aspects of the same thing. In each case, to accept the divine testimony is to acknowledge God's claim and thereby achieve one's own salvation. Just as in 1 Jn 5:11 the content of the testimony is defined as being that "God gave us eternal life", in his Son, so too the thought of Jn 3:33 ff. culminates in the statement that he who believes in the Son—and hence accepts God's word, v. 34—has eternal life (v. 36). The Father speaks in the Son's revelation, which is of itself a valid testimony, but can still be considered as the two-fold testimony given by the Son and the Father (cf. 8:14 with 17f.). The testimony of God to which Jesus appeals (5:32, 37; 8:18) may be seen in Scripture or in the "works" which he is enabled to do; but it is also recognizable, and clearest of all in the very words he speaks (cf. 6:63; 7:17; 8:47; 12:47f.; 14:10b). As revealer, Jesus is most intimately united to his Father, and to disregard him is also to

[106] The image here simply means "to confirm", cf. Arndt and Gingrich, *Lexicon*, s. v. 2c. The confirmation which faith gives to God is explicit personal commitment.

disregard the Father (cf. 5:23; 8:50; 12:44f.). But to accept his testimony is to acknowledge the truth of God's words and the certainty of his promises, and thus to allow them to bear fruit.

3:34	ὃν γὰρ ἀπέστειλεν ὁ θεὸς τὰ ῥήματα τοῦ θεοῦ λαλεῖ, οὐ γὰρ ἐκ μέτρου δίδωσιν τὸ πνεῦμα.	For he whom God has sent speaks the words of God; for he sets no measure as he gives the Spirit.

The divine envoy is no more than God's spokesman, the mediator of his life-giving words to a world estranged from God, to a humanity on whom the anger of God has rested up to now (v. 36); for this very reason the call and the claim of this unique revealer and saviour cannot be disregarded. He speaks the words of God and no more, but he does so with full authority. Behind this is the old Jewish axiom, that a man's envoy is like himself,[107] which is attested for Jesus in the Synoptics (Mk 9:37; Lk 9:48; Mt 10:40) and also used by the Johannine Jesus, with even stronger emphasis (12:44f.; 13:20; cf. 15:21; 17:18; 20:21). But the legal principle here is the vehicle of a much profounder truth. The "envoy" is the "Son" (vv. 35f.) who is and remains most intimately united to the Father. The Father has not merely given Jesus authority to speak (12:49), he speaks himself in Jesus (cf. 14:10). The sender is here so completely one with the envoy that to "see" the latter is to "see" the former (12:45), to hear the words of Jesus is to hear the words of God. Thus "speaking the words of God" with which God's prophets had been charged takes on a new and unique meaning on the lips of the eschatological envoy, the "Son", as the evangelist has profoundly grasped in the light of his Christology. This is the key to the following clause, "for he sets no measure as he gives the Spirit". God gives the Spirit in unlimited fullness to this last envoy, who speaks the words of God as no one has done before. The rabbis were convinced that the prophets received the Spirit in different measures ("as weighed out").[108] But the testimony of the Baptist has already affirmed that the Spirit descended on Jesus at the baptism, to remain fully active upon him (1:33f.). Jesus has the perfect fullness of the Spirit, and hence he can "baptize with holy Spirit" (1:34), speak words which are Spirit and life (6:63b, cf. 68), and impart the Spirit to believers, as from a superabundant source (7:39).

Hence it has sometimes been thought that the subject of the clause is not God[109] but his envoy, who speaks his words and with them pours out

---

[107] See Billerbeck, vol. I, p. 590, and vol. II, p. 558.

[108] *Ibid.*, vol. II, p. 431, and Schlatter, *ad loc.*

[109] After δίδωσιν, 𝔎 D Θ pm a ff^2 vg add ὁ θεός; sy^c ὁ πατὴρ . . . τῷ υἱῷ.

the Spirit superabundantly.[110] In view of the explanatory particle (γάρ) one would then have to interpret as follows: that he speaks the words of God is recognizable from the fact that he imparts the Spirit in (eschatological) fullness. This is of course true and in line with Johannine thought (cf. also 1 Jn 3:24; 4:13), but does not seem to be directly asserted here, where the evangelist is proving that God speaks in the words of his envoy (vv. 33, 34a). And this is precisely the point which is elucidated in the clause in question, which says that God himself makes the words of his envoy inspired and divine words through the fullness of the Spirit bestowed upon him. V. 35 goes on to say that God (the Father) has placed "everything" at his disposal, that is, the whole truth which is to be revealed. The "everything" of v. 35 corresponds to the "without measure" of v. 34. By bestowing on his envoy the fullness of the Spirit, God has entrusted to him the fullness of salvific knowledge which is to be revealed to men, so that it only remains for men to believe in the Son to attain eternal life (v. 36). Taken in this way, the verses give us a deep insight into the Christological and "trinitarian" thought of the evangelist. That which unites the Father and the Son for the Son's work of revelation and salvation is the Spirit, whom the Father communicates fully to the Son, and whom the Son pours out in his words for the salvation of men—even though the Spirit is only given in fact after Jesus's glorification. It follows that the other thought, already expressed by Origen, is also implied: "The redeemer who is sent to speak the words of God does not give the Spirit only in part."[111] This is a "trinitarian" thinking which remains centred on the history of salvation and can still consider the "Spirit" as God's gift to the Messiah, enabling him as the perfect bearer of the Spirit to bestow "baptism in the Spirit" on men (cf. 1:33). There is no reason, therefore, to excise τὸ πνεῦμα (not found in B* sys) as a "non-Johannine addition".[112]

3:35	ὁ πατὴρ ἀγαπᾷ τὸν υἱόν, καὶ πάντα δέδωκεν ἐν τῇ χειρὶ αὐτοῦ.	The Father loves the Son, and has placed everything in his hands.

The reason for the total communication of the Spirit is the love of the Father for the Son. When the evangelist comes to speak of the unfathomable mystery of Jesus's union with God, he always uses the absolute "the Father" and "the Son", because this is the only way in which he can

---

[110] So Origen, *In Joh.*, Frg. 48, Cyril of Alexandria, Lagrange; cf. Dodd, *Interpretation*, pp. 310f., 410 (who is inclined to it, but does not decide).

[111] *In Jo.*, Frg. 48.

[112] Bultmann, p. 119, n. 1.

indicate the ultimate metaphysical source of the common thought and action of God and Jesus. Here he stresses the love of the Father (as in 5:20; 15:9f.; 17:23f., 26), because it is of the nature of love to give and to give without measure (cf. 3:16; 13:1; 14:31; 1 Jn 3:1, 16f.; 4:10). The perfect δέδωκεν is either timeless, like the present δίδωσιν in v. 34, or envisages the act of loving and giving by which the Father entrusted "everything" to the Son as he sent him into the world. The Semitic phrase, "to give something into the hands of another"[113] means in general the conferring of power and authority. In the mission of Jesus, this ultimately means the salvific "power over all flesh" which is given to the Son and becomes effective after his glorification—the power to give eternal life to the men entrusted to him (17:2, cf. 13:3). But this presupposes his authority as revealer, which discloses the way of salvation to those who are receptive to it. As in 13:3, the statement is couched in the most general terms, to comprise the whole process of salvation, from the giving of revelation to the giving of life by the Son. Hence, too, it is unnecessary to find overtones of ancient cosmological and mythological speculations in the phrase[114] or to take this Johannine logion on the Son as a re-interpretation of an original "Son of Man" logion, which spoke of the Lord of spirits giving him power to judge.[115] It is rather the Johannine way of expressing the authority and "equipment" of the revealer and redeemer as he is sent into the world, and the terms "Father" and "Son" point to the authentic Johannine origin. In terms of Christology, it should be noted that the phrase does not speak of the immanent self-communication of the Father to the Son within the Trinity, but of the giving of knowledge and power when the Son is sent as saviour, although on profounder consideration the former appears to be the presupposition of the fullness of knowledge and power communicated to the Son. What the Son possesses in a unique manner from the Father—knowledge of the Father's being (cf. 17:6), life (5:26, cf. 6:57) and glory (17:5, 22)—he can transmit to those who believe in him, so that they may partake of it after their fashion. We hear, as it were, an answer to this in the words of the Logos hymn: "We have all received of his fullness" (1:16).

3:36 ὁ πιστεύων εἰς τὸν υἱὸν ἔχει ζωὴν αἰώνιον· ὁ δὲ ἀπειθῶν τῷ

He who believes in the Son has eternal life, but he who diso-

[113] It is "old Hebrew" (Schlatter, *ad loc.*, with instances). The change from ἐν τῇ χειρί (3:35) to εἰς τὰς χεῖρας (13:3) is irrelevant; the underlying Hebrew is בְּיַד.

[114] Cf. Bultmann, pp. 119f., n. 3. The previous "the Father loves the Son", i.e., the personal relationship in keeping with Johannine Christology, makes any mythological reminiscence unlikely from the start.

[115] Schulz, *Untersuchungen*, pp. 126f. That "the apocalyptic Son of Man" became "the

υἱῷ οὐκ ὄψεται ζωήν, ἀλλ' ἡ ὀργὴ τοῦ θεοῦ μένει ἐπ' αὐτόν.	beys the Son shall not see life, but the anger of God remains upon him.

The kerygmatic summons which results directly from this is: "He who believes in the Son has eternal life." Faith, as understood by John, is all that is needed on the part of man, if he is to share the promised salvation of the revealer, but it is faith in the revealer himself, because he is bearer and mediator of the divine life. The synoptic summons to "repent" and to "believe in the Gospel" (Mk 1:15) is repeated in John, in as much as the Johannine "faith in the Son" involves obedient submission to the saviour from heaven (cf. the contrast in v. 36b), acceptance of his revelation and commands (cf. the λαμβάνειν in 3:11, 32f.; 12:48; 17:8; also 8:31, 51; 15:7, 14) and the "following" of Jesus (8:12). The "repentance" (of which John does not speak) by which men turn from sin and from all that is opposed to God, and turn to God and the doing of his will, takes place when they unite themselves with the Son who leads them out of the darkness of this world into the heavenly world of light and life (cf. 12:46; 14:3, 6). Thus what the Johannine faith primarily produces is union with the person of the revealer sent by God, and hence salvation. The "soteriological principle", which recurs again and again in one form or another,[116] gives expression to this truth. And this is the essential difference between Gnosis (in the sense of Gnosticism) and faith. Through Gnosis, man turns in upon himself; through faith, he is united to the redeemer. In the Hermetic Gnosis we read: "He who knows is both good and pious and already divine" (*Corpus Hermeticum* X, 9); in Christian faith, however, the believer adheres to the Son of God who has come into the world (πιστεύειν εἰς αὐτόν) and who is his way and bridge to heaven. John always uses the verb to speak of "faith"—ἡ πίστις occurs only in 1 Jn 5:4. Faith is not something abstract, but a vital, personal attitude (cf. excursus vii).

But this faith which unites the believer with Christ the Son of God brings with it the immediate assurance of salvation: he who believes in him "has eternal life" (cf. 20:31). The ζωὴ αἰώνιος which in the Synoptics is still a purely eschatological concept, reserved for the future (Mk 10:17 parr.; 10:30 parr.; Lk 10:25; Mt 25:46) becomes in John the gift of present salvation. The adjective αἰώνιος, which is sometimes omitted, characterizes rather the intrinsic quality, the divine nature of this true life, though it also implies the permanence and indestructibility of something that lasts "for ever" (6:51, 58; 8:51f.; 11:26), since this is

---

Hellenistic Son of God" (even before John) is an unwarranted assumption, and that John took over such (freshly minted) Son of God logia is even less likely.

[116] 3:15f.; 5:24ff.; 6:40, 47; 8:12, 51; 11:25f.; 12:46; 14:6, 10f.; 20:31; 1 Jn 5:13.

also a quality of this true, divine life.[117] Many reasons can be adduced for his projection of the Johannine eschatology into the present. The decisive reason behind the basic "soteriological principle" is certainly the Christological. Salvation is present in Christ to the believer, the divine life is immediately accessible in him. This is indicated by the ἐν αὐτῷ of 3:15 (which is to be referred to ἔχῃ . . ., see *ad loc.*), and by the ἐν τῷ ὀνόματι αὐτοῦ of 20:31. With Christ and his person, through him and his mediation, the believer gains the divine life which he has lost. By believing "in him", by "receiving him" as the personal bearer and mediator of divine life (1:12; cf. 5:43; 13:20—a Johannine expression), he enters into fellowship with him and allows himself to be led back by him to fellowship with the life of God.

This does not mean that faith must be in the nature of an act of personal confidence in Jesus as Saviour.[118] The decisive element is rather the acceptance of his testimony or revelation (3:33). But the personal union with "the Son" brought about by faith remains the essential presupposition of the assurance of salvation: he who "has" the Son "has" life (1 Jn 5:12). In this Christological perspective the actual details of the application of salvation, which include baptism and the Eucharist, are not directly contemplated, any more than the question of whether the earthly Jesus already gives life (without the sacraments) or only the exalted and glorified Lord (cf. 7:39; 17:2). The important thing is that to bind oneself to the Son in faith is to take the decisive step, and to "pass from" the realm of death into the realm of divine life which Jesus throws open (5:24; cf. 1 Jn 3:14). In Jesus the eschatological hour has come (5:25; cf. 4:23), salvation is there, the divine life is present (cf. 1 Jn 1:2), and the one "work" demanded is to believe in this eschatological envoy and saviour (cf. 6:29). By believing in him man attains salvation at once and for all eternity, and hence the present tense of "has eternal life" is to be taken strictly. It is not merely a promise, though it is also a promise since this life is of unfailing power (cf. the ἕξει of 8:12; also 1 Jn 2:25). It is not affirmed, on the other hand, that the believer on earth already possesses the perfection of life, so that it is impossible to speak of an eschatological future. The assertions about the present possession of divine life are perfectly compatible with those which speak of a future "resurrection to life" (5:29), on the last day, when Jesus raises up those who believe in him (6:39, 40, 44, 54). The Johannine notion of life demands that the whole man, including his body,

---

117 On the statistics of the usage see Mussner, ΖΩΗ, pp. 48f.; on the significance of the attribute see Sasse, "αἰών", pp. 208f.; Mussner, pp. 177f.

118 On the nature of Johannine faith see Schnackenburg, *Der Glaube im vierten Evangelium*, pp. 1–21; also excursus vii below.

should attain to divine life, as is also presupposed in 11:25f.; 12:25, and not just that the immortal "soul" should live with God. The oneness of life of the risen Jesus with his own (cf. 14:19) is realized gradually, first through the meeting of the disciples on earth with their risen Lord, then by their coming to the place where he is (cf. 12:26; 13:36; 14:2f.; 17:24), and finally by their own resurrection. But the decisive factor is the transition to the realm of divine life, which takes place in faith in the Son.

The second part of the verse illustrates the same truth from the negative side, in keeping with the Johannine style (cf. 3:18; 1 Jn 5:12 etc.), and thereby makes the kerygmatic call more urgent. Unbelief is disobedience to the Son and means exclusion from the realm of divine life. "Not to see life" is the same as "not to see the kingdom of God" (cf. 3:3) and recalls the synoptic "enter into life" (Mk 9:43, 45 par.). As long as and in so far as men in their unbelief reject the bringer of life, they cannot now and in the future share in the life of God.[119] To persist in unbelief is to remain in death—worse, it is to remain under the judgment of God. The "anger of God" rests upon those who disobey the Son. In the O.T. and Judaism the term occurs frequently and in various forms, but it is used by John only here, in the sense of God's eschatological judgment being already at work. Here too we can see how all decision is transposed into the present, according to the special eschatological viewpoint of John. The unbeliever passes judgment on himself by the very fact that he does not believe in the one person who can rescue him from disaster, from the sphere of darkness and death (cf. 3:19ff.). Through his own fault, Jesus's mission of salvation becomes his doom (cf. 9:39ff.), the word of revelation and life becomes his judge (12:48). The hour of decision which has been brought about for all men by the coming of the eschatological Saviour, becomes for the unbeliever the hour of condemnation, which the future judgment will only make manifest (cf. 5:29). At the same time a division is brought about among men, between believers and unbelievers (cf. 3:19), which confirms the verdict of God on the "world" which has turned away from him (cf. 9:39). From a somewhat different viewpoint, John is expressing what Paul has to say about the two-fold function of the "evangelium"—to save and to judge, to reveal both salvation and the anger of God (Rom 1:17f.). Both speak of a "present" judgment, which is in fact the eschatological verdict of God[120]—a judgment which the revelation brought by Jesus or the preaching of the Church does no more than make

[119] The future may be considered as logical (in so far as the participle contains a condition) or as temporal (in so far as the state of estrangement continues); in fact both elements are connected.

[120] On the present and future character of the divine wrath see Stählin, "ὀργή", pp. 430ff.; MacGregor, "The Concept of the Wrath of God in the NT", esp. pp. 104f.; Blank, *Krisis*, pp. 74f.

manifest, since it already rested upon mankind in secret. Paul goes on to develop his kerygmatic call to pagans and Jews alike (Rom 1–2), while John addresses each individual whom the word of the revealer and life-bringer "from above" reaches. In both, humanity is inexorably and finally placed before the decision as to whether it will believe or not in the only saviour, whether it will accept the salvation offered by God or make his verdict of death come true.[121]

3:13 καὶ οὐδεὶς ἀναβέβηκεν εἰς τὸν οὐρανὸν εἰ μὴ ὁ ἐκ τοῦ οὐρανοῦ καταβάς, ὁ υἱὸς τοῦ ἀνθρώπου.

And no one has ascended to heaven except him who has descended from heaven, the Son of Man.

The second part of the kerygmatic discourse makes a fresh start, but still links up with (καί) the first part, which spoke of the heavenly revealer "coming from above", by saying that no one has ascended to heaven except him who has come down from heaven. The object of the eschatological revelation is not to give instruction on the hidden things of heaven, but to mediate salvation, which consists in gaining access to the world of God, the heavenly kingdom of light and life (cf. 3:3, 5). This thought had already been led up to by vv. 35 f., where the mention of the unrestricted power of the Son (vv. 35 f.) to give eternal life to believers (v. 36 a) was already an adequate indication of the revealer's mission (v. 34). The ascent of the only envoy truly come from heaven continues this line of thought and puts the salvific intention of God in the sending of his Son beyond all doubt (vv. 16 f.). If, nonetheless, there is a "judgment", this is the fault and the effect of unbelief, since to refuse to believe in the unique Son of God is to condemn oneself (v. 18). First come the fundamental statements about the ascent of the Son of Man to the heavenly world, which led him, and had to lead him, through the "exaltation" on the Cross (v. 14), so that he could give life to all who believe in him (v. 15). It was not for his own sake that the Son of Man set out on his way of *katabasis* to this earth and *anabasis* to the heavenly world, but to accomplish God's universal salvific will with regard to a world doomed to death.

When one reads vv. 13 ff. in the context of this proclamation of salvation, one does not feel the difficulties which are posed for exegesis by the immediate collocation of vv. 13 and 12. The negation in v. 13 is generally taken to be apologetical, condemning the effort (of apocalyptic seers or Gnostics) to ascend to heaven and receive revelations of heavenly things. But the central idea, that the ascent takes place in order to receive revelations or to bring tidings from above, is not found here (contrast 1:18).[122] Hence

[121] For μένει M al be e sy^{p} Ir^{Lat} read μενεῖ. The uncertainty is due to the lack of accents in the majuscules (so too 14:17), the preference for the future to assimilation to ὄψεται.

[122] Lagrange (cf. also Zahn, Schick) tries to meet the difficulty by treating the phrase as a

other commentators understand the context to mean that Jesus now begins to disclose the "heavenly things" which were mentioned in v. 12—his own entry into the heavenly world and the ensuing possibility of believers' following him there.[123] The perfect ἀναβέβηκεν is taken either as the perfect in a general statement ("can ascend") or as an anachronism due to the standpoint of the evangelist. But it cannot be a general statement, since the aorist καταβάς makes the context historical,[124] and the Johannine Jesus never speaks anachronistically as a rule (the only possible exception is 4:38; see *ad loc.*). Nonetheless, the explanation is correct for v. 13, except that a later redactional collocation of v. 12 and v. 13 (due to the association between τὰ ἐπουράνια and "ascending", εἰς τὸν οὐρανόν) is more likely than a revelation of the "heavenly things" in the setting of the Nicodemus episode, especially after the sceptical question of v. 12.

The evangelist certainly understands the theme as part of the ἐπουράνια mentioned by Jesus at the end of the Nicodemus episode; but it is the continuation of the discourse on the envoy who "comes from above", who is referred to in the emphatic "he who has come down from heaven". He alone, who came down once in the course of history (aorist ὁ καταβάς), has really entered the heavenly world, and now dwells there continually (perfect ἀναβέβηκεν), at the goal of all longings for salvation. The designation of "Son of Man" at the end is fully deliberate, since this Christological title is used in John in connection with the thought of ascent (6:62), "exaltation" (3:14; 12:34) and "glorification" (12:23; 13:31). It also designates Jesus during his stay on earth (1:51; 9:35; 12:34), but from the point of view of his heavenly origin and his return to heaven for the full accomplishment of his saving work (cf. 6:27; 13:31). It is the earthly Jesus seen in the light of his future power of salvation. This "heavenly man", who merely ascends to "where he was before" (6:62), is enabled by his ascent to lead to salvation those who have joined themselves to him in faith, as is made still clearer in the following verse.

Thus the Johannine Son of Man concept is endowed with a significance and a richness beyond that of its origins (probably Jewish apocalyptic, cf. Dan 7:14 and Enoch) and which presupposes a development within the Christology of the Church. The most ancient Son of Man logia in the Synoptics point to his future coming in power (at the parousia), others include his work on earth, and others again the thought of his divinely-ordained suffering and death. But the future glory

---

"condensed expression": "No one has ascended to heaven (and brought tidings); only one (has brought tidings): he who has descended from heaven, the Son of Man"; but in the instances adduced by Lagrange, Jn 3:27; Mt 12:4; Lk 4:27; Rev 21:27 the matter, in which εἰ μή indicates the exception, has already been named.

[123] This explanation is ingeniously developed by Odeberg, pp. 72–98 and was taken over by Bultmann and Wikenhauser. The "earthly" theme of "birth from above" (foundation of salvation) is said to be followed by the "heavenly": entry into the heavenly world along with the Son of Man (fullness of salvation).

[124] On such general propositions cf. Funk, *Greek Grammar*, para. 344; the texts cited (including Rom 9:19) allow of no historical exceptions.

is never linked with pre-existence in the Synoptics, though pre-existence could have been suggested by Dan 7:14. Thus the Johannine concept, which includes the Crucifixion as "exaltation" and initial "glorification" (though omitting the express mention of the parousia as the "coming in glory" strictly speaking), represents the final and most mature development of the set of thoughts connected with this title. Cf. further, excursus v.

If the evangelist puts forward his "kerygmatic discourse" as his own testimony, in the name of and according to the mind of the revealer and saviour who has "returned home" in the meantime, the words "who is in heaven"[125] found after "the Son of Man" in many non-Alexandrine manuscripts could be original, referring to the Son of Man's remaining with God after his re-ascent, as in 1:18 (see *ad loc.*). But it is an unnecessary addition, and possibly a later gloss, though well supported in the textual tradition.[126] If the words are supposed to be uttered by the earthly Jesus, they raise difficulties. The Johannine Jesus does not speak of himself as being at once on earth and in heaven (not even in 1:51, see *ad loc.*), but reserves the ascent of the Son of Man and his glorification for the future (6:62; 12:23, 32; cf. 17:1).

The clause was adduced by many of the Fathers to prove the doctrine of the two natures in Christ. Augustine's comment is: "Hic erat carne, in coelo erat divinitate, immo ubique divinitate";[127] so too Cyril of Alexandria[128] and also modern exegetes.[129] But the title "Son of Man" remains linked to the history of salvation, as was perhaps sensed by the translators of the old Latin and Syriac versions who have "who was in heaven"[130] or "who is from heaven.[131]

3:14	καὶ καθὼς Μωϋσῆς ὕψωσεν τὸν ὄφιν ἐν τῇ ἐρήμῳ, οὕτως ὑψωθῆναι δεῖ τὸν υἱὸν τοῦ ἀνθρώπου,	And as Moses raised up the serpent in the desert, so too must the Son of Man be raised up,

The ascent of the Son of Man to heaven, the return of the Son to the Father (cf. 13:1; 16:28; 20:17) begins with his "exaltation" on the Cross, where its power to save believers is disclosed. Jesus himself says,

---

125 The words are omitted only by $P^{66\ 75}$ B ℵ L W 083 33 1241 sa Tat (according to the commentary of Ephraim and the cod. Ven.) Or Did Cyr. The editors are divided: the phrase is included in the text by Tischendorf, Weiss, Vogels, Lagrange (with hesitation), Bover; it is omitted by Westcott and Hort, von Soden, Merk. So too the exegetes: Schanz, Zahn, Schlatter, Bauer, Büchsel, Loisy, Hoskyns, Strathmann and Barrett are in favour of it; Tillmann, Bultmann, Wikenhauser, Schick and F.-M. Braun, with others, are against it.

126 All the strands of tradition attest it except the rather closely-knit Alexandrian group. From the variants, it would seem that the text caused difficulty, which would explain its omission. On the other hand, a gloss could easily have been composed on the model of 1:18.

127 *In Jo.*, tr. XII, 8 (*Corpus christianorum* 36, p. 125).

128 *In Jo. Ev.*, II (*PG* 73, col. 249).

129 Cf. Lagrange, Hoskyns.

130 e $sy^{c\ pal}$ (also Tat).

131 0141 sy^{s}.

12:32, "When I am raised up from the earth, I shall draw all men to me". The present text stresses the need (δεῖ) of this exaltation if all believers are to be given eternal life, and the crowd's answer to the words of Jesus just quoted contain a formulation of the very same type (12:34). This is all the more remarkable as the answer is supposed to reflect the words of Jesus (πῶς λέγεις σύ), though Jesus had not actually spoken in these terms (but cf. 12:23f.). It is legitimate to conclude that we have here a brief kerygmatic formula which the evangelist uses to express an important thought of Jesus, a Johannine counterpart, as it were, to the prediction of the Passion in the Synoptics (Mk 8:31 parr.), which also expresses the divinely-ordained necessity of the Cross in the history of salvation.[132]

This is also the easiest explanation of the present tense, where one would rather have expected an ἔδει, given the standpoint of the evangelist (cf. the perfect ἀναβέβηκεν in v. 13). The timelessness of the divine plan is unaffected by its execution in time. A similar timeless δεῖ is found in 20:9, where we read that after the actual resurrection of Jesus the two disciples at the tomb did not know ὅτι δεῖ αὐτὸν ἐκ νεκρῶν ἀναστῆναι. Hence the δεῖ does not make it necessary to assign these words to the dialogue with Nicodemus. Even if the discourse comes from the evangelist and is meant to be taken as such, the rule that Son of Man logia only occur on the lips of Jesus is not infringed, since the evangelist is thinking in any case of a saying of Jesus (cf. 12:34).

If v. 14b reflects in "Johannine" form a standard theme of ancient Christian preaching (based on Jesus's own testimony), it is very instructive with regard to Johannine theology. First we have the typological application of the story told in Num 21:8f., from which the motif "as Moses raised up the serpent in the desert" is taken. This piece of typology, which was frequently echoed in post-Apostolic times,[133] occurs only here in the N.T. and is probably derived from the evangelist's own theological reflection.[134] The example of Cain, to illustrate the hatred that is equivalent to murder, is given in 1 Jn 3:12, 15 in a similar type of sentence (καθώς-clause), and is likewise unique. But what is the "typical" element in the incident in the desert? In the O.T. narrative, the brazen serpent is fixed to a stake (strictly, a "sign") by God's command, for the Israelites to look at, to enable them to survive in spite of being bitten by the snakes. John exploits three points which he sees as intrinsically connected: the "ex-

---

132 Cf. Grundmann, "δεῖ", pp. 24f.

133 *Barnabas*, 12:5–7; Justin, *Apol.*, 60; *Dial.*, 91; 94; 112; Tertullian, *Adv. Marc.*, III, 18; Cyril of Jerusalem (*PG* 23, col. 797); Gregory of Nyssa (*PG* 44, col. 413). But this typological interpretation offers many variations and modifications, cf. Daniélou, *Sacramentum futuri*, pp. 144ff.

134 Contrast Manson, "The Argument of Prophecy" who (following J. Rendel Harris) supposes the existence of a primitive Christian collection of *Testimonia*. These cannot perhaps be excluded for really "Messianic" texts, but in this case it is improbable that John had any such collection before his eyes. Wis 16:5 and the rabbinical treatment of Num 21:8f. (cf. Billerbeck, col. II, pp. 425f.) are no real preludes to Jn 3:14f.

altation", its salvific power and the divine plan behind all (δεῖ). The other features should not be interpreted allegorically. The point of the comparison is neither the stake nor the serpent, but the "exaltation". And this is linked with the thought that salvation for many comes from this "exaltation". Even the fact that the mortally wounded "look upon" the stake is not mentioned, and hence can hardly be exploited in favour of a theory of the meaning of "faith". (At most, one could compare the "looking upon" the pierced body of Jesus in 19:37). Rabbis and Jewish mystics speculated on this "looking".[135] John does not do so, and hence does not allow us to confine "faith" to confidence of salvation *(fides fiducialis)*.

By considering the Crucifixion, in the light of this typology, as a salvific "exaltation", which also becomes the "glorification" of the Son of Man (cf. 8:28; 12:34 with 12:23; 13:31), the evangelist takes a most important step in Christology. In earlier Christian theology, the Crucifixion marked the lowest point of humiliation, which was only followed later by the "exaltation" which led to Jesus's installation as Lord at the right hand of God (cf. Acts 2:33–36; 5:30f.; Phil 2:8–11).[136] But John sees the Cross itself as "exaltation", as the beginning of the salvific Lordship of Christ (cf. the two-fold νῦν in 12:31 and the κέκριται of 16:11), as the "glorification" by the Father, which is manifested in Christ's power to give life to all who belong to him (cf. 17:1f.). John does not speak of a Son of Man who is going to a Passion and death which would be a "humiliation", as do the Synoptics; for John, the Pauline "scandal" of the Cross is not overcome only by the subsequent resurrection, but by the majesty and saving power

[135] Cf. *Mishnah, Rosh ha-shana*, III, 8b: "Does a serpent kill, or does a serpent give life? On the contrary, when the Israelites were wise with regard to the things above and when their hearts served their Father in heaven, they were always healed." The Jewish mystics explained looking at the serpent as looking upon evil in order to turn away from it and direct their hearts to God, cf. the examples in Odeberg, pp. 108f. In spite of a similarity of terminology, to "raise oneself" and "contemplate" the good (spiritually) in *C. Herm.*, IV, 5, 11b (cited by Odeberg, p. 100) is something quite different, and brings out, in fact, the fundamental difference between Gnostic "vision" and Christian "faith". Bultmann too recognizes that the notions of the Gnostic sect of the Ophites concerning the serpent have nothing to do with the Johannine typology (p. 109, n. 1).

[136] The "Exaltation" Christology of these texts is not, however, connected with the "Son of Man" but with Ps 110: 1, the installation at the right hand of God and the title of Kyrios (cf. Acts 2:33–36; only the title of Kyrios in Phil 2:11). How far there is a connection with "Son of Man" is highly controversial, cf. Cullmann, *Christologie*, pp. 178–84, 190f.; E. T.: pp. 179–88, 192; Schulz, *Untersuchungen*, pp. 104–9; Schweizer, *Erniedrigung und Erhöhung*, pp. 33–38 (has recourse to the notion of the "just man" humiliated and exalted, cf. 21–33); Hahn, *Christologische Hoheitstitel*, pp. 112–25 (against any original connection between "Son of Man" and "Exaltation", the latter being mainly derived from Ps 110:1, cf. pp. 126–32). The line of Christology developed in the text was also seen by Vergote, "L'exaltation du Christ en croix selon le quatrième évangile", esp. p. 23; on the exact development of the thought in John see Thüsing, *Erhöhung*, pp. 31–35.

of the Cross itself. The "hour" fixed by the Father for his death (cf. 7:30; 8:20), on which his gaze is fixed (cf. 12:23; 13:1; 17:1), is now—in contrast to the Synoptics (cf. Mk 14:41; Lk 22:53)—only superficially the hour of darkness (cf. 13:30) and of disturbance (cf. 12:27). In reality it is the hour of his passing from this world to the Father (13:1) and the hour of his glorification (12:23; 17:1). The impulse to this new interpretation of the "raising up" as "glorification" may have been found by the evangelist in Is 52:13, where it is said of the Servant of the Lord that ὑψωθήσεται καὶ δοξασθήσεται σφόδρα. Since this text is also probably behind Phil 2:9, we can observe how it has been developed in the scriptural theology of John, who has also enriched it with the typology of the brazen serpent. Though the "exaltation" also means the Crucifixion, the Crucifixion itself, in the Johannine perspective, is already so rich in theological meaning that it at once implies the "glorification".[137]

3:15	ἵνα πᾶς ὁ πιστεύων ἐν αὐτῷ ἔχῃ ζωὴν αἰώνιον.	that all who believe may have in him eternal life.

Salvation is effected by the Son of Man raised up on the Cross and by him alone. When he is "raised up from the earth" he will "draw all" to himself (12:32). The certainty of his work of salvation is founded on God's plan (δεῖ, v. 14), the goal of which (ἵνα) is the giving of life to believers. It is also assured by the union of the Son with the Father who having been glorified through the Son, now glorifies him by giving eternal life to all who have been entrusted to the Son (17:2; cf. 13:31f.). That the Son of Man becomes mediator of salvation is expressly said in the words ἐν αὐτῷ, which do not depend on ὁ πιστεύων but on ἔχῃ, and are placed before it for emphasis. The indication of the object of faith by ἐν would be completely singular in John, who always uses πιστεύειν εἰς. (The dative τῷ ὀνόματι is used in 1 Jn 3:23, the only certain instance). It would also be an exception in the whole usage of the N.T., apart from Mk 1:15. But ἔχειν ἐν occurs several times in the Johannine writings (14:30; 16:33; 20:31; cf. 1 Jn 4:16). "By him" and "in him" the believer gains eternal life, that is, through his person and through fellowship with him.[138] The Son of Man is his guide to salvation, on whom he can rely, though not juridically (contrast 14:30) or in any merely superficial sense, but because he has been given fellowship in his life (cf. 15:4–7; 17:23; 1 Jn 2:24; 3:24; 4:13). Hence the ἐν also indicates this intrinsic union or leads up to it, cf. 1 Jn

---

[137] Contrast Thüsing, pp. 3–12 ("The only content of the Johannine ὑψωθῆναι which can be ascertained with certainty is, therefore, the crucifixion of Jesus", p. 12).

[138] This ἐν should not be taken in a purely "mystical" sense; even in 20:31 the ἐν τῷ ὀνόματι αὐτοῦ still points to the person of Jesus Christ, or stresses that life is imparted through union with him in faith (πιστεύοντες).

5:11, which says that the eternal life given us by God is present for us "in his Son". In the arrangement of the text suggested in these pages (vv. 13ff. after vv. 31–36), the hearers had already heard (v. 36) that he who believes in the Son has eternal life. Now they learn how this is possible. By joining himself to the Son of Man, by giving himself to the Son and being united with him, the believer receives eternal life from him who has been crucified and glorified.

This point is eliminated by the variants which give a personal object to πιστεύειν instead of reading ἐν αὐτῷ,[139] though πιστεύειν often occurs in John without any object being expressed.[140] Given the Christological character of Johannine faith, this is not surprising. The context often shows where faith is to be directed, and it is always orientated to Christ, the Son (of God), even where it has a special meaning (as for instance in 20:8, 25, faith in the resurrection of Jesus). Further, πιστεύειν by itself is used for preference to designate Johannine faith in the full sense (cf. 1:7; 4:41, 53; 5:44; 6:36 etc.).

Emphasis is also laid on "eternal life". Just as the serpent "raised up" in the desert saved bodily life by God's will, so too the Son of Man raised up on the Cross gives eternal life to his own (for "eternal life" see commentary on v. 36). This notion of rescue is taken up in the following section.[141] — *See excursus v.*

3:16	Οὕτως γὰρ ἠγάπησεν ὁ θεὸς τὸν κόσμον, ὥστε τὸν υἱὸν τὸν μονογενῆ ἔδωκεν, ἵνα πᾶς ὁ πιστεύων εἰς αὐτὸν μὴ ἀπόληται ἀλλ' ἔχῃ ζωὴν αἰώνιον.	For God loved the world so much that he gave his only-begotten Son, so that none who believe in him may perish but may have eternal life.

In a sentence which has become memorable for all time, the kerygmatic discourse sums up the whole Christian message of redemption. The plan of salvation which is realized in the way of the Son of Man through the Cross into glory, stems ultimately only from God's incomprehensible love for the "world", that is, for the world of men, which is estranged from him, bereft of divine life and the object of his anger (cf. v. 36). God himself bridges the chasm caused by men's sin (so too Rom 5:8–10, using the concept of "reconciliation"). The best commentary is provided by 1 Jn 4:9f., which agrees with Jn 3:16 in form and content. There the central thought stands

---

[139] εἰς αὐτόν is read by ℵ Θ ℜ, many minuscules and most versions; ἐπ' αὐτόν by A; ἐπ' αὐτῷ by P^{66} L; ἐν αὐτῷ is attested by P^{75} B W N 083 al. c and some vg MMS. This last reading is rightly adopted by all modern editors.

[140] 1:7, 50; 3:12, 18b; 4:41, 42, 53; 5:44; 6:36, 47, 64; 9:38; 10:25f.; 11:15, 40; 12:39; 14:11b, 29; 16:31; 19:35; 20:8, 25, 29, 31b.

[141] The addition μὴ ἀπόληται ἀλλ' in D Θ Ψ pm lat sy^s is certainly an intrusion from v. 16; it does not fit in with ἐν αὐτῷ.

out still more clearly; that of the prevenient, merciful love of God, which takes the form of sending his only-begotten Son into the world and of delivering him up to death in expiation for sin. In the Gospel, the thought of God's immense love probably explains also the change from "Son of Man" to "Son", since the "Son" is the most cherished and precious gift that God can bestow upon the world. Hence the choice of words is certainly deliberate: "he gave" (ἔδωκεν) his Son, "his only Son", as the order of the words emphasizes. The translation "he delivered up" presupposes παρέδωκεν in the Greek, the standard term in early Christianity for Jesus's being delivered up to be crucified,[142] probably a reminiscence of the expiatory sufferings of the Servant of the Lord (Is 53:6, 12).[143] John only uses the compound verb for Judas's betrayal,[144] his ἔδωκεν is primarily intended to indicate the sending of the Son into the world (cf. v. 17), though this is, of course, the first act of the drama of the Crucifixion, the profoundest mystery of God's love (cf. 1 Jn 4:10). Thus the expiatory death, as the supreme manifestation of God's love, may already be implied, but the perspective has been shifted from the "exaltation" of the Son of Man to the entry of the Son of God into the "world". In the Johannine theology of incarnation and mission, the greatness of God's act is manifest in the very bridging of the chasm between God and the "world". Here, as whenever the mission of the Son is spoken of, the notion of "world" is neither quite neutral nor quite negative. The "world" is not simply the place where men live, but sinful mankind which has turned away from God. Still, it is not yet the specific term for mankind in so far as it rejects the divine envoy and pursues him with enmity and hatred. It is the "world" far from God and yet profoundly longing for him and sensing its need for redemption, the "world" which is the object of God's infinite love and mercy.[145] God has manifested this love (cf. 1 Jn 4:9) in a historical act (ἠγάπησεν), the mission of the Son and his delivery to death,

[142] So also many exegetes for 3:16, e.g., Schanz, Calmes, Loisy, Lagrange, Wikenhauser, Braun, Schick. Bauer is doubtful: "Has John perhaps taken over a saying which originally meant that God gave his Son to death out of love for the world, and filled it with his own spirit?" *(ad loc.)*.

[143] Cf. Büchsel, "δίδωμι", Schelkle, *Die Passion Jesu*, pp. 70–72; Romaniuk, *L'amour du Père et du Fils dans la sotériologie de s. Paul*, esp. pp. 88–95. Sometimes the simple form is found, but always in the phrase δοῦναι τὴν ψυχήν (Mk 10:45 par. Mt 20:28) or ἑαυτόν (Gal 1:4; 1 Tim 2:6; Tit 2:14; cf. 1 Macc 2:50; 6:44) or with ὑπέρ (Lk 22:19). For the Johannine usage of διδόναι see also 6:32, "My Father gives you the true bread from heaven". Jesus is *the* gift of God to mankind.

[144] 6:64, 71; 12:4; 13:2, 11, 21; 18:2, 5; 21:20; in a technical legal sense 18:30, 35, 36; 19:11, 16.

[145] On the concept of "world" cf. Sasse, "κόσμος", pp. 888f., 894ff.; also Schnackenburg, *Letters of St John*, excursus vi. On positive and negative assessment of the world Odeberg, pp. 115–29 offers copious material from rabbinical, Hermetic and Mandaean writings, and from the *Odes of Solomon*.

which are immovable facts of history, as is also indicated by the unusual indicative after ὥστε.[146] The Son is again described as ὁ μονογενής, as in 1:14 (see *ad loc.*). The only-begotten is also the uniquely loved. It is this Son, most intimately united to him and supremely loved,[147] his own and only Son, that God has given to the world to snatch it from destruction. The evangelist now describes still more fully (cf. v. 15) the purpose of God's loving act. It is the giving of "eternal life", which is supremely important and indeed indispensable, since it saves men from "perishing". The Johannine way of thinking in sharply-contrasted dualistic categories brings out the situation of man in full clarity: it is either "life" or "destruction", "rescue" or "judgment" (v. 17). Hence "destruction" is the same as judgment, eternal rejection. According to the Jewish notion, which is retained unchanged in the Synoptics, the place of destruction is Gehenna (hell), where the whole man, "body and soul", perishes in the state of death to which he is condemned (Mt 10:28). John takes up the expression "to perish" (cf. 17:12; also 10:10, 28; 12:25), but gives it a presential meaning, as he does with the correlative concept of "eternal life". Destruction already hangs over man (cf. v. 36) and he can only escape from his catastrophic situation by believing in the Son of God.

3:17	οὐ γὰρ ἀπέστειλεν ὁ θεὸς τὸν υἱὸν εἰς τὸν κόσμον ἵνα κρίνῃ τὸν κόσμον, ἀλλ' ἵνα σωθῇ ὁ κόσμος δι' αὐτοῦ.	For God did not send his Son into the world to judge the world, but that the world may be saved by him.

The evangelist explains further (γάρ) and emphasizes that the only purpose of the sending of the Son of God into the world was to save it. Is this typical Johannine antithesis (οὐ . . . ἀλλ' ἵνα)[148] merely to bring out still more strongly the saving love of God, or has it also a polemical or apologetical purpose? If one compares the Samaritans' exultant proclamation of "the Saviour of the world" (4:42) or the similar phrase in 1 Jn 4:14, it would seem that the evangelist is merely trying to win over the

[146] In the New Testament the only other occurrence is Gal 2:13; occasionally in classical literature, e.g., Epictetus, *Diss.*, I, 11, 4; IV, 11, 19 cf. Bauer, *ad loc.*; Funk, *Greek Grammar*, para. 391, 2; instances from the papyri in Mayser, *Grammatik*, vol. II, 3, p. 97, lines 6–10.

[147] For the precise meaning in 3:16 the Jewish parallels are important. Here Israel is called the "first-born" of God, cf. *Ps. Sol.*, 18:4, "Thy chastisement falls upon us as upon a first-born only son (υἱὸν πρωτότοκον μονογενῆ)"; *Ex. Rabbah*, 19: "R. Nathan (c. 160) said: As I made Jacob the first-born . . . so too I shall make the King, the Messiah, the first-born, see Ps 89:28, I will make him the first-born" (Billerbeck, vol. II, p. 426). The difference is that the Jewish parallels merely make a comparison and portray God's choice and love, whereas the real Son, uniquely beloved, is meant in John.

[148] Cf. 1:8; 9:3; 11:52; (without οὐ) 13:18; 14:30f.: 1 Jn 2:19. Cf. Schweizer, *Ego eimi*, p. 91 (no. 8); Ruckstuhl, *Literarische Einheit*, p. 194 (no. 8).

world, with all its apparatus of saviours and redeemers, by announcing positively to it the Christian message of salvation (see my commentary on 1 Jn 4:14). A polemical effort on the part of John to distinguish the Christian redeemer "from certain contemporary figures which put themselves forward as judges"[149] is most unlikely. We should rather suspect a defensive attitude in face of unbelieving Judaism with which Jesus is constantly coming into conflict in John; we hear the same tone on two other occasions (8:15; 12:47; cf. also 5:30; 8:26). Perhaps Jews of the time of the evangelist reproached Christians with the fact that Jesus reacted with harshness and threats of judgment when faced with the representatives of unbelief among his people. The universal salvific will of God, which is stressed here (ἵνα σωθῇ ὁ κόσμος) also distinguishes Christianity from Gnosticism, where salvation is confined to men capable of receiving it (the Gnostics).[150] In contrast to all forms of dualism John affirms that God wills the salvation and not the destruction of the "world", the well-being of all men and not just that of a privileged section.

3:18	ὁ πιστεύων εἰς αὐτὸν οὐ κρίνεται· ὁ δὲ μὴ πιστεύων ἤδη κέκριται, ὅτι μὴ πεπίστευκεν εἰς τὸ ὄνομα τοῦ μονογενοῦς υἱοῦ τοῦ θεοῦ.	He who believes in him is not judged. But he who does not believe is already judged, because he has not believed in the name of the only-begotten Son of God.

The notion of judgment is further elucidated in these verses and its special Johannine characteristics are brought out fully. The "realized eschatology" which is involved in the fact that the eschatological revealer and redeemer has already come,[151] is nowhere so palpable as here. Judgment takes place here and now, and is determined by faith or unbelief with regard to the only-begotten Son of God. But the thought of v. 17 remains dominant throughout. God for his part has no desire to "judge", but only to "save". If, nevertheless, there is a "judgment", this is only due to the refusal of men to believe in his Son. Judgment is only the dark, reverse side of God's eschatological act of love and redemption, and the unbelief which draws down judgment upon itself remain an impenetrable enigma with which the evangelist grapples again and again (cf.

---

[149] Bauer, *ad loc.*; he gives three examples of it and also three examples to the contrary. The strongest verbal parallel to Jn 3:17 is *Cornutus*, 16 (on Hermes as Logos): οὐ γὰρ πρὸς τὸ κακοῦν καὶ βλάπτειν, ἀλλὰ πρὸς τὸ σῴζειν μᾶλλον γέγονεν ὁ λόγος.

[150] According to *C. Herm.*, I, 22f., Poimandres comes only to the good and holds aloof from the wicked. The classification of men as "pneumatic", "psychic", and "hylic" belong to a later stage of Gnosticism, cf. Jonas, *Gnosis*, vol. I, pp. 212f.

[151] See on this point (and on the following in general) Blank, *Krisis*, esp. pp. 91–108.

3:19ff.; 5:39–47; 6:36–47; 8:23f.,43–47; 9:39ff.; 10:25f.; 13:37–43; 15:22ff.). "Judgment" is here used in the purely negative sense of reprobation, condemnation to punishment or death. This narrower sense, alongside that of judgment passed upon the good and the wicked "to render to every man according to his works" (Rom 2:6f.; cf. 2Cor 5:10; Rom 14:10) is already to be met with in early Christianity before John, and also in Judaism, under the form of the "wrath of God (in judgment)".[152] The new and disturbing element in the Johannine affirmation is that he who does not believe is already judged and remains (note the perfect) under sentence of death, finally, "eschatologically", as long as, and in so far as, he refuses to believe in the person of the Son of God as life-bringer and to accept life from him. Thus unbelief becomes self-condemnation. By taking this decision, man deprives himself of the "last" possibility of escaping from the realm of death (cf. 5:24). There is no parallel in rabbinical literature to this immediate eschatological "judgment".[153] Though the thought is given such terrifying urgency, its presentation in 3:18 must be carefully noted. First the promise of salvation is made to the believer. He "will not be judged", hence he never comes up for judgment (5:24; cf. 1 Jn 3:14). Only then is it said that he who refuses to believe is "already judged"; the reason given in 18b is also in the perfect, which indicates a persistent state. "Judgment" has taken place *ipso facto* by the act of unbelief. Thus the salvific will of God and the possibility of man's salvation preponderate, and the door is not closed even to the unbeliever. Whether and how long he remains in the sphere of death and condemnation depends upon man. To the very end the Johannine Jesus, in spite of all the disbelief he has met with, urges men "to believe in the light" as

---

[152] Cf. Mt 5:21f.; 12:18, 20 (= Is 42:1, 3 LXX); also Mt 7:1f.; 11:22, 24; 12:41f.; Jud 9; 2 Pet 2:11. The Bible prefers to speak in this case of the divine "wrath", cf. Mt 3:7 par. Lk 3:7; Rom 5:9; 1 Thess 1:10 etc. The concept and vocabulary can now be fruitfully studied in the Qumran texts, cf. *1 QS*, 2:15, "May the anger of God and the zeal of his judgment flame out against him unto eternal destruction"; 4:12f.; *1 QM*, 11:14, "and to show the justice of the judgment of thy truth among all the children of man"; also 6:3, 5; 11:16; 12:5; 14:5; 19:2; *1 QH*, 2:24; 3:27f., 4:26f.; *Dam.*, 1:2f.; 3:8f.; 5:16; 20:15. The usage of LXX is different, where κρίσις is mostly used to translate "right" מִשְׁפָּט (still found in Mt 23:23); cf. Büchsel, "κρίσις", pp. 942–3.

[153] The passage from *Gen. Rabbah* cited by Odeberg (p. 137) has only a remote resemblance: "R. Jannai and R. Simeon both said, There is no Gehenna; it is the Day that burns the wicked. . . R. Jehuda ben Elai said, Neither a Day nor Gehenna, but a fire that comes forth from the bodies of the wicked and burns them . . . (Is 33:11 follows as proof)." The Mandaean literature speaks both of the preservation of the elect from judgment and of the judgment passed by the wicked on themselves, cf. *Ginza*, 183, 11f.: "They shall be struck by their own blows and my blows need not strike them." See further Odeberg, pp. 135ff.; Bauer; Bultmann, *ad loc.* The notion was at least in germ in the dualistic thinking which dominated the epoch, but was Christianized by John by means of the antithesis of faith and unbelief.

long as they have it (12:36), and the unbelief of the crowds does not prevent some of them from coming to believe (cf. 12:42). The thought of judgment has become formally kerygmatic in John. It has become an immediate summons, challenging men to decision here and now. But John's kerygmatic thinking does not exclude a future judgment. The decision taken by the unbeliever will be formally ratified, before the eyes of the world, at the last judgment (5:29), by the Son of Man (5:27); or, as 12:48 says, the word of the revealer which the unbeliever rejected will be his judge on the last day. This is not an artificial harmonization, produced by an "ecclesiastical redaction" operating with the old "dramatic" eschatology. The present judgment does not deprive man of his further capacity to take a decision, though it can lead to the "hardening" of his heart (see commentary on 9:39 and 12:39f.), and it does not prevent God from completing his action in the future, by making his "judgment" manifest to all the world. The "anger of God" (v. 36) is not merely a way of describing the bleak and hopeless situation of man when he takes control of his own destiny. It is above all an affirmation about the rights and the power of the personal God, to whom man's whole life is subject, to whom he must account for all his actions, on whom he is dependent for his final destiny. But the Johannine theology can help to avoid too naive ideas of the "last judgment". It is nothing but the divine acknowledgment of the condition brought about by human decision, and the merciless disclosure of an existence long since vowed to destruction, already a victim of "death".

3:19	αὕτη δέ ἐστιν ἡ κρίσις, ὅτι τὸ φῶς ἐλήλυθεν εἰς τὸν κόσμον καὶ ἠγάπησαν οἱ ἄνθρωποι μᾶλλον τὸ σκότος ἢ τὸ φῶς, ἦν γὰρ αὐτῶν πονηρὰ τὰ ἔργα.	But this is judgment, that the light came into the world and men loved darkness more than light, for their works were evil.

From the fundamental insight, that the unbeliever pronounces the eschatological verdict on himself by his present decision, the evangelist turns (δέ) once more (cf. v. 16f.) [154] to the historical process and recognizes that men in fact have preferred darkness to light (aorist). "Darkness" appears here, as in 1:5b, as the personified power of evil, in contrast to the "light", which the "Son" really is in person—a usage also current in the texts of Qumran, except that there is nothing like the "Son" to correspond to the personal power of the "light", though the "Prince of lights" (*1 QS*,

[154] The movement of thought is typically Johannine: association of thought which takes up and develops further the last concept (κέκριται—κρίσις; so too vv. 19–20 φῶς); αὕτη—ὅτι is characteristic of Johannine style; the same form of transition in 17:2–3.

3:20) offers a faint resemblance. The evangelist has already spoken of his own sad experience (1:10f.; 3:11, 32). Now he expresses himself on the dark background of unbelief (vv. 19d–21). Such an attitude on the part of men means a judgment (κρίσις), [155] that very judgment (cf. the article, referring back) which unbelief itself brings about (v. 18). "Judgment" does not indicate, by a shift of meaning, merely the division among men following the coming of the light (though a division did take place); v. 19 deals only with men who have shut their eyes to the light, and the two classes of men become visible only when unbelief is explained (vv. 20f.). Jesus is not sent to judge the world (v. 17), and still the judgment is there (v. 17), an affirmation made even more drastic in 9:39, which says that Jesus has come "to pronounce judgment" (εἰς κρίμα). The meaning in both cases is that in fact, though not through his fault, a judgment is brought about by his revelation. But it is also affirmed indirectly in 3:19 ff. (as it is directly in 1:12 and 3:33) that there were some exceptions to the general attitude, some men who responded to the light (v. 21). The verdict of the evangelist in v. 19 is not meant to be purely historical; the judgment takes place (ἐστίν, not ἦν) wherever men prefer darkness to light and do not believe in the Son of God. "Men" (οἱ ἄνθρωποι) are envisaged, and not just the Jews of Jesus's time. The evangelist records his own and his communities' experience along with that of Jesus. The retrospect gives the impression that the judgment has already taken place. But this cannot mean that the punishment has already been inflicted, but only that a decision has been taken by which the men in question have placed themselves on the side of the "Prince of this world", on whom judgment has been passed by the death and victory of Jesus on the Cross (cf. 12:31; 16:11). The purpose of the evangelist is not to combat the traditional eschatology, but to display the personal responsibility of unbelievers and the horror of their act in its true colours. There is still a difference between the definitive verdict on the "Prince of this world" who is already "cast out" (cf. 12:31) and the judgment on unbelief, which only remains effective as long as unbelief persists (cf. 8:24) and never constitutes an irresistible compulsion (cf. 12:35f., 42, 46ff.). The verdict on past history goes hand in hand with the present call to decision, which is the real purpose of this kerygmatic discourse, as the ending (v. 21) also indicates. The coming of the light (more precisely, the fact that it has come—note the perfect) is still a perpetual challenge to men, asking then to choose faith and salvation or unbelief and judgment. As a revelation directed to believers, the discourse explains why the one bringer of salvation is confronted with so much unbelief, and also calls for the holiness of life without which no one "comes to the light". Echoes of the thought

[155] Cf. Arndt and Gingrich, *Lexicon*, s. v.; Büchsel, "κρίνω", pp. 939, 942f.

and language of parts of the prologue (or of the Logos-hymn) are unmistakable (cf. 1:4f., 9ff.), but the evangelist also evokes the exhortatory passages in 1 John, where a life "in the light" is demanded by faith and appears as its necessary consequence (1:7; 2:8–11).

Unbelief, the choice of "darkness" in preference to the "light", is attributed to the "evil works"[156] of men. There appears to be a certain tension between this "moral" explanation of unbelief and the passages which affirm that no one can come to Jesus unless the Father "draws" him (6:44), or unless it is "granted" him by the Father (6:65). But the contradiction is only apparent. Those who are granted the grace of faith are not deprived of personal responsibility for their decision (cf. 6:66–70). And it is not said that those who come to the light, with their works which are "done in God" (v. 21), do so by their own strength. The profound mystery of the cooperation of God and man in the act of faith is not fully illuminated by these lines of thought, which start from two different points of theological reflection. Jesus's revelation, that the Father "draws" to the Son everyone whom he "gives him" (6:37, 44), and the resulting theological insight, that faith is the free gift of God, are not called in question by an assertion on another level, to the effect that unbelief is due to moral fault. The reflections of 3:19ff. on the enigmatic rejection of the "light" by men are occasioned, in fact, by personal experience (v. 19b) and seek to explain how in spite of all God's efforts to save (v. 16f.) and the clear (v. 32) and unquestionable (cf. 8:45f.) revelation of the Son, men could still close their hearts to the "light". God for his part has done everything to save men from the darkness, and his envoy has manifested himself before them in his words and works (cf. 10:37f.; 15:22ff.). The fault can only be on the side of men. Their inexplicable "hatred" (v. 20; cf. 15:24) rises up from the abyss of a heart darkened by sin. It is the consequence of a total perversion and moral corruption.[157] When, on the other hand, v. 21 describes those who come to the "light" as men who have acted in accordance with God's will and are ready to display their works as "done in God", this does not mean that the ultimate grounds of their faith have been uncovered, but simply indicates that they were

[156] "Evil works" is a rare expression in the New Testament; elsewhere only Jn 7:7; Col 1:21; 2 Jn 11; cf. Heb 6:1; 9:14 "dead works"; 2 Pet 2:8 "lawless works". Still, it is "ancient Hebrew" (Schlatter, *ad loc.* also with rabbinical examples), as is now confirmed by the Qumran texts; cf. *1 QS*, 2:5 (evil deeds); 2:7 (darkness of your works); 4:23; *1 QH*, 1:27 (works of deceit) with many similar phrases. For the concept cf. *1 QM*, 15:9, "For they are a community of iniquity and all their works are done in darkness."

[157] Chrysostom, *Hom.*, XXVIII, 2f. stigmatizes the heathens' vices as the main hindrance to their conversion to Christianity (*PG* 59, col. 164) and then warns Christians against "vainglory" (κενὴ δόξα) as the most dangerous attitude of all (*PG* 59, col. 166). Augustine, *In Jo.* tr. XII (*Corpus christianorum*, pp. 128f.) stresses the need of repentance and conversion and also of confession of sins.

better disposed towards faith. V. 21 does not intend to provide a full and positive explanation of faith. Verses 20 and 21 should rather be taken as a unit, an explanation of the thesis that the "evil works" (v. 19c) are the culpable background of unbelief.

3:20	πᾶς γὰρ ὁ φαῦλα πράσσων μισεῖ τὸ φῶς καὶ οὐκ ἔρχεται πρὸς τὸ φῶς, ἵνα μὴ ἐλεγχθῇ τὰ ἔργα αὐτοῦ·	For everyone who does evil hates the light and does not come to the light, that his deeds may not be displayed as evil.

In explaining unbelief as due to evil works, the evangelist employs the opposition of light and darkness which he used symbolically and allegorically in v. 19 (cf. also 1 Jn 2:11). Christ, the light of revelation and life (cf. 1:4, 9) which enlightens the darkness of the cosmos (8:12; 9:5; 12:35f.), is hated and shunned by evil-doers. This is based on the thought of sunlight or the light of day (cf., in a different way, 11:9f.), which thieves and other criminals do not welcome, from fear of being detected. The same idea is often found in the O.T., and also in classical Greek literature.[158] The metaphorical use of "light" and "darkness" for good and evil is developed in late Judaism and becomes predominant in the texts of Qumran.[159] In Jn 3:20f. the allegorical language forms only a very transparent veil for the reality intended. He who does evil "hates the light", that is, Christ, the holy and sinless (cf. 8:46f.); he who has God for his father, must love him (cf. 8:42). At first sight, the evangelist seems to offer only a psychological explanation of unbelief. The evil-doer shuns the light for fear of having his works "displayed"[160] (in their malice). But underlying this psychological portrayal there is a deeper explanation of

[158] In the Old Testament: Job 24:13–17; 38:12f.; Is 29:15; Jer 49:9; Ps 11:2; 91:5; as yet hardly in a transferred sense, but see Prov 2:13; Is 5:20; cf. Aalen, *Licht und Finsternis*, pp. 71 ff.; for the profane usage see Bauer's parallels, *ad loc.*

[159] Cf. *Enoch*, 41:8; 58:6; 108:11, 14 (the spirits of the good, who belong to the race of light, and those who are born in darkness); *Syriac Apoc. Bar.*, 18:2; *Test XII*, *Nepht.*, 2:10; *Lev.*, 19:1; *As.*, 5:2f.; *Joseph*, 20:2; *Benj.*, 5:3, "Where there is reverence for good works and light in the mind, even darkness fleeth." Cf. Percy, *Untersuchungen*, pp. 66f.; Aalen, *Licht und Finsternis*, pp. 178–83. On the Qumran texts see also Nötscher, *Terminologie*, pp. 93ff. The Mandaean texts (esp. *Book of John*, Lidzbarski, pp. 203, 19ff.; *Ginza*, pp. 285, 30ff.) are based on the Gnostic concept of the world: the wicked bury themselves in darkness, sink into the depths, love the dwelling-place of darkness. But in this they are farther away from Jn 3:20f., cf. Percy, *Untersuchungen*, pp. 53f.

[160] 'Ελέγχειν is here used of evil works as φανεροῦσθαι is of good ones (v. 21). Thus it does not mean "examine" or "rebuke" but "bring to light", cf. Eph 5:11, 13; Ignatius, *Phil.*, 7:1; Hermas, *Vis.*, I, 1, 5; Diognetes, 2:8; so sometimes also in profane Greek (Arndt and Gingrich, *Lexicon*, s. v. 1). In Septuagint usage, where it mostly translates יכח, it may still have a forensic sense: the wicked are brought to justice for their crimes. Thus the mean-

the principles involved, which is developed by Jesus when speaking of children of God and of the devil (8:42–47). The men who reject God's envoy and his words are a different type of being, foreign to God (3:31; 8:23). When the light of revelation falls upon them, they themselves are unmasked for what they are, and not just their works. Thus their "hatred" has a psychological explanation and is also rooted in a profounder level of their being; it comes from a general attitude for which they are themselves responsible and which is totally corrupt. This is why they do not "come to the light", which in John is a synonym for "believing" (5:40; 6:35, 37, 44, 45; 7:37). In the same way, in 5:40–47, Jesus throws light on the hidden depths of the heart and unmasks the unbelieving Jews as men who do not seek God but their own vainglory, so estranged from God by nature that they cannot believe God's envoy.

3:21	ὁ δὲ ποιῶν τὴν ἀλήθειαν ἔρχεται πρὸς τὸ φῶς, ἵνα φανερωθῇ αὐτοῦ τὰ ἔργα ὅτι ἐν θεῷ ἐστιν εἰργασμένα.	But he who does the truth comes to the light, that it may be manifested that his works are done in God.

But the evangelist now turns from this gloomy picture. As frequently in 1 John, the bright picture of the opposing attitude is drawn against the dark background. "He who does the truth" comes to the light. This turn of phrase, which expresses morally good action done according to God's will, is Semitic, and is found several times in the texts of Qumran.[161] This "truth", which covers everything that belongs to God (cf. commentary on 1 Jn 1:8), is totally opposed to the "lie", the falsehood and wickedness which comes from the devil (8:44; 1 Jn 2:21; cf. also Rom 1:25; 2 Thess 2:9f.). Those who are loyal to God and strive to do his will (cf. 1 Jn 2:17b) have the disposition which also enables them to hear and accept the words of God's envoy, which are the truth as such, the truth that comes from God (cf. 8:43, 45 ff.). The truth of God is present in Christ (cf. 14:6), but only those are open to it who are "of the truth" (18:37; cf. 1 Jn 2:21; 3:19) and act accordingly.

In their own way, this is also what the members of the community of Qumran strive for. They describe themselves frequently as "sons (or servants) of the truth" (*1 QS*, 4:5f.; *1 QM*, 17:8; *1 QH*, 6:29; 7:30; 9:35; 10:27; 11:11), and the opposition between "truth" and "wrong-doing" is brought out particularly strongly at *1 QS*, 4:17, where we read: "Wrong-doing is an abomination to the truth, and all the ways

---

ing in John becomes transparent: the words of the revealer are judge (see on v. 19). Büchsel, "ἐλέγχω", p. 471, n. 8, prefers to keep "reprimand, correct".

161 *1 QS*, 1:5; 5:3; 8:2; cf. *1 QpHab*, 7:11f.; the same phrase also in 1 Jn 1:6 (see there, with further references). "Works of truth", except in the doubtful passage *1 QH*, 13:4, are linked only with God.

of truth are an abomination to wrong-doing". The division between those who behave according to the truth of God and the evil-doers is noted in *1 QS*, 5:10f. He who joins the community of those who have "dedicated themselves freely to his truth and to executing his good pleasure" must "separate himself from all men of iniquity". However, the "truth" is not considered as something within the reach of man, but as the gracious gift and revelation of God, particularly in the Thanksgiving Hymns. It is God who brings forth "the truth" of the upright (*1 QH*, 4:45), who purifies the just from their guilt so that "all their deeds may be in thy truth" (*1 QH*, 6:8f.) and strengthens the heart in his doctrines and his truth, so that they may be led along the paths of justice (*1 QH*, 7:14). It is difficult to decide how far man is predetermined, according to the sect, to walk in the "truth" or in wrong-doing (cf. *1 QS*, 4:24f.), but it is unlikely that personal responsibility is denied. Their mentality closely resembles that of John. On the "dualism" of "light" and "darkness", see commentary on 1:5.

The psychological point of view seems to be once more in the foreground: those whose actions are in accordance with God's will feel themselves drawn to the "light", so that their works may be clearly seen. But the underlying thought is that of "being of the truth", and, as at Qumran, the gratuitous character of faith is not thereby excluded. The main intention is to demonstrate the intrinsic connection between "doing the truth" and "coming to the light", but this final verse also contains an exhortation and a call to action. The point of the ἵνα-clause is not that the works of him who "does the truth" should be clearly seen, but that it should be clearly seen that they are "done in God", that is, in accordance with God and his will.[162] Under the light, that is, when the person and words of the revealer show everything in its true colours, it will be clearly seen that[163] these works are "true", that they are in conformity with God's nature. Theologically, this implies that there is a kinship between the "children of God" (cf. 11:52) and the Son of God sent as revealer and redeemer, and also that there is an intrinsic relationship between moral behaviour and faith—a fundamental conviction from which 1 Jn also argues (cf. 1:6f.; 2:3f., 9ff.; 3:14, 19; 5:2f.).

Thus the "kerygmatic discourse" has reached the end. The concluding sentences in particular prove beyond doubt that Nicodemus is no longer being addressed. It is a discourse which discloses and brings home the significance of the Christian revelation, but it is also a summons, a strengthening of faith and a moral exhortation. It is best understood as a proclamation composed by the evangelist which makes use of a lofty style such as is usual in a revelation discourse. It contains the whole

---

[162] The ἐν θεῷ which is singular in this connection, means either close connection with God, i.e. "in fellowship, in accord with . . ." (cf. Oepke, "ἐν", p. 535, 27ff.), or the norm, the regulating circumstances, i.e. "in keeping with God's will, in a manner agreeable to God", as is possible for the Hebrew בְּ (cf. Köhler and Baumgartner, *Lexicon*, s. v. 7; also Arndt and Gingrich, *Lexicon*, s. v. III, 2).

[163] As in 1 Jn 2:19, the ὅτι is factual and explicative, going with φανεροῦσθαι.

Johannine kerygma in succinct form. It is in the same terse and forceful language as we find in many passages of 1 Jn, with the same characteristics of thought and strong similarities of style. Only the copious exhortations in which the message is exploited and applied to the reader is missing in the Gospel. But the beginnings of such exhortation are there, and the latent intention of making the message a challenge and an obligation can be felt throughout. — *See excursus vi.*

CHAPTER V

Baptisms in Judea:
Last Testimony of John the Baptist (3:22–30)

This section takes up once more the thread of the evangelist's narrative. After his stay in Jerusalem for the Passover (2:13–25), during which the dialogue with Nicodemus took place (3:1–12), Jesus goes to Judea where he (or his disciples) baptize (3:22; 4:2). Some time later he leaves (4:1 ff.) and retires through Samaria (4:4–42) to Galilee (4:43–54). Jesus's working in Judea is mentioned only because it is the occasion of the complaints of John's disciples (v. 26) and hence for John's last testimony (vv. 27–30). This is the main object of the evangelist's interest. The topographical and historical details have often been called in question by the critics, but they are so concrete and so lacking in tendentiousness that there seems to be no reason why they should be fictitious. We may suspect that the evangelist used the testimony of John the Baptist to his disciples to confront the disciples of John in his own day, when they were vying with the preachers of Christianity (see commentary on 1:6–8 and 15). But the answer which the great desert preacher gave his followers, in his own and in a later day, is also of positive value for the evangelist's portrayal of Christ. This final testimony to Jesus as the Messiah is, in the mind of the evangelist, the legacy bequeathed by the great Baptist, the precursor of Jesus, to all later ages.

3:22	Μετὰ ταῦτα ἦλθεν ὁ Ἰησοῦς καὶ οἱ μαθηταὶ αὐτοῦ εἰς τὴν Ἰουδαίαν γῆν, καὶ ἐκεῖ διέτριβεν μετ' αὐτῶν καὶ ἐβάπτιζεν.	After that, Jesus came with his disciples into the land of Judea, and there he stayed with them and baptized.

"After that", certainly not long after the Passover week, Jesus goes with his disciples (cf. 2:12, 17, 22) to the Judean countryside (γῆ = χώρα, 11:54). The precise place is not mentioned. The scene of John's earlier baptisms was beyond the Jordan. Jesus probably stayed on the west bank, though he need not have tied himself to any particular spot.

During this period he was baptizing, that is, his disciples were, as the correction in 4:2 says. The remark is surprising, since the Synoptics mention only Jesus's command to baptize after the Resurrection (Mt 28:19; cf. Mk 16:16). One may not conclude either that the information is unhistorical or that Jesus had the same aims as John, till a separation came about.[1] The baptism of those who came to Jesus is not improbable in the context of the movement launched by John,[2] whose example Jesus may have followed: he always acknowledged the value of John's baptism (cf. Mk 11:30–33 parr.; Lk 7:29f.; Mt 21:32). But baptism must have meant something different to him. His message, as summed up in Mk 1:14f., goes beyond the eschatological call to repentance preached by John, since he understands his mission as something incomparably loftier and unique. And he does not act in common with John when baptizing. John had withdrawn to the north (v. 23). Jesus can have given this baptism merely a preparatory character; it meant only joining him and being ready to hear his call, which is why he soon gave it up altogether. The Fathers of the Church were already preoccupied with the significance of this baptism during the earthly work of Jesus.[3] It cannot be equivalent to the baptism of John, and neither can it be connected with the later Christian baptism. To the mind of the evangelist, it cannot yet be the baptism in the Spirit (cf. 7:39); and Jesus can hardly have practised a mere baptism of penance like John, since all our other sources are silent on the point. It would also have been contrary to the preaching of John, as understood by John (cf. 1:26, 33). From the way it is mentioned, however, no particular importance is attached to this baptism. It merely serves to introduce a dispute between a Jew and John's disciples. But it is also improbable that the evangelist has invented the baptism and the whole scene, merely to read a lesson to the followers of the Baptist in his own day.[4] Possibly some disciples of Jesus, coming as they did from the school of John, continued to baptize

[1] So Goguel, *Jean-Baptiste*, pp. 86–95; similarly Stauffer, *Jesus, Geschichte und Gestalt*, pp. 61–5, esp. p. 62: "At the very time that the Baptist was arrested as a fanatic for the law, his favourite disciple Jesus left him and broke officially with the law." Contrast Bornkamm, *Jesus von Nazareth*, p. 45, E. T.: p. 54, who says that Jesus did not begin his own work as a disciple of John and did not continue directly the work of the Baptist.

[2] Cf. Beasley-Murray, *Baptism in the New Testament*, pp. 67–71.

[3] Tertullian, *De bapt.*, 11, 4 (*Corpus christianorum* 1, p. 286) says that it cannot have been the Christian sacrament of baptism; so too Chrysostom, *In Jo. hom.*, 29, 1 (*PG* 59, col. 167). This, however, is the opinion of Augustine, esp. in *Ep.*, 44, 10 (Goldbacker, vol. II, 1–2, pp. 117f.) and *Ep.*, 265, 5 (Goldbacker, vol. II, 4, pp. 642f.), intent as he is on showing that Jesus himself baptizes when baptism is given (by the disciples). Many later theologians and exegetes followed Augustine (Maldonatus, Calmes, Belser, cf. Lagrange, *ad loc.*).

[4] Cf. Hoskyns, pp. 226–8: the evangelist is thinking of old Palestinian and contemporary Greek (pagan) baptisms, both of which he joins to contrast them with the "baptism in the

in the spirit of their former master in order to gain new followers for Jesus (cf. 4:1), and Jesus tolerated the practice. As they practised it, it remained a baptism of repentance, but at the same time, it admitted to the group of those who wished to join Jesus.[5] This type of baptism therefore would have had a character of its own, appropriate to the time of preparation for the public ministry of Jesus. Nothing is said, be it noted, of Jesus preaching or teaching. For the moment, Jesus is still gathering disciples. It is only when John is imprisoned that Jesus comes forward with his message before the people (cf. Mk 1:14).

3:23	ἦν δὲ καὶ ὁ Ἰωάννης βαπτίζων ἐν Αἰνὼν ἐγγὺς τοῦ Σαλείμ, ὅτι ὕδατα πολλὰ ἦν ἐκεῖ, καὶ παρεγίνοντο καὶ ἐβαπτίζοντο·	But John too was baptizing, at Aenon near Salim, because water was plentiful there and people came and were baptized.

In the fourth Gospel, the baptism of John also appears as a means of preparing men for fellowship with the Messiah and of moving them to follow him. The disciples who remained with John did not share this opinion, as is clear from v. 26; and according to many critics, neither did John himself. But in this case, the account of his bearing witness to Jesus as the Messiah must be dismissed as totally unhistorical (contrast Mt 11:2 ff.). No matter what critical view is taken, the relationship of the Baptist to Jesus remains unexplained and inexplicable.[6] It may, in fact, be problematical, historically speaking, but in the fourth Gospel it follows at any rate a consistent course. The Baptist continues his work; his service of the Messiah (cf. 1:31) is not yet ended. But he moves to another site a good deal further north. What impelled him to go? The evangelist seems to suggest that he did not wish to hinder Jesus from coming forward in the most important part of Judea, the country near Jerusalem. But the matter remains obscure.[7]

Aenon is indicated precisely as near Salim, which brings us, fairly certainly, to northern Samaria, south of Betshan. The name Aenon (probably the Aramaic *'enawan*, contracted to *'enān*) point to a place with springs, which suits the explana-

---

Spirit" given by Jesus (cf. 3:34!), though he does not thereby falsify history.—But Jesus permits his disciples to continue. Hence their baptism can hardly stand for Hellenistic practices of baptizing with water.

[5] So already Chrysostom (*PG* 59, col. 167): the disciples were to lead many to the saving doctrine of Jesus; so too many modern exegetes like Schanz, Knabenbauer, Lagrange, Tillmann, Schick, Strathmann, Beasley-Murray, *Baptism*, p. 72.

[6] Cf. Kraeling, *John the Baptist*, pp. 123–57, esp. pp. 145f.: the veil of history has been drawn tight and it is useless to try to lift it.

[7] Olmstead, *Jesus in the Light of History*, thinks that John the Baptist left the territory of Herod Antipas because of his quarrel with him. But then how did he come to be arrested?

tion that "water was plentiful there". Some eight miles south of Betshan (Scythopolis) there is, in fact, a group of five springs, of which the largest is called Ed-Der. This agrees with Eusebius (*Onomasticon*, 40), who puts Aenon eight Roman miles south of Betshan, and also knows of a place called Salim. Whether this Salim is to be identified with Tell er-Ridra or with Umm el-'Amdān which is nearer the springs,[8] does not matter. The place where baptism could be given is near where the road from Jerusalem to Betshan, via Samaria, dips towards the valley of the Jordan. This site is preferable to the present Salim east of Nablus (Neapolis, New Sichem).[9] The exact localization in 3:23 could be connected with the fact that later disciples of John continued to work there,[10] but this does not mean that the indication has been transposed from the time of the evangelist back into the time of Jesus.

Thus the place where John was baptizing was a good distance away from Jesus. People were still coming to him for baptism, but we are not told that he sent them to Jesus, which is strange in the context of the fourth Gospel. Even the fourth Gospel, therefore, displays John as working to some extent independently, even after the baptism of Jesus.

3:24	οὔπω γὰρ ἦν βεβλημένος εἰς τὴν φυλακὴν ὁ Ἰωάννης.	For John had not yet been imprisoned.

The remark interposed by the evangelist, that John was not yet imprisoned, is important for the relationship with the Synoptics. Everything here narrated took place before Jesus came publicly forward, as described in the Synoptics (Mk 1:14f. parr.). The fourth evangelist supposes that the end of John's life is known, and he only aims at putting certain matters in a certain light. This is also characteristic of his portrayal of Jesus's work.

3:25	Ἐγένετο οὖν ζήτησις ἐκ τῶν μαθητῶν Ἰωάννου μετὰ Ἰουδαίου περὶ καθαρισμοῦ.	A quarrel then arose between the disciples of John and one of the Jews, on the question of purification.

The next remark is also brief, and merely serves to explain why John's disciples complained to their master. In the context, all it can mean is that a Jew, perhaps from Judea where Jesus was baptizing (v. 22), had an argument with the disciples of John on the comparative values of the baptism of Jesus and that of John. This follows from the fact that we

---

[8] For the last named Abel, *Géographie*, pp. 142 and 447; Kopp, *Heilige Stätten*, p. 171 (after W. F. Albright), E. T.: *Holy Places*, p. 135: "As elsewhere on the plain, prospecting and excavating have not been carried out here either."

[9] Kopp, p. 172, with n. 146, E. T.: p. 136, n. 86. On the site of the two places in question cf. Wright and Filson, *The Westminster Historical Atlas to the Bible*, Pl. IX.

[10] So Kundzinš, *Topologische Überlieferungsstoffe*, pp. 25–7, 73–5.

then find the disciples of John (καὶ ἦλθον, v. 26) discussing the fact that Jesus is drawing greater crowds. They must have learned of this from the Jew in question. This Jew ("Jews" in several important MSS)[11] provoked the disciples to contradiction. They started the argument (ἐκ, "from the side of", cf. Arndt and Gingrich, *Lexicon*), which turned on "purification". If the sites of the two baptisms lay far apart, conjectures like 'Ιησοῦ or τῶν 'Ιησοῦ, which would involve the disciples of John in a direct conflict with Jesus or his disciples, are out of place. The remark would cause no difficulties in the Johannine narrative, were it not for καθαρισμός. Baptism is βαπτισμός or βάπτισμα (a word not used by John, however), and καθαρισμός designates Jewish ritual in 2:6. But in view of the fact that the fourth evangelist speaks of "cleansing" and "clean" when envisaging the effects of Jesus's words and deeds as realized in Christian baptism (cf. especially the overtones in 13:10f.; also 15:3; 1 Jn 1:7, 9), it is quite possible that he understood the subject of καθαρισμός (in general, without the article) as the question of the power of the various baptisms to confer intrinsic purity and absolve sins, especially as the word was well known to the early Church in this sense.[12] The background of contemporary history is again visible here; we catch a glimpse of the conflict between the Church and the disciples of John. Given the style of the fourth Gospel, there could also be a suggestion of the superiority of the new covenant over the O.T. and Judaism (cf. 2:6).

3:26	καὶ ἦλθον πρὸς τὸν 'Ιωάννην καὶ εἶπαν αὐτῷ, 'Ραββί, ὃς ἦν μετὰ σοῦ πέραν τοῦ 'Ιορδάνου, ᾧ σὺ μεμαρτύρηκας, ἴδε οὗτος βαπτίζει καὶ πάντες ἔρχονται πρὸς αὐτόν.	They went to John and said to him, "Rabbi, the man who was with you beyond the Jordan, the one to whom you bore witness, there he is baptizing and everyone is going to him."

The disciples of John complain of Jesus's successful baptizing but without challenging the testimony of their master. What they thought of Jesus remains obscure. But perhaps the question is wrongly put, since the evangelist, who formulated the complaint (cf. the typical οὗτος as in 1:7; 3:2), perhaps only meant to depict their small-minded jealousy (cf. also the hyperbolical πάντες). John's disciples have not yet grasped the meaning of his testimony, which he now takes up, to show them that

---

11 P[66] ℵ* Θ G 565 λ φ al. lat sy[c] sa bo Orig. This was, no doubt, because the plural was more common and the man is not further described (the singular in John only here and 4:9; 18:35). In spite of the strong support, the reading is certainly secondary (P[75] has the singular).

12 Cf. Heb 1:3; 2 Pet 1:9; also 2 Cor 7:1; Eph 5:26; Tit 2:14; Heb 9:14, 22f.; 10:2. See further Hauck, "καθαρός", pp. 429f.

events since then have been directed by God and confirm John's testimony. His humility and generosity stand out brilliantly against their narrowmindedness.

3:27	ἀπεκρίθη Ἰωάννης καὶ εἶπεν, Οὐ δύναται ἄνθρωπος λαμβάνειν οὐδὲ ἓν ἐὰν μὴ ᾖ δεδομένον αὐτῷ ἐκ τοῦ οὐρανοῦ.	John answered, with the words, "No one can have anything unless he is given it from heaven.

John begins his answer to his disciples with a religious principle which could be misunderstood outside the concrete situation: "No one[13] can have anything unless it is given him from heaven (i.e., from God)." The idea becomes clearer if one does not take δίδοσθαι ἐκ as the opposite of λαμβάνειν, as is usually done, but in the sense of "being empowered to do something". The construction διδόναι with the infinitive is common,[14] and the expressions in 6:65 and 19:11 are exact parallels. We can see, therefore, the hand of the evangelist here, and there is no need to postulate a special source for 3:27; the expressions are Semitic.[15] From the context, the meaning is that Jesus[16] could not have attracted so many men to him[17] if God had not given him power to do so. John's testimony (v. 28) is thereby confirmed and his desires (v. 29) fulfilled. Jesus is the Messiah, because the crowds flock to him and he gathers his community (v. 29). The principle of v. 27 is formed for the particular occasion, and does not mean that in general success is a sign of divine approval.

3:28	αὐτοὶ ὑμεῖς μοι μαρτυρεῖτε ὅτι εἶπον, Οὐκ εἰμὶ ἐγὼ ὁ Χριστός, ἀλλ' ὅτι Ἀπεσταλμένος εἰμὶ ἔμπροσθεν ἐκείνου.	You yourselves must bear me witness that I said 'I am not the Messiah, I am only sent before him'.

---

[13] Ἄνθρωπος is used here in a vague sense for τις, which also happens in classical Greek, but is far more frequent on Semitic soil; so too in the New Testament cf. Arndt and Gingrich, *Lexicon*, s. v. 3; Funk, *Greek Grammar*, para. 301, 2; οὐ — ἄνθρωπος is probably a Semitism.

[14] Cf. Mt 13:11; (19:11); Lk 1:74; Jn 5:26; Acts 2:4; 4:29; 14:3; Rom 15:5; Eph 3:16; 2 Tim 1:18; Rev 3:21; 6:4 etc. Combinations with ἵνα in John must also be placed here.

[15] On οὐ — ἄνθρωπος cf. note 13 above; δίδοσθαι ἐκ, Niphal or Hophal of נתן with מִן; οὐρανός is the well-known circumlocution for God. See the examples in Schlatter, *ad loc.*

[16] Cyril of Alexandria, Augustine, Thomas Aquinas; among moderns, Lagrange and Braun make the sentence refer to the Baptist: John will not presume to draw men to himself whom God has not given him. But this does not fit well as an answer to v. 26. The idea which Lagrange wished to avoid, that all success is sanctioned by God, is expressed indirectly with regard to Jesus in v. 29; hence v. 27 too must refer to Jesus.

[17] Λαμβάνειν, according to the linguistic explanation given above must mean "take". If one disregards the correlatives λαμβάνειν — δίδοσθαι, many far-fetched explanations are ruled out. The additional ἀφ' ἑαυτοῦ after λαμβάνειν in D Θ 33 also becomes superfluous.

After this appraisal of Jesus and his God-given success, John explains why he has no further hopes in his own regard. His disciples must admit that he denied that he was the Messiah (1:20) and that he had put himself forward only as precursor and herald of the Messiah (cf. 1:23). Like the first testimony of John, this too, in the eyes of the evangelist, had its relevance for the contemporary followers of John. The ἐκεῖνος (Jesus) is characteristic of the style of the evangelist.[18]

3:29	ὁ ἔχων τὴν νύμφην νυμφίος ἐστίν· ὁ δὲ φίλος τοῦ νυμφίου, ὁ ἑστηκὼς καὶ ἀκούων αὐτοῦ, χαρᾷ χαίρει διὰ τὴν φωνὴν τοῦ νυμφίου. αὕτη οὖν ἡ χαρὰ ἡ ἐμὴ πεπλήρωται.	It is the bridegroom that has the bride. But the friend of the bridegroom who stands there and listens to him, is overjoyed at the voice of the bridegroom. This is my joy, and it is complete.

The Baptist illustrates his attitude by an image which alludes to Jewish marriage customs and reveals Semitic sensibilities. It can hardly be a later invention. In its form it is a short parable with allegorical traits, a type often found in the Jewish *mashal*. By the friend of the bridegroom John understands himself (cf. 29c). Hence he certainly thinks of Jesus as the bridegroom. It is true that the image of bridegroom and bride is not found in Jewish writings as an allegory for the Messiah and the Messianic community;[19] but on the lips of the Baptist, "bride" need not have been an allegory for the community. He is depicting his own relationship to Jesus, for which he uses the image of the bridegroom and his friend. The "friend of the bridegroom" is one of the two groomsmen who were entrusted with special functions at a Jewish marriage, their chief duty being to lead the bride to the bridegroom and keep watch outside the bridal chamber.[20] The "voice of the bridegroom" probably means the triumphal shout by which the bridegroom announced to his friends outside that he had been united to a virginal bride.[21] This is the voice which John "hears" and which causes him to rejoice heartily—a striking picture of unselfishness quite acceptable to Semitic feeling, and chosen by John to express his joy on behalf of Jesus. This joy is the point

---

[18] See Ruckstuhl, *Literarische Einheit*, pp. 194 and 204 (no. 17).

[19] The image is used only for the relationship of Yahweh with his people, (after Hosea, and then in the allegorical interpretation of Song) but not of the Messiah and the Messianic community, cf. Jeremias, "νύμφη", pp. 1094f.

[20] See Billerbeck, vol. I, pp. 45f. and 500ff.; Derrett, "Water into Wine", pp. 82ff. For the confidential role of the "groomsman", *Tos. Keth.*, 1, 4 is particularly instructive (Billerbeck, vol. I, pp. 45f.).

[21] See Schlatter, *ad loc.*; Jeremias, "νύμφη", pp. 1094, 7ff.

of the comparison, as the final clause shows: the Baptist, who wishes to be no more than the friend of the bridegroom, sees his hopes fulfilled.

The parabolic character is further illustrated by a trait which cannot be found in the actual situation. The voice of the bridegroom which is heard by the friend, can only be understood in the framework of the parable, since the Baptist could not actually hear Jesus at the moment (ἀκούειν with genitive). The evangelist, however, and his Christian readers must certainly have interpreted the "bride" as the Messianic community. The primitive Church undoubtedly also understood the "bridegroom" in the little parable of Mk 2:19f. parr. as a direct allusion to Jesus the Messiah. Metaphors and similes like Jn 3:29f. could easily give rise to the allegory of the Church as the bride of Christ which is found in other texts of the N.T.

In this interpretation, the parable has nothing to do with the notion of the "sacred marriage" (ἱερὸς γάμος) of pagan Hellenism, which was an element of the mystery religions and, in a different way, of Gnosticism. The friend of the bridegroom, who plays a central role in the image of v. 29, does not figure at all in the Gnostic myth of the marriage of the Soter with Sophia. The erotic element does not appear at all in the parable (contrast *Odes of Solomon*, 3; 38:11; 42:8f.).[22]

3:30	ἐκεῖνον δεῖ αὐξάνειν, ἐμὲ δὲ ἐλαττοῦσθαι.	He must grow greater, while I grow less.

John ends with a short saying in which he signals the (divinely-willed) necessity of the "growth" of Jesus (ἐκεῖνος) and his own "decrease" (δεῖ). The growth and decrease do not refer directly to the number of followers, but to the power and influence which each exercises.[23] But we should also note the interpretation given by the Church Fathers, who saw here an image of the waxing and waning of the sunlight; the terms can be verified in this sense.[24] The saying corresponds to the moment in the history of salvation. John is still working, but his time is running out. Jesus has not launched out into his full activity (of proclaiming and teaching), but he is on the point of doing so. Something new is on foot,

---

[22] On the "hieros gamos" cf. Bousset, *Hauptprobleme der Gnosis*, pp. 267ff.; Norden, *Die Geburt des Kindes*, pp. 67ff.; Reitzenstein, *Mysterienreligionen*, pp. 34ff., 99f., 245ff.; Criticism in Schmid, "Heilige Brautschaft", cols. 528ff., esp. 546ff.; Bultmann too, pp. 126f., n. 2 does not accept this explanation from comparative religion.

[23] The verbs occur in this sense in classical literature, cf. Liddell and Scott, vol. I, p. 277, s. v. II–III, p. 528, s. v. II, 1.

[24] For αὐξάνειν Arndt and Gingrich, *Lexicon*, s. v. cites the calendar of Antiochus (c. A.D. 200) for 25 December, for ἐλαττοῦσθαι Dio Cassius, 45, 17. On the waxing of the moon, cf. also Aristotle, *Anal. post.*, 78b, 6. This explanation is adopted by Bauer, Bultmann and Wikenhauser.

the work of John is accomplished.[25] The primitive Church, building on certain sayings of Jesus (cf. Mk 2:21f. parr.; Mt 11:11f.; Lk 16:16) understood this change as marking the turning-point at which the old age gave way to the new. The Baptist may well have had some sense of this newness, which God's plan of salvation brought with it. In any case, his last words, as recorded by the fourth evangelist, testify to his human grandeur and his prophetic insight.

---

[25] It is possible that John was imprisoned soon after. Some MSS have a note to this effect after v. 36 (2145 e sy^{hmg}).

CHAPTER VI

Jesus Reveals Himself in Samaria (4: 1—42)

1. This long passage, which is a redactional unity, is of itself no more than a description of an episode on the return journey of Jesus from Judea to Galilee. But the evangelist takes a special interest in this incident in Samaria. This is probably due to a number of reasons: a) in the context of the Gospel narrative, the faith of the half-pagan Samaritans who accept Jesus so whole-heartedly and welcome him to their homes (4:40f.) stands out all the more strikingly against the background of the superficial, miracle-hungry faith of the Jerusalem crowds (2:23–25), the bewilderment of the spiritual élite (Nicodemus, 3:1–12) and the suspicious attitude of the Pharisees (4:1–3). Faith is wanting or inadequate among Jesus's own people, but the response among the non-Jewish world is quick and eager; b) Here is where Jesus, in the course of his self-revelation, can disclose his mission as saviour of the world (4:42; cf. 3:17). This universalism permeates the whole Gospel, and the readers, mostly gentile Christians, can see a striking example of it here; c) We may perhaps go further and suspect that the author has a special interest in the mission to Samaria, which the primitive Church, and the "Hellenist" Philip in particular (Acts 8), took up at an early date. Fair-sized Christian communities must have continued to exist in Samaria, and the incident transmitted in Jn 4 may have first been recounted there. The evangelist himself, who once more displays good local knowledge, may have worked there for a time. The intermediate section, 4:35–38, shows a very marked interest in missionary work. We could thus see the actual setting in the life of the communities in which the tradition was handed on. Is it the same as that which is also reflected in the traditions and interests behind many passages in Lk (cf. Lk 9:52–56; 10:30–37; 17:11–19)? d) This narrative provided a good occasion for treating a theme which was important to the Johannine communities, the liturgical worship. In connection with the place of worship, an obvious question with which the Samaritans were constantly preoccupied (v. 20), Jesus

gives a sublime revelation about the nature of the true worship of God, which must have been particularly comforting and helpful for communities on the high spiritual level which the fourth Gospel presupposes. The words addressed by Jesus to the simple Samaritan woman (vv. 23f.) are also addressed to his believers of later days, who are already practising the Christian form of worship and are open to a deeper understanding of it.

2. The structure of the passage is clear, and the elements well-organized. The evangelist is not concerned with the pastoral and pedagogical methods by which Jesus influences the woman, but with the gradual self-revelation of Jesus. As regards the woman, Jesus intends to lead her to faith; and in her fellow-countrymen also, the evangelist depicts the progress of their faith (v. 42). Hence revelation and faith, as in 2:11, 22; 3:11, are the two points of view which dominate the narrative as such. How revelation makes a stronger and stronger impact and how faith is led upwards can be seen from the following key-words: v. 9, Ἰουδαῖος—v. 11, κύριε—v. 12, μείζων τοῦ πατρὸς ἡμῶν Ἰακώβ;—v. 19, προφήτης—vv. 26, 29, ὁ χριστός—v. 42, ὁ σωτὴρ τοῦ κόσμου. The structure is almost dramatic.[1] At the climax of Jesus's self-revelation to the woman, when he proclaims himself the Messiah (v. 26), the dialogue breaks off, the disciples arrive, the woman leaves her jug and runs to the village. The intervening scene with the disciples (vv. 31–38) heightens the tension, till the end of the story is reached with the men of Sychar confessing their faith in the saviour of the world.

3. This skilful construction, however, is no reason for doubting the historicity of the narrative. One might be more inclined to take the Samaritan woman as an allegorical figure, representing the "adulterous", apostate Samaritan nation, and this seems to be suggested by the strange story of the woman's life (vv. 17f.).[2] But one must be cautious with one's verdict in this difficult question. The woman plays a personal role of some importance in the narrative, since it is she who summons her fellow-citizens (vv. 28–30), and the evangelist certainly intends their faith and confession to be taken historically, like the coming of the "Greeks" later (12:20 ff.). Unless all individuals in John are to be taken as "symbols"[3] the Samaritan must be regarded primarily as an individual. It is also possible that the woman became a symbol of the Samaritan

---

[1] Cf. Windisch, "Der Johanneische Erzählungsstil", pp. 178ff.; L. Schmid, "Die Komposition der Samaria-Szene, Joh 4:1–42".

[2] So many moderns, very decidedly Strathmann; but see Bauer, pp. 75f. ("much of this is possible, but none of it sure"); Bultmann, p. 138, n. 4.

[3] So Kraft, "Die Personen des Johannesevangeliums"; contrast Oehler, "Typen oder allegorische Figuren im Johannesevangelium?"

nation in the eyes of the evangelist, on account of the peculiarities of her life-story.

4. The impression of the presence of a deeper symbolism always arises in John from the fact that the narrative also includes theological themes which are intrinsically connected with it. This is a characteristic of the evangelist, and it may have influenced him in the actual choice of his themes. In the present section three themes are dealt with: the "living water" which Jesus and Jesus alone can give (vv. 10–14); the "adoration in Spirit and truth" (vv. 20–24); "the labours of sowing and the joy of harvest" (vv. 35–38). The first theme, the question of what the revealer gives and promises believers, runs through the whole Gospel and is constantly elucidated under different images (the wine at Cana, ch. 2; the bread of life, ch. 6, etc.). The second theme (worship) already appeared in the background of 2:13–22. The third theme (missionary work) is suggested by the narrative itself (work in Samaria) and is only set in a broader perspective. But these themes, which are to some extent independent, must not obscure the fact that the evangelist always has the self-revelation of Jesus in mind as his main theme. His Christ is radiant with a new majesty here, and we can already see its ultimate source: the unity of Jesus with him who sent him (v. 34).

Introduction (4:1–5)

4:1	Ὡς οὖν ἔγνω ὁ κύριος ὅτι ἤκουσαν οἱ Φαρισαῖοι ὅτι Ἰησοῦς πλείονας μαθητὰς ποιεῖ καὶ βαπτίζει ἢ Ἰωάννης,	When then the Lord learned that the Pharisees had heard that Jesus was winning and baptizing more disciples than John
4:2	—καίτοι γε Ἰησοῦς αὐτὸς οὐκ ἐβάπτιζεν ἀλλ' οἱ μαθηταὶ αὐτοῦ—	—though Jesus himself did not baptize, but only his disciples—
4:3	ἀφῆκεν τὴν Ἰουδαίαν καὶ ἀπῆλθεν πάλιν εἰς τὴν Γαλιλαίαν.	he left Judea and set off again for Galilee.

The evangelist explains Jesus's departure from Judea as a withdrawal in face of the Pharisees. Learning that the Pharisees had heard of his success, he breaks off his activity and leaves. The Pharisees had already called John to account for his baptizing (1:24), but there has been no mention up to this of these influential persons taking up an unfriendly attitude to Jesus. The evangelist attributes the departure simply to the decision of "the Lord".[4] He sees Jesus as under the law of "the hour" which the Father has fixed for him (cf. 2:4), and presumably thinks that Jesus is trying to avoid for the present an open conflict with the leading circles of Judaism, in keeping with his Father's will. The suspicious Pharisees must have been greatly troubled to see Jesus winning more candidates for baptism and more followers[5] than John. In a parenthesis the evangelist, or more probably, the redaction[6] notes that it was not Jesus himself but his disciples who baptized (see commentary on 3:22).

4:4	ἔδει δὲ αὐτὸν διέρχεσθαι διὰ τῆς Σαμαρείας.	He had to take the way through Samaria.
4:5	ἔρχεται οὖν εἰς πόλιν τῆς Σαμαρείας λεγομένην Συχὰρ πλησίον τοῦ χωρίου ὃ ἔδωκεν Ἰακὼβ τῷ Ἰωσὴφ τῷ υἱῷ αὐτοῦ·	So he came to a place in Samaria called Sychar, near the piece of land which Jacob had given to his son Joseph.

The ἔδει shows a certain urgency. Otherwise Jesus could have taken the more easterly route along the valley of the Jordan, though this was hot and difficult and was mostly avoided.[7] According to Josephus, the quick way was through Samaria, by which it was possible to reach Jerusalem from Galilee in three days.[8] Taking the usual route, Jesus comes to the famous well of Jacob, also an important geographical point, because here the road forks, one branch curving westwards towards Samaria (Sebastiyeh) and western Galilee, the other running north-east towards Bethshan and the lake of Gennesaret. Seen from the well of

---

[4] This is one of the few places in the narrative in which Jesus is called ὁ κύριος; the only other places are 6:23; 11:2; 20:20. In the present text Tat (ar and neerl) ℵ D Θ 565 λ al. lat (except f q) sy^c p hmg bo read ὁ Ἰησοῦς (Tischendorf, Bover); 6:23 and 11:2 are suspect, as possibly redactional additions; 20:20 is probably to be explained by 20:2, 18. The risen Jesus is seen by the community as "the Lord" in a special sense (cf. also 20:25; 21:7, 12). Since 4:1 is certainly part of the gospel narrative, perhaps ὁ Ἰησοῦς was the original reading or the evangelist's expression; the redaction may have been already responsible for replacing it by ὁ κύριος, when v. 2 was added (see below).

[5] The "disciples" must be taken in a wider sense here (but contrast v. 2), as in 6:60f., 66; 7:3; 8:31; 9:27f. This is the effect of a later usage, whereby all believers were looked on as μαθηταί (cf. Acts). Cf. Rengstorf, "μαθητής", pp. 462f.; Schulz, *Nachfolgen und Nachahmen*, pp. 137–44.

[6] Signs of redactional composition in v. 2 are: καίτοι γε is singular, Ἰησοῦς without the article is at least remarkable, if not a criterion of the style of the redaction (cf. also 4:44; 12:16), as Jeremias, "Johanneische Literarkritik", pp. 44f., tries to prove. The intrinsic reasons for a subsequent emendation by the "redaction" are readily understood.

[7] Cf. Dalman, *Orte und Wege Jesu*, pp. 249–56; on the ordinary route through Samaria, *ibid.*, pp. 222f., E. T.: *Sacred Sites*, pp. 209–15, 212.

[8] *Vita*, 52, 269.

Jacob, Mount Garizim lies to the south-west and Mount Ebal to the north-west. The place called Sychar by the evangelist (Vg. Sichar) is mostly identified with the present village of Askar, a little more than half a mile north-east of the well of Jacob. The identification is probably correct, a copyist's mistake for Shechem, as Jerome supposed,[9] being unlikely, since the displacement of this ancient biblical name by Sychar would be inexplicable.

The ancient city of Shechem was destroyed in 128 B.C. by John Hyrcan. The new foundation of Neapolis (Nablus, about a mile and a half from the ancient Shechem) was not yet in existence in the time of Jesus. Excavations at Balata (begun by E. Sellin) have revealed the ruins of the ancient Shechem, but it is uncertain when the village came into existence. It is somewhat nearer the well of Jacob, but need hardly be considered for Sychar, since the narrative of the evangelist presupposes a large town (πόλις) and one somewhat farther away (cf. vv. 28–31). Hence the evangelist did, in fact, probably mean Sychar, the identification of which with Askar is also supported by an early tradition.[10] Though the settlement of Askar only exists since Arab times,[11] it may well be on the site of the ancient Sychar, and is possibly even linked to the older settlement through the changed name.[12]

It was deduced from Gen 48:22; Jos 24:32 that Jacob gave his son Joseph the land at Shechem which he had bought from the sons of Hamor (Gen 33:19). The site of Joseph's grave, which is not mentioned in John, is uncertain.[13]

Jesus's dialogue with the Samaritan woman (4:6–26)

a) The meeting with the Samaritan woman (4:6–9)

4:6	ἦν δὲ ἐκεῖ πηγὴ τοῦ Ἰακώβ. ὁ οὖν Ἰησοῦς κεκοπιακὼς ἐκ τῆς ὁδοιπορίας ἐκαθέζετο οὕτως ἐπὶ τῇ πηγῇ· ὥρα ἦν ὡς ἕκτη.	Jacob's well was there. And Jesus, tired from travelling, sat down without more ado by the well. It was about the sixth hour.

[9] *Ep.*, 108, 16 (Hilberg, p. 322); *Quaest. in Gen*, 48, 22 (*PL* 23, col. 1004); cf. Kopp, *Heilige Stätten*, p. 205, E. T.: *Holy Places*, p. 159.

[10] Cf. Kopp, *ibid.*, pp. 203ff., E. T.: p. 155. On the Jewish tradition see also below, n. 14. A map in Kopp, p. 157 or Hartmann, *Encyclopedic Dictionary of the Bible*, which also gives a good photograph taken from Gerizim (pl. XXII).

[11] Cf. Albright "Recent Discoveries", p. 160. Hence he argues for a misspelling for Shechem (Sichem).

[12] Cf. Kopp, p. 208, E. T.: p. 165, who thinks an early change of name possible (for discussion of the fragmentary indication on the Madaba map, see German text, pp. 205–10). Delcor holds a similar view, cf. "Vom Sichem der hellenistischen Epoche zum Sychar des Neuen Testaments".

[13] On the tradition about the "land" or "plot of ground" which Jacob gave his son Joseph,

The well of Jacob, which is still to be seen today in the same place where it was shown to earlier pilgrims, is undoubtedly genuine, though it is not mentioned in the O.T.[14] It is a fine installation, with a cylindrical shaft seven feet in diameter and 106 feet deep driven into the rock and fresh subsoil water at the bottom (like Isaac's well in Gen 26:19), ringed by a wall on top.[15] There are two holes through which a bucket can be lowered (v. 11) and the water lies near the bottom of the shaft. Jesus, tired from his journey, sits down without ceremony (οὕτως) by the well (on the ground)[16] or on the edge of the well. The time given, about midday, explains his being tired and thirsty (v. 7).

4:7	Ἔρχεται γυνὴ ἐκ τῆς Σαμαρείας ἀντλῆσαι ὕδωρ. λέγει αὐτῇ ὁ Ἰησοῦς, Δός μοι πεῖν.	A Samaritan woman arrived to draw water. Jesus said to her, "Give me a drink",

A Samaritan woman (ἐκ τῆς Σαμαρείας, of Samaritan descent), comes to draw water. Two things are remarkable here, that the woman chooses the hottest hour of the day, and that she does not go to the source at Ain Askar (if Sychar is Askar) or Ain Defne at Balata. Lagrange thinks that the spring at Askar did not always flow, or that the woman lived closer to the well of Jacob. Her coming at midday is generally explained by her desire, as a notorious sinner, not to have to meet other women. The evangelist does not delay on such points. He is concerned with the meeting with Jesus and the ensuing conversation, which Jesus begins of his own accord with a request for water.

4:8	οἱ γὰρ μαθηταὶ αὐτοῦ ἀπεληλύθεισαν εἰς τὴν πόλιν, ἵνα τροφὰς ἀγοράσωσιν.	for his disciples had gone to the town, to buy food.

As an afterthought, the evangelist remarks that the disciples had gone in the meantime to buy provisions in the town. Once again, we must not ask why they all went off together; but their disappearance and re-

see Billerbeck, vol. II, pp. 432f.; Dalman, *Orte und Wege*, p. 228, E. T.; *Sacred Sites*, p. 214, is sceptical about the present site of Joseph's tomb, while Kopp, p. 200, E.T.: p. 115, is confident.

[14] Billerbeck, vol. II, pp. 431f., thinks that the spring called Sykhar or Sokher in the rabbinical writings may be Jacob's well. The name may perhaps be already found in *Jub.*, 34:4 ("King of Sakir"), also in *Test. Jud.*, 6, 3 (Μαχήρ, a deformation for Σακίρ, as is read by the Jewish midrash, see Charles, vol. II, p. 75 and 237; cf. Kopp, p. 205.

[15] Cf. Dalman, *Orte und Wege Jesu*, pp. 226–9; E. T.: *Sacred Sites*, pp. 212–5; Lagrange on 4:6 and 4:11.

[16] Cf. the reading ἐπὶ τῇ γῇ in P[66]*, which, however, is probably merely a slip; the corrector wrote πη over it.

appearance (v. 27) need not be considered a piece of stage-setting manipulated by the evangelist. Things could have happened that way.

4:9	λέγει οὖν αὐτῷ ἡ γυνὴ ἡ Σαμαρῖτις, Πῶς σὺ Ἰουδαῖος ὢν παρ' ἐμοῦ πεῖν αἰτεῖς γυναικὸς Σαμαρίτιδος οὔσης; (οὐ γὰρ συγχρῶνται Ἰουδαῖοι Σαμαρίταις.)	The Samaritan woman said to him, "How can you, a Jew, ask me for a drink, since I am a Samaritan woman?" The Jews have, in fact, no dealings with the Samaritans.

Jesus's request astonishes the woman, since he is a Jew and he addresses a Samaritan woman. Relationships between Jews and Samaritans were mostly unfriendly, because the Samaritans were considered since the exile as a mixed race of semi-pagans (cf. 2 Kgs 17:24–41), though the mood could vary. Since John Hyrcan (135–104 B.C.) who conquered Shechem and destroyed the temple on Mt Garizim, relations were particularly strained. In the time of Jesus there were frequent clashes (cf. Lk 9:52 ff.), which sometimes caused bloodshed,[17] when the Galileans passed through Samaria. The strict Jewish rules which practically identified Samaritans with heathens were probably already in existence.[18] Hence the woman has real reason to feel surprised. The evangelist, who is obviously well acquainted with the situation, explains further to his readers that the Jews had no dealings with the Samaritans.[19] As the sentence is missing in some MSS,[20] it may be a later interpolation.

b) Jesus's gift of living water (4:10–15)

4:10	ἀπεκρίθη Ἰησοῦς καὶ εἶπεν αὐτῇ, Εἰ ᾔδεις τὴν δωρεὰν τοῦ θεοῦ καὶ τίς ἐστιν ὁ λέγων σοι, Δός μοι	Jesus answered her with the words, "If you knew the gift of God and who it is who says

[17] A serious clash in the year A.D. 52 is mentioned by Josephus, *Ant.*, XX, 118–36; *Bell.*, II, 232–46.

[18] On the many rules of the Mishnah see Billerbeck, vol. I, pp. 538 ff.; on the development, first easing and then growing tense again, cf. Jeremias, *Jerusalem zur Zeit Jesu*, vol. II B, pp. 224–31. He shows that strict segregation was the rule till R. Aqiba (d. 135).

[19] Daube, "Jesus and the Samaritan Woman: The Meaning of συγχράομαι", tries to prove that the only possible translation is: "They do not use (vessels) in common with the Samaritans"; he is followed by Barrett, *ad loc.* But in this case an object would seem to be indispensible after συγχρῶνται; and the other sense seems to be adequately proved, cf. Arndt and Gingrich, *Lexicon*, s. v. 2; Moulton and Milligan, col. 616 s. v. However, underlying the general statement may be the idea that the Jews feared to defile themselves by taking food and drink from Samaritans; cf. Jeremias, p. 230, esp. n. 45.

[20] ℵ* D a b d e j. The remark is omitted by Tischendorf, loyal to his codex Sinaiticus, and considered a gloss by many commentators.

πεῖν, σὺ ἂν ᾔτησας αὐτὸν καὶ ἔδωκεν ἄν σοι ὕδωρ ζῶν.	to you, 'Give me a drink', you would have asked him and he would have given you living water."

Jesus utters a mysterious word which raises the conversation at once to a higher level. It is a revelation which, as in the dialogue with Nicodemus (3:3), announces the theme which is to be developed in what follows. There is a masterly transition from the outward situation to the inner confrontation of man with the revealer. If the woman knew the "gift of God" and the stranger who asks her for a drink of ordinary water, the roles would be exchanged. She (the σύ is emphatic) would do the asking and become beneficiary. According to the chiastic structure of the sentence, which goes from the "gift of God" to the person of the speaker, and from the speaker back to the "living water", "the gift of God" must be the "living water" which Jesus can give, the true "water of life" which is not a gift on the natural, earthly plane but a heavenly gift from God.[21] From this standpoint, it is not Jesus who is in need of anything, but the woman; and she is confronted with the one person who can satisfy the deepest needs of man.

Δωρεά is a comprehensive term for everything that God bestows on man for his salvation. For the rabbis, it was above all the Torah,[22] for the primitive community the Holy Spirit (Acts 2:38; 8:20; 10:45; 11:17), for Paul the divine gift of righteousness (Rom 5:17) or salvation or grace in general (2 Cor 9:15; Eph 3:7; 4:7; cf. Heb 6:4, the heavenly gift). In non-Christian religions too δωρεά is in general the gift of God, which is defined more closely according to the particular character of the religion in question. Thus in the Hermetic Gnosis it is the power to see God and become like him.[23] John begins with a general term which is to be defined more exactly as the discourse proceeds.

The fresh spring water from the well is a symbol of what Jesus can and will give. What this precisely is cannot be determined from the imagery, and it would be one-sided to define it at once as Jesus's words, divine life, the Holy Spirit or baptism.

---

[21] The "gift of God", therefore, does not directly mean Jesus (against Odeberg, p. 152, who thinks it is the same assertion as 3:16); the καί is not epexegetic (against Schweizer, *Ego eimi*, p. 161, n. 122).

[22] See the examples in Odeberg, pp. 150ff.; but the rabbis knew other "gifts of God", e.g. peace, liberation, the land of Israel, grace (*Gen. Rabbah*, 6, 7).

[23] Cf. *C. Herm.*, IV, 5: "All who have gained a share in the gift of God are immortal instead of mortal"; X, 9: "Knowledge (γνῶσις) is the goal of science (ἐπιστήμη), but science is a gift of God"; in *Asclepius*, 18, the spirit or the mind (*sensus*, *mens* = νοῦς) is the "heavenly gift which alone makes men happy"; *Frg.* (in Stobaeus), II A, 6 (Nock and Festugière, vol. III, p. 5): "Only few men can gain knowledge of the truth, those to whom God has given the power to see God (τὴν θεοπτικὴν δύναμιν)."

Water provides almost endless symbolism for the Oriental, to whom it appears as the most indispensable factor in life—purifying, stilling thirst, giving and renewing life and fruitfulness—which could easily be applied to the higher needs and blessings of man. In many cults, especially in Egypt and Babylon, water played a role as a libation for the dead, as water of life and source of youth. There was an extensive baptist movement arising from the desire to be cleansed from earthly stains or guilt. The other world was also supposed to be rich in sources of life and healing waters.[24] But it would be far-fetched to apply such ideas here. The water which Jesus offers is his present gift, which quenches all thirst and leads to eternal life (v. 14).

What is basic here is the link with O.T. imagery. There God himself is "the fountain of living waters" (Jer 2:13; 17:13).[25] His worshippers can drink from "the river of his delights" (Ps 36:8). The image is transferred from God to Wisdom (Bar 3:12; Ecclus 15:3; 24:30 ff.; cf. also Wis 7:25; Song 4:15; *Enoch* 48:1; 49:1), applied to the Torah[26] and the Holy Spirit[27] by the rabbis, and to the Logos by Philo.[28] Thus the figurative expression on the lips of Jesus can have become for the evangelist a symbol of all that Jesus meant to him. And in using the symbolism, he may have been taking into account, as with the concept of Logos, the mentality and religious desires of his readers. In the Gnostic *Odes of Solomon*, the image is used in a way which resembles very closely the language of John, though applied only to Gnosis as the means of quenching all thirst.[29] But for John, salvation is to be sought elsewhere: only in Jesus, his revelation and the divine life which he communicates.

"Living water" is one of the many images by which Jesus designates himself or his gifts in John, along with "bread", "vine", "door", "way" and so on. The metaphor of the bread from heaven gives an important pointer for the explanation of the "living water": that the gift is closely related to the giver. Jesus is the living and life-giving bread, and Jesus

---

[24] Copious material from comparative religion in Ninck, *Die Bedeutung des Wassers in Kult und Leben der Alten*; Bonnet, "Die Symbolik der Reinigung im ägyptischen Kult"; Karge, *Rephaim*, pp. 557ff.; Bauer, *Johannesevangelium*, pp. 68f.; Thomas, *Mouvement baptiste, passim*; Bultmann, *Johannes*, pp. 133–6.

[25] The image is used in *Enoch*, 96:6; *Dam.*, 8:21; cf. 3:16; 6:3f. (applied to the Torah). For the Old Testament see Reymond, *L'eau, sa vie et sa signification dans L'Ancien Testament*; also Daniélou, "Le symbolisme de l'eau vive".

[26] See Billerbeck, vol. II, pp. 435f.; for the image of v. 14 see also *Yalkut Shimoni*, II, 480 (in Odeberg, p. 160), "The words of the Torah are received (into the heart of man) till the Torah becomes a flowing spring."

[27] See Billerbeck, vol. II, pp. 434f.; this symbolism was used at the feast of Tabernacles (rite of drawing water), see on 7:37ff.

[28] The Logos is the "source of wisdom" (*Fuga*, 97), and wisdom is in turn the source from which the Logos flows like a stream (*De somn.*, II, 242). Philo frequently compares wisdom with water or a source elsewhere.

[29] Cf. *Odes of Solomon*, 6:11 (10) ff., "All the thirsty upon earth were given to drink of it, and thirst was relieved and quenched: for from the Most High the draught was given ... 18 (17) and they lived by the water of life for ever"; 11:6f.: "And speaking waters touched my lips from the fountain of the Lord plenteously, and I drank and was inebriated with the living water that doth not die"; cf. also 30:1ff. It is improbable that these passages depend directly on Jn 4:10ff., since the metaphor of drinking is applied differently, cf. *Odes*, 4:10; 28:15; 38:17. See Braun, *Jean le Théologien*, pp. 242f. But the texts from the Gnostics

gives this bread; in the same way, knowledge of his person cannot be separated from knowledge of his gift of "living water". To know him in his being as God's "Word" of revelation and salvation is to understand his gift, which is revelation and life. Only the revealer who has become flesh, who is divine light and life (cf. 1:4; 8:12; 11:25; 14:6), can pass on this life (5:25f.; 6:57), in the word which he attests (5:25; 6:63; 8:51) and in the sacraments (3:5; 6:53f.). Thus the assertion which is meant to give the woman food for thought at the moment and to provoke her to further questions, also becomes a word of revelation for later believers. It urges them to recognize the true gift of God and its only giver, or again, to recognize who speaks the word of God and to ask him for his gifts.

4:11	λέγει αὐτῷ ἡ γυνή, Κύριε, οὔτε ἄντλημα ἔχεις καὶ τὸ φρέαρ ἐστὶν βαθύ· πόθεν οὖν ἔχεις τὸ ὕδωρ τὸ ζῶν;	She said to him, "Sir, you have nothing to draw water in, and the well is deep. Where can you have the living water from?

The woman is moved by Jesus's words but has not grasped their profounder meaning. Hearing Jesus's offer of "living water", she misunderstands it as a promise of something earthly and natural—the sort of misunderstanding which has already occurred with Nicodemus (3:4). She is interested in the "living water" but can only think of the water in the well of Jacob. Still, she now addresses the stranger respectfully as "sir", and asks him "whence" he can procure this water without a vessel to draw it in. For the evangelist, this question as to the "whence" is important. The same innocent question, which has such grave overtones, was heard in the miracle at Cana (2:9) and in the dialogue with Nicodemus (3:8). Its full meaning is revealed in 7:27f.; 8:14; 9:29f.; 19:9. It is the question of where the revealer and his gifts come from. John answers dialectically that men "know" (7:28), in a superficial, worldly sense (cf. 6:42) and yet do "not know" (8:14), that is, his true heavenly origin. They are helpless and confused before his coming and his revelation (19:9). Where his hearers are ready to believe, Jesus reveals that he and his gifts are "from above" (3:3, 7, 31), "from heaven" (3:31; 6:31 ff.). Thus the Christian reader already knows "whence" Jesus has the living water.

---

against whom Hippolytus writes probably allude to Jn 4:14, cf. *Ref.*, 5:9 (Naassenes); 19:21 (Sethians); 27:2 (Baruch-Book of Justin); they use the significant term ζῶν ὕδωρ ἁλλόμενον. The "living water" in the Mandaean writings is the running water of Mandaean baptism, of which the candidate drinks three handfuls (Lidzbarski, *Mand. Liturgien*, p. 27), which guarantees his ascent to life. See Rudolf, *Die Mandäer*, vol. II, pp. 61–66, 125f.

4:12	μὴ σὺ μείζων εἶ τοῦ πατρὸς ἡμῶν Ἰακώβ, ὃς ἔδωκεν ἡμῖν τὸ φρέαρ καὶ αὐτὸς ἐξ αὐτοῦ ἔπιεν καὶ οἱ υἱοὶ αὐτοῦ καὶ τὰ θρέμματα αὐτοῦ;	Surely you are not greater than our father Jacob who gave us the well and used it to drink from, as did his sons and his flocks?"

The Samaritan still wonders whether Jesus may not be thinking of another spring. Is he not content with the excellent well of Jacob? Her remark may be meant to sound mocking; but though the question expects the answer no, it may also suggest that she may have some suspicion of the greatness of Jesus. The Samaritans held the patriarchs in high honour, and the expression "our father Jacob" implies a claim to be specially linked with the builder of the well as their forefather.[30] The description of Jacob's giving "us" the well and of his drinking from it, along with his sons and flocks, is not found in the O.T. and could have come from popular tradition in the locality. The theme of "digging the well" is of some importance in the Qumran texts.[31]

4:13	ἀπεκρίθη Ἰησοῦς καὶ εἶπεν αὐτῇ, Πᾶς ὁ πίνων ἐκ τοῦ ὕδατος τούτου διψήσει πάλιν·	Jesus answered her with the words, "All who drink this water will be thirsty once more.
4:14	ὃς δ' ἂν πίῃ ἐκ τοῦ ὕδατος οὗ ἐγὼ δώσω αὐτῷ, οὐ μὴ διψήσει εἰς τὸν αἰῶνα, ἀλλὰ τὸ ὕδωρ ὃ δώσω αὐτῷ γενήσεται ἐν αὐτῷ πηγὴ ὕδατος ἁλλομένου εἰς ζωὴν αἰώνιον.	But whoever drinks the water which I give him will never be thirsty again. The water which I give him will become in him a spring with water flowing for eternal life."

As in the Nicodemus episode, 3:5, Jesus now states more clearly that he is not thinking of "this" water in the well of Jacob, but that he is ready to give a completely different sort of water, which quenches all thirst for ever. This second revelation, which is couched in very well-balanced phrasing, gives further information on Jesus's gift. V. 14 takes

---

[30] According to Josephus, *Ant.*, XI, 341, the Samaritans claimed to be descended from Ephraim and Manasseh; in *Pesiqta*, 11 (98a) R. Meïr mentions that the Samaritans called Jacob their father, see Schlatter, *ad loc.* On their high esteem for the patriarchs and God's covenant with them see MacDonald, *The Theology of the Samaritans*, pp. 234 f., 242 ff., 296 ff. etc.

[31] See *Dam.*, 3:16; 6:3–9; 19:34. According to 6:4, the "well" is the law; those who dug it are the penitents of Israel. The "staff" with which they dug is the "searcher of the law" (6:7), whom many identify with the "Teacher of Righteousness". Hence it is a midrash, but the use of the metaphor is noteworthy.

the form of a negative followed by a positive statement which is a feature of Johannine style. Three points are to be noted: 1, that the water is able to quench thirst for ever; 2, it becomes a source which flows in man; 3, the water springs up εἰς ζωὴν αἰώνιον. The first theme is also found in the Wisdom literature, though pointing in a different direction. In Ecclus 24:21 Wisdom says, "Those who eat me will hunger for more, and those who drink me will thirst for more", which means that they will desire only Wisdom. This yearning is only fulfilled in eternity, cf. *Enoch*, 48:1, "Around (the fountain of righteousness) there were many fountains of wisdom, and all the thirsty drank of them and were filled with wisdom."[32] In so far as the image expresses hunger and thirst for justice (cf. Mt 5:6), it has still deeper roots in the O.T., e.g. Is 55:1–3, "Ho, every one who thirsts, come to the waters; and he who has no money, come, buy and eat . . . Hearken diligently to me, and eat what is good, and delight yourselves in fatness. Incline your ear and come to me; hear, that your soul may live." The images of hunger and thirst, satisfaction and refreshment, are also used in Is 49:10; 58:11; Jer 31:25; Amos 8:11f.; Ps 107:5, 9. In Jn 6:32 ff., 48 ff. the image of bread completes that of water (ch. 4) and both are used together in 6:35, "He who comes to me shall not hunger, and he who believes in me shall never thirst." Thus the Johannine Jesus takes up this imagery, but in relating it to himself as the present revealer and saviour, gives it a new and deeper meaning. He is already giving the water of salvation and the bread of eternal life to all who believe in him.

The Gnostic *Odes of Solomon* also speak jubilantly of the quenching of thirst in terms which recall Jn 4,[33] and also of being inebriated (11:7f.), finding rest (30:2f., 7), and of the sweetness of the water (28:15; 30:4), which last are not in John. Thirst for the true life is strongly felt in Gnosis, but satisfied in other ways, as for instance by knowledge or even ecstatic experiences of the soul. It remains possible that the fourth evangelist wished to take such moods and yearnings into account.

The living water given by Jesus becomes a source within man, as Philo says of the Logos[34] and a later midrash of the divine Torah.[35] Jesus's gift

---

[32] The image is also found in the *Qumran Hodayoth* (*1 QH*, 4:11); "They (the glib liars) keep the drink of knowledge from the thirsty, and give them vinegar for their thirst." "Knowledge" or "intelligence" refers to the correct interpretation of the Torah, cf. Nötscher, *Terminologie*, pp. 43ff. The metaphor of "drinking" for learning the Torah is also used by the rabbis.

[33] See the texts above, n. 29.

[34] See Philo, *De post.*, 129, where the divine Logos is compared with the river of paradise "by reason of the unbroken flow of the constant streams of words and doctrines ever sweet and fresh, by which it brings nourishment and growth to souls that love God"; see also *De somn.*, II, 246ff.

[35] See the statement quoted above on v. 10 (above n. 26).

takes in and penetrates the whole man.[36] All his gifts become forces which abide and work within man, like the ζωή (6:53; 1 Jn 3:15), the λόγος of God or of Jesus (5:38; 8:37; 1 Jn 1:10; 2:14), the ἀλήθεια (1 Jn 1:8; 2 Jn 2), the πνεῦμα τῆς ἀληθείας (14:17), the χρῖσμα (1 Jn 2:27) and the σπέρμα of God (1 Jn 3:9). Finally, Jesus affirms that this source flows unceasingly and unendingly. The water is said to "spring up,[37] bubble up", to bring out the supernatural "vitality" of the divine forces bestowed on man, the undiminished vigour and freshness which no new needs can impair (cf. 14 a). The words εἰς ζωὴν αἰώνιον do not fit in well with the metaphor, since they cannot have a locative sense. They must be understood in terms of time and finality. Permanence is suggested by the parallel εἰς τὸν αἰῶνα, v. 14 a, the end in view by the corresponding statement about the bread of life, 6:27, μένουσαν εἰς ζωὴν αἰώνιον cf. also 4:36; 12:25. The divine gift brought by Jesus retains its vigour unthreatened by decay, to remain "for ever", a Johannine notion which recurs constantly.[38] Hence "eternal life" here also takes on a futurist tinge (cf. 3:36b; 1 Jn 2:25). The synoptic usage still makes itself felt and the eschatological outlook is retained.[39] But the eschatological gift is already given by the revealer at the present moment.

Jesus's gift of living water has now been adequately described. It is a divine gift brought by Jesus from the heavenly world and given to men to quench fully and for ever their most radical "thirst for life", penetrating and permeating man, unfolding its vital powers and continuing to work unfailingly till eternal life. If we ask finally what concrete gift is meant, it does not matter much whether we think of the Holy Spirit (like most Fathers and many modern exegetes[40]) or of divine life, since for John both are intimately connected. The Spirit is the creator of life (6:63a), and hence Jesus, who communicates eternal life, is described as possessing the Spirit (1:32f.; 3:34) baptizing in the Spirit (1:33) and

[36] Jn 7:38 is not a parallel, since the source from which the water flows must be the body of Jesus (see *ad loc.*).

[37] Elsewhere in the New Testament ἅλλεσθαι is used only of the "jumping" of the cripples who were healed Acts 3:8; 14:10 (so Is 35:6 LXX). The metaphor is used in another way Jg 14:6, 19; 15:14; 1 Sam 10:10 (LXX) of the Spirit of God who "leaps" upon the men of God; in Wis 18:15 of the word of God.

[38] Εἰς τὸν αἰῶνα in connection with divine life 6:51, 58; 8:51, 52; 10:28; 11:26; of Christ's remaining 8:35 (12:34); of the Paraclete's remaining 14:16.

[39] A similar image of water in an eschatological context is that of Ezek 36:25, "I shall pour pure water upon you that you may be clean", which is used in *1 QS*, 4:21 as follows: "He (God) will pour the Spirit of truth upon him like waters of purification." Here water is a symbol of the Holy Spirit as in Is 44:3; Joel 3:1f. Another metaphorical use in *1 QpHab*, 11:1f.: "And after that knowledge shall be revealed to them like the waters that fill the sea." These superficial parallels only show the flexibility of the symbolism of water.

[40] Mussner, ΖΩΗ, pp. 112f., maintains that it refers to the Spirit; other Catholic exegetes (Schanz, Durand, Lagrange, Braun) think of the divine life (sanctifying grace) or of both together.

pouring out streams of living water (7:38). But believers are also said to "receive" the Spirit (7:39; cf. 14:17; 20:22; 1 Jn 2:27; 3:24; 4:13). The ζωή mediated by the πνεῦμα, however, is the great gift of salvation, representing an active and vital reality in man, so that the image of the source welling up unfailingly could also be applied to it. It is also possible to explain it as revelation or the words of Jesus, since it is through the words of the revealer that Spirit and life come to believers (5:24; 6:63, 68; 8:51).

4:15 λέγει πρὸς αὐτὸν ἡ γυνή, Κύριε, δός μοι τοῦτο τὸ ὕδωρ, ἵνα μὴ διψῶ μηδὲ διέρχωμαι ἐνθάδε ἀντλεῖν.

The woman said to him, "Sir, give me this water, so that I need not be thirsty or come to draw water here."

Like Nicodemus (3:9), the woman continues to misunderstand, and asks for the magic water which is to quench all thirst (cf. the request for bread 6:34), so that she can be freed from the need of fetching water. It seems as though Jesus's efforts have been in vain.

c) The disclosure of her life-story by the revealer (4:16-19)

4:16 Λέγει αὐτῇ, Ὕπαγε φώνησον τὸν ἄνδρα σου καὶ ἐλθὲ ἐνθάδε·

He said to her, "Go and call your husband and come (back) here."

But Jesus gives the conversation a turn which continues it in the sense at which he is aiming. Knowledge of the woman's life underlies his simple request to summon her husband. This superhuman knowledge is part of the picture of the revealer in John (cf. commentary on 1:48; 2:24f.). Exegetes were formerly inclined to marvel at the masterly pedagogy of Jesus. But his efforts are not primarily directed at bringing the woman to abandon her sinful way of life. He is trying to make her more receptive to revelation, to lead her to believe in him (cf. vv. 19, 26, 29), which will of course also bring about a decisive change in her way of life (cf. 3:21).

4:17 ἀπεκρίθη ἡ γυνὴ καὶ εἶπεν αὐτῷ, Οὐκ ἔχω ἄνδρα. λέγει αὐτῇ ὁ Ἰησοῦς, Καλῶς εἶπες ὅτι Ἄνδρα οὐκ ἔχω·

The woman answered with the words, "I have no husband." Jesus said, "You are right when you say, 'I have no husband.'

4:18 πέντε γὰρ ἄνδρας ἔσχες, καὶ νῦν ὃν ἔχεις οὐκ ἔστιν σου ἀνήρ· τοῦτο ἀληθὲς εἴρηκας.

You have had five husbands, and now the man you have is not your husband. Here you have told the truth."

When she answers evasively that she has no husband, Jesus shows her how well he knows her life-story. She has had five husbands (in succession) and is now living with a man who is not her husband. The Jews held that a woman could only marry twice, or three times at most,[41] and with the strict views of Orientals on morality, the Samaritans must also have considered such frequent re-marriage as dishonourable and illegitimate. V. 29 supposes further that the woman is aware of her guilt and of the low opinion which her fellow-citizens have of her.

The unusual life-story of the Samaritan has led many exegetes to suppose that she is a symbolic figure, representing the people of Samaria and the religious apostasy of this hybrid nation by the usual image of marital infidelity. There is the further detail that according to 2 Kgs 17:24 ff., Sargon, king of Assyria, deported the inhabitants of Samaria after the capture of the city in 722 B.C. and settled part of five tribes from the eastern part of his empire there. These continued to worship their old gods. Even when after a plague of lions had been sent to punish them, they turned to the worship of Yahweh, their worship of the true God on Mt Garizim was considered unlawful by the Jews. The analogy, however, is not exact; 2 Kgs 17: 29 ff. mentions five foreign peoples, but seven gods, which were all worshipped together, and Yahweh along with them. Since the worship of Yahweh alone survived in the time of Jesus, it is hard to believe that the evangelist wished to designate it as "concubinage", which would be a very strange application of the ancient image from Hosea (cf. also v. 22, "You worship what you do not know"). In what follows, especially vv. 29, 39, 42, the evangelist takes the Samaritan and her previous life as the history of an individual; hence the symbolic interpretation, at least if given in isolation as the only one, is inacceptable.[42]

In spite of her wayward life, the Samaritan still has her religious questions and yearnings. This is not unusual, and Jesus's efforts correspond to what we know from the Synoptics. Here in John Jesus is seen as the same Saviour, seeking those who are lost, even in the non-Jewish world. He reveals his glory in the deep gloom of human weakness and misery, wherever he finds men at least ready to believe.

The modern "existential" interpretation, that revelation discloses the being of man (Bultmann), is also read into the text. It is not revelation as such but Jesus, the revealer, who brings to light of his own accord the woman's life-history, to make her see things clearly and give her an impulse towards faith. Nonetheless, his revelation also has a "critical" function (cf. 3:19 ff.; 5:40–47; 8:43–47).

4:19	λέγει αὐτῷ ἡ γυνή, Κύριε, θεωρῶ ὅτι προφήτης εἶ σύ.	The woman said to him, "Sir, I see that you are a prophet.

The Samaritan, who must have been astonished at the stranger's knowledge of her hidden past, concludes that he is a prophet (cf. Lk 7:39).

[41] See Billerbeck, vol. II, p. 437.

[42] Howard is critical of the symbolic interpretation (*Fourth Gospel*, pp. 182f.); so too Bultmann, p. 138; Barrett, *ad loc.*

The Synoptics also testify that this was the most general verdict pronounced among the people when they saw a man of God at work. The term was applied to John the Baptist (cf. Lk 1:76; Mt 14:5; Mk 11:32 parr.) and to Jesus himself (Mt 21:11, 46; Lk 7:16). It is in this general sense that "prophet" is to be understood here (cf. also 9:17). To judge by the absence of the article, the Samaritan is not thinking of *the* (Messianic) prophet (like 6:14; 7:40, 52 *var. lect.*), though the Messiah as expected by the Samaritans had prophetic traits, after Deut 18:15, 18. Nothing is said of the woman's emotional reactions; the evangelist is not concerned with her psychology or feelings, but with her growing faith. Hence her next words are not to be taken as a manoeuvre, steering the conversation away from a painful subject, but as a continuation of the dialogue, in which a religious question is discussed.[43]

d) Adoration in "Spirit and truth" (4:20–24)

4:20	οἱ πατέρες ἡμῶν ἐν τῷ ὄρει τούτῳ προσεκύνησαν· καὶ ὑμεῖς λέγετε ὅτι ἐν Ἱεροσολύμοις ἐστὶν ὁ τόπος ὅπου προσκυνεῖν δεῖ.	Our fathers worshipped on this mountain, and you people say that the place where God should be worshipped is in Jerusalem."

The Samaritan puts before the "prophet" the age-old problem debated between Samaritans and Jews, as to where God should be worshipped (cf. 2 Kgs 17:28–41). Since the Samaritans worshipped on Mt Garizim (Hebrew גְּרִיזִים) which rose in front of the speakers' eyes at the well of Jacob, the question readily suggested itself. According to the Samaritan tradition, the place at which the Israelites were to build an altar after their entry into Canaan (Deut 27:4–8) was not Mt Ebal but Mt Garizim, which is found here in the Samaritan Pentateuch instead of Ebal. How the building of the temple of Yahweh on Mt Garizim came about is not quite clear,[44] but it must have existed at least since the beginning of the Hellenistic era, till it was destroyed in 128 B.C. by John Hyrcan. But even

[43] Hoskyns's interpretation undoubtedly goes too far: since it is the task of the prophet to determine the place of forgiveness, she asks him to indicate the true place to adore God.

[44] After Nehemias drove the son of a high priest from Jerusalem because he had married the daughter of the Persian governor Sanballat of Samaria (Neh 13:28), the latter may have thought of founding his own place of worship. But in the Persian era the temple of Jerusalem was favoured as a place of worship and the Samaritans seem to have continued to go there, though reluctantly. Josephus, *Ant.*, XI, 321–4, relates that the Samaritans asked and were granted permission to build their own temple by Alexander the Great. In this connection he names people whose names coincide to a remarkable extent with those of Neh 13:28, especially the high priest Manasses, who was son-in-law of the governor "Sanballetes" (*Ant.*, XI, 302f.). Is Josephus making a mistake by placing people of a hundred years earlier in the time of Alexander? Or does he perhaps know that the temple was only built after

after this, the Samaritans did not give up their place of worship and refused to make the pilgrimage to Jerusalem.[45]

4:21 λέγει αὐτῇ ὁ Ἰησοῦς, Πίστευέ μοι, γύναι, ὅτι ἔρχεται ὥρα ὅτε οὔτε ἐν τῷ ὄρει τούτῳ οὔτε ἐν Ἱεροσολύμοις προσκυνήσετε τῷ πατρί.

Jesus said to her, "Believe me, madam, the hour is coming when you shall worship the Father neither on this mountain nor in Jerusalem.

Jesus answers with a word of revelation which points on to the future. The "hour is coming" when both places of worship will lose their significance. This Johannine expression (cf. 5:25, 28; 16:2, 25, 32) has a religious and eschatological sense, and is defined more closely in v. 23 by the words νῦν ἐστιν. With the person of Jesus, this day is already dawning, and a new type of worship is signalled in which the place where it is offered is unimportant. Then—which means from now on—the Samaritans will also pray to the "Father", that is, to God as revealed to them by Jesus, and the old shrines will not matter. This prophetic word with which Jesus turns to the woman, with a plea for confidence (πίστευέ μοι)[46] contains a consoling promise for the Samaritans who have suffered so much contempt from the Jews.

4:22 ὑμεῖς προσκυνεῖτε ὃ οὐκ οἴδατε· ἡμεῖς προσκυνοῦμεν ὃ οἴδαμεν, ὅτι ἡ σωτηρία ἐκ τῶν Ἰουδαίων ἐστίν.

You worship what you do not know, we worship what we know, for salvation comes from the Jews.

But before he develops this thought, Jesus remarks that the Jews still have precedence in the history of salvation. The Samaritans (ὑμεῖς) do not possess true knowledge of God; their worship rather grew out of national and political ambitions. The Jews (ἡμεῖς) are the legitimate worshippers of God, and "salvation", that is, the Messiah, stems from the

---

the Persian era? Cf. Schürer, *Geschichte*, vol. II, p. 21, E. T.: vol. II, i, p. 7; Noth, *Geschichte Israels*, p. 319; E. T.: pp. 354f.; Abel, *Histoire de la Palestine*, vol. I, pp. 360–9.

[45] Apart from Jn 4:20, we know this from Josephus, *Ant.*, XVIII, 85–87, telling of the false prophet who tried to gather the Samaritans on Mt Garizim, ὃ ἁγνότατον αὐτοῖς ὀρῶν ὑπείληπται, and the Passover which has been celebrated by the Samaritans on Mount Garizim, with long interruptions, down to the present day. See Jeremias, *Die Passafeier der Samaritaner*, pp. 5–52 (illustrated description); pp. 55–66 (history of the liturgy); Gaster, *Passover, its History and Traditions*, pp. 77–83.

[46] Πιστεύειν with dative has not its usual Johannine sense here (of believing someone as witness); it means "to trust". Though the usage of πιστεύειν is consistent, it allows of some exceptions, cf. 2:24, ("trust oneself to someone"), 9:18 (πιστεύειν περί).

Jews.[47] In spite of the supposedly "anti-Jewish" character of John, the idea is not very surprising. The Gospel also uses οἱ Ἰουδαῖοι in a neutral sense, when speaking of Jewish institutions and historical characteristics.[48] Judaism as such is not rejected, but only the unbelieving Jewish leaders of the day.[49] The Gospel displays no hatred of the Jewish people, though it regards them with a certain aloofness. The role of Israel in the history of salvation is not denied, but considered as a stage which has been left behind; in this sense, 1:17 provides a commentary on our present text. In the situation as he found it, Jesus had to overcome the woman's repugnance to the "Jews" (v. 9). The text probably also had a contemporary, possibly missionary significance, as removing the scandal of the Messiah from Israel. Converted Samaritans had to recognize that they were once schismatics and that it was only in Christ that they had been made part of the people of salvation.

There is no justification, therefore, for the effort of critics to eliminate v. 22b as a gloss and to understand ἡμεῖς of Christians, for whom Jesus is made to speak as in 3:11.[50] The ἀλλά at the beginning of the next verse also tells against this view, since it calls attention to the change in situation since v. 22, which is in fact a sort of transition, leading from the announcement of the eschatological age in v. 21 to its actual presence in v. 23.

4:23	ἀλλὰ ἔρχεται ὥρα, καὶ νῦν ἐστιν, ὅτε οἱ ἀληθινοὶ προσκυνηταὶ προσκυνήσουσιν τῷ πατρὶ ἐν πνεύματι καὶ ἀληθείᾳ· καὶ γὰρ ὁ πατὴρ τοιούτους ζητεῖ τοὺς προσκυνοῦντας αὐτόν.	But the hour is coming and it is here now, when the true worshippers will worship the Father in Spirit and truth. And such are the worshippers whom the Father demands.

Jesus now tells the Samaritan more clearly that the true worship of God is beginning "now", that is, with himself (cf. 5:25). The words τῷ πατρί also show that the promise of v. 21 is being taken up once more and put more clearly. Jesus uses the term "Father", not just because it is his usual way of speaking of God in the fourth Gospel, but because he is

---

[47] Σωτηρία only occurs here in John, but cf. ὁ σωτὴρ τοῦ κόσμου 4:42; 1 Jn 4:14. The Johannine doctrine is that the σωτήρ comes from Judaism, but to be saviour of the world, including the gentiles. Here John is close to the theology of Luke, cf. Lk 1:69, 71, 77; Acts 4:12; 13:26, 46f.; cf. also Paul in Rom 1:16; 11:11.

[48] Cf. the designation of the Jewish feasts as τῶν Ἰουδαίων 2:13; 5:1; 6:4; 7:2; 11:55; also 2:6; 18:20; 19:40, 42. A neutral use of the term also in 7:11; 11:19, 31, 33, 36, 45; 12:9, 11, though transitions to a derogatory use can also be noted.

[49] Hence the statement of v. 22 does not contradict the texts where Jesus denies that the unbelieving Jews have any real knowledge of God (7:28b; 8:19, 55).

[50] Cf. Loisy, Bauer, Bultmann, *ad loc.*; Odeberg, pp. 170f.; Hoskyns takes the opposite view.

describing the new relationship of the true adorer to God (cf. 1:12; 3:5f.; 1 Jn 3:1f.). The Johannine Jesus often speaks of "God",[51] but here he is inviting men who seek God to an unheard-of intimacy with the "Father". In a very succinct and pregnant phrase, Jesus describes true (ἀληθινός) adoration as that which is performed in "Spirit and truth". The pair of words,[52] in which the emphasis is on πνεύματι, means the same thing in both of its elements. A spiritualistic understanding, as though Jesus was contrasting the material place of worship with a purely interior worship of God in the mind of man, is excluded by the concept of *pneuma*, which according to v. 24 can only mean the Spirit of God, as it mostly does in the Johannine writings.[53] The "truth" also means, in Johannine theology, the divine reality revealed by Jesus, which believers are called to share in. After the dialogue with Nicodemus, it is easy to understand that the true adorers "in Spirit and truth" are those who are "born of the Spirit" (cf. 3:3–8). Of himself, earthly man can have no access to God and his heavenly realm (cf. 3:31); and if he is to pray effectively, he must also be enabled to do so by God, by being filled with his Spirit. In true worship there is an encounter with God for which God must make man capable by his grace. This is now also illustrated in a surprising way by the texts of Qumran.[54]

Speaking of the last days, *1 QS*, 4:20f. says: "Then God will purify all the deeds of man by his truth and he will cleanse the frame of man. He will eradicate the perverse spirit from within his flesh, and cleanse him by holy spirit from all his wicked deeds. He will pour out on him the spirit of truth like purifying water..." The community of Qumran, which is certain of this promise of the eschatological spirit of purification, already considers itself as the initial stage of this purified humanity, and believes that God has already filled it with holy spirit. In the ritual for entry into the community we read, *1 QS*, 3:6 ff., "By the spirit of counsel for the ways of man, all his iniquities shall be absolved, and he shall see the light of life; and by the holy spirit for unity in his truth, he shall be purified from all his iniquities." According to *1 QS*, 9:3–6, the community sees itself as a "holy house for Aaron" and a "house of the community for Israel" (cf. also 8:5f.), and speaks of "the sacrifice of the lips like a sweet odour rightly offered", and of "perfect behaviour like an agreeable sacrifice

[51] Cf. 4:10; 5:42, 44; 6:46; 8:40, 42; 11:4, 22, 40. The idea of Jesus's Father is not at once involved in the theme of divine worship (cf. the θεός in v. 24); the occurrence of the designation must therefore be connected with the nature of the adoration.

[52] The phrases χάρις καὶ ἀλήθεια 1:14, 17; ἀλήθεια καὶ ζωή 14:6; ἐν ἔργῳ καὶ ἀληθείᾳ 1 Jn 3:18; ἐν ἀληθείᾳ καὶ ἀγάπῃ 2 Jn 3 are comparable. The πνεῦμα is also characterized by ζωή (6:63) as well as by ἀλήθεια (14:17; 15:26; 16:13; 1 Jn 4:6; 5:6).

[53] But the Hellenistic spiritualizing is found in Philo, cf. *Quod deter.*, 21: "Genuine worship is that of a soul bringing simple reality (ἀλήθεια) as its only sacrifice"; *Vita Mos.*, II, 108; " The true oblation, what else can it be but the devotion of a soul which is dear to God?"; cf. also *Spec. leg.*, I, 271; *Plant.*, 108.

[54] See Schnackenburg, "Die Anbetung in Geist und Wahrheit (Joh 4,23) im Lichte von Qumrân-Texten"; also Gärtner, *The Temple and the Community in Qumran and the New Testament*, pp. 44ff., 119f.

freely offered". These cultic terms are used to express the community's pure worship of God, consisting of praise of God and of life according to his commandments. Hence the members wish to be "a foundation of holy spirit for eternal truth, to expiate the guilt of sin and the malice of crime, and to win blessing for the land". This is confirmed by the Thanksgiving Hymns, where the speaker (mainly, no doubt, the "Teacher of Righteousness") expresses the same thoughts on his own behalf. See for instance *1 QH*, 16:11f., "I know that no one is righteous except through thee, and through the spirit which thou hast given me, I have besought thee to bestow thy graces fully on thy servant, purifying me by thy holy spirit and bringing me (into the covenant) by thy grace, according to the multitude of thy mercies", or 17:26, "I will praise thee, O Lord, for thou hast poured out (thy) holy spirit upon thy servant..."; cf. also 7:6f.; 12:11f.; 13:18f.; 14:25; fr. II, 9, 13. The speaker asks for further gifts of spirit and truth: "Because I know these things, I find words on my lips, to pray and (to supplicate...), to seek (holy) spirit and to hold fast to the truth of thy covenant" (16:6f.). Thus praise of God and a perfect life are made possible by the holy spirit which the speaker believes he has received; but they are also a response to the grace of God.

Jesus's revelation on the true worship of God is well illustrated by the Qumran texts, but it goes beyond them, since Jesus proclaims that the eschatological fulfilment has come. a) If man is to adore God "in Spirit and truth", he must first be filled and penetrated by the Spirit of God. This is fully and effectively true of believers in Christ since their birth from God in baptism, where they receive power to become children of God (1:12f.; 1 Jn 3:1f.), are born "from above" through the Spirit of God (3:3, 5f.) and are thus enabled to lead a holy, indeed a sinless life which shows itself in love (1 Jn 2:29; 3:9; 4:7; 5:1, 18). b) This immediate, eschatological gift of the Spirit has come about through Jesus Christ (1:17). Hence true adoration in the Spirit is only possible in union with Christ. His glorified body is the holy temple of God (2:21); true worship is performed in him. To this extent, the ἐν πνεύματι of John is akin to the ἐν Χριστῷ of Paul.[55] In any case true and acceptable adoration is only possible through Jesus, the revealer and bringer of life (cf. 4:26; 6:63f.). c) Worship of God in the N.T. is directed to the Father, by whom the children of God are loved and chosen, whom they gratefully praise with all the familiarity of children and whom they serve according to his will. d) The worship offered in Spirit and truth is performed by the *community* of believers. The true adorers are not individualists but God's flock, gathered into one by the Son of God (cf. 6:37ff.; 10:1–18, 26–29) and continuing to gather to itself all the scattered children of God (cf. 10:16; 11:52). As the N.T. people of God, it is not subject to the limitations imposed by the history of salvation on the ancient temple of Jerusalem, whose rites it replaces by a worship in Spirit and truth founded on Christ which makes no difference between Jews, Samaritans and gentiles. As the

[55] See Horst, Προσκυνεῖν, p. 306; Schweizer, "πνεῦμα", p. 438, 7.

community of Christ, it is given the Spirit of God and charged with the new worship. e) The new worship is neither mere lip-service nor a purely interior cult. Bloody sacrifices cease at once, but the externals of worship are not totally rejected.[56] They are continued on a higher level in a sacramental and more spiritualized way. The new sacrificial gift is the glorified flesh and blood of the risen Lord (cf. 6:51c, 62f.).[57] Above all, such adoration must be effective in the keeping of the commandments, in fulfilling Jesus's commandment of charity (13:35). True adoration demands the "doing of the truth" (cf. 3:21; 1 Jn 1:6).

These are the adorers whom the Father wants and seeks for (ζητεῖ,[58] v. 23b), which also implies that the woman must allow God to find her, that is, by responding to Jesus who is speaking to her. Having laid bare her sinful life, Jesus wishes to bring her to accept God's pardon from him and to serve the Father with a pure heart, in Spirit and truth. For this, she must believe in Jesus, the revealer and saviour. Thus the dialogue culminates in the self-revelation of Jesus as the Messiah (v. 26).

4:24	πνεῦμα ὁ θεός, καὶ τοὺς προσκυνοῦντας αὐτὸν ἐν πνεύματι καὶ ἀληθείᾳ δεῖ προσκυνεῖν.	God is Spirit, and those who worship him must worship in Spirit and truth."

Jesus now explains further why this adoration must be inspired by the grace and the Spirit of God and must be the response of a pure heart. It is because of the nature of God. "God is spirit", which is a reminder that God is different from all that is earthly and human. It is not a definition of God's essence, but it expresses the transcendence and holiness of God. In John, πνεῦμα means all that belongs to God and the heavenly world, in contrast to all that is earthly and human. To be born merely from the "flesh" is to remain a prisoner of the world of the flesh which is doomed to perish, to be deprived of access to the higher realm of the spirit which is divine and heavenly. There is need of a new creation, which God himself must bring about by his power, if man is to be raised up to meet God and to belong to him. Man himself must (δεῖ) become a different being, a man

---

[56] It is different in Gnosticism, where only the mystic worship is of value, cf. *Odes of Solomon*, 20:2ff.: "To him I offer the sacrifice of his thought. For his thought is not like (the thought) of the world nor the thought of the flesh, nor like them that serve carnally. The sacrifice of the Lord is righteousness, and purity of heart and lips."

[57] Cf. Hoskyns, p. 245: "True worship is directed to the flesh and blood of Jesus."

[58] No doubt ζητεῖν here means primarily "to wish, demand", but the Father also "seeks" such adorers—through the Son. In that particular situation Jesus sought the woman (cf. v. 27); the word is used of religious searching in 1:38; 5:44; negatively 6:24, 26; cf. also 8:21; 13:33; 20:15. Odeberg says (173) that "the ἀνάβασις of the worship is met by a κατάβασις", and terms Jn 4:23 the counterpart to 3:16.

transformed by the Spirit, if he is to worship God adequately. What is decisive is not the place where worship is offered, but the man who worships and the way in which he can adore.

The spirituality of God, which is spoken of here, is part of the O.T. concept of God. God is not formally called "spirit" in the O.T., but he reveals himself by the way his Spirit rules over creation and history (Neh 9:20; Is 63:14), by his activity in giving and restoring life and well-being which extends even to the eschatological new creation (Ezek 36:27; 39:29). By the power of his Spirit he is greater than "man" or "flesh" (Is 31:3; see commentary on Jn 3:6 ff.), but calls all living things to serve him (cf. Is 34:16) and imposes his commandments on man by his holy Spirit (cf. Ps 51:12 ff.; Is 59:21; 63:10). It is the eschatological outlook above all which links Jn 4:23f. with the O.T. prophecy of the last days. Compared with this, the formal parallels which can be adduced from the religious environment of Christianity are merely superficial. There are similar sayings in Stoicism;[59] but here πνεῦμα is still thought of in connection with the material world, as the power which penetrates all things and holds them together. It is different again in Gnosticism, where God's transcendence is intensified till it is absolutely dissociated from the world and utterly unattainable, or is accessible only to the Gnostic, as is now well illustrated by the new finds from Nag-Hammadi. In the *Apocryphon of John*, God is frequently described as the "invisible Spirit"; he is "the (true) God, the Father of the all, the holy (Spirit), the invisible, he who is above the all, he who exists in his immortality; he is in pure light on which no eye can look" (22:19–23:2); "his aeon is immortal, he is in repose and reposes in silence" (26 : 6 ff.). Only Christ, "whom the invisible Spirit has set as God over the all" (32 : 12 ff.), reveals the ascent to the kingdom of lights and makes it possible for men, but only for those "who are of the race which does not waver. Those on whom the spirit of life descends, after they have united themselves with the power, will be saved and made perfect; and they will be worthy to ascend to those great lights . . ." (65:1 ff.). In the *Gospel of Truth* we read: "But those who are to receive the doctrine, the living ones who are inscribed in the book of the living, receive the doctrine, and only they. They receive themselves from the hand of the Father, they turn back to him again. Because the perfection of the all is in the hands of the Father, it is necessary that the all should ascend to him" (21). Everything here is developed in terms of the secret and exclusive doctrines of Gnosticism. The "Spirit" bestows on the elect the Gnosis which saves him: "As for knowledge of the Father and the revelation of his Son, he (the Spirit) gave them (the Gnostics) the power to experience it" (30).[60] The gulf between the Christian and the Gnostic doctrine of redemption is particularly clear in this meeting of Jesus with the Samaritan, where the true revealer and saviour speaks.

e) Jesus reveals himself as the Messiah (4:25–26)

4:25	λέγει αὐτῷ ἡ γυνή, Οἶδα ὅτι Μεσσίας ἔρχεται, ὁ λεγόμενος	The woman said to him, "I know that the Messiah is com-

[59] Cf. Chrysippus, *Frg.*, 10 (von Arnim, vol. II. p. 112, 31 f.): θεὸς . . . σῶμα, πνεῦμα ὢν νοερὸν καὶ ἀίδιον; Cleanthes, *Frg.*, 1009 (*ibid.*, p.299, 11 ff.): πνεῦμα νοερὸν καὶ πυρῶδες, οὐκ ἔχον μὲν μορφήν, μεταβάλλον δ'εἰς ὅ βούλεται καὶ συνεξομοιούμενον πᾶσιν (Quoted by Kleinknecht, "πνεῦμα", p. 353, 31–35).

[60] The translation of the *Gospel of Truth* according to Schenke, that of the *Apocryphon of John* according to Till.

Χριστός· ὅταν ἔλθῃ ἐκεῖνος, ἀναγγελεῖ ἡμῖν ἅπαντα.

ing, who is called Christ. When he comes he will tell us everything."

The Samaritan has not grasped Jesus's revelation, and hopes for the Messiah who will "tell us everything". She has failed to understand that Jesus is telling her that the present hour is that of fulfilment, of the coming of him who makes the true adoration of God possible. To some extent, this is an example of a "Johannine misunderstanding"; she is looking to the future, while Jesus speaks of the present. But her religious yearnings are sincere, she has also perhaps some intimation of the mystery of Jesus, and this provides him with the occasion of revealing himself to her as the expected Messiah (v. 26). In him she can find the fulfilment of her hopes, and the Samaritans along with her.

The Messianic expectations of the Samaritan are in accord with what we know from Samaritan sources. The Messiah is called *Ta'eb*, that is, he who returns;[61] in the light of Deut 18:18, he is regarded as the prophet who is to appear at the end, succeeding to the great prophet Moses. The importance of this text in the hopes of the Samaritans may be seen from the fact that it is added to the tenth commandment of the decalogue in their Pentateuch.[62] Their *Ta'eb* was regarded above all as a political leader, the restorer of the kingdom of Israel, like the Davidic Messiah of the Jews, though on account of his connection with Moses he was of the tribe of Levi. Hence, being himself a priest, he was also to restore the true worship.[63] His role as prophetic revealer or teacher, which was sometimes contested, was deduced from Deut 18:18. Thus the *Memar Markah* (a Samaritan source, third or fourth century A.D.), IV, 12 says that he will reveal the truth.[64] The existence of Messianic hopes among the Samaritans is also confirmed by Josephus, who tells how someone came forward, under Pontius Pilate, and promised to show the Samaritans where Moses had buried the sacred vessels on Mt Garizim; the armed intervention of Pilate, however, quelled the disturbance at once (*Ant.*, XVIII, 85-87). The absence of the article before Μεσσίας is strange; Odeberg (p. 187) suspects that it goes back to an original *Ta'eb* (so too Bultmann); if so, the woman's ὁ λεγόμενος Χριστός would mean, "he who is called Messiah (by you Jews)". But the phrase is probably a comment of the evangelist, like 1:41.[65]

4:26 λέγει αὐτῇ ὁ Ἰησοῦς, Ἐγώ εἰμι, ὁ λαλῶν σοι.

Jesus said to her, "I am he, I who am speaking to you."

---

[61] The translation can hardly be "he who leads back", cf. Merx, *Der Messias der Samaritaner*, pp. 42f.

[62] See Gaster, *The Samaritans*, pp. 185–90, esp. p. 187.

[63] On the Samaritan expectation of the Ta'eb, see Montgomery, *The Samaritans*, pp. 242–50; Merx, pp. 42f.; Gaster, pp. 90ff.; Odeberg, *Fourth Gospel*, pp. 181ff.; MacDonald, *The Theology of the Samaritans*, pp. 362–71.

[64] MacDonald, pp. 364f. (on *Memar Markah* cf. pp. 42f.).

[65] See Schnackenburg, "Messiasfrage", p. 241.

Jesus presents himself to the Samaritan as the expected Messiah, using the formula of revelation ἐγώ εἰμι. "The Messiah" can be easily supplied from the context. But in the mind of the evangelist, it must already suggest the absolute terms in which Jesus reveals his divine being (cf. 6:20; 8:24, 28, 58; 13:19).[66] Jesus is not compelled by the situation to give this answer (cf. 9:37), but reveals himself of his own accord to the Samaritan. With this the dialogue has reached its climax, as Jesus brings the Samaritan, who is also a representative of her people, to believe in him as the Messiah. And the themes of the water of life, and of adoration in Spirit and truth, are not left in isolation from the self-revelation of Jesus. He is the giver of the living water, he is also the "place" of the new worship of God, which is made possible by him and henceforth realized in him. The success of his missionary effort remains uncertain for the moment, since the disciples arrive and the conversation is broken off. But the Samaritan goes to call her fellow-countrymen, and they follow her eagerly. Jesus knows that the field is ripe for the harvest (v. 35f.), and the Samaritans finally come to believe in him without reserve as the "saviour of the world" (v. 42).

Interlude: Jesus's conversation with his disciples (4:27–38)

Introduction (4:27–30)

The following verses conclude the encounter of Jesus with the Samaritan and prepare for the two subsequent scenes, the interlude in which Jesus speaks of the "missions" to his disciples, and the grand finale in which the people of Sychar take Jesus to their hearts and believe in him (vv. 39–42). The Christological interest is maintained in these introductory verses, by means of the awed amazement of the disciples (v. 27) and the woman's appealing to her countrymen to go out to meet this mysterious man.

4:27	Καὶ ἐπὶ τούτῳ ἦλθαν οἱ μαθηταὶ αὐτοῦ, καὶ ἐθαύμαζον ὅτι μετὰ γυναικὸς ἐλάλει· οὐδεὶς μέντοι εἶπεν, Τί ζητεῖς; ἤ, Τί λαλεῖς μετ' αὐτῆς;	At that moment his disciples arrived, and they were astonished to see him talking to a woman. But no one asked him, "What do you seek?", or, "What are you talking of?"

Just then,[67] the disciples return from the town with their purchases (v. 8). Thus the conversation concludes impressively with Jesus's word of

[66] There will be an excursus later on the ἐγώ εἰμι formula.

[67] Instead of ἐπὶ τούτῳ Tat sy read ἐν τῷ λαλῆσαι; b j *statim*; vg *continuo*.

revelation (cf. 8:58); the woman's reactions are not described. The astonishment of the disciples is due to the fact that Jesus is talking to a woman, as is clear from the formulation (γυναικός without the article or any other qualification). They are not taken aback, like the Samaritan (v. 9) to see him disregarding the barriers of race. They are thinking of the reserve imposed on all Jews, and a rabbi in particular, with regard to the female sex.[68] But they do not criticize Jesus's behaviour. They merely wonder what Jesus can have been aiming at (τί ζητεῖς) in the conversation, and what was the subject (τί λαλεῖς μετ'αὐτῆς) of the discussion. Ζητεῖν in John hardly ever means a vague "wish", but "to seek", "to strive for", and in the second question τί can hardly mean "why", but "what"—as the parallelism with the first τί already suggests.[69] This short comment of the evangelist[70] underlines the reverent attitude of the disciples towards Jesus, and the two questions show the interest which the disciples take in the conversation—and keep the reader's interest alive. The awe of his friends makes the mystery of the revealer stand out more strongly.

4:28	ἀφῆκεν οὖν τὴν ὑδρίαν αὐτῆς ἡ γυνὴ καὶ ἀπῆλθεν εἰς τὴν πόλιν καὶ λέγει τοῖς ἀνθρώποις,	The woman left her jug there and went off to the town, where she told everybody,

The woman comes once more (οὖν) into the picture, as she hurries away to call her countrymen. There is no need to see anything in the abandonment of the water-jar[71] except that she wants to reach home quickly and unimpeded, to return with the people. The narrator is concerned only with the news which she spreads in the town.

4:29	Δεῦτε ἴδετε ἄνθρωπον ὃς εἶπέν μοι πάντα ὅσα ἐποίησα· μήτι οὗτός ἐστιν ὁ Χριστός;	"Come and see a man who has told me everything I have done. Is he perhaps the Messiah?"

The woman is full of the idea that she should bring others out to see the mysterious stranger at the well (δεῦτε, ἴδετε); it would be out of place, therefore, to draw conclusions as to her own belief. The strongest argument, she feels, is that the stranger knew of her past life, and hence must

---

[68] See Billerbeck, vol. II, p. 438 *ad loc.*; Moore, *Judaism*, vol. II, pp. 269f.

[69] John uses λαλεῖν with the accusative object (in the neutral) remarkably often, 30 times in all.

[70] Μέντοι is characteristic of Johannine style, cf. Schweizer, *Ego eimi*, p. 93 (no. 17); Ruckstuhl, *Literarische Einheit*, p. 204 (no. 26).

[71] Chrysostom: she was so inflamed by the words of Jesus that she forgot the purpose of her journey (*Hom.*, 34, 1: *PG* 59, col. 193).

certainly have prophetic gifts (cf. vv. 17–19)—which is also a sign that the evangelist does not restrict the significance of her life-story merely to that of a symbol. The question as to whether the man is the Messiah or not, is put merely tentatively; the μήτι does not demand absolutely a negative answer,[72] but can express a cautious opinion. It is meant to cause reflection (cf. v. 39), and the reader is thereby reminded of Jesus's self-revelation (v. 26).

4:30	ἐξῆλθον ἐκ τῆς πόλεως καὶ ἤρχοντο πρὸς αὐτόν.	They left the town and made for him.

The woman succeeds, in fact, with her countrymen. They all set out from the town (historic aorist) and make their way (imperfect) to the well of Jacob.

Interlude: Jesus speaks of missionary work (4:31–38)

The approach of the Samaritans signals a success for the work of Jesus as revealer. Jesus's conversation with his disciples in the meantime clearly has a missionary character and looks beyond the promising "harvest" that is at hand to the future mission of the Church. Just as Jesus is now fulfilling the mandate of his Father, so he too sends out his disciples to continue his work (v. 38). In the words addressed to his disciples he depicts the hidden work of the Father and his own visible success as sowing and harvest (vv. 35f.) and the metaphor of the harvest is retained for the later era which he opens up by his earthly work (v. 34). The terminology of vv. 37f. is enough to show that the missionary interests of the Church make themselves strongly felt here ("sowing and harvesting", "sending out", "labouring"); in addition, there is probably an interest in the mission in Samaria (see commentary on v. 38). The transition from the time of Jesus's work to that of the Apostles is made, not very smoothly, by the rather awkward parenthesis of v. 37. But there is no compelling reason to consider vv. 37f. as an addition made by the redactors or a later gloss, still less to assert that the whole theme (vv. 35–38) is from another pen.[73] The thread of the narrative, interrupted in v. 30, is not simply taken up again in v. 39. On the contrary, this verse recounts the faith of the Samaritans, and v. 40 links up once more with v. 39 (οὖν). The section vv. 39–42 is not just to round off the story, but to deal with the theme of "faith", founded first on the woman's amazing news, and then on the

---

[72] Cf. Funk, *Greek Grammar*, para. 427, 2 (more or less "perhaps"), cf. also 7:26 (μήποτε). According to Bultmann, p. 142, n. 4, from the standpoint of those addressed.

[73] So Odeberg, p. 190.

words of the revealer himself (cf. v. 39 with 41 f.). The section, like the preceding dialogue with the Samaritan, is dominated by a theme which in vv. 37 f. evokes interests outside the immediate situation. This explains the structure and movement of vv. 31–38. The disciples' urging Jesus to eat leads to his speaking of the food which consists of doing his Father's will (vv. 31–34); this is what makes him look at the harvest at hand (vv. 35 f.) and then take in the later missionary work of his disciples (vv. 37 f.). The interpretation is rendered more difficult by two proverbial phrases (vv. 35 a and 37), which become intelligible when it is noted that they serve as transitions.

4:31 Ἐν τῷ μεταξὺ ἠρώτων αὐτόν οἱ μαθηταὶ λέγοντες, Ῥαββί, φάγε. — Meanwhile, his disciples invited him to eat, saying, "Rabbi, take something to eat".

The disciples' offer of food is normal in the situation, since Jesus is exhausted and the disciples have bought provisions in the meantime (cf. vv. 6–8). But like Jesus's request to the Samaritan, the disciples' invitation to eat serves merely as the occasion for his revealing a profounder truth. But this does not affirm Jesus's superiority to bodily needs, a divine mode of existence not subject to earthly conditions, much less a Gnostic contempt for the material.[74] There is hardly even an echo of the thought of Mt 4:4, since there is no antithesis between earthly bread and the word of God. The Johannine Jesus merely resists the urging of his disciples by making a positive affirmation about the "food" which he has to "eat", and this food is of a completely different nature.

4:32 ὁ δὲ εἶπεν αὐτοῖς, Ἐγὼ βρῶσιν ἔχω φαγεῖν ἣν ὑμεῖς οὐκ οἴδατε. — But he said to them, "I have food to eat which you do not know of".

The "food"[75] is not in the nature of a gift of God or inner strength given by the Father. It is only a way of describing the great interest which dominates the mind of Jesus and claims him totally; the whole expression "to have food to eat" becomes a metaphor. Jesus has nothing special to

[74] Contrast the attitude of Thomas in *Acts of Thomas* (Bonnet, p. 106): "And as they dined and drank, the Apostle tasted nothing, so that they that were about said unto him: wherefore art thou come here, neither eating nor drinking? But he answered them saying: I am come here for somewhat greater than food or drink and that I may fulfil the King's will"; also cited by Behm, "βρῶμα", p. 642, n. 60.

[75] Βρῶσις means the same as βρῶμα (v. 34), cf. 6:27, 55, and hence is the food, not the eating, which is why φαγεῖν is added; it is found elsewhere with this meaning, cf. Arndt and Gingrich, *Lexicon*, s. v. 3.

sustain him, as the disciples mistakenly believe, but he must put himself completely at the disposition of his Father. Ἔχειν with the infinitive means "to have to do something" (cf. Lk 12:50), not, however, under coercion, but by an inward compulsion (cf. Acts 23:17 ff.; 2 Jn 12; 3 Jn 13),[76] as follows from the ἵνα-clause in v. 34. But the Greek phrase is ambiguous and can give rise to the misunderstanding of the disciples in v. 33. The metaphor of eating to describe mental effort, here dedication to the divine will, is not unusual.[77] In another way, men are also called upon to "eat" and "drink" in a metaphorical sense, by "coming to Jesus", by "believing" in the "bread from heaven" (cf. 6:35, 50, 51 a). But the disciples have no idea of this "food" of Jesus; they constantly find themselves bewildered by the mystery of his work, which stems from his unity with the Father and from his charge (cf. 2:17; 5:17; 9:4; 11:7–10).

4:33	ἔλεγον οὖν οἱ μαθηταὶ πρὸς ἀλλήλους, Μή τις ἤνεγκεν αὐτῷ φαγεῖν;	His disciples asked each other, "Has someone perhaps brought him food?"

The disciples fall at once into a crude misunderstanding. They ask one another—again not daring to address Jesus—"Surely he cannot have been given food?" Such misunderstandings of Jesus's revelation occur, not merely among the wider public (Nicodemus, 3:4; the Samaritan, 4:15) and unbelievers (cf. 6:52; 7:35; 8:22, 57) but even among his disciples even in their last hours with him (cf. 14:8; 16:17 f., 30). As heavenly revealer Jesus is strange and incomprehensible to all men (cf. 3:31 f.). At the same time, these Johannine misunderstandings also take the conversation a step further. They enable Jesus to explain his revelation, to express it more forcibly and decisively.[78]

4:34	λέγει αὐτοῖς ὁ Ἰησοῦς, Ἐμὸν βρῶμά ἐστιν ἵνα ποιήσω τὸ θέλημα τοῦ πέμψαντός με καὶ τελειώσω αὐτοῦ τὸ ἔργον.	But Jesus said to them, "My food is to do the will of him who sent me and to carry out his work.

The style and rhythm of the saying (three stichs) already mark it as a word of revelation. The whole life of Jesus is centred on and grows out of the effort to do the will of him who sent him. The expression, "to do the

[76] Cf. Arndt and Gingrich, *Lexicon*, s. v. 6, b.

[77] The image is used of the Torah, Prov. 9:5; Ecclus 24:21; of moral endeavour, Philo, *Leg. all.*, I, 97 (τὸ γὰρ φαγεῖν σύμβολόν ἐστι τροφῆς ψυχικῆς . . .); of studying the Torah and of good works *Qoh. Rabbah*, 2:24 (see Behm, "ἐσθίω", p. 689, 5–13.

[78] Cf. 3:5 with 3:3; 6:53 with 6:51 b; 8:23 f. with 8:21; 14:9 f. with 14:7; 16:19–22 with 16:16.

will of God",[79] which is frequent in the O.T., Judaism and primitive Christianity, is mostly found in John in connection with the typical Johannine designation of God as the Father: it is the Father who has sent Jesus.[80] Theologically, the affinities with Heb 10:5–9 are noteworthy. There Christ's total dedication (in the sacrifice of the Cross) is based on Ps 40:7–9, but his readiness to do the will of God is already expressed by Christ at his entry into the world (v. 5). The decisive element in his act of redemption is the dedication of his will, his obedience towards God, which dominates his whole life and culminates in the sacrificial offering of his body. So too here Jesus tells his disciples that he is exhausting his strength in order to do God's will perfectly. The second phrase, καὶ τελειώσω αὐτοῦ τὸ ἔργον, seems to be merely a variation of the same thought,[81] perhaps to bring out still more strongly the persistance in the fulfilment of the divine task of redemption, which is carried out to the end (cf. 17:4; 19:30, where, however, τετέλεσται is used, from τελέω). The singular τὸ ἔργον means the whole "work" which Jesus has to do on earth, and is to be distinguished from the ἔργα, the individual tasks which he has to accomplish. But of course both "the works" and "the work" of Jesus's whole life on earth are at one in being based on the will of the Father. Τελειοῦν probably also signifies that Jesus is to bring to completion the work begun by the Father,[82] so that the two "work together" in perfect unity (cf. 5: 17, 19).

If τελειώσω is taken in this way,[83] it links up very well with v. 36. The "sower" is then the Father, and the "harvester" the Son. No doubt v. 34 is a statement of a general principle which covers the whole earthly work of Jesus. But even in particular cases Jesus's work is done in obedience to the will of his Father, which leads here to the expression of gratitude in v. 36.

---

[79] Cf. Mk 3:35 par. Mt; Mt 7:21; Eph 6:6; Heb 10:7, 9 (= Ps 39:8f. LXX); 10:36; 13:21; 1 Jn 2:17. On Judaism see Billerbeck, vol. I, p. 467.

[80] On the lips of Jesus 24 times with πέμπειν, 15 times or 17 times with ἀποστέλλειν; cf. Haenchen, "Der Vater, der mich gesandt hat". For the concept in Paul see Gal 4:4; Rom 8:3.

[81] In the first member of the phrase $P^{66\ 75}$ B C D Θ L Ψ W 083 λ 33 565 1241 al. read ποιήσω (adopted by Westcott and Hort, von Soden, Lagrange, Merk and Bover); ℵ 𝔎 al. ποιῶ (adopted by Tischendorf, Weiss, Vogels and Nestle). The present seems to bring out better the present nature of the action; it is also possible that the following τελειώσω is not to be taken as aorist subjunctive but as future, cf. 15:8 and Funk, *Greek Grammar*, para. 369, 3. Hence ποιῶ should be preferred, as the *lectio difficilior*.

[82] τελειοῦν can have various shades of meaning. "Perfected" unity (17:23) and love (cf. 1 Jn 2:5; 4:12, 17, 18) indicate the "perfection" of a state or attitude; the "fulfilment" of a work means rather its final accomplishment (cf. 19:28, where speaking of the scripture, instead of the usual πληρωθῇ, it is said ἵνα τελειωθῇ with regard to τετέλεσται). But it is Jesus's "being accomplished" that leads to this "accomplishment". See also du Plessis, ΤΕΛΕΙΟΣ, p. 174.

[83] Cf. Thüsing, *Erhöhung*, pp. 51 and 54.

Theologically, the saying is important. Jesus lives entirely from his inner union with the Father, receives from him the command to act and submits himself obediently. He is so full of a sense of mission and so zealous for his Father's interests that worldly things and needs sink into insignificance. His union with the Father does not appear here as mystical and metaphysical, but rather as unity of will and fellowship in work, though deeper reasons may be sensed. All that he does is inspired by his love and his obedient submission to his Father, which, however, does not exclude oneness of being with him, but rather presupposes it. His obedient service and his work for the salvation of men is at the same time an example for his disciples, who are to take it up and continue it (cf. 13:15f.).

4:35–38. Harvest and mission. This section causes difficulties and has led to a variety of interpretations. Since the Samaritans are approaching while Jesus speaks, v. 35b can hardly be anything but an allusion ("look!") to this spiritual harvest-field (the fields are "white", ripe for harvest). The present success is seen by Jesus as a highly promising sign for the future mission. Such a broadening of the perspective is not an isolated instance in John. The evangelist's interest in the gathering in of the "scattered children of God" can be recognized in 11:52, and Jesus himself speaks in 10:16 of his sheep from "other folds". The image of (missionary) "fruit" occurs again in 12:24, and as in ch. 4, the "Greeks" enquiring for Jesus are a promising sign. Finally, in the high priestly prayer (17:20f.) Jesus also directs his gaze towards future believers, likewise in connection with the mission of his disciples (the aorist is used in both cases, cf. 4:38 and 17:18). In all these cases, the earthly Jesus is already inspired by the certainty of his future exaltation and power to give life to believers. Thus we try to give a positive explanation which will take into account the progression from the immediate situation to the experience of the early Christian mission.

4:35	οὐχ ὑμεῖς λέγετε ὅτι Ἔτι τετράμηνός ἐστιν καὶ ὁ θερισμὸς ἔρχεται; ἰδοὺ λέγω ὑμῖν, ἐπάρατε τοὺς ὀφθαλμοὺς ὑμῶν καὶ θεάσασθε τὰς χώρας ὅτι λευκαί εἰσιν πρὸς θερισμόν.	Do you not say, 'Another four months and the harvest is here'? But now, I tell you, look at the fields before your eyes, and see how they are white for the harvest.

Jesus, full of the thought of his work, expresses his joy at seeing the future harvest already taking shape (vv. 35b–36a). To impress on his disciples the remarkable character of the event, he contrasts it with ordinary experience: normally, the harvest takes longer to ripen. The phrase οὐχ ὑμεῖς λέγετε (35a) corresponds clearly to his own affirmation ἰδοὺ λέγω ὑμῖν (35b).[84] The question introduced by οὐ is not unusual,[85] and always refers to something which is supposed known. The disciples say, or rather, might say that the harvest only comes after four months' waiting. The sentence is Semitic in idiom,[86] and can be either a statement evoked by the occasion or a general proverb. Which it is cannot be decided by the formulation (for instance, by the ἔτι[87]). The existence of such a proverb cannot be proved, but is not impossible. Even though six months were normally counted between sowing and harvest,[88] the interval could also be given as four months, counting from the farmer's last sowing till the beginning of the harvest, that is, the shortest period of waiting between his labours.[89] Jesus is not concerned with the time it takes the seed to ripen, but with the waiting imposed on the farmer, which is not necessary in his own case.

The question of whether it is a proverb or general rule, or a reference to the actual time of the year is of importance only for the chronology of the life of Jesus. In the second case, the scene would have to be placed in December or January.[90] But the evangelist certainly had not this question in mind, though subsequent calculations are not ruled out (cf. 2:20). The text cannot be used as a firm pointer for the chronology of Jesus's ministry.

Jesus tells his disciples to look—"lift up your eyes"[91]—and contemplate the white fields, ready for harvest. The fields probably mean the approaching Samaritans (in their white garments), who demonstrate vividly to the disciples that Jesus's harvest-field is ready. Unlike the farmer, he has not to wait a long time for the harvest.[92]

4:36	ἤδη ὁ θερίζων μισθὸν λαμβάνει καὶ συνάγει καρπὸν εἰς ζωὴν	The reaper is already receiving his reward and gathering a

[84] The expression is hardly to be omitted with λ 565 pc Orig.

[85] Cf. 6:42, 70; 7:19, 25, 42; 8:48; 9:8; 10:34; 11:37, 40; 14:10; 18:26; 19:10.

[86] Coordination instead of subordination; on the present construction see Beer and Meyer, *Hebräische Grammatik*, paras. 112, 121, 1b. Schlatter, *ad loc.*, cites Jer 51:33 as an example.

[87] This should be kept with all modern editors; its absence in D L φ pm sy^c is easily explained by the similarity with the preceding ὅτι (i.e., haplography).

[88] See Billerbeck, vol. II, pp. 439f.

[89] Sowing could be delayed by rain; the harvest began at the end of April or the beginning of May, cf. Schlatter, *ad loc.* The saying often adduced from *Pal. Ta'an.*, I, 64a (Billerbeck, vol. II, p. 440 under *d*), to exclude a possible proverb, refers to the time of growth, not to the farmer's waiting between his two operations.

[90] Cf. Holzmeister, *Chronologia*, pp. 144–8.

[91] This is a Semitic idiom, "ancient Hebrew", cf. Gen 13:14; 1 Chr 21:16; Is 60:4; Zech 2:1; Mt 17:8; Lk 6:20; 16:23; Jn 6:5.

[92] Some editors of the text (Weiss, Bover) and exegetes take ἤδη with this clause; but in Johannine usage ἤδη is usually at the beginning (3:18; 4:51; 7:14; 9:22; 13:2; 15:3; 19:28, 33), and is clearly at the end only in 9:27. In P[75], however, there is a stop after ἤδη.

αἰώνιον, ἵνα ὁ σπείρων ὁμοῦ χαίρῃ καὶ ὁ θερίζων.	crop for eternal life, so that the sower may rejoice along with the reaper.

He already experiences the joy of harvest home. Continuing to speak figuratively, he clearly means himself when he speaks of the "reaper". The mention of "receiving reward" and "gathering the crop" is merely to depict the harvest in progress and the joy of the reaper. The reception of the reward hardly refers here to the metaphor of payment of wages (cf. Mt 20:8 ff.). The reward is probably the gathering of the harvest itself; the καί, therefore, gives the precise explanation of the reward. Otherwise the sequence would be very strange: one does not expect payment before the work is done. Jesus's "reward" is simply the joy of harvest (36c); his life and his work are so completely identified (v. 34) that his only desire is to see the "harvest". Καρπός is from the terminology of the mission, as in 12:24; cf. Paul in Rom 1:13; 1 Cor 9:7; Phil 1:22.[93] The work of Jesus on earth, and still more, the sacrifice of his death (12:24) lead to a rich missionary harvest, a growing community of believers (cf. also 14:12); the harvest strictly speaking begins only with his exaltation (cf. 11:52; 12:32; 17:2).

The "harvest" is an eschatological metaphor, already used in the O.T., both for the judgment of the nations (Joel 4:13) and the gathering of the scattered Israelites (Is 27:12), and likewise in apocalyptic.[94] Both appear in the parable of the weeds among the wheat (Mt 13:30, 39–42), the judgment alone in Rev 14:15f. (after Joel 4:13). But the use of Joel 4:13 in Mk 4:29 already shows that the coming of salvation is in the foreground, and the logion Mt 9:37f. par. Lk 10:2 (Q) further demonstrates how close this eschatological "harvest" was in the mind of Jesus. The mission becomes an eschatological event: Jesus gathers the people of God, to lead it to the kingdom of God, and sends out his disciples to help with this work or to continue it. The fourth evangelist sees things in the same perspective as early Christianity, but projects the eschatology even more fully into the present: with Jesus the eschaton is already there (cf. 4:23), the time of harvest has come, and Jesus himself is already starting to gather in the crop. But the outlook still takes in the future, the harvest goes on, the mission takes up the work of Jesus and continues it. The eschatological perspective is also displayed in the concept of "eternal life". The believers whom Jesus gains in Samaria are a harvest or fruit "for eternal life". This means that Jesus imparts to them eternal life

---

[93] The metaphor is otherwise used predominantly of the success of moral effort or of the work of the Spirit in man (Gal 5:22), cf. Hauck, "καρπός", pp. 617f.

[94] *4 Esdr*, 4:28–32; *Syriac Apoc. Bar.*, 70:2; rabbinical examples in Billerbeck, vol. I, pp. 672f.

(cf. 3:16, 36; 5:24 etc.) and thus leads them to eternal life (cf. 12:25). Hence the εἰς is final, possibly also local (in conjunction with συνάγειν), cf. Mt 3:12; 13:30.[95] Even where the image is spatial, the presential character of ζωή is not excluded (cf. 5:24; 1 Jn 3:14).

Harvest as the gathering of the yield means joy; it is already a typical image in the O.T. (Is 9:2; Ps 126:5f.). Jesus too has such joy, but with the special note, that here the sower is to rejoice along with[96] the reaper. Who is the sower? If it were not for v. 37, it could be Jesus himself, who is active in sowing as well as reaping.[97] But the contrast between sower and reaper in v. 37, the co-operation between Jesus and him who sent him according to v. 34, and finally, the combination of two persons under ὁμοῦ (v. 36), leave no option but to think of the Father. Then the ἵνα-clause contains the further thought of the Father sharing with Jesus the joy of harvest. As they worked together at the sowing (v. 34), so too they can now rejoice in common at the harvest. Elsewhere too in John it is the Father who "gives" believers to Jesus and "draws" them to him (cf. 6:37 ff., 44, 65; 10:29; 17:6), while Jesus only takes up the Father's work and completes it. The idea expressed in v. 34 is probably still at work here.

This analysis is not compatible with the interpretation which takes the θερίζων as the disciples.[98] From v. 36 on, the harvest is already being reaped, and even a very slight postponement of the harvesting would spoil the whole point of 36c. The interpretation in question is arrived at by working back from v. 38. But there the future is envisaged, a perspective to which the evangelist provided himself with a transition in v. 37. If one keeps in mind the progressive nature of the thought, the exegesis in question is also unnecessary.

4:37	ἐν γὰρ τούτῳ ὁ λόγος ἐστὶν ἀληθινὸς ὅτι Ἄλλος ἐστὶν ὁ σπείρων καὶ ἄλλος ὁ θερίζων.	Here, indeed, the proverb is true, 'One man sows and another reaps'.

Linking up with the preceding, Jesus explains (γάρ), by means of a proverb (λόγος), that sower and reaper are not the same. The singular with the article is generic,[99] and the sense is that what one man sows,

[95] So Mussner, ΖΩΗ, p. 177: to bring the harvest into the barns of eternal life; cf. also Dodd, *Interpretation*, p. 146, who thinks that the underlying thought in John is that of the two ages (this world and the world to come).

[96] Ὁμοῦ does not mean "in the same way" but "in union with". The adverb expresses local (or personal proximity), along with and near to, cf. Arndt and Gingrich, *Lexicon*, p. 572.

[97] So for instance Loisy, Bauer, Strathmann, Wikenhauser; Preisker, "μισθός", p. 702, 25 ff.

[98] Cf. Bultmann, p. 146, Schick.

[99] Cf. Funk, *Greek Grammar*, paras. 252, 263.

another reaps. Thus the verse performs the function of a transition: in v. 36, the Father was the sower and Jesus the reaper, but now other sowers and reapers are envisaged. The rule that one man sows and another reaps remains valid, reliable,[100] even in the future.

4:38	ἐγὼ ἀπέστειλα ὑμᾶς θερίζειν ὃ οὐχ ὑμεῖς κεκοπιάκατε· ἄλλοι κεκοπιάκασιν, καὶ ὑμεῖς εἰς τὸν κόπον αὐτῶν εἰσεληλύθατε.	I have sent you to reap what you have not laboured on. Others have laboured, and you have come in to enjoy the fruits of their labour."

Jesus explains to his disciples what their missionary situation is: since he sent them out, they too may reap; but they must remember that others have laboured before them. The aorist is to be taken seriously (ἀπέστειλα); Jesus places himself mentally in the future, when he has already sent out his disciples. Nothing is said in John of a first mission during the earthly work of Jesus, an omission which is hardly accidental, in spite of the fragmentary character of the narrative. As long as Jesus is dwelling in this cosmos, he is the only one who works, in union with his Father (cf. 5:17, 19; 7:3; 9:4; 10:25, 32, 37; 14:10). The disciples only begin their missionary work after his departure, when they have been sent out by the risen Lord (20:21) and are guided and supported by the Holy Spirit (cf. 15:26f.; 16:7–11). In itself, the time of Jesus is distinguished from the time of the Church; but Jesus's view already takes in the coming time of fruitfulness, in which he, as the exalted Lord, draws all men to him (12:32), does still greater works through his disciples (cf. 14:12) and gathers the one flock of believers (cf. 10:16; 17:21). Hence the aorist ἀπέστειλα, which recurs in 17:18, must be explained in terms of prophetic prevision.[101] The mission is only conferred after the Resurrection (20:21, with the present πέμπω), but 4:38 already looks back on this act (cf. the following perfect). The evangelist is not trying, so to speak, to insert a saying of the risen Lord into the discourse at the well of Jacob.

[100] Ἀληθινός, before which important witnesses read the article (P[66] ℵ 𝔎 D Θ pm), must here be practically the same as ἀληθής, merely stressing more strongly still the certainty of the proverb, cf. Arndt and Gingrich, *Lexicon*, s. v. 2. On ἀληθινός in this sense of "sure, exact, correct" cf. 8:16; 19:35. It is remarkable that the whole v. 37 is missing in P[75]. But this is easily explained by the fact that the copyist's eye jumped from ὁ θερίζων at the end of v. 36 to the same word at the end of v. 37. On the literary analysis see also Ruckstuhl, *Literarische Einheit*, pp. 235f.

[101] The reading of ℵ D is ἀπέσταλκα, probably by assimilation to the following perfects. Strictly speaking, one would expect the *futurum exactum*, which apart from a few exceptions can only be expressed in Greek by the periphrasis of the *perf. part.* and ἔσομαι (Funk, *Greek Grammar*, paras. 65, 1b; 352); this is not used in the New Testament, and is superfluous here in the context, cf. the following perfects. A very similar aorist 15:8.

It is the earthly Jesus who speaks, fully conscious of his future exaltation and of the salvation which he will effect through his disciples.

If this point is missed, and the text explained as the conferring of a mission at the present juncture, one has to fall back, like the Fathers and many later exegetes,[102] on the untenable explanation that the "others" who laboured before the disciples are the prophets, John the Baptist and eventually Jesus. But the inclusion of the prophets and John the Baptist is very far from mind of the evangelist. Jesus alone accomplishes the eschatological work of salvation; Moses (5:46) and John the Baptist (1:19–34; 5:33f.) only bear testimony to him. And Jesus's work is continued by his envoys, in his name and in his stead (cf. 13:20; also 13:16; 15:20). The view now propounded by Thüsing,[103] that the "others" are Jesus and the Father, is excluded above all by the expression "labour" (κοπιᾶν). This might hold good for Jesus (cf. 4:6), but it would be quite out of place for the Father.

In contrast to Jesus, the disciples will be able to reap a harvest where others have already laboured. Κοπιᾶν and κόπος are terms perhaps introduced by Paul[104] for missionary work (cf. 1 Thess 3:5; 1 Cor 3:8; 15:10; Col 1:29 etc.), and also for activity in the community (cf. 1 Thess 5:12; 1 Cor 16:16; Acts 20:35; 1 Tim 4:10; 5:17). Since the term is used here in a technical, missionary sense (contrast 4:6), there is reason to believe that this text is coloured by the actual missionary interests of the evangelist in his own day. This becomes even clearer when we examine the "others". Predecessors of Jesus may be excluded (see above); and Jesus himself (possibly in conjunction with his Father) cannot be intended. Jesus speaks of himself as "sending out" the disciples, and the roles are kept distinct. Jesus is the sender, "others" perform the labour, and the disciples addressed by Jesus are the harvesters, who benefit by the labours of the "others". The saying has a mysterious sound, as though the readers should know who are meant. The simplest explanation is that of O. Cullmann,[105] who suggests that the evangelist is thinking of concrete conditions of the Christian mission, in particular in Samaria.

We know from Acts 8 that Philip, one of the "seven", and possibly other "Hellenists" did missionary work in Samaria (cf. 8:4). The "Apostles in Jerusalem" (8:14) sanctioned and completed the work by sending Peter and John, who imposed hands on the neophytes and communicated the Holy Spirit (8:14–17). The fourth evangelist,

---

[102] Origen, *In Jo.*, XIII, 50 (Preuschen, p. 277), Chrysostom, *Hom.*, 34, 2 (*PG* 59, col. 119), Theodore of Mopsuestia (Vosté, *CSCO* 116, p. 67), Augustine, *Tr.* XV, 32; (*Corpus christianorum*, 36 p. 163), Thomas Aquinas (Cai p. 123). Among moderns cf. Maldonatus, Lagrange, Tillmann, F.-M. Braun.

[103] *Erhöhung*, pp. 54f. Bultmann, p. 147, considers this interpretation but rejects it.

[104] Cf. von Harnack, "Κόπος", esp. pp. 4f.; Hauck, "κόπος".

[105] "Samaria and the Origins of the Christian Mission"; he thinks that the Johannine groups were linked both with Qumran and the disciples of the Baptist and with the group of which Stephen was a member. Cullmann argues from the opposition of these groups to the Jerusalem temple; but he overlooks important differences between them. Schlatter had already referred to Acts 8 (*ad loc.*, p. 134).

here as elsewhere close to the Lucan tradition (cf. also Lk 9:52–56; 10:33–37; 17:11 19; Acts 1:8; 9:31), could have paid special attention to this mission in Samaria, though why exactly, we do not know. Is his presentation inspired by the fruitfulness of the mission in Samaria, where he had connections, or by the work of the preachers from the ranks of the Hellenists, with whom he himself was associated? The latter is suggested by the tone of the passage, which emphasizes the labours of the "others" and gives the older disciples food for thought. But that he himself belonged to this rather shadowy circle (and was thus brought into contact with heterodox groups in Judaism, possibly also with the Essenes of Qumran), remains purely hypothetical.

"Entering into the labours of others" is a metaphor for taking up their work and reaping the benefit of their labours. What the "doctrine" of the passage precisely refers to in the concrete we can no longer tell, but it contains a reminder which is of permanent importance for missionary theology. All missionary work is in unbroken continuity with the mission and work of Jesus, and every missionary builds on the labours of his predecessors. As regards the procedure of the fourth evangelist, we can see that his perspective shifts from Jesus to the "time of the Church", and that this latter is simply the prolongation and fructifying of the time of Jesus, and indeed that both times are basically one, just as the exalted Lord continues and completes his earthly work, though in a different way. And vice versa, the evangelist can show the bearing of the words of the earthly Jesus on later problems and the needs of his own day, as is also apparent in many other texts (cf. the Baptist episodes; also 13:8 ff.; 19:34–37 etc.).

With this interpretation we have decided against various other views: a) that by "sowers" and "reapers" in v. 36 Jesus means himself; b) that the "reapers" in v. 36 are the disciples; c) that the "others" of v. 38b refer to Jesus and the Father. Another view of the whole context can be taken if with many Fathers and Lagrange one interprets it as follows: vv. 36–38 are a digression; v. 35a is a proverb, according to which the disciples are urged in v. 35b to see the harvest with the eyes of the spirit. The following verses are only development of the image of the harvest: the reapers gain their reward, but should remember that the sowers laboured before them. V. 36 is, therefore, only a general principle, of which the actual application is given in v. 38. This explanation fails to do justice to the concrete situation. What is the point of this general instruction on missionary work here? The facts are rather that Jesus starts from the actual situation and then looks out on the future, which in turn provides an occasion for giving the disciples some basic instruction on their mission.

Conclusion: the faith of the Samaritans (4:39–42)

After the interlude with the disciples, where the metaphor of the harvest has already made it clear to the reader that Jesus will find faith among the Samaritans, the final section takes up once more the thread of the narrative (cf. v. 30) and brings the story to its end. It contains a theology of faith where the evangelist demonstrates that full faith can only be attained in the encounter with Jesus and by hearing his words. The motive of faith is all the loftier, the more exclusively faith adheres to the word of the revealer; the content of faith grows as it grasps better the eschatological and soteriological significance of Jesus. Here faith in Christ reaches a climax in confessing Jesus as the universal saviour of the world.

4:39	Ἐκ δὲ τῆς πόλεως ἐκείνης πολλοὶ ἐπίστευσαν εἰς αὐτὸν τῶν Σαμαριτῶν διὰ τὸν λόγον τῆς γυναικὸς μαρτυρούσης ὅτι Εἶπέν μοι πάντα ὅσα ἐποίησα.	But many Samaritans of the town believed in him on account of the words of the woman who testified, "He told me everything I have done."

The testimony of the woman was enough to bring many of the people of the town to believe in Jesus.[106] In stating this at once, the evangelist shows that his interest is not confined to the purely historical. This initial faith, which is illustrated by their readiness to believe (cf. v. 30, "they came to him") is to become more widespread (v. 41, πολλῷ πλείους), firmer (42a) and deeper (42b) through Jesus's own work as revealer. The superhuman knowledge of Jesus to which the woman testifies is only the starting-point, and the woman herself is merely a means of bringing people into contact with Jesus, just as the disciples of John were directed to Jesus by their master and led one another to Jesus (cf. 1:35–51). The question of Messiahship is already involved in this process (cf. v. 29; so too 1:41, 45). But the firm and clear answer is given to the would-be believers when they encounter and stay with Jesus himself.

4:40	ὡς οὖν ἦλθον πρὸς αὐτὸν οἱ Σαμαρῖται, ἠρώτων αὐτὸν μεῖναι παρ' αὐτοῖς· καὶ ἔμεινεν ἐκεῖ δύο ἡμέρας.	When, therefore, the Samaritans came to him, they asked him to stay with them. And he stayed there two days.

The people who have come from Sychar to the well of Jacob invite the "Jew" to their homes without misgivings. Theologically, this means that faith overcomes any scandal that may be given by the external circumstances of the revealer's origin (contrast 6:42; 7:27, 41f., 52) and listens to Jesus as the eschatological envoy of God. Historically, however, the evangelist's interest in the Samaritans is unmistakable. He is emphasizing their readiness to believe in contrast to the "Jews" of Jerusalem (cf. 2:18, 20; 4:1–3) and to the people of Galilee (4:44; cf. 6:30f., 41, 52). Jesus accedes to the request of the Samaritans to stay with them, but

---

[106] εἰς αὐτόν is missing in ℵ* 482 a e Orig *(partim)*; this is possibly the original, since John often uses the absolute πιστεύειν. In fact, however, Messianic faith is meant.

only for two days.[107] The stay in Samaria is only a road-side halt for Jesus, the movement of whose way is directed by the Father, even in its timing (cf. "Jesus's hour" 2:4; 7:30; 8:20 etc.).

4:41	καὶ πολλῷ πλείους ἐπίστευσαν διὰ τὸν λόγον αὐτοῦ,	And many more believed in him on account of his words.

Jesus's own word, which the evangelist signals by διὰ τὸν λόγον αὐτοῦ is still more effective in arousing faith. This affirmation is part of the theology of revelation and of "the word" of Jesus, which the evangelist develops throughout his work. The λόγος of Jesus is of divine origin (7:16; 12:49; 14:10; 17:6, 8, 14, 17) and falls on fruitful ground where men are "of God" (cf. 8:47a; 18:37; negatively 8:37, 43, 47b.). The "word of revelation" (cf. 5:24; 8:31, 51f.; 12:48) or the words of revelation (ῥήματα, always in the plural, 3:34; 6:63, 68; 8:47; 12:47f.; 14:10; 15:7; 17:8) do not merely give knowledge of divine and hidden things. They are charged with divine Spirit and divine life (6:63, 68), they unite with God and bestow salvation. Our present text is particularly concerned with the motive of faith (διὰ τ. λ.). The content of Jesus's preaching is not stated, but may be gathered from the confession in v. 42. It is the salvation brought by Jesus to the whole world, and not just to the Jews. Nothing is said of σημεῖα being wrought by Jesus in Sychar. Here too the Samaritans in question are exemplary models of faith, since they do not need signs and wonders (contrast v. 48) but believe at once in response to Jesus's word (contrast 10:38; 14:11).

4:42	τῇ τε γυναικὶ ἔλεγον ὅτι Οὐκέτι διὰ τὴν σὴν λαλιὰν πιστεύομεν· αὐτοὶ γὰρ ἀκηκόαμεν, καὶ οἴδαμεν ὅτι οὗτός ἐστιν ἀληθῶς ὁ σωτὴρ τοῦ κόσμου.	And they told the woman, "It is no longer on account of your words that we believe. We have heard him ourselves and we know that he is in truth the saviour of the world."

Even those who had given credence to the woman now testify explicitly that their faith is no longer based on what the woman said. Her λαλιά fades away before the λόγος of Jesus, not because it was mere "talk" or "chatter",[108] but because it was only the superficial echo in human words

[107] Bultmann, p. 148, n. 2, thinks that the evangelist "perhaps" meant to allude to the precept attested in *Did.*, 11:5, that a wandering preacher should not stay longer than two days in any given community. But it is unlikely that the evangelist would try to show Jesus troubling himself about such a point of discipline.

[108] This is often the meaning of the word in ordinary Greek; but in the New Testament and early Christian literature it is found in a neutral sense, cf. Arndt and Gingrich, *Lexicon*, s. v.

of what was only really disclosed in the self-revelation of Jesus. When the Samaritans affirm, "We ourselves have heard", they wish to signal the impression made on them by Jesus's words. The evangelist does not intend to make a fundamental distinction between Jesus's own word, his direct testimony to himself, and the preaching of others, between a faith which grasps its object directly and a faith resting on authority.[109] The woman had no mandate or authority to preach, while the authorized preachers merely transmit the words of Jesus (cf. 13:20; 17:20), united with the Spirit in giving testimony to him (15:26f.; cf. 14:26; 17:20f.).

The confession of faith which the Samaritans utter is of special importance—"He is the Saviour of the world".[110] Here the climactic series of designations given to Jesus in ch. 4 reaches it culmination-point. The title is chosen deliberately by the evangelist, and on several grounds. 1) Jesus is "Saviour" in the Messianic sense, since he answers the hopes of Samaritans as well as Jews. It is true that the Samaritans regarded their *Ta'eb* above all as a political leader, the future protector of their worship, rather than as a religious teacher, much less a redeemer. But just as in John Jesus's Messiahship surpasses all the expectations of Judaism, so too the hopes of the Samaritans are fulfilled in an undreamt-of way. 2) Jesus is the Saviour of the "world". His self-revelation has taught the Samaritans that the true saviour sent by God does not belong to one people alone, does not set up a special form of worship in Samaria or Juda (vv. 21–24) but bestows salvation on the whole world. 3) The evangelist also chooses the title with an eye to his readers. Purely historically speaking, it is unlikely that the Samaritans chose this well-known phrase, even though to the mind of the evangelist they have progressed beyond their limited Messianic hopes. The title σωτήρ was not a current title of the Messiah in Judaism.[111] It was transferred from Yahweh to Jesus by the Christian community (cf. Lk 1:47; 2:11; Acts 5:31; 13:23; Phil 3:20; the pastoral epistles). The full designation of Jesus as ὁ σωτὴρ τοῦ κόσμου is confined to John (4:42; 1 Jn 4:14), where it corresponds to the thought so frequently emphasized there, that God sent his Son for the salvation of the "world" (3:17; 12:47; cf. 1:29; 3:16f.; 6:33, 51;

The mention of the λαλία of Jesus in 8:43 is made from the standpoint of the interlocutors, who fail to recognize his words for what they are, the λόγος from God. Rengstorf, *Anfänge*, p. 15, n. 10, understands the word in the positive sense of a profession of faith, on the basis of the faith in the god Asclepius which was widely confessed (cf. Aristides, *Or.*, 42 λαλία εἰς 'Ασκληπιόν); but a note of contempt is unmistakable in the present text.

[109] So Bultmann, p. 149.

[110] The addition of ὁ χριστός 𝔎 D Θ pl it is certainly secondary, a reminiscence of v. 29. The "saviour of the world" here takes the place of the title of Messiah, which is given a universalist interpretation on the lips of the Samaritans.

[111] This is true in spite of Is 19:20; Zech 9:9. Cf. Staerk, *Soter;* I, p. 133: Dibelius and Conzelmann, *Die Pastoralbriefe*, p. 75.

1 Jn 2:2; 4:9). But the title "Saviour of the world" also played a part in Hellenism,[112] and the evangelist probably felt that it was well adapted for the public preaching of the Gospel. Clearly, he does not wish it to be understood in the sense in which it was used in his syncretistic environment. He uses it of Jesus in a special and exclusive way. It is doubtful whether he means it antithetically, that Jesus and no other is the true "Saviour of the world". As no ἐγώ εἰμι saying is attached, it is probably merely to be taken in a positive, kerygmatic sense.

The title occurs in emperor worship, being used with particular frequency of Hadrian, though it was also used of earlier emperors.[113] We should not assume that our text contains polemics against the divine honours paid to the emperors; this particular title is not found in Revelation, which combats the cult of the emperors. The god of healing, Asclepius, was also given this title;[114] the cult flourished in Asia Minor (there was a shrine of Asclepius in Pergamum). But in spite of some pointers in this direction, it is not certain that John wished to campaign against this cult, especially in the present text where no healings are mentioned.

In content, the title is akin to that of "Kyrios";[115] it too contains an element of majesty and royalty. The Saviour of the world exercises a saving sovereignty over the world (cf. also 17:2; 18:37).

The historicity of the narrative in Jn 4:1–42

Critical research has often considered the narrative in 4:1–42 as a purely literary composition of the evangelist without historical value.[116] The main reasons are:

1. The conversion of the Samaritans by Jesus is contradicted by other sources. a) The most important is the undeniably authentic saying of Jesus that he was sent only to the lost sheep of the house of Israel (Mt 15:24), with the order to the disciples, not to go to the Samaritans

[112] See Wendland, "Σωτήρ"; Lietzmann, *Der Weltheiland;* Dibelius and Conzelmann, pp. 74–77 (with further lit.).

[113] Weber, *Untersuchungen zur Geschichte des Kaisers Hadrianus*, pp. 225f., 229; Otto, "Augustus Soter"; Lohmeyer, *Christuskult und Kaiserkult*, and previous note. According to W. Bousset, *Kyrios Christos*, p. 243, the title here is to be explained by the worship of the emperors; but it suffices to accept a universalist tendency, such as is expressed elsewhere by the mention of the cosmos, cf. 1:29; 3:17; 8:12; 12:46f.; 1 Jn 2:2; 4:14. So too Cullmann, *Christologie*, p. 251, E. T.: pp. 241f.

[114] See Dölger, "Ὁ σωτήρ"; Rengstorf, *Anfänge*, pp. 13ff.; supposes deliberate polemics against the cult of Asclepius.

[115] This is suggested in particular by the Lucan use of the title, cf. Lk 2:11; Acts 5:31 (with 2:36); but also Phil 3:20. The influence of the worship of the emperors is unmistakable later in the Pastoral Letters. Cf. Bousset, *Kyrios Christos*, pp. 240–6 (too one-sided); Dibelius and Conzelmann, *Pastoralbriefe* (emphasize the complexity of the content); Cullmann, *Christologie*, pp. 245–52, E. T.: pp. 238–45.

[116] The arguments are collected in Bauer, pp. 75f.

(Mt 10:5f.). But as the pericope of the Syro-Phoenician woman shows, the economy of salvation by which Jesus's work was directed did not prevent his making exceptions in particular cases. It is true that the evangelist's unmistakable interest in the Samaritan mission (4:38) has led him to present the episode as an event of major importance; but the historical possibility of the story is not thereby excluded. That Jesus's programme did not include preaching in Samaria is indirectly confirmed by the fact that he stayed there only two days and hastened on to Galilee. The fourth evangelist does not speak of any prolonged activity in Samaria. b) The hostile attitude of a Samaritan village, as narrated in Lk 9:52–56, renders the narrative of Jn 4 improbable. But this is just an episode, like the events of Jn 4, though pointing in a different direction. c) The spiritual situation of Samaria before the Christian mission (Acts 8) does not tell in favour of great receptivity for the faith, since "men were enslaved by other powers there" (Bauer). This is true in general. But the conversion of a single Samaritan locality, as narrated in Jn 4, could provide an exceptional case. The evangelist, in fact, only thinks of it as a promising sign of a coming change in the mentality of the Samaritans. It is only the impression that might be given of a fundamental readiness to believe on the part of the Samaritans that should be attributed to the evangelist. d) Justin, who came from Samaria, testifies that nearly all his fellow-countrymen still venerated Simon (*Dialog.*, 120; *Apol.*, 25, 3; cf. 56, 1). This shows the difficulties of the Christian mission in Samaria. But if it were pressed too far, it would undermine the veracity of Acts 8. The conversion of a single locality, as narrated in Jn 4, is as little open to doubt as the existence of Christian communities or groups in Samaria in apostolic times. It is also possible that the Samaritan mission suffered set-backs in the second century, with the progress of Gnosticism.

2. The symbolic character of the narrative makes its historical value suspect. The possible symbolism of the five marriages of the woman at the well of Jacob has already been discussed (see commentary on v. 18). But it has also been shown that the evangelist wished the woman to be understood as an individual (see commentary on vv. 28f. and 42a). The evangelist obviously combines the two things, seeing in the historical figure the "typical" picture of the religious story of the Samaritan people. The case is similar to that of other narratives in John, especially the major miracles of the cure of the man born blind and the raising of Lazarus.

3. There are similar incidents in the O.T. (cf. Gen 24:11–20; 1 Sam 9:11; 1 Kgs 17:10) and even in Indian legend (the meeting of the disciple of the Buddha, Ananda, with the girl of Jandala as she is drawing water). This shows the legendary character of the story, which is part of folklore. These comparisons are confined to the setting (a conversation at a well),

and are no more decisive than many ostensible parallels invoked in comparative religion. What really matters in Jn 4 are the religious themes which are discussed, and the conversion of the Samaritans to the Christian faith. This kernel guarantees the independence of the narrative. But even the setting—the countryside round Jacob's well and Jesus's journey from Judea to Galilee through this territory—is not incredible. More we cannot say about this episode, which the evangelist has, no doubt, re-moulded in the telling to adapt it to his purposes.

CHAPTER VII

Return to Galilee: The Second Miracle at Cana (4:43–54)

With the passage 4:43–54, the evangelist rounds off the whole section dealing with the beginnings of revelation. Jesus's way takes him back to Galilee, where the first "sign" was given (2:1–11) and it is in the same place, Cana, that Jesus performs his second "sign", a healing at a distance which saves the son of a royal official from death. The miracle of the wine is expressly recalled at the beginning of the story, and the healing at a distance is signalled at the end as the "second sign". There are also intrinsic links which connect 4:43–54 with the preceding narrative. Jesus has reached the goal for which he set out in 4:1 ff., and the attention is concentrated on the reception given to Jesus by his countrymen in Galilee (cf. v. 44). Just as the crowds in Jerusalem believed only on account of the marvellous signs (2:23), so too the Galileans believe only on account of all they saw during the Passover (v. 45). Just as the disciples appeared as representatives of faith at the first miracle at Cana (2:11), so too the royal official now comes to believe, with all his household (v. 53). Here the mass of the people persists in an inadequate, superficial type of faith tied to miracles (v. 48), while in Jerusalem the leading circles remain sceptical and aloof with regard to Jesus (cf. 2:18 ff.; 3:11; 4:1). All this constitutes a "pre-view" of the rest of the Gospel, which will only verify more fully what the reader senses in the opening section, that in Galilee Jesus will be deserted by the people (6:66), in Jerusalem he will meet open hostility and threats to his life (5:18; 7:19 f.), so that in the "city of God" Jesus is walking on perilous ground (chs. 7–10), where, however, the destiny of the envoy of God, the Messiah, is to be decided (chs. 11–12).

There should, therefore, be a break after chapter 4, and the healing recounted at the end of it should not be taken along with the similar miracle in ch. 5,[1] quite apart from the question of reversing the order of chs. 5 and 6. The question of literary criticism has a bearing on the ex-

[1] On which see below at the end of the section.

planation of the present passage, but will be discussed only at the end. The exegesis itself will show that these questions of composition and redaction cannot be avoided.

The return to Galilee (4:43–45)

4:43	Μετὰ δὲ τὰς δύο ἡμέρας ἐξῆλθεν ἐκεῖθεν εἰς τὴν Γαλιλαίαν·	But after the two days there, he went on from there to Galilee.

The story goes on without a break after the Samaria episode; after his two days there (v. 40), Jesus sets out for Galilee. The time given so exactly can scarcely have a symbolical meaning,[2] but simply indicates Jesus's eagerness to return to Galilee (cf. 4:4 ἔδει).

4:44	αὐτὸς γὰρ Ἰησοῦς ἐμαρτύρησεν ὅτι προφήτης ἐν τῇ ἰδίᾳ πατρίδι τιμὴν οὐκ ἔχει.	For Jesus himself affirmed that a prophet has no honour in his own country.

To explain or justify his action (γάρ) a proverb is cited which Jesus himself is said to have appealed to, and which is also found in profane literature.[3] The idea that one's native city is the slowest to accord recognition can only refer here to Galilee; πατρίς must be taken in a different sense than in the synoptic parallels, meaning homeland. According to 1:45f.; 6:42; 7:3, 41, 52 (cf. also Ναζωραῖος, 18:5, 7; 19:19), there can be no doubt that the fourth Gospel regards Galilee as Jesus's homeland. Jerusalem, which a number of modern exegetes[4] take to be Jesus's native city according to the fourth Gospel (so too Origen and Theodore of Mopsuestia) is rather the city of God in which the destiny of the Messiah is to be played out, as in the Lucan tradition. Apart from Galilee as Jesus's earthly homeland, with Bethlehem as his birthplace, cf. 7:42, the fourth evangelist only considers the heavenly origin of Jesus, which is unknown to the Jews (cf. 7:27f.; also 3:13, 31; 8:23; 18:37); as frequently in the Septuagint and profane literature, ἰδίᾳ here is merely the equivalent of the

---

[2] Against Boismard, *Du baptême à Cana*, p. 107, who finds here, as in 2:1, an allusion to the resurrection of Jesus. No doubt Hos 6:2 says, "after two days he heals us" (יְחַיֵּנוּ i.e., brings us to life); but this is still not the two days of Jn 4:43.

[3] Dion Chrysostom, 30 (47), 6; Apollonius of Tyana, *Ep.*, 44 (Conybeare, vol. II, p. 436); Epictetus, *Diss.*, III, 16, 11 (Oldfather, vol. II, pp. 106f.). Quoted by Arndt and Gingrich, *Lexicon*, s. v.

[4] Schanz, Belser, Wendt, Hoskyns, Barrett; Dodd, *Interpretation*, p. 352; Feuillet, "La signification théologique du second miracle de Cana", pp. 67f.

possessive pronoun.[5] In view of 4:1, the proverb could here mean that Jesus expects no great gains in his homeland of Galilee, which is precisely what he wants, in order to avoid exposing himself prematurely to the attentions of the authorities in Jerusalem.[6] This explanation—of a question which Augustine already discussed[7]—would be in line with the movement of the Gospel (cf. 7:3–8 for a later instance) and with the Johannine theology of an "hour" fixed for Jesus (see commentary on 2:4). However, according to 4:48 and ch. 6, Jesus clearly does wish to operate on a large scale and to win the people to believe. Thus there is much to be said for the idea that the verse is a redactional gloss, inserted in view of what actually happened to Jesus (cf. 6:42),[8] though the linguistic pointers are not definite.[9] Finally, it is also possible that the evangelist wished to give a gentle reminder, questioningly as it were, of the saying of Jesus of which he was aware, and then record the actual behaviour of the Galileans. No definite certainty can be arrived at.

Another question is the relationship of this quotation to the saying of Jesus given by the Synoptics in the Nazareth episode (Mk 6:4; Mt 13:57; Lk 4:24). The wording does not coincide with that of Mark/Matthew or with the form given by Luke; but it is closer to the former with τιμὴν οὐκ ἔχει (cf. ἄτιμος), though not so trenchantly put (cf. οὐκ—εἰ μή).

There could be an echo of the Lucan δεκτός in Jn 4:45 (ἐδέξαντο); but Luke has adapted the saying to the context (by οὐδεὶς προφήτης, cf. the subsequent examples, 4:25–27) and probably modified the original formulation. There seems, then, to be no literary dependence; John has taken the saying from oral tradition.[10] The saying circulated in various forms, as is also confirmed by P. Oxy., I, 6 (Klostermann, *Apocr.*, II, p. 19) and logion 31 of the *Gospel of Thomas*, where it is found in a longer, two—membered (more original?) form, "No prophet is welcome in his native city (village, in *Gospel of Thomas*), no physician heals those who know him". Finally one could ask whether 4:44 does not contain a rudimentary trait of the tradition of the "rejection in Nazareth", which is also alluded to, apparently, in 6:42.

---

[5] Cf. Ezra 5:8, εἰς τὴν ἰδίαν πόλιν, with Neh 2:1 (both LXX); further examples in Deissmann, *Bibelstudien*, pp. 120f.; Arndt and Gingrich, *Lexicon*, s. v. 2; Funk, *Greek Grammar*, para. 286; Mayser, *Grammatik*, vol. II, 2, pp. 73f.

[6] Cf. Bauer, Strathmann, *ad loc.*

[7] *In Jo.* tr. XVI, 1ff. (*Corpus Christianorum* 36, pp. 164ff.); he makes use of the question, however, only for homiletic purposes.

[8] So Bernard, *ad loc.*; Hirsch, *Studien*, p. 55 (giving other reasons); Jeremias, "Johanneische Literarkritik", p. 44, who sees a sign of it in the fact that Ἰησοῦς is without the article.

[9] The use of the article with Ἰησοῦς seems inconsistent, quite apart from the uncertainty of the text in some places. In v. 44 the following terms are very Johannine: αὐτὸς γάρ, cf. 2:25; 4:42, 45; 6:6; also μαρτυρεῖν in the sense of "affirm, confirm" with a following ὅτι, cf. 1:32, 34; 3:28; 4:39; 7:7 (12:17 the text is uncertain); 1 Jn 4:14. The οὖν could look back beyond v. 44 to v. 43, but could link up with v. 43 directly (if v. 44 was missing), cf. 4:5 with 4; 4:40 with 39; 7:3 with 2; 7:15 with 14 etc.; but it could finally also be the redactor's link, if he added v. 44 (cf. Hirsch).

[10] Cf. Noack, *Zur joh. Tradition*, pp. 64, 94f.

4:45 ὅτε οὖν ἦλθεν εἰς τὴν Γαλιλαίαν, ἐδέξαντο αὐτὸν οἱ Γαλιλαῖοι, πάντα ἑωρακότες ὅσα ἐποίησεν ἐν Ἱεροσολύμοις ἐν τῇ ἑορτῇ, καὶ αὐτοὶ γὰρ ἦλθον εἰς τὴν ἑορτήν.

When, then, he reached Galilee, the Galileans received him well, because they had seen everything that he had done in Jerusalem during the feast. For they too had gone to the feast.

The reader has been told nothing so far of the Galileans' attitude to Jesus—not even after the first miracle at Cana. Hence the evangelist now notes that they did in fact "receive" Jesus (δέχεσθαι occurs only here; under the influence of the proverb, v. 44?), but only because they had seen all that he had accomplished in Jerusalem. This derogatory judgment is confirmed by Jesus's words in v. 48; the response of the Galileans is as inadequate as that of the people of Jerusalem (2:23). Hence "receive" only means a welcome of a superficial type, not that "acceptance" (λαμβάνειν τινά) which designates genuine faith (1:12; 5:43; cf. 3:11, 32f.; 12:48; 13:20; 17:8). This is only an apparent correction of the saying quoted by Jesus in v. 44; its real meaning is already confirmed. If ch. 4 is followed immediately by ch. 6, we can trace clearly the fall into unbelief, 6:66, through the remarks in 6:2–26–30–42. But in between comes the story of the healing at a distance, in which the theme of faith is again treated from the positive aspect.

The second miracle of Cana: healing of the son of the official (4:46–54)

This story, in which a child at the point of death is healed at a distance by a word spoken by Jesus, has all the characteristics of a Johannine miracle: a very grave crisis, a remarkable cure, an exact verification and also a deep symbolic or theological significance. It is linked with the first miracle at Cana by the localization and the enumeration, and also resembles it in as much as no explanatory words of revelation are attached. But it is not hard to see the theological significance which the evangelist attributes to it. The faith which adheres to Jesus and his words is the way to life. Jesus can give life by his word, but he demands faith as the presupposition of his gift. Thus we have an "illustration" of the truth affirmed in 3:15f., 36, even though the life restored in the first place is only physical. But it gives the true believer the assurance that Jesus also gives divine and immortal life. This theme is then most fully and luminously developed at the raising of Lazarus (cf. 11) where the "glory" of Jesus as giver of life radiates still more brilliantly (cf. 11:4, 40). The same truths are brought out at the miracle of healing at the pool of Bethesda, with the revelation discourse which follows (ch. 5); but basically it is the dominant theme of the whole Gospel (cf. 20:31).

There is, therefore, no doubt as to the Johannine character of the pericope. But special problems are raised by the comparison with the synoptic story of the centurion of Capernaum, which could be concerned with the same historical event. A certain tension within the narrative itself also raises the question as to whether the evangelist has not drawn on a special source for this story (as for the first miracle of Cana) and worked on it in his own special way. But we shall leave these problems of sources and of the history of tradition till the end of the running commentary. In any case, the final redaction must have found a consistent meaning in the narrative as it stands.

4:46	Ἦλθεν οὖν πάλιν εἰς τὴν Κανὰ τῆς Γαλιλαίας, ὅπου ἐποίησεν τὸ ὕδωρ οἶνον. καὶ ἦν τις βασιλικὸς οὗ ὁ υἱὸς ἠσθένει ἐν Καφαρναούμ.	He came then once more to Cana in Galilee, where he had turned the water into wine. And there was a certain royal official whose son was ill in Capernaum.

It must be assumed from the itinerary that Jesus reached Cana via Nazareth. The evangelist is interested in the placing of the healing at the scene of the first "sign", as his explicit back-reference shows. Possibly an earlier narrative (in a source at the disposition of the evangelist) put the meeting of the father and Jesus near Capernaum, which had been mentioned in 2:12. The sick child is in Capernaum, at the north of the lake of Gennesaret, hence a considerable distance away. It cannot be proved that the Cana tradition is connected with the districts being strongly populated by Christians in the first century;[11] and it can also hardly be explained merely by the tendency to put the miracle at a greater distance from the speaker and so enhance it.[12] The "royal official"[13] who is in anguish about his child in Capernaum, is one of the staff of "King" Herod Antipas. "King" was the popular name for the tetrarch.[14] The term can mean a court official or—less probably—a military man.[15] In the latter case he

[11] So Kundzinš, *Topologische Überlieferungsstoffe*, p. 25.

[12] So Bultmann, *Geschichte der synoptischen Tradition*, p. 242; E. T.: *Synoptic Tradition*, p. 227; Strathmann, *ad loc.;* Schweizer, "Die Heilung des Königlichen", p. 65; Haenchen, "Johanneische Probleme", p. 28.

[13] The reading βασιλίσκος D (a) may be due to the early Latin translation *regulus*; at any rate, it is secondary.

[14] Cf. Mk 6:14 par. Mt; *Gospel of Peter*, 1:2; also Cicero, *Verr.*, 4:27; but the correct title of "tetrarch" in Josephus, *Ant.*, XVII, 188; XVIII, 27, 36 etc.; inscriptions on the islands of Cos and Delos, cf. Schüler, *Geschichte*, vol. I, p. 432; so too Mt 14:1; Lk 3:19; 9:7.

[15] In Josephus, οἱ βασιλικοί (always pl.) are mostly non-Jewish mercenaries (*Ant.*, XV, 289; XVII, 266, 270, 281 etc.), but can also be court officials (*Ant.*, X, 123), as in inscriptions, cf. Bauer, *ad loc.;* Arndt and Gingrich, *Lexikon*, s. v.

would most likely be a pagan.[16] In v. 48, no doubt, Jesus seems to include him among the Jews of Galilee; but this may be merely an impression evoked by the evangelist (cf. v. 45). Otherwise the evangelist does not seem to take any interest in whether he is a Jew or not.[17]

4:47	οὗτος ἀκούσας ὅτι Ἰησοῦς ἥκει ἐκ τῆς Ἰουδαίας εἰς τὴν Γαλιλαίαν ἀπῆλθεν πρὸς αὐτὸν καὶ ἠρώτα ἵνα καταβῇ καὶ ἰάσηται αὐτοῦ τὸν υἱόν, ἤμελλεν γὰρ ἀποθνήσκειν.	He heard that Jesus had come from Judea to Galilee, and went and asked him to come down and cure his son, who was on the point of death.

The verse bears marks of Johannine writing, cf. οὗτος (so too 1:7; 3:2; 5:6; 9:3), the remark about the journey from Judea to Galilee (cf. v. 54) and the phrase ἤμελλεν γὰρ ἀποθνήσκειν (cf. 11:51; 12:33; 18:32). The official has travelled the sixteen miles[18] from Capernaum to Cana to call Jesus to his child, who was on the point of death (cf. Lk 7:2). It appears from v. 52 that the child was suffering from a grave fever.

4:48	εἶπεν οὖν ὁ Ἰησοῦς πρὸς αὐτόν, Ἐὰν μὴ σημεῖα καὶ τέρατα ἴδητε, οὐ μὴ πιστεύσητε.	Jesus said to him, "Unless you people see signs and portents, you will refuse to believe."

Jesus's denunciation of a faith which clings to miracles is addressed to the official, but it envisages the Galileans as a whole (cf. v. 45). The craving for miracles is characterized as a wish for σημεῖα καὶ τέρατα,[19] a pair of words which occurs only here in John but which is found regularly in the Septuagint and in the rest of the N.T. It is a denunciation of a faith which relies exclusively on the spectacular, the visible, external elements of the miracle (cf. 2:23; 6:2, 14). But John also recognizes a genuine faith on the basis of "signs", a faith inspired by the believer's profounder insight, cf. 2:11; 6:26; 12:37; 20:30. The purely sensational is not a valid motive of faith. The grave doubt expressed by Jesus (οὐ μή)

---

[16] See Josephus, *Ant.*, XVII, 198.

[17] The exegetes are divided. Many think of a Jewish official of the court, others, on account of the synoptic "Centurion from Capernaum", of a pagan, cf. Bernard, Hoskyns, Strathmann, Barrett.

[18] See Dalman, *Orte und Wege*, pp. 113f. E. T.: *Sacred Sites*, p. 105.

[19] τέρας, which corresponds to the Hebrew מוֹפֵת means a particularly startling miracle (cf. Acts 2:19 quoting Joel 3:3); in the New Testament (except Acts 2:19) only with σημεῖα. The double expression is common in LXX (some 26 times); in the New Testament, common in Acts, but found also in other places, Mk 13:22 parr.; Rom 15:19; 2 Cor 12:12; 2 Thess 2:9; Heb 2:4.

brings a peculiar tension into the rest of the story, since on the one hand the official believes the mere word of Jesus (v. 50) and comes, on the other hand, to full faith (v. 53b) only when he has verified exactly the healing at a distance (v. 53a). In the present context, the words are equivalent to a trial of faith, like Jesus's reaction to his mother's request at the first miracle of Cana (2:4) or to Martha later on (11:23f.).

4:49	λέγει πρὸς αὐτὸν ὁ βασιλικός, Κύριε, κατάβηθι πρὶν ἀποθανεῖν τὸ παιδίον μου.	The official said to him, "Sir, come down before my boy dies."

The father, however, is not discouraged and repeats his request still more urgently. The imminent danger of death is dramatically underlined. The double affirmation that death is near (vv. 47, 49) has its counterpart in the triple affirmation that the child will live (vv. 50, 51, 53). The contrast is deliberate, and shows the wish to depict the miracle as a recall from death to life.

4:50	λέγει αὐτῷ ὁ Ἰησοῦς, Πορεύου· ὁ υἱός σου ζῇ. ἐπίστευσεν ὁ ἄνθρωπος τῷ λόγῳ ὃν εἶπεν αὐτῷ ὁ Ἰησοῦς καὶ ἐπορεύετο.	Jesus said to him, "Go, your son will live". The man believed the word Jesus said to him, and went away.

Jesus now pronounces the efficacious word, in a form which recalls that of 1 Kgs 17:23, where the prophet Elijah says to the widow of Zarephath, after reviving her dead son, "See, your son lives". No doubt, there is no special word in Hebrew for "be cured"; but the Greek-speaking readers are invited to recognize clearly Jesus's life-giving power, as he restores life by his word alone, in contrast to the ancient prophet. The official believes the word of Jesus, as is expressly stated; he sets off for home, full of confidence in this word. Thus he seems to have attained a degree of faith higher than that of the Galileans, who believe only what they "see" (v. 48).

4:51	ἤδη δὲ αὐτοῦ καταβαίνοντος οἱ δοῦλοι αὐτοῦ ὑπήντησαν αὐτῷ λέγοντες ὅτι ὁ παῖς αὐτοῦ ζῇ.	He was still on his way down when his servants came to meet him, to tell him that his son would live.
4:52	ἐπύθετο οὖν τὴν ὥραν παρ' αὐτῶν ἐν ᾗ κομψότερον ἔσχεν· εἶπαν οὖν αὐτῷ ὅτι Ἐχθὲς ὥραν ἑβδόμην ἀφῆκεν αὐτὸν ὁ πυρετός.	He then asked them when his son had begun to be better. They told him, "Yesterday at the seventh hour the fever left him."

Hence the following scene, which takes place the next day as the man is returning home, is all the more remarkable, since it attaches importance to the exact verification of the miracle and thus, after all, favours once more the motive supplied by the external experience of miracles (cf. v. 53). After the servants' news, there can be no doubt that the sudden cure of the sick child was due to Jesus's word. The same tendency to guarantee the fact of the cure by unimpeachable witnesses also dominates the story of the man born blind, ch. 9; it is compatible, no doubt, with the lofty and spiritualized concept of "sign" which is that of the evangelist. But after v. 48, it is strange to find so much stress laid on the exact verification of the healing at a distance. The statement of the servants is understandable at once; here too no symbolic significance is to be attached to the time given.

4:53	ἔγνω οὖν ὁ πατὴρ ὅτι ἐν ἐκείνῃ τῇ ὥρᾳ ἐν ᾗ εἶπεν αὐτῷ ὁ Ἰησοῦς, Ὁ υἱός σου ζῇ, καὶ ἐπίστευσεν αὐτὸς καὶ ἡ οἰκία αὐτοῦ ὅλη.	Then the father recognized that it was the time at which Jesus had said to him, "Your son will live." And he became a believer, and all his household.

What follows seems still more awkward. Apparently it is only when he is sure that Jesus's word from afar healed his child miraculously that the official comes to full faith (πιστεύειν used absolutely). Is this not a weak type of faith, which corresponds to the attitude blamed by Jesus in v. 48 and is no longer on the level of faith in the mere word of Jesus (v. 50)? Since the faith which the official and his household have attained is certainly the full faith in Jesus as the Messiah, it must be considered as the final stage of the development of the official's faith, in which development the "faith in the word" of v. 50 is only a phase, though an important one. But the reader has to ask himself whether the official has really gone beyond the attitude blamed by Jesus in v. 48. It could also be taken to mean that the official first sought for the sign, and then, if only by means of a sign, found Jesus himself.[20] But the difficulty of v. 48 still remains, and is not removed by suggesting that the evangelist was perhaps interested in recording the conversion of this eminent family.[21] The literary genesis of this piece of narrative must also be examined (see below).

---

[20] So Schweizer, "Die Heilung des Königlichen", esp. pp. 69f.

[21] Zahn, *ad loc.* thinks that the conversion of the man and his household must have caused a great stir in Galilee and makes a number of hypotheses. On such conversions of households, see Acts 10:44–48; 11:14 (Cornelius); 16:15 (Lydia); 16:31f. (the prison governor); 18:8 (Crispus); Rom 16:3 (Prisca and Aquila); 1 Cor 1:16 (Stephanas); Phm 2 (Philemon).

4:54	Τοῦτο δὲ πάλιν δεύτερον σημεῖον ἐποίησεν ὁ Ἰησοῦς ἐλθὼν ἐκ τῆς Ἰουδαίας εἰς τὴν Γαλιλαίαν.	This was the second sign, wrought by Jesus as he came from Judea to Galilee.

The final remark of the evangelist underlines the need for literary criticism, since this cure at Capernaum is called the "second sign", though the evangelist mentions further "signs" (2:23; cf. 4:45) in Jerusalem after the first "sign" at Cana (2:11). It does not appear from the text that the evangelist wished to stress the Galilean miracles in contrast to those at Jerusalem. The last phrase, "as he came from Judea to Galilee" seems rather to be another item from an itinerary. And the enumeration of the Galilean signs is not taken further (cf. 6:2).

Literary criticism

The difficulties noted in the narrative call for the solution which has been often put forward,[22] namely that the evangelist took over the story in substance from a source which also contained the first Cana miracle, and inserted it into his narrative with some redactional additions. It may be further assumed that in the source the healing at a distance followed closely upon the miracle of the wine, being the "second sign", but that the evangelist put it at the end of his presentation of Jesus's journey to Jerusalem and back to Galilee. He was dissatisfied with the narrative itself, a simple miracle-story with the typical verification of the cure,[23] and he expressed his criticism by means of the logion of v. 48. He decided to give the story here, only when accompanied by this criticism of a superficial faith in the spectacular, so that he could propound further his understanding of true and full faith (cf. vv. 39, 42). The royal official believed the mere word of Jesus (v. 50). But the evangelist did not wish to omit the verification of the cure as given in the source, since in his concept of "sign" the historical reality of the event is just as important as the profound Christological significance. Hence he inserted v. 48 at an early point, as an admonition to strive for genuine faith, but then told the story as he found it. If the evangelist inserted v. 48 of his own accord, it became necessary to repeat the man's request in v. 49, in order to link up with the following. The difficulty created for the narrative by v. 48 is not thereby removed, but becomes more intelligible in the light of the evangelist's procedure.

---

[22] Schweizer, "Die Heilung"; Haenchen, "Johanneische Probleme", pp. 23–31; Schnackenburg, "Zur Traditionsgeschichte von Joh 4:46–54" (with further disscussion).

[23] Cf. Bultmann, *Synoptische Tradition*, p. 240, E. T.: p. 225. Two impressive healings at a distance are ascribed to rabbi Chanina ben Dosa (c. A.D. 70); see Fiebig, *Jüdische Wundergeschichten*, pp. 20ff. In spite of some noteworthy contacts, the main difference remains, that the rabbi heals by prayer, Jesus by his word.

Apart from the enumeration in v. 54, the following points also support the assumption that the evangelist is here using a miracle-story from a σημεῖα-source:

a) Like the story of the marriage feast at Cana, that of the healing of the son of the official contains hardly any characteristics of Johannine style.[24] No doubt there is the οὖν *historicum*, but v. 46 a is probably the evangelist's setting of the story, and it is a word which he could easily insert elsewhere as well.

b) The journey noted in 2:12, which now serves merely to link the miracle of the wine at Cana with the cleansing of the temple at Jerusalem, could have been originally (in the source) the introduction to the second miracle. The new story (4:46b) linked up with the goal of the journey of 2:12, since the official's son lay sick in Capernaum. He may have been thought of as meeting Jesus on the road, at some distance from Capernaum.[25] If this is correct, it was the evangelist who decided to situate the conversation at the scene of the first miracle, Cana, a procedure understandable on several grounds: not so much to enhance the miracle by lengthening the distance, as to make the connection between the two stories clearer. They had come one after the other in the source, but had now been separated by the journey to and from Jerusalem.

We must then assume that anything in 4:46–54 which refers to the long journey in between or presupposes Cana as the meeting-place must be attributed to the evangelist. He is directly responsible, therefore, for vv. 46 a–47 a from ἀκούσας to Γαλιλαίαν, in 47 b for καταβῇ καί, in 51 a for ἤδη δὲ αὐτοῦ καταβαίνοντος, in v. 52 for ἐχθές, in v. 54 for the final words, after ὁ Ἰησοῦς.

c) The question arises as to whether the σημεῖα-source did not contain further miracles, on which the evangelist has also drawn. In view of 6:2 (signs wrought on the sick), it could be assumed that further healing-miracles followed the two Galilean miracle-stories. The synoptic account of the cure of Peter's mother-in-law (Mk 1:29 ff. parr.) which took place in Capernaum, comes to mind. In any case, 6:2 presupposes more miraculous healings in Galilee, and the enumeration is also not continued.

With regard to the other miracles recounted in John, we are also justified in asking whether they may not have been taken from the same source. See Introduction, ch. iv, 3.

Other solutions based on literary criticism are unconvincing. If the existence of a "basic document" is assumed, two possibilities arise. Either

[24] Cf. Schweizer, *Ego eimi*, p. 100; id., "Die Heilung", p. 65, n. 5; Ruckstuhl, *Literarische Einheit*, pp. 217f.; Schnackenburg, "Zur Traditionsgeschichte von Joh 4:46–54".

[25] Wilkens, *Entstehungsgeschichte*, p. 27, suspects that 2:12a originally read the imperfect κατέβαινεν instead of κατέβη; the observation that 2:12 could be the introduction of the second "Cana Miracle" was made as early as Wellhausen, pp. 23f.; Spitta, *Das Johannesevangelium als Quelle der Geschichte Jesu*, pp. 65f.; see also Bultmann, pp. 79, 85.

the miracle-story was part of the document, or it comes from a redactional effort to complete the document. In neither case can the difficulties be accounted for, unless further redactional touches are assumed. Then the question is who were responsible for them. And the stylistic criteria are neglected.[26] It is unlikely that there will be much support for the newer hypothesis put forward by M.-É. Boismard, who ascribes the substance of the story to the evangelist, and vv. 48, 49 (which we allot to the evangelist) to a redactor, as also the "scene-shifting" in vv. 51–53. The redactor is said to be none other than Luke.[27]

Comparison with the synoptic tradition of the "centurion of Capernaum"

A historical problem of no small interest arises when Jn 4:46–54 is compared with the synoptic tradition of the "centurion of Capernaum" (Mt 8:5–13; Lk 7:1–10). Has the same event been presented in different ways in the three accounts, or must one maintain that there were two different healings at a distance? Nearly all modern Protestant commentaries assume more or less definitely one event behind the two stories,[28] and hence, since the two synoptic accounts also vary considerably, consider the three narratives as varying forms of the one tradition. Catholic authors on the other hand, except for a few hesitant judgments,[29] postulate a different incident for John. The point calls for investigation.

Let us examine first the contacts between the two traditions. In the Synoptics as in John we have a healing at a distance by Jesus's authoritative word, even though Luke does not give the words of healing explicitly. Hence it is a special type of cure, of which there is only one other example, the cure of the daughter of the Syro-Phoenician woman (Mk 7:24–30; Mt 15:21–28).[30] A healing at a distance, however, where Jesus

---

[26] Spitta, *Johannesevangelium*, pp. 76f., says that the pericope was not part of the "basic document" and assigns it (along with 2:1–12 and ch. 21) to the "redaction" (cf. 68ff.); vv. vv. 48f. and 52f. are said to be still later redactional touches. According to Hirsch, *Studien*, p. 9, the pericope was part of the original Gospel, according to Macgregor and Morton, pp. 77f. cf. 93f., it belonged to the primary source (J^1).

[27] On Boismard, "S. Luc et la rédaction du Quatrième Évangile", see Schnackenburg, "Zur Traditionsgeschichte", pp. 67–70.

[28] Except Zahn, pp. 273f.

[29] Cf. Wikenhauser, p. 117: "It cannot be excluded that the three accounts describe the same event"; Feuillet, "La signification théologique", p. 65: "Peut-être aura-t-il (sc. l'évangeliste) assigné à ce miracle le rôle dévolu dans les Synoptiques . . . à la guérison du serviteur du centurion."

[30] Hence Bultmann, *Synoptische Tradition*, p. 39, E. T.: p. 38, regards both accounts as "variants" and in fact as "ideal scenes", i.e., "community products". But Haenchen,

does not meet the sick person at all,[31] is important enough not to be multiplied without necessity. For the case under discussion there are in fact important coincidences, which we recount briefly:

a) The sick person is in Capernaum, which is all the more significant because the fourth evangelist is clearly far more interested in Cana, where he makes the meeting of Jesus with the child's father take place (4:46f.). We mention merely incidentally that the miracle took place rather early in the Galilean ministry of Jesus, since Matthew and Luke probably followed other principles in the order of the pericopes.[32]

b) In both cases the anxious petitioner is in the service of "King" Herod Antipas. According to Matthew and Luke he is a "centurion", according to John a βασιλικός, by which one can also understand a military man, though a court official is more likely.

c) The sick person is very close to the petitioner, in Matthew a παῖς, in Luke a δοῦλος, in John, however, a υἱός (on which see below).

d) The petitioner takes the initiative in order to gain Jesus's help, though the way differs in each case. Luke and John agree in speaking of an ἐρωτᾶν on the part of the petitioner (Lk 7:3; Jn 4:47).

e) In all three accounts stress is laid on the faith of the petitioner, though with notable difference of interests.

f) Luke (7:2) and John (4:47) agree in saying that the patient was "on the point of dying".

g) Matthew (8:13) and John (4:52–53a) agree in verifying the time at which the healing took place, though greater emphasis is laid on this in John.

Along with these pointers to the identity of the event there are, however, a number of notable differences, which have often been brought forward[33] but which we list once more here. The most important is probably the shift in the objective of the narrative. The central interest in the Synoptics is the famous saying of the centurion, where he declares that it is not necessary for Jesus to enter his house, a word of command being sufficient, as he illustrates from his own profession. This attitude evokes a special word of praise from Jesus for his faith. In John, the royal official insists that Jesus should come, and it is Jesus who of his own accord utters the word which heals from afar. But the literary analysis has shown that

---

"Johanneische Probleme", pp. 23f., n. 1, has showed the structural differences between the two accounts. He shows that Jesus's answer in Mt 8:7 can hardly be taken as an astonished question, expressing reluctance, as it is often taken to be.

[31] This is how it differs from Lk 17:11–19; cf. also Jn 9:6f.

[32] Matthew has inserted the story into his cycle of miracles chs. 8–9, Luke has also connected it with miracles after the sermon on the mount, but envisaging already the question of the Baptist and Jesus's answer in 7:18–23.

[33] See, e.g., Lagrange, pp. 128f.

Jesus's word of reproach in v. 48 was probably tacked on to the narrative at a later stage, and that the repetition of the father's request (v. 49) only became necessary on account of the insertion. The original narrative, as read perhaps in a source by the evangelist, likewise retained the immediate departure of the father at Jesus's word (v. 50). Though it did not contain his great profession of faith, it then attached great value to the exact verification of the healing at a distance. Thus the scope of the narrative would have also differed considerably in the source drawn upon by John, though the course of events was narrated in substantially the same way (except for the centurion's own statement in the synoptic narrative). The main question which remains is whether tradition could take such different ways in transmitting the same event.

The other variations are not so important, but may be mentioned briefly:

a) In the Synoptics, the petitioner is a "centurion", in John an "official". But this is not a grave difficulty (see above).

b) In the two synoptic accounts the centurion is a pagan, well disposed towards Judaism according to Luke. John gives the impression that he is a Jew, though this is not affirmed directly; but the words addressed to him in v. 48 seem to treat him as representative of the Galileans (cf. v. 45). His paganism is essential to the synoptic narrative, as is clear above all from the final statement, Mt 8:10; Lk 7:9, and as is further emphasized in Matthew by the added logion (only in Matthew) of the influx of the pagans to the eschatological banquet (Mt 8:11 f.; cf. Lk 13:28 ff.). At least the emphasis which Matthew and Luke lay on the faith of the pagan is missing in John. But we must take the intention of the fourth evangelist into consideration. In the course of his narrative what was important to him here was the attitude of the Galileans (cf. vv. 43–45, 47 a, 54 b). Once more, the source may have left the question of the man's religion open, or even have affirmed that he was not a Jew.

c) According to Matthew and Luke the meeting takes place in Capernaum, in John in Cana. Considering how firmly tradition in general transmits concrete topological items, this might be thought to be an important point. However, minor "blurring" also occurs elsewhere.[34] But we have seen above that the fourth evangelist probably imported the mention of Cana into his geographical framework, to begin and end the first section of Jesus's public ministry in the same place (cf. 2:11 with 4:46 a, 54) and so give it a certain unity. In all three accounts the sick person is in Capernaum.

---

[34] Cf. 6:24 (Capernaum) with the corresponding text of Mk 6:53 (Mt 14:34) (the plain of Gennesaret); 12:9 (corresponding to Mt 21:1) (Bethany) with Mk 11:1 par. Lk 19:29 (Bethphage-Bethany).

d) Whether the sick person was a "child" or a "slave" is of itself unimportant for the narrative. In the Synoptics, one might think that the ambiguous παῖς[35] of Matthew was defined clearly in Luke as "slave" ("servant"). Was this perhaps due to the mention of δοῦλος in the comparison (also in Mt 8:9), since in 7:7 Luke once more seems to show knowledge of an original παῖς? We also come upon παῖς in Jn 4:51, though in this tradition it is defined as meaning "son". Here too we could see a "blurring" in the tradition, which can be explained and justified by the unimportance of the matter from the point of view of the objective of the narrative.

e) It is also impossible to reconcile the nature of the illness as given by Matthew (paralysis) and John (fever). Basically, the position is as in the previous point. But there is also the factor that Matthew goes his own way in describing illnesses.[36] In the present case, the fever mentioned by John would seem to fit the facts better, as the danger of death is acute, as Lk 7:2 also says.

f) Only John says that the servants met the father while he was still on his way home and told him of the sudden improvement of the sick child. This is to some extent in conflict with the final remark of Lk 7:10, but does not present a serious difficulty, since Luke, given the structure of his narrative, could hardly have ended it otherwise and only means to establish briefly the miraculous healing. This verification, which is indispensable to a miracle-story, is again formulated differently in Mt 8:13, where it is not only closer to the Johannine narrative but also leaves room for the scene on the way home.

We are left, it seems, with divided feelings after this investigation. Similarities and divergencies are equally apparent and the verdict as to whether one or more events are involved seems to be left to the judgment of the individual commentator. But if we consider the history of tradition and its forms, another major element enters into the discussion. This is the considerable amount of divergence which exists between the two Synoptics themselves, even though they are unquestionably narrating the same episode. One difference that cannot be harmonized away is that in Matthew the centurion himself addresses Jesus directly, while in Luke he treats with Jesus, twice, by means of messengers. The petition of the Jewish elders recommending the good pagan (Lk 7:3–5) could have been passed over by Matthew (though it alters considerably the opening of the

[35] In Matthew παῖς can mean "son" as well as "child" (cf. 17:18 with 15) and "servant" (14:2, court officials).

[36] In the summary account 4:24 he mentions along with "possessed" also "lunatics and cripples" (παραλυτικούς). He seems to have a liking for these last two terms (cf. 17:15 with Mk 9:17f.). In 8:6 Matthew has possibly interpreted the original δεινῶς βασανιζόμενος concretely as being crippled. In 12:22 he also departs from Lk 11:14.

story). But the second mission, that of the "friends" (Lk 7:6), is remarkable and cannot be reconciled with the parallel account in Matthew. The words which the centurion addresses directly to Jesus in Matthew are now passed on almost word for word by his friends, in the form of a message. The procedure in Luke is obviously secondary, a subsequent manipulation which robs the scene of the spontaneity which it had in Matthew. The divergency of the Lucan presentation cannot be missed, and without going into the possible reasons for it,[37] we must take cognizance of the fact that tradition has proceded in this way.

These considerations make it difficult to exclude the possibility that the Johannine account, especially in the form which we assume it had in the probable source, deals with the same event, and the resemblances noted above make the assumption even highly probable. The actual event, the healing at a distance, is untouched by the narrational divergencies, and many of the circumstances point to the same illness. Only a few of the important details are to some extent blurred, and then the various interpretations and "applications" given by each narrator, or by the evangelists using their narrative, give the impression that we are dealing with different events. But once the peculiarities of the literary genre which is involved have been noted, it will be difficult to admit that there two different events are in question.

The theological objective of the fourth evangelist

Finally, let us examine more closely the aims pursued by the evangelist in the adoption and redaction of this episode. As we have already seen, he was preoccupied above all with the subject of faith, for which the narrative, as he found it, must have seemed very helpful. But since the tradition had anchored the miracle firmly in Galilee, he did not wish to have a representative of paganism come forward at that precise place. Galilee is for him the earthly homeland of Jesus, and the Galileans, Jesus's fellow-countrymen, always provide him with protection and support against the authorities in Jerusalem. They welcome him (4:45), and later he also finds safety among them (cf. 7:1). Further, the evangelist has just presented the Samaritans as representatives of the non-Jewish world, with their confession of the "Saviour of the world". In Galilee, he is concerned with the problem of full and genuine faith; from this point of view, however, he puts Jesus's countrymen on the same footing as the

---

[37] Haenchen, "Johanneische Probleme", p. 27, surmises that the version used by Luke came from Jewish-Christian circles who were trying "to turn a story in praise of the faith of Gentile Christianity into another in which the Gentiles could only be considered when they could show that they had merited well of Israel". This is not completely convincing.

people of Jerusalem (4:45). But with the example of the "royal official", he clearly means to demonstrate what they too could attain if they brought good will to bear. They too should leave behind the stage of the "faith that sees" (v. 45) and come like the royal official to faith in the word of Jesus (v. 50) and to the full Messianic faith (v. 53).

But the evangelist is also interested in presenting a "sign", as he understands it. The cure of someone mortally ill manifests Jesus's power of giving "life" (cf. vv. 50, 51, 53). This Christological symbolism also holds his attention at the healing of the man born blind (ch. 9, Jesus the light of the world) and the raising of Lazarus (ch. 11, Jesus the resurrection and the life). At the same time, the factual reality of the event is to be made clear, as is true of all the major miracles in John. It is precisely in the "flesh" of his earthly coming that the incarnate Logos reveals the underlying divinity and his significance for man. His "works" become unimpeachable witnesses, to which belief cannot be refused (cf. 5:36; 10:25, 38; 14:11; 15:24) and at the same time "signs" which manifest his glory (cf. 2:11; 11:4, 40). This way of understanding the "signs" is also apparent in 6:2. After the multiplication of the loaves, Jesus reproaches the Jews with seeking him, not because they have seen "signs" (note the plural) but because they have eaten their fill of bread. Hence there is a way of seeing "signs" which the Johannine Jesus desires and approves of. But if the "signs" are not grasped in faith, they are nothing but outward "miracles", and this is what the evangelist expresses in 4:48 in the phrase "signs and portents".

When the healing at a distance is understood as "restoration to life", it comes very close to the miracle of ch. 5, where the concept of Jesus as life-giver is further developed in the revelation discourse which is attached (cf. 5:21–26). But there are reasons which forbid us to link the second miracle of Cana with the healing of the paralytic in Jerusalem.[38] 1. In the narrative sequence the story is connected with the preceding (cf. 4:43–46), and 4:54 points back to 2:11. 2. The miracle in Jerusalem is called a "work", not a "sign" (cf. 5:17, 19; 7:21), and though this hardly constitutes an objective distinction, it tells against their being associated as parallels in the mind of the evangelist.[39] 3. Further healings in Galilee are mentioned in 6:2, and in general it seems that ch. 6 should follow ch. 4

[38] As does Dodd, *Interpretation*, pp. 318f.; and esp. Feuillet, "La signification théologique".

[39] Van den Bussche, "La structure de Jean I–XII", starts with the distinction between "signs" and "works" to separate the "section of the signs" (chs. 2–4) from the "section of the works" (chs. 5–10), which latter he regards as a higher degree of revelation (p. 88); see also the volumes of his commentary entitled "the book of signs" (Jn 1–4) and "the book of works" (Jn 5–12). But this is not objectively justified, since the miracles continue to be regarded as "signs" in the "book of works" (cf. 6:14, 26; 9:16; 12:18, 37). A different distinction must be drawn between σημεῖον and ἔργον; see further excursus iv.

(on which see later). 4. The notion of restoring to life gives a connection not merely with ch. 5, but with all that Jesus says and does. It is a viewpoint which dominates the whole Gospel (cf. commentary on 3:36, 15f.). Jesus already spoke of his gift of "life" under the image of water in 4:11–14. 5. In contrast to ch. 5, the notions of forgiveness of sin (cf. 5:14) and of judgment (5:22f., 27–30) are missing.

Hence 4:43–54 should be considered as the conclusion of the first part of the ministry of Jesus, in which the evangelist begins to depict Jesus as the Messiah sent by God, the heavenly revealer who gives life to men. Here too the forces of faith and unbelief are seen at work, and the reader can sense the future development. — *See excursus vii.*

EXCURSUSES

EXCURSUS I

The Origin and Nature of the Johannine Concept of the Logos

It is impossible to take up here the whole wide-ranging discussion on the origin of the Logos-doctrine in John,[1] and we must content ourselves with a general orientation based on a selective treatment. The exegesis of the prologue (or the Logos-hymn) should already have shown that the closest parallels in thought are to be found in Jewish Wisdom speculation, though it should also be clear that the Johannine Logos-doctrine is on another plane, by reason of the personal character of the Logos, his real personal pre-existence and above all his incarnation. The question also arises as to why the Christian hymn does not keep to the notion of "Wisdom", which is twice mentioned in the Synoptics with reference to Jesus (Lk 7:35 = Mt 11:19; Lk 11:49; cf. Mt 23:34) and is probably to be presupposed in many of his sayings, especially in the Logia-tradition common to Matthew and Luke.[2] Its influence on many sayings and narrative elements of John is also probable.[3] The primitive Church was

---

[1] Some lit.: Aall, *Der Logos*, 2 vols.; Krebs, *Der Logos als Heiland im ersten Jahrhundert*, with older lit. and an appendix on Reitzenstein; Leisegang, "Logos"; Vosté, *De Prologo Johanneo et Logo*; Tobac, "La notion de Christ-Logos dans la littérature johannique"; Grether, *Name und Wort Gottes im Alten Testament*; Dürr, *Die Wertung des Göttlichen Wortes im Alten Testament und im antiken Orient*; Kleinknecht, "Der Logos im Griechentum und Hellenismus"; Procksch, "Wort Gottes im Alten Testament"; Kittel, "Wort und Reden im Neuen Testament"; Middleton, "Logos and Shekina in the Fourth Gospel"; Asting, *Die Verkündigung des Wortes im Urchristentum*, pp. 267–74; Bury, *The Fourth Gospel and the Logos-Doctrine*; Dupont, *Essais*, pp. 13–58; Schubert, "Einige Beobachtungen zum Verständnis des Logosbegriffs im frührabbinischen Schrifttum"; Dodd, *Interpretation*, pp. 263–85; Robert, "Logos. La Parole divine dans l'Ancien Testament"; Mondésert, "Logos. La Parole divine à l'époque néotestamentaire"; Starcky, "Logos. La Parole divine dans le Nouveau Testament"; Schulz, *Komposition*, pp. 7–69; Braun, "Messie, Logos et Fils de l'Homme".

[2] Feuillet, "Jésus et la Sagesse divine d'après les évangiles synoptiques"; id., *Études Johanniques*, pp. 88–99, who also discusses the question of whether the disciples of Jesus are to be understood as modelled on the disciples of Wisdom (*ibid.*, pp. 99–117).

[3] Cf. 3:12, 31; 4:14; 6:33ff.; 7:34, 37f.; 8:12, 25; 10:14; 15:1ff. A good deal of this is

familiar with a Christology inspired by Wisdom speculation (cf. 1 Cor 1:24; 10:4; Col 1:15 ff.) and couched in terms of such literature (cf. Heb 1:2f.). But the hymn adopted by John in his prologue uses the title 'Logos', and, it should be noted, in the absolute sense—not, for instance, ὁ λόγος τοῦ θεοῦ as in Rev. 19:13. This needs some explanation, especially as the notion of Logos played a considerable role in the history of thought since early Greek philosophy. What was the immediate occasion of the choice of this highly resonant term? There were probably many reasons, as for other widely used expressions which were also adopted by primitive Christianity (e.g., σωτήρ, κύριος, ἐπιφάνεια). But to ascertain the main reason for the choice, to determine the primary interest of the author of the hymn, should throw light on the important question of the general religious and cultural background.

1. The "Logos" in Greek philosophy

The philosophical concept of "Logos" reflects the determinate structure of thought and the intelligible unity of being (cf. Heraclitus, Fragments 1 and 2). It then came to mean, especially in Stoicism, the rationality and order of the universe and the corresponding moral attitude of men (ὀρθὸς λόγος). It was an attempt to define the world and its processes as a set of unified relationships, and to determine man's place in the general structure of reality. There can be little doubt that the Johannine concept is very different,[4] as may also be seen from the concept of the "world" in John and its relationship to the Logos. While the Logos of philosophy penetrates and sustains the cosmos, which to the mind of the Greeks remains a well-ordered and harmonious whole, in Jn 1:10 the "world" appears as something negative which opposes itself to the Logos. It is also instructive that the early Christian apologists with some philosophical training (Justin, Tatian, Athenagoras and Theophilus of Antioch) go outside the doctrine of John when they treat of the Logos.[5] The doctrine of the λόγος σπερματικός is already taken up by Justin;[6] the distinction between the λόγος ἐνδιάθετος and the λόγος προφορικός appears in Theophilus of Antioch.[7] The Logos is used, as in Greek

---

more problematical than Feuillet thinks (*Études*, pp. 72–88). On the miracles see also Ziener, "Weisheitsbuch und Johannesevangelium", *Biblica* 39 (1958), pp. 37–60.

[4] Dyroff, "Zum Prolog des Johannesevangeliums" tried once more to demonstrate the connection with Heraclitus, but without arousing conviction; cf. Menoud, *L'Évangile de Jean*, p. 52.

[5] Cf. Barbel, *Christos Angelos*, pp. 18 ff.; Emery, "Il Logos nel pensiero dei Padri Apostolici"; Holte, "Logos Spermatikos", esp. pp. 124 ff.

[6] Justin, *Apol.*, 5, 2 ff.; 46, 1–5; *App.*, 8:1–3; 10:1–8; 13:1–6.

[7] Theophilus of Antioch, *Ad Autolycum*, II, 10 and 22 (*PG* 6. cols. 1064, 1088).

philosophy, though with a Christian colouring, to provide the starting-point for a general understanding of reality, including man and his nature. Nothing of the sort can be found in the restricted perspective of John, which is entirely concentrated on Christ as the Logos.

2. *The theology of the Word of God in the Bible*

Once Greek thought has been excluded as the origin of the Logos concept in John, the obvious thing to do is to look for it in the Bible. And there was in fact a theology of "the word of God" which had been developed in the O.T.,[8] based on the account of creation and on the event of revelation, and continued in some poetical passages which lead on to the Wisdom literature of late Judaism. The word of God is not merely a creative and conservational force (cf. Ps 33:6, 9; 147:15–18; Is 40:26; 48:13; Wis 9:1), but the bearer of salvation and new life (cf. Ps 107:20; Ezek 37:4f.; Is 40:8; 55:10f.; Wis 16:12). The word of God uttered at creation, through the mouth of the prophets (cf. Jer 1:4, 11; 2:1 etc.) and in the law (cf. Ps 119:38, 41, 105, etc.) has a number of functions which may very well be compared with those attributed to the Logos of John. But the Logos-doctrine of John cannot be derived from these alone,[9] though they may have influenced it indirectly—through speculation on Wisdom and the Torah.

The "theology of the word of God" may also be recognized under a new guise in the N.T., in which the words and message of Jesus were endowed with the same dignity, and indeed with eschatological import and force. To hear his word and to accept it in faith is to hear the word of God (cf. Lk 5:1; 8:21; 11:28)—a concept most fully developed in John (cf. 5:24; 8:51; 12:48; 14:24; 15:3; 17:14, 17). But the words of the revealer (sometimes called τὰ ῥήματα, 3:34; 6:63, 68; 8:47; 12:47f.; 14:10; 15:7; 17:8) are not identical with the revealer as "the Word". He is not called the Logos absolutely because he utters the word or words of God; on the contrary, his words rather have the force of God's words because he is the Logos, that is, the divine revealer and redeemer. It cannot be objected that ὁ λόγος is used absolutely in the explanation of the parable of the sower (Mk 4:14–20 parr.), since this is a technical term for the missionary and preaching activity of the early Church (cf. 1 Thess 1:6; 2:13; 1 Cor 1:18; 15:2; 2 Cor 1:18; 5:19 etc.). In the last resort, of course, when the good news of Jesus Christ is

---

[8] See Grether, *Name und Wort Gottes;* Dürr, *Die Wertung;* Procksch, "Wort Gottes"; Ringgren, *Word and Wisdom;* Eichrodt, *Theologie*, vol. II, pp. 40–48; Robert, "Logos".
[9] So B. Weiss, *Lehrbuch*, pp. 606ff.

proclaimed, he himself is the eschatological "word of God" to men (cf. 2 Cor 1:19f.; Heb 1:2), but this is not a title of Christ, except in the prologue of John (and 1 Jn 1:1; Rev 19:13 comes from another tradition). Hence the N.T. "word of God theology" must also be ruled out as the origin of this remarkable title.[10]

3. *"Word of God", Wisdom, Torah and Memra Yahweh in Judaism*

Where the O.T. spoke of the "word of God", later Jewish theology preferred other terms, though not exclusively. How closely God's "word" and "wisdom" are allied may be seen from Wis 9:1f., "O God of my fathers and Lord of mercy, who hast made all things by thy word, and by thy wisdom hast formed man, to have dominion over the creatures thou hast made..." But this is a clear instance of the transition in the Wisdom literature from the "word of God" to "wisdom", which occurred most often when man was spoken of. Hence in the *Slavonic Enoch*, 30:8, God says: "When all was completed, my Wisdom bade me create man", while in 33:4 he says, with regard to creation in general, "My thought is my counsellor, my word is active and my eyes gaze upon all things". When, therefore, the Logos-hymn describes the sovereign action of the Word in terms of Wisdom, particularly in relation to men, this constitutes a later stage of development, and it is not clear why the author then recurs again to the term "word", and not the "word of God" but to the term "the Logos", used absolutely. Thus the Wisdom speculation provides the aptest parallels in thought, but leave the term chosen by the Christian hymn unexplained.

This is also true of the "Torah theology", which also tended more and more to explain the earlier "word of God" as the Torah. In Ps 119 the "word of God" and the "law" are still juxtaposed as synonyms (cf., along with the texts cited above, vv. 17f., 35 ff., 43f., 148 ff. etc). But on the whole it has become a hymn of praise to the Torah, which is regarded as the word of God which gives guidance and blessing. In Baruch, "Wisdom", which "lived among men" (3:37) is explained as the "law": "She is the book of the commandments of God, and the law that endures for ever. All who hold her fast will live..." (4:1); cf. Prov. 8: 33 ff.; Wis 6:18; Ecclus 24:23 ff. When rabbinism speaks of the Torah as the prologue does of the Logos,[11] giving the Torah similar attributes and

---

[10] A different view in Zahn, *Einleitung*, vol. II, pp. 545ff. (547: "The general presuppositions and analogies are contained in the words of Jesus himself"); cf. Asting, *Verkündigung*, pp. 274–8, 293–6.

[11] Cf. Billerbeck, vol. II, pp. 353–8; vol. III, pp. 129ff.

salvific functions, this is a development within Judaism which has adopted the Torah instead of the word of God or Wisdom. In this context a return to the "word" seems strange. Some scholars maintain, however, that this was done deliberately, as a Christian antithesis to the Jewish "law", adducing Jn 1:17 as proof.[12] All the terms in which Judaism attributed pre-existence and majesty to the Torah were applied to the Logos and turned into assertions about Christ: "In him, the eternal word of God, the word of creation, the word of the law, has not merely been handed on (ἐδόθη) but has come to be (ἐγένετο). He is not merely the preacher and transmitter of a Torah, he is Torah in person, a new Torah."[13] But it remains questionable whether this antithesis, supposedly worked out by the evangelist, explains adequately the choice of the term Logos used absolutely. The title of Logos is not retained in v. 17, where Jesus Christ is named as antithesis to Moses; the contrast to νόμος is not λόγος but χάρις and ἀλήθεια. Once more, there are parallels in content, and there may be overtones of an antithesis to the cult of the Torah. But this does not explain the term Λόγος.

We may exclude completely, as is now sufficiently obvious,[14] the appeal to the *Memra d^eAdonai* (the word of the Lord) in the Aramaic translations of the Bible. This has nothing to do with speculation on hypostasization, but merely a periphrasis for God, to avoid irreverence. It should also be recalled that personifications of God's wisdom—or Spirit or word—are not really hypostasizations.[15] Wisdom literature has still no inkling of the personal character of the Logos.

4. *The Logos in Philo*

The pregnant expression ὁ λόγος, which is missing in the Jewish writings hitherto examined, occurs extremely frequently in Philo of Alexandria, the religious philosopher of Hellenistic Judaism,[16] whose ideas are drawn

---

[12] Bornhäuser, *Das Johannesevangelium eine Missionsschrift für Israel*, pp. 5–14; Kittel, "Wort und Reden", pp. 138f.

[13] Kittel, p. 139, 2–10.

[14] Cf. Billerbeck, vol. II, pp. 302–33 (excursus "Memra Jahves"); Contrast Middleton, "Logos", p. 129, who holds for a personification of the divine word in many places and thinks that the Johannine Logos is connected with it. Starcky, "Logos", takes an intermediate position (col. 472).

[15] Cf. Moore, *Judaism*, vol. I, p. 415: "It is an error to see in such personification an approach to personalization. Nowhere either in the Bible or in the extra-canonical literature of the Jews is the word of God a personal agent or on the way to become such."

[16] Cf. Leisegang, "Logos", cols. 1072–8; Bréhier, *Les idées philosophiques et religieuses de Philon d'Alexandrie*, pp. 83–111; Wolfson, *Philo*, pp. 226–94; also Sagnard, *La gnose, valentinienne*, pp. 598–602; Jonas, *Gnosis*, vol. II, I, pp. 74ff.; Jervell, *Imago Dei*, pp.

from many streams of thought. His philosophy is chiefly influenced by Plato, through Middle Platonism, and by the Stoics. His religion comes from his ancestral faith, and he is sincerely concerned to combine the two. We need not quote here the texts dealing with the Logos in terms similar to those of the Logos-hymn, since many have already been cited in the course of the commentary, and the material has been adequately collected elsewhere.[17] The Logos-doctrine of Philo is intended to bridge the gulf between the purely spiritual God and the material world, and also to explain the presence and action of God in the soul.[18] Hence the Logos is given divine attributes: he is the "first-born of God", the "image of God", "second God". The divine functions of creating, sustaining and governing the world are transferred to the Logos, but he also shares in the work of the salvation of men. It is understandable that many scholars have been and still are inclined to hold that the Johannine Logos resembles closely and even depends on this feature of Jewish Hellenism, all the more so since it may be shown that Philo influenced early rabbinical writing to some extent.[19] Philo took the step which we must assume the author of the Logos-hymn also took: he identified divine Wisdom, as it appears in the later books of the O.T., with the Logos[20] and hence established the connection between the term used in the Jewish Bible and that of Hellenistic philosophy. It is easy to see why: a way of opening out to the Hellenistic world had to be found. The same must be true of the Logos-hymn and the Johannine prologue.

But it is another question, whether the author of the hymn (or the evangelist) was dependent on Philo when choosing the absolute use of the title of Logos, which has "a Hellenistic tone".[21] There are considerable objections to such an assumption, above all, the great differences between the concept of the Logos in John and in Philo:

1. The Logos in Philo remains an intermediate power between God and creation, though it is hard to define his position exactly. He is not an "intermediate being" like one of the Gnostic emanations;[22] but Philo

---

53–60; Hegermann, *Die Vorstellung vom Schöpfungsmittler im hellenistischen Judentum und Urchristentum*, pp. 67–87.

[17] Cf. Feine, *Theologie*, pp. 327ff.; Dodd, *Interpretation*, pp. 276f.

[18] Cf. *De opif.*, 146; *De poster.*, 122: *Immut.*, 134; *De somn.*, II, 249 etc.

[19] Cf. Schubert, "Beobachtungen".

[20] Cf. *Leg. all.*, I, 65; II, 86; *Heres*, 127 with 234 etc.; also Wolfson, *Philo*, pp. 253–61; Jervell, *Imago Dei*, p. 69; Hegermann, *Vorstellung*, pp. 75f., 78f., 86f.

[21] Starcky, "Logos", col. 492.

[22] Cf. Wolfson, *Philo*, pp. 261–89, who takes, however, a rather onesided view: "If his Logos and powers and ideas are in some respects employed by God as intermediaries they are selected by Him for that task not because of the need to bridge some imaginary gulf between Him and the world, but rather, as Philo himself suggests, for the purpose of setting various examples of right conduct to men" (p. 289).

does in fact insert the Logos between God and creation in his effort to preserve and bridge the distance between them, for which he uses the notion of exemplary cause which is not found in John. Philo, for instance, on Gen 1:27, affirms that God did not make man *as* his image but *after* his image, which he says means that the Logos was the image of God, and man the image of the Logos.[23] In John the Logos is really the creator (along with God) of all things (see commentary on 1:3).

2. The Logos in Philo is not strictly divine, as he explains in his commentary on Gen 31:13. "He that is truly God is One, but those that are improperly so called are more than one. Accordingly the holy word in the present instance has indicated Him who is truly God by means of the articles, saying, 'I am the God', while it omits the articles when mentioning him who is improperly so called, saying, 'Who appeared to thee in the place' not 'of the God', but simply 'of God'. Here it gives the title of 'God' to his chief word."[24]

The disquisitions on the Logos, which are partly in metaphorical language, leave his relationship to God obscure (cf. *Conf.*, 146). The decisive point is the personal nature of the Logos, as grasped by John in the light of the incarnation. For the evangelist, the Logos is truly Son of God, while for Philo he is the "eldest" or "firstborn" son, in contrast to the world which is the "younger son" (*Immut.*, 31).

3. The role which the Logos plays in salvation according to Philo differs essentially from the functions of the Johannine Logos. According to Philo, the Logos governs the world and the souls of the just in particular, in which he dwells and moves as in a city, bringing them bliss and regaling them as God's cupbearer:[25] he is the mediator or teacher of (mystic) union with God.[26] The Johannine Logos, however, is the historical revealer and redeemer, to whom men must be united in faith; his "glory" was hidden in the flesh, but believers receive grace upon grace from his fullness. Even with regard to Philo and his spiritualized religion, the incarnation remains an insuperable barrier and provides an infallible criterion.

Philo, then, discloses a Hellenistic Judaism in which Wisdom speculation was combined with the notion of the Logos. But he had no direct influence on the Christian hymn, which had a similar cultural background, but was marked from the start by the Christian faith in its own special way.

---

[23] *Heres.*, 231; cf. *De opif.*, 139.

[24] *De somn.*, I, 229f. The anarthrous θεός in Jn 1:1c has a different meaning, see *ad loc.*

[25] Cf. *De poster.*, 122; *De somn.*, II, 247ff.

[26] Cf. Bréhier, *Idées philosophiques*, pp. 101–7, 230–7; Goodenough, *By Light, Light*, pp. 235–64; Völker, *Fortschritt und Vollendung bei Philo von Alexandrien*, pp. 158–98.

5. The Logos and the Gnostic Myth

Recent research on Gnosis claims to have discovered and analysed, behind the confused mass of systems with their series of aeons and emanations, their multifarious nomenclature and extravagant fantasies, the phenomenology of a consistent attitude to existence. Anthropological in interest and dualistic in colouring, it prompted a restless search for redemption and taught a basically uniform way of salvation, "Gnosis", in fact, which penetrated, affected or moulded to its purpose the various realms of thought and piety of the Hellenistic age.[27] It was a widespread "religion" with a definite view of the world,[28] by which even Judaism and Christianity are said to have been influenced. As regards our present question, this means that Jewish Wisdom speculation, with its myth of pre-existent Wisdom descending on earth and seeking a "place of rest", is only a variant of an old pagan myth; and it means further, that the Christian doctrine of redemption has elaborated this myth in its own way, by applying it to the historical Messiah, Jesus of Nazareth, and hence reaching its Christology of a pre-existent divine being who came down from heaven, became man in Jesus Christ and re-ascended in triumph. This is a question of supreme importance for the fourth Gospel, and it will be discussed in detail later (excursus vi). Here we are only interested in the assertion that the Logos-hymn also goes back to this ancient myth, whence it borrowed the figure and the name of the "Logos". According to R. Bultmann, the main representative of this view which has become so widespread in Germany, this same figure is met with "in various manifestations and under various names . . . But almost without exception, it is known by the title or name of Λόγος, except that this is often replaced by Νοῦς, especially in philosophical writers, a title with the same meaning to the minds of the Greeks".[29] In Gnosis strictly speaking, this figure is often enlarged or split up, but even where the Λόγος (or Νοῦς or Ἄνθρωπος) has been reduced to a minor figure in the list of aeons, his real and original significance can always be recognized.[30] For this reconstruction from late sources, Bultmann then claims great (pre-Christian) antiquity, affirming that it influenced the Logos-hymn, which "presents Jesus and his work in terms of Gnostic mythology".[31] Verification is rendered difficult by the question of sources, since later sources are also called in to prove the existence of older views, and we cannot be

---

[27] Cf. esp. Jonas, *Gnosis*, vol. I, pp. 94–210.

[28] Cf. Quispel, *Gnosis als Weltreligion;* Wilson, *Gnostic Problem;* Grant, *Gnosticism and Early Christianity.*

[29] Cf. Intro. to prologue, part 3; also Bauer, excursus, pp. 6–10; Wikenhauser, pp. 55f.

[30] Bultmann, pp. 9–14, esp. 11.

[31] *Ibid.*, 12.

sure of the extent to which post-Christian literature drew on John itself for the title of Logos. We confine ourselves to sifting the material and drawing some conclusions.

a) The title of Logos in Gnostic literature

In the non-Christian Gnosis of Hermetism, the Logos figures in the cosmogony of the "Poimandres" (*Corpus Hermeticum*, I, 5f.), and in the tractate on regeneration (*Corpus Hermeticum*, xxxiii, 21). These passages have already been discussed briefly (Introduction, p. 137). They show no very great affinities with the Johannine Logos. In the developed cosmogony of the Poimandres (of which there is no trace in John), the occurrence of Λόγος is perhaps to be explained by Jewish influences (Gen 1). It is used along with Νοῦς, which is the predominant term in the rest of the Hermetic literature.

Mandaean literature provides rich non-Christian material, which has preserved ancient Gnostic views, in spite of the lateness of the actual writings. Among the many envoys and titles which it furnishes, there is a Yokabar, "the first word . . . who passed through the worlds, came, split open the firmament and revealed himself".[32] This mythological figure is also described in part of the *Book of John* as a being of light *(Yokabar-Ziwa)*, clothed with brightness, who comes to the world "to plant the plantation of life", and to be for man "a leader from the place of darkness to the place of light".[33] This is an old stratum of tradition, as may be seen from the fact that the figure occurs frequently in the Mandaean liturgies (see Lidzbarski, index). In the liturgy of baptism, the catechumen praises Yokabar-Ziwa as "the messenger of life and the word of the first men of established righteousness "(Lidzbarski, p. 16, 11). He is also called "the word of life, who came from the house of life to just and believing men" (*ibid.*, p. 35, 6f.), and "the great, first word" (*ibid.*, p. 59, 2). This messenger "from the house of life" is also mentioned frequently in the *Canonical Prayerbook*.[34] Here is a passage, from Lady Drower's translation, which is strongly reminiscent of John: "I am the Word of the First Life. Pre-existent am I to all 'uthras, For the Life created me and blessed me And gave me strength, benison and goodness, — And sent me to bless my mystic brethren, All the 'uthras; to speak and to be obeyed. And I came and blessed them And gave them strength, benison and goodness, just as my Father Had given them to me."[35] Here, however, one may suspect that Christian influences have

[32] Lidzbarski, *Johannesbuch der Mandäer*, XXV; cf. *Mand. Liturgien*, pp. 16, 11.
[33] Lidsbarski, pp. 219f. [34] Drower, *Canonical Prayerbook*, pp. 18f., 50, 261, 287.
[35] *Ibid.* p. 261 (the beginnings of the lines in the poetic part are indicated by large capitals).

been at work, as seems to have been the case in the language of prayer in particular.[36] But the fact remains that "the Word (of life etc.)" is not an uncommon designation for mythical figures with changing names in Gnosis: Adakas (*Prayer Book*, 293), Mahzian (*ibid.*, 294), Yawar-Ziwa (*Ginza*, 289, 9–11; 291, 13), Anosh (*Ginza*, 295, 15 ff.).

The *Odes of Solomon* also speak frequently of the "Word" as the Gnostic redeemer, and he is the theme of Ode 12: "And he caused his knowledge to abound in me because the mouth of the Lord is the true Word and the door of his light." (v. 3). This word hastens through the worlds (v. 5), gives speech to the silent (v. 8) and finally finds a dwelling-place among men (v. 12); "Blessed are they who have understood everything by means of (the Word) and have known the Lord in his truth" (v. 13). In 16:19 the writer alludes to the creative activity of God's Word: "The worlds were made by his word and by the thought of his heart." His redemptive work is described in 41:11–14 in the following terms: "His word is with us in all our way, the Saviour who makes alive and does not reject our souls" (v. 11). The next verse clearly has a Christian tinge: "the man who was humbled, and exalted by his own righteousness" (v. 12). Hence the Odes could depend on John to some extent (cf. Introduction, pp. 144ff.), but they still seem to reflect the existence of a pre-Christian myth of the "Word" (cf. Ode 12).

The situation is more or less the same in the case of the Coptic Gnostic writings from Nag-Hammadi. The *Gospel of Truth* includes passages in which the "Word" is ascribed cosmic and soteriological functions. The introduction has already been cited (pp. 147f. above); cf. further 23:18, "His (the Father's) wisdom (σοφία) meditates the Word, his instruction utters it, his knowledge has revealed it"; 23:34 ff., "So the Word of the Father goes forth in (into?) the All, as fruit of his heart and image (?) of his will". The "Word" which sustains the All (24:3) is also in the heart of the Gnostic (26:5). But an incarnation is also envisaged, as a result of Christian preaching ("the Word took bodily form", 26:8) and is seen as bringing confusion and division among the "vessels" (men): some were emptied and others were filled (26:10 ff.). The Johannine prologue could also have influenced ch. 37; but there seems to be an ancient myth behind the passage which reads: "Every one of his (the Father's) words is the work of his one (or, unique) will through the revelation (or, manifestation) of his Word. Since they are the depth (βάθος) of his thought, the λόγος, who went forth first, has revealed them and a corresponding νοῦς. The unique λόγος is in silent grace" (trans. after W. Till, partly uncertain).

---

[36] Cf. Rudolf, *Die Mandäer*, vol. I, p. 106, with references to Lidzbarski, *Mand. Liturgien*, pp. 65ff.

Here we have "depth", "procession", νοῦς and a primordial "silence", and emanations of which the λόγος is the first. These are Gnostic ideas and expressions. In the *Apocryphon of John*, 31, there is a series of emanations which "came forth in silence"; and then we read: "His (the invisible Spirit's) will embodied itself, he came and appeared, he came with mind and light, with which to praise him. The Logos follows the will; for through the Logos, Christ has created all things".[37] The Christian element in these texts, especially the *Apocryphon of John*, seems to be very superficial.[38]

Since we have these original texts, it is hardly necessary to investigate the Gnostic systems as presented by the Fathers. The Logos is well documented as one of the many creative emanations, sometimes linked with Sophia, especially in Valentinian Gnosis.[39] But ancient Gnostic myths may also be reflected in the language of Church writers whose orthodoxy and Christian perspectives in theology are beyond question, as may be seen from Ignatius of Antioch. As H. Schlier has demonstrated, the statement in *Magn.*, 8:2, that Jesus Christ, the Son of God, is αὐτοῦ λόγος ἀπὸ σιγῆς προελθών, reflects a set of concepts which is not derived from John, but is native to Gnosis.[40] The material which Schlier had then (1929) at his disposition has now been increased by the Coptic Gnostic texts cited above. Schlier could then point to the pair of aeons which came first in the system of Valentinus, σιγή and βυθός, from which he deduced a more ancient stage in which the divine sphere in general was designated as σιγή. The new texts only confirm this view.

We may end our survey of the material here, but we have still to ask what it means with regard to the origin of the Johannine concept of the Logos.

b) The facts and their implications

The texts give us no reason to doubt the existence of an ancient Gnostic myth which used the term "Word" for the envoy from the heavenly

[37] According to Papyrus Berolinensis 8502, translated by Till, p. 192; cf. Giversen, *Apocryphon Johannis*, pp. 58f. (Cod. II of Nag-Hammadi, pl. 55, 3–11) with commentary, pp. 173ff. Cod. III of Nag-Hammadi does not read "the word" but "a word", cf. Krause and Labib, *Die Drei Versionen*, p. 62 (Cod., p. 10, line 17). Giversen, p. 174, considers that the last clause, "Christ has created all things by the Logos" as interpolated, after Jn 1:1–3.

[38] See on the *Apocrypon Johannis*, van Unnik, *Evangelien aus dem Nilsand*, pp. 81–92, esp. 92, "Here everything points to the fact that the origin of Gnosis is to be sought outside Christianity, and that a system already in existence was later enriched with Christian elements"; Wilson, *Gnostic Problem*, pp. 149–71, esp. p. 154; "This might seem once more to point to a pre-Christian Jewish Gnosticism which has been but slightly Christianized."

[39] Cf. Sagnard, *La gnose valentinienne*, pp. 240ff.; 311–5; 481–94 (Heracleon).

[40] Schlier, *Religionsgeschichtliche Untersuchungen*, pp. 36–39.

world, among other terms by which his functions in the creation of the cosmos and the salvation of men were expressed. The term was given a typically Gnostic meaning, summing up the view of cosmogony and soteriology which was prevalent everywhere in Gnosis, though under an extreme variety of forms. This ancient myth has little or nothing in common with the notion of creation in Judaism and Christianity. It is intent on producing a cosmogony which will explain the origin of a material world which is evil, and of the malignant situation through which man is at the mercy of this evil world. The "Word" is a beneficent power, which is also, and above all, saviour of men, in so far as they are receptive to it. It is a mythical way of speaking of the Gnosis imparted to man from the inner core of his essential nature, from the homeland and the goal of his pneumatic "self". The "Word" then comes to designate the Gnostic "Saviour-Envoy", though as a rule along with other mythical names and figures. It would be hard to prove that Logos was the original or most prevalent designation; for this there is only the problematical argument, that "the Word" occurs again and again among the various names given by the various systems, and hence it must be the substratum of all and the original designation of the Gnostic envoy. But this is no more than a postulate.

It is true that when we compare this Gnostic figure with the Logos of Greek philosophy on the one hand, and the Logos of John on the other, it is much closer to the latter, in so far as it plays a role in creation (or cosmogony) as well as in redemption. But we have also noted that this is also true of Wisdom in Judaism and of the Logos in Philo. Are we then to understand that the author of the Christian hymn adopted the thought of the Wisdom texts, while taking the title of Logos from the Gnostic myth? It is most unlikely that he would turn for the title to a current of thought from which he is otherwise worlds apart—both as regards the origin of the world and the nature of salvation. It is much more likely that he had other reasons to choose the title, especially the importance of the "word of God" in the Bible, and the use of the (absolute) designation of Logos in Hellenistic Judaism, as in Philo. There may also have been the simple reason that the masculine noun Logos appeared to the author of the hymn (and to the evangelist) as more fitting than the feminine noun Sophia to present his pre-existing and incarnate Christ.[41] He may, of course, have also been influenced more remotely by the use of the term in Gnostic circles, Christian and pagan, just as Ignatius of Antioch was. This may in fact be a pointer to a milieu like that of the Bishop of Antioch.

It cannot be urged that the personal character of the Gnostic envoy proves the Gnostic origin of the concept of the Logos as a person in John.

---

[41] Bauer, *Johannesevangelium*, p. 7.

Superficially, the Gnostic saviour may seem to be more clearly and definitely a person than the Jewish Wisdom or Torah, or the Logos of Philo. In reality, it is only a mythical figure and hence far less a person. The "personification" of the Jewish entities—which was, however, not a real personification—would have been going in the same direction as the Christian author who was looking for a suitable terminology to depict his Christ. But it has been sufficiently demonstrated in the commentary that the personal character of the Christian Logos was dictated by Christian belief in the historical coming of Jesus as the Christ-Logos, and that this faith was the only possible source of the personal character being asserted so definitely.[42]

The ultimate reason why the scholars in question appeal to Gnosticism as the determinant factor in the choice of the title Logos in John is probably not the coincidence in terminology. It is rather the effort to explain the "mythical language" in which the Johannine Christology is clothed by means of the Gnostic myth which is also said to have given its essential stamp to the pre-Johannine Christology of the primitive Church, as in the hymn of Phil 2:6–11, and in the Pauline and Deutero-pauline writings.[43] But this is a much wider problem, in theology and comparative religion, and the Gnostic origin of the title Logos would contribute to its solution—if this could be affirmed with certainty of the Johannine hymn. But there is no such certainty. We have tried to show the elements of truth in this hypothesis: the existence of an ancient myth in which, among others, the expression "the Word" was used. But direct dependence on this myth with regard to the Johannine hymn is not proved, and hence the fundamental problem of the roots of Johannine Christology still remains an open one.

The Johannine hymn to the Logos is, in the main, much closer to Jewish and primitive Christian thinking than to Gnosticism, and this must have been the main reason for the choice of the title Logos. The concept could have been worked out, like that of Philo, under the guidance of Hellenistic Jewish thought, to provide a Greek expression adequate to combine the two notions of the "word of God" and "Wisdom" or the Torah.[44]

---

[42] Cf. also Langkammer, "Zur Herkunft des Logostitels im Johannesprolog".

[43] Cf. Bultmann, p. 11 with n. 1; *Theologie,* pp. 174ff., E. T.: vol. I, pp. 164–83.

[44] Cf. Dodd, *Interpretation*, p. 278: ". . . the author started from the Jewish idea of the Torah as being at once the Word of God and the divine Wisdom manifested in creation, and found, under the guidance of Hellenistic Jewish thought similar to that of Philo, an appropriate Greek expression which fittingly combined both ideas"; cf. also the final remark of Robert, "Logos", cols. 496f.

EXCURSUS II

Pre-Existence

There can be little doubt that the testimony of John the Baptist to the pre-existence of Jesus is meant to convey the Christian faith. Apart from the historical question of whether such a confession is possible or probable on the lips of John—which we answered by seeing in it a Christian interpretation of his testimony to the Messiah—it raises a question in the history of religion. What were the conditions which could give rise to the notion or conviction that a man really existed prior to his birth, prior, indeed, to the creation of the world? The notion of pre-existence was certainly not completely novel, an idea dropped down straight from heaven; but the immediate attachments of the Christian confession are not a matter of indifference. Here too, as in the question of the origin of the title of Logos, we are chiefly concerned with the hypothesis that the Christian faith took over a Gnostic myth and presented its Christology at least in the outward cloak of Gnostic mythological language. Are the Jewish presuppositions enough to explain the Christian belief in the pre-existence of the redeemer, not, of course, in the sense of a mere application of a proposition of Jewish theology, but as the transcendent elaboration of a Jewish idea? Or is one confined from the start to the ancient and ultimately pagan myth? The discussion will cover in part the relationship between Johannine theology and Gnostic myth (see excursus vi).

1. The notion of pre-existence in Judaism

There were a certain number of things so important in Jewish theology that they were held to have existed before the creation of the world, and Scripture proofs were adduced for each of them. For the most part, it is a pre-existence in the thought and plans of God, but it cannot be reduced simply to an "ideal pre-existence"; precise examination and distinctions are called for here. The conviction of the pre-existence of the soul penetrated only gradually into Judaism, where it never became universal, under the influence of Hellenistic Platonism, first affecting Hellenistic Judaism and later, more or less after the middle of the third century A.D., Palestinian rabbinism. But the doctrine is not relevant here, since the Johannine Logos possesses a special pre-existence reserved to him alone. The pre-existence of the Messiah presents a special problem, though it was seen for the most part in the same perspective as the other entities which existed before creation. We meet a very singular view, which has been the subject of much discussion and controversy, in the "Parables" of the *Book of Enoch*, where the figure of the "Son of Man" or "the Elect" is found. He does not seem to fit into the usual categories of "ideal" pre-existence in the mind of God or of the "preparation" and "appointment" of the coming last things. We must examine the texts more closely.

a) The Jewish doctrine of the pre-existence of certain entities

According to a Jewish theological tradition which has been transmitted in various forms, seven things existed "before the creation of the world". According to *Pes.*, 54a Bar (quoted on 1:1) these were: the Torah, penance, the Garden of Eden, Gehenna, the Throne of Glory, the Sanctuary and the Name of the Messiah.[1] The divergent tradition in *Gen. Rabba*, 1, 2b, is noteworthy: "Six things preceded creation; some of them were (really) created, some of them came into the mind of God, to be created later. The Torah and the throne of glory were (really) created; the Torah, see Prov 8:22; the throne of glory, see Ps 93:2 . . . The Fathers and Israel and the sanctuary and the name of the Messiah came into God's mind, to be created . . ."; this is followed by a discussion as to whether the Torah or the throne of glory was first to be created.[2] The traditions run parallel, and coincide in basing the pre-existence of the Torah on Prov 8:22. But the special emphasis on the Torah (and the heavenly "throne of glory") as being really created before the world shows a special trend. In the first form of the tradition, penance follows the Torah, for the very good reason that God must have foreseen the infringement of the Torah when he created it, and hence created at once the remedy which was so highly prized in Judaism, namely, penance.[3] Thus this ancient Tannaitic tradition seems to regard pre-existence as "ideal", that is, as only in the mind of God, while the second, later tradition, which gives a privileged place to the Torah (and the "throne of glory", cf.

[1] See the text in Billerbeck, vol. I, p. 974, or vol. II, p. 335; Epstein, *Pesahim*, p. 265.

[2] Billerbeck, vol. I, p. 974; Freedman, vol. I, p. 6.

[3] Cf. Moore, *Judaism*, vol. I, pp. 526f., and vol. III, p. 161.

Jer 17:12 or Ps 93:2), accords it the reality of actual being. This is undoubtedly due to the influence of Wisdom speculation. *Gen. Rabba*, 1 (beginning) comments as follows: the Torah was an instrument in the hand of God, just as an architect uses a plan to execute his work.[4] On account of the similarity of this interpretation with that of Philo—the Logos as exemplary cause—it has been suggested that the author of this midrash was perhaps acquainted with the ideas of Philo.[5] The pre-existence of the Torah, like that of the throne of glory, attains more concrete reality here, though it falls short of the real, personal pre-existence of the Johannine Logos.

Here the main concern of Jewish thought is to trace created and temporal things, all beings and all happenings, to the thought of God. This is given clear expression in the texts of Qumran: "From the God of knowledge comes all that is and will be. Before they were, he established their whole design; and when they exist, according to their fixed laws, they fulfil their work according to his glorious design, unalterably" (*1 QS*, 3:15f.). Men in particular are included in this eternal plan of God, as the first Thanksgiving Hymn says: "In the wisdom of thy knowledge, thou hast fixed for them a way of life before they came to be: all things came to pass according to thy word, and without thee nothing was done" (*1 QH*, 1:19f.). Particular attention is then paid to the election of Israel with all its attendant privileges: "Blessed be the God of Israel for all his holy plan and for his works of truth ... Thou [hast redeemed] us for thyself as an eternal people, and wrought marvels for us in the inheritance of the light in thy fidelity" (*1 QM*, 13:2, 9f.) This theology of "predetermination" could naturally lead to giving the Torah above all a special place in "protology", as may be seen from rabbinical speculation. On Job 20:4, quoted as follows in the midrash, "It (Wisdom) knows what exists from eternity", R. Hama ben Hanina says: "All the creatures made on each day of creation asked each other: what works did God bring forth in you?" Working backwards, he comes to ask finally: whom could the works of the first day ask? And the answer is: "Is it not the Torah, which preceded the making of the world"?[6] The Torah was said to have come into existence exactly 974 generations or 2000 years before the creation of the world,[7] and lay on God's knees as he sat on the throne of glory.[8] Everything is depicted so vividly and concretely that it is certain that pre-existence in the mind of God was taken seriously.

---

[4] Billerbeck, vol. III, p. 356; Freedman, vol. I, p. 1.

[5] Moore, *Judaism*, vol. I, p. 265, with further references.

[6] *Gen. Rabbah*, 8 (6a) in Billerbeck, vol. II, p. 353; Freedman, vol. I, p. 56.

[7] Cf. Billerbeck, vol. II, pp. 354f.

[8] *Midr. Ps.*, 90:12 (196a) in Billerbeck, vol. I, pp. 974f.

Another component is supplied by eschatology. Not only are the events predetermined by God, the good things of the world to come are prepared beforehand. The *Fourth Book of Esdras* is quite clear: "For you paradise is opened, the tree of life is planted, the age to come is prepared, plenty is provided, a city is built, rest is appointed, goodness is established and wisdom perfected beforehand" (8:52). The same view may be seen behind the saying of the king ("Son of Man") in Mt 25:34, "Come, O blessed of my Father, inherit the kingdom prepared for you from the foundation of the world".[9] Hence it can be said that eschatological things "appear" or "show themselves"; they are already in heaven but now come forth from concealment (cf. *4 Esdr.*, 7:26, 35f.; 13:36; *Syriac Apocalypse of Baruch* 51:7f.; 73:1). The doctrine of the pre-existence of the blessings of salvation serves to make the certainty of salvation more vivid. "It cannot be denied that the texts adduced signify the real pre-existence of the blessings of salvation; they are not merely planned, they are really there."[10]

It is only natural that these pre-existing realities should include the bringer of salvation or "the name of the Messiah", the latter being one of the seven things created before the world (see above). This is explained as follows in the *Midrash on Ps 90*, 12 (196a): God has before him the name of the Messiah "engraved on a precious stone above the altar" of the heavenly sanctuary, as he sits on the throne of glory. This is, of course, only the "ideal" pre-existence of the Messiah,[11] an existence in God's mind as part of the plan of salvation which guarantees that the saviour or helper will one day really appear on earth. But the apocalyptic texts, as we shall see, go beyond this at certain points (cf. *Enoch*, *4 Esdras*).

It has already been noted that the doctrine of the pre-existence of the soul (hence too of the soul of the Messiah) has a different origin, in Platonic Hellenism. It is unlikely that Wis 8:20; 9:15 presuppose it, but it is found in Philo (*Gig.*, 12–15; *Somn.*, I, 138f.) and is attributed to the Essenes by Josephus (*Bellum*, II, 154f.). It was later adopted by many of the rabbis.[12] Real pre-existence was then ascribed to the soul of the Messiah; the late midrash, *Pesiqta Rabbathi* (beginning of 10th cent.) says that his soul was called into existence, like those of all men, at the beginning of creation, to dwell then with God in heaven.[13] But these are speculations which both for chronological and theological reasons cannot be used as comparisons in the present question, since this distinction

[9] See also *Enoch*, 25:7; 103:3; *4 Esdr.*, 7:14; 13:18; *Syriac Apoc. Baruch*, 48:49; 52:7; 84:6; see Volz, *Eschatologie*, pp. 114f.

[10] Volz, *Eschatologie*, p. 116.

[11] Cf. Billerbeck, vol. II, pp. 334f.; Volz, *Eschatologie*, p. 206.

[12] Cf. Billerbeck, vol. II, pp. 341–6.

[13] *Ibid.*, pp. 347ff.

between soul and body is completely foreign to the Johannine thinking on Christ the Logos. It appears, nonetheless, that Judaism was open to various concepts of pre-existence.

In the course of the commentary, we have sufficiently stressed the concept of pre-existence with regard to divine Wisdom or the Torah. It was a realistic way of depicting God's plan for creation and human history, in terms of personification. It was not a real personification nor a real pre-existence "outside" God, but still the category of a purely "ideal" pre-existence does not quite suit it. God uses Wisdom or the Torah as the instrument or blueprint of his creation. Wisdom is his "counsellor" and "helper". Such speculations could, as we have seen, have been drawn on by the primitive Christian hymn for its doctrine of the Logos, though here the notion of pre-existence is again different from that of which we have been speaking. But notions of disparate origin could easily be confused in Judaism.

b) The pre-existent "Son of Man" in apocalyptic

In the "Parables" of *Enoch* (chs. 37–71), the pre-Christian origin of which has been contested, but not yet seriously shaken,[14] the coming bringer of salvation is presented as "the elect" or "the righteous" or again, as the "Son of Man", of whom a number of statements are made which point to his heavenly pre-existence. Some scholars deny that this is more than an "ideal" pre-existence, in terms of the ordinary Jewish notions (see above), while others affirm it vigourously, like E. Sjöberg,[15] followed by S. Mowinckel.[16] The latter view seems imperative when one examines the texts. The statements about the "Son of Man" are more

---

[14] In general, the "Parables" are dated to the first century B.C. The notion that this part of *Enoch* comes from Jewish Christian circles of the second century A.D. received some impetus from the fact that other parts of *Enoch* were found in Qumran, but nothing from the Parables, cf. Milik, *Dix Ans de découvertes dans le Désert de Juda*, pp. 30f. Grelot, in *Recherches de Science religieuse* 46 (1958), pp. 18ff., also points to *Jub.*, 4:17–23, where all the literature ascribed to Enoch is mentioned, but not the Parables. But this argument from silence is not conclusive; the section, which is different in content, could have been incorporated later. Possibly chs. 70–71 indicate the literary "seam", cf. Sjöberg, *Der Menschensohn im äthiopischen Henochbuch*, pp. 147–89, esp. p. 166: "This provides no sure evidence against the originality of chs. 70–71; it is still possible that they are original. But in a work of the complexity of *Enoch* it cannot again be excluded that one or both of the chapters may be secondary additions. The theme here dealt with, the assumption of Enoch, is not touched on in the Parables. The two chapters form, therefore, an appendix in any case." See also Eissfeldt, *Einleitung*, p. 839, E. T.: pp. 619 f.

[15] *Menschensohn*, pp. 83–101.

[16] Mowinckel, *He that Cometh*, pp. 370–3; cf. also Coppens and Dequecker, *Le Fils de l'homme et les Saints du Très-Haut, Daniel, VII dans les Apocryphes et dans le Nouveau Testament*, pp. 81f. (see the bibliography there, pp. 55f. and 73f.).

fully developed than in Dan 7, and cover much the same ground as those about the "Elect", so that it is merely a matter of variation in terminology.[17] The main texts are as follows:

39:7f. "I saw his dwelling-place under the wings of the Lord of Spirits. And all the righteous and elect before him shall be strong as fiery lights ... There I wished to dwell, and my soul longed for that dwelling-place: and there heretofore hath been my portion, for so hath it been established concerning me before the Lord of Spirits."

48:3 "Before the sun and the signs were created, before the stars of the heaven were made, his name was named before the Lord of Spirits."

6 "And for this reason hath he been chosen and hidden before him, before the creation of the world and for evermore."

52:9 "And all these things shall be denied and destroyed from the face of the earth, when the Elect One shall appear before the face of the Lord of Spirits"; cf. 69:29 on the "Son of Man".

62:7 "For from the beginning the Son of Man was hidden, and the Most High preserved him in the presence of his might, and revealed him to the elect" (Charles).

In 48:3 the "naming of his name" probably means no more than the pre-temporal election of the "Son of Man"; but 48:6 adds that the Son of Man was "hidden" before God. He then has a dwelling-place "under the wings of the Lord of Spirits" (39:7) till he finally "appears" at the end (cf. 38:2; 52:9; 69:29) and "stands" before the Lord of Spirits. The notion that the Son of Man existed from the beginning, but dwelt hidden in heaven "in the presence of the might of God" and was then revealed only to the elect, is then expressed more clearly in 62:7.

This interpretation is supported by *4 Esdr.* 13, which also shows that the view in question was not completely singular. Here too, before his eschatological appearance, the bringer of salvation is already dwelling with the Most High (cf. vv. 26, 52); Esdras is rapt up to heaven "to dwell with my Son (originally "servant")[18] and thy fellows, till the times are at an end". The future bringer of salvation, whatever his name, already possesses a real existence hidden with God.[19]

---

[17] See the grouping in Coppens and Dequecker, *Le Fils de l'homme*, pp. 78ff.

[18] For the "my Son" of the Latin, Syriac and Ethiopian versions the two Arabic MSS read "my servant", which is adopted, correctly, by the Revised Standard Version. The alteration is easily explained among Christian copyists (the middle term being the Greek παῖς with its two meanings, Volz, *Eschatologie*, pp. 204f.).

[19] So too Volz, *Eschatologie*, pp. 204f., who also refers to certain tendencies in this direction in the translations of the Septuagint.

We have already pointed out that in apocalyptic the eschatological blessings are already "prepared" in heaven, and it could be argued that the texts just quoted merely transfer this notion to the person of the bringer of salvation. But his personal pre-existence is something more than this, and seems to have another origin. Nothing is said in the texts of how he originally came to be, as for instance that this inhabitant of heaven was made before the rest of creation: the field of vision does not take in protology. But it has been suggested that there is a connection between the "Son of Man" and the "Primordial Man" of ancient oriental myth, (who is to be distinguished from Adam).[20] The hypothesis is primarily based on the similarity of their eschatological functions,[21] which, however, had further characteristics of their own in Judaism. The idea may be basically connected with the ancient myth, but Jewish apocalyptic had no notion of this. "Judaism, then, was completely unaware that the Son of Man was really the Primordial man. What it had to say about the Primordial Man was connected with the biblical figure of Adam as he is presented in the rabbinic legend of Adam."[22] Hence if Judaism had once been influenced by such mythical representations, they had long since been merged into its faith in God the creator. Jewish apocalyptic, with its expectation of the "Son of Man", is already clearly striking out on its own, and hence the notion of pre-existence connected with this figure is of importance in its own right. It shows at any rate that Judaism was capable of absorbing various notions of pre-existence and exploiting them for the benefit of its own theology.

2. Pre-existence in Gnosticism

With Gnosticism, we are in a completely different world of thought. To understand the notion of pre-existence to which it gave rise, we must recall that Gnosis is an anthropology, stemming from a certain understanding of existence, which strives to free man from the constraint of his earthly state in the cosmos and enable him to find his true "self", his

---

[20] Cf. the survey of the theories in Staerk, *Die Erlösererwartung in den östlichen Religionen*, pp. 422–35. He then goes on to accept this hypothesis, as does Mowinckel, *He that Cometh*, pp. 420–37, in a modified form. But more recent research counsels more caution, cf. Moe, "Der Menschensohn und der Urmensch"; Coppens and Dequecker, *Le Fils de l'homme*, pp. 67ff., Colpe, *Die religionsgeschichtliche Schule*, pp. 149–53 ("Son of Man—and also Gnostic Anthropos—cannot be considered as the terms of an evolution launched by the Indo-iranian myth. The intermediate links are missing", p. 152); Schenke, *Der Gottmensch in der Gnosis*, pp. 144–54 (some indirect influence, but with great restrictions, pp. 151f.). See further excursus v and vi.

[21] Cf. Mowinckel, *He that Cometh*, pp. 427–31, and 436.

[22] *Ibid.*, p. 346.

real nature, once more. For this it develops a cosmology in mythological language, which ascribes to the pneumatic kernel of man's being an origin and "homeland" in the supreme region of eternal and purely spiritual being, a "heavenly" pre-existence in the pleroma, while the material, perishable nature of his body is a product of "the world", and the "soul" linked to the body represents the mixing of spiritual and material which as a cosmogony (by means of various emanations and gradations) has led to the "world's" coming forth from the ultimate spiritual principle.[23] Hence only the pneuma dwelling in the deepest recesses of the soul has "pre-existence"; and this is also what distinguishes the doctrine at this point from the Greek notion, according to which the pre-existent soul is imprisoned in the body and recommences its immortal life after separation from the body. Gnosticism sees the *pneuma*, the "spark" from the heavenly world of light, as sinking deeper and deeper into the corporal and material world,[24] an exile yearning from afar to return to its homeland. The return is accomplished by the "soul" (here understood as the essential kernel of its being) when it wakes from its "sleep" and remembers its true home, as is described most impressively in the "Song of the Pearl" (Hymn of the Soul) in the *Acts of Thomas*, 108–113.[25] But this is only a mythological way of depicting the "Gnosis" of the man who is capable of attaining it, which is self-knowledge, or rather, knowledge of the "self". And the return to "where he was before" is only a way of saying that he has regained his "essential" or true existence.[26]

Here then we only have self-redemption by Gnosis described in mythical language. Since cosmology and anthropology correspond, since man as microcosm reflects the relationships of the macrocosm, a cosmogony is presented as a way of understanding the real nature of "man", whose nature is to be understood in the light of its origin. This purpose was also served by the myth of Ἄνθρωπος, the cosmological "primordial man", who then also becomes ἄνθρωπος, the human being in his actual con-

---

[23] Cf. Jonas, *Gnosis*, vol. I, pp. 178–90; Schlier, "Der Mensch im Gnostizismus".

[24] Cf. *C. Herm.*, I, 14–17 and Haenchen, "Aufbau und Theologie des Poimandres", esp. pp. 173–6.

[25] Greek text ed. by Bonnet, pp. 219–24; transl. from the Syriac version by Bornkamm, pp. 498–503; James ("Song of the Soul"), pp. 411–15; see Jonas, *Gnosis*, vol. I, pp. 320–7; Adam, *Die Psalmen des Thomas und das Perlenlied als Zeugnis vorchristlicher Gnosis*, pp. 55–75; Klijn, *The Acts of Thomas*, pp. 273–81 (considered Christian-Syrian).

[26] Cf. the "essential (οὐσιώδης) man" in *C. Herm.*, I, 15 and the "essential birth", *ibid.*, XIII, 14; also *Asclepius*, 7 and 8 (Nock and Festugière, vol. I, pp. 304–5). That knowledge of self is redemption, is the basic conviction of Gnosis, cf. *C. Herm.*, I, 19: ὁ ἀναγνωρίσας ἑαυτὸν ἐλήλυθεν εἰς τὸ περιούσιον ἀγαθόν. With the help of such knowledge, man attains to "perfection" and "apotheosis", cf. *C. Herm.*, IV, 4; XIII, 10, 22; the Naassenes in Hippolytus, *Ref.*, V, 8, 38 (Wendland, p. 96, 7): ἀρχὴ γάρ . . . τελειώσεως γνῶσις ἀνθρώπου.

dition.[27] In this perspective, the two figures merge into one: the macrocosmic "primordial man" also stands for historical man, while the life and destiny of man are described in the image painted of the primordial man. The Anthropos myth is then used in particular to explain the redemption of man: submerged in the material world from which he needs to be set free, man is to find himself once more and free himself through knowledge of his nature and origin. The "Song of the Pearl" (see above) provides a good example of this ambivalence: the king's son from the east, who sets out to fetch the precious pearl from Egypt is "the 'primordial man' who comprises all humanity, seeking to win back his 'soul', that is, himself"[28]; but this "Man" who comprises within himself all the souls to be redeemed is at the same time the prototype who represents also each individual soul. Each Gnostic can see his own destiny mirrored in his, and his own redemption prefigured. A similar function may also be noted in the "Son (of God)" in the *Odes of Solomon*.[29]

Hence assertions about pre-existence in Gnosis differ fundamentally in meaning from those which occur in Biblical thought, which is centred on history and the history of salvation. One can only speak of "pre-existence" in Gnosis in an improper sense; there is no horizontal view which takes in a succession of ages, an existence before the world and time, which becomes historical and is afterwards regained. There is only the present task of coming to oneself, of being oneself "substantially", that is, of becoming aware of one's own true self by means of Gnosis. The myth unfolded in historical sequence is only an aid to the imagination, the recourse to the "pre-existence" of the soul (or its essential core) is only a means of assuring oneself of the essential nature of man. In contrast to Gnosis, the Bible affirms that man and the world came to be by a true act of creation, which implies a real beginning of existence and an antecedent pre-temporal state, while in the Gnostic cosmogony the whole process is fluid and the distinctions are blurred. Further, the Bible distinguishes sharply between God and the world, so that "ideal" pre-existence in the mind of God cannot possibly be confused with the temporal existence of created things, whereas in Gnosis God himself changes into the world or man,[30] so that the ("pre-existent") self of man is identical with the divine substance.[31] Finally, there is a genuine eschatology in the Bible, which provides new perspectives for the understanding of "pre-existence" (see above). But in Gnosis the process of "returning" or "ascending once

[27] Cf. Haenchen, "Poimandres", p. 174. [28] Jonas, *Gnosis*, vol. I, p. 321.

[29] Cf. Abramowski, "Der Christus der Salomo-Oden", esp. pp. 52–62.

[30] Cf. Haenchen, "Poimandres", p. 170, and, very emphatically, Jervell, *Imago Dei*, pp. 131 ff. ("Self-multiplication of the godhead").

[31] Jervell, pp. 130f.: "The inner man, the Self, must be in some way identical with the divine substance; otherwise no knowledge would be possible."

more" to the heavenly home (even when foreseen only after death) is only ostensibly temporal or eschatological; in reality, it is the soul's becoming aware of itself, the divinization of man.

It is in this general context of thought that the individual statements of Gnosticism must be examined, when pre-existence is pre-supposed or affirmed. This is true above all of the typical question about the origin and goal of man, as for instance in the *Acts of Thomas*, 15: "... who I was, and who and how I now am, that I may become again what I was."[32] The Gnostic is not concerned with temporal pre-existence as such, but only with the nature of man which is expressed in this term; something that is elsewhere couched for preference in spatial categories (above—below; *Excerpts from Theodotus*, 78:2, "... where we were, whither we have been cast down, whither we hasten"), can also be put in terms of time. This explains the enigmatic logion which is found in the *Gospel of Thomas* (logion 19): "Jesus said: Blessed is he who was before he came into being", and in the *Gospel of Philip*: "The Lord said, Blessed is he who is before he came into being. For he who is, both was and shall be" (logion 57).

The subject is true, substantial existence, which is found only in those who are not confined to their present earthly state but participate in spiritual and eternal being; "the merely material man ... belongs only to this world, and has neither past nor future".[33] The meaning of the logion is brought out more clearly in the "Nature of the Archons" (Codex II of Nag-Hammadi in Labib's enumeration), where Norea, the wife of Noah, represents the Gnostics, and asks whether she too belongs to the material world. The answer is: "You and your children belong to the Father who has existed from the beginning. Therefore the powers shall not approach them, because of the spirit of truth who dwells in them. All who have learnt this way are immortal among mortal man."[34] This explains the "way" of the saviour in the systems which make use of this type of myth: he comes from "pre-existence" in the heavenly world of light and descends into the death-dealing material cosmos of darkness, to re-ascend once more when redeemed by Gnosis. Gnostic "pre-existence" remains mythical, and as such is perhaps believed in. But it only attains significance in so far as it is an indication of the higher true existence of the Gnostic.

---

[32] Bonnet, p. 121; Bornkamm, p. 450.

[33] Wilson, *The Gospel of Philip*, p. 117.

[34] According to the translation of Schenke in Leipoldt and Schenke, *Koptisch-gnostische Schriften*, p. 78; the passage was used by Gärtner in *The Theology of the Gospel of Thomas*, pp. 199f.

3. *Pre-existence in John*

The pre-existence of the Johannine Christ is affirmed in the prologue and in the testimony of the Baptist (1:30; cf. 15), by Jesus himself in 6:62 ("where he was before"), 8:58 ("before Abraham was, I am"), in the high priestly prayer (17:5, 24) and indirectly in many other texts where his pre-existence is assumed (cf. 6:33, 50f., 58; 7:28f.; 8:14, 23, 26, 42; 10:36; 16:28). In comparison with Jewish and Gnostic texts, all these assertions have a special character of their own, though certain contacts may also be recognized.

The similarity between the pre-existent Logos of John and the "Wisdom" of Judaism has already been noted, and the real, personal existence of the Logos, to which there is no counterpart in Jewish thought, has also been sufficiently stressed (cf. excursus i). As we expanded the scope of our enquiries, we came upon the apocalyptic figure of the "Son of Man", which must be accorded a special type of pre-existence in the context of Jewish thought. It is worth noting that the notion of pre-existence in John is sometimes also linked with the title of "Son of Man" (cf. 3:13; 6:62). It is true that the Son of Man theology in John has left the Jewish heritage far behind, and rather represents a development and transformation of the (eschatological) assertions of primitive Christianity with regard to the Son of Man (cf. excursus v). But we can still see the common root, or at least one of the sources on which John drew. What is missing in Judaism is the notion of the ascent, corresponding to the descent of the Son of Man, which opens for believers the way to the heavenly world. The coming of Wisdom to men from heaven offers no real basis of comparison.

But the correspondence between descent and ascent in the Gnostic myth seems to bring the Johannine notion of the pre-existent redeemer more into line with Gnostic thought, and other allied traits might be his divine nature and his union with those who follow him. But the impression is illusory, as is apparent when one observes the real facts. The Johannine Christ is not an image and prototype of the soul; nothing is ever said of the pre-existence of humanity which is to be redeemed. The way of Christ the Logos from pre-existence to incarnation is proper to him and reserved to him; it is affirmed only to bring out the uniqueness of the revealer and bringer of life. The privileged position of the redeemer brings us once more closer to Judaism, where pre-existence is confined to certain agents of salvation. There is, however, an echo of Gnostic terminology in Jn 8:14, where Christ proclaims that he knows the whence and whither of his way. It could be objected that this is due to the distinctive Christian doctrine of redemption, which led to the re-moulding of the Gnostic myth and to its being applied and restricted to the historical figure of the redeemer. But the process was rather the opposite: the Christian redeemer, whose pre-existence was part of the faith, is here presented even to Gnostics as the true fulfilment of their longing for redemption. Since it was he who had truly come down from heaven, he could lead all men up to the heavenly world (cf. 3:13).

If we consider the actual statements about pre-existence, they are rather Jewish than Gnostic in character. In the testimony of the Baptist, two earthly figures are compared, John and Jesus, and one of them, Jesus, is said to take precedence of the other, "because he was before me". This historical view of pre-existence, which is envisaged perfectly realistically, does not fit into the pattern of Gnostic thought, but is not incompatible with Jewish principles (cf. the statements about the resurrection of prophets of earlier times[35]), though in the sense here intended only possible as a confession of the Christian faith. The text which speaks of Abraham is still clearer (8:58). The context speaks of the patriarch's looking forward to the day of Jesus (the Messiah) (v. 56), and this idea finds support in Jewish tradition, according to which God revealed to Abraham the distant future.[36] Jesus can use the occasion to outbid all Jewish expectations with his claim to have been in existence before Abraham. For Jewish ears this is, of course, a blasphemy (cf. v. 59), since it recalls the divine "I am" of Exod 3:14; but the statement remains in the line of thought engendered by Israel's history, though the claim of the Johannine Christ transcends such thought. Must the evangelist have drawn his inspiration for such affirmations of pre-existence from the Gnostic myth? It is true that Judaism was very far from thinking of the Saviour as pre-existent and divine,[37] but here the Christian faith only transcends Jewish thinking in the same way as it does for the whole concept of the Messiah.

But it is also possible to demonstrate the positive sources of the Johannine assertions on pre-existence: they originate in the Christology of the primitive Church previous to John. Paul provides at least one example of how a Jew could arrive at affirmations of pre-existence from meditating on texts of Scripture. He explains the rock which accompanied the Israelites in the desert as Christ, and strange though this interpretation may seem, it becomes intelligible when one knows that Philo had already referred the rock to Wisdom (*Leg. alleg.*, II, 86; *Quod det.*, 115–118). The

---

[35] Cf. Mk 6:15; 8:28 parr.; the opinion also existed that the Messiah was King David returned from the dead, cf. Billerbeck, vol. II, pp. 335–9.

[36] Cf. Billerbeck, vol. II, p. 525f.

[37] On the Son of Man in *Enoch*, Sjöberg, *Menschensohn im Henochbuch*, p. 94: "The subordination of the Son of Man under God is taken for granted in the Parables. Like all other beings of heaven and earth, the Son of Man depends on God, is called into being by God and has his dignity only by divine decree." But his dignity raises him not merely above men, but above angels.

same line of thought, Wisdom speculation, also underlies, no doubt, other Pauline assertions with regard to pre-existence: 1 Cor 8:6 (creative activity attributed to Wisdom); Rom 10:6f. (if one may see in the quotation from Deut 30:12ff. an allusion to Wisdom, in the sense of Bar 3:29f.); Gal 4:4 (if the text is based on Wis 9:10, 17). "The notion of the pre-existence of Jesus—which Paul takes for granted—came to him in terms of Wisdom speculation"; his assertions are based "on a Jewish exegetical tradition which had no knowledge of a redeemer-myth, but had a strongly developed doctrine on the Wisdom of God".[38] One cannot, of course, go back directly to Paul from John; but the reference to Wisdom speculation is also palpable in Heb 1:3 (cf. Wis 7:25f.) and there are good reasons for suspecting its presence in the (pre-Pauline) hymn of Col 1:15ff.[39] When the Logos hymn, in its own fashion, draws inspiration from the same source, it must be regarded as tributary to a tradition which was widespread in primitive Christianity. The fourth evangelist followed the same lines, though in his hands the assertions on pre-existence took on a new emphasis and a deeper meaning as he developed them in the sense of his Christology. Passages like 6:62; 8:14, 58; 17:5, 24 are probably to be attributed to his theological reflection.

There remains, of course, the possibility that previous to John, the Gnostic myth had been adopted by Hellenistic Christianity. But in the light of the actual development of Christology, we are obliged to ask whether the Christian community did not arrive at its affirmation of the pre-existence of Christ by another route. If, in keeping with Jewish ideas, they first thought of Jesus as exalted to the right hand of God (Acts 2:36; 5:31; 13:33) and retained this "Christology of exaltation" in the (pre-Pauline) hymn of Phil 2:6–11, attributing to the heavenly Kyrios the same dignity as God, it would then be more likely that the attribution of pre-existence to their Christ was the fruit of further reflection. The state of "humiliation" was preceded by the stage of divine glory.[40] But these questions lie outside the scope of our present investigations. It seems certain, at any rate, that John took up the Christology of the primitive Church and developed it further; this primary interest does not exclude the fact that at a secondary stage, when formulating his thought, especially when speaking of "the descent and ascent of the Son of Man" (cf. excursus v), he also approximated to Gnostic usage.

---

[38] Schweizer, "Die Herkunft der Präexistenzvorstellung bei Paulus", p. 69.

[39] See esp. Hegermann, *Die Vorstellung vom Schöpfungsmittler*, pp. 93–101, 125f.

[40] Cf. Schweizer, *Erniedrigung und Erhöhung*, pp. 99ff., 174ff.

EXCURSUS III

The Titles of Jesus in John 1

When we look back at ch. 1, we are struck by the number of titles which are attributed to Christ in this short space. But it is not surprising, when we recall the basic Christological purpose of the fourth Gospel. It is worth while pausing to consider further these Christological titles, their connection with one another and their possible background.

1. List of titles

In the order in which they occur in John 1, we find the following titles:

the Logos, vv. 1, 14;
God, vv. 1 c, 18b (in a great part of the MSS);
life and light, vv. 4, cf. 5, 9;
the Only-begotten (ὁ μονογενής), vv. 14d, 18b (sometimes without the article);
(the) Son, v. 18 (in some MSS);
the lamb of God, vv. 29, 36;
the Son of God, vv. 34 (in the majority of the MSS), 49;
the Elect of God, v. 34 (in part of the MSS, a special and preferable reading);
the Messiah, v. 41, cf. equivalently 45;
king of Israel, v. 49;
the Son of Man, v. 51.

In addition, there are some descriptions which can hardly be counted as titles, though they indicate important Christological or Messianic functions:

the greater (in rank) who comes after the Baptist, vv. 15, 27, 30;
he who exists before the Baptist, vv. 15, 30;
he who is in the bosom of the Father, v. 18;
he who baptizes with Holy Spirit, v. 33.

In view of the testimony given by the Baptist before the embassy from Jerusalem, it may be asked whether his refusal to be identified with certain Messianic figures is not indirectly a testimony to Jesus's identity with them. This is obviously true of the designation of Messiah (vv. 20, 25); but it is shown later in the Gospel that Jesus was believed to be "the prophet" (6:14; 7:40, 52 *var. lect.*), and it seems, at least according to ch. 7, that Jesus accepts this title, if it is rightly understood (as it is not in ch. 6).[1] "Elijah", however, does not occur again; hence if the theme is Messianic, it is not adopted into Johannine theology, which is easily understood when one remembers that in Mark and Matthew John is allotted the role of Elijah as precursor of the Messiah.[2]

Finally, we must note the form of address, "rabbi" (1:38, 49), which occurs fairly often in the Gospel (3:2; 4:31; 6:25; 9:2; 11:8). It alternates with the frequently used κύριε (cf. 6:34 with 25; 6:68 with 13:6, 9), and of itself is non-committal, since it is used by various classes of speakers and was a term in general use. But when used by the disciples, it has a special significance, as may be seen in particular from the words of Jesus in 13:13, "You call me 'Master' and 'Lord', and you do well to do so, because I am." The majesty of Jesus is already experienced by the disciples in his life on earth and is reflected in their attitude and in this reverent form of address in particular. And Jesus explicitly says that his authority is also friendship, (13:16; 15:20), on which he insists at the Last Supper (cf. 15:15). The question then arises as to whether κύριος is

---

[1] It may be true that in 7:40f. the popular opinion that Jesus is really "the Prophet" or "the Messiah" simply means in both cases that he is the eschatological saviour, the variation merely depicting "the vagueness of Messianic theology" (Bultmann, pp. 230f., n. 6). But the intention of the evangelist is to depict Jesus as "the (Messianic) Prophet" as well as "the Messiah". This is also true of 7:52 *var. lect.* The evangelist finds no difficulty in the fact that the Messiah must come from Bethlehem (v. 42), because he certainly knows of Jesus's birth in Bethlehem, nor in the misgivings of the rulers that "the Prophet does not come from Galilee" (v. 52). The questions or objections raised in ch. 7 (see also v. 27) are answered by the evangelist in a positive sense for his picture of Christ. Teeple, *The Mosaic Eschatological Prophet* seems to give too little weight to these passages when he sees Jesus in the fourth gospel as merely superior to Moses (95f.) and allows the expectation of "the Prophet", according to Deut 18:5, only as a popular opinion (cf. pp. 90, 109). Contrast Cullmann, *Christologie*, p. 36, E. T.: p. 37, and esp. Hahn, *Christologische Hoheitstitel*, p. 397.

[2] Cf. J. Jeremias, "Ἠλ(ε)ίας", pp. 938f.; Trilling, "Die Täufertradition im Matthäusevangelium", esp. pp. 279–82. The opinion that Jesus in John is understood as "Elijah" (in the sense of the Messiah), since this is the logical consequence of 1:21, 25 (as for "the Messiah" and "the Prophet"), is propounded by Robinson, "Elijah, John and Jesus: An Essay in Detection", esp. p. 270. But the conclusion is certainly unwarranted. Since the Messianic expectations with regard to Elijah play no further part in John, the point must be that it is merely polemics, to deprive the Baptists of the title of Elijah (in the sense of Messiah), cf. Richter, "Bist Du Elias?", *Biblische Zeitschrift* 6 (1962), pp. 238–42.

not given a profounder meaning after the Resurrection. Mary Magdalen addresses Jesus as ῥαββουνί, but this is clearly part of the process of recognition, as she meets once more her well-known "master". Thomas says, "My Lord and my God!" (20:28), which is also to some extent an expression of the fact that he recognizes Jesus: but it is above all a confession of his majesty and divinity. Finally, the expression is given a definite pregnancy in the epilogue, ch. 21 (cf. vv. 7, 12 and its frequent use as a form of address). But it never attains the theological significance which it has in Paul and the Christian churches for whom he speaks. In John, "the Lord" is not used specifically to speak of the exalted ruler, installed in power at the right hand of God, the Lord of his community. Hence the designation cannot be included among the titles of Christ in John.

On further inspection, only a few titles prove to be added in the rest of the Gospel after ch. 1: "the Saviour of the world" (4:42), a confession of the universal significance of Jesus which is in place in the chapter on Samaria; "the holy one of God" (6:69), a Messianic title chosen no doubt to exclude political and material implications (cf. 6:14f.). But then Jesus's self-designation as "the Son" occurs with impressive frequency. This however, was already adumbrated in ch. 1, as was the divine and majestic ἐγώ εἰμι (especially the absolute use in 8:24, 28, 58; 13:19) by the attribute of θεός and the incarnation of the Logos, his "pitching his tent" among men. Then there are the metaphors which are attached to these theophany formulae. They depict the Johannine Christ by means of expressive symbols (the "bread of life" or the "bread from heaven", the "light of the world", the "true shepherd", the "door", the "way", the "resurrection and the life", the "true vine") and hence help to portray him more fully. But one can hardly take these metaphors as attributes of Christ in the strict sense, though they do have this character in liturgical usage, like "lamb of God". On the whole, our first impression is confirmed, that the diapason of the praise of Christ is sounded in the first chapter, where so many high titles are bestowed.

2. *Theological significance*

Can any particular intention of the evangelist be recognized in the number and the order of the titles of Christ in ch. 1? There is certainly nothing systematic about them, but they reveal certain interests. It cannot, for instance, be maintained that the list of titles is meant to lead up to a climax in the "Son of Man" (v. 51), as though this were the loftiest and most important. The title plays a considerable role in John (cf. excursus v), but not to such an extent that the other Christological affirmations are combined and absorbed in it. It has, on the contrary, a special meaning of its own, in so far as it evokes the "descent" of the redeemer and his "ascent" into heaven to lead "his own" thither, and portrays the revealer on earth as in perpetual communication with heaven. Hence the Son of Man logion has been placed deliberately at the end of ch. 1, just as the central Christological affirmation of v. 18 comes as the conclusion of the prologue and the transition to the Gospel narrative. The logion signals the beginning of the revelation in words and "signs" which is to follow, where Christ's union with heaven as he works on earth is visibly displayed (cf. ὄψεσθε) to believers. It may also show the Son of Man as the representative of Jacob (Israel), but it certainly shows him as the fulfilment of the Messianic hopes of Israel (cf. v. 49), in a way which surpasses all expectation. Finally, it gives the "realized" eschatology of the fourth evangelist, who interprets in his own way the eschatological affirmations of the Synoptics with regard to the Son of Man. As so often in John, one may assume that various motives were at work; but the main reason for these words to the newly-won disciples is certainly to call attention to the full revelation of the Messianic glory of Jesus which is about to begin—a glory, however, which is accessible only to faith (cf. 2:11), the "Messianic secret" in the Johannine sense.

We have already discussed the significance of the prologue, with its assertions about the Logos, his pre-existence and divinity, his functions in creation and salvation (see Introduction to the Prologue). The next section, on John's testimony and its result, the coming of the first disciples to Jesus (1:19–51), has an importance of its own and forms a complete episode, in spite of its being linked up with the narrative as a whole. It is concerned above all with Jesus's Messiahship, as appears negatively from John's refusal to claim any direct Messianic significance for himself, and positively from his pointing to the loftier figure who comes after him (vv. 27, 30). The Baptist takes on the task of presenting Jesus to Israel as the Messiah expected by the chosen people (v. 30). He justifies his testimony by the fact that Jesus is bearer and giver of the Spirit, he who always possesses the Spirit in its fullness, and is hence the Messiah, who, however, also "baptizes" men with this Spirit (v. 33). And in fact the decisive question which is discussed by John's disciples among themselves and which they put before Jesus is whether he is the Messiah (cf. vv. 41, 45, 49). It is the question which preoccupies these representatives of a lively religious movement in Judaism, just as it appears later as the focus of popular discussion (cf. especially chs. 7 and 9).[3]

But a further point becomes clear when one examines the Baptist's testimony more closely: it is that it is meant to interpret the Messiahship

[3] Cf. Schnackenburg, *Messiasfrage*, pp. 240–64, esp. 247 ff.

of Jesus in the sense of the full Christian profession of faith. Hence John speaks unambiguously of Jesus's pre-existence and of his expiatory death for the salvation of the whole world. Neither the stereotyped statements on Jesus's pre-existence (1:15, 30) nor the profoundly symbolic appellation of "the lamb of God" (v. 29) can be well understood on the level of sheer history. But they can be readily grasped as theological interpretations of the evangelist. A similar process may be observed in Matthew, as for instance when after Jesus's walking on the waters the disciples pay homage to their master as "Son of God" (14:33), in palpable contrast to Mark, where the disciples are represented as being still unresponsive and lacking in understanding (6:52); or when Simon Peter confesses Jesus as "Son of the living God" (Mt 16:16), going further than in Mk 8:29. We can recognize here a procedure adopted by the primitive Church, which linked its profession of faith to the narrative of the past, or rather, displayed the permanent truths of faith which were immanent to the historical testimony. Hence one should not try to eliminate from the title "lamb of God" the element of the universally expiatory death, even though this must have lain outside the actual horizon of John the Baptist (see commentary). One must rather try to understand how faith in Christ could crystallize and become articulate, without departing from its proper and original reality. One can then understand that the titles used of Christ in John are deliberately chosen, and that the author drew on the treasures of biblical theology and liturgy whose development was enshrined in the hymns to Christ, of which the Logos-hymn is only one example.

Another instance is the confession of Nathanael, whose praise of the "king of Israel" is intelligible on the lips of the "true Israelite" (cf. v. 49 with 47) and historically possible, though perhaps not at once at his first encounter with Jesus. But here too the addition of "Son of God" shows Christian interpretation at work, which without losing sight of the historical foundation, brings out what is of importance to the faith and provides at the very beginning a text which paves the way for the proclamation of faith envisaged at the end (20:31). It also fulfils one of the main aims of early Christianity and of the fourth Gospel: that of presenting Jesus as the promised Messiah whom Israel hoped for from among its sons, and at the same time, as the eschatological saviour who surpasses all expectations and can be confessed only in new categories. The addition of the Son of Man saying in v. 51 would then correspond to the same interests. The last word on Jesus cannot be left to Nathanael, well though he speaks. The self-revelation of Jesus—or God's revelation of himself in Jesus—is far more than any human knowledge, no matter how striking (cf. v. 48); it is a proclamation of salvation which has been brought from heaven and is disclosed in the words and works of the Son of Man on earth, something "greater" than can be achieved by human insight and religious expectation.

It seems, therefore, that the Christological titles are deliberately grouped by the evangelist to serve his theological reflection and his mode of presentation.

3. Liturgical background?

Still another question occurs in view of the stereotyped form of the many titles and Christological designations of Jesus in Jn 1. Do they not come from liturgical usage as it was gradually fixed in the primitive Church? To avoid mere speculation and to find some concrete data, we must examine the Revelation of St John, part of whose actual setting must have been the liturgy, as is clear from its celestial hymns, its many forcible and pregnant formulae (cf. Rev. 1:5;[4] 1:8, 17f.; 5:5; 12:4; 19:11, 13, 16 etc.) and its doxologies.[5] It is true that the apocalyptic genre of the writing, and the peculiarities of the language and thought must make us very cautious of admitting literary relationships between John and Revelation; and this caution is justified and reinforced by an examination of the titles of Christ. Nonetheless, we may assume that the books come from a milieu common to both, since there remain many contacts and echoes in terminology, which call for some attention with regard to the titles of Christ occurring in Jn 1.

A connection has often been assumed between the (absolute) title of Logos in the prologue and the name of Christ, "the Word of God", in the parousia of Rev 19:13. But the completeness of the title here, which points more definitely to the biblical background, and the content which is given it by the context, show that the name chosen for the future conqueror has a different connotation than the Johannine Logos. The apocalyptic horseman has a warlike character, which seems to be linked with his name, since it is said that a sharp sword issues from his mouth to strike the nations (v. 15, cf. Is 11:4). This is entirely foreign to the prologue, and goes back to another tradition (cf. Wis 18:15f.) which assigned the functions of judging and punishing to the "Word of God". But the liturgical usage of the title is suggested by the occurrence of another epithet in the immediate context, "King of kings and Lord of lords" (Rev 19:16; cf. 17:14), and then there could be at least a super-

---

[4] Cf. Holtz, *Die Christologie der Apokalypse des Johannes*, pp. 55–61.

[5] Cf. Torrance, "Liturgie et Apocalypse"; Delling, "Zum gottesdienstlichen Stil der Johannesapokalypse"; Läuchli, "Eine Gottesdienststruktur in der Johannesoffenbarung"; Shepherd, *The Paschal Liturgy and the Apocalypse.*

ficial connection, if common or similar terms were used in divine worship. It is a feature of liturgical terms that they can take on various meanings according to the various settings in which they are employed. Hence the "Word of God" could sometimes be considered in terms of creation and redemption, and at others in terms of its all-conquering power and its function in judgment (cf. also Jn 12:48).

There is a remarkable analogy to support this assumption in "lamb of God", Jn 1:29, 36, when compared with the "lamb" or "ram" (ἀρνίον) of Revelation.[6] Once more, neither terminology nor content coincide completely. A derivation and explanation of the "lamb of God" in the Gospel which links it with apocalyptic notions seemed, in our opinion, mistaken. But however one thinks of the derivation of the "lamb" in Revelation,[7] the notion contains traits of majesty and lordship (cf. Rev 5:8, 12; 6:16; 7:17; 17:14) which brings it within the ambit of apocalyptic Messianism. It remains, nonetheless, the lamb which even in the glory of heaven still appears "as slaughtered" (Rev 5:6; cf. 5:12; 13:8)—which may be a reminiscence of the paschal lamb—and it is the lamb in whose blood the martyrs have washed their clothes (Rev 7:14), which is an indication of its soteriological function (cf. also 12:11). The liturgical symbol combines various traits into the one image of which it makes use. The "lamb of God" in John lacks all the traits of the conquering warrior which appear in apocalyptic, but certainly retains its connection with the paschal lamb. The melting-pot for the various associations—and the matrix for new concepts and connections—could well be a symbol of the "lamb of God" in use in the liturgy. The fourth evangelist may have been stimulated by such language and have exploited it in his own way for the benefit of his Christology.

No such connections can be pointed to with regard to the other titles of Christ in Jn 1. The N.T. speaks of Jesus as king in various ways. John admits "king of Israel" as a title of honour (1:50; 12:13) and stresses the kingly claim of his Christ as revealer of divine truth, in Jesus's answer to Pilate (18:37). But "king of the Jews" he finds dubious or in need of interpretation, and not a proper title (cf. 18:33f.; 19:3). Here he diverges from the other N.T. writers, in whom "king of Israel" only occurs in the mocking words of the Jews under the Cross (Mk 15:32, par. Mt 27:42). Though the seer of Patmos upholds the kingly dignity of the scion of David (cf. Rev 3:7; 5:5; 22:16), he uses the title of king for Jesus only in the formula "King of kings" (17:14; 19:16), as the great kings of the east styled themselves in ancient times, a title inherited by the Roman em-

[6] See the careful investigations of Holtz, *Die Christologie*, pp. 39–47, who thinks that the "lamb" means the paschal lamb; cf. also pp. 78ff.

[7] On the various attempts (from apocalyptic or Is 53) see Holtz, pp. 41–43.

perors. It is not certain that the title of king was applied to Christ in the liturgy by the primitive Church, as it was to God, cf. 1 Tim 1:17; 6:15; Rev 15:3. "Son of God" as title of Christ occurs only once in Rev (2:18). The "Son of Man" plays a bigger part (1:13; 14:14) but quite unlike his role in John; he is "the form under which Christ appears when dealing with his community".[8] These titles in John appear to be rather the result of theological reflection and the effort to express the faith rather than of liturgical usage.

The ἐγώ-εἰμι sayings may form another link with the liturgy, since such utterances of the heavenly Lord are also heard in Rev (1:8, 17; 2:23; 21:6; 22:13, 16). But we shall deal with these later, since the preparatory nature of this section of the self-revelation of Jesus precludes their occurring in Jn 1. In spite of the critical reserves which must be made about the liturgical background, the multiplicity of the titles of Christ in Jn 1 remains striking; the similar phenomenon in Revelation is probably to be explained at least to some extent by reason of the liturgy. Hence we may conclude that there are some grounds for suspecting the presence of liturgical influences, but no more than that. On the whole, it is probable that the Christological interests of the evangelist played a preponderant role. His desire to give expression to his faith was probably the dominant factor in the grouping of the pregnant titles of Christ in Jn 1.

---

[8] *Ibid.*, p. 134; cf. the whole section, pp. 116–37.

EXCURSUS IV

The Johannine "Signs"

The term "sign", which appears for the first time in 2:11, is a theological one, deliberately chosen by the evangelist, with a meaning which must be assessed in relation to the whole Gospel. The use of the term is not quite uniform and it poses many problems which are still the subject of lively controversy today.[1] We shall first take up the question of vocabulary, then discuss the main problems and finally try to see what is the special relevance of the concept of "sign" in Johannine theology, keeping in mind throughout the presuppositions and procedure of the evangelist.

1. Vocabulary

The term occurs 17 times in John mainly in the sense in which it appears in the final comment of the evangelist, 20:30: "Jesus did many other signs before his disciples, which are not written down in this book. But these have been written that you may believe..." The signs are important works of Jesus, performed in the sight of his disciples, miracles, in fact, which of their nature should lead to faith in "Jesus the Messiah, the Son of God". The remark may be the conclusion of a "σημεῖα-source" which contained only a limited number of "signs" (cf. Introduction, ch. iv, 3); it can hardly refer to the Resurrection narratives immediately preceding it, since the apparitions are not described as "signs" nor would such a description tally with the views of the evangelist (see below). "Before the disciples" is not a proof that the signs are the apparitions, since it is true

---

[1] Lit.: Cerfaux, "Les miracles signes messianiques de Jésus et oeuvres de Dieu, selon l'Évangile de s. Jean"; Charlier, "La notion de signe (σημεῖον) dans le Quatrième Évangile"; Mollat, "Le semeion johannique"; Riga, "Signs of Glory. The Use of 'Semeion' in St John's Gospel"; Rengstorf, "σημεῖον", pp. 241–57; S. Hofbeck, Σημεῖον.

of the public miracles at which the disciples were present, and hence has a special significance. The "signs" can speak and testify to later believers only in so far as the disciples see them with believing eyes and recognize Jesus's glory in them (cf. 2:11 above).

If this is the correct interpretation of the final statement, one can easily see what are the σημεῖα in which the evangelist is chiefly interested. They are the major miracles which are not merely mentioned but described in some detail. It has been long customary to count seven of these (is the number accidental?—the parabolic discourses with ἐγώ εἰμι also add up to seven): the miracle of the wine at Cana, the Cana miracle of the healing at a distance, the healing at the pool of Bethesda, the multiplication of the loaves, the walking on the waters, the cure of the man born blind and the raising of Lazarus. The first two are explicitly designated as "signs" (2:11; 4:54), as are also the miracle of the loaves (cf. 6:14, 26), the cure of the blind man (cf. 9:16) and the raising of Lazarus (12:18; cf. 11:47). The cure at Bethesda is not expressly termed a "sign" (ch. 5), but it is treated as an important ἔργον (7:21; cf. 5:20, 36). In view of the close connection between these concepts (see 2 below), the revelation discourse following the miracle and the importance of the miracle itself, we are certainly justified in considering it a "sign" in the sense of the evangelist. Serious doubt is possible only with regard to the walking on the waters. We miss the designation as σημεῖον (it is unlikely that the plural of 6:26 includes the miracle), a clear indication of its public character (unless the "knowledge" of the crowd in 6:22, 25 can be appealed to), and the explanation of the undoubtedly miraculous event. The question must be left open for the moment.

But there is another element in the vocabulary of the evangelist. He often speaks of Jesus's σημεῖα in general, without any indication of their precise nature (cf. 2:23; 3:2; 6:2, 14 *[var. lect.]*, 26; 7:31; 9:16; 11:47; 12:37; cf. 10:41). The σημεῖα described above are mostly included, but the summaries sometimes indicate miracles, especially healings, which do not form part of the "signs" described in detail or which go beyond them, 2:23; 3:2; 6:2. Is this an older usage taken over by John from a written source or oral tradition, or is he simply extending his own to take in a wider field and show that there were many other miracles besides those recounted in detail which demonstrate Jesus as the doer of "signs" (cf. 7:31; 9:16; 10:41; 11:47; 12:37)? There is at least one place in which it is clear that a ready-made concept has been taken over. This is 4:48 where σημεῖα καὶ τέρατα occurs, a well-known phrase from the O.T. (Septuagint) which has been retained in the N.T., especially in Acts. It has a somewhat pejorative sense here in John, and if one then examines some further texts, the context indicates that the σημεῖα summarized at 2:23 (cf. 6:45) and 6:2 are considered of less value, not indeed in themselves, but in their effects. Men believed simply because they saw "signs". But the intention and expectation of the Johannine Jesus when working his "signs" is quite different, as may be seen from his reproach to the Jews in 6:26, "You do not seek me because you have seen signs. . ." Thus the "signs" should have led men to deeper insight, as the evangelist also implies when he speaks of "so many signs" which Jesus had wrought and which still had not moved men to believe (12:37). Thus there is a tension, and indeed a discontinuity in the Johannine concept of "sign", which is in need of explanation. Either the evangelist took over a rather neutral concept, to which he then opposed his own deeper understanding of it, or he used a concept consistent in itself and combined with it an intrinsic theological tension.[2] Perhaps the two explanations should be combined. In one of his sources, no doubt, he found the general notion already in existence, but not the subject of theological reflection. This notion he used in his narrative. But he developed a more profound theological concept, which he often used unequivocally (for the major miracles), and against which he elsewhere measured the people's understanding of the "signs". In this way he could illustrate the problems posed by Jesus's work as revealer and show the various stages of men's faith. But in any case we have before us a concept of "sign" which has a distinctive theological contour and which leads us to the heart of Johannine theology.

Finally, we must mention a use of "sign" which is outside the framework considered above—the "sign" which men ask for. This occurs twice in John, once after the cleansing of the temple (2:18) and then after the multiplication of the loaves, when Jesus summons the Jews in Capernaum to believe in him (6:30). The demand is made by sceptics, or, as the evangelist sees them, unbelievers, and in both cases the context leaves no doubt as to the type of sign they demand—a preternatural event to accredit Jesus's mission (2:18), a "sign from heaven" (6:30), and hence a spectacular marvel. Here the evangelist is at one with the synoptic tradition, which also contains such incredulous demands for a sign (Mk 8:11f.; Mt 12:38; 16:1; Lk 11:16, 29), and in the fourth Gospel Jesus reacts in the same way, with a flat refusal of such a "sign (from heaven)" as is demanded by men, by "this generation" (Mk 8:12), by a "wicked and unfaithful generation" (Mt 12:39; 16:4). There is no continuity between this very negative concept of sign and the positive understanding of it in the fourth Gospel. The Johannine "signs" in the full and deepest sense are wholly the work of Jesus, indissolubly linked to his work of revelation

[2] This was seen by Haenchen in his literary analysis of 4:46–54, but perhaps the theological concept of "sign" as understood by the evangelist himself was not sufficiently taken into account; see Haenchen, "Johanneische Probleme", p. 29; id., "Der Vater, der mich gesandt hat", pp. 208f.; also Schnackenburg, "Zur Traditionsgeschichte von Joh. 4:46–54", pp. 65f.

under his Father's mandate, and can only be accepted and understood in faith. But are they not also meant to arouse faith? This brings us to a new problem, which is already signalled by the fact that the evangelist uses "signs" and "works" side by side.

2. "Signs" and "works"

The great miracles in John can be called either "signs" or "works". Thus by the nature of things the two expressions can be applied to the same objects, and the question is why does the evangelist, whose style is matured and whose choice of words is deliberate, now use one term and now another. The difference cannot be explained by the use of various sources or on other grounds of literary criticism, since the terms are interchanged for no apparent reason within a given chapter (cf. 7:3 with 31; 9:3f. with 16; 10:25, 32, 37f. with 41; 12:37 with 15:24). And it is not done for the sake of varying the expression, since the two words do not occur close together, and are reserved in each case for given contexts. Various thoughts and aspects must have been associated with "signs" and "works" in the evangelist's mind, and it should be instructive with regard to his theology to see what they were.

Something is gained at once, perhaps, by merely noting the chapters in which the two expressions occur. Apart from the final remark in 20:30, the occurrences of σημεῖα are spread throughout chs. 1–12; the ἔργα in the sense of the marvels performed by Jesus first appear in ch. 5 and then recur throughout as far as the farewell discourses inclusively (14:10 ff.; 15:24; cf. 17:4, in the singular). In a investigation of the structure of John,[3] H. van den Bussche has suggested that chs. 2–4 are the "section of the signs", chs. 5–10 the "section of the works", which are followed by the "last journey to Jerusalem", chs. 11–12. He thinks he can observe a progression from the "signs" to the "works". The former, whose origin he sees in the mighty works of the book of Exodus, announced the Messianic times and disclosed the Messianic function of Jesus, who performed them. The "works" (from ch. 5 on) revealed a deeper meaning in the "signs", in so far as they established the unity of being and action between God and his Son.[4] Van den Bussche is correct in stating that the "works" are always related to the will of the Father and to the mission of the Son and hence are a realization of "*the* work" (in the singular) which the Son has to accomplish on earth (4:34; 17:4).[5] But the division between

---

[3] "La structure de Jean I–XII". [4] *Ibid.*, pp. 80f.

[5] See Thüsing, *Erhöhung*, pp. 58–63; but he seems to concentrate too much on the time of exaltation (on the basis of 5:20), cf. on 5:36 (p. 61): "But then the ἔργα which are to be

works and signs can hardly be that given by van den Bussche, since the raising of Lazarus is characterized as a "sign" and reveals the glory of the Son of God or God himself (cf. 11:4, 40). The evangelist never sees Christ except as one with the Father (cf. also 2:11 with 1:51). The contrast between chs. 2–4 as the "section of the signs" and 5–10 as the "section of the works" is the most questionable point of all, since the latter chapters still speak of the "signs" (6:2, 14 etc). It would be better to consider chs. 2–12 as the "Book of Signs" (C.H. Dodd, *Interpretation*, pp. 297 ff.), though we should prefer to include 1:19–51, as the introduction to this part.

If one considers the various contexts in which the "works" of Jesus are mentioned, it will be seen that they often have the function of bearing testimony to Jesus as the envoy of God (5:36; 10:25, 37f.; 14:11; 15:24). They testify reliably (10:38; 14:11) and convincingly (15:24) that Jesus is sent by the Father (5:36; cf. 9:4) or that the Father "is in Jesus" (cf. 10:38; 14:11). Jesus's works are done "in the name of the Father" (10:25), which in John means not just to carry out a charge or follow an inner impulse, but to work together with him (cf. 4:34; 5:17, 19). It signifies in fact that the Father works through the Son, as Jesus himself says: "The Father, who abides in me, performs his works" (14:10). Thus the "works" are part of the notion of "mission", in the profound Johannine meaning of the sending of the Son by the Father.[6] And one can also see why the works are meant to arouse faith, or, if confronted with disbelief which opposes the testimony of the works, can disclose the sin of disbelief (cf. 10:25f.; 15:24).

The "signs" are also supremely relevant for Christology, but under another aspect. They also stimulate reflection (cf. 3:2; 7:31; 9:16; 11:47), but as visible and marvellous happenings (2:23; 6:2, 14). But they are ineffective in bringing about the full Christian faith if they are perceived only externally or sought for as sensations (cf. 4:48). They only disclose their meaning when they are greeted with faith and when their inner meaning is grasped under the outward event (cf. 3:11; 6:26; 11:4, 40). Hence the notion of testimony is not combined with that of sign. Their significance for faith is different. They "show" the true believer the glory of Christ as he works on earth, but where faith is weak and inadequate they show only the visage of the marvellous and hence

---

done must be the same as the μείζονα ἔργα of giving life and judging, or must at least be connected with them. These would be the real testimonies. Thus the works of the exalted Lord, not of the earthly Jesus, would be envisaged." He goes on to say (p. 62) that 5:36 means both the works of the exalted Lord and the earthly Jesus.

[6] See Haenchen, "Der Vater, der mich gesandt hat"; he does not examine the difference in usage of "signs" and "works". See also Rengstorf, "σημεῖον", pp. 246ff. (has recourse to the Exodus tradition); Riga, "Signs of Glory", pp. 416–23.

do not lead to full faith (12:37). It might be said that the "works" are more markedly "Messianic", while the "signs" are completely orientated to Christology, though the two can never be completely disjoined in John.

The various perspectives which are opened up by the "works" and the "signs" can be seen more clearly when one notes that the "signs" are restricted to the public work of Jesus on earth. They end with 12:37, with a retrospect of Jesus's work as revealer (as "light of the world") and are not mentioned again except at 20:30. The "works" build up into the "work" of Jesus, which he consummates with his death on the Cross (cf. 17:4; 19:30). Further, Jesus also promises his disciples that those who believe in him will accomplish the works which he has done, and even greater ones (14:12). But nothing is said of the disciples' performing "signs", and this is certainly not accidental. The only satisfactory explanation of these data is that the "signs" are an expression of Jesus's activity as revealer, as exercised by him on earth in his incarnation. From this point of view, they are on a level with his words, while his "works", as motive for faith, are less than Jesus's bare word (cf. 10:38; 14:11). The "signs" are, as it were, already an articulate revelation and when Jesus speaks his words of self-revelation, the "signs" only become more vivid and clear in their quality of "sign" (cf. 6:35, 48, 51; 9:5; 11:25f.). It is true that they only begin to speak to the believer, in so far as he sees and understands the significance of the sign. They are ordained to faith in the same way in which revelation awaits the response of faith.

If this view is correct, it is clear why the apparitions of the risen Lord can hardly be taken as "signs". They are no longer part of Jesus's self-revelation to the world but have an entirely different character. They are Christophanies before the disciples (cf. 14:22 and the term ἐμφανίζειν). They also lack the "material" quality which belongs to all the earlier signs. For the same reason, it is better not to include the walking on the waters among the signs, though it takes place during the time of Jesus's public work and is attached directly to another great "sign". The evangelist gives no pointers, but he may have considered the walking on the waters as a special "sign" for the disciples. It would still form an exception in the whole series.[7]

[7] An extension of the concept of "sign" to take in the cross of Jesus cannot be justified, as is attempted by Mollat, "Le semeion johannique", p. 209 ("La notion de semeion domine aussi le récit de la Passion") and esp. by Charlier, "La notion de signe", pp. 444–7. Jn 3:14 does not provide a proof, because the brazen serpent is not designated as a "sign" by John, nor does 12:33, because the evangelist's remark, that Jesus has just signified (σημαίνων) the sort of death he is to die (v. 32), does not depict the cross itself as a "sign". Otherwise the martyrdom of Simon Peter would be a "sign" by reason of 21:19, unless one maintains that the author of the epilogue had no feeling for the theological language of the evangelist (cf. Charlier, p. 446, n. 1). No doubt the death of Jesus has the significance of a "sign" in John, as we have to understand it; but the linguistic usage of John is different.

With these conclusions in mind, we should now be able to estimate the place of the "signs" in Johannine theology, and more precisely, in the Christology.

3. The theological significance of the "signs"

Let us begin with the first "sign", which was done by Jesus at the marriage feast of Cana. It is not illustrated by a word of revelation which might disclose the deeper meaning of the event (see above). But the three statements in 2:11 seem to be intrinsically connected. The "sign" as such indicates that "Jesus revealed his glory", and this becomes visible to his disciples through faith. This explanation is confirmed by the raising of Lazarus, where Jesus says to Martha, before the open tomb, as he is about to pronounce his mighty life-giving word, "Did I not tell you that if you believe you will see the glory of God?" (11:40). Here it is the glory of God, in 2:11 the glory of Jesus, but this only means that God's power is present and active in Jesus, that God is the origin and goal of all Jesus's own glory. The raising of Lazarus also manifests the glory of Jesus, as the opening sentences of the story show: "This illness is not unto death, but for the glory of God, that the Son of God may be glorified through it" (11:4).[8] In Jesus's work the glory of God or his own glory becomes manifest, when it is grasped with the eyes of faith. This power to "unveil" may be noted in all the "signs", though not always with the same definiteness. It is most marked where the symbolism is already apparent from the type of miracle wrought and when it is underlined still further by the words of Jesus, as at the multiplication of the loaves, the cure of the blind man and the raising of Lazarus.

But one must be careful not to refer this doctrine at once to a (Platonizing) concept of image. The "signs" are not "forms" or figurative processes which have a symbolic value and can thus summon up a profounder picture; they are not "things and events in this world" which "derive what reality they possess from the eternal ideas they embody".[9] The revelation of the "glory" of God points in another direction. The miracle of the loaves in particular, with the revelation discourse which follows, shows that the evangelist is firmly rooted in biblical and Messianic thought, as do the other miracles. The Johannine "signs" are akin to the miracles of the Exodus, as presented in the book of Wisdom (though

[8] On which see Thüsing, *Erhöhung*, pp. 229ff.; on the usage of "glory" and "to glorify" see also pp. 240–4.

[9] Dodd, *Interpretation*, p. 143.

this can hardly have been the immediate model for the miracles in John).[10] One may add the Jewish notion that the miracle of the manna was to be repeated in the days of the Messiah (cf. commentary on 6:31).[11] And we should also note the prophetic promise that the glory of God was to be revealed over Jerusalem and the peoples in the end of days (emphasized particularly in Is 60 ff.). The eschatological envoy of God does not yet bring the cosmic glory, but he gives glimpses of it in his "signs", as is clear from the miracle at Cana, at the cure of the blind man, which portrays Jesus as the "light of the world" (9:5) and at the raising of Lazarus, which is of itself a future eschatological event but which is already given reality by Jesus in the "sign". We should not, therefore, overlook the Messianic and eschatological significance of the Johannine "signs",[12] which still remains close to the synoptic understanding of Jesus's miracles.

But the Johannine concept of "sign" goes far beyond the (Messianic) significance attached to the synoptic miracles. The Christological perspective of the evangelist makes it something completely new. Some idea of his concentration on Christology may be gathered from the fact that in 12:41 it is the glory of Jesus which Isaiah saw, when he had the vision of Yahweh on his lofty throne in heaven (Is 6:1). And in the light of the Son of Man logion of 1:51, the assertion of 2:11 becomes even more intelligible: the Son of Man on earth is the place of God's presence and action; God's eschatological action is realized in him. This Christological principle affects even the interpretation of the demand for a sign which comes from the synoptic tradition, a demand which, as we saw, contains a different concept of "sign". The enigmatic prophecy of Jesus at the purging of the temple, by which he counters the Jews' demand for credentials by promising a different sort of sign (the destruction and rebuilding of the temple), is fulfilled, according to the commentary of the evangelist (2:21), in Jesus's own person, by the resurrection of his body. Jesus's answer in ch. 6 is still clearer: he himself in person, as he reveals himself in his words and "signs" is the true sign from heaven given by God, the "bread of life" which came down from heaven, surpassing from every point of view the manna given by Moses (6:32–35). This is the true quality of "sign" in the miracle of the loaves, which the Jews have seen (cf. 6:36) and still have not really seen (with believing eyes, cf. 6:26). The bread he gives to men displays the giver himself as the bread

[10] See Ziener, "Weisheitsbuch und Johannesevangelium".

[11] See Billerbeck, vol. II, p. 481; Volz, *Eschatologie*, p. 388.

[12] See Richardson, *The Miracle Stories of the Gospel*; Kallas, *The Significance of the Synoptic Miracles;* Vögtle, "Jesu Wunder einst und heute"; Delling, "Botschaft und Wunder im Wirken Jesu". Matthew had already begun to interpret the Marcan miracle stories from a particular theological aspect, cf. Held, *Überlieferung und Auslegung im Matthäusevangelium*, pp. 155–287.

of life come down from heaven. All the great miracles designated as "signs" focus the attention entirely on the worker of them and manifest the majesty and saving power bestowed upon him.

This Christological perspective also dominates the "realized" eschatology of the fourth evangelist. Though there is no direct connection, a comparison with the "sign of Jonah" mentioned in Mt 12:39f. par. Lk 11:29f. is instructive. In the more original version given by Luke, it probably means the parousia of Christ, which will be a "sign" for the Jews, though a sign of judgment for the unrepentant.[13] But in keeping with the eschatology of the fourth evangelist, Christ himself as actually present is the "judgment" which according to God's plan brings about the separation between believers and non-believers (cf. 9:39). Jesus himself, it is true, is not designated as "sign" in John, but this is the meaning of his person, as disclosed in the "sign" of the healing of the blind man. All the signs, in fact, which display Jesus as giver of life, give positive assurance of the presence of eschatological salvation in his person: the healing of the official's son at Capernaum, the cure of the cripple at the pool of Bethesda and the raising of Lazarus. The "life" which Jesus gives to these men, on whom the gates of the underworld have practically closed, is symbol and pledge of the "eternal life" awaited in the age to come, still understood by the Synoptics as the future life with God, but seen by John as already present in Jesus and communicated by him to believers in the immediate present. Since the "signs" reveal Jesus as "the resurrection and the life", they also show that his gift of life is actually present. In as much as they show physical life being restored to the healed, they also represent the restoration of the spiritually dead to the divine life which Jesus bears within him and which he imparts to believers (cf. 5:25f.).

But there is another problem connected with this. Is it the chief purpose of the Johannine "signs" to point forward to the saving work of the exalted Lord[14] or, as present signs, wrought during the earthly life of Jesus, are they meant to manifest the actual glory and saving power of the incarnate Christ? The "signs" are indissolubly linked with the person of Christ, whose work as revealer on earth necessarily leads to his "exaltation" and "glorification" and reaches its goal in the salvific action of the exalted Lord. The closeness of this connection, which becomes a unity in the person of Christ, could seem to make the question

---

13 See Jeremias, "'Ιωνᾶς", pp. 411f.; Vögtle, "Der Spruch vom Jonaszeichen"; Rengstorf, "σημεῖον", pp. 231f. A different view again, but not convincing, in Glombitza, "Das Zeichen des Jona".

14 They would then be more closely connected with the symbolic actions of the prophets (see in text under 4); but not with apocalyptic portents, which are all signs of disasters (cf. Mk 13:4 parr.).

superfluous or show that it is wrongly put. But it is still to some extent justified, especially with regard to the interpretation of the "hour" of Jesus mentioned at the miracle of Cana (2:4). Does this first "sign" already indicate the exaltation and glorification of Jesus at the end of his earthly path, where the Messianic blessings (the precious wine of Jesus) have their true reality? Or does it signal the "hour" which now strikes of his earthly work as revealer, since it is precisely in this work of the incarnate Christ that his own and his Father's glory is revealed to believers? It is undoubtedly possible to interpret Jesus's words as meaning: "What I now do is not my definitive work but only a 'sign' of it",[15] and this view might be supported by the way ἡ ὥρα μου is used elsewhere—though the usage is not quite uniform. But the other texts do not lend support to the view that "sign" points forward to the future. The "signs" are closely linked to the work of Jesus on earth (see above) and their main purpose is to bring out the revelation of Jesus's glory which is actually taking place, which is the glory of the only-begotten of the Father in the time of his incarnation (1:14). To affirm this is not to deny that his saving power of bestowing the divine life on believers (cf. 17:2) only comes into play effectively after the hour of his "glorification" (cf. 12:23, 32; 13:31f.; 17:1); but this is taken for granted by John, who writes after the glorification of Jesus, at a time when the divine Spirit of life is being poured out on believers (cf. 7:39). The "signs" are not meant to throw light on the historical process through which Jesus passed as Saviour, but simply to awaken faith in Jesus's being "the Christ, the Son of God" (20:30f.). They manifest the significance of the person of Jesus as such for salvation. They are limited to the time of Jesus's earthly activity to draw attention to the unique revelation brought once for all by the Saviour, the Son of God incarnate, and to throw light on its eschatological significance. Thus the later heralds of the faith can only recount, attest and recall the revelation given by Jesus in "signs" (and words), which becomes thereby "present" in their own day. It is presupposed implicitly that he who once wrought these "signs" on earth has in the meantime been glorified, that he still lives and still effects the salvation of believers. But his revelation, as a historical and eschatological event, is closed, and it only remains to explain it further, disclose its riches and explicitate its full truth (cf. the Paraclete sayings, especially 14:26; 16:13f.)

Thus we are led finally to assume an intrinsic connection between the incarnation and the revelation of Jesus Christ in "signs" which it introduces and renders possible. This is also confirmed by the type and structure of the "signs" themselves. It has been noted long ago that in

[15] Thüsing, *Erhöhung*, p. 94.

spite of their symbolic character they have a solidly "material" aspect, involving very definite corporeal realities and firmly anchored in time and space. That they actually took place, that they can be attested and that they are beyond doubt is of the same decisive importance to the evangelist as their symbolic force. They too (as "works") are to be "testimonies" whereby faith is proclaimed and unbelief convicted, and thus they have a sort of juridical validity, as is especially clear in the repeated cross-examinations of the man born blind (cf. 9). This characteristic of the Johannine "signs", which is so obvious that it does not need to be pursed in detail, has an unmistakable analogy in the person of the incarnate Logos himself. The sublimity with which the spiritual nature and the godhead of the Logos are affirmed in the prologue hymn is equalled by the firmness with which the fact of his becoming flesh is stated. In the same way, the "signs" have a material form under which they become visible, while they contain within a profoundly spiritual, that is to say, Christological meaning. Thus the similarity in structure cannot be accidental, because the "signs" are wrought by the Son of God become man, and by him alone; and they reveal his saving power and glory, so that their sole function is to be a medium whereby his nature is signified.

Thus the Christological significance proves to be the most important element of the Johannine "signs", the most characteristic of their properties and the heart of their theology. Finally, we might ask whether they are not very like the sacraments, which could be seen as performing the same function of "sign" after the glorification of Jesus as did the "signs" during his work on earth. There is indeed a certain analogy, which we may find unmistakable, but this is hardly true in the perspective of the evangelist. The sacraments, which are the representation and application of the salvific work of Jesus (see commentary on 6:53–58), presuppose the "signs" performed during Jesus's earthly life and communicate the salvation (the divine "life") which the "signs" demonstrate as present in the person of Jesus by virtue of their character of sign. But the sacraments are never called "signs" and are not what John understands by "signs". They are symbols and instruments of salvation. But they are not signs of revelation or revelation effected in signs, such as are performed by the incarnate Logos, the Son of Man on earth. But this is precisely the Johannine notion of "sign", as it appears in the Gospel.[16]

16 So substantially also Rengstorf, "σημεῖον", pp. 248f.; see also on "sign" and "faith", pp. 249ff.

Excursus IV

The sources of the Johannine concept of "sign"

The very peculiarity of this theological concept, for which the responsibility must be attributed to the evangelist, has caused the question of its origin to recede into the background. But as it has its interest for the setting of Johannine thought, the discussion of the question must engage us briefly. We have already seen that the Hellenistic notion of image, contrasting the spiritual form or idea with the material reality in which the idea is embodied, is not the proper framework in which to understand the Johannine "sign". It has not left the biblical way of thought so far behind that one has to switch over to the purely Hellenistic, possibly philosophical realm.

First of all, the links with the synoptic tradition are still clearly recognizable. John takes up the Jews' demand for a sign, as we have seen, judges it as do the Synoptics, but opposes it with his own answer. His σημεῖα correspond, more or less, to the synoptic description of the δυνάμεις of Jesus, but for these he uses the terms σημεῖα or ἔργα. There is, of course, the old biblical phrase σημεῖα καὶ τέρατα, which occurs once in Mark and Matthew (Mk 13:22 par.) for the prodigies performed by the seducer of the last days, once in John (4:48), and several times in Acts, where it is used in a favourable sense. This does not explain the specific use of the term in John. Nevertheless, we are justified in assuming that John used a Christian source which had σημεῖα for the miracles of Jesus, instead of the synoptic δυνάμεις, with the same general sense. This usage, which was not yet the object of theological reflection, seemed to us to be reflected in several passages of John. The evangelist found it suitable, but clearly did not wish to take it over without considerable reflection. Hence he used it in a deeper sense of his own and inserted it into his Christological perspectives. In doing so he adopted, though not at first-hand, the old biblical concept, the Hebrew אות, which also has the meaning of "sign".

But one may also ask whether John was not still more strongly inspired by the O.T. אותות in his profound theological concept of the σημεῖον, in spite of his giving it his own original Christological interpretation. K. H. Rengstorf in particular has emphasized that the Johannine "signs" are "in principle, of the same type as the classical σημεῖα of the O.T., the Egyptian 'signs' of the days of Moses".[17] He considers that the Septuagint uses σημεῖον to interpret אות, "to call attention to the self-revelation of the one God as the God of Israel, within the framework of the O.T. concept of God".[18] Other scholars have rather insisted on the objective parallels between the Johannine "signs" and the miracles of the Exodus

---

[17] "σημεῖον", pp. 256, 3f. [18] *Ibid.*, pp. 32ff.

(see above). The relationship must be admitted, at least to some extent, since the Johannine ἐγώ εἰμι also seems to take up the formula of the O.T. theophanies (which are discussed later). But just as Exod 3:14 and the events of Sinai and the Exodus are not in themselves an adequate explanation of the "I am" of John, so too the miracles of the Exodus alone do not suffice to explain the Johannine "signs".

Probably the symbolic actions of the prophets must also be taken into consideration. As recent research has shown, these are not to be regarded as purely pedagogic adjuncts to preaching, or the acting out of an oracle orientated to the future. The symbol was "a creative prefiguration of the future",[19] a revelation which projected efficaciously into the present the future events over which God disposed. Thus they are highly important for the process of revelation, as is brought out by C. A. Keller in the dissertation where he defines the word OTH as "revelatory sign".[20] If we may take it that "the prophetic symbolic act is simply an intensified form of prophetic speech",[21] the affinity with the Johannine "signs" in the eschatological revelation of Jesus becomes certain. Here too, of course, the level of meaning must be transposed to that of the N.T. revelation, and the original connotation transcended, to attain the heights of Johannine theology. Jesus is not just a "prophet" who prefigures the future creatively and efficaciously. He is the divine revealer who has himself appeared upon earth, and whose work is the effective realization of salvation. Hence his "signs" are not manifestations of the glory to come, or at least not primarily so—they never have the character of signs of doom—but of the divine glory which is already present in him and already working efficaciously on believers, though it is only in the future that it will be fully efficacious. But the "revelatory character" of the symbol is shared by the Johannine and the prophetic "signs", and it was probably this biblical line of thought which led the evangelist to "discover" and develop their symbolic character.

If we may link up the Johannine concept of "sign" both with the great signs which took place at the Exodus and with the symbolic actions of the prophets, we can understand more readily the peculiar combination of symbolism and real event in the Johannine presentation. It is improbable, however, that the evangelist reached his notion of "sign" by working on and combining various ready-made elements of thought. It is more probable that in the course of his meditation on the Gospel tradition he sought to grasp the profounder meaning of the great miracles in the light of his faith in Christ. Here he may have been helped

---

[19] Von Rad, *Theologie*, vol. II, p. 109, E. T.: vol. II, p. 96; cf. Fohrer, *Die symbolischen Handlungen der Propheten*.

[20] *Das Wort 'OTH als "Offenbarungszeichen" Gottes*. [21] Von Rad, *ibid*.

by his reminiscences of the O.T., which may have been the occasion of his own characteristic conception. Our review of the O.T. "signs" allows us to affirm no more than this, which is put forward merely as a debatable hypothesis.

EXCURSUS V

The "Son of Man" in the Fourth Gospel

The fourth Gospel has a very characteristic approach to the Son of Man theology and it is therefore important to survey the whole range of the evangelist's thought and expression on this matter and to discuss its problems. Such a study does not merely concern Johannine theology and its background, but the whole present-day debate on the "Son of Man", where, in point of fact, relatively little attention is paid to the Johannine data.[1] The peculiar character of the fourth Gospel certainly means that the Johannine logia cannot be invoked to determine the burning question as to whether Jesus himself used the title as a vehicle of his own self-understanding. They remain, nonetheless, of considerable importance for the development and influence of the Son of Man theology adopted—or as some scholars hold, initiated—by the primitive Church. Did the evangelist retain this designation on the lips of Jesus simply because he knew of it from existing tradition, or was his Son of Man theology occasioned by other impulses, due to contacts with Jewish or Gnostic circles? Did he combine traditional Christian elements with another conception, creating something quite new in theological thought? Here too the question of the Gnostic myth of the redeemer once more becomes acute. Does it re-appear in the Son of Man theology, disguised with a different name? Before we turn to this difficult problem, however, it will be well to gain a comprehensive view of the relevant logia in John, and to inquire whether there are not other texts in the Gospel which are also inspired by the notion of the "Son of Man".

---

[1] Special literature: Iber, *Überlieferungsgeschichtliche Untersuchungen zum Begriff des Menschensohns im Neuen Testament;* Schulz, *Untersuchungen zur Menschensohn-Christologie im Johannesevangelium;* Cullmann, *Christologie*, pp. 189–92, E. T.: pp. 184–7; Sidebottom, "The Ascent and Descent of the Son of Man in the Gospel of John"; id., "The Son of Man as Man in the Fourth Gospel"; id., *The Christ of the Fourth Gospel*, pp. 69–136; Hahn, *Hoheitstitel*, pp. 39ff.; Schnackenburg, "Der Menschensohn im Johannesevangelium" (on which this excursus is based.).

Excursus V

1. The Johannine perspective

The title "Son of Man" is found thirteen times in John:

1:51 The angels of God ascend and descend on the Son of Man.
3:13 Only the Son of Man who has descended from heaven has ascended thither.
3:14 Like the serpent in the desert of which he is the antitype, the Son of Man must be raised up.
5:27 The "Son" has power to sit in judgment because he is the "Son of Man".
6:27 The Son of Man will give the food that remains for eternal life.
6:53 Men must eat the flesh of the Son of Man and drink his blood, if they are to have life in them.
6:62 The Son of Man will ascend to heaven.
8:28 The Jews will raise up the Son of Man.
9:35 Jesus asks whether the man born blind and healed by him believes in the Son of Man.
12:23 The hour has come for the Son of Man to be glorified.
12:34c The Son of Man must be raised up (cf. v. 32).
12:34d The people ask who this Son of Man is.
13:31f The Son of Man is now glorified.

Do these texts give a uniformly consistent picture, or do they contain disparate concepts from various traditions, applied and inserted into their context in different ways? We may begin by dividing the material into groups:

3:13; 6:62 the Son of Man descended from heaven who ascends there again;
3:14; 8:28; 12:34c the "exaltation" of the Son of Man;
12:23; 13:31f. the "glorification" of the Son of Man.

The three groups form a consistent picture, because "exaltation" and "glorification" are closely connected (cf. 12:23 with 32 and 34c), and the "hour" of exaltation and glorification is that of the "ascent" (cf. 3:13 with 14; also 12:31 with 13:31f [νῦν]).[2]

The three texts from the discourse on the bread of life and the bread from heaven likewise form a unity, since they link the statements about the bread which Jesus is in person and which he gives believers or the partakers of the Eucharist (v. 53). "The bread which has come down from heaven", which gives life to the world (vv. 33, 51) is precisely the Son of Man, who also "ascends to where he was before" (v. 62). It is this Son of Man who will give food which has abiding power for eternal life

[2] Thüsing, *Erhöhung*, pp. 253–88.

(v. 27). But this links up with the preceding group: it is the exalted and glorified Son of Man, who has descended from heaven and re-ascended, who gives divine and eternal life—as the bread from heaven in person, and then with the eucharistic bread. The whole discourse presupposes the descent as well as the exaltation and glorification which takes place at the ascent; the two aspects are indispensable in both parts—the parabolic discourse on the personal bread from heaven and the application to the Eucharist, vv. 53–58. The three Son of Man logia are not merely extrinsic links, they provide key-words for the understanding of the whole.

A different appraisal seems to be called for in the two texts where the crowd, or someone from the crowd, asks who is the Son of Man (9:35; 12:34d). The question is concerned with the Messiah (12:34b), who in the mind of the evangelist is none other than the Son of Man. The question of the Messiah is the general basis on which the evangelist gives his particular doctrine of the Son of Man (cf. ch. 1; also excursus i). Hence the people's questions about the Son of Man are not extraneous to this line of thought. There is an indirect connection with 8:28, where it is said that the unbelieving Jews will know, after the exaltation of the Son of Man, that Jesus is he whom he claims to be (ἐγώ εἰμι).

At first sight, there seems to be something strange about 1:51, which speaks of the Son of Man on earth being in constant communication with God. But the explanation given in the commentary allows us to apply this text also to the descending and re-ascending Son of Man. The background of descent and ascent is not yet disclosed. The Son of Man on earth speaks only of his relationship to the heavenly world, with which the angels ascending and descending on him keep him in constant communication. It is only in the following revelation discourses that the reader learns that the Son of Man was once in heaven and returns there again. But for the evangelist the logion already points in this direction and forms a preparation for later assertions. This first Son of Man logion also has another important aspect, in as much as it says that the Son of Man will disclose himself to believers, in further revelations. The counterpart to this is the assertion that the Son of Man remains an enigma to unbelievers or to the weak of faith (cf. 8:28; 12:34d). It might be said that the "Son of Man" in John has the same function as the "Messianic secret" in Mark.

Finally, the allusion to the Son of Man as judge, in 5:27, is singular. The absence of the article shows that a traditional concept has been adopted, which, however, is made to serve the purpose of a Johannine context, which speaks of the "Son" and present salvation or condemnation.[3] The terminology of the judgment links up with 12:31 f., accord-

[3] Cf. Iber, *Untersuchungen*, pp. 133–8; Blank, *Krisis*, pp. 120–43, 158–64.

ing to which the "Prince of this world" is judged at the exaltation of the Son of Man (cf. 16:11). Thus the old eschatological concept of the Son of Man as judge is merged into the Johannine theology.

To sum up: all thirteen texts in John which speak of the Son of Man form a consistent and well-knit whole. The Son of Man is the Johannine Messiah, the giver of life (the "true bread of life", ch. 6) and judge. He alone can and does exercise these functions in his actual activity, because he is the Son of Man who has come down from heaven and ascends there again. The roots may be different, but the concept of "Son of Man" in John is a unity.

Apart from these logia, which probably belong to a definite "theme of tradition",[4] are there other texts in John which contain the concept under different terms? It has often been suggested that "Son of Man" is merely a special form of the notion of the "Primordial Man" *(Urmensch)* and that the old "Anthropos" myth shows through the Johannine thought.[5] This opinion would be reinforced if it could be shown that the evangelist understood "Son of Man" in all or many of the places where Jesus is designated as "Man" in John.[6] The "ecce homo" in particular is appealed to. Is there any truth in this? The trial of Jesus in John undoubtedly has overtones. To the theologically minded evangelist it probably represented another and greater "trial" on a cosmic scale. Jesus, who is falsely accused as "King of the Jews", is truly king, not after the fashion of this world, however, but in the realm of "truth" (cf. 18:36). The Roman judge, who presents him as king derisively, only has power over him "from above" (19:11), and actually displays to the Jews the true king whom they have rejected (cf. 19:13f.).[7] Here too, as throughout the Gospel, the Jewish Messiah is shown in his true greatness as revealer and as redeemer of the world, ruling and conquering more magnificently than the Jews expected or the Roman judge could understand. At most, one could find in the "ecce homo" an indirect allusion to the "Son of Man", in so far as this title also designates the Messiah in the Johannine sense (cf. 12:34). But there is not the least suggestion that Jesus is the archetypal "Man" in the sense of any "Anthropos" myth. According to the context, however, the primary meaning of the scene is again different.

---

[4] See Schulz, *Untersuchungen*, pp. 96–124.

[5] Schaeder, "Der Mensch im Prolog des vierten Evangeliums", pp. 306–41; Dodd, *Interpretation*, pp. 241–9; Cullmann, *Christologie*, pp. 144f., E. T.: pp. 142f.; Sidebottom, and others; but Kraeling, *Anthropos and Son of Man*, rejected any influence of the Anthropos myth on John, pp. 167ff. and attacked the position of Schaeder (pp. 170ff.); see further Moe, "Der Menschensohn und der Urmensch" and excursus vi below.

[6] So esp. Sidebottom, "The Son of Man".

[7] See Blank, "Die Verhandlung vor Pilatus, Joh 18:28—19:16 im Lichte johanneischer Theologie".

Pilate dismisses "this man" contemptuously; immediately afterwards, the Jews themselves accuse him of "claiming to be Son of God" (19:7)—and this, in truth, is what he is!

If we examine the other passages in which Jesus is termed "man",[8] it becomes less and less possible to see behind them an allusion to the "Son of Man". The word is mostly used by others to speak of Jesus, either not knowing his name (4:29; 5:12) or belittling him (9:16a, 24; 11:47, 50; 18:14, 17, 29) or in a rather neutral sense (9:11, 16b). Some texts, however, show that "this man" gives rise to reflections (cf. 4:29; 7:46; 9:16b), and once Jesus speaks of himself in the same way (8:40), but with no special emphasis or merely to invite reflection. The sharp contrast between "man" and "God" in 10:33 (cf. "Son of God" in vv. 34 ff.) may be compared with the "ecce homo" scene, 19:5 and 7. The Scripture proof in 10:34 is concerned with Ps 82:6, in which earthly potentates are ironically called "gods" and "sons of the Most High". But it is not a psalm in which the term "son of man" occurs, as in Ps 8:5; 80:17. Schaeder's hypothesis, that 1:6 was part of an original hymn to Enosh, and that the application to John the Baptist was secondary,[9] is not well founded, since 1:6–8 is undoubtedly a piece of prose inserted into the Logos hymn. Hence to postulate a recondite allusion to the υἱὸς τοῦ ἀνθρώπου behind the frequent designations of Jesus as (ὁ) ἄνθρωπος would be very forced.

Other supposed allusions to the Son of Man are not much more plausible. C. H. Dodd explains Jesus's description of himself as the "true vine" (15:1) as a reference to Ps 80, where Israel is the vine planted by God's right hand (vv. 15f.) and where in v. 16 the Septuagint has a "son of man", not in the Hebrew, bringing "'Vine' and 'Son of Man' into direct parallelism".[10] Their equivalence would extend to their corporate sense, so that Jesus as the Son of Man would be the true Israel, a concept also supposed to underly 1:51.[11] The O.T. background of the imagery of the vine seems unquestionable; but it is highly doubtful that the incorrect reading in question had any significance for John. We found ourselves unable to admit a corporate sense for "Son of Man" in 1:51. The role of the eschatological revealer is much rather an exclusive one, even when he acts as leader and saviour of the new "Israel".

This is also true of the ἐγώ εἰμι of Jesus, which might also be seen as an allusion to the Son of Man, especially in the context of ch. 6. But no direct reference can be traced; none of the three Son of Man logia in ch. 6 is formulated in terms of ἐγώ εἰμι. It is true that the Bread of Life which

---

[8] 4:29; 5:12; 7:46; 8:40; 9:11, 16ab, 14; 10:33; 11:47, 50; 18:14, 17, 29; 19:5.

[9] "Der Mensch im Prolog", pp. 326–9.

[10] *Interpretation*, pp. 411, 245, n. 1.

[11] *Ibid.*, pp. 245f.

has come down from heaven is identical with the Son of Man, but the aspect of "Son of Man" is not connected directly with the ἐγώ εἰμι utterance. This is also true of 8:28, where the ἐγώ εἰμι might be thought to take up the "Son of Man" of the clause immediately preceding ("when you have raised up the Son of Man"), except for the fact that the absolute ἐγώ εἰμι occurred earlier, in v. 24, where the Son of Man is not mentioned. The ἐγώ εἰμι of v. 28 clearly takes up that of v. 24, and hence the exaltation of the Son of Man merely indicates the moment (τότε) at which the unbelieving Jews will come to know Jesus's true being.

It is likewise highly improbable that the "I am the door" of 10:9 can be connected with 1:51, as Sidebottom, after Odeberg, assumes.[12] The imagery of the ἐγώ εἰμι saying is much more likely to come from the parabolic discourse 10:1–5 (in particular vv. 1 f.), and to have been given an independent development, in contrast to v. 7, in order to bring out Jesus's unique role as saviour, as in the parallel saying about the "way" in 14:6. This aspect is not considered in the Son of Man saying in 1:51. All these concepts are no doubt connected in the Johannine Christology, but they display no particular affinity with the title of "Son of Man".

Thus apart from the Son of Man logia themselves, there seem to be no grounds for assuming that the concept of the Son of Man has greatly influenced the fourth Gospel. Hence too one will refuse to follow Sidebottom in particular in his search for the possible O.T. bases of the equation of "Son of Man" and "Man" in a comprehensive and archetypal sense.[13] Sidebottom holds that the well-known expression in Ezekiel, the "son of man" by which God addresses the prophet (pp. 73 ff.), and other similarities (75 ff.) are highly significant for the Johannine concept, and appeals further (after Dodd) to Ps 80, to Ps 8 (p. 78) and Wis 2 (pp. 81 f.), with a cross-reference to Is 53. But this is very shaky ground on which to base the transition from "son of man" to "Man" (pp. 84–98) and finally to invoke the Anthropos myth as the ultimate source (pp. 99–111). Even the premise which he states in the following terms is questionable: "If John, then, was influenced in his use of the Christian term Son of Man by any speculation about Man, it was most probably through that form of it which was entertained in the Wisdom circles of Judaism" (p. 111).

From the point of view of method, it is more correct to consider the Son of Man logia in themselves and to look for the context to which they approximate most closely. Here again a comparison with the Synoptics is suggested.

---

[12] *The Christ of the Fourth Gospel*, p. 124.

[13] "The Son of Man", pp. 231–5; id., *The Christ of the Fourth Gospel*, pp. 69–83 (to which the page-references in brackets in the text refer).

2. The Johannine Son of Man and the synoptic tradition

The Johannine Son of Man is more closely allied to the synoptic tradition than might appear at first sight. The clearest link is the recourse to the Son of Man of Daniel in 5:27. This has been ascribed to a subsequent ecclesiastical redaction by Bultmann and others,[14] but with no compelling reason, since the traditional "futurist" eschatology has been made entirely subservient to the "realized" eschatology of the Johannine context (cf. vv. 22 and 30),[15] and the realized eschatology is by no means nullified by vv. 28–29. With this assertion of the Son of Man's role as judge, the fourth evangelist is in accord with the synoptic logia Lk 12:8 par.; Mk 8:38 parr.; 13:26 parr.; 14:62 parr.; Lk 11:30 par.; 12:40 par.; 17:24, 26, 30 par.; Mt 13:41; 19:28; 25:31; Lk 18:8; 21:36, that is, the sayings about the future, and in particular about judgment, which must be considered as the most ancient and original stratum of the synoptic tradition.[16] But most of the other Johannine logia on the Son of Man are also closely linked with the eschatological Son of Man sayings. The whole group of concepts connected with "elevation" and "glorification" can be attached to these. The "glorification" of the Son of Man links up with the synoptic "coming in glory" (Mk 8:38 parr.; 13:26; Mt 25:31). It is true that the fourth evangelist sees the future manifestation of the glory of Jesus as already taking effect and accomplished in principle in his "elevation". But this is a perspective which is already opened up by the words of Jesus in the synoptics before the Sanhedrin (Mk 14:62 parr.), and which is made clearer in the theology of Luke (cf. Lk 22:69; 23:42f.; 24:26 εἰσελθεῖν εἰς τὴν δόξαν αὐτοῦ; Acts 7:55f.). Likewise, it cannot be doubted that the Johannine concept of the "exaltation" takes up the synoptic "sitting at the right hand of God" (cf. Mk 10:37 par.; 14:62 parr.; Mt 25:31; Acts 2:33f.; 5:31; 7:55f.), though it does not treat it as a second stage following the "humiliation" of the Cross, but rather understands the Crucifixion itself as "exaltation" (3:14; 8:28; 12:32, 34). The fourth evangelist is aware of the traditional view, but his profounder theological contemplation has modified it for the benefit of his Christology.

Further, when speaking of the "exaltation" in connection with the crucifixion of Jesus, John shows that he is familiar with the second group

---

[14] pp. 196f. (further opinions *ibid.*, p. 197, n. 1).

[15] Cf. Iber, *Untersuchungen*, pp. 128–47; Léon-Dufour, "Trois Chiasmes Johanniques", pp. 253f.; Blank, *Krisis*, pp. 158–64. Another view in Boismard, "L'Évolution du thème eschatologique", pp. 514–8, who finds two levels in 5:19–25 and 26–30, explaining the first as a "relecture" of the second.

[16] Cf. Tödt, *Der Menschensohn in der synoptischen Überlieferung;* E. T.: *Son of Man in the Synoptic Tradition;* Hahn, *Hoheitstitel*, pp. 13–53. We cannot now go into the discussion relaunched by E. Schweizer.

of Son of Man logia in the Synoptics, the predictions of the Passion. The saying of 3:14 in particular (cf. also 12:34c) is unmistakably akin to the fundamental predictions of the suffering and death of the Son of Man. The Son of Man "must" (the δεῖ of the divine plan) "suffer . . . be killed and rise again after three days", as we read in the Synoptics (Mk 8:31 parr.) or "be raised up", as John says, compressing the historical sequence into a single act (3:14). But one may go still further. There are good reasons for assuming that the prophecy of the vicarious expiation of the Servant of the Lord (Is 53) is behind the synoptic predictions of the Passion, though the point is disputed.[17] But the same "Servant Song" was probably also the inspiration of the fourth evangelist in his Christology of "exaltation and glorification", and indeed the very first verse of the song (52:13), "Behold, my servant . . . ὑψωθήσεται καὶ δοξασθήσεται σφόδρα." Here the two dominant Johannine concepts occur together with the same meaning; the theological progress of John, with regard to previous Christology, such as that of the hymn Phil 2:6–11, where v. 9 also speaks of the "exaltation", consists in his regarding the hour of the "exaltation" on the Cross as already that of the "glorification" (cf. 12:23f. with 32, 34c; 13:31f.; 17:1f.). Here too the evangelist's theology links up with the Passion sayings of the Synoptics and their O.T. background and provides a development based on the underlying texts of Scripture.

But it is equally noteworthy that the Son of Man logia in John show no direct connections with the third group of Son of Man logia in the Synoptics, those which speak of the present work on earth of the Son of Man. The Johannine Jesus is, of course, considered as Son of Man while on earth, much more emphatically than in the Synoptics, since he is the Son of Man who has come down from heaven (3:13) and who is in constant communication with heaven through the angels which ascend and descend upon him (1:51). But the Johannine logia have no contacts, in form or content, with the synoptic logia which proclaim that the Son of Man has power on earth to forgive sins, (Mk 2:10), that he is lord of the Sabbath (Mk 2:28), that he has nowhere to lay his head (Lk 12:58) and so on. Even 1:51, the Son of Man logion most strongly related to the present, is much more in line with the futurist assertions of the Synoptics,

---

[17] See esp. Mk 9:12, where the appeal to scripture and the old-fashioned word ἐξουδενηθῇ recall Is 53:3; the same sense is given by Mk 8:31 parr. and Lk 17:25. Cf. Jeremias, "παῖς θεοῦ", p. 704; Michaelis, "πάσχω", pp. 913ff.; contrast Tödt, *Menschensohn*, pp. 151–7, who thinks that the underlying text is Ps 118:22. But the influence of Is 53 (vv. 10ff.) is undeniable, at least for Mk 10:45b par., cf. Lohse, *Märtyrer und Gottesknechte*, pp. 117–22; Hahn, *Hoheitstitel*, pp. 57ff. The whole question is well presented in the light of the use of scripture in the early Church by Lindars, *New Testament Apologetic*, pp. 77–88 (on John p. 83).

especially the logion about "seeing" (ὄψεσθε) the Son of Man sitting at the right hand of God and coming with the clouds of heaven (Mk 14:62 parr.). We must conclude that it was not through the synoptic tradition that the fourth evangelist arrived at his affirmations relating to the presence of the Son of Man, but by his own processes of theological reflection on the data. Here the Synoptics and John go their separate ways, after having been on common ground first with regard to their development of the sayings about the future and then, though already displaying a certain variety, with regard to the sayings on the Passion of the Son of Man.

Thus the author of John shows that he has certain contacts with these older traditions. And he does not lose sight of the historical foundation, as may be seen from his attitude to the people's notion of the Son of Man. The two questions about this "Son of Man" show that he was aware that it was not a usual title of the Messiah. According to the objection which Justin puts on the lips of his Jewish interlocutor, Trypho,[18] the Jew had expected the glorious "Son of Man" according to Dan 7, but not a Messiah who died an ignominious death under the curse of the law. The situation is similar in the Gospels, and here John agrees with the Synoptics in so far as it too shows Jesus using the title of Son of Man to express a self-understanding which surpasses the expectations of the Jews and provokes their contradiction. The Johannine Jesus, however, does not confine himself to this title, but also uses other modes of expression to speak of himself.

But along with the traditional background of the Son of Man logia in John, there are certain traits which go to make up their special characteristics in John, above all, the dominant thought of the descent and ascent of the Son of Man, and of his exaltation and glorification which are connected with it. Can this theological development be ascribed to the evangelist, or must one have recourse to a tradition derived from another source? A theological development of synoptic logia and thoughts can be observed elsewhere in John, so that one is entitled to suspect its presence here also.

The re-interpretation of the Messianic preaching of John the Baptist is Christologically important. The saying about the "stronger" who is to come after, and whose shoe-laces the Baptist feels unworthy to loosen, Mk 1:7, is interpreted of the pre-existence of Jesus. Here, as with the "Son of Man", a concept from the Messianism of Jewish apocalyptic has been made to serve the ends of Johannine Christology, which is concerned with the salvation to be found in the pre-existent Logos, present in the Incarnation, known as the unique Son of God who has been sent by the Father (cf. 1:14, 18).

[18] Justin, *Dial.*, 32, 1.

The new "eschatological" view is also to be seen in the adoption and rendering of the synoptic phrase, "enter into the kingdom of God". The expression occurs only in the Nicodemus episode (3:5, cf. v. 3). But the context, which speaks of "birth from above", presupposes the Johannine concept of the realms "above" and "below" (cf. 3:12, 13, 31; 8:21), and hence the phrase must mean, "enter into the heavenly realm above", the divine kingdom of life and light. Here too a traditional expression from eschatology and apocalyptic has been taken up and re-interpreted in terms of Johannine thought.

Other arguments could also be adduced to show that John is giving a new interpretation to existing primitive Christian tradition, though it remains possible that he also received impulses from his environment. As regards the Son of Man logia at any rate, one must not overlook the obvious link with the synoptic tradition, though it may have been given a strikingly new interpretation in John. The only question to be asked about the background of the Son of Man theology in John is whether the evangelist, as well as drawing upon the common Christian tradition, was also exposed to other influences. This means, in fact, whether he has adopted the (Gnostic) redeemer myth into his conception of the Son of Man.

3. The Son of Man sayings and the myth of the redeemer

The existence of an ancient Anthropos myth cannot be doubted. Copious material had already been gathered from non-Christian and Christian Gnostic sources, though not sufficiently sifted according to date or properly distributed according to its relevance to a myth of a supreme all-embracing God or an archetypal man *(Urmensch)*, to the (god) Anthropos or speculation on Adam, or according to its Gnostic or non-Gnostic presuppositions.[19] But now with the texts from Nag-Hammadi we have at our disposal an early Christian Gnostic literature which displays very fully and in a wide variety of forms the notion of a divine being who was called "Man", "First Man", "Perfect Man" and the like. The material has been so fully presented by H.-M. Schenke[20] that there is no need to cite the texts in full here. The Anthropos does not always have the same place in the hierarchy of the Gnostic gods; he can present himself in various guises, now as the supreme God, then again as the second God or the redeemer. But these are only variations of the one

[19] Cf. Colpe, *Religionsgeschichtliche Schule;* Schenke, *Der Gott "Mensch" in der Gnosis;* see further excursus vi.

[20] *Der Gott "Mensch"*, pp. 6–15.

fundamental concept, that the supreme God presents himself as the Anthropos (who is his "image"); and the Anthropos is the prototype who represents the origin, way and goal of man, his fall and redemption, the return of man to the being and all-embracing unity of God. H.-M. Schenke distinguishes two types of doctrine about the God "Man". In the first type, as represented by the *Apocryphon of John*, God himself is the "Primordial Man", according to whose image the "primordial man" of earth comes to be, and "the image of the divine *Urmensch*, remaining to some extent upon the earthly *Urmensch*, is the divine and essential element in earthly man". In the second type found in other texts, after the image of God beside God, a second heavenly *Urmensch* appears, who descends into the earthly *Urmensch* and becomes its higher principle.[21] But the various forms of the myth only make it clearer that we have to do with speculations on the nature of man, which make use of cosmogonies and their myths, and ideas on the macrocosm and the microcosm —the latter being a sort of anthropology.

What interests us here is whether the "Son of Man" occurs in such contexts, whether his place here is original, and whether it could have influenced the Johannine notion of the "Son of Man". The "Son of Man" is in fact often named in Christian Gnostic systems. We give here a brief survey of the occurrences known before the discovery of the Nag-Hammadi texts[22]:

In the system of Ptolemy, Irenaeus, *Adv. Haer.*, I, 6, 3 (Harvey, vol. I, pp. 113f.);

In the system of Marcos, *ibid.*, I, 8, 14 (Harvey, vol. I, p. 150); Hippolytus, *Ref.*, VI, 51, 4 (Wendland, p. 184, 2);

Among the Ophites or Naassenes, Irenaeus, *Adv. Haer.*, I, 28, 1 and 3 (Harvey, vol. I, pp. 227f. and 232f.); Hippolytus, *Ref.*, V, 6, 4 (Wendland, p. 78, 6); V, 7, 33 (Wendland, p. 87, 5); X, 9, 1 (Wendland, p. 268, 13);

In Monoimos, Hippolytus, *Ref.*, VIII, 12, 2ff.; 13, 3f. (Wendland, pp. 232f.); X, 17, 1f. (Wendland, pp. 278f.).

In all these texts the "Son of Man" is literally conceived of as son of the Anthropos, the highest Gnostic godhead or the universal God. Hence the Gnostics understood "Son of Man" in the light of "Man" as a name for God, and considered him to be his first product or primary image. He was the archetypal "Man" on whom earthly man is modelled. As regards the content of the idea, this figure can have very little to do with Jewish apocalyptic.

The case is somewhat different with the Jewish Christians of the pseudo-Clementine writings. Here the memory of the earthly Jesus still dominates

[21] *Ibid.*, pp. 64f.

[22] Cf. Iber, *Untersuchungen*, pp. 11–17.

and his eschatological return is expected; the use of the title points back to the primitive Christian tradition of Palestine. This is linked up secondarily with certain Gnostic views, in particular those about the "true prophet", who was first incorporated in Adam and then returned in various forms throughout the ages till his supreme manifestation in Jesus. Hence, as "true prophet" Adam is once called "son of Man", a title otherwise reserved for Jesus.[23] Gnostic influence can be seen in the insertion of "Son of Man" into the series of syzygies; as a counterpart to the "tempter" (Satan, the evil principle), the "Son of Man" (Jesus) embodies the good prophetic spirit who has been passing through mankind since Adam.[24] Here too the presence of the "Son of Man" is not originally due to Gnosticism.

From the Nag Hammadi texts we may consider the *Apocryphon of John*, which in two places speaks of the "Son of Man". In the first text, which is more or less the same in the various forms in which we have the *Apocryphon*, we read: "A voice came from the height of the lofty aeons: 'The Man exists and the Son of Man'".[25] "The Man" undoubtedly means the supreme godhead, the "Son of Man" his image (produced by him and Barbelo), who is then the model for the first earthly man, Adam, as appears from the passages which follow. In the second text we read: "When Adam recognized the image of his own First Knowledge, he begot the figure of the Son of Man. He called him 'Seth' according to the manner of birth in the aeons."[26] This must mean the Gnostic, who is himself "Son of Man" corresponding to the "Son of Man" of the pleroma of the aeons. This is obviously the Gnostic concept of the archetypal or primordial Man *(Urmensch)*, who appears here under the title of "Son of Man". This type of thinking is completely alien to John. Hence the *Apocryphon of John* also provides merely a superficial resemblance to the Christian texts. In reality, it contains speculation on "Man" as the supreme godhead, whose image is incorporated in earthly man.

---

[23] *Pseudo-Clementine Hom.*, III, 22, 3 (Rehm, p. 64, 20f.) says of Adam: ὡς υἱὸς ἀνθρώπου ἄρσην ὢν . . . προφητεύει. Here the expression is transferred from Jesus to Adam, both being seen together as "the true prophet"; but the meaning of υἱὸς ἀνθρώπου is affected by the Gnostic understanding of the "Son of Anthropos". Elsewhere, as in the Gospels, Son of Man is a designation of Jesus, e.g., *Recog.*, I, 60 (*PG* 1, col. 1240 B): John the Baptist is greater than all *filiis mulierum* but not *filio hominis*. The eschatological expectation of the "Son of Man" is attested in the account given by Hegesippus about James, the brother of the Lord, in Eusebius, *Hist. eccles.*, II, 23, 4–18, esp. 13. See further Schoeps, *Theologie und Geschichte des Judenchristentums*, pp. 78–82, 98–108; Iber, *Untersuchungen*, pp. 17–23; Cullmann, *Christologie*, p. 149, 194, E. T.: pp. 146, 189; Strecker, *Das Judenchristentum in den Pseudoklementinen*, pp. 145–53.

[24] *Pseudo-Clementine Recog.*, III, 61 (*PG* 1, col. 1308 c); cf. Iber, *Untersuchungen*, pp. 23ff.

[25] So codex II, p. 14, line 13ff. (Krause and Labib, pp. 148f.).

[26] *Ibid.*, p. 24, line 35 to p. 25, line 2 (179).

Finally, we may glance at the *Gospel of Philip*. In logion 54, Jesus is designated as "Son of the Man": "Even so came (the) Son of the Man (as dyer)." The primitive Gnostic thinking on the supreme godhead as the "Man", on his "Son" and on his descendants the Gnostics, is rendered very precisely in logion 102 (p. 124; the beginning of the sentence is lost with the end of p. 123), " . . . and the true (ἀληθινός) man and the Son of the Man and the descendants (σπέρμα) of the Son of the Man". It is these "descendants" of the "Son of the Man", the Gnostics, who are also envisaged in logion 120: "There exists the Son of the Man, and the son of the Son of the Man. The Lord is the Son of the Man, the son of the Son of the Man is he who is created by the Son of the Man." Here the "Son of the Man" is identified with the "Lord", that is, with Jesus Christ, by whom further "sons" are "created" (or "begotten", *ibid.*). It is clear that the title of "Son of Man", known from the Gospel tradition, is referred to Jesus, but given a Gnostic sense and exploited in favour of the Gnostics.

As far as we know, the expression "Son of Man" has not been found in any Gnostic texts which are free from Christian influences. The conclusion is unavoidable, that Gnosticism had the concept of the God "Man" at a very early date, but only took over the term "Son of Man" from Christianity and interpreted it in the light of the concept in question. One cannot but agree with Schenke's verdict: "Through the medium of Christianity, the title of the saviour, Son of Man, made its way into Gnosis, where it took on a meaning in theological speculation which it was devoid of in the Church."[27]

It follows that John cannot have derived the title of "Son of Man" from Gnosticism. And in fact his "Son of Man" has nothing to do with the archetypal "primordial man" and the godhead "Man". It comes from the Christian tradition. It remains, of course, possible that for the descent and ascent of his Christ he drew on Gnostic notions. But it cannot be affirmed that such notions were inspired by the title of "Son of Man". And this tells against the probability of his having borrowed from Gnosis its myth of the redeemer descending from heaven and re-ascending. If he did, he took the title "Son of Man" from another tradition and then submitted it to the sort of "Gnosticizing" which we have been able to point to in the Christian Gnostic texts. But since he shows no traces of Gnostic thought as such, the supposition remains without foundation. It is much more likely that the Johannine "Son of Man" is connected with Wisdom speculation.[28] As in the Wisdom literature, the "Son of Man" appears on earth (cf. Bar 3:37f.) and reveals heavenly things (cf. Wis 9:16f.); he moves between

---

[27] "Der Mensch im Prolog", p. 154.

[28] Cf. Braun, "Logos et Fils de l'Homme"; esp. pp. 144ff.; id., *Jean le Théologien*, vol. II, p. 227.

heaven and earth, the realm "above" and the realm "below" (cf. Bar 3:29) and brings men divine revelation for their salvation. But the origin of the characteristic traits of the Johannine "Son of Man" is a question which we shall have to discuss in a wider framework (excursus vi).

EXCURSUS VI

The Gnostic Myth of the Redeemer and the Johannine Christology

We have been confronted repeatedly—when dealing with the question of the origin of the title Logos in John, with the notion of pre-existence and the ideas connected with the "Son of Man"—by the problem of whether and to what extent the Johannine Christology has been influenced by the Gnostic myth of the redeemer. We came to the conclusion (which prejudices the issue to some extent) that the Gnostic origin of the title Logos is improbable, that the notion of pre-existence has other presuppositions than those of Gnosticism and that the Johannine Son of Man is based primarily on the tradition of the primitive Church. But we also saw that this did not fully solve the problem, since John could also have been to a subordinate degree influenced by the Gnostic redeemer myth, and in particular, might have been adopting a Gnostic pattern with the notion of the "descent of the Son of Man" and his "ascent" to the heavenly world. This question will be treated more fully in this excursus.

Such an investigation has important bearings theologically. As is well known, R. Bultmann assumes the presence of the "Gnostic redeemer-myth" and derives the "revelation discourses" from a Gnostic source and thus claims to explain the mythological" language of the evangelist, while understanding his real intention otherwise—as a presentation of the "eschatological revelation" of Jesus Christ, which must, therefore, be understood "existentially" (cf. Introduction, ch. x, *ad fin*). The early existence of the "redeemer myth" is important for this view, even though the existential interpretation itself is also based on other theological presuppositions and could ultimately do without this special thesis. If it were true, however, the fourth evangelist himself would provide an early example of "de-eschatologizing" (operating on an apocalyptic eschatology) and of "de-mythizing", of which the existential interpretation might be the logical outcome. The Johannine "eschatology" will be discussed later. But it is undoubtedly linked very closely and intrinsically with the Christology. And for the latter it is important to decide whether the evangelist intends his expressions to apply directly to the matter in hand or only "improperly". Is he merely making use of figurative language, of a received myth, of a traditional scheme of representation, while in reality he pursues a deeper purpose which concerns even present-day man with his changed picture of the universe and his new understanding of existence? But we must distinguish further. There is no need to stress the fact that an expression like the "descent and ascent of the Son of Man" is linked with an outmoded cosmology. Like other assertions of the Bible, it needs to be detached from this framework and brought into harmony with our more modern view of the world. This spatial category would then be part of the language of symbol and imagery which religion probably cannot entirely dispense with, even for our modern scientific view of the world. But "existence theology" goes further. It includes the person of the redeemer himself in the process of re-interpretation and refuses to consider his *personal* significance, as mediator of salvation, for the "redemption" of man. It is merely his life and death that are considered as an act of revelation, as the "eschatological event", which is significant for all men, even at the present day. The details of the interpretation are still a matter of keen debate and various solutions are given. But all these efforts are at one in attributing to the evangelist a theological intention which goes far beyond the face value of his expressions. This attempt is facilitated if it can be proved that the fourth evangelist took over a "Gnostic redeemer-myth", but becomes correspondingly more difficult if the Johannine Christology (and theology in general) must be regarded as in continuity with the tradition of the primitive Church. For then a radically "existential interpretation" is faced with the difficult task of proving that primitive Christianity as a whole, including John, had a different intention at heart than can be derived from its Christological formulae and confessions when taken in their obvious sense. And then the variation in Christological language is not such as to justify at once the search for a profounder "constant" behind it which would be its "real" intention (the "new understanding of existence").[1] The hermeneutical problem is not eliminated by the present enquiry, but at least the historical basis, how primitive Christianity understood its faith in Christ, can be made clear.

We shall first discuss the existence and antiquity of the alleged "Gnostic redeemer-myth", then compare it with the Christology of John and finally try to determine positively the historical presuppositions of the Christological language of the evangelist.

1. The Gnostic myth of the redeemer

For many years, chiefly under the influence of the studies of R. Reitzenstein and his theory of the "Iranian Redemption Mystery" (1921), the Gnostic "redeemer-myth" was treated as an ancient and consistent entity, appearing in Gnosticism as the doctrine of the "redeemed redeemer", though in various forms. In view of the difficulties of the Old Persian texts, and of the comparison of the literary testimonies of Gnosticism, it is understandable that the N.T. exegetes who were interested in comparative religion had to rely to a great extent on the judgment

[1] Cf. R. Bultmann, "Christologie des Neuen Testaments"; Braun, "Der Sinn der neutestamentlichen Christologie" (on John esp. p. 370); cf. also Hejdanek and Pokorný, "Jesus, Glaube, Christologie".

of the historians of religion. A firm conviction grew up about the existence of an early "redemption or redeemer myth" in which the "primordial Man" also took on the role of redeemer, in as much as after his fall into matter (or his fragmentation in the world under the various elements) he delivered himself again (or gathered his scattered members), returned to the divine world or total unity and delivered at the same time (with himself and in himself) the men who were amenable to his redemption. The history of these researches has now been written by C. Colpe,[2] who also undertakes a purely historical investigation of the thesis. This is in fact an urgent task, since this element of religious history is supposed to have given rise to important concepts in the N.T., including Pauline theology (the Body of Christ, the first and second Adam).[3] For the Iranian texts, which have a considerable bearing on the origins of the "redeemer myth", the N.T. scholar must rely on the students of comparative religion. The main question is whether the ancient Iranian myths contain a view of redemption such as may be found in later Gnostic texts, and in particular, in Manicheism.

The material from which Reitzenstein started, the Parthian hymns, the Arabian account in the *Fihrist* and the Avestan *Hadoxt-Nask*, has been newly presented and investigated by C. Colpe.[4] It appears that there is a doctrine of redemption of the Gnostic type in these texts, but that it reflects later views of Parseeism or Manicheism. For the key question of Gnosis, whether belief in redemption is already found in ancient Iran, C. Colpe investigates the figure of Gayomart, which is supposed to be the genesis of the Gnostic notion of "Primordial Man". His conclusion is as follows: "The comparison between the *Urmensch* ('Primordial Man') of the ancient Avesta and of Gnosticism can only be attempted in the light of reconstructions based partly on Pehlevi texts and partly on other Gnostic traditions (. . .) and then only to arrive at a preliminary stage of Gnosticism which is perhaps entirely absent from the ancient Avesta."[5] In this connection he also examined the possible relationship between Gayomart and the "Son of Man" of late Judaism, and notes that Gayomart

---

[2] Colpe, *Die religionsgeschichtliche Schule*, pp. 9–68.

[3] Käsemann, Schlier and others derive the concept of the "Body of Christ" from the Gnostic myth; this well-known thesis has now been examined from the point of view of comparative religion by Schenke, *Der Gott "Mensch" in der Gnosis*, with negative results, cf. pp. 155f. On the parallel "Adam and Christ" see Cullmann, *Christologie*, pp. 175ff., E. T.: p. 173 (via Gnostic speculation on Adam-Anthropos); criticism in Vögtle, "Der Menschensohn und die paulinische Christologie"; E. Schweizer in *Evangelische Theologie* 23 (1963), p. 108 (on Brandenburger); O. Michel in *Theologische Literaturzeitung* 89 (1964), pp. 271ff.

[4] *Die religionsgeschichtliche Schule*, pp. 69–139.

[5] See p. 143; cf. the whole section, pp. 140–70.

has an eschatological role only in the Pehlevi texts, which means no more than that he is the first-fruits of the resurrection. He finds no trace of his acting as judge, like the "Son of Man" (*Enoch*, 46–48; 62 f.; 69).[6] Other specialists also reject the Gayomart hypothesis for the origin of the redeemer myth.[7] The case of Yima is not very different, as Colpe shows. Neither the Son of Man nor the Gnostic Anthropos can be regarded "as the final stages of an evolution launched by the Indo-Iranian myth; the intermediate links are missing".[8] H.-M. Schenke comes to very similar results: to link the myth of the original giant, in which the world is made from the dead or slaughtered giant, with the doctrine of Mani on the "Primordial Man", a number of intermediate stages would have to be assumed, but they cannot be verified.[9]

Taking as his starting-point the figure of Manvahmed instead of the "Primordial Man", G. Widengren has tried to trace Manichean notions back to the religion of Zarathustra.[10] Manvahmed is described as follows: "Manvahmed proceeded from the Primal Light, the essence and abode of the Father of Greatness ... Moreover, it is the security and seal of the soul, a guarantee of the salvation of the soul whose higher 'self' it constitutes. The saviour, the Great Manvahmed, clearly stands out as the higher principle in man, and, at the same time, as his helper in bringing salvation. Manvahmed is the 'element of light' in mankind and, as such, both something outside and inside the human soul."[11]

Here we are certainly at the heart of the Gnostic doctrine of redemption. As C. Colpe says, Manvahmed "may be clearly identified with the *nous* of the Greek or the light-*nous* of the Coptic texts".[12] Widengren finds this Manichean notion verified as early as in the "Great Vohu Manah" of the Avesta, particularly in *Yasna*, 49:10, "This, O Mazdah, thou storest up in thy house, Manah Vohu and the souls of the righteous ones." With H. S. Nyberg, he interprets the passage to mean that the Vohu Manah, the heavenly, cosmic *manah*, is put on the same level as the souls, which have their individual *manah*.[13] But Vohu Manah is also a mythical person, closely connected with his father, Ahura Mazda. He then compares Pehlevi texts, from the Denkart, where Vohu Manah is often spoken of as coming into souls, and concludes from the similarity that the Manichean

---

[6] See pp. 150 f.

[7] Cf. Duchesne-Guillemin, *Ohrmazd et Ahriman*, pp. 77 f. (quoted by Colpe, p. 150, n. 2); Schenke, *Der Gott "Mensch" in der Gnosis*, pp. 17 ff. (against W. Bousset). Schenke, however, admits some influence of the myth of the primeval giant on Zoroastrian speculations about Ormuzd himself (p. 19).

[8] See pp. 151 f. [9] See pp. 19 f., cf. also pp. 21 ff.

[10] Widengren, *The Great Vohu Manah and the Apostle of God.* [11] See p. 18.

[12] See p. 96. Colpe describes the Vohu Manah as *salvator salvandus* (p. 95).

[13] See p. 44.

concept is derived unchanged from an ancient Iranian source.[14] This explains the notions of the "descent and ascent" of the redeemer and of his "sending", which are frequent in the texts.

Widengren sums up his findings as follows: "We have been able to ascertain in the Avesta the existence of an ancient doctrine, according to which man has a part of a cosmic Mind, Vohu Manah, within him, his own individual *manah* being fundamentally identical with the universal principle, which is a collective body, constituted by all the existent *manah-s* of all human beings, dead and living. This cosmic Manah is a mythical being, but also the centre of a speculative theory on man and his relation to the divine world, surrounding Ahura Mazdah. Vohu Manah as a person besides his collective body acts as a saviour towards the members of this body, namely the single *manah*-s. As to their phenomenological structures, these conceptions are, on the whole, the same as those in Mani's religion . . ."[15]

The appearance of the Vohu Manah in the Avesta is noteworthy, but the question remains as to whether the (Gnostic) notion of redemption which Widengren attaches to it, basing himself on later texts, was already there, or whether the notion was only combined with it in the course of its development. When the Manichean hymns are examined, it is also noteworthy that Manvahmed only occurs here and there among a large number of other and more general titles, which suggests that "here too it is only one of the redeemer godheads among others".[16] This justifies once more the suspicion that while Manicheism uses ancient Iranian material, it has imposed its own Gnostic interpretation on it, as can be observed in the case of the "Primordial Man".

In this very difficult question, it will be necessary in the future to be much more precise about the contents as well as the dating of doctrines. Thus C. Colpe distinguishes three types of Gnostic doctrine about redemption, all of which express the basic Gnostic notion of "redemption" but which differ as regards a "redeemer myth". (1) For the revelation of redemptive knowledge, all that is needed is a prophet to proclaim it, and he can be called or "sent" in various ways. (2) The Gnostic redeemer in the strict sense does indeed descend, but only through the heavens as far as the realm of the "Powers", without reaching earth. (The Manvahmed is of this type). (3) Between these two types there is the "docetic" redeemer who appears on earth with only a phantom body (especially in the Christian systems).[17] And in fact the Hermetic writings and many Christian Gnostic groups manage to do without a mythological redeemer; even in the *Apocryphon of John* Christ appears merely as the revealer of a secret doctrine, the bringer of true knowledge which as such has redemptive power. Hence it becomes clearer that the whole movement known as "Gnosis" was primarily concerned with redemption through "knowledge of the essence" of man, and that it then tended to develop—not indeed

[14] See pp. 46–49. [15] See p. 72. [16] Colpe, p. 97. [17] See p. 198.

necessarily, but still, for preference—a "redeemer myth". In view of recent research, it cannot be affirmed that it was only stimulated to do so by the Christian message of the historical coming of Jesus Christ as redeemer, though Christianity gave further impulses and modifications to its "redeemer myth". But it is equally difficult to maintain that Gnosis presented Christianity with a ready-made and consistent myth of a redeemer. It would certainly be premature to ask when and how the Gnostic redeemer-myth or the various forms of it arose.[18] Our effort here was merely to show how difficult it is to speak of a "Gnostic Redeemer Myth" prior to Christianity in a clear and definite form.

2. The comparison with the Johannine Christology

When one compares Johannine Christology with the Gnostic myth of redemption one notes first of all that certain essential aspects of the latter are missing in John. Christ is not the prototype of man in need of redemption; he is not a "Primordial Man", neither *salvator salvatus* nor *salvandus*. He has no typical significance as "man", as we showed in our investigation of the title of "Son of Man" (excursus v). There is no trace of the "Paradisaical Man" in John and the protological role of Christ is not reflected in it. His activity as mediator of creation, which appears only in the Logos hymn (1:3, 10b), is anything but a cosmogony intended to explain the nature of man. It is an affirmation of his divine dignity and power, which is exercised on a new level in the work of redemption of which it is one of the foundations. Hence too there is no speculation on the essential kernel of man's "self", which would correspond, for instance, to the concept of Manvahmed. The notion also put forward in connection with the "Son of Man", that he is a collective personality containing or representing the whole of mankind to be redeemed, is totally misconceived (see commentary on 1:51). There is no question of denying that John is also concerned with the redemption of mankind and its return to the heavenly world. On the contrary, its Christology is completely orientated towards soteriology. But for the evangelist, the question of salvation presents itself differently. It means escaping the wrath of God's judgment, leaving the realm of death which is constituted precisely by the "wrath" of God, estrangement from God (cf. 3:36 with 5:24) and passing over into the realm of divine life, to which man enters by par-

[18] Colpe has promised further discussion of the point. His remark is important: "There is far more justification in asking about how 'man' becomes redeemer in Gnosis than in asking how the 'redeemer becomes man' . . . If these two questions are kept in mind, man's becoming redeemer and man's descent, the priority of Gnosticism will probably not be affirmed so readily."

ticipation in the life of God, by fellowship with God (cf. 14:6, 9f.; 20:31). The Gnostic redeemer myth and the Johannine Christology are two different worlds: religious philosophy (in mythical language) opposed to biblical religion (in the sense of man's being bound to a personal God), myth to history, Gnosis to faith. The Christian message is not just a variant of Gnostic thought, with myth turned into history and the redeemer who once "appeared" figuratively on earth now seen as taking "flesh" only in the historical Jesus. It is something entirely different and new. Christ in John remains the Messiah, the eschatological saviour of the Jews, except that he is so in a way which transcends absolutely the human hopes of Israel. The expressions in John which are reminiscent of Gnosis should not be allowed to blur the radical difference in the notion of redemption and the basis on which the figure of the redeemer is drawn.

The radical difference between biblical beliefs as regards redemption and the Gnostic doctrine must be kept clearly in mind, if one is not to fall victim to a new Gnostic misunderstanding in the interpretation of the N.T. If the "existential interpretation" is pushed so far that all personal relationship with God is eliminated in favour of the relationship between man and man, it is hard to see how this way of understanding the biblical revelation can still be distinguished from man's taking cognizance of himself on strictly human terms, which is ultimately "Gnosis". In contrast to the Gnostic distortion of the Christian faith in his day, the author of 1 John appealed to or evolved the formula, Ἰησοῦν Χριστὸν ἐν σαρκὶ ἐληλυθότα (4:2). He meant this to be much more than an affirmation of the historicity of the redeemer or a challenge to the Gnostic devaluation of the bodily and material. As the whole epistle shows, he is thinking of the "scandal" of the incarnation, which signals a way of redemption utterly foreign to that of Gnosis (see *The Letters of St John*, excursus iii).

Is the situation adequately described by saying that John merely borrows imagery and language from Gnosticism, without taking over its doctrine of redemption? This is the question of affinities with Gnosticism in terminology and categories. As regards the titles of Christ, only "Logos" and "Son of Man" could possibly be Gnostic in origin. But we saw that there was no proof in either case. Other relationships were much more likely for "Logos", while for "Son of Man" a Gnostic origin was excluded. The position is not very different with "Son", "Son of God" and even Μονογενής. Though Gnosticism, of course, often speaks of certain godheads and mythical figures having a "Son" or "Sons" there is every reason to believe that here too, as in the case of "Son of Man", John is in the line of primitive Christology and its development, and this belief becomes a certainty on closer investigation.[19] This leaves only the ἐγώ εἰμι sayings

[19] The title "the Son of God" and the absolute "the Son" will be discussed later; cf. in the meantime Dodd, *Interpretation*, pp. 250–62; Cullmann, *Christologie*, pp. 305–11, E. T.: pp. 270ff.; Davey, *The Jesus of St John* (main thesis: the Johannine Christology is based on the synoptic tradition); Sidebottom, *The Christ of the Fourth Gospel*, pp. 149–65; Hahn,

and the imagery of the "parabolic discourses" to be derived from Gnosticism, but recent research does not favour this assumption.[20] The Gnostic thesis can hardly be maintained on the basis of the titles of Christ.

Let us consider, therefore, the functions ascribed to Christ in John or rather his "way", as it is depicted there. There are two characteristic expressions, the "descent and ascent" of the Son of Man and the "sending" of the Son or his "coming" into the world. Such languages is very commonly used in the Gnostic texts to speak of the redeemer or envoy. The Mandaean and Manichean literature, the *Odes of Solomon*, the Gnostic *Acts of the Apostles* and the Coptic Gnostic writings offer copious material, which we need not cite here.[21] This cannot be due to Christian influences, at least not for the most part. It stems from the Gnostic way of seeing the heavenly world above as sharply distinguished from the earthly world below. The "fall" is described as the submersion of the fragments of divine light under matter and "redemption" as their return to the pleroma; the redeemer descends (through the spheres of the planets) and ascends triumphantly again, thus representing the way and goal of the soul which is to be redeemed—the divine element in man.

Is this Gnostic, dualist picture of the world the only possible explanation for the Johannine expressions? It must first be noted that the Bible already contains a similar scheme of spatial representation, in the contrast between "heaven" and "earth", even though they are not separated by a dualistic opposition, but held together by the thought of God, as when for instance Jesus says that heaven is God's throne and the earth his foot-stool (Mt 5:34f.). But in later Judaism, the effect of the "dualistic" understanding of the world and existence which was penetrating everywhere in Hellenism was to separate "heaven" and "earth", "above" and "below", by placing them in sharp contrast. No doubt, Jewish thought remained true to its historical and "horizontal" perspective ("this world and the world to come"), but the spatial and vertical category was also there, and particularly marked in discussion of heaven or the heavens as God's dwelling-place, in the hopes of revelation from certain men who were taken up into heaven, or where ecstatic visions were sought (apocalyptic, mysticism). But even rabbinical Judaism did not

---

Christologische Hoheitstitel, pp. 319–333 (p. 330: "In this respect, the gospel of John is an interesting example of the development of traditions which we can find at an earlier stage in the synoptics"); Schnackenburg, "Sohn Gottes".

[20] Cf. Zimmermann, "Das absolute ἐγώ εἰμι"; Schulz, *Komposition*, pp. 70–131. The latter allows of some notable Gnostic influence only for the imagery of the vine and the shepherd, cf. Borig, *Der wahre Weinstock*.

[21] See Bultmann, "Mandäische und manichäische Quellen", pp. 105 ff.; Bornkamm, *Mythos und Legende in den apokrypen Thomas-Akten*, pp. 9 ff.; Widengren, *The Great Vohu Manah*, *passim*; Schmithals, *Das kirchliche Apostelamt*, pp. 103–80.

completely exclude this line of thought, in its frequent speculation on the heavenly world.[22]

Many examples could be adduced to show that Jewish thought could move between the poles of "above" and "below" (see commentary on 3:12). The *Sifre* on Deut 32:2, 306 (132 a), compares the beings which were created "from heaven" (from heavenly substances) with those which were created "from earth" (from earthly substances); man's soul is said to be from heaven and his body from earth. "If man keeps the law and does the will of his Father in heaven, he is like the creatures from above ... But if he does not keep the law and do the will of his Father in heaven, he is like the creatures from below." In *Gen Rabba*, 8 (6c) we have the doctrine that God has put "four sorts of things from above" and "four sorts of things from below" in man,[23] which reflects the development of a Hellenistic anthropology of spirit and body in rabbinism.[24] There is also an important passage in the *Palestinian Targum*, quoted by J. Ramón Diaz, where Joseph is blamed because "he left the grace (or the mercy—חֶסֶד) from above for the grace from beneath, and the grace which had accompanied him from his father's house, and his confidence in the chief butler: he trusted in the flesh, the flesh which passes away and tastes the cup of death".[25]

But the establishment of such categories does not help much; we must examine the matter more closely.

The notion of the "ascensio" figures largely in apocalyptic, where great men of the early days and of biblical history are taken up to heaven (Enoch, Moses, Isaiah, Baruch),[26] and a passage like Jn 3:13 might be directed against such speculations. But the decisive element of "descent" is missing, as also in Jewish mysticism, where there is no trace of pre-existence being linked to it.[27]

In the Wisdom literature, however, the thought of Wisdom's descent upon earth can be verified. In Wis 7:7 Solomon says, "Therefore I prayed, and understanding was given me; I called upon God, and the spirit of wisdom came to me (ἦλθεν μοι)." Further on we read, "In every generation she passes into holy souls (μεταβαίνουσα) and makes them friends of

---

[22] According to Schlatter, *Der Evangelist Johannes*, p. 92, "in the view of the universe taken by the Pharisees, 'heaven' was filled with a large number of imaginary objects, with the heavenly temple and the heavenly Jerusalem and the heavenly princes who formed God's council, and the heavenly abode of souls." But more precise distinctions are needed here; cf. Bietenhard, *Die himmlische Welt im Urchristentum und Spätjudentum;* Traub, "οὐρανός", pp. 511 f.

[23] See the texts in Billerbeck, vol. II, pp. 430 f.

[24] Cf. Sjöberg, "Ruaḥ im palästinischen Judentum", pp. 376 f.; Meyer, "σάρξ im Judentum", p. 117.

[25] "Palestinian Targum", pp. 78 f.

[26] Cf. esp. the Enoch literature: *Enoch*, 14:8ff.; 39:3ff.; 52:1ff.; 71; *Slavonic Enoch*, 1:8f. (expounded in chs. 3–21); also *Jub.*, 4:21; *Greek Apoc. Bar.*, 2–17; *Ascensio Is.*, 3:9.

[27] Odeberg, *The Fourth Gospel*, p. 73. But it is interesting that later on the terminology of "ascending" to the Merkabah was dropped in favour of a mystical and paradoxical way of speaking of "descending" to it; cf. Scholem, *Die jüdische Mystik*, p. 50, and the whole section, pp. 47–58.

God, and prophets" (v. 27). That Wisdom comes from on high follows from the fact that she dwells with God (8:3) and sits by his throne (9:4). "Send her forth from the holy heavens, and from the throne of her glory send her" (9:10). Even more clearly, in mythological language, Wisdom herself describes her coming to earth and finding rest among the people of Israel in Ecclus 24:3–12, "I came forth from the mouth of the Most High, and covered the earth like a mist. I dwelt in high places, and my throne was in a pillar of cloud. Alone have I made the circuit of the vault of heaven and have walked in the depths of the abyss" (vv. 3 ff.). She finds a resting place at last in Israel (vv. 7 ff.). The same ideas are expressed in Bar 3:29–38, where the terminology approximates to that of John. V. 29 asks, "Who has gone up to heaven (τίς ἀνέβη εἰς τὸν οὐρανόν), and taken her, and brought her down from the clouds (κατεβίβασεν)?"—a passage which is often, though probably incorrectly, cited as a parallel to Jn 3:13 (see *ad loc.*). The passage ends with, "Afterwards she appeared upon earth (ἐπὶ τῆς γῆς ὤφθη) and lived among men", as part of Israel's glory. The notion of Wisdom herself ascending to heaven is not included, and the passage to this effect in *Enoch*, 42:1, has a different meaning, namely that Wisdom found no resting-place on earth and returned to her place. This is not a redemptive "ascent" but a disappointed withdrawal. Thus Wisdom literature suggests the notion of the descent of Wisdom, but does not link it with that of the ascent as a salvific act.

There are also passages in rabbinical literature which link up closely "descent" and "ascent". They deal with the Shekina, though with marked differences of approach. *Sukka*, 5 a, says that the Shekina never descended and that neither Moses nor Elijah ever went up on high, that is, to heaven.[28] This is at most a sample of "vertical" thinking. H. Odeberg provides further material. According to *Aboth d^e Rabbi Nathan*, 34, the Shekina descends ten times into the world, and ascended by ten stages, when withdrawing from the temple—which is again a punishment. The same thought is also expressed in other passages.[29] This type of speculation, therefore, does not provide a real parallel to the descent and salvific ascent of the redeemer.

From all this it appears that Judaism shows examples of thinking in spatial and vertical categories, and at times of the notion of descent and ascent, but that that of the redeemer, as given in John, cannot be found there. Terminologically, therefore, the Gnostic redeemer myth, in one form or another, may be considered as a noteworthy parallel; but we have not yet examined the ideas which were current before John in Christian thinking and their possible influence on the formation of the evangelist's

---

[28] See in Billerbeck, vol. II, p. 425.

[29] Odeberg, pp. 90–93; also in Billerbeck, vol. III, pp. 172f.

vocabulary (see 3 below). That the Gnostic "parallels" do not reveal the roots of Johannine thought is already evident from the difference in content noted above, and from the titles given to Christ. This is even clearer when we consider finally the mission of the "Son" who is sent into the world by the Father. For the "sending" of the redeemer or his "coming" into the world there are many parallels in Gnostic literature. But there is no need to have recourse to them to explain the expressions in question. "To send" and "to come" are common in the Bible, and the notion of the mission of the pre-existent Son of God is already expressed in Paul (Gal 4:4; Rom 8:3), in a perspective of a history-centred salvation which is rooted in Jewish thought. Other traits of the Johannine description of the Son must also be taken into account which have no counterparts in the Gnostic "envoy". Above all, in John Jesus appears as the obedient "Son", with no other intention but that of carrying out his Father's will (cf. 4:34; 5:30c; 6:38; 7:18; 8:29; 9:31 ff.; 12:49f.; 15:10), and ready to sacrifice his life (10:17f.; cf. 12:27f.; 18:11). The judicial function which he claims (5:22f., 27, 30b) is also alien to the Gnostic envoy.[30] At most, therefore, there are certain echoes in terminology, but the idea itself is totally different.

3. *The presuppositions of Johannine Christology*

If we start with the assumption, as for the titles of Christ, that John based himself on the Christology already current in the primitive Church and developed it in his own way, we find that the notion of descent and ascent is not an absolute novelty. The hymn in Phil 2:6–11, which is in substance certainly earlier than Paul, describes three successive modes of being of Christ or Christological stages: first, existence in the "form of God" (pre-existence, v. 5), then the human mode of existence resulting from the "emptying out" and the acceptance of the "form of a slave" (v. 7) even to the "humiliation" of death on the Cross (v. 8), and finally his glorious installation as Lord of the universe, which supposes once more his presence in heaven (vv. 9–11). The three stages are as well defined as in John, though in different terms. The diptych of "humiliation and exaltation" is much more strongly underlined, which points to a Jewish background.[31] To this the new and special stage of real (godlike) pre-existence has been added, the precise description of which does not

[30] What Bultmann offers as parallels in "Mandäische und manichäische Quellen", pp. 136 ff. are weak and in fact misleading; contrast the judicial function of the apocalyptic "Son of Man" with which Jn 5:27 links up.

[31] Cf. Schweizer, *Erniedrigung und Erhöhung*, pp. 53–86; earlier, Rawlinson, *The New Testament Doctrine of Christ*, pp. 31–9; also Hahn, *Hoheitstitel*, pp. 112–25, 189–93, who often speaks of a "Christology on two levels", esp. pp. 265–8.

concern us here. But this again has led to the "exaltation" being modified in a not unimportant way. It is now a "super-exaltation" (ὑπερύψωσεν, v. 9), the setting-up of a sovereignty of cosmic import which in the thought of the hymn was not yet possessed in this way by the pre-existent Christ. This view, centred on the history of salvation and linked with theocratic concepts (enthronement as Lord, divine rule over the world) can hardly be derived from Gnostic notions. It reveals a biblical and Jewish way of thinking, for which, as we have seen, the notion of pre-existence is not impossible or remote, though it had not hitherto been applied to the Messiah in this way. But there is an important link between the thought presented in the hymn of Phil 2 and the Johannine Christology, the notion of "exaltation". In Jn 3:14 it follows the assertion of the "ascent" of the Son of Man so immediately that one can only conclude that for John the "ascent" takes the form of "exaltation", which means that we have here part of the primitive Christian heritage of the evangelist. No doubt he has re-interpreted and re-moulded it, (as he has done with the concept of "Son of Man") by making the "exaltation" of Jesus already take place on the Cross (see commentary on 3:14), but still the continuity and development of the Christian root is unmistakable. If then the "ascent" of the Son of Man is the "exaltation" (and "glorification") in John, it is probable that the author, viewing the "exaltation" as a vertical process in space, went from this to speak of "ascending".

Another principle was also at work, which may still be observed in 20:17. Here the risen Lord speaks only of "ascending". The corresponding "descent" is not mentioned, and this is certainly not accidental or merely due to the situation. The explanation is to be found in the ancient kerygma of resurrection and "ascension". No doubt the most ancient kerygma of the resurrection does not mention expressly Jesus's being "taken up" to heaven (but cf. Acts 3:21), but the thought had to take root, once Jesus was raised from death to life (Mk 16:6), to sit at the right hand of God (cf. Mk 14:62) and be established as universal Lord (cf. Mt 28:18; Acts 2:34 ff.). From this Luke developed his picture of the "bodily ascension" of Jesus, which he designated chiefly by the term ἀναλαμβάνεσθαι (Acts 1:2, 11, 22; cf. Lk 9:51) but once by ἀναβαίνειν (Acts 2:34 a), an expression which readily suggested itself (cf. also Rom 10:6, after Deut 30:12). John does not adopt the realistic and objectivating mode of presentation used by Luke, nor the linear view of the post-paschal event which distributed it into successive temporal phases, but the shares the objective theological thought of the "going to the Father" (cf. 13:1; 14:28; 16:5, 28; 17:11, 13), and in 20:17 expresses it in the form of "ascending".[32] This is spoken of in another ancient Christian hymn as

[32] See Thüsing, *Erhöhung*, pp. 263–75.

ἀνελήμφθη ἐν δόξῃ (1 Tim 3:16) and once in Luke as εἰσελθεῖν εἰς τὴν δόξαν αὐτοῦ (Lk 24:26), while John simply speaks of the "glorification" of Jesus (7:39; 12:23; 13:31f.; 17:1, 5). We may conclude that the set of concepts in which the post-paschal event of the enthronement of Jesus in heaven was enshrined was in some measure responsible for the Johannine expression "ascend", and so another of its roots in primitive Christianity has been discovered.

John does not speak of a "super-exaltation" of Christ. On the contrary, he considers the "glorification" of Jesus as the recovery of the glory which he possessed with the Father before the creation of the world (17:5, 24). But the notion that he now exercises a Lordship which was not his in this form in his pre-existence, is not absent. It is merely given a new Christological angle. After the glorification by the Father, the Son is to glorify the Father in turn, by communicating eternal life to believers. It is only then that he makes full and effective use of his ἐξουσία "over all flesh" and so in fact exercises his Lordship as saviour (cf. 17:1f.).[33] Thus the parallel between the pre-existence of Christ and his state of glory after the exaltation is more marked in John. Theoretically, one might say that he was led to this position by the conceptual schema of "descent and ascent". But the opposite process is also thinkable, that his Christological perspective of Jesus's recovering his former glory (and now being able to radiate it to the redeemed) produced the correlatives of "descent and ascent". The second alternative becomes more probable when one recalls that the real interest of the evangelist is the communication of divine life to a "world" of men in the grip of death. The Christological is ultimately, we must remember, in the service of the theological: God loved the world so much that he gave his only Son, so that the world could be given eternal life through him (3:16). For this, the Son has to take the way of "exaltation" to attain his glory where those who believe in him can rejoin him (cf. 14:3f.; 17:24). Since this is the divine plan, the goal of Christ's way becomes of special importance and dominates the thinking of the evangelist, as may be seen for instance from 6:62, "When, then, you see the Son of Man going up to where he was before". Attention is focussed on the pre-existence of Christ, since this alone provides the full explanation of his majesty and dignity, his power and authority. This was also the main reason, as we saw, for the prologue (or the Logos hymn) being prefixed to the Gospel (see Intro. to prologue). Johannine Christology is not modelled on a set pattern of mythological speculation about a redeemer descending from heaven and returning there again. It is rather the desire to establish clearly the Christian revealer's power to save that leads to the

---

[33] *Ibid.*, pp. 190f.

emphasis on his pre-existence, so that now his "way" is seen more clearly to begin from "above" and to return there once more.

Confirmation of this view may be had from the revelation discourse which develops most largely the theme of the "descent from heaven" and the "ascent" thither—the discourse on the bread of life in ch. 6. Why does it affirm so emphatically that "the bread of God is that which comes down from heaven and gives life to the world" (v. 33; cf. 41, 42, 50, 51, 58)? Because it deals with the question of salvation and intends to prove that hitherto men had not had the true divine life, enduring and imperishable, not even through the manna, the "heavenly" gift which Israel received through Moses in the blessed days of its desert wanderings. For this, he who was really in heaven had to come, he who "descended" and as such, being above all earthly things (3:31) and invested with the fullness of divine authority (3:35) and of the Spirit (3:34), is alone able to impart the Spirit and life of God, though only fully effectively when he has "ascended" again (6:62). This, then, was the starting-point for reflection on the origin and nature of Jesus, and for the development of the notion of "descent". It was dictated, as we can see, by authentic and primordial Christian interests and the course it took remains in continuity with its Jewish pre-suppositions.

The notion of "descent", however, as we have already seen, is also prepared for by Jewish Wisdom speculation, which is also the main source of the notion of pre-existence as applied to Christ, as has been proved for Paul by E. Schweizer in particular.[34] The same line of thought was probably also at work in the discourse on the bread of life, Jn 6, since Wisdom likewise invites men to eat her bread and drink her wine (Prov 9:1–6), to eat their fill of her produce (Ecclus 24:19 cf. 21; 51:24).[35] Thus the trains of thought converge: in the prologue, the Logos possesses real pre-existence, is active at creation like Wisdom, and later dwells among men, without mention of a "descent". According to the discourse on the bread, the true bread of life descends from heaven, and like Wisdom, Jesus invites men to come to him to hunger no more, to believe in him to thirst no more (6:35). Must not John have drawn his inspiration from the same source when he spoke of the "descent"? No doubt, he goes on to link "descent and ascent" with the "Son of Man" (3:13; cf. 6:62). But in Johannine Christology, the most diverse impulses and aspects are merged into a consistent composition: along with the notion of the "Son of Man" there is also that of the "Son" who is sent by the Father and returns to him, and that of the Logos of the Wisdom type who was with God and

---

[34] Schweizer, "Die Herkunft der Präexistenzvorstellung bei Paulus"; id., *Erniedrigung und Erhöhung*, pp. 99f.

[35] Cf. Feuillet, *Études Johanniques*, pp. 72–76.

pitched his tent among men. The evangelist may and must be credited with the final amalgamation of the various elements.

There remains the similarity of terms and categories with the Gnostic myth of the redeemer. But it is well to remember that the descent and ascent of the soul was spoken of in Hellenism long before the existence of any developed form of Gnosis,[36] though the redeemer myth, strictly speaking, is not known prior to Gnosis. It may be supposed, therefore, that the fourth evangelist, in his effort to import the Christian message into his Hellenistic environment, paid some attention to it in his choice of terms. But his message was not derived from it, since he developed it on the basis of Jewish and early Christian presuppositions. There may be assimilation to the Gnostic redeemer myth, but the root or source is not there. If the evangelist was prepared to listen to the questions put by Gnosticism, he gave, nonetheless, a completely different and authentically Christian answer.

---

[36] Cf. Schweizer, *Erniedrigung und Erhöhung*, pp. 151–5.

EXCURSUS VII

The Notion of Faith in the Fourth Gospel

Jn 4 treats of faith, as man's response to Jesus's revelation, from many aspects and with considerable urgency. Throughout the whole of the Gospel one can recognize the supreme importance which the evangelist accords to faith. If one comes to it from the Synoptics, one is struck at once even by the mere numerical frequency with which the verb "to believe" occurs in John (98 times, against 11 times in Matthew, 14 in Mark, 9 in Luke), though without the substantive "faith", which only occurs once in the Johannine writings outside Revelation, in 1 Jn 5:4. In the Pauline writings, we meet the verb 54 times, and the substantive 142, so that faith is equally emphasized by Paul and John, though the accents are different. Then "faith" in John has developed largely in meaning and nature beyond the Synoptics, in which it remains more closely linked to the situation (faith at miracles of healing) or is understood as a charismatic force (Mk 11:22 parr.), whereas in John it appears as a fundamental and comprehensive decision and attitude towards the eschatological envoy of God and his saving revelation. In a word: faith in John has attained a markedly theological eminence, in which it resembles that of Paul. But in contrast to Paul, for whom faith in the crucified and risen Lord is all-important, John brings faith into his account of the earthly work of Jesus and makes it unfold in the encounter with the redeemer during his life in this world, though its bearing on the time after Easter is always made apparent, and is explicitly stated in the concluding sentence, Jesus's answer to Thomas (20:29).

The evangelist is thus enabled to describe exactly the coming and the growth of faith, the motives it springs from and the dangers it runs (as also those of unbelief), and at the same time bring out the fundamental soteriological significance of faith as the one thing demanded for salvation. Paul opposes faith to the "works of the law" as the one way of salvation, demonstrated by free redemption in grace through the blood of Jesus. But this antithesis is echoed at most once in John (cf. 6:29 with 28), and in its place, faith is positively presented as the one answer of man which is in keeping with the eschatological revelation and can lead to salvation. These differences spring from theological perspectives and historical conditions, and need not detain us longer. It is enough to note that Paul and John accord the same theological importance to faith, which shows that they are in accord as to the nature of the Christian way of salvation. The kinship of Pauline and Johannine theology is also apparent from the fact that these two great Christian thinkers do not specifically mention the μετάνοια which is urged so strongly in the preaching of Jesus in the Synoptics. They have clearly merged the call to repentance with that to faith, and have derived from faith only one further basic imperative of Christian existence, charity. In Paul, faith is to become effective in love (Gal 5:6); in John, fraternal charity becomes the one "new commandment" of Christ (13:34f.; 15:12f., 17; 1 Jn *passim*; faith and love together, 1 Jn 3:23). Faith and love sum up for John all the demands imposed on the disciple of Christ. This is the fruit of a profound and concentrated theological effort.[1]

So many aspects come to light when we examine the Johannine concept of faith[2] that it is not possible to treat them all in an excursus. We shall merely try to stress the special characteristics of Johannine faith and to situate this fundamental demand of the last evangelist in its historical setting, to find as it were the *Sitz im Leben* or actual background of Johannine Christianity. We shall begin with a survey of the linguistic usage (vocabulary) and then extend our observations to take in equivalent or allied terms (field of thought), so that we can then grasp the "nature" of Johannine faith, understand the evangelist's interest in the call to faith, the awakening of faith and the pedagogy of faith, and finally strive to sound the depths of his theological conception of faith.

1. *Vocabulary*

The following list will give a survey of Johannine usage:

πιστεύειν εἰς with acc.: 1:12; 2:11, 23; 3:16, 18a 18bβ, 36; 4:39, 6:29, 35, 40; 7:5, 31, 38, 39, 48; 8:30; 9:35, 36; 10:42; 11:25, 26a, 45, 48; 12:11, 36, 37, 42, 44 *(bis)*, 46; 14:6 *(bis)*, 12; 16:9; 17:20 (36 times).

---

[1] Cf. Schnackenburg, *Die Sittliche Botschaft des Neuen Testaments*, pp. 255–60, E. T.: *The Moral Teaching*, pp. 316–22.

[2] Special literature on Johannine faith: Weber, *Die Vollendung des neutestamentlichen Glaubenszeugnisses durch Johannes;* Schlatter, *Der Glaube im Neuen Testament*, pp. 176–221, 486–520, 595–600; Huby, "De la connaissance de foi dans s. Jean"; Schnackenburg, *Der Glaube im vierten Evangelium;* Braun, "L'accueil de la foi selon s. Jean"; Bonningues, *La foi dans l'évangile de s. Jean;* Mollat, "La foi dans le quatrième évangile"; Philips, "Faith

πιστεύειν with dat.: 2:22; 4:21, 50; 5:24, 38, 46 *(bis)*, 47 *(bis)*; 6:30; 8:31, 45, 46; 10:37, 38 *(bis)*; 12:38 (in an O.T. quotation); 14:11a (18 times).

πιστεύειν ὅτι . . . : 4:21 *(vid. supr.)*; 6:69; 8:24; 11:27, 42; 13:19; 14:10, 11a *(vid. supr.)*; 16:27, 30; 17:8, 21; 20:31a (13 times).

πιστεύειν used absolutely: 1:7, 50; 3:12 *(bis)*; 15:18bα; 4:41, 42, 48, 53; 5:44; 6:36, 47, 64a, 64bβ; 9:38; 10:25, 26; 11:15, 40; 12:39; 14:11b, 29; 16:31; 19:35; 20:8, 25, 29 *(bis)* 31b (30 times).

πιστεύειν with neuter acc.: 11:26b (once)

Special construction and non-religious usage: 2:24; 9:18.

The construction used oftenest is πιστεύειν εἰς, which seems to be the key-expression for the Johannine thought on the subject. Unfortunately, scholars differ as to its interpretation. Some, especially among the older Protestant exegetes, see in it a confident dedication of oneself to the person of Jesus which leads to salvation; others, especially among Catholic exegetes, see in it the recognition of Jesus's claim, an assent which can be expressed in the form of articulate (credal) statements.[3] In this approach, confessional interests dictated by different concepts of faith seem to predominate; it should be avoided as far as possible, so that the principles and categories of John itself may be clearly seen.

It is important to note, to begin with, that faith, followed by εἰς with the accusative, is directed almost exclusively to the person of Jesus, the only exception being 14:1, where Jesus speaks of God as the object in which the disciples believe (or should believe). This exception should certainly be explained by the situation of leave-taking. The disciples are to draw from their faith or confidence in God the strength and motive for their faith in Jesus, because their hearts could be "troubled" by his Passion. Hence in the high priestly prayer Jesus commends his disciples to the immediate care of the Father during this time (17:11 ff.). Elsewhere, faith is always directed to Jesus, and this is the most marked characteristic of Johannine faith. To believe means to accept the self-revelation of Jesus and to attach oneself to this unique mediator of salvation to attain eternal life (3:36 etc.).

We are justified, therefore, in speaking of a personal allegiance to Jesus Christ, a dedication of oneself; but the element of confidence is not essential to this. It should not, indeed, be excluded, in view of the

---

and Vision in the Fourth Gospel"; Decourtray, "La conception johannique de la foi"; Bultmann, "πιστεύω", pp. 224–30; Grundmann, "Verständnis und Bewegung des Glaubens im Johannesevangelium"; Schlier, "Glauben, Erkennen und Lieben nach dem Johannesevangelium"; Willocx, *La notion de foi dans le quatrième évangile* (with comprehensive bibliography); Vanhoye, "Notre foi, oeuvre divine, d'après le quatrième évangile".

[3] See Schnackenburg, *Der Glaube*, pp. 1 ff., 6–11; Willocx, *La notion de foi*, pp. 70–80.

underlying Hebrew הֶאֱמִין and the biblical notion of faith in general.[4] It is certainly implied in Jesus's appeal to the Samaritan (4:21) and in 14:1, cited above. But it does not play a decisive role in John. A survey of the vocabulary rather makes it certain that in John "to believe in Jesus" means above all to acknowledge his claims for his own person. 1. In many texts, πιστεύειν εἰς is on the same footing as a ὅτι-clause, cf. 4:39 with 42; 11:45 with 42; 14:12 with 11; 17:20b with 8 and 21d. 2. Several of the formulae attached to πιστεύειν εἰς show that it is a matter of acknowledging certain claims of Jesus. This is clear from εἰς τὸ ὄνομα αὐτοῦ, 1:12; 2:23, and even more so from εἰς τὸ ὄνομα τοῦ μονογενοῦς υἱοῦ τοῦ θεοῦ, 3:18; note also εἰς ὃν ἀπέστειλεν ἐκεῖνος, 6:29, εἰς τὸ φῶς, 12:36, and εἰς τὸν υἱὸν τοῦ ἀνθρώπου, 9:35. 3. Sometimes a passage which takes the place of πιστεύειν εἰς shows that it is a matter of acknowledging the claims of Jesus. In 7:31 the sentence ὁ Χριστὸς ὅταν ἔλθῃ κτλ is clearly meant to be an explanation of ἐπίστευσαν εἰς αὐτόν. We may also compare 7:48 with 52; 11:25f. with the confession of v. 27; 10:42 with 41c. 4. Finally, it sometimes follows from the whole situation that πιστεύειν εἰς means an attitude of acceptance. The faith demanded by Jesus in 6:35d consists of acknowledging him as the bread of life (v. 35b); 6:40 belongs to the same context. Disbelief is primarily the denial of the Messiahship of Jesus (cf. 6:64 with 41f.; 7:5, 26f., 31, 41). Hence too the soteriological texts of 3:16, 18, 36; 5:24 etc. are not to be taken in the sense of a *fides fiducialis*. Faith in Jesus is named merely as the presupposition or condition of "the Son's" giving life to believers, and this faith is the same as that invariably called for elsewhere in the Gospel, the acceptance and acknowledgment of this unique mediator of salvation.

When πιστεύειν is used absolutely, the form second in frequency, the content can mostly be determined by the context, especially in 1:7, 50; 3:15, 18bα; 4:41, 42; 5:44; 6:36, 47; 9:38, 10:25, 26; 12:39; 14:11b; 16:31; 20:8, 25, 29 (bis) 31. The context is unclear or completely unhelpful in 4:48, 53; 6:64a, 64bα; 11:15, 40; 14:29. A special object must be supposed in 3:12; 19:35. When we supply what is implicit in these texts, it appears once more that they also involve a claim on the part of Jesus, which the believer is to acknowledge. Often the absolute πιστεύειν means the Johannine faith in the fullest sense (cf. 20:31), as in 1:7; 3:15, 18; 4:41, 53; 6:47; 9:38; 11:40 etc.

We must note particularly πιστεύειν with the dative, which has often been said to be essentially the same as π. εἰς with the accusative. This view is supported by the interchangeability of בְּ and לְ after הֶאֱמִין But the equivalence can be established only for 1 Jn 3:23, (τῷ ὀνόματι) compared with Jn 1:12; 3:18c; 20:31b (εἰς τὸ ὄνομα). The texts where

[4] On the notion of faith see Weiser, "πιστεύω".

the dative, like the accusative, refers to Jesus (4:21; 5:38, 46b; 6:30; 8:31, 45, 46; 10:37, 38a) or his words (2:22; 4:15; 5:47b) are explained by Bultmann as meaning that in the kerygma, the Christ who is preached encounters men and speaks to them himself.[5] This interpretation, which appeals to the "kerygma" as such, and hence is a theological development (not justified by the text), recognizes correctly that where the dative is used the words of Jesus are involved. This follows from the explicit mention in 2:22; 4:50 and 5:47b, and is also clear from 10:37f. and 14:11, where the dative of the person indicates, along with the "works", the motive of faith, and in fact the higher motive: he who does not believe the mere word of Jesus should at least believe his works. However, along with Jesus and his words, other persons and things appear as the object of πιστεύειν with the dative: the Father who sent Jesus (5:24), the Scriptures (2:22), Moses (5:46) or his writings (5:47), the works of Jesus (10:38). The only reasonable explanation of this usage is to be found in the section on μαρτυρία, (5:31–47). The dative designates the witness or the testimony, and here everyone and everything appealed to testify to Jesus. In the list of witnesses, 5:31–36, John the Baptist (where the image of the lamp takes the place of "believe him") is followed by the works (v. 36), the Father himself (v. 37), the Scriptures (vv. 39f.) or Moses and his writings (vv. 46f.). But Jesus himself is also a witness to his revelation. His own testimony is already fully valid of itself (8:14) and to believe his mere word is the highest degree of faith from the point of view of motive (see above). All the datives used of Jesus can be consistently explained in this way (cf. especially 5:38, 46b in the list of witnesses), even 8:31, where in view of v. 30 one might be included at first to make it synonymous with πιστεύειν εἰς.

It is also of great importance theologically that Johannine faith is always referred to witnesses and testimony. John insists on the "foundations of the faith" which enable the seeker to give a rational assent to the message of Christ; but the motivation is not purely rational, it is in keeping with the nature of N.T. revelation. It provides sufficient light for the reason but still does not spare man the need for his personal decision, for submitting to God as he reveals himself in Christ, for the obedience of faith (cf. 3:36b). This feature appears throughout the whole of the N.T. revelation, and is merely more strongly marked in John. But the Johannine concept of testimony[6] has some traits of its own:

---

[5] In "πιστεύω", p. 224, 38f.

[6] Cf. Trépanier, "Contribution à une recherche de l'idée de témoin dans les écrits johanniques"; Strathmann, "μαρτυρία", pp. 502ff.; Vergote, *Het getuigenis-thema in het vierde evangelie;* Vanhoye, "Témoignage et vie en Dieu selon le quatrième évangile"; de la Potterie, "La notion de témoignage dans S. Jean"; Brox, *Zeuge und Märtyrer*, pp. 70–92; Blank, *Krisis*, pp. 198–226.

the gradation of the witnesses and testimony (see commentary on 5:31–47), Jesus's own testimony, seen in the closest unity with that of the Father, as fully sufficient and indeed the supreme and decisive testimony (see commentary on 8:14–18); and the ensuing "Christological concentration". Jesus is not merely the one object of faith because the full revelation is given in him. He is also the source in which the believer finds the deepest motive and the surest foundation of his faith, because he is attested by God, attests himself in God and is continually attested as such in the apostolic testimony (cf. 1 Jn 5:9 with the commentary and excursus *ad loc.*).

Finally, the texts where πιστεύειν is followed by a ὅτι-clause confirm the fact that for John Jesus Christ is the one "object" and "content" of faith. All these texts proclaim Jesus as the Christ and Son of God or contain Christological formulae which take up an aspect of the fundamental confession (6:69; 11:27; 20:31 a) to develop it and explore its depths. Thus for instance we hear that Jesus is in the Father and the Father in him (14:10, 11), or that he has come forth from God (16:27; cf. 30) or that the Father has sent him (11:42; 17:8, 21). Particular significance must be attached to the two-fold occurrence of the formula ἐγώ εἰμι in the absolute sense (8:24; 13:19). This is the most pregnant expression of Jesus's claim to be the divine revealer in the strict sense, the eschatological presence of God in his self-disclosure. It demands, therefore, from the believer only that he accepts this claim of Jesus and hence Jesus himself as the eschatological revealer and saviour. This confirms once more our interpretation of π. εἰς (cf. 6:29); this "faith in Jesus" to which the promise of salvation is attached is the same faith which is made explicit in the ὅτι-clause. Only once does such a ὅτι-clause contain a rather special content, in a text where the πιστεύειν itself has not the usual ring of Johannine "faith" (see above and *ad loc.*). This is 4:21, where Jesus says to the Samaritan that the hour is coming when the Samaritans will worship the Father neither on Mt Gerizim nor in Jerusalem. But even here the content is still connected with the person of Jesus (cf. 4:23).

2. *Associated terms*

The personal union of the believer with the revealer is also expressed by other terms which can stand for the Johannine faith. In the prologue the phrase "they did not accept him", 1:11, is taken up by the evangelist in 12 with "but those who received him" (ἔλαβον for the compound παρέλαβον), and this expression "to receive him"—remarkable in Greek for a personal relationship—is peculiar to John and serves as a stylistic criterion (see *ad loc.*). It occurs again in the same sense in 5:43 and 13:20;

the synoptic parallels to 13:20 all have δέχεσθαι. It may, therefore, be only a peculiarity of style, but its closeness to Johannine faith is clear from the equivalents, "to receive our testimony" (3:11), "to receive my words" (12:48; 17:8). To "receive" Jesus's words and "accept" them inwardly is to accept the revealer himself along with his revelation and so to "believe" as John understands it. The text of the prologue suggests the idea of someone approaching, as does 5:43. But this image of Jesus "coming" to men has its counterpart, that of believers "coming to him". As is particularly clear in ch. 6, ἔρχεσθαι πρός can be a synonym for πιστεύειν. In v. 35 it is parallel to πιστεύειν εἰς, and the expression is retained in the following (vv. 37, 44f., 65). It can be seen from the context that the metaphor in v. 37 is that of a flock. The Father entrusts to the Son those who are to belong to his flock of believers, and "will lead them to him". But the Son drives no one away who "comes" to him (as he is "drawn" by the Father, cf. vv. 44f.); he keeps him and saves him from perishing (6:38; cf. also 17:12). John understands the relationship of faith to Jesus as a very personal one, but he does not forget that believers form a united fellowship around Jesus and indeed that this community of believers is intended and predestined by God. Where the moral element in the decision of faith is prominent, the evangelist can also speak of "coming" to Jesus, under the symbolism of light in 3:20f. ("to come to the light") or depicting the negative aspect ("you refuse to . . .") in 5:40. And again, Jesus can give the invitation, "Whoever thirsts, let him come to me and drink" (7:37) and the subsequent ὁ πιστεύων εἰς ἐμέ (whatever its antecedent) confirms the meaning "to believe" for "to come". In the light of this usage, possibly the "coming" of the first disciples (1:40, 47f.) or of other men (cf. 3:2, 26; 4:30) to Jesus may imply something more than a mere physical approach. "To follow" is part of the same field of thought (cf. 1:37f., 41, 44). In 8:12 it means the following in faith which is always possible, and in the parable of the shepherd (10:4, 5, 27) to listen with faith to Jesus the shepherd (10:3, 8, 16, 27).[7]

Hence faith also can be described as "hearing" the voice or the words of Jesus (cf. also 5:24; 6:45; 8:43, 47; 12:47; 18:37), in the sense of "obeying" (cf. the negative 3:36b). Here we see how faith on the part of man corresponds to Jesus's revelation which is chiefly given in words. But "hearing" must be an inward hearing; it means "learning" from the Father (6:45) and accepting, keeping and following out the words of the revealer (cf. 8:51f.; 14:23f.; 15:20; 17:6). Believers must "abide in" the word of Jesus (8:31)—a text which links up at once with the moral

[7] On "following" as a synonym for believing, see Schulz, *Nachfolgen und Nachahmen*, pp. 172–6.

element in faith, the "keeping of the commandments" of Jesus, the working out of faith in love.

Other verbs which are associated with faith are "to see" (6:40; 12:45) and especially "to know". "To see" Jesus in faith points to the peculiar character of Christian revelation, namely that men "see" the Father in him, and only in him (14:9). The verb γινώσκειν is used particularly often, and its close relationship to πιστεύειν has often been noted and studied.[8] It occurs 56 times in John, sometimes parallel to "believe" (cf. 14:7 with 10; 17:8b with c; 17:21d with 23c; also 6:69?) sometimes as a "higher" degree of faith or a stage of its development (cf. 8:28 with 24; especially 10:38; also 12:16; 13:7; 14: 20). In 6:69, Cyril of Alexandria[9] and Augustine[10] already tried to find the movement *a fide ad intellectum;* but this intellectualistic interpretation of γινώσκειν must be rejected, if only by reason of the biblical concept of "knowing",[11] which is also retained in John (cf. especially the reciprocal "knowledge" in 10:14f., and the "knowledge of God" in 8:55; 14:7; 16:3; 17:25; the negative with οἶδα 8:19, 55; 15:21). "Knowledge" in John has many aspects and relationships. In proximity to "faith" it must often indicate a greater clarity of faith (cf. 6:69; 10:38; 14:20), though not in the sense of a clearer rational understanding, but rather as "faith's own understanding".[12] We must always remember that "to know" in biblical thought is always an act which institutes or reinforces fellowship. Hence "faith" can certainly grow into "knowledge" and it is surely no accident that the latter term occurs more frequently in the farewell discourse in ch. 14 and the high priestly prayer in ch. 17. But the very fact that faith brings about fellowship with the revealer and life-giver means that it at once contains such knowledge. The two concepts complete one another: faith opens out to an ever deeper knowledge, a closer union with the person "known", to greater love of him; "knowledge", at least on earth, is bound up with faith and hence preserved from the misunderstandings of mysticism or Gnosticism. Elsewhere "knowledge" retain its own proper meaning. It refers to other objects and truths than Jesus Christ and his

---

[8] Richter, *Das Verhältnis der Begriffe* πιστεύειν *und* γινώσκειν *im Evangelium und in den Briefen des Johannes;* Schnackenburg, *Der Glaube*, pp. 11–17; Bultmann, "πιστεύω", pp. 228ff.; Willocx, *La notion de foi*, pp. 152–73.

[9] *Ad loc.* (*PG*, col. 628).

[10] *In Jo.*, tr. XXVII, 9 (*Corpus Christianorum*, p. 274); so also Thomas Aquinas, *ad loc.* (Cai, p. 189), Schanz and others.

[11] Cf. Bultmann, "γινώσκω", pp. 696–700, 711ff.; Botterweck, "*Gott erkennen*" *im Sprachgebrauch des Alten Testaments;* Féret, *Connaissance biblique de Dieu;* de la Potterie, "Οἶδα et γινώσκω. Les deux modes de la connaissance dans le quatrième évangile"; Schlier, "Glauben, Erkennen, Lieben".

[12] R. Bultmann, "γινώσκω", p. 713, 21, E. T.: *Gnosis*, p. 50.

revelation. In the relationship of the Son and the Father there can be no question of faith, but only of "knowledge". Faith gives eternal life, the "knowledge" of the one true God which leads to fellowship is eternal life (17:3).

Johannine faith is also strongly centred on confessing. The term ὁμολογεῖν is rare in the Gospel (1:20, of the Baptist; elsewhere only in 9:22; 12:42) but there are in fact a large number of confessions of faith, and in the epistles stereotyped confessional formulae are introduced by ὁμολογεῖν (1 Jn 2:23; 4:2f., 15; 2 Jn 7). The evangelist attaches importance to the various confessions of faith which he records of various individuals (Nathanael, 1:49; Simon Peter, 6:68f.; the man born blind, 9:38; Martha, 11:27; Thomas, 20:28) or of groups (the people of Sychar, 4:42; also the Galileans after the multiplication of the loaves, 6:14). He selects and varies carefully the titles of Jesus, his intention being to give examples, since faith in Jesus should be professed by means of confessions (cf. 12:42). Johannine faith is intrinsically ordained to confessing; it is a faith to be expressed in Christological confessions, which must persevere in face of unbelief (in the Gospel) and heresy (in 1 John) and is also probably meant to be developed in the liturgy (cf. excursus iii). Here we see part of the historical background of the Johannine concept of faith, though it is not a complete explanation of it.

Finally, Johannine faith is most intimately connected with discipleship. The faith of the Twelve, the disciples in the stricter sense, is stressed at the very beginning (2:11); the evangelist continues to concern himself with their faith, even in the supper room (6:67 ff.; 13:19; 14:1, 10 ff., 29; 16:27, 30f.; 17:8), and then again after the Resurrection (20:8, 25–29). It is important to note that there is also a wider concept of discipleship in Jn (cf. 4:1; 6:60, 66; 7:3; 8:31; 9:28; 19:38) which means practically the same as "to believe in Jesus" in the full sense of the word. This "discipleship" which consists of faith points clearly to the time of the Church, after Easter (cf. the usage in Acts)[13] and merely serves to confirm the basically theological and exemplary sense of Johannine faith. "Following" in the sense of making the full act of faith (see above) provides the connecting link. We can also see from the "example of the disciples", however, including the Twelve, what full and genuine faith should be: adhering decidedly to Jesus, remaining steadfastly with him, even when the "scandal" of his words has to be overcome (cf. 6:60f., 66), abiding in his word (8:31) and, an important point, openly professing faith in him (cf. 9:28–38; 19:38). "Discipleship" of Christ in this sense is an active faith which is exercised in deeds as well as in words and which perseveres in fraternal charity (13:34f.; 15:8).

[13] See K. H. Rengstorf, "μαθητής", pp. 426f.

Thus the words associated with faith, its affinities with other important concepts, throw more light on the nature of the Johannine faith. It is the reception of the revelation proclaimed by Jesus, the personal acceptance of this unique revealer and saviour, personal union with him in a growing understanding, open confession and active love according to his commandments and example.

3. Faith and salvation

The Johannine faith, which is thus centred on Christ, gains its true significance only from the promise of salvation which Christ makes to believers. It is mostly expressed in the formula, "He who believes in the Son has eternal life" (3:36a; cf. 3:15, 16; 6:40, 47; 20:31; 1 Jn 5:13). Behind this is the idea of total liberation from the realm of death (cf. 3:36b.; 8:24). The believer, though he suffers physical death, does not die the death of estrangement from God which would put an end to his true existence (cf. 11:25f.). Or, to put it differently, he does not come under the wrath of God's judgment or his sentence of death (3:18; 5:24). The believer has passed or crossed over from the realm of death to the realm of divine life (5:24; 1 Jn 3:14). The same thought is expressed under the symbol of light, which is closely connected with "life". He does not remain in darkness (12:46), he has become a "son of light" (12:36) and "will have the light of life" (8:12). All these expression depict the transition from misery and ruin to salvation and well-being, a transition which is accomplished in the decision of faith and which is permanently effective; the decision is one which is valid to the end, really definitive, "eschatological". Whatever be the verdict on the concepts here employed,[14] they give an impressive picture of the deliverance of man, the fundamental change in his situation in terms of disaster and well-being. All that is demanded of man is faith, as it has been described above according to the mind of John; this is the decisive step. Thus Johannine faith has a soteriological as well as a Christological character; the aspects are equally important and closely allied.

A comparison with the Synoptics on the one hand and with Paul on the other again allows us to see more clearly the theological purposes and emphases which are here involved. In the earlier evangelists, the significance of faith for salvation is given only in a subdued tone, as it were. It is to be heard especially in Jesus's answer to those he has healed, "Your faith has saved you" (Mk 5:34 parr.; 10:52 parr.; Lk 17:19), a formula which actually refers to the bodily healing but already has, in

---

[14] See esp. F. Mussner, ΖΩΗ, pp. 52–56, 93–98; Blank, *Krisis*, pp. 91–100, 127–34.

particular for the believing readers of later times, the deeper meaning of the salvation of the whole man. Luke also uses it for the word of pardon which Jesus speaks to the sinful woman (7:50), and he introduces the mention of the faith that saves into the explanation of the parable of the sower (8:12); it is found in Mark only in the secondary ending (16:16). On the whole the Synoptics preserve faithfully the memory of Jesus's reserve in demanding direct faith in his person, though they make it clear from their whole presentation that the saving faith in Jesus Christ, the Messiah and Son of God, of which the community was certain after Easter, is based on and justified by the words and conduct of the earthly Jesus. It is proclaimed openly by Jesus in John; faith in Jesus as the Son of God is demanded as explicitly as Jesus speaks of his divine Sonship.

Paul presents to faith the death and resurrection of Christ as the salvific events (Rom 4:24f.; 10:9) in which God has accomplished his gratuitous deliverance, and from this enlarges on the Christian way of salvation as the antithesis to the Jewish way based on the works of the law. It has been asserted that John is not concerned with the question of the way of salvation when he speaks of faith, but is fighting for the true understanding of salvation itself.[15] This is correct, in so far as the antithesis has disappeared and he is concerned rather with the positive significance of faith. But he too still affirms that the Christian way of salvation is in virtue of faith, though the positions which he rejects are different. He opposes it to Judaism, in so far as it denies the Messiahship of Jesus, and above all to the various concepts of salvation current in Hellenism, in particular, no doubt, the Gnostic doctrine that man must free himself by Gnosis and essential insight and so escape from the bonds of matter, the oppression of the lower world or worlds, re-discovering his true self and ascending into the heavenly world of light and life. Faith, and in the concrete, faith directed to the historical redeemer Jesus Christ, become the antithesis of a Gnosis immanent to man and disjoined from history (cf. 1 John). John did not merely bring out (exactly like Paul) the central function of faith within the Christian message of salvation, as the one decision and attitude demanded of man, and affirm its critical significance in eliminating other ways of salvation, but he also (like Paul for his day) confronted his own times and his own situation with the challenge of faith and formulated it accordingly.

When we consider the promise of salvation made to believers, it is noteworthy that eternal life is promised as a gift in the present life. John does not look like Paul mainly to the eschatological future, to the judgment of God in which the believer is definitively made righteous and saved (though righteousness is already effective and a new existence is

[15] Bultmann, "πιστεύω", p. 225, 12ff.

given in Christ); he concentrates on the salvation already acquired in the present (though this too only displays its full glory at the end). This new accentuation—for that is all it is—is probably occasioned by the nature of the audience for which the Gospel was destined and the cultural environment, among other factors. Where the Jewish heritage and Jewish thought cease to predominate, there is less interest in the last act of the cosmic process and more in the immediate renewal of human existence, in the essential life of man. John meets this quest and yearning by preaching a Christ who confers on believers a birth from above (3:3 ff.) and divine, eternal life which delivers them from the baneful realm of death and can never be lost if they remain united to the heavenly envoy and life-giver, in his word and in his love. Every substantial element of the Christian doctrine of salvation is preserved, even the future "resurrection to life" after death (5:29; 6:39f.); but all the emphasis is on the present possession of the life and strength which is imparted and constantly sustained by the divine envoy and bringer of divine life (5:26). Here as in Paul a new understanding of existence is expressed, though the categories and presuppositions are somewhat different. John has reinterpreted the Christian message for his readers, but the basic attitude which he demands is still the same, faith in Christ, the Messiah and the Son of God.

4. The genesis and growth of faith; the testing and the triumph of faith

But it is chiefly the community of believers that John addresses on the subject of their faith (20:30f.). He is aware that their faith in Christ does not go unchallenged. It is true that it is only from the great epistle that we learn that heretics and seducers have penetrated their ranks (1 Jn 2:18 ff.) and are spreading their propaganda energetically in the world (4:1–6). But simular circumstances must be assumed for the readers of the Gospel and their environment. The evangelist aims at strengthening and deepening the Christian faith (20:30f.), first by recalling the clear self-revelation of Jesus and then by showing his readers the nature and characteristics of genuine faith.

A number of examples serve to show how faith is prepared for by the testimony of others (the first disciples, 1:35–51; the people of Sychar, 4:29f., 39f.) and brought about and developed by the encounter with Jesus himself. The latter is decisive; it is only when speaking to Jesus that the disciples of John are fully convinced of the Messiahship of Jesus and the scepticism of Nathanael is broken down; the Samaritans affirm that their faith is based on Jesus's own word, and only make their full profession of faith in Jesus as "saviour of the world" when they have met him in person (4:41f.). The man born blind likewise arrives at a full confession of his faith only in face of Jesus (9:38). The Samaritan woman is an example of how Jesus leads men gradually to faith in his Messiahship. It is always this personal encounter with Jesus in the Gospel that seems to give the final impulse to faith; when he is present confidence grows, faith finds in him new strength and inspiration, and attains greater depth and solidity, as can also be seen in the case of Martha (11:21–27, 40) and Thomas (20:27 ff.). Here the evangelist is speaking of actual encounters with the Son of God during his life on earth; but, as he gives us to understand by the final words of the risen Lord to Thomas (20:29) and the last verses of the Gospel (20:30f.), such an encounter still remains possible even for later readers, not by direct "sight" of Christ whose coming is a matter of history, but by hearing the apostolic testimony (cf. 17:20). The exalted Lord still continues to address his community, and it is still possible to follow him in faith (8:12) and, as we may legitimately presume, personal encounter and fellowship are likewise possible.

The genesis and growth of faith, its trials and its triumphs, its human inadequacy which can still gain firmness from Jesus, its constant fragility which can still be overcome by the memory of Jesus's word (cf. 13:19; 14:29; 16:4), in a word, the whole dynamism of the life of faith is certainly portrayed by the evangelist, and his chief means of doing so is the faith of the disciples. He is preoccupied with it throughout the whole of the Gospel; much of the earthly work of their master was obscure and enigmatic to the disciples, but they come to understand it in the light of the Resurrection, as the evangelist twice affirms by the comments which he inserts (2:22; 12:16). The final understanding of the words of Jesus is only given them by the Paraclete, the Holy Spirit, who teaches them all things and reminds them of all that Jesus has said to them (14:26)—the Spirit of truth who leads them to the full truth of the revelation of Christ (16:13). This is clearly meant to be addressed to later believers as well, who are to regard the testimony of Jesus's earthly companions and that of the Paraclete as a single unity (cf. 15:26f.).[16] The constant mistakes and slowness of the disciples (cf. 4:33; 14:5, 8; 16:17 ff., 29 ff.), the feeble grasp they have of his way (cf. 11:8, 16; 18:10f.), their naive contradiction of their master's words (cf. 13:37; 16:29f.)—all this is a typical example of the human way of thinking, which Jesus, nonetheless, bears with patiently. They still have the will to believe, the basic attitude of faith, which is steadfast under trials and assaults, as is clear from the "crisis" after the multiplication of the loaves, where Simon

[16] See Mussner, "Die johanneischen Parakletsprüche und die apostolische Tradition", esp. p. 67.

Peter utters the decisive word, "To whom should we go? You have the words of eternal life" (6:68). This confirms once more that faith is ultimately personal union with the revealer, and still clings to his words, even when they seem unintelligible and repugnant (cf. 6:61 ff.).Faith is called upon to overcome the scandal of Jesus's words and way.

Hence too Jesus acknowledges the faith of his disciples. In spite of their persistent misapprehensions he can tell them in the supper room, "The Father himself loves you, because you have loved me, and have believed that I came forth from God" (16:27), which is again an indication of the character of total, personal dedication of faith, because it is joined to "love". In the high priestly prayer Jesus also speaks without reserves of the faith of his disciples (17:8; cf. v. 25). They have done the essential, since they have accepted (ἔλαβον) the words of revelation which the Father entrusted to the Son, they have retained and obeyed the word of God (v. 6, τετήρηκαν), they have recognized in Jesus the envoy of God. Willingness to accept Jesus and his words, to hear and to obey, was always there, and has enabled them to persevere steadfastly with Jesus (cf. the confrontation with the "world", 17:14, 25). And Jesus, who strove to "make his Father's name known" (17:26) and wills to make it known in the future, is the educator of his disciples, leading them on to a deeper and more solid faith (cf. 1:50f.; 6:6; 9:2 ff.; 11:15) and strengthening them for the shattering experience of his Passion (13:19; 14:1, 29; 16:31f.).

Thus faith can exist more or less fully, as can be manifested in various ways: by the strength of faith (cf. the waverings of the people especially ch. 7; 9; 10:21, 41f.; 11:45; 12:11, 34), its motives (the works and the words of Jesus 10:37f.; 14:11f.), its content (cf. the various judgments on Jesus) and the outward confession and exercise of faith (cf. 9:22; 12:42; 19:38). Since only the full Messianic and Christological confession is acknowledged as real faith in Jesus, many men remain in the preliminary stages or on the outskirts of faith and need to come to a clear decision if they are not to fall back once more into unbelief (cf. 6:66 with 64, and the other groups in Jerusalem). Jesus's call for faith brings about the crisis in which all sham and frailty in faith is brought to light and all unbelief unmasked (cf. 6:14, 26, 42, 60, 64; 8:31–59; 9:16, 24–34).

The motives are particularly important for the type of faith which emerges. As has already been shown in the excursus on the Johannine "signs", there is a superficial faith based on miracles which Jesus rejects as inadequate (4:48), because it fails to understand the language of the "signs" and does not penetrate to real faith in him, the envoy of God (cf. 6:26, 36). Jesus accepts a faith which is based on his "works" as testimony to his mission, but regards it as on a lower level than a faith which assents to his word alone (10:37f.; 14:10f.). What is decisive always is that the believer grasps the significance of the person of Jesus in the economy of salvation; and hence the highest form of faith is that which accepts Jesus himself in his testimony (8:14), which recognizes his divine origin in his words and in his "doctrine" (cf. 7:16f.). For this is a direct response to the person of the revealer, a recognition of the Father in the Son, a ratification of God's revelation which makes itself known in the words of the one revealer who comes down from heaven (3:33f.). So too in later times men are called on to accept the testimony of the apostolic word (cf. 20:29) in which the eschatological revelation of Jesus is taken up and handed on (cf. 1 Jn 1:1–3).

The trials which faith undergoes are of great importance in the education, strengthening and development of faith. This is probably the way in which the evangelist understood Jesus's delay in responding at once to those who asked for help: Jesus's answer to his mother at the marriage feast of Cana possibly (2:3f.), but certainly his first reaction to the royal official's plea and the bare, unsupported affirmation, "Your son will live" (4:48, 50), and then very clearly Jesus's answer to Martha, which is too sublime for her to understand (11:25f.). But once more it is the faith of the disciples which displays at its fullest the stimulating and discriminatory function of trials. Even before the multiplication of the loaves the evangelist calls attention to the purpose which Jesus has in mind (6:6); and in the great crisis of faith which follows, when Jesus's words of revelation are a stumbling-block which brings many down, Jesus utters the astringent words to the Twelve, "Do you not also want to go?" (6:68) This is the moment in which their whole life of faith is at stake, and which they survive successfully through the confession of Simon Peter.

The severest test of faith, the Passion of Jesus, seems to be judged from another theological point of view by the evangelist (in accord with the Synoptics). It is the hour of darkness when the "prince of this world" is given power over all but Jesus himself (cf. 13:27, 30; 14:30) and even the loyal little flock of believers is scattered (16:32); he sees it therefore as a factor in the history of salvation. Jesus uses his farewell discourses to bring his disciples safely through this time of grave trouble and to lead them into a new future of faith. Only "the disciple whom Jesus loved" holds out steadfastly under the Cross (19:26f.), and he too is the first to understand the signs of the Resurrection, when he "saw and believed" (20:8). Thus he appears as the ideal embodiment of the believer who knows his Lord, who perseveres by his side, who recognizes him in his hidden manifestation (as again in the epilogue 21:7) and hence also is given the promise that he will "remain" till the Lord comes (cf. 21:22f.)—all of which, no doubt, constitutes on a deeper level a lesson for the believing community. The fourth Gospel is full of "instructions on the faith" which are concerned not only with the object of faith but also with the life of faith itself, as it is demanded of the harried Christian community in the midst of a world of unbelief.

5. Faith as grace

The grim reality of unbelief, which preoccupies the evangelist as much as faith and torments him with its strange nature, motives and manifestations, also led him, no doubt, to his profoundest view of faith, that it is grace. On the face of it, it might appear contradictory that the Johannine Jesus continues undeterred to put his summons to faith before all men, till the last moment of his public ministry, though unbelief has provoked his opponents to inexorable hatred and mortal enmity (11:47–53) and a decisive movement towards faith is scarcely to be expected any longer from the people (cf. 12:35f.), while on the other hand he considers believers as a flock entrusted to him by the Father (cf. 6:37 ff.), men who are "of God" and hear his voice with faith (cf. 8:47; 10:27; 18:37). But this seeming contradiction is explained by the theological perspective of the evangelist, even though he does not go so far as to lose sight of the tension between divine predestination and the freedom of decision of man's will.

We observe firstly that assertions on faith as grace are only found in contexts which deal with the incomprehensibility of unbelief. The main text is a consideration which intervenes in the great revelation discourse on the bread from heaven in ch. 6. After the fundamental revelation of vv. 32–35 Jesus affirms: "But I tell you that you have seen and still do not believe" (v. 36). Then comes a passage in which Jesus stresses that he rejects no one whom the Father leads to him, but that he protects him, gives him eternal life and will raise him up on the last day (vv. 37–40). The intention of Jesus is obviously to explain the hard fact of unbelief in his hearers and to disclaim responsibility for it. All he does is to execute the will of him who sent him, and he takes all who come to him into his flock of believers—which is the image already underlying his words here. After the unbelieving murmurs of the Jews (vv. 41f.) he starts afresh and now speaks more clearly of the action of the Father: "No one can come to me unless the Father who sent me draws him" (v. 44). The Scripture quotation which follows and its application are not easy to understand; but the fundamental notion, that the Father who "draws" men is absolutely at the beginning of "coming" to Jesus in faith, is expressed clearly enough. Jesus affirms once more, "But there are some of you who do not believe" (v. 64a) and continues, "Hence I said to you, No one can come to me unless it is granted him by the

Father" (v. 65). The "granting" or "giving" is merely another Johannine expression (cf. commentary on 3:27) for the fact that the power to be united to Jesus in faith, and union with Jesus in faith, must come from God.

Ch. 8 is not different. Jesus rebukes his hearers sharply for their unbelief, indeed, reproaches them with being children of the devil (v. 44). That is why they cannot understand his language or really hear his words (v. 43). Why do they not believe him? "Because you are not of God", answers Jesus (vv. 46f.). It may be debated whether this refers to their being, their predestination or their moral quality. But John has recourse to this "being from God"[17] once more only when moved by the tormenting question of why the Jews do not believe the truthful and sinless envoy of God.

Ch. 10 speaks of the flock of believers entrusted to Jesus. The first part, the parabolic discourse, shows that the flock belongs to their shepherd (τὰ ἴδια πρόβατα, v. 3f.) and stresses their union with him (vv. 14f.); towards the end of the discourse it becomes clear that the real owner of the flock is the Father (vv. 17f.), but this is only really explicitly stated in a further controversy with the Jews whom Jesus accuses of refusing to believe (v. 25). It is because they are not his sheep that they do not believe and do not listen to his voice (vv. 26f.). But the sheep who follow Jesus have been given him by the Father, and no one can snatch them from his hand—which is the sense of v. 29, however the text is read (see *ad loc.*). This interpretation is confirmed by the words of Jesus in the high priestly prayer, "They were yours and you gave them to me" (v. 6, cf. vv. 9f., 24a.). The teaching is uniform throughout. Certain men, given to the Son by the Father, constitute the flock of believers. These are also meant when the evangelist speaks of the "children of God" scattered throughout the world whom Jesus will gather together (11:52) or when Jesus speaks of "those who are of the truth" and who hear his voice (18:37). All this suggests the idea of predestination. The community of believers sees itself as a flock which belongs to God because he has chosen and predestined it (cf. also 1 Jn 2:19). But faith is only spoken of explicitly as grace where unbelief is made the subject of reflection.

Side by side with these there is another set of assertions in which unbelief is said to be due to moral failings. Men's attachment to evil prevents their coming to the "light" (3:19ff.); they seek their own glory and not the glory which comes from the one God (5:44); their passions and actions show that they are children of the devil (8:44), and in the end they are struck with blindness for their wilful refusal to see (9:39f.). The problem of the "hardening of the heart" to which this line of thought leads need not detain us here (cf. 12:39 ff.). In any case, such hardening

---

[17] See commentary on 1 Jn 5:19 in Schnackenburg, *Letters of St John*.

is also self-induced according to the evangelist (9:40; 12:42f.). There is no excuse for refusing to believe in the Son of God who has given proof of his mission in words and works (cf. 15:22 ff.). Such refusal, when considered and deliberate, is *the* great sin (16:9).

The evangelist has made no effort to reconcile systematically divine predestination and the moral guilt of man, nor does he see any contradiction in the fact that faith is the free decision of man's will and at the same time and essentially, the free grace of God. He does not see the two things on the same plane. He knows from the call of the divine revealer that faith is a decision; but he comes to understand that God himself must "draw" men and lead them to Jesus, only by his own meditation on unbelief. At the same time, the insight thus gained enables him to avert misunderstanding (such as is hinted at for instance in 6:29). The decision of faith is not a human achievement like the Jewish works of the Law, but simply the fitting answer, made possible by the grace of God, to the revelation given by Jesus. Here too the fundamental truth of the new order of grace is valid: grace and truth came through Jesus Christ (1:17). Ultimately, therefore, membership of the community of believers, the blessing of belonging to the flock of Christ, is simply a reason for praising the Father (cf. 17:6 ff.).

BIBLIOGRAPHY

BIBLIOGRAPHY OF CITED WORKS

I. SOURCES

Achelis, H., *Hippolyts kleinere exegetische und homiletische Schriften*, GCS 1 (1897).

Aland, K., *Synopsis quattuor Evangeliorum* (1964).

Arnim, H. von, *Stoicorum veterum fragmenta*, vol. II: *Chrysippi fragmenta logica et physica* (1903).

Avigad, N., and Yadin, Y., *A Genesis Apocryphon* (1956).

Baehrens, W. A., *Origenes Werke*, vol. III: *Homilien zu Samuel 1, zum Hohelied und zu den Propheten, Kommentar zum Hohelied in Rufins und Hieronymus' Übersetzung*, GCS 33 (1925).

Bardy, G., and Sender, J., *Théophile d'Antioche, Trois Livres à Autolycus*, Texte grec et introduction de G. Bardy, traduction de J. Sender, Sources chrétiennes 20 (1948).

Barthélemy, D., and Milik, J. T., *Discoveries in the Judaean Desert*, vol. I: *Qumran Cave I* (1955).

Batiffol, P., *Le Livre de la Prière d'Aseneth*, Studia patristica 1–2 (1889–90).

Beer, G., Holtzmann, O., Rengstorf, K. H., and Rost, L., *Die Mischna* (1912 ff.).

Billerbeck, P., *Kommentar zum Neuen Testament aus Talmud und Midrasch*, 4 vols. (1922–28).

Bonner, C., *The Homily on the Passion by Melito Bishop of Sardes*, Studies and Documents, 12 (1940).

Bonnet, M., "Acta Thomae", *Acta Apostolorum Apocrypha*, ed. by R. A. Lipsius and M. Bonnet, vol. II, 2 (1903), pp. 99–288.

Bonsirven, J., *Textes rabbiniques des deux premiers siècles chrétiens* (1955).

Bornkamm, G., "The Acts of Thomas", *New Testament Apocrypha*, ed. by E. Hennecke, W. Schneemelcher and R. M. Wilson, vol. II (1965), pp. 425–533.

Bover, J. M., *Novi Testamenti Biblica graeca et latina* (3rd ed., 1953).

Bulhart, V., *Tertulliani Opera*, vol. V, CSEL 70 (1942).

Burrows, M., *The Dead Sea Scrolls of St. Mark's Monastery*, vol. I: *The Isaiah Manuscript and the Habakkuk Commentary*, vol. II: *The Manual of Discipline* (1950–51).

Cai, R., *S. Thomae Aquinatis super Evangelium s. Joannis Lectura* (5th ed., 1952).

Camelot, P. T., *Ignace d'Antioche, Polycarpe de Smyrne, Lettres. Martyre de Polycarpe*, Texte grec, traduction française, Sources chrétiennes (2nd ed., 1951).

Charles, R. H., *The Greek Versions of the Testaments of the Twelve Patriarchs* (1908; repr. 1960).

— *The Apocrypha and Pseudepigrapha of the Old Testament in English*, 2 vols. (1913).

Cohn, L., and Wendland, P., *Philo of Alexandria. Opera*, 7 vols. (1896–1930); vol. VII: *Indices*, by J. Leisegang (1926–30).

Conybeare, F. C., *Philostratus. The Life of Apollonius of Tyana, the Epistles of Apollonius and the Treatise of Eusebius*, 2 vols., Loeb Classical Library (1912).

Corssen, P., "Die monarchianischen Prologe zu den Evangelien", *Das Muratorische Fragment und die monarchianischen Prologe zu den Evangelien*, ed. by H. Lietzmann, KT 1 (1902).

Danby, H., *The Mishnah*, translated from the Hebrew, with introduction and brief notes (1933).

Devreesse, R., *Essai sur Théodor de Mopsueste*, Studi e Testi 141 (1948), pp. 287–419: Greek Fragments of Theodor of Mopsueste's Commentary on John.

Drower, E. S., *The Haran Gawaitha and the Baptism of Hibil-Ziwa* (1953).

— *The Canonical Prayerbook of the Mandaeans* (1959).

Duensing, H., *Epistula Apostolorum nach den aethiopischen und koptischen Texten*, KT 152 (1925).

— "Epistula Apostolorum" *New Testament Apocrypha*, ed. by E. Hennecke, W. Schneemelcher and R. M. Wilson, vol. I (1963), pp. 189–227.

Epstein, I., *The Babylonian Talmud*, translated with notes, 34 vols., with index vol. (1935–52).

Freedman, H., and Simon, M., *Midrash Rabbah*, translated into English, 10 vols. (2nd ed., 1951).

Funk, F. X., and Bihlmeyer, K., *Die Apostolischen Väter* (1924).

Geffcken, J., *Die Oracula Sibyllina*, GCS 8 (1902).

Gibson, M. D., *The Commentaries of Isho'dad of Merv, Syriac and English*, vol. I: *Gospels translated*, vol. II: *Matthew and Mark in Syriac*, vol. III: *Luke and John in Syriac*, Horae Semiticae 5–7 (1911).

Giversen, S., *Apocryphon Johannis*, Text, Translation, Introduction and Commentary (1963).

Glück, A., *Gaudentius. Tractatus*, CSEL 69 (1936).

Goldbacker, A., *Augustini opera*, vol. II, 1–2 *Epistulae*, CSEL 34 (1895–98), vol. II, 4 *Epistulae*, CSEL 57 (1911).

Goldschmidt, L., *Der babylonische Talmud*, German translation, 12 vols. (1929 ff.).

Grobel, K., *The Gospel of Truth.* Translation with Commentary (1960).

Guarienti, A., *Catena aurea in quattuor evangelia*, vol. II (1953), pp. 321–593: *Evangelium Johannis.*

Guillaumont, A., and others, *The Gospel according to Thomas*, Text and Translation (1959).

Hadas, M., *Aristeas to Philocrates*, Text and English Translation (1951).

Hartel, W., *Cypriani opera*, 3 vols., CSEL 3 (1868–71).

Harvey, W. W., *S. Irenaei Libri quinque adversus haereses*, 2 vols. (1857).

Hausmann, K., *Ein neuentdeckter Kommentar zum Johannesevangelium* (1930).

Helm, R., *Eusebius-Jerome Chronicle*, GCS 47 (1956).

Hilberg, J., *Hieronymi opera*, vol. I, 2 *Epistulae*, CSEL 55 (1912).

Holl, K., *Epiphanius*, vol. I, GCS 25 (1915); vol. II, GCS 31 (1922).

Husselman, E. M., *The Gospel of John in Fayumic Coptic* (1962).

James, M. R., *The Apocryphal New Testament*, Newly Translated (1924).

Janssen, R., *Das Johannesevangelium nach der Paraphrase des Nonnus Panopolitanus*, TU 23, 4 (1903).

Jeremias, J., "An unknown Gospel with Johannine Elements. Papyrus Egerton 2", *New Testament Apocrypha* ed. by E. Hennecke, W. Schneemelcher and R. M. Wilson, vol. I (1963), pp. 94–7.

Jülicher, A., Matzkow, W., and Aland, K., *Itala. Das Neue Testament in altlateinischer Überlieferung*, vol. IV: *Johannesevangelium* (1963).

Kasser, R., *Papyrus Bodmer III: Évangile de Jean et Genèse I-IV, 2, en bohairique*, Text and French Translation, CSCO 117 and 118 (1958).

— *L'Évangile selon Thomas* (1961).

Kittel, R., *Biblia hebraica* (4th ed., 1949).

Klostermann, E., *Apokrypha*, vol. I: *Reste des Petrusevangeliums, der Petrusapokalypse und des Kerygma Petri*, KT 3 (1903), vol. II: *Evangelien*, KT 8 (1904).

Krause, M., and Labib, P., *Die drei Versionen der Apocryphen des Johannes im koptischen Museum zu Altkairo* (1962).

Kroymann, A., *Tertulliani opera*, vol. III, CSEL 47 (1906).

— *Tertulliani opera*, vol. II, 2, CSEL 70 (1942).

Kurfess, A., "Christian Sibyllines", *New Testament Apocrypha*, ed. by E. Hennecke, W. Schneemelcher and R. M. Wilson, vol. II (1965), pp. 703–45.

Lambert, G., "Le Manuel de Discipline du désert de Juda. Étude historique et traduction intégrale", NRT 73 (1951), pp. 938–75. Reprinted in *Analecta Lovaniensia Biblica et Orientalia*, Series II, 23 (1951). Page-references refer to this edition.
Leipoldt, J., and Schenke, H.-M., *Koptisch-gnostische Schriften aus den Papyrus-Codices von Nag-Hammadi* (1960).
Leloir, L., *Saint Éphrem. Commentaire de l'Évangile Concordant, version Arménienne.* Text and Latin translation, 2 vols., CSCO (1953–54).
— *Éphrem, Commentaire de l'évangile concordant. Texte syriaque* (Chester Beatty 709), edited and translated, Chester Beatty Monographs 8 (1963).
Lidzbarski, M., *Ginza. Der Schatz oder das grosse Buch der Mandäer*, German translation (1925).
— *Mandäische Liturgien*, German translation (1920).
— *Das Johannesbuch der Mandäer*, German translation (1915).
Lietzmann, H., *Das Muratorische Fragment und die monarchianischen Prologe zu den Evangelien*, KT 1 (2nd ed., 1933).
Lipsius, R. A., and Bonnet, M., *Acta Apostolorum Apocrypha*, 2 vols. (1891–1903; repr. 1959).
Lohse, B., *Die Passa-Homilie des Bischofs Meliton von Sardes*, Textus Minores 24 (1958).
Lohse, E., *Die Texte aus Qumran*, Hebrew and German (1964).
Malinine, M., Puech, H.-C., and Quispel, G., *Evangelium Veritatis* (1956).
Malinine, M., Puech, H.-C., Till, W., and Quispel, G., *Evangelium Veritatis XVII–XVIII* (1961).
Martin, V., *Papyrus Bodmer II, P 66* (1956).
Martin, V., and Barns, J. W. B., *Papyrus Bodmer II, Supplément*, New edition, with photographic reproduction of complete manuscript (1962).
Martin, V., and Kasser, R., *Papyrus Bodmer XV, P 75* (1961).
Ménard, J. E., *L'Évangile de Vérité*, translation into Greek (1962).
Merk, A., *Novum Testamentum graece et latine* (8th ed., 1958).
Migne, J. P., *Patrologia Graeca*, 161 vols. (1857–66).
— *Patrologia Latina*, 217 vols. (1878–90).
Moesinger, G., *Ephraim. Evangelii Concordantii expositio* (1876).
Morin, D. G., *Liber Comicus* (1893).
Nestle, E., and Aland, K., *Novum Testamentum Graece* (25th ed., 1963).
Niese, B., *Flavii Iosephi opera*, 7 vols. (1877–1904; repr. 1962).
Nock, A. D., and Festugière, A.-J., *Corpus Hermeticum*, 4 vols. (1945–54).
Odeberg, H., *3 Enoch or The Hebrew Book of Henoch* (1928).
Oldfather, W. A., *Epictetus. The Discourses, Manual, and Fragments*, translated by W. A. Oldfather, 2 vols., Loeb Classical Library (1926–28).
Parmentier, L., *Theodoret. Historia Ecclesiastica*, GCS 19 (1911).
Petschenig, M., *Ambrosii opera*, vol. VI: *Explanatio Psalmorum Duodecim*, CSEL 64 (1919).
Preisendanz, K., *Papyri graecae magicae*, 2 vols. (1928–31).
Preuschen, E., *Origen*, vol. IV: *Commentarius in Johannem*, GCS 10 (1903), pp. 1–480 and p. 574: fragments.
Pusey, P. E., *Sancti patris nostri Cyrilli arch. Alexandrini in d. Joannis evangelium*, 3 vols. (1872).
Quasten, J., *Monumenta eucharistica et liturgica vetustissima*, Florilegium patristicum 7 (1935).
Rabin, C., *The Zadokite-Documents* (2nd ed., 1958).
Rahlfs, A., *Septuaginta*, 2 vols. (1935).
Rehm, B., *Die Pseudoclementinen*, vol. I: *Homilien*, GCS 42 (1953).
Reuss, J., *Johannes-Kommentare aus der griechischen Kirche*, TU 89 (1965).
Roberts, C. H., *An Unpublished Fragment of the Fourth Gospel in the John Ryland's Library* (1935).
Sagnard, F. de, *Clément d'Alexandrie, Extraits de Théodote.* Texte grec, introduction et traduction, Sources chrétiennes 23.
Sande Bakhuyzen, W. H. van de, *Der Dialog des Adamantius* Περὶ τῆς εἰς θεὸν ὀρθῆς πίστεως, GCS 4 (1901).

Schäferdiek, K., "The Acts of John", *New Testament Apocrypha*, ed. by E. Hennecke, W. Schneemelcher and R. M. Wilson, vol. II (1965), pp. 188–259.
Schmidt, C., *Gespräche Jesu mit seinen Jüngern nach der Auferstehung, Epistula Apostolorum . . . nach einem koptischen Papyrus*, TU 43 (1919).
Schmidt, C., and Till, W., *Koptisch-gnostische Schriften*, vol. I, GCS 45 (2nd ed., 1954).
Schenke, H.-M., "Das Evangelium nach Philippus", German translation, *TLZ* 84 (1959), pp. 1–26.
Schneemelcher, W., "The Gospel of the Egyptians", *New Testament Apocrypha*, ed. by E. Hennecke, W. Schneemelcher and R. M. Wilson, vol. I (1963), pp. 166–78.
Schwarz, E., *Eusebius, Kirchengeschichte* (2nd ed., 1952).
Scott, W., *Hermetica*, 4 vols. (1924–36).
Sedlaček, I., *Dionysius bar Salibi, in Apocalypsim, Actus et Epistolas Canonicas Commentarii*, CSCO 2, 53 and 60 (1909–10).
Soden, H. von, *Die Schriften des Neuen Testaments in ihrer ältesten erreichbaren Textgestalt*, 4 vols. (1902–13).
Stählin, O., *Clement of Alexandria*, vol. I: *Protrepticus, Paedagogus*, GCS 12 (1905), vol. II: *Stromata, Book 1–6*, GCS 15 (1906), vol. III: *Stromata, Book 7–8, Excerpta ex Theodoto, Eclogae propheticae, Quis dives salvetur, Fragments*, GCS 17 (1909).
Sukenik, E. L., *The Dead Sea Scrolls of the Hebrew University* (1955).
Testuz, M., *Papyrus Bodmer X–XII* (1959).
— *Papyrus Bodmer XIII*, with French Translation (1960).
Till, W., "Das Evangelium der Wahrheit, Neue Übersetzung des vollständigen Textes", *ZNW* 50 (1959), pp. 165–85.
— *Die gnostischen Schriften des koptischen Papyrus Berolinensis 8502*, TU 60 (1955).
— *Das Evangelium nach Philippos*, Text and German Translation (1963).
— "Apocryphen Johannes'", *Evangelien aus dem Nilsand*, ed. by W. C. van Unnik (1960), pp. 185–214.
Tischendorf, C., *Novum Testamentum Graece*, 2 vols. (8th ed., 1869–72).
Vaillant, A., *Le Livre des Secrets d'Hénoch*, Texte slave et traduction française (1952).
Vogels, J., *Novum Testamentum graece et latine* (4th ed., 1955).
Völkner, W., *Quellen zur Geschichte der christlichen Gnosis* (1932).
Vosté, J.-M., *Theodori Mopsuesteni Commentarius in Evangelium Johannis Apostoli*, vol. I: Text, CSCO, 115; vol. II; French translation, CSCO 116 (1940).
Weiss, B., *Das Neue Testament, Handausgabe*, 3 vols. (1894–1900).
Wendland, P., *Hippolytus*, vol. III, GCS 26 (1916).
Wernberg-Möller, P., *The Manual of Discipline* (1957).
Westcott, B.F., and Hort, F. J. A., *The New Testament in the original Greek*, vol. I: Text; vol. II: Introduction and Appendix (1881; 2nd ed. of vol. II, 1896).
Wettstein, J., *Novum Testamentum Graecum editionis receptae cum Lectionibus variantibus... necnon commentario pleniore . . . opera et studio Joannis Jacobi Wetstenii* (1451–52; reprint 1962).
Whittaker, M., *Die apostolischen Väter*, vol. I: *Der Hirt des Hermas*, GCS 48 (1956).
Widengren, G., *The Great Vohu Manah.*
Willems, R., *Aurelii Augustini in Johannis evangelium tractatus CXXIV*, Corpus Christianorum, Series latina 36 (1954–58).
Willis, J. A., "Johannes Scotus Eriugena: Annotationes in Johannem", *Classica et Mediaevalia* 14 (1953), pp. 233–6.
Wilson, R. M., *The Gospel of Philip*, Translation and Notes (1962).
Wordsworth, J., and White, H. J., ed., *Novum Testamentum Domini nostri Jesu Christi secundum editionem S. Hieronymi*, vol. I: *Evangelia* (1895).

II. LITERATURE ON THE GOSPEL OF ST JOHN

Abbott, E. A., *Johannine Vocabulary* (1905).
— *Johannine Grammar* (1906).
Aland, K., "Papyrus Bodmer II. Ein erster Bericht", *TLZ* 82 (1957), cols. 161–84.

Bibliography

Albright, W. F., "Recent Discoveries in Palestine and the Gospel of St. John", *The Background of the New Testament and its Eschatology*, in honour of C. H. Dodd, ed. by W. D. Davies and D. Daube (1956), pp. 153–71.

Allen, E. L., "The Jewish-Christian Church in the Fourth Gospel", *JBL* 74 (1955), pp. 88–92.

Ausejo, S. de, "Es un Himno a Cristo el Prólogo de San Juan?", *Estudios Biblicos* 15 (1956), pp. 223–77, 381–427.

— "El concepto de 'carne' aplicado a Cristo en el IV Evangelio", *Sacra Pagina. Miscellanea biblica Congressus internationalis catholici de re biblica*, vol. II (1959), pp. 219–34.

Bacon, B. W., *The Fourth Gospel in Research and Debate* (1910).

— *The Gospel of the Hellenists* (1933).

Bailey, J. A., *The Traditions common to the Gospels of Luke and John* (1963).

Baldensperger, W., *Der Prolog des vierten Evangeliums, sein polemisch-apologetischer Zweck* (1898).

Barrett, C. K., "The Old Testament in the Fourth Gospel", *JTS* 48 (1947), pp. 155–69.

— "The Holy Spirit in the Fourth Gospel", *JTS* 1 (1950), pp. 1–15.

— "The Lamb of God", *NTS* 1 (1954–55), pp. 210–18.

— *The Gospel according to St John*, A Commentary on the Greek Text (1955).

— "The Theological Vocabulary of the Fourth Gospel and the Gospel of Truth", *Current Issues in New Testament Interpretation*, Essays in Honor of O. A. Piper (1962), pp. 210–23, 297f.

Bauer, W., "Johannesevangelium und Johannesbriefe", *Theologische Rundschau* 1 (1929), pp. 135–60.

— *Das Johannesevangelium*, Handbuch zum Neuen Testament 6 (3rd ed., 1933).

Baumbach, G., *Qumran und das Johannesevangelium* (1957).

Baur, F. C., "Die Komposition und der Charakter des Johannesevangeliums", *Tübinger Theologisches Jahrbuch* (1844).

Becker, H., *Die Reden des Johannesevangeliums und der Stil der gnostischen Offenbarungsrede*, ed. by R. Bultmann, FRLANT 68 (1956).

Becker, U., *Jesus und die Ehebrecherin. Untersuchungen zur Text- und Überlieferungsgeschichte von Joh 7:53 – 8:11.* Beihefte ZNW 28 (1963).

Behm, J., "Der gegenwärtige Stand der Erforschung des Johannesevangeliums", *TLZ* 73 (1948), pp. 21–30.

Belser, J. E., *Das Evangelium des Johannes übersetzt und erklärt* (1905).

Benoît, P., "Marie Madeleine et les Disciples au tombeau selon Jean 20 : 1–18", *Judentum, Urchristentum, Kirche*, Festschrift für J. Jeremias (1960), pp. 141–52.

Bernard, J. H., *A Critical and Exegetical Commentary on the Gospel according to St John*, 2 vols., International Critical Commentary (1928).

Betz, O., *Der Paraklet. Fürsprecher im häretischen Spätjudentum, im Johannesevangelium und in neu gefundenen gnostischen Schriften* (1963).

Birdsall, J. N., *The Bodmer Papyrus of the Gospel of John*, 18 pp. (1960).

— "John 10 : 29", *JTS* 11 (1960), pp. 342–4.

Blank, J., "Die Verhandlung vor Pilatus, Joh. 18:28 – 19:16 im Lichte johanneischer Theologie", *BZ* 3 (1959), pp. 60–81.

— "Der johanneische Wahrheitsbegriff", *BZ* 7 (1963), pp. 163–73.

— *Krisis. Untersuchungen zur johanneischen Christologie und Eschatologie* (1964).

Blinzler, J., "Eine Bemerkung zum Geschichtsrahmen des Johannesevangeliums", *Biblica* 36 (1955), pp. 20–35.

Bludau, A., *Die ersten Gegner der Johannesschriften*, Biblische Studien 22, 1–2 (1925).

Boismard, M.-É., "Le Chapitre 21 de Saint Jean", *RB* 54 (1947), pp. 473–501.

— "A propos de Jean 5 : 39", *RB* 55 (1948), pp. 5–34.

— "Dans le sein du Père, Joh. 1 : 18", *RB* 59 (1952), pp. 23–39.

— "Problèmes de critique textuelle concernant le Quatrième Évangile", *RB* 60 (1953), pp. 347–71.

— *Le Prologue de saint Jean* (1953).

— "Le Papyrus Bodmer II", *RB* 64 (1957), pp. 363–98.

— "De son ventre couleront des fleuves d'eau", *RB* 65 (1958), pp. 522–46.

— "L'Évolution du thème eschatologique dans les traditions johanniques", *RB* 68 (1961), pp. 507–24.
— "Saint Luc et la rédaction du Quatrième Évangile", *RB* 69 (1962), pp. 185–211.
— "Les traditions johanniques concernant le Baptiste", *RB* 70 (1963), pp. 5–42.
— "Review of V. Martin and J. W.-B. Barns, Papyrus Bodmer II, Supplément", *RB* 70 (1963), pp. 120–33.
— "Le lavement des pieds", *RB* 71 (1964), pp. 5–24.
— *Du baptême à Cana, Jean 1:1 – 2:11* (1965).
Bonningues, M., *La foi dans l'évangile de Saint Jean* (1955).
Bonsirven, J., "Les arameïsmes de S. Jean l'Évangéliste", *Biblica* 30 (1949), pp. 405–31.
Borig, R., "*Der wahre Weinstock*", *Untersuchungen zu Joh 15 : 1–10* (unprinted dissertation, Würzburg 1964).
Bornhäuser, K., *Das Johannesevangelium eine Missionsschrift für Israel*, Beiträge zur Förderung der christlichen Theologie 2, 15 (1928).
Bousset, W., "Ist das vierte Evangelium eine literarische Einheit?", *Theologische Rundschau* 12 (1909), pp. 1–12, 39–64.
Bouyer, L., *Le quatrième Évangile* (3rd ed., 1956); E. T.: *The Fourth Gospel*, trans. by P. Byrne (1964).
Bover, J. M., "Χάριν ἀντὶ χάριτος, Joh. 1 : 16", *Biblica* 6 (1925), pp. 454–60.
— "Authenticidad de Joh. 5 : 3b–4", *Estudios Biblicos* 11 (1952), pp. 69–72.
Braun, F.-M., "L'Expulsion des vendeurs du Temple", *RB* 38 (1929), pp. 178–200.
— *Évangile selon Saint Jean*, La Sainte Bible 10 (1946).
— "Qui ex Deo natus est, Joh. 1 : 13", *Aux sources de la tradition chrétienne*, Mélanges M. Goguel (1950), pp. 11–31.
— "L'arrière-fond judaïque du quatrième Évangile et la Communauté de l'alliance", *RB* 62 (1955), pp. 5–44.
— "L'accueil de la foi selon saint Jean", *Vie Spirituelle* 92 (1955), pp. 344–63.
— "Hermétisme et Johannisme", *Revue Thomiste* 55 (1955), pp. 22–42, 259–99.
— "L'arrière-fond du Quatrième Évangile", *L'Évangile de Jean*, Recherches Bibliques 3 (1958), pp. 179–96.
— *Jean le Théologien et son évangile dans l'église ancienne*, Études Bibliques (1959).
— "Messie, Logos et Fils de L'Homme", *La venue du Messie*, Recherches Bibliques 6 (1962), pp. 133–47.
— "Saint Jean, la sagesse et l'histoire", *Neotestamentica et Patristica*, in honour of O. Cullmann (1962), pp. 123–33.
— *Jean le Théologien*, vol. II: *Les grandes traditions d'Israël et l'accord des écritures selon le quatrième Évangile*, Études Bibliques (1964).
Brenz, J., *In d. Johannis evangelium exegesis* (1528).
Bretschneider, C. T., *Probabilia de evangelii et epistularum Johannis apostoli indole et origine* (1820).
Bromboszcz, T., *Die Einheit des Johannesevangeliums* (1927).
Brooks, O. S., "The Johannine Eucharist", *JBL* 82 (1963), pp. 293–300.
Brown, R. E., "The Qumran Scrolls and the Johannine Gospel and Epistles", *CBQ* 17 (1955), pp. 403–19, 559–74.
— "The Problem of History in John", *CBQ* 24 (1962), pp. 1–14.
— "The Gospel of Thomas and St. John's Gospel", *NTS* 9 (1962–63), pp. 155–77.
Brown, S., "From Burney to Black. The Fourth Gospel and the Aramaic Question", *CBQ* 26 (1964), pp. 323–39.
Büchsel, F., *Das Evangelium nach Johannes*, Das Neue Testament Deutsch (1934).
Buck, H. M., *The Johannine Lessons in the Greek Gospel Lectionary* (1958).
Bultmann, R., "Der religionsgeschichtliche Hintergrund des Prologs zum Johannesevangelium", *Eucharisterion*, Festschrift H. Gunkel (1923), vol. II, pp. 3–26.
— "Die Bedeutung der neuerschlossenen mandäischen und manichäischen Quellen für das Verständnis des Johannesevangeliums", *ZNW* 24 (1925), pp. 100–46.
— "Untersuchungen zum Johannesevangelium", *ZNW* 29 (1930), pp. 169–92.
— *Das Evangelium des Johannes*, Kritisch-evangelischer Kommentar zum Neuen Testament (10th ed., 1941); *Ergänzungsheft* (1950; rev. ed., 1957).

Bibliography

Burney, C. F., *The Aramaic Origin of the Fourth Gospel* (1922).

Bury, R. G., *The Fourth Gospel and the Logos Doctrine* (1940).

Buse, I., "The Cleaning of the Temple in the Synoptics and in John", *The Expository Times* 70 (1958–59), pp. 22–4.

Bussche, H. van den, "De betekenis van 'het uur' in het vierde Evangelie", *Collationes Brugenses et Gandavenses* 2 (1952), pp. 5–16.

— "Het wijnwonder te Cana, Joh. 2 : 1–11", *Collationes Brugenses et Gandavenses* 3 (1953), pp. 1–33.

— "La structure de Jean I-XII", *L'Évangile de Jean*, Recherches Bibliques 3 (1958), pp. 61–109.

— *Het vierde evangelie*, 4 vols. (1959–60); E. T.: *The Gospel of the Word* (1967).

Cadbury, H. J., "The Ancient Physiological Notions underlying Joh. 1 : 13a and Heb. 11 : 11", *The Expositor* 9 (1924), pp. 430–9.

Calmes, T., *Évangile selon Saint Jean* (2nd ed., 1906).

Calvin, J., *In Evangelium secundum Joannem Commentarius* (1553).

Carpenter, J. E., *The Johannine Writings. A Study of the Apocalypse and the Fourth Gospel* (1927).

Carroll, K. L., "The Fourth Gospel and the Exclusion of Christians from the Synagogue", *The Bulletin of the John Ryland's Library* 40 (1957), pp. 19–32.

Castellini, G., "De Joh 1 : 13 in quibusdam citationibus patristicis", *Verbum Domini* 32 (1954), pp. 155–7.

Cerfaux, L., "Les miracles, signes messianiques de Jésus et œuvres de Dieu, selon l'Évangile de s. Jean", *L'attente du Messie*, Recherches Bibliques (1954), pp. 131–8.

Ceroke, C. P., "Jesus and Mary at Cana. Separation or Association?", *Theological Studies* 17 (1956), pp. 1–38.

— "The Problem of Ambiguity in John 2 : 4", *CBQ* 21 (1959), pp. 316–40.

Chapman, J., *John the Presbyter and the Fourth Gospel* (1911).

Charlier, J. P., *Le signe de Cana* (1959).

— "La notion de signe (σημεῖον), dans le Quatrième Évangile", *Revue des Sciences Philosophiques et Théologiques* 43 (1959), pp. 434–48.

Clark, K. W., "The Text of the Gospel of John in Third Century Egypt", *Novum Testamentum* 5 (1962), pp. 17–24.

Colwell, E. C., *The Greek of the Fourth Gospel* (1931).

Comeau, M., *S. Augustin exégète du quatrième évangile* (1930).

Connick, C. M., "The Dramatic Character of the Fourth Gospel", *JBL* 67 (1948), pp. 159–69.

Cooke, F. A., "The Cleansing of the Temple", *The Expository Times* 63 (1951–52), pp. 321 f.

Corell, A., *Consummatum est. Eschatology and Church in the Gospel of St John* (1958).

Cortès Quirant, J., "Las Bodas de Canâ. La respuesta de Cristo a su Madre, Joh. 2 : 4", *Marianum* 20 (1958), pp. 155–89.

Craig, C. T., "Sacramental Interest in the Fourth Gospel", *JBL* 58 (1939), pp. 31–41.

Cullmann, O., "Der johanneische Gebrauch doppeldeutiger Ausdrücke als Schlüssel zum Verständnis des vierten Evangeliums", *Theologische Zeitschrift* 4 (1948), pp. 360–72.

— "Εἶδεν καὶ ἐπίστευσεν. La vie de Jésus objet de la 'vie' et de la 'foi' d'après le quatrième Évangile", *Aux sources de la tradition chrétienne.* Mélanges M. Goguel (1950), pp. 52–61.

— "Samaria and the Origins of the Christian Mission", *The Early Church* ed. by A. J. B. Higgins (1956), pp. 188–92.

Daube, D., "Jesus and the Samaritan Woman. The Meaning of συγχράομαι", *JBL* 69 (1950), pp. 137–47.

Davey, F. N., "The Fourth Gospel and the Problem of the Meaning of History", in E. C. Hoskyns, *The Fourth Gospel*, ed. by F. N. Davey (1940; 2nd rev. ed., 1947), pp. 107–128.

Decourtray, A., "La conception johannique de la foi", *NRT* 91 (1959), pp. 561–76.

Derrett, J. D. M., "Water into Wine", *BZ* 7 (1963), pp. 80–97.

Dillon, R. J., "Wisdom, Tradition and Sacramental Retrospect in the Cana Account, Jn 2 : 1–11, *CBQ* 24 (1962), pp. 268–96.

Dodd, C. H., *The Interpretation of the Fourth Gospel* (1953).
— "A l'arrière-plan d'un dialogue johannique", *Revue d'Histoire et de Philosophie Religieuse* 37 (1957), pp. 5–17.
— *Historical Tradition in the Fourth Gospel* (1963).
Dubarle, A. M., "Le signe du Temple, Joh. 2 : 19", *RB* 48 (1939), pp. 21–44.
Dunkerley, R., "Lazarus", *NTS* 5 (1958–9), pp. 321–7.
Dupont, J., *Essais sur la christologie de S. Jean* (1951).
Durand, A., *Évangile selon saint Jean*, Verbum salutis 4 (25th ed., 1938).
Dyroff, A., "Zum Prolog des Johannesevangeliums", *Pisciculi.* Festschrift Dölger (1939), pp. 86–93.
Eckhardt, K. A., *Der Tod des Johannes als Schlüssel zum Verständnis der johanneischen Schriften* (1961).
Edwards, H. E., *The Disciple Who Wrote These Things* (1953).
Edwards, R. A., *The Gospel according to St. John, its Criticism and Interpretation* (1954).
Eisler, R., "Das Rätsel des Johannesevangeliums", *Eranos-Jahrbuch* 3 (1935), pp. 323–511.
Enz, J. J., "The Book of Exodus as a Literary Type for the Gospel of John", *JBL* 76 (1957), pp. 329–42.
Faulhaber, D., *Das Johannesevangelium und die Kirche* (1935).
Faure, A., "Die alttestamentlichen Zitate im vierten Evangelium und die Quellenscheidungshypothese", *ZNW* 21 (1922), pp. 99–121.
Feuillet, A., "L'Heure de Jésus et le Signe de Cana", *Ephemerides Theologicae Lovanienses* 36 (1960), pp. 5–22.
— "La signification théologique du second miracle de Cana", *RSR* 48 (1960), pp. 62–75.
— *Études Johanniques* (1962).
— "Les adieux du Christ à sa Mère, Jn 19 : 25–27, et la maternité spirituelle de Marie", *NRT* 86 (1964), pp. 469–89.
Filson, F. V., "Who Was the Beloved Disciple", *JBL* 68 (1949), pp. 83–88.
Fischel, H. A., "Jewish Gnosticism in the Fourth Gospel", *JBL* 65 (1946), pp. 157–74.
Frangipane, D., "Et gratiam pro gratia, Joh. 1 : 16", *Verbum Domini* 26 (1948), pp. 3–17.
Gaechter, P., "Maria in Kana, Joh. 2 : 1–11", *ZKT* 55 (1931), pp. 351–402.
— "Der formale Aufbau der Abschiedslehre Jesu", *ZKT* 58 (1934), pp. 155–207.
— "Die Form der eucharistischen Rede Jesu", *ZKT* 59 (1935), pp. 420–41.
— "Strophen im Johannesevangelium", *ZKT* 58 (1934), pp. 155–207; 59 (1935), pp. 419–41; 60 (1936), pp. 99–120, 403–23.
Gardner-Smith, P., *Saint John and the Synoptic Gospels* (1938).
Gärtner, B., *John 6 and the Jewish Passover*, Coniectanea Neotestamentica 17 (1959).
Gaugler, E., "Die Bedeutung der Kirche in den johanneischen Schriften", *Internationale Kirchliche Zeitschrift* 14 (1924), pp. 97–117, 181–219; 15 (1925), pp. 27–42.
Geerlings, J., *Family 13 – The Ferrar Group: The Text according to John* (1962).
Gennaro, J., *Exegetica in prologum Joannis sec. maximos Ecclesiae Doctores antiquitatis christianae* (1952).
George, A., "L'heure de Jean XVII", *RB* 61 (1954), pp. 392–7.
Glasson, T. F., "John 1 : 9 and a Rabbinic Tradition", *ZNW* 49 (1958), pp. 288–90.
Goodenough, E. R., "John a primitive Gospel", *JBL* 64 (1945), pp. 145–82.
Goodwin, C., "How did John treat his sources?", *JBL* 73 (1954), pp. 61–75.
Grant, R. M., "The Origin of the Fourth Gospel", *JBL* 69 (1950), pp. 305–22.
Grässer, E., "Die antijüdische Polemik im Johannesevangelium", *NTS* 11 (1964–65), pp. 74–90.
Green, H. C., "The Composition of St. John's Prologue", *The Expository Times* 66 (1955–56), pp. 315–8.
Green-Armytage, A. H. N., *John Who Saw. A Layman's Essay on the Authorship of the Fourth Gospel* (1952).
Grelot, P., "Jean 7 : 38, eau du rocher ou source du Temple?", *RB* 70 (1963), pp. 43–51.
Grill, J., *Untersuchungen über die Entstehung des vierten Evangeliums*, 2 vols. (1902–23).
Grundmann, W., "Verständnis und Bewegung des Glaubens im Johannesevangelium", *Kerygma und Dogma* 6 (1960), pp. 131–54.
Gryglewicz, F., "Der Evangelist Johannes und die Sekte von Qumran", *Münchener Theologische Zeitschrift* 10 (1959), pp. 226–8.

Guilding, A., *The Fourth Gospel and Jewish Worship* (1960).

Gutjahr, F., *Die Glaubwürdigkeit des irenäischen Zeugnisses über die Abfassung des vierten kanonischen Evangeliums* (1904).

Gyllenberg, R., "Die Anfänge der johanneischen Tradition", *Neutestamentliche Studien für R. Bultmann, ZNW* 21 (1954), pp. 144–7.

Haenchen, E., "Aus der Literatur zum Johannesevangelium 1929–56", *Theologische Rundschau* 23 (1955), pp. 295–335.

— "Johanneische Probleme", *ZTK* 56 (1959), pp. 19–54.

— "Der Vater, der mich gesandt hat", *NTS* 9 (1962–63), pp. 208–16.

— "Probleme des johanneischen Prologs", *ZTK* 60 (1963), pp. 305–34.

Haring, N. M., "Historical Notes on the Interpretation of John 13 : 10", *CBQ* 13 (1951), pp. 355–80.

Harnack, A. von, "Über das Verhältnis des Prologs des vierten Evangeliums zum ganzen Werk", *ZTK* 2 (1892), pp. 189–231.

— "Das 'Wir' in den johanneischen Schriften", *Sitzungsberichte der Preussischen Akademie der Wissenschaften zu Berlin* (1923), pp. 96–113.

— "Zur Textkritik und Christologie der Schriften des Johannes", *Sitzungsberichte der Preussischen Akademie der Wissenschaften zu Berlin* (1915), pp. 534–73, reprinted in *Studien zur Geschichte des Neuen Testaments und der alten Kirche*, vol. I (1931).

Hartingsveld, L. van, *Die Eschatologie des Johannesevangeliums* (1962).

Higgins, A. J. B., *The Historicity of the Fourth Gospel* (1960).

Hirsch, E., *Studien zum vierten Evangelium* (1936).

— *Das vierte Evangelium in seiner ursprünglichen Gestalt verdeutscht und erklärt* (1936).

— "Stilkritik und Literaranalyse im vierten Evangelium", *ZNW* 43 (1950–51), pp. 128–43.

Hofbeck, S., Σημεῖον. *Der Begriff des "Zeichens" im Johannesevangelium unter Berücksichtigung seiner Vorgeschichte* (Unprinted dissertation, Würzburg 1963).

Hoffmann, J., *Das Johannesevangelium als Alterswerk. Eine psychologische Untersuchung* (1933).

Holzmeister, U., "Nathanael fuit ne idem ac S. Bartholomaeus Apostolus?", *Biblica* 21 (1940), pp. 28–39.

Hoskyns, E. C., *The Fourth Gospel* ed. by F. N. Davey, 2 vols. (1940; 2nd rev. ed., 1947).

Houssiau, A., "Le milieu théologique de la leçon εγγεννηθη, Joh. 1 : 13", *Sacra Pagina. Miscellanea biblica Congressus internationalis catholici de re biblica* (1959), vol. II, pp. 170–88.

Howard, W. F., *The Fourth Gospel in Recent Criticism and Interpretation*, Revised by C. K. Barrett (4th ed., 1955).

Howton, J., "Son of God in the Fourth Gospel", *NTS* 10 (1963–64), pp. 227–37.

Huby, J., "De la connaissance de foi dans S. Jean", *RSR* 21 (1931), pp. 385–421.

Janssens, Y., "Héracléon. Commentaire sur l'Évangile selon saint Jean", *Muséon* 72 (1959), pp. 101–51, 277–99.

Jeremias, J., "Die Berufung des Nathanael", *Angelos* 3 (1928), pp. 2–5.

— "Johanneische Literarkritik", *Theologische Blätter* 20 (1941), pp. 33–46.

— "Joh 6 : 51c–58 redaktionell?", *ZNW* 44 (1952–53), pp. 256–7.

— *Die Wiederentdeckung von Bethesda, Joh 5 : 2*, FRLANT 59 (1949).

Jervell, J., "Er kam in sein Eigentum. Zu Joh 1:11", *Studia Theologica* 10 (1956), pp. 14–27.

Jocz, J., "Die Juden im Johannesevangelium", *Judaica* 9 (1953), pp. 129–42.

Johnston, E. D., "The Johannine Version of the Feeding of the Five Thousand, An Independent Tradition?", *NTS* 8 (1961–62), pp. 151–4.

Joüon, P., "L'Agneau de Dieu", *NRT* 67 (1940), pp. 318–21.

Kahlefeld, H., *Der Hymnus vom Wort*, Christliche Besinnung 5 (1952).

Käsemann, E., "Ketzer und Zeuge. Zum johanneischen Verfasserproblem", *ZTK* 48 (1951), pp. 292–311.

— "Aufbau und Anliegen des johanneischen Prologs", *Libertas Christiana*, Festschrift für F. Delekat (1957), pp. 75–99.

Kilpatrick, G. D., "John 4 : 51 παῖς or υἱός?", *JTS* 14 (1963), p. 393.

Klijn, A. F. J., "Papyrus Bodmer II, Joh 1–14, and the Text of Egypt", *NTS* 3 (1956–57), pp. 327–34.

Knabenbauer, J., *Evangelium secundum Joannem*, Cursus Scripturae Sacrae (2nd ed., 1906).
Köster, H., "Geschichte und Kultur im Johannesevangelium und bei Ignatius von Antiochien", *ZTK* 54 (1957), pp. 56–69.
Kraft, E., "Die Personen des Johannesevangeliums", *Evangelische Theologie* 16 (1956), pp. 18–32.
Kragerud, A., *Der Lieblingsjünger im Johannesevangelium* (1959).
Kuhn, K. G., "Johannesevangelium und Qumrantexte", *Neotestamentica et Patristica*, Festschrift O. Cullmann (1962), pp. 111–22.
Kundzinš, K., *Topologische Überlieferungsstoffe im Johannesevangelium*, FRLANT 39 (1925).
— "Charakter und Ursprung der johanneischen Reden", *Acta Universitatis Lithuanensis* 1,4 (1939), pp. 185–293.
— "Zur Diskussion über die Ego-Eimi-Sprüche im Johannesevangelium", *Charisteria Joh. Köpp Octogenario oblata* (1954), pp. 95–107.
Kurfess, A., "Zu Joh. 2 : 4", *ZNW* 44 (1952–53), p. 257.
Lagrange, M.-J., *Évangile selon saint Jean*, Études bibliques (3rd ed., 1927).
— "Le réalisme historique de l'Évangile selon saint Jean", *RB* 46 (1937), pp. 321–41.
Lamarche, P., "Le Prologue de Jean", *RSR* 52 (1964), pp. 497–537.
Langkammer, H., "Die Zugehörigkeit des Satzteiles ὃ γέγονεν in Joh. 1 : 3–4 bei Hieronymus", *BZ* 8 (1964), pp. 295–8.
— "Zur Herkunft des Logostitels im Johannesprolog", *BZ* 9 (1965), pp. 91–4.
Laurentin, A., "*We attah-kai nun*. Formule caractéristique des textes juridiques et liturgiques, à propos de Jean 17 : 5", *Biblica* 45 (1964), pp. 168–97, 413–32.
Leal, J., "La hora de Jesús, la hora de su Madre", *Estudios Eclesiásticos* 26 (1952), pp. 147–68.
Lee, E. L., "St. Mark and the Fourth Gospel", *NTS* 3 (1956–57), pp. 50–8.
Léon-Dufour, X., "Le signe du temple selon saint Jean", *RSR* 39 (1951), pp. 155–75.
— "Trois chiasmes johanniques", *NTS* 7 (1960–61), pp. 249–55.
Lietzmann, H., "H. von Sodens Ausgabe des Neuen Testaments. Die Perikope von der Ehebrecherin", *ZNW* 8 (1907), pp. 34–47.
— "Bemerkungen zu H. von Sodens Antikritik", *ZNW* 8 (1907), pp. 234–7.
Lightfoot, R. H., *St John's Gospel*, edited by C. F. Evans (1956).
Loewenich, W. von, *Das Johannesverständnis im zweiten Jahrhundert*, Beihefte *ZNW* 13 (1932).
Lohse, E., "Wort und Sakrament im Johannesevangelium", *NTS* 7 (1960–61), pp. 110–25.
Loisy, A., *Le quatrième Évangile, Les épîtres dites de Jean* (2nd ed., 1921).
Lozano, J., *El concepto de verdad en San Juan* (1964).
Lütgert, W., "Die Juden im Johannesevangelium", *Neutestamentliche Studien für G. Heinrici* (1914), pp. 147–54.
Luther, M., *Evangelienauslegung*, ed. by E. Mülhaupt, vol. IV: *Das Johannesevangelium*, ed. by E. Ellwein (1954).
MacGregor, G. H. C., and Morton, A. Q., *The Structure of the Fourth Gospel* (1961).
— "The Eucharist in the Fourth Gospel", *NTS* 9 (1962–63), pp. 111–9.
Maldonatus, J., *Commentarius in quattuor evangelia*, ed. by J. M. Raich, vol. II: *in Lucam et Joannem* (1874).
Manson, T. W., "The Fourth Gospel", *The Bulletin of the John Ryland's Library* 30 (1946–47), pp. 312–29.
Marmorstein, A., "Iranische und Jüdische Religion. Mit besonderer Berücksichtigung der Begriffe 'Wort', 'Wahrheit' und 'Glorie' im Vierten Evangelium und in der rabbinischen Literatur", *ZNW* 26 (1927), pp. 231–42.
Massaux, É., "Le Papyrus Bodmer II, P[66] et la critique néotestamentaire", *Sacra Pagina. Miscellanea biblica Congressus internationalis catholici de re biblica*, vol. I (1959), pp. 194–207.
Maurer, C., *Ignatius von Antiochien und das Johannesevangelium*, ATANT 18 (1949).
May, E., *Ecce Agnus Dei! A Philological and Exegetical Approach to John 1 : 29, 36* (1947).
Mehlmann, J., "De mente S. Hieronymi circa divisionem versuum Joh. 1 : 3s", *Verbum Domini* 33 (1955), pp. 86–94.

— "A Note on John 1 : 3", *The Expository Times* 67 (1955–56), pp. 340–1.
Meinertz, M., "Die Nacht im Johannesevangelium", *Theologische Quartalschrift* 133 (1953), pp. 400–7.
Melanchthon, P., *Enarratio in Evangelium Joannis*, Edition C. J. Bretschneider, vol. 15 (1848), cols. 1–440.
Ménard, J. E., "L'Interprétation patristique de Joh. 7 : 38", *Revue de l'Université de Ottawa* 25 (1955), pp. 5–25.
Mendner, S., "Johanneische Literarkritik", *Theologische Zeitschrift* 8 (1952), pp. 418–34.
— "Die Tempelreinigung", *ZNW* 47 (1956), pp. 93–112.
— "Zum Problem Johannes und die Synoptiker", *NTS* 4 (1957–58), pp. 282–307.
— "Nikodemus", *JBL* 77 (1958), pp. 293–323.
Menoud, P.-H., *L'Évangile de Jean d'après les recherches récentes* (2nd ed., 1947).
— "L'Évangile de Jean d'après les recherches de Bultmann à Barrett", *L'Évangile de Jean*, Recherches Bibliques 3 (1958), pp. 11–40.
Merlier, O., *Le Quatrième Évangile. La question johannique* (1961).
— *Itinéraire de Jésus et Chronologie dans le Quatrième Évangile* (1961).
Metzger, B. M., "The Bodmer Papyrus of Luke and John", *The Expository Times* 73 (1962), pp. 201–3.
Meyer, H. A. W., *Das Evangelium des Johannes: kritischer und exegetischer Kommentar* (1834; 5th ed., 1896).
Meyer, P. W., "A Note on John 10 : 1–18", *JBL* 75 (1956), pp. 232–5.
Michaelis, W., "Joh. 1 : 51, Gen. 28 : 12 und das Menschensohn-Problem", *TLZ* 85 (1960), cols. 561–78.
Michl, J., "Bemerkungen zu Joh. 2 : 4", *Biblica* 36 (1955), pp. 492–509.
— "Der Sinn der Fusswaschung", *Biblica* 40 (1959), pp. 697–708.
Middleton, R. D., "Logos and Shekina in the Fourth Gospel", *Jewish Quarterly Review* 29 (1938–39), pp. 101–33.
Mitton, C. L., "The Provenance of the Fourth Gospel", *The Expository Times* 71 (1960), pp. 337–40.
Mollat, D., "La foi dans le quatrième évangile", *Lumen Vitae* 2 (1955), pp. 515–31.
— "Le semeion johannique", *Sacra Pagina. Miscellanea biblica Congressus internationalis catholici de re biblica*, vol. II (1959), pp. 209–18.
— "Rassegna di lavori cattolici su S. Giovanni dal 1950 al 1960", *Rivista Biblica* 10 (1962), pp. 64–91.
— *L'Évangile de Jean*, Bible de Jérusalem (2nd ed., 1960); E. T.: *Jerusalem Bible* (1966).
Moody, D., "God's only Son. The Translation of John 3 : 16 in the Revised Standard Version", *JBL* 72 (1953), pp. 213–9.
Moule, C. F. D., "A Note on 'under the fig tree' in John 1 : 48, 50", *JTS* 5 (1954), pp. 210–1.
— "The Individualism of the Fourth Gospel", *Novum Testamentum* 5 (1962), pp. 171–90.
Mowinckel, S., "Die Vorstellungen des Spätjudentums vom heiligen Geist als Fürsprecher und der johanneische Paraklet", *ZNW* 32 (1933), pp. 97–130.
Mowry, L., "The Dead Sea Scrolls and the Background for the Gospel of St. John", *The Biblical Archeologist* 17 (1954), pp. 78–94.
Müller, T., *Das Heilsgeschehen im Johannesevangelium* (1961).
Mussner, F., ΖΩΗ. *Die Anschauung vom "Leben" im vierten Evangelium unter Berücksichtigung der Johannesbriefe* (1952).
— "Die johanneischen Parakletsprüche und die apostolische Tradition", *BZ* 5 (1961), pp. 56–70.
Nagel, W., "Die Finsternis hat's nicht begriffen, Joh. 1 : 5", *ZNW* 50 (1959), pp. 132–7.
Niewalda, P., *Sakramentensymbolik im Johannesevangelium?* (1958).
Noack, B., *Zur johanneischen Tradition* (1954).
Nunn, H. P. V., *The Authorship of the Fourth Gospel* (1952).
Odeberg, H., *The Fourth Gospel*, vol. I (1929).
Oehler, W., "Typen oder allegorische Figuren im Johannesevangelium?", *Evangelische Theologie* 16 (1956), pp. 422–7.
Omodeo, A., *Saggio di Commentario al IV Evangelio*, 1:1 – 3:21 (1932).
Orbe, A., *Estudios Valentinianos*, vol. II: *En los origines de la exegesis juánea, Joh. 1:3* (1955).

Osty, E., "Les points de contact entre le récit de la Passion dans saint Luc et saint Jean", *Mélanges J. Lebreton*, vol. I (1951), pp. 146–54.

Overbeck, F., *Das Johannesevangelium. Studien zur Kritik seiner Erforschung*, ed. by A. Bernoulli (1911).

Parker, P., "Bethany beyond Jordan", *JBL* 74 (1955), pp. 257–61.

— "Two Editions of John", *JBL* 75 (1956), pp. 303–14.

— "John the Son of Zebedee and the Fourth Gospel", *JBL* 81 (1962), pp. 35–43.

Peinador, M., "La respuesta de Jesús a su Madre en las bodas de Caná", *Ephemerides Mariologicae* 8 (1958), pp. 61–104.

Percy, E., *Untersuchungen über den Ursprung der johanneischen Theologie* (1939).

Philips, G. H., "Faith and Vision in the Fourth Gospel", *Studies in the Fourth Gospel*, ed. by F. L. Cross (1957), pp. 83–96.

Pölzl, F. X., and Innitzer, T., *Kurzgefasster Kommentar zum Evangelium des heiligen Johannes bis zum Beginn der Leidensgeschichte* (4th ed., 1928).

Porter, C. L., "Papyrus Bodmer XV (P 75) and the text of Codex Vaticanus", *JBL* 81 (1962), pp. 363–76.

Potter, R. D., "Topography and Archaeology in the Fourth Gospel", *Studia Evangelica. Papers Presented to the International Congress on The Four Gospels in 1957*, TU 73 (1959), pp. 329–37.

Potterie, I. de la, "De interpunctione et interpretatione versuum Joh. 1 : 3–4", *Verbum Domini* 33 (1955), pp. 193–208.

— "De punctuatie en de exegese van Joh. 1 : 3–4 in de traditie", *Bijdragen. Tijdschrift voor Filosofie en Theologie* 16 (1955), pp. 117–35.

— "Een nieuwe papyrus van het vierde Evangelie, Papyrus Bodmer II", *Bijdragen. Tijdschrift voor Filosofie en Theologie* 18 (1957), pp. 119–28.

— "L'Évangile de Jean et la Gnose", *L'Évangile de Jean*, Recherches Bibliques 3 (1958), pp. 197–208.

— "La notion de témoignage dans saint Jean", *Sacra Pagina. Miscellanea biblica Congressus internationalis catholici de re biblica*, vol. II (1959), pp. 193–208.

— "Οἶδα et γινώσκω. Les deux modes de la connaissance dans le quatrième évangile", *Biblica* 40 (1959), pp. 709–25.

— *Getuige van het Woord. Inleiding op de geschriften van Johannes* (1961).

— "Naître de l'eau et naître de l'Esprit", *Sciences Ecclésiastiques* 14 (1962), pp. 417–43.

Quispel, G., "Nathanael und der Menschensohn, Joh. 1 : 51", *ZNW* 47 (1956), pp. 281–3.

Rahner, H., "Flumina de ventre Christi. Die Patristische Auslegung von Joh. 7 : 37–8", *Biblica* 22 (1941), pp. 269–302, 367–403.

Raney, W. H., *The Relation of the Fourth Gospel to the Christian Cultus* (1933).

Rengstorf, K. H., *Die Anfänge der Auseinandersetzung zwischen Christusglaube und Asklepiosfrömmigkeit* (1953).

Reuss, J., "Die Erklärung des Johannesevangeliums durch den Patriarchen Photius von Konstantinopel", *BZ* 6 (1962), pp. 279–82.

Ribera, F. de, *Commentarius in Joannis evangelium* (1623).

Richter, *Das Verhältnis der Begriffe πιστεύειν und γινώσκειν im Evangelium und in den Briefen des Johannes* (1887).

Richter, G., "Bist Du Elias? Joh. 1 : 21", *BZ* 6 (1962), pp. 79–92, 238–56; 7 (1963), pp. 63–80.

Riga, P., "Signs of Glory. The Use of 'Semeion' in Saint John's Gospel", *Interpretation* 17 (1963), pp. 402–24.

Robinson, J. A. T., "The Parable of John 10 : 1–5", *ZNW* 46 (1955), pp. 233–40.

— "The Destination and Purpose of St. John's Gospel", *NTS* 6 (1959–60), pp. 117–31.

— "The New Look on the Fourth Gospel", *Studia Evangelica. Papers Presented to the International Congress on The Four Gospels in 1957*, TU 73 (1959), pp. 338–50.

— "The Relation of the Prologue to the Gospel of St John", *NTS* 9 (1962–63), pp. 120–9.

Ruckstuhl, E., *Die literarische Einheit des Johannesevangeliums* (1951).

Sabbe, M., "Tempelreiniging en tempellogion", *Collationes Brugenses et Gandavenses* 2 (1956), pp. 289–99, 466–80.

Sahlin, H., *Zur Typologie des Johannesevangeliums* (1950).

Sanders, J. N., *The Fourth Gospel in the Early Church* (1943).
— "Those Whom Jesus Loved. St John 11 : 5", *NTS* 1 (1954–55), pp. 29 ff.
Schaeder, H. H., "Der Mensch im Prolog des vierten Evangeliums", in R. Reitzenstein and H. H. Schaeder, *Studien zum antiken Synkretismus*, pp. 306–41.
Schanz, P., *Commentar über das Evangelium des heiligen Johannes* (1885).
Schick, E., *Das Evangelium nach Johannes*, Echter-Bibel (1956).
Schlatter, A., *Die Sprache und Heimat des vierten Evangelisten*, Beiträge zur Förderung christlicher Theologie 6, 4 (1902).
— *Der Evangelist Johannes, wie er spricht, denkt und glaubt* (1930).
Schlier, H., "Im Anfang war das Wort. Zum Prolog des Johannesevangeliums", in H. Schlier, *Die Zeit der Kirche* (3rd ed., 1962), pp. 274–87.
— "Glauben, Erkennen und Lieben nach dem Johannesevangelium", *Einsicht und Glaube*, Festschrift G. Söhngen (1962), pp. 96–111; reprinted in H. Schlier, *Besinnung auf das Neue Testament* (1964), pp. 279–93.
Schmid, J., "Joh. 1 : 13", *BZ* 1 (1957), pp. 118–25.
Schmid, L., "Die Komposition der Samaria-Szene, Joh. 4: 1–42", *ZNW* 28 (1929), pp. 148–58.
Schmidt, K. L., "Der Johanneische Charakter der Erzählung vom Hochzeitswunder in Kana", *Harnack-Ehrung. Beiträge zur Kirchengeschichte ihres Lehrers A. von Harnack zu seinem 70ten Geburtstag dargebracht von einer Reihe seiner Schüler* (1921), pp. 32–43.
Schnackenburg, R., *Der Glaube im vierten Evangelium* (1937).
— *Das erste Wunder Jesu* (1951).
— "Logos-Hymnus und johanneischer Prolog", *BZ* 1 (1957), pp. 69–109.
— "Die 'situationsgelösten' Redestücke in Joh. 3", *ZNW* 49 (1958), pp. 88–99.
— "Das vierte Evangelium und die Johannesjünger", *Historisches Jahrbuch* 77 (1958), pp. 21–38.
— "Neuere englische Literatur zum Johannesevangelium", *BZ* 2 (1958), pp. 144–54.
— "Die Anbetung in Geist und Wahrheit, Joh. 4 : 23 im Lichte von Qumrantexten", *BZ* 3 (1959), pp. 88–94.
— "Die Sakramente im Johannesevangelium", *Sacra Pagina. Miscellanea biblica Congressus internationalis catholici de re biblica*, vol. II (1959), pp. 235–54.
— "Die Messiasfrage im Johannesevangelium", *Neutestamentliche Aufsätze*, Festschrift für J. Schmid (1963), pp. 240–64.
— "Zur Traditionsgeschichte von Joh. 4 : 46–54", *BZ* 8 (1964), pp. 58–88.
Schneider, J., "Zur Komposition von Joh. 10", Festschrift für A. Fridrichsen, *Coniectanea Neotestamentica* 11 (1947), pp. 220–5.
Schniewind, J., *Die Parallelperikopen bei Lukas und Johannes* (1914; 2nd ed., 1958).
Schubert, K., "Einige Beobachtungen zum Verständnis des Logosbegriffs im frührabbinischen Schrifttum", *Judaica* 9 (1953), pp. 65–80.
Schulz, A., "Das Wunder zu Kana im Lichte des Alten Testaments", *BZ* 16 (1922), pp. 93–6.
Schulz, S., *Untersuchungen zur Menschensohn-Christologie im Johannesevangelium* (1957).
— *Komposition und Herkunft der johanneischen Reden* (1960).
Schürmann, H., "Joh. 6 : 51c. Ein Schlüssel zur grossen johanneischen Brotrede", *BZ* 2 (1958), pp. 245–62.
— "Die Eucharistie als Representation und Applikation des Heilsgeschehens nach Joh. 6 : 53–58", *Trierer Theologische Studien* 68 (1959), pp. 30–45, 108–18.
Schwartz, E., *Über den Tod der Söhne Zebedäi*, Abhandlungen der Königlichen Gesellschaft der Wissenschaften zu Göttingen (1903 and 1904).
— "Aporien im vierten Evangelium", *Nachrichten von der königlichen Gesellschaft der Wissenschaften zu Göttingen* (1907), pp. 342–72; (1908), pp. 115–48, 149–88, 497–560.
Schweizer, E., *Ego eimi . . . Die religionsgeschichtliche Herkunft und theologische Bedeutung der johanneischen Bildreden, zugleich ein Beitrag zur Quellenfrage des vierten Evangeliums*, FRLANT 56 (1939).
— "Die Heilung des Königlichen, Joh. 4 : 46–54", *Evangelische Theologie* 11 (1951–52), pp. 64–71.
— "Der Kirchenbegriff im Evangelium und den Briefen des Johannes", *Studia Evangelica. Papers Presented to the International Congress on the Four Gospels in 1957.* TU 73 (1959), pp. 363–83.

— *Erniedrigung und Erhöhung bei Jesus und seinen Nachfolgern*, ATANT 28 (2nd ed., 1962).
Scott, E. F., *The Crisis in the Life of Jesus. The Cleansing of the Temple and its Significance: Joh.* 2 : 12–22 (1952).
Sidebottom, E. M., "The Son of Man as Man in the Fourth Gospel", *The Expository Times* 68 (1957), pp. 231–5, 280–3.
— "The Ascent and Descent of the Son of Man in the Gospel of John", *Anglican Theological Review* 2 (1957), pp. 115–22.
— *The Christ of the Fourth Gospel* (1961).
Sigge, T., *Das Johannesevangelium und die Synoptiker.* Neutestamentliche Abhandlungen 16, 2–3 (1935).
Smith, D. M., "The Sources of the Gospel of John. An Assessment of the Present State of the Problem", *NTS* 10 (1963–64), pp. 336–51.
Smith, R. H., "Exodus Typology in the Fourth Gospel", *JBL* 81 (1962), pp. 329–42.
Snape, H. C., "The Fourth Gospel, Ephesus and Alexandria", *The Harvard Theological Review* 47 (1954), pp. 1–14.
Soden, H. von, "H. von Sodens Ausgabe des Neuen Testaments. Die Perikope von der Ehebrecherin", *ZNW* 8 (1907), pp. 110–24.
Soltau, W., *Das vierte Evangelium in seiner Entstehungsgeschichte dargelegt*, Sitzungsberichte der Heidelberger Akademie der Wissenschaften 6 (1916).
— Sparks, H. F. D., "St. John's Knowledge of Matthew. The Evidence of John 13 : 16 and 15 : 20", *JTS* 3 (1952), pp. 58–61.
Spicq, C., "Le Siracide et la structure littéraire du prologue de S. Jean", *Mémorial Lagrange* (1940), pp. 183–95.
Spitta, F., *Das Johannesevangelium als Quelle der Geschichte Jesu* (1910).
Stählin, G., "Zum Problem der johanneischen Eschatologie", *ZNW* 33 (1934), pp. 225–59.
Stange, E., *Die Eigenart der johanneischen Produktion* (1914).
Stauffer, E., "Agnostos Christos. Joh 2 : 24 und die Eschatologie des vierten Evangeliums", *The Background of the N. T. and its Eschatology*, Studies in honour of C. H. Dodd (1956), pp. 281–99.
— "Historische Elemente im vierten Evangelium", *Bekenntnis zur Kirche*, Festgabe für E. Sommerlath (1960), pp. 33–51.
Strachan, R. H., *The Fourth Gospel, its Significance and Environment* (3rd ed., 1941).
Strathmann, H., *Das Evangelium nach Johannes*, Das Neue Testament Deutsch (1951).
Tasker, R. V. G., "The Text of the Fourth Gospel used by Origen in his Commentary on John", *JTS* 37 (1936), pp. 146–55.
— "The Chester Beatty Papyrus and the Caesarean Text of John", *Harvard Theological Review* 30 (1937), pp. 157–64.
Teeple, H. M., and Walker, F. A., "Notes on the Plates in Papyrus Bodmer II", *JBL* (1959), pp. 148–52.
— "Qumran and the Origin of the Fourth Gospel", *Novum Testamentum* 4 (1960), pp. 6–25.
— "Methodology in Source Analysis of the Fourth Gospel", *JBL* 81 (1962), pp. 279–86.
Temple, S., "A Key to the Composition of the Fourth Gospel", *JBL* 80 (1961), pp. 220–32.
Thüsing, W., *Die Erhöhung und Verherrlichung Jesu im Johannesevangelium*, Neutestamentliche Abhandlungen 21, 1–2 (1960).
Tillmann, F., *Das Johannesevangelium* (4th ed., 1931).
Titus, E. L., "The Identity of the Beloved Disciple", *JBL* 69 (1950), pp. 323–8.
Tobac, E., "La notion de Christ-Logos dans la littérature johannique", *Revue d'Histoire Ecclésiastique* 25 (1929), pp. 213–38.
Toledo, F. de, *In Sacrosanctum Joannis evangelium commentarii* (1589).
Torrey, C. C., "The Aramaic Origin of the Fourth Gospel", *Harvard Theological Review* 16 (1923), pp. 305–44.
Trépanier, B., "Contribution à une recherche de l'idée de témoin dans les écrits johanniques", *Revue de l'Université d'Ottawa* 15 (1945), pp. 5–63.
Unnik, W. C. van, "The Purpose of St John's Gospel", *Studia Evangelica, Papers Presented to the International Congress on the Four Gospels in 1957*, TU 73 (1959), pp. 382–411.
Vanhoye, A., "Témoignage et vie en Dieu selon le quatrième évangile, *Christus* 2 (1955), pp. 150–71.

— "Notre foi, œuvre divine, d'après le quatrième évangile", *NRT* 86 (1964), pp. 337–54.
Vawter, B., "The Johannine Sacramentary", *Theological Studies* 17 (1956), pp. 151–66.
— "What Came to Be in Him was Life", *CBQ* 25 (1963), pp. 401–6.
Vergote, A., *Het getuigenis-thema in het vierde evangelie* (Unprinted dissertation, Louvain 1950).
— "L'exaltation du Christ en croix selon le quatrième évangile", *Ephemerides Theologicae Lovanienses* 28 (1952), pp. 5–23.
Vogels, H., "Die Tempelreinigung und Golgotha, Joh. 2 : 19–22", *BZ* 6 (1962), pp. 102–7.
Vosté, J.-M., *De Prologo Johannis et Logo* (1928).
Weber, H. E., *Die Vollendung des neutestamentlichen Glaubenszeugnisses durch Johannes* (1912).
Weiss, B., *Das Evangelium des Johannes; kritischer und exegetischer Kommentar* (1880; 4th ed., 1902).
Wellhausen, J., *Das Evangelium Johannis* (1908).
Wendt, H. H., *Die Schichten im vierten Evangelium* (1911).
Westcott, B. F., *The Gospel according to St John* (1882; rev. ed., 1908).
Wetter, G. P., *Der Sohn Gottes. Eine Untersuchung über den Charakter und die Tendenz des Johannesevangeliums*, FRLANT 26 (1916).
Wikenhauser, A., *Das Evangelium nach Johannes* (2nd ed., 1957).
Wiles, M. F., *The Spiritual Gospel. The Interpretation of the Fourth Gospel in the Early Church* (1960).
Wilkens, W., *Die Entstehungsgeschichte des vierten Evangeliums* (1958).
— "Die Erweckung des Lazarus", *Theologische Zeitschrift* 15 (1959), pp. 22–39.
— "Evangelist und Tradition im Johannesevangelium", *Theologische Zeitschrift* 16 (1960), pp. 81–90.
Willocx, F.-M., *La notion de foi dans le quatrième évangile* (Unprinted dissertation, Louvain 1962).
Windisch, H., "Die johanneische Weinregel, Joh. 2 : 10", *ZNW* 14 (1913), pp. 248–57.
— "Der Johanneische Erzählungsstil", *Eucharisterion*, Festschrift für H. Gunkel, vol. II (1923), pp. 174–213.
— *Johannes und die Synoptiker* (1926).
— "Die fünf johanneischen Paraklet-Sprüche", *Festgabe für A. Jülicher* (1927), pp. 110–37.
— "Angelophanien um den Menschensohn auf Erden. Ein Kommentar zu Joh. 1 : 51", *ZNW* 30 (1931), pp. 215–33.
Zahn, T., *Das Evangelium des Johannes* (5th ed., 1921).
Ziener, G., "Weisheitsbuch und Johannesevangelium", *Biblica* 38 (1957), pp. 396–418; 39 (1958), pp. 37–60.
— "Johannesevangelium und urchristliche Passafeier", *BZ* 2 (1958), pp. 263–74.
Zimmermann, H., "Papyrus Bodmer II und seine Bedeutung für die Textgeschichte", *BZ* 2 (1958), pp. 214–43.
— "Das absolute ἐγώ εἰμι als die neutestamentliche Offenbarungsformel", *BZ* 4 (1960)", pp. 54–69, 266–76.
Zwaan, J. de, "John Wrote in Aramaic", *JBL* 57 (1938), pp. 155–71.

III. OTHER LITERATURE

Aal, A., *Der Logos*, vol. I: *Geschichte der Logosidee in der griechischen Literatur* (1896); vol. II: *Geschichte der Logosidee in der christlichen Literatur* (1899).
Aalen, S., *Die Begriffe "Licht" und "Finsternis" im Alten Testament, im Spätjudentum und im Rabbinismus* (1951).
Abel, F.-M., *Géographie de la Palestine*, 2 vols., Études Bibliques (1933–38).
— *Histoire de la Palestine. Depuis la conquête d'Alexandre jusqu'à l'invasion arabe*, 2 vols., Études Bibliques (1952).
Abramowski, R., "Der Christus der Salomo-Oden", *ZNW* 35 (1936), pp. 44–69.
Adam, A., "Erwägungen zur Herkunft der Didache", *Zeitschrift für Kirchengeschichte* 68 (1957), pp. 1–47.

— *Die Psalmen des Thomas und das Perlenlied als Zeugnis vorchristlicher Gnosis* (1959).

— "Die ursprüngliche Sprache der Salomo-Oden", *ZNW* 52 (1961), pp. 141–56.

Aland, K., "Zur Liste der griechischen neutestamentlichen Handschriften", *TLZ* 78 (1953), cols. 466–96.

— "The Present Position of New Testament Textual Criticism", *Studia Evangelica. Papers Presented to the International Congress on the Four Gospels*, TU 73 (1959), pp. 717–31.

— "Neue neutestamentliche Papyri, II", *NTS* 9 (1962–63), pp. 303–13; 10 (1963–64), pp. 62–79; 11 (1964–65), pp. 14–21.

— *Kurzgefasste Liste der griechischen Handschriften des Neuen Testaments*, vol. I (1963).

Allegro, J. M., "Further Messianic References in Qumran Literature", *JBL* 75 (1956), pp. 174–87.

Allen, J., *The Early Church and the New Testament* (1951).

Altaner, B., *Patrology*, trans. by H. C. Graef (1960).

Aragon, J.-L. d', *L'Église dans la Bible* (1962).

Arndt, W., and Gingrich, F., ed., *A Greek-English Lexicon of the New Testament and other Early Christian Literature.* A translation and adaptation of the 4th ed. of W. Bauer's Griechisch-Deutsches Wörterbuch zu den Schriften des Neuen Testaments und der übrigen urchristlichen Literatur (1957).

Asting, R., *Die Verkündigung des Wortes im Urchristentum* (1939).

Audet, J.-P., *La Didaché*, Études Bibliques (1958).

— "L'hypothèse des testimonia. Remarques autour d'un livre récent: P. Prigent, Les Testimonia dans le christianisme primitif: L'Épître de Barnabé I–VI et ses sources", *RB* 70 (1963), pp. 381–405.

Barbel, J., *Christos Angelos* (1941).

Bardy, G., "Cérinthe", *RB* 30 (1921), pp. 344–73.

— "Jean, le Presbytre", *DBS*, vol. IV (1949), cols. 843–7.

Barrett, C. K., *The Holy Spirit and the Gospel Tradition* (1947).

Barrois, A., "Béthanie", *DBS*, vol. I (1928), cols. 968–70.

— "La métrologie dans la Bible", *RB* 40 (1931), pp. 185–213.

— *Manuel d'archéologie biblique*, vol. II (1953).

Baudissin, W. W., "Gott schauen in der alttestamentlichen Religion", *Archiv für Religionswissenschaft* 18 (1915), pp. 173–239.

Bauer, J., "Πῶς in der griechischen Bibel", *Novum Testamentum* 2 (1957–58), pp. 81–91.

Bauer, W., *Rechtgläubigkeit und Ketzerei im ältesten Christentum* (1934).

Baumgartner, W., "Der heutige Stand der Mandäerfrage", *Theologische Zeitschrift* 6 (1950), pp. 401–10.

Baur, F. C., *Kritische Untersuchungen über die Kanonischen Evangelien* (1847).

Baus, K., *Von der Urgemeinde zur frühchristlichen Grosskirche.* Handbuch der Kirchengeschichte, ed. by H. Jedin, vol. I (1962); E. T.: *From the Apostolic Community to Constantine*, Handbook of Church History, ed. by H. Jedin and J. Dolan, vol. I (1965).

Beasley-Murray, G. R., *Baptism in the New Testament* (1962).

Beer, G., and Meyer, R., *Hebräische Grammatik*, vol. II (1955).

Behm, J., "αἷμα", *TWNT*, vol. I (1933), pp. 171–6.

— "βρῶμα, βρῶσις", *TWNT*, vol. I (1933), pp. 640–3.

— "ἐσθίω", *TWNT*, vol. II (1935), pp. 686–93.

Bengel, J. A., *Gnomon Novi Testamenti* (1742).

Benoît, P., "Inspiration", *Initiation biblique*, ed. by A. Tricot and A. Robert (3rd ed., 1954), pp. 6–45; E. T.: *Guide to the Bible*, vol. I (2nd ed., 1960).

— "Rapports littéraires entre les épîtres aux Colossiens et aux Éphésiens", *Neutestamentliche Aufsätze*, Festschrift für J. Schmid (1963), pp. 11–22.

Betz, J., "Christus – petra – Petrus", *Kirche und Überlieferung*, Festschrift für J. Geiselmann (1961), pp. 1–21.

Betz, O., "Die Geburt der Gemeinde durch den Lehrer", *NTS* 3 (1956–57), pp. 314–26.

Beyer, K., *Semitische Syntax im Neuen Testament*, vol. I, 1 (1962).

Bianchi, U., *Il dualismo religioso* (1958).

Bibliography

Bieler, L., *ΘΕΙΟΣ ΑΝΗΡ*, vol. I (1935).
Bieneck, J., *Sohn Gottes als Christusbezeichnung bei den Synoptikern* (1951).
Bietenhard, H., *Die himmlische Welt im Urchristentum und Spätjudentum* (1951).
Billerbeck, P., *Kommentar zum Neuen Testament aus Talmud und Midrasch*, 4 vols. (1922–28)
Black, M., *An Aramaic Approach to the Gospels and Acts* (2nd ed., 1954).
Blank, J., *Meliton von Sardes, vom Passa* (1963).
Blinzler, J., "Chronologie des Neuen Testamentes", *LTK*, vol. II (1958), cols. 422–5.
— "Brotbrechen", *LTK*, vol. II (1958), cols. 706–7.
— *Der Prozess Jesu* (3rd ed., 1960); E. T.: *The Trial of Jesus*, trans. by J. and F. McHugh (1959).
Bloch, J., *On the Apocalyptic in Judaism* (1952).
Boismard, M.-É., "Critique textuelle et citations patristiques", *RB* 57 (1950), pp. 388–408.
— "Lectio brevior, potior", *RB* 58 (1951), pp. 161–8.
— "L'Apocalypse", *Introduction à la Bible*, ed. by A. Robert and A. Feuillet, vol. II: *Nouveau Testament* (1959), pp. 709–42; E.T.: *Introduction to the New Testament* (1965).
Bonnet, H., "Die Symbolik der Reinigung im ägyptischen Kult", *Angelos* 1 (1925), pp. 103–21.
Bornkamm, G., *Mythos und Legende in den apokryphen Thomas-Akten*, FRLANT 49 (1933).
— "πρέσβυς, πρεσβύτερος", *TWNT*, vol. VI (1959), pp. 651–80.
— "Glaube und Geschichte in den Evangelien", *Der historische Jesus und der kerygmatische Christus*, ed. by H. Ristow and K. Matthiae (1960), pp. 281–8.
— *Jesus von Nazareth* (1956); E. T.: *Jesus of Nazareth* (1962).
Botterweck, G. J., "*Gott erkennen*" *im Sprachraum des Alten Testaments* (1951).
Bousset, W., *Die Evangelienzitate Justins des Märtyrers in ihrem Wert für die Evangelienkritik* (1891).
— *Hauptprobleme der Gnosis*, FRLANT 10 (1907).
— *Kyrios Christos. Geschichte des Christusglaubens von den Anfängen des Christentums bis Irenaeus*, FRLANT 21 (2nd ed., 1921).
Brandenburger, E., *Adam und Christus* (1962).
Braun, F.-M., *La Mère des Fidèles* (1953).
— "Essénisme et Hermétisme", *Revue Thomiste* 54 (1954), pp. 523–58.
— "Messie, Logos et Fils de l'Homme", *La venue du Messie*, Recherches Bibliques 6 (1962), pp. 133–47.
— "Qumran und das Neue Testament", *Theologische Rundschau* 28 (1962), pp. 97–234; on John pp. 192–234.
Braun, H., *Spätjüdisch-häretischer und frühchristlicher Radikalismus*, vol. I (1957).
— "Der Sinn der neutestamentlichen Christologie", *ZTK* 54 (1957), pp. 341–77.
— "Qumran und das Neue Testament", *Theologische Rundschau* 28 (1962), pp. 192–234.
Bréhier, É., *Les idées philosophiques et religieuses de Philon d'Alexandrie* (3rd ed., 1950).
Brownlee, W. H., "Biblical Interpretation among the Sectaries of the Dead Sea Scrolls", *Biblical Archeologist* 14 (1951), pp. 54–76.
— *The Dead Sea Manual of Discipline*, Supplementary Studies of the Bulletin of the American Schools of Oriental Research, 10–12 (1951).
— "John the Baptist in the New Light of the Ancient Scrolls", *The Scrolls and the New Testament*, ed. by K. Stendahl (1958), pp. 33–53.
Brox, N., *Zeuge und Märtyrer* (1961).
Büchsel, F., "δίδωμι", *TWNT*, vol. II (1935), p. 168.
— "ἐλέγχω", *TWNT*, vol. II (1935), pp. 470–3.
— "ἡγέομαι", *TWNT*, vol. II (1935), pp. 909–10.
— "κρίνω, κρίσις. Der Gerichtsgedanke im Neuen Testament", *TWNT*, vol. III (1938), pp. 936–43.
— "μονογενής", *TWNT*, vol. IV (1942), pp. 745–50.
Bultmann, R., "ἀληθινός", *TWNT*, vol. I (1933), pp. 249–51.
— "Christologie des Neuen Testaments", *Glauben und Verstehen*, vol. I (1933), pp. 245–67; E. T.: *Essays Philosophical and Theological*, vol. I (1955).
— "γινώσκω, γνῶσις", *TWNT*, vol. I (1933), pp. 688–715; E. T.: *Gnosis*. Bible Key Words 5 (1952).

— "Neues Testament und Mythologie", *Beiträge zur evangelischen Theologie* 7 (1941), pp. 27–69, reprinted in *Kerygma und Mythos*, vol. I, pp. 15–48; E. T.: *Kerygma and Faith* (1963).
— "πιστεύω", *TWNT*, vol. VI (1959), pp. 197–230.
— *Theologie des Neuen Testaments* (1953); E. T.: *Theology of the New Testament*, translated by K. Grobel, 2 vols. (1952–55).
— *Das Verhältnis der urchristlichen Christusbotschaft zum historischen Jesus*, Sitzungsberichte der Heidelberger Akademie der Wissenschaften (3rd ed., 1962).
— *Geschichte der synoptischen Tradition* (4th ed., 1961 with supplementary fascicule); E. T.: *The History of the Synoptic Tradition*, trans. by J. Marsh (1963).
Burney, C. F., *The Poetry of our Lord* (1925).
Burrows, M., *More Light on the Dead Sea Scrolls* (1958).
Busse, E., *Der Wein im Kult des Alten Testaments* (1922).
Buzy, D., *Évangile selon Saint Matthieu* (1950).
Cajetan, Thomas de Vio, *Tentacula novi testamenti* (1523–24).
Camelot, P. T., "Didache", *LTK*, vol. III (1959), cols. 369–70.
Camerarius, J., *Commentarius in Novum Foedus* (1642).
Campenhausen, H. von, *Die Idee des Martyriums in der alten Kirche* (1936).
— *Kirchliches Amt und geistliche Vollmacht in den ersten drei Jahrhunderten* (2nd ed., 1963).
Carmignac, J., "Le retour du Docteur de Justice à la fin des jours?", *Revue de Qumran* I (1958), pp. 235–48.
— "Notes sur les Peshârîm", *Revue de Qumran* 3 (1961–62), pp. 505–32.
— "Les affinités qumraniennes de la onzième Ode de Salomon", *Revue de Qumran* 3 (1961–62), pp. 71–102.
Casel, O., "Art und Sinn der ältesten christlichen Osterfeier", *Jahrbuch für Liturgiewissenschaft* 14 (1938), pp. 1–78.
Chevallier, M.-A., *L'Esprit et le Messie dans le Bas-Judaïsme et le Nouveau Testament* (1958).
Cladder, H., "Cerinth und unsere Evangelien", *BZ* 14 (1917), pp. 317–32.
Clark, K. M., "The Effect of Recent Textual Criticism upon New Testament Studies", *The Background of the New Testament and its Eschatology*, in honour of C. H. Dodd, ed. by W. D. Davies and D. Daube (1956), pp. 27–51.
Colpe, C., "Mandäer", RGG, vol. IV (1960), cols. 709–12.
— *Die religionsgeschichtliche Schule. Darstellung und Kritik ihres Bildes vom gnostischen Erlösermythus*, FRLANT 78 (1961).
Colwell, E. C., "The Significance of Grouping of New Testament Manuscripts", *NTS* 4 (1957–58), pp. 73–92.
— "Method in Locating a Newly-discovered Manuscript within the MS Tradition of the Greek New Testament", *Studia Evangelica. Papers Presented to the International Congress on the Four Gospels in 1957*, TU 73 (1959), pp. 757–77.
Colwell, E. C., and Riddle, D. W., *Prolegomena to the Study of the Lectionary Text of the Gospels* (1933).
Congar, Y. M.-J., "Inspiration des Écritures canoniques et apostolicité de l'Église", *Revue des Sciences Philosophiques et Théologiques* 45 (1961), pp. 32–42.
Conybeare, F. C., "Ein Zeugnis Ephräms über das Fehlen von C. 1 und 2 im Texte des Lukas", *ZNW* 3 (1902), pp. 192–7.
Conzelmann, H., "Jesus Christus", *RGG*, vol. III (1959), cols. 619–53.
— *Die Mitte der Zeit* (3rd ed., 1960); E. T.: *The Theology of St. Luke*, translated by G. Buswell (1960).
— *Die Apostelgeschichte* (1963).
Coppens, J., "Le don de l'Esprit d'après les textes de Qumran", *L'Évangile de Jean*, Recherches Bibliques 3 (1950), pp. 209–23.
Coppens, J.,and Dequeker, L., *Le Fils de l'homme et les Saints du Très-Haut en Daniel VII dans les Apocryphes et dans le Nouveau Testament* (1961).
Cross, F. M., *The Ancient Library of Qumran and Modern Biblical Studies* (1958).
Cullmann, O., "ὁ ὀπίσω μου ἐρχόμενος", *Coniectanea Neotestamentica* 11 (1947), pp. 26–32.
— *Die Tauflehre des Neuen Testaments* (1948); E. T.: *Baptism in the New Testament*, trans. by J. K. S. Reid, Studies in Biblical Theology 1 (1950).

— "πέτρα", *TWNT*, vol. VI (1959), pp. 94–100.
— *Petrus: Jünger, Apostel, Märtyrer* (2nd ed., 1960); E. T.: *Peter: Disciple, Apostle, Martyr. A Historical and Theological Study*, trans. by F. V. Filson (1953).
— *Urchristentum und Gottesdienst* (2nd ed., 1950); E. T.: *Early Christian Worship*, trans. by J. S. Todd and J. B. Torrance (1953).
— "The Significance of the Qumran Texts for Research into the Beginnings of Christianity", *JBL* 74 (1955), pp. 213–26.
— *Christologie des Neuen Testaments* (1957); E. T.: *The Christology of the New Testament*, trans. by S. C. Guthrie and C. A. M. Hall (1959).
Cumont, F., *Les religions orientales dans le paganisme romain* (1906; 4th rev. ed., 1929); E. T.: *The Oriental Religions in Roman Paganism* (1911).
Dalberg, P., *Die Theologie der hellenistisch-jüdischen Missionsliteratur unter Ausschluss von Philo und Josephus* (1954).
Dalman, G., *Die Worte Jesu*, vol. 2: *Einleitung* (2nd ed., 1930); E. T.: *The Words of Jesus considered in the Light of Post-Biblical Jewish Writings and the Aramaic Language*, vol. I: *Introduction and Fundamental Ideas*, trans. by D. M. Kay (1902).
— *Grammatik des jüdisch-palästinensischen Aramäisch* (2nd ed., 1905).
— *Jesus-Jeshua, Die drei Sprachen Jesu: Jesus in der Synagoge, auf dem Berge, beim Passahmahl, am Kreuz* (1922); E. T.: *Jesus-Jeshua* (1929).
— *Orte und Wege Jesu* (3rd ed., 1924); E. T.: *Sacred Sites and Ways. Studies in the Topography of the Gospels*, trans. by P. P. Levertoff (1935).
Daniélou, J., *Origène* (1948).
— *Sacramentum Futuri* (1950).
— *Théologie du Judéo-Christianisme* (1958); E. T.: *The Theology of Jewish Christianity*, trans. by J. A. Baker (1964).
— "Le symbolisme de l'eau vive", *RSR* 32 (1958), pp. 335–46.
— "Bulletin d'Histoire des Origines Chrétiennes I", *RSR* 47 (1959), pp. 63–124.
— "Odes de Salomon", *DBS*, vol. VI (1959), cols. 677–84.
— "Bulletin d'Histoire des origines Chrétiennes II", *RSR* 49 (1961), pp. 564–620.
Davies, W. D., *Christian Origins and Judaism* (1962).
Deissmann, A., *Bibelstudien* (1895); E. T.: *Bible Studies* (1901).
Delcor, M., "Vom Sichem der hellenistischen Epoche zum Sychar des Neuen Testaments", *Zeitschrift des Deutschen Palästina-Vereins* 78 (1962), pp. 34–48.
Dell, A., "Matthäus 16 : 17–19", *ZNW* 15 (1914), pp. 1–49.
Delling, G., "καταλαμβάνω", *TWNT*, vol. IV (1942), p. 10.
— "πλήρωμα", *TWNT*, vol. VI (1949), pp. 283–309.
— "'βάπτισμα, βαπτισθῆναι", *Novum Testamentum* 2 (1957–58), pp. 92–115.
— "Zum gottesdienstlichen Stil der Johannesapokalypse", *Novum Testamentum* 3 (1959), pp. 107–37.
— "Botschaft und Wunder im Wirken Jesu", *Der historische Jesus und der kerygmatische Christus*, ed. by H. Ristow and K. Matthiae (1960), pp. 389–402.
Devreesse, R., "Chaînes exégétiques grecques", *DBS*, vol. I (1928), cols. 1084–1233.
Dey, J., Παλιγγενεσία. Neutestamentliche Abhandlungen 17, 5 (1937).
Dibelius, M., *Jesus* (2nd ed., 1949); E. T.: *Jesus*, trans. by C. B. Hedrick and F. C. Grant (1963).
Dibelius, M., and Conzelmann, H., *Die Pastoralbriefe* (3rd ed., 1955).
Dieterich, A., *Eine Mithrasliturgie* (3rd ed., 1923).
Dodd, C. H., *The Bible and the Greeks* (1935; 2nd ed., 1954).
— *According to the Scriptures* (1952).
Dölger, F. J., "ὁ σωτήρ", *Antike und Christentum* 6 (1950), pp. 241–75.
Doresse, J., *Les livres secrets des gnostiques d'Egypte* (1958); E. T.: *The Secret Books of the Egyptian Gnostics* (1960).
Dörrie, H., and Duchesne-Guillemin, J., "Dualismus", *Reallexikon für Antike und Christentum*, vol. IV (1959), cols. 334–50.
Doskocil, W., *Der Bann in der Urkirche* (1958).
Duchesne-Guillemin, J., *Ohrmazd et Ahriman* (1953).
Duplacy, J., "Où en est la critique textuelle du Nouveau Testament?" *RSR* (1959).

— "Citations patristiques et critique textuelle du Nouveau Testament", *RSR* 47 (1959), pp. 391–400.
— "Bulletin de critique textuelle du Nouveau Testament I", *RSR* 50 (1962), pp. 242–63.
Dupont, J., *Gnosis. La connaissance religieuse dans les épîtres de S. Paul* (1949).
Dürr, L., *Die Wertung des göttlichen Wortes im Alten Testament und im antiken Orient* (1938).
Eckermann, J. C. R., *Theologische Beiträge*, vol. V (1796).
Eichrodt, W., *Theologie des Alten Testaments*, vol. I (5th ed., 1957); vols. II–III (4th ed., 1961); E. T.: *Theology of the Old Testament*, vol. I, trans. by J. A. Baker (1961), vol. II (1967).
Eissfeldt, O., *Einleitung in das Alte Testament* (3rd ed., 1964); E. T.: *The Old Testament. An Introduction* (1965).
Elliger, K., *Studien zum Habakuk-Kommentar vom Toten Meer* (1953).
Emery, S., "Il Logos nel pensiero dei Padri Apostolici", *Studia Patav.* 1 (1954), pp. 400–24.
Enchiridion Biblicum. Documenta ecclesiastica Sacram Scripturam spectantia (3rd ed., 1956).
Erasmus, D., *Paraphrases in quattuor Evangelia*, edition J. Clericus, vol. VII.
Evanson, E., *The Dissonance of the Four Generally Received Evangelists* (1792).
Fabbi, F., "La condiscendenza divina nell'ispirazione biblica", *Biblica* 14 (1933), pp. 330–47.
Farmer, W. R., *Maccabees, Zealots and Josephus* (1956).
Fascher, E., ΠΡΟΦΗΤΗΣ (1927).
— *Textgeschichte als hermeneutisches Problem* (1953).
Féderlin, L., *Béthanie au delà du Jourdain* (1908).
Feine, P., *Theologie des Neuen Testaments* (8th ed., 1951).
Feine, P., and Behm, J., *Einleitung in das Neue Testament* (1950).
Fendt, L., "Der heutige Stand der Forschung über das Geburtsfest Jesu am 25. Dezember und über Epiphanias, *TLZ* 78 (1953), pp. 1–10.
Féret, H.-M., *Connaissance biblique de Dieu* (1955).
Festugière, A.-J., *La révélation d'Hermès Trismégiste*, 4 vols. (1945–54).
Feuillet, A., "Jésus et la Sagesse divine d'après les évangiles synoptiques", *RB* 62 (1955), pp. 161–96.
Fiebig, P., *Jüdische Wundergeschichten des neutestamentlichen Zeitalters* (1911).
Flusser, D., "The Dead Sea Sect and Pre-Pauline Christianity", *Aspects of the Dead Sea Scrolls*, Scripta Hierosolymitana 4 (1958), pp. 215–66.
Foerster, W., *Von Valentin zu Herakleon. Untersuchungen über die Quellen und die Entwicklung der valentinianischen Gnosis*, Beihefte ZNW 7 (1928).
— "ἐξουσία", *TWNT*, vol. II (1935), pp. 559–71.
— "Das Wesen der Gnosis", *Die Welt als Geschichte* 15 (1955), pp. 100–14.
— "Der heilige Geist im Spätjudentum", *NTS* 8 (1960–61), pp. 117–34.
Fohrer, G., *Die symbolischen Handlungen der Propheten* (1953).
Frank, H., "Epiphanie", *LTK*, vol. III (1959), cols. 942–4.
Friedrich, G., "εὐαγγέλιον", *TWNT*, vol. II (1935), pp. 705–35.
— "προφήτης: Johannes der Täufer", *TWNT*, vol. VI (1959), pp. 838–42.
Funk, R. W., ed., *A Greek Grammar of the New Testament and other early Christian literature.* A Translation and a revision of F. Blass and A. Debrunner's Grammatik des neutestamentlichen Griechisch (1961).
— "The Wilderness", *JBL* 78 (1959), pp. 205–14.
Gaechter, P., *Maria im Erdenleben* (2nd ed., 1954); E. T.: *Light on Mary's Life* (1966).
Galling, K., *Biblisches Reallexicon*, Handbuch zum Alten Testament I, 1 (1937).
Galot, J., *Marie dans l'Évangile* (1958).
Gärtner, B., "טַלְיָא als Messiasbezeichnung", *Svensk Exegetik Årsbok* 18–19 (1953-54), pp. 98–108.
— *The Temple and the Community in Qumran and the New Testament* (1965).
— *The Theology of the Gospel of Thomas* (1961).
Gaster, M., *The Samaritans, their History, Doctrines and Literature* (1925).
Gaster, T. H., *Passover, its History and Traditions* (1958).
Geiselmann, J. R., *Jesus der Christus* (1951).

Geyser, A. S., "The Youth of John the Baptist", *Novum Testamentum* 1 (1956), pp. 70–75.
Giblet, J., "Prophétisme et attente d'un Messie-Prophète dans le Judaïsme", *L'Attente du Messie*, Recherches Bibliques (1954), pp. 85–130.
Giversen, S., "Nag Hammadi Bibliography", *Studia Theologica* 17 (1963), pp. 139–87.
Glombitza, O., "Das Zeichen des Jona", *NTS* 8 (1961–62), pp. 359–66.
Gnilka, J., "Die essenischen Tauchbäder und die Johannestaufe", *Revue de Qumran* 3 (1961), pp. 185–207.
— *Die Verstockung Israels. Isaias 6 : 9–10 in der Theologie der Synoptiker* (1961).
Gögler, R., *Zur Theologie des biblischen Wortes bei Origenes* (1963).
Goguel, M., *Jean-Baptiste* (1928).
— *La vie de Jésus* (1932); E. T.: *The Life of Jesus*, trans. by O. Wyon (1933).
Goodenough, E. R., *By Light, Light. The Mystic Gospel of Hellenistic Judaism* (1935).
Goppelt, L., *Typos* (1939).
— *Christentum und Judentum im ersten und zweiten Jahrhundert*, Beiträge zur Förderung christlicher Theologie 2, 55 (1954).
Grant, R. M., *The Bible in the Church* (1948).
— *Gnosticism and Early Christianity* (1959).
— "Scripture and Tradition in St Ignatius of Antioch", *CBQ* 25 (1963), pp. 322–35.
Gressmann, H., *Der Messias*, FRLANT 43 (1929).
Grether, O., *Name und Wort Gottes im Alten Testament*, Beihefte ZAW 64 (1934).
Grillmeier, A., "Die theologische und sprachliche Vorbereitung der christologischen Formel von Chalkedon", *Das Konzil von Chalkedon*, vol. I (1941), pp. 5–202.
— "Aloger", *LTK*, vol. I (1957), cols. 363–4.
Grotius, H., *Annotationes in libros evangeliorum* (1641).
Grundmann, W., "δεῖ, δέον, ἐστί", *TWNT*, vol. II (1935), pp. 21–5.
— "κράζω, ἀνακράζω, κραυγή, κραυγάζω", *TWNT*, vol. III (1938), pp. 898–904.
— *Die Geschichte Jesu Christi* (1957).
Guillet, J., "Les exégèses d'Alexandrie et d'Antioche. Conflit ou malentendu?", *RSR* 34 (1947), pp. 257–302.
Gutbrod, W., "Ἰουδαῖος im Neuen Testament", *TWNT*, vol. III (1938), pp. 376–84.
Gutwenger, E., "Papias, eine chronologische Studie", *ZKT* 69 (1947), pp. 385–416.
Haag, H., "Ebed-Jahwe Forschung 1948–58", *BZ* 3 (1959), pp. 174–204.
Haenchen, E., "Gab es eine vorchristliche Gnosis?", *ZTK* 49 (1952), pp. 316–49.
— "Aufbau und Theologie des Poimandres", *ZTK* 53 (1956), pp. 149–91.
— *Die Apostelgeschichte* (3rd ed., 1959).
— "Literatur zum Thomasevangelium", *Theologische Rundschau* 27 (1961), pp. 147–78, 306–38.
— "Literatur zum Kodex-Jung", *Theologische Rundschau* 30 (1964), pp. 39–82.
Hahn, F., *Christologische Hoheitstitel. Ihre Geschichte im frühen Christentum* (1963).
Hahn, F., Lohff, W., and Bornkamm, G., *Die Frage nach dem historischen Jesus* (1962).
Harnack, A. von, *Die Chronologie der altchristlichen Literatur bis Eusebius*, vol. I (1897).
— "κόπος (κοπιᾶν, οἱ κοπιῶντες) im frühchristlichen Sprachgebrauch", *ZNW* 27 (1928), pp. 1–10.
— *Studien zur Geschichte des Neuen Testaments und der alten Kirche*, vol. I: *Zur neutestamentlichen Textkritik* (1931).
Hartmann, L., ed., *Encyclopaedic Dictionary of the Bible*, trans. from the Dutch (1963).
Hauck, F., "δέκα", *TWNT*, vol. II (1935), pp. 35–6.
— "καθαρός. Rein und unrein im Neuen Testament", *TWNT*, vol. III (1938), pp. 427–30.
— "καρπός", *TWNT*, vol. III (1938), pp. 617–8.
— "κοπός", *TWNT*, vol. III (1938), pp. 827–9.
Heard, R. G., "Papias Quotations from the New Testament", *NTS* 1 (1954–55), pp. 130–4.
— "The old Gospel Prologues", *JTS* 6 (1955), pp. 1–16.
Hegermann, H., *Jesaja 53 in Hexapla, Targum und Peschitta* (1954).
— *Die Vorstellung vom Schöpfungsmittler im hellenistischen Judentum und Urchristentum* (1961).
Heinemann, I., *Philons griechische und jüdische Bildung* (1932, reprint 1962).

Hejdanek, L., and Pokorný, P., "Jesus, Glaube, Christologie", *Theologische Zeitschrift* 18 (1962), pp. 268–82.

Held, H. J., *Überlieferung und Auslegung im Matthäusevangelium* (1960).

Hempel, J., "Der Symbolismus von Reich, Haus und Stadt in der biblischen Sprache", *Wissenschaftliche Zeitschrift der E. M. Arndt Universität Greifswald*, Reihe 4 (1954–55), pp. 123–30.

Higgins, A. J. B., *The Lord's Supper in the New Testament*, Studies in Biblical Theology 6 (1952).

Hölscher, G., *Die Hohenpriesterlisten bei Josephus und die evangelische Chronologie*, Sitzungsberichte der Heidelberger Akademie der Wissenschaften 3 (1939–40).

Holl, K., "Der Ursprung des Epiphanienfests", *Gesammelte Aufsätze*, vol. II (1928), pp. 123–54.

Holte, R., "Logos Spermatikos. Christianity and Ancient Philosophy according to St. Justin's Apologies", *Studia Theologica* 12 (1958), pp. 109–68.

Holtz, T., *Die Christologie der Apokalypse des Johannes* (1962).

Holtzmann, H. J., *Lehrbuch der historisch-kritischen Einleitung in das Neue Testament* (3rd ed., 1892).

— *Lehrbuch der neutestamentlichen Theologie*, vol. II (2nd ed., 1911).

Holzmeister, U., *Chronologia Vitae Christi* (1933).

Horner, G. W., *The Statutes of the Apostles* (1904).

Horst, J., προσκυνεῖν (1932).

Huby, J., and Léon-Dufour, X., *L'Évangile et les Évangiles* (2nd ed., 1954).

Hudel, A., *Die religiösen und sittlichen Ideen des Spruchbuches* (1914).

Huppenbauer, H. W., *Der Mensch zwischen zwei Welten*, ATANT 34 (1959).

— "Belial in den Qumrantexten", *Theologische Zeitschrift* 15 (1959), pp. 81–9.

Hurter, H., *Nomenclator literarius theologiae catholicae*, vol. II (3rd ed., 1906).

Iber, G., *Überlieferungsgeschichtliche Untersuchungen zum Begriff des Menschensohnes im Neuen Testament* (unprinted dissertation, Heidelberg 1953).

Iersel, B. M. F. van, "*Der Sohn*" *in den synoptischen Jesusworten* (1961).

Imschoot, P. van, "Sagesse et l'Esprit dans l'Ancien Testament", *RB* 47 (1938), pp. 23–49.

Jansenius, C., *Commentariorum in suam concordiam ac totam historiam evangelicam partes IV* (1577).

Jastrow, M., *A Dictionary of the Targumim, the Talmud Babli and Yerushalmi and the Midrashic Literature*, 2 vols. (Reprint 1950).

Jellicoe, S., "The Hesychian Recension Reconsidered", *JBL* 82 (1963), pp. 409–18.

Jeremias, G., *Der Lehrer der Gerechtigkeit*, Studien zur Umwelt des Neuen Testaments 2 (1963).

Jeremias, J., *Jesus als Weltvollender* (1930).

— *Die Passahfeier der Samaritaner*, Beihefte ZAW 59 (1932).

— "ἀμνός, ἀρήν, ἀρνίον", *TWNT*, vol. I (1933), pp. 342–5.

— "'Ηλ(ε)ίας", *TWNT*, vol. II (1935), pp. 930–47.

— "'Ιωνᾶς", *TWNT*, vol. III (1938), pp. 410–3.

— "Μωυσῆς", *TWNT*, vol. IV (1942), pp. 852–78.

— "νύμφη, νύμφιος", *TWNT*, vol. IV (1942), pp. 1092–9.

— "παῖς θεοῦ", *TWNT*, vol. V (1954), pp. 676–713.

— "πάσχα", *TWNT*, vol. V (1954), pp. 895–903.

— "ποιμήν", *TWNT*, vol. VI (1959), pp. 484–98.

— "'Αμνός τοῦ Θεοῦ — παῖς Θεοῦ", *ZNW* 34 (1935), pp. 115–23.

— "Kennzeichen der ipsissima vox Jesu", *Synoptische Studien*, Festschrift A. Wikenhauser (1954), pp. 89–93.

— *Die Abendmahlsworte Jesu* (3rd ed., 1960); E. T.: *The Eucharistic Words of Jesus*, trans. by A. Ehrhardt (1955).

— *Unbekannte Jesusworte* (3rd ed., 1963); E. T.: *Unknown Sayings of Jesus*, trans. by R. H. Fuller (1957).

— *Die Kindertaufe in den ersten vier Jahrhunderten* (1958).

— *Jerusalem zur Zeit Jesu*, 2 vols. (2nd ed., 1958).

— *Die Gleichnisse Jesu* (6th ed., 1962); E. T.: *The Parables of Jesus*, trans. by S. H. Hooke (1963).
— "An Unknown Gospel with Johannine Elements. Papyrus Egerton 2", *New Testament Apocrypha* ed. by E. Hennecke, W. Schneemelcher and R. M. Wilson, vol. I (1963), pp. 94–7.
Jervell, J., *Imago Dei* (1960).
Johansson, N., "*Parakletoi*". *Vorstellungen von Fürsprechern für die Menschen vor Gott in der alttestamentlichen Religion, im Spätjudentum und im Urchristentum* (1940).
Johnston, G., "Spirit and Holy Spirit in the Qumran Literature", *New Testament Sidelights, Studies in Honor of A. C. Purgy* (1960), pp. 27–42.
Jonas, H., *Gnosis und spätantiker Geist*, vol. I: *Die mythologische Gnosis*, FRLANT 51 (1934), vol. II, 1: *Von der Mythologie zur mystischen Philosophie*, FRLANT 63 (1954).
— *The Gnostic Religion, the Message of the Alien God and the Beginnings of Christianity* (1958; 2nd rev. ed., 1963).
Jonge, M. de, *The Testament of the Twelve Patriarchs* (1953).
Joüon, P., "Respondit et dixit", *Biblica* 13 (1932), pp. 309–14.
Jülicher, A., and Fascher, E., *Einleitung in das Neue Testament* (7th ed., 1931).
Kallas, J., *The Significance of the Synoptic Miracles* (1961).
Karge, P., *Rephaim* (2nd ed., 1925).
Karpp, H., "Die Bibel in der mittelalterlichen Kirche", *Theologische Rundschau* 29 (1963), pp. 301–34.
Käsemann, E., "Das Problem des historischen Jesus", *ZTK* 51 (1954), pp. 125–53.
Kasser, R., *L'Évangile selon Thomas* (1961).
Keller, C. A., *Das Wort 'ōth als Offenbarungszeichen Gottes* (1946).
Kenyon, F. G., *The Text of the Greek Bible. A Students Handbook* (2nd ed., 1949).
Kirchgässner, A., *Erlösung und Sünde im Neuen Testament* (1950).
Kittel, G., "ἔρημος, ἐρημία, ἐρημόω, ἐρήμωσις", *TWNT*, vol. II (1935), pp. 654–7.
— "Der neutestamentliche Gebrauch von δόξα", *TWNT*, vol. II (1935), pp. 250–5.
— "Wort und Reden im Neuen Testament", *TWNT*, vol. IV (1942), pp. 100–40.
Kittel, H., *Die Herrlichkeit Gottes*, Beihefte ZNW 16 (1934).
Klausner, J., *Jesus of Nazareth* (3rd ed., 1947).
Kleinknecht, H., "Der Logos im Griechentum und Hellenismus", *TWNT*, vol. IV (1942), pp. 76–89.
— "πνεῦμα im Griechischen", *TWNT*, vol. VI (1959), pp. 333–57.
Klijn, A. F. J., "A Survey of the Researches into the Western Text of the Gospels and Acts", *Novum Testamentum* 3 (1959), pp. 161–73.
— *The Acts of Thomas* (1962).
Knackstedt, J., "De duplici miraculo multiplicationis panum", *Verbum Domini* 41 (1963), pp. 39–51, 140–53.
— "Die beiden Brotvermehrungen im Evangelium", *NTS* 10 (1963–64), pp. 309–35.
Koch, R., *Geist und Messias* (1950).
Köhler, L., and Baumgartner, W., *Lexicon in Veteris Testamenti Libros* (1953).
Kopp, C., *Das Kana des Evangeliums* (1940).
— *Die heiligen Stätten der Evangelien* (1959); E. T.: *The Holy Places of the Gospels*, trans. by R. Walls (1963).
Köster, H., *Synoptische Überlieferung bei den Apostolischen Vätern*, TU 65 (1957).
Kraeling, C. H., *Anthropos and Son of Man* (1927).
— *John the Baptist* (1951).
Kraft, B., "Barnabasbrief", *LTK*, vol. I (1957), cols. 1256–7.
Krebs, E., *Der Logos als Heiland im ersten Jahrhundert*, Freiburger Theologische Studien 2 (1910).
Kretschmar, G., "Zur religionsgeschichtlichen Einordnung der Gnosis", *Evangelische Theologie* 13 (1953), pp. 354–61.
Kuhn, K. G., "Die in Palästina gefundenen hebräischen Texte und das Neue Testament", *ZTK* 47 (1950), pp. 209 ff.
Kümmel, W. G., "Jesus und der jüdische Traditionsgedanke", *ZNW* 33 (1934), pp .105–30.

— "Futuristische und präsentische Eschatologie im ältesten Christentum", *NTS* 5 (1958–59), pp. 113–26.

— *Das Neue Testament. Geschichte und Erforschung seiner Probleme*, Orbis academicus (1958).

— *Einleitung in das Neue Testament*, founded by P. Feine and J. Behm (14th ed., 1965); E. T.: *Introduction to the New Testament*, trans. by A. J. Mattill (1966).

Kuss, O., "Zur Frage einer vorpaulinischen Todestaufe", *Münchener Theologische Zeitschrift* 4 (1953), pp. 1–17.

Lagrange, M.-J., *La Méthode historique* (1903); E.T.: *Historical Criticism and the Old Testament*, trans. by E. Meyers (1905).

— *Le Messianisme chez les Juifs*, Études Bibliques (1909).

Lambert, G., "Le Manuel de Discipline du désert de Juda. Étude historique et traduction intégrale", *NRT* 73 (1951), pp. 938–75, Reprinted in *Analecta Lovaniensia Biblica et Orientalia*, Series VI, 23 (1951). Page-references refer to this edition.

Lampe, G. W. H., "The Holy Spirit in the Writings of St. Luke", *Studies in the Gospels*, Essays in Memory of R. H. Lightfoot (1957), pp. 159–200.

Lapide, Cornelius A., *Commentarius in quattuor evangelia*, 4 vols., ed. by A. Padovani (4th ed., 1935).

Läuchli, S., "Eine Gottesdienststruktur in der Johannesoffenbarung", *Theologische Zeitschrift* 16 (1960), pp. 359–78.

Lauring, R. B., "The Problem of two Messiahs in the Qumran Scrolls", *Revue de Qumran* 4 (1963–64), pp. 39–52.

Leipoldt, J., and Schenke, H., *Koptisch-gnostische Schriften aus den Papyrus-Codices von Nag-Hamadi* (1960).

Leisegang, H., "Logos", *Paulys Realencyclopädie der klassischen Altertumswissenschaft*, ed. by G. Wissowa and W. Kroll, vol. XIII (1926), cols. 1035–81.

Léon-Dufour, X., "L'Évangile selon Saint Matthieu", *Introduction à la Bible*, ed. by A. Robert and A. Feuillet, vol. II: *Nouveau Testament* (1959), pp. 163–95; E. T.: *Introduction to the New Testament* (1965).

— "Récits de la Passion", *DBS*, vol. VI (1960), cols. 1419–91.

— *Les Évangiles et l'histoire de Jésus* (1963).

Liddell, H. G., and Scott, R., *A Greek-English Lexicon* (9th ed., 1940).

Liebermann, S., *Hellenism in Jewish Palestine* (1950).

Lietzmann, H., *Der Weltheiland* (1909).

Lightfoot, J. B., *St Paul's Epistle to the Colossians and to Philemon* (14th ed., 1904).

— *Horae Hebraicae et Talmudicae in quattuor Evangelistas* (2nd ed., 1648).

Lindars, B., *New Testament Apologetic. The Doctrinal Significance of the Old Testament Quotations* (1961).

Lohmeyer, E., *Christuskult und Kaiserkult* (1919).

— *Das Evangelium des Markus* (1937).

— "Vom urchristlichen Abendmahl. Das Mahl in der ältesten Christenheit", *Theologische Rundschau* 9 (1937), pp. 273–312.

Lohse, B., *Das Passafest der Quartadecimaner* (1953).

Lohse, E., *Märtyrer und Gottesknecht. Untersuchungen zur urchristlichen Verkündigung vom Sühntod Jesu Christi*, FRLANT 64 (1955).

Lubac, H. de, *Exégèse médiévale. Les quatre sens de l'Écriture*, 4 vols. (1959–64).

— *Histoire et Esprit. L'intelligence de l'Écriture d'après Origène* (1950).

MacDonald, J., *The Theology of the Samaritans* (1964).

MacGregor, G. H. C., "The Concept of the Wrath of God in the New Testament", *NTS* 7 (1960–61), pp. 101–9.

Macuch, R., "Alter und Heimat des Mandäismus nach neuerschlossenen Quellen", *TLZ* 83 (1957), pp. 401–8.

Maier, J., *Die Texte vom Toten Meer, Übersetzung und Anmerkungen*, 2 vols. (1960).

Manson, W., *Jesus the Messiah. The Synoptic Tradition of the Revelation of God in Christ with special Reference to Form-criticism* (1943).

— "The Argument of Prophecy", *JTS* 46 (1945), pp. 129–36.

Marcus, R., "Pharisees, Essenes and Gnostics", *JBL* 73 (1954), pp. 157–61.

Massaux, É., *Influence de l'Évangile de saint Matthieu sur la littérature chrétienne avant saint Irénée* (1950).
— "État actuel de la critique textuelle du Nouveau Testament", *Nouvelle Revue Théologique* 75 (1951), pp. 703–26.
— "Quelques variantes importantes de Papyrus Bodmer III et leur accointance avec la gnose", *NTS* 5 (1958–59), pp. 210–12.
May, H. G., "Cosmological Reference in the Qumran Doctrine of the Two Spirits and in Old Testament Imagery", *JBL* 82 (1963), pp. 1–14.
Mayeda, G., *Das Leben-Jesu-Fragment Papyrus Egerton 2 und seine Stellung in der urchristlichen Literaturgeschichte* (1946).
Mayer, R., and Reuss, J., *Die Qumranfunde und die Bibel.*
Mayser, E., *Grammatik der griechischen Papyri aus der Ptolemäerzeit*, 2 vols. (1906–34).
Meinertz, M., *Einleitung in das Neue Testament* (5th ed., 1950).
Meistermann, B., *Guide de la Terre Sainte* (2nd ed., 1923).
Mercier, J., "Wild, Jean", *DTC*, vol. XV (1950), cols. 3538–9.
Merx, A., *Der Messias oder Ta'eb der Samaritaner*, ZAW *(Beihefte)* 17 (1909).
Metzger, B. M., *Annotated Bibliography of the Textual Criticism of the New Testament, 1914–39* (1955).
— "Recent Developments in the Study of the Text of the Bible", *JBL* 78 (1959), pp. 13–20.
— *Chapters in the History of New Testament Textual Criticism* (1963).
— *The Text of the New Testament* (1964).
Meyer, R., "Προφήτης. Prophetentum und Propheten im Judentum der hellenistischen Zeit", *TWNT*, vol. VI (1959), pp. 813–28.
— "σάρξ, im Judentum", *TWNT*, vol. VII (1964), pp. 109–118.
— "κόλπος", *TWNT*, vol. III (1938), pp. 824–6.
Michaelis, W., *Einleitung in das Neue Testament* (3rd ed., 1961).
— "ὁράω", *TWNT*, vol. V (1954), pp. 315–68.
— "πάσχω", *TWNT*, vol. V (1954), pp. 903–23.
Michel, O., "ναός", *TWNT*, vol. IV (1942), pp. 884–95.
— "Spätjüdisches Prophetentum", *Neutestamentliche Studien für R. Bultmann* (1954), pp. 60–6.
Milik, J. T., *Dix ans de découverte dans le Désert de Juda* (1957); E. T.: *Ten Years of Discovery in the Judean Desert* (1959).
Moe, O., "Der Menschensohn und der Urmensch", *Studia Theologica* 14 (1960), pp. 119–29.
Molin, G., *Die Söhne des Lichtes. Zeit und Stellung der Handschriften vom Toten Meer* (1954).
Molitor, J., "Die Armenische Bibelübersetzung", *LTK*, vol. II (1958), cols. 397–8.
Mommsen, T., "Papianisches", *TNW* 3 (1902), pp. 156–9.
Mondésert, C., "Logos. La Parole divine à l'époque néotestamentaire", *DBS*, vol. V (1957), cols. 465–79.
Montgomery, J. A., *The Samaritans, the Earliest Jewish Sect. Their History, Theology and Literature* (1907).
Moore, G. F., *Judaism in the First Centuries of the Christian Era, the Age of Tannaim*, 3 vols. (1927–30).
Moulton, J. H., and Howard, M., *A Grammar of New Testament Greek*, vol. II (1929).
Moulton, J. H., and Milligan, G., *The Vocabulary of the Greek Testament Illustrated from the Papyri and other Non-Literary Sources* (1949).
Mowinckel, S., *He That Cometh*, trans. by G. W. Anderson (1956).
Munck, J., "Presbyters and Disciples of the Lord in Papias", *Harvard Theological Review* 52 (1959), pp. 223–43.
Mussner, F., "Der historische Jesus", *Der historische Jesus und der Christus unseres Glaubens*, ed. by K. Schubert (1962), pp. 103–28.
Nagel, W., "Epiphanienfest", *RGG*, vol. II (1958), cols. 530–1.
Neill, S., *The Interpretation of the New Testament 1861–1961* (1964).
New Testament in the Apostolic Fathers, by a Committee of the Oxford Society of Historical Theology (1905).
Nilsson, M. P., *Geschichte der griechischen Religion*, 2 vols. (2nd ed., 1961); E. T.: *A History of Greek Religion*, trans. by F. J. Fielder (1925; 2nd ed., 1949).

Ninck, M., *Die Bedeutung des Wassers in Kult und Leben der Alten* (1921).
Norden, E., *Agnostos Theos. Untersuchungen zur Formgeschichte religiöser Rede* (1913).
— *Die Geburt des Kindes* (1924).
Noth, M., *Geschichte Israels* (2nd ed., 1953); E. T.: *History of Israel*, trans. by S. Godman and rev. by P. R. Ackroyd (2nd ed., 1960).
Nötscher, F., *Das Angesicht Gottes. Schauen nach biblischer und babylonischer Auffassung* (1924).
— *Biblische Altertumskunde* (1940).
— *Zur theologischen Terminologie der Qumran-Texte*, Bonner Biblische Beiträge 10 (1956).
— *Gotteswege und Menschenwege in der Bibel und in Qumran*, Bonner Biblische Beiträge 15 (1958).
— "Geist und Geister in den Texten von Qumran", *Mélanges bibliques rédigés en l'honneur de A. Robert* (1957), pp. 305–15.
— "Schicksalsglaube in Qumran und Umwelt", *BZ* 3 (1959), pp. 205–34; 4 (1960), pp. 98–121.
— "Heiligkeit in den Qumranschriften", *Revue de Qumran* 2 (1959-60), pp. 163–81, 315–44.
Oepke, A., "ἐν", *TWNT*, vol. II (1935), pp. 534–9.
Olmstead, A. T., *Jesus in the light of History* (1942).
O'Neill, J. C., *The Theology of Acts in its Historical Setting* (1961).
Otto, W., "Augustus Soter", *Hermes* 45 (1910), pp. 448–60.
Otzen, B., "Die neugefundenen hebräischen Sektenschriften und die Testamente der zwölf Patriarchen", *Studia Theologica* 7 (1953), pp. 125–57.
Perler, O., *Der Nous bei Platon und das Verbum bei Augustinus als vorbildliche Ursache der Welt* (1931).
Pernot, H., *Les quatre Évangiles nouvellement traduits et annotés* (1943).
Pétrement, S., *Le dualisme chez Platon, les Gnostiques et les Manichéens* (1947).
Pfleiderer, O., *Urchristentum, seine Schriften und Lehren, in geschichtlichem Zusammenhang beschrieben*, 2 vols. (2nd rev. ed., 1902).
Philonenko, M., *Les interpolations chrétiennes des Testaments des Douze Patriarches et les manuscripts de Qumran* (1960).
Plessis, P. J. du, ΤΕΛΕΙΟΣ. *The Idea of Perfection in the New Testament* (1961).
Plöger, O., *Theokratie und Eschatologie* (1959).
Polman, A. D. R., *Het Woord Gods bij Augustinus* (1955).
Pontet, M., *L'exégèse de S. Augustin prédicateur* (1944).
Preisker, H., "μισθός im Neuen Testament", *TWNT*, vol. IV (1942), pp. 702–5.
Prigent, P., *Les Testimonia dans le christianisme primitif. L'Épître de Barnabé I-XVI et ses sources*, Études Bibliques (1961).
Procksch, O., "Wort Gottes im Alten Testament", *TWNT*, vol. IV (1942), pp. 89–100.
Prümm, K., *Religionsgeschichtliches Handbuch für den Raum der altchristlichen Umwelt* (2nd ed., 1954).
Pryke, J., "John the Baptist and the Qumran Community", *Revue de Qumran* 4 (1963–64), pp. 483–96.
Quasten, J., *Patrology*, 3 vols. (1950, 1953, 1960).
Quispel, G., *Gnosis als Weltreligion* (1951).
— "Jüdische Gnosis und jüdische Heterodoxie", *Evangelische Theologie* 14 (1954), pp. 474–84.
Rad, G. von, "Kabhod im Alten Testament", *TWNT*, vol. II (1935), pp. 240–5.
— *Theologie des Alten Testaments*, 2 vols. (1957–65); E. T.: *Old Testament Theology*, 2 vols. trans. by D. Stalker (1961–66).
Radermacher, L., *Neutestamentliche Grammatik*, Handbuch zum Neuen Testament 1 (2nd ed., 1925).
Rahner, H., "Antiochenische Schule", *LTK*, vol. I (1957), cols. 650–2.
— "Kerinthos", *LTK*, vol. VI (1961), col. 120.
Rahner, K., *Über die Schriftinspiration*, Quaestiones disputatae 1 (1958); E. T.: *Inspiration in the Bible*, trans. by C. H. Henkey and rev. by M. Palmer, Quaestiones Disputatae 1 (2nd rev. ed., 1964).

Ramón Diaz, J., "Palestinian Targum and New Testament", *Novum Testamentum* 6 (1963), pp. 75–80.
Rawlinson, A. E. J., *The New Testament Doctrine of Christ* (3rd ed., 1949).
Reicke, B., "Official and Pietistic Elements of Jewish Apocalypticism", *JBL* 79 (1960), pp. 137–50.
Reitzenstein, R., *Poimandres. Studien zur griechisch-ägyptischen und frühchristlichen Literatur* (1904).
— *Das Mandäische Buch des Herrn der Grösse und die Evangelienüberlieferung*, Sitzungsberichte der Österreichischen Akademie der Wissenschaften in Wien (1919).
— *Das iranische Erlösungsmysterium* (1921).
— *Die hellenistischen Mysterienreligionen nach ihren Grundgedanken und Wirkungen* (3rd ed., 1927).
Rengstorf, K. H., "μαθητής", *TWNT*, vol. IV (1942), pp. 417–64.
— "σημεῖον", *TWNT*, vol. VII (1964), pp. 199–261.
Renié, J., "Une antilogie évangélique", *Biblica* 36 (1955), pp. 223–6.
Resch, A., *Ausserkanonische Paralleltexte zu den Evangelien*, TU 10, 3 (1896).
Reuss, E., *Die Geschichte der heiligen Schriften des Neuen Testaments* (6th ed., 1887).
Reuss, J., *Matthäus-, Markus- und Johannes-Katenen* (1941).
— "Non(n)os von Panopolis", *ZTK*, vol. VII (1962), col. 1028.
Reymond, P., *L'eau, sa vie et sa signification dans l'Ancien Testament* (1958).
Richardson, A., *The Miracle Stories of the Gospel* (1941).
Rigaux, B., "L'historicité de Jésus devant l'exégèse récente", *RB* 65 (1958), 481–522.
Ringgren, R., *Word and Wisdom* (1947).
Ristow,H., and Matthiae, K., ed., *Der historische Jesus und der kerygmatische Christus* (1960).
Robert, A., "Logos. La Parole divine dans l'Ancien Testament", *DBS*, vol.V (1957), cols. 442–65.
Robert, A., and Feuillet, A., ed., *Introduction à la Bible*, vol. II: *Nouveau Testament* (1959); E. T.: *Introduction to the New Testament* (1965).
Roberts, C. H., "The Christian Book and the Greek Papyri", *JTS* 50 (1949), pp. 155–68.
Robinson, J. A. T., "Elijah, John and Jesus: An Essay in Detection", *NTS* 4 (1957–58), pp. 263–81.
Robinson, J. M., *The New Quest of the Historical Jesus* (1959).
Romaniuk, R., *L'amour du Père et du Fils dans la sotériologie de saint Paul* (1961).
Rössler, D., *Gesetz und Geschichte. Untersuchungen zur Theologie der jüdischen Apokalyptik und der pharisäischen Orthodoxie* (1960).
Rowley, H. H., "The Baptism of John and the Qumran Sect", *New Testament Essays* (1959), pp. 218–29.
Ruckstuhl, E., *Die Chronologie des Letzten Mahles und des Leidens Jesu* (1963).
Rudolph, K., *Die Mandäer*, vol. I: *Prolegomena: Das Mandäerproblem;* vol. II: *Der Kult*, FRLANT 92 and 93 (1960–61).
Sagnard, F., *La Gnose Valentinienne et le témoignage de saint Irénée* (1947).
Sasse, H., "αἰών, αἰώνιος", *TWNT*, vol. I (1933), pp. 197–209.
— "κόσμος", *TWNT*, vol. III (1938), pp. 867–96.
Schäfer, K. T., *Grundriss der Einleitung in das Neue Testament* (2nd ed., 1952).
— "Der Ertrag der textkritischen Arbeit seit der Jahrhundertwende", *BZ* 4 (1960), pp. 1–18.
Schauf, W., *Sarx. Der Begriff 'Fleisch' beim Apostel Paulus unter besonderer Berücksichtigung seiner Erlösungslehre* (1924).
Scheidweiler, F., "Paradoxie in der neutestamentlichen Christologie", *ZNW* 49 (1958), pp. 258–64.
Schelkle, K. H., *Die Passion Jesu in der Verkündigung des Neuen Testaments* (1949).
Schenke, H.-M., *Der Gott "Mensch" in der Gnosis* (1962).
— "Die Arbeit am Philippus-Evangelium", *TLZ* 90 (1965), pp. 321–32.
Schermann, T., *Die allgemeine Kirchenordnung, frühchristliche Liturgien und kirchliche Überlieferung;* vol. I: *Die allgemeine Kirchenordnung des 2. Jahrhunderts* (1914).
Schlatter, A., *Der Glaube im Neuen Testament* (4th ed., 1927).
Schlier, H., *Religionsgeschichtliche Untersuchungen zu den Ignatiusbriefen* (1929).

— "ἀμήν", *TWNT*, vol. I (1933), pp. 339–42.
— "Der Mensch im Gnostizismus", *Anthropologie Religieuse*, ed. by C. J. Bleeker (1955), pp. 60–76; E.T.: "Man in Gnosticism", *The Relevance of the New Testament* (1967), chapter 5.
— *Der Brief an die Epheser* (1957).
Schmauch, W., "In der Wüste", *In Memoriam E. Lohmeyer* (1951), pp. 202–23.
Schmaus, M., *Die psychologische Trinitätslehre des heiligen Augustinus* (1927).
Schmid, J., "Barnabas", *Reallexikon für Antike und Christentum*, vol. I (1950), cols. 1207–17.
— "Evangelium", *LTK*, vol. III (1959), cols. 1255–59.
— *Das Evangelium nach Markus* (3rd ed., 1954).
— "Heilige Brautschaft", *Reallexikon für Antike und Christentum*, vol. II (1954), cols. 528–64.
— *Das Evangelium nach Lukas* (3rd ed., 1955).
— *Begegnung der Christen*, Festschrift für O. Karrer (2nd ed., 1960), pp. 347–59.
— "Jona", *LTK*, vol. V (1960), col. 1113.
— "Mandäismus", *LTK*, vol. VI (1961), cols. 1343–7.
— "Oden Salomons", *LTK*, vol. VII (1962), 1094–5.
Schmidt, K. L., *Der Rahmen der Geschichte Jesu* (1919).
— "Die Stellung der Evangelien in der allgemeinen Literaturgeschichte", *Eucharisterion für H. Gunkel*, vol. II (1923), pp. 50–134.
Schmithals, W., *Das Kirchliche Apostelamt* (1961).
Schmitt, J., "Nazareth", *DBS*, vol. VI (1958), cols. 318–63.
— "Les écrits du Nouveau Testament et les textes de Qumran", *RSR* 29 (1955), pp. 381–401; 30 (1956), pp. 55–74, 261–82.
Schnackenburg, R., *Das Heilsgeschehen bei der Taufe nach dem Apostel Paulus* (1950).
— "Die Erwartung des 'Propheten' nach dem Neuen Testament und den Qumran-Texten", *Studia Evangelica. Papers Presented to the International Congress on the Four Gospels in 1957*, TU 73 (1959), pp. 622–39.
— "Formgeschichte", *LTK*, vol. IV (1960), cols. 211–3.
— "Zum Verfahren der Urkirche bei ihrer Jesusüberlieferung", *Der historische Jesus und der kerygmatische Christus*, ed. by H. Ristow and K. *Matthiae* (1960), pp. 439–54.
— *Die sittliche Botschaft des Neuen Testaments* (2nd ed., 1962); E. T.: *The Moral Teaching of the New Testament*, trans. by J. Holland-Smith and W. J. O'Hara (2nd ed., 1967).
— "Zur formgeschichtlichen Methode in der Evangelienforschung", *ZKT* 85 (1963), pp. 16–32.
— "Sohn Gottes", *LTK*, vol. IX (1964), cols. 851–4.
— *Die Kirche im Neuen Testament* (1961); E. T.: *The Church in the New Testament*, trans. by W. J. O'Hara (1965).
— *Die Johannesbriefe* (2nd rev. ed., 1963); E. T.: *The Letters of St. John*, trans. by W. J. O'Hara (in preparation).
Schneemelcher, W., "The Gospel of the Egyptians", *New Testament Apocrypha*, ed. by E. Hennecke, W. Schneemelcher and R. M. Wilson, vol. I (1963), pp. 166–78.
Schneider, J., *Doxa* (1932).
Schniewind, J., *Euangelion* (1927–31).
Schoeps, H. J., *Theologie und Geschichte des Judenchristentums* (1949).
— *Urgemeinde, Judenchristentum, Gnosis* (1956).
Scholem, G. G., *Die jüdische Mystik in ihren Hauptströmungen* (1957); E. T.: *Major Trends in Jewish Mysticism* (1961).
— *Jewish Gnosticism, Merkabah Mysticism and Talmudic Tradition* (1960).
Schubert, K., *Die Religion des nachbiblischen Judentums* (1955).
— "Die Messiaslehre in den Texten von Chirbet Qumran", *BZ* 1 (1957), pp. 177–97.
— *Die Gemeinde vom Toten Meer* (1958).
— ed., *Der historische Jesus und der Christus unseres Glaubens* (1962).
— "Die Entwicklung der Auferstehungslehre von der nachexilischen bis zur frührabbinischen Zeit", *BZ* 6 (1962), pp. 177–214.

— "Die jüdischen Religionsparteien im Zeitalter Jesu", *Der historische Jesus und der Christus unseres Glaubens*, ed. by K. Schubert (1962), pp. 15–101.
Schulz, A., *Nachfolgen und Nachahmen* (1962).
Schulz, S., "Die Bedeutung neuer Gnosisfunde für die neutestamentliche Wissenschaft", *Theologische Rundschau* 26 (1960), pp. 209–66, 301–34.
— "Salomo-Oden", *RGG*, vol. V (1961), cols. 1339–42.
Schürer, E., *Geschichte des Jüdischen Volkes im Zeitalter Jesu Christi*, 3 vols. (4th ed., 1901–11); E. T.: *A History of the Jewish People in the Time of Jesus Christ*, trans. by J. MacPherson and others from the 2nd German edition (1898–1905).
Schürmann, H., "Die Anfänge der christlichen Osterfeier", *Theologische Quartalschrift* 131 (1951), pp. 414–25.
— *Der Paschamahlbericht Lk 22: Eine quellenkritische Untersuchung*, Neutestamentliche Abhandlungen, 19, 5 (1953).
Schweitzer, A., *Geschichte der Leben-Jesu-Forschung* (6th ed., 1951); E. T.: *The Quest of the Historical Jesus. A Critical Study of its Progress from Reimarus to Wrede*, trans. by W. Montgomery (3rd ed., 1963).
Schweizer, E., "Die Herkunft der Präexistenzvorstellung bei Paulus", *Evangelische Theologie* 19 (1954), pp. 65–70.
— "Römer 1 : 3f. und der Gegensatz von Fleisch und Geist vor und bei Paulus", *Evangelische Theologie* 15 (1955), pp. 563–71.
— "πνεῦμα, πνευματικός", *TWNT*, vol. VI (1959), pp. 387–450.
— *Gemeinde und Gemeindeordnung im Neuen Testament* (1959); E. T.: *The Church Order in the New Testament*, trans. by F. Clarke (1961).
— "σάρξ im Neuen Testament", *TWNT*, vol. VII (1964), pp. 123–45.
Scott, R. B. Y., "Weights and Measures of the Bible", *Biblical Archeologist* 22 (1959), pp. 22–40.
Seemann, H., "Aufgehellte Bibelworte", *Benediktinische Monatschrift* 28 (1952), pp. 230–2.
Seesemann, H., "οἶνος", *TWNT*, vol. V (1954), pp. 163–7.
Seitz, O. J. F., "Two Spirits in Man. An Essay in Biblical Exegesis", *NTS* 6 (1959–60), pp. 82–95.
Shepherd, M. H., *The Paschal Liturgy and the Apocalypse* (1960).
Silbermann, L., "Unriddling the Riddle", *Revue de Qumran* 3 (1961–62), pp. 323–64.
Simon, M., "Retour du Christ et reconstruction du Temple dans la pensée chrétienne primitive", *Aux Sources de la tradition chrétienne*, Mélanges Goguel (1950), pp. 247–57.
— *Les sectes juives au temps de Jésus* (1961).
Sjöberg, E., *Der Menschensohn im äthiopischen Henochbuch* (1946).
— *Der verborgene Menschensohn in den Evangelien* (1955).
— "Neuschöpfung in den Toten-Meer-Rollen", *Studia Theologica* 9 (1955), pp. 131–6.
— "Ruaḥ im palästinischen Judentum", *TWNT*, vol. VI (1959), pp. 373–87.
Smalley, B., *The Study of the Bible in the Middle Ages* (2nd ed., 1952).
Smits, A. C., Oud-testamentische Citaten in het Nieuwe Testament, vol. II (1955).
Soden, H. von, *Die Schriften des Neuen Testaments in ihrer ältesten erreichbaren Textgestalt hergestellt auf Grund ihrer Textgeschichte*, vol. I, 1 (2nd ed., 1911).
Spicq, C., *Esquisse d'une histoire de l'exégèse latine au Moyen Âge* (1944).
Staab, K., "Katenen", *LTK*, vol. VI (1961), cols. 56–7.
Staerk, W., *Soter*, vol. I: *Der biblische Christus* (1933).
— *Die Erlösererwartung in den östlichen Religionen* (1938).
Stählin, "ὀργή. Der Zorn des Menschen und der Zorn Gottes im Neuen Testament", *TWNT*, vol. V (1954), pp. 419–48.
Starcky, J., "Logos. La Parole divine dans le Nouveau Testament", *DBS*, vol. V (1957), cols. 479–96.
Stauffer, E., *Die Theologie des Neuen Testamentes* (3rd ed., 1947); E. T.: *New Testament Theology*, trans. by J. Marsh (1955).
— "Probleme der Priestertradition", *TLZ* 81 (1956), pp. 135–50.
— *Jesus, Gestalt und Geschichte* (1957); E. T.: *Jesus and his Story*, trans. by D. M. Barton (1960).

Stegmüller, F., *Repertorium biblicum medii aevi*, 7 vols. (1950–62).
Stein, B., *Der Begriff kebod Jahwe und seine Bedeutung für die alttestamentliche Gotteserkenntnis* (1939).
Stein, E., *Die allegorische Exegese des Philo aus Alexandreia* (1929).
Steinmann, J., *Saint Jean-Baptiste et la spiritualité du désert* (1955).
Strathmann, H., "μάρτυς, μαρτυρέω, μαρτυρία, μαρτύριον im Neuen Testament", *TWNT*, vol. IV (1935), pp. 492–510.
Strauss, G., *Schriftgebrauch, Schriftauslegung und Schriftbeweis bei Augustin* (1959).
Strecker, G., *Das Judenchristentum in den Pseudoclementinen*, TU 70 (1958).
Streeter, B. H., *The Four Gospels* (1924; 7th ed., 1951).
Strobel, A., "Der Termin des Todes Jesu", *ZNW* 51 (1960), pp. 69–101.
Suggs, M. J., "The Use of Patristic Evidence in the Search for a Primitive New Testament Text", *NTS* (1957–58), pp. 139–47.
Sundberg, W., *Kushta I: The Descending Knowledge* (1953).
Tasker, R. V. G., *The Old Testament in the New Testament* (2nd ed., 1954).
Taylor, V., *The Gospel according to St Mark* (1952).
— *The Names of Jesus* (1953).
Teeple, H. M., *The Mosaic Eschatological Prophet* (1959).
Thomas, J., *Le mouvement baptiste en Palestine et Syrie, 150 av. J.-C. – 300 ap. J.-C.* (1935).
Thyen, H., "Die Probleme der neueren Philo-Forschung", *Theologische Rundschau* 23 (1955), pp. 230–46.
Tödt, H. E., *Der Menschensohn in der synoptischen Überlieferung* (1959); E. T.: *The Son of Man in the Synoptic Tradition* (1965).
Torrance, T. F., "Liturgie et Apocalypse", *Verbum Caro* 11 (1957), pp. 28–40.
Torrey, C. C., *Our Translated Gospels. Some of the Evidence* (1937).
Traub, H., "οὐρανός", *TWNT*, vol. V (1954), pp. 509–36.
Trilling, W., "Die Täufertradition im Matthäusevangelium", *BZ* 3 (1959), pp. 271–89.
Unnik, W. C. van, "The 'Gospel of Truth' and the New Testament", *The Jung Codex, a Newly Discovered Gnostic Papyrus*. Three Studies by H. C. Puech, G. Quispel and W. C. van Unnik. Trans. and ed. by F. L. Cross (1955), pp. 79–129.
— *Evangelien aus dem Nilsand* (1960); E. T.: *Newly Discovered Gnostic Writings*, trans. by H. H. Hoskins (1960).
— "Die jüdische Komponente in der Entstehung der Gnosis", *Vigiliae Christianae* 15 (1961), pp. 65–82.
Vaux, R. de, *Les institutions de l'Ancien Testament*, 2 vols. (1960); E. T.: *Ancient Israel. Its Life and Institutions*, trans. by J. McHugh (1961).
Vermès, G., "A propos des Commentaires bibliques découverts à Qumran", *Revue d'Histoire et de Philosophie Religieuse* 35 (1955), pp. 95–103.
Vielhauer, P., "Apocalyptic", *New Testament Apocrypha*, ed. by E. Hennecke, W. Schneemelcher and R. M. Wilson, vol. II (1965), pp. 608–42.
Vogels, H. J., *Handbuch der Textkritik des Neuen Testaments* (2nd ed., 1955).
Vögtle, A., "Der Spruch vom Jonaszeichen", *Synoptische Studien*, Festschrift Wikenhauser (1954), pp. 230–77.
— "Ekklesiologische Auftragsworte des Auferstandenen", *Sacra Pagina, Miscellanea biblica Congressus internationalis de re biblica*, vol. II (1959), 280–94.
— "Der Menschensohn und die paulinische Christologie", *Congressus Internationalis Catholicus Studiorum Paulinorum*, vol. I (1961), pp. 199–218.
— "Jesu Wunder einst und heute", *Bibel und Leben* 2 (1961), pp. 234–54.
— "Die Genealogie Mt 1 : 2–16 und die matthäische Kindheitsgeschichte", *BZ* 8 (1964), pp. 45–58, 239–62; 9 (1965), pp. 32–49.
Völker, W., *Quellen zur Geschichte der christlichen Gnosis* (1932).
— *Fortschritt und Vollendung bei Philo von Alexandrien* (1938).
Volz, P., *Die Eschatologie der jüdischen Gemeinde im neutestamentlichen Zeitalter* (2nd ed., 1934).
Vööbus, A., *Early Versions of the New Testament* (1954).
Wagner, G., *Das religionsgeschichtliche Problem von Römer 6 : 1–11* (1962).
Walther, G., *Jesus, das Passalamm des Neuen Bundes* (1950).

Weber, W., *Untersuchungen zur Geschichte des Kaisers Hadrianus.*
Weiser, A., "πιστεύω. Der alttestamentliche Begriff", *TWNT*, vol. VI (1959), pp. 182–97.
Weiss, B., *Lehrbuch der biblischen Theologie des Neuen Testamentes* (7th ed., 1903).
Weiss, J., *Das Urchristentum* (1917).
Wellhausen, J., *Einleitung in die drei ersten Evangelien* (2nd ed., 1911).
Wendland, P., "Σωτήρ", *ZNW* 5 (1904), pp. 335–53.
— *Die urchristlichen Literaturformen* (2nd ed., 1912).
Wenschkewitz, H., "Die Spiritualisierung der Kultusbegriffe Tempel, Priester und Opfer im Neuen Testament", *Angelos* 4 (1932), pp. 70–230.
Wernberg-Möller, P., *The Manual of Discipline* (1957).
— "A Reconsideration of the Two Spirits in the Rule of the Community, 1 QS 3 : 13–4 : 26" *Revue de Qumran* 3 (1961), pp. 413–41.
Wibbing, S., *Die Tugend- und Lasterkataloge im Neuen Testament und ihre Traditionsgeschichte unter besonderer Berücksichtigung der Qumrantexte* (1959).
Widengren, G., *The Great Vohu Manah and the Apostle of God* (1945).
Wikenhauser, A., *Einleitung in das Neue Testament* (3rd ed., 1958); E. T.: *New Testament Introduction*, trans. by J. Cunningham (1958).
Williams, C. S. C., *Alterations to the Text of the Synoptic Gospel and Acts* (1951).
Wilpert, J., *Die Malereien der Katakomben Roms*, 2 vols. (1903).
Wilson, R. M., *The Gnostic Problem* (1958).
Windisch, H., *Der Barnabasbrief*, Handbuch zum Neuen Testament, Ergänzungsband 6, 3 (1920).
Winter, P., *On the Trial of Jesus* (1961).
Wolff, H. W., *Jesaja 53 im Urchristentum* (3rd ed., 1952).
Wolfson, H. A., *Philo, Foundations of Religious Philosophy in Judaism, Christianity and Islam*, vol. I (1948).
Woude, A. S. van der, *Die messianischen Vorstellungen der Gemeinde von Qumran* (1957).
— "Le maître de Justice et les deux Messies de la Communauté de Qumrân", *La secte de Qumrân et les origines du christianisme*, Recherches Bibliques 4 (1957), pp. 121–34.
Wrede, W., Das Messiasgeheimnis in den Evangelien (1901).
Wright, G. E., and Filson, F. V., *The Westminster Historical Atlas to the Bible* (2nd ed., 1947).
Wright, L. E., *Alterations to the Words of Jesus as quoted in the Literature of the Second Century* (1952).
Yadin, Y., "A Note on DSD IV, 20", *JBL* 74 (1955), pp. 40–43.
Zahn, T., *Forschungen zur Geschichte des neutestamentlichen Kanons und der altkirchlichen Literatur*, vol. VI (1900).
— *Einleitung in das Neue Testament*, 2 vols. (3rd ed., 1907); E. T.: *Introduction to the New Testament*, 3 vols. (1909).
Zapletal, V., *Der Wein in der Bibel*, Biblische Studien 20, I (1920).
Zerwick, M., *Graecitas biblica exemplis illustratur* (3rd ed., 1955).
Ziener, G., *Die theologische Begriffssprache im Buch der Weisheit* (1956).
— "Die Brotwunder im Markusevangelium", *BZ* 4 (1960), pp. 282–5.
Zuntz, G., "On the Hymns in Corpus Hermeticum XIII", *Hermes* 83 (1955), pp. 68–92.

INDICES

TEXTUAL INDICES

I OLD TESTAMENT

II NEW TESTAMENT

III EARLY CHRISTIAN WRITINGS

IV. JEWISH WRITINGS

A. APOCRYPHA AND PSEUDEPIGRAPHA

C. RABBINIC TEXTS

V. MANDAEAN WRITINGS

VI. CLASSICAL AND HELLENISTIC WRITINGS

INDEX OF AUTHORS

See also Bibliography

Index of Authors